GRAFTED ARTS

This book focuses on Maratha military rulers and British East India Company officials who used the arts to engage in diplomacy, wage war, compete for prestige, and generate devotion as they allied with (or fought against) each other to control western India in the eighteenth century. This book conceptualizes the artistic combinations that resulted as ones of "graft" – a term that acknowledges the violent and creative processes of suturing arts, and losing and gaining goods, as well as the shifting dynamics among agents who assembled such materials.

By tracing grafted arts from multiple perspectives – Maratha and British, artist and patron, soldier and collector – this book charts the methods of empire building that recast artistic production and collection in western India and from there across India and in Britain. This mercenary method of artistry propagated mixed, fractured, and plundered arts. Indeed, these grafted arts – disseminated across India and Britain over the nineteenth century to aid in consolidating empire or revolting against it entirely – remain instigators of nationalist agitation today.

HOLLY SHAFFER is an assistant professor of history of art and architecture at Brown University with a focus on eighteenth- and nineteenth-century British and South Asian arts and their intersections.

COVER IMAGES

FRONT *British Soldier in an Indian Landscape* (detail), Britain and Maharashtra, late 18th or early 19th century. Bharat Itihas Sanshodhak Mandal, Pune

BACK *Shiva and Parvati* (detail), Poona, Lucknow or Jaipur, ca. 1800. British Museum, London, Edward Moor Collection

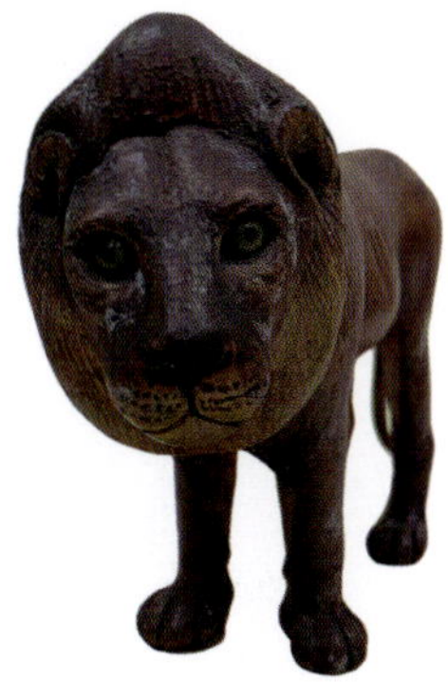

GRAFTED ARTS

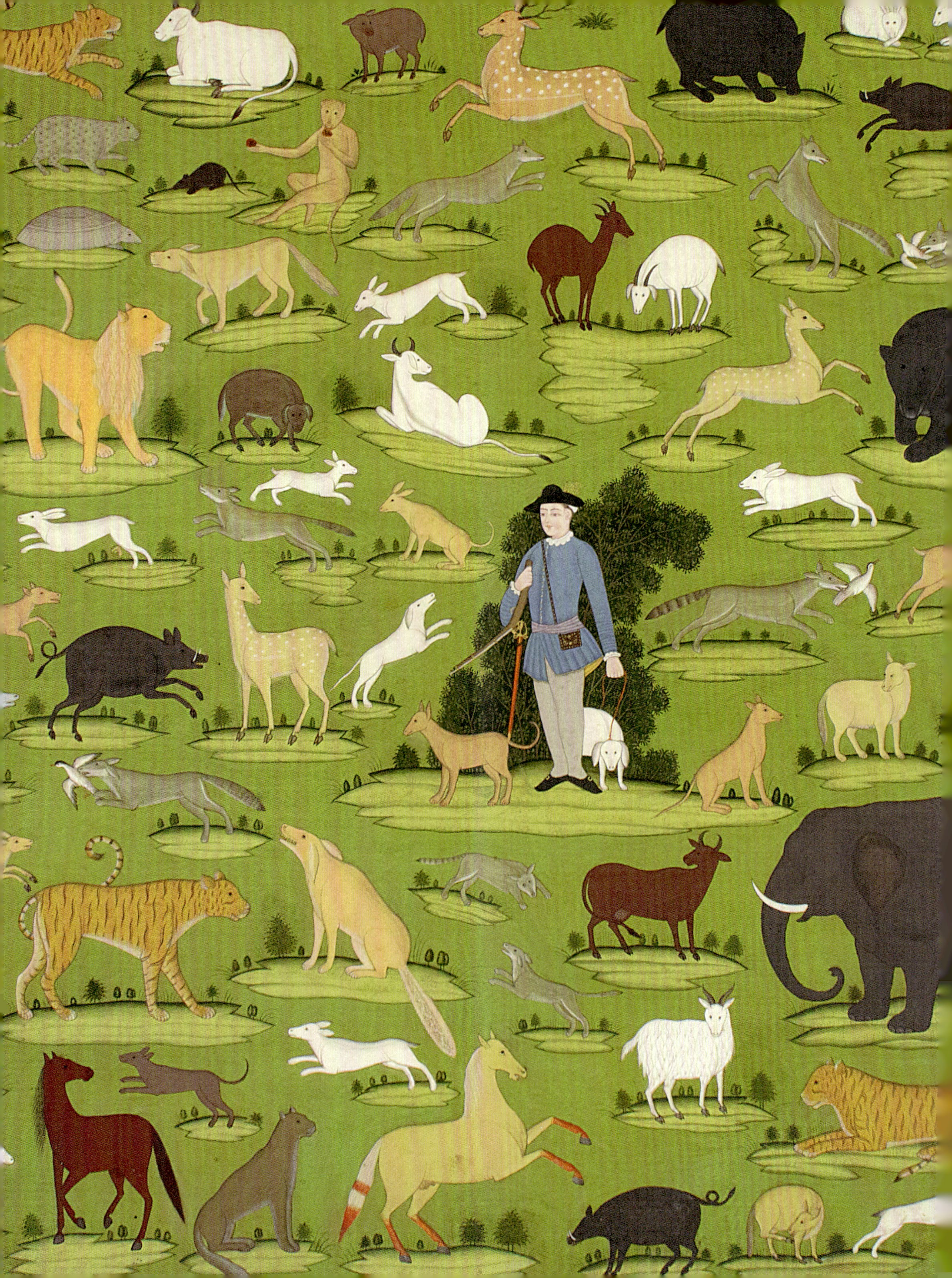

GRAFTED ARTS

Art Making and Taking in the Struggle for Western India ❦ 1760–1910

HOLLY SHAFFER

PAUL MELLON CENTRE FOR STUDIES IN BRITISH ART
Distributed by Yale University Press ❦ New Haven and London

For Andrew and Hugh

Awarded the Edward Cameron Dimock, Jr. Prize in the Indian Humanities by the American Institute of Indian Studies and published with the Institute's generous support.

AIIS Publication Committee:
Sarah Lamb (Co-Chair), Anand A. Yang (Co-Chair), Chanchal Dadlani, Diane Mines, Tulasi Srinivas, Tariq Thachil

First published in 2022 by the Paul Mellon Centre for Studies in British Art
16 Bedford Square, London, WC1B 3JA
paul-mellon-centre.ac.uk

ISBN 978-1-913107-28-4 HB
Library of Congress Control Number: 2021948034

British Library Cataloguing-in-Publication Data
A catalogue record for this book is available from the British Library

Designed by Bobby Birchall, Bobby&Co.
Origination by DL Imaging
Printed in China through World Print Ltd

FSC www.fsc.org MIX Paper from responsible sources FSC® C014688

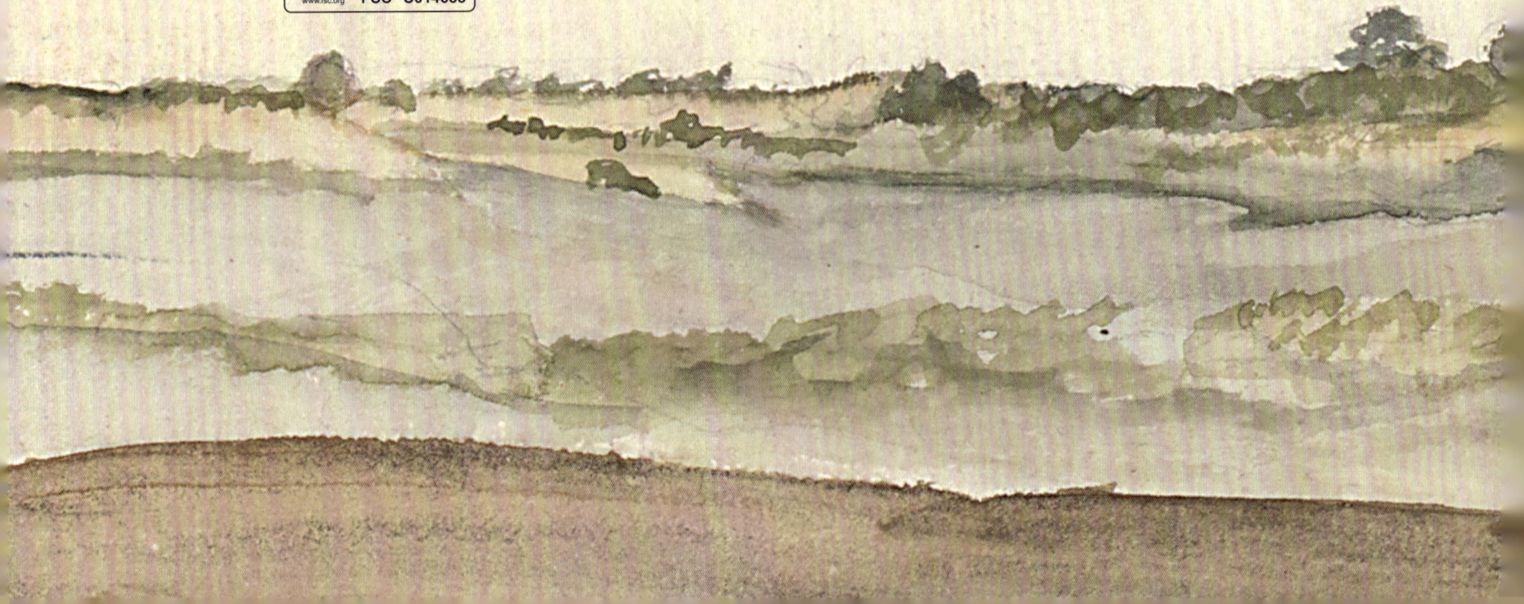

Contents

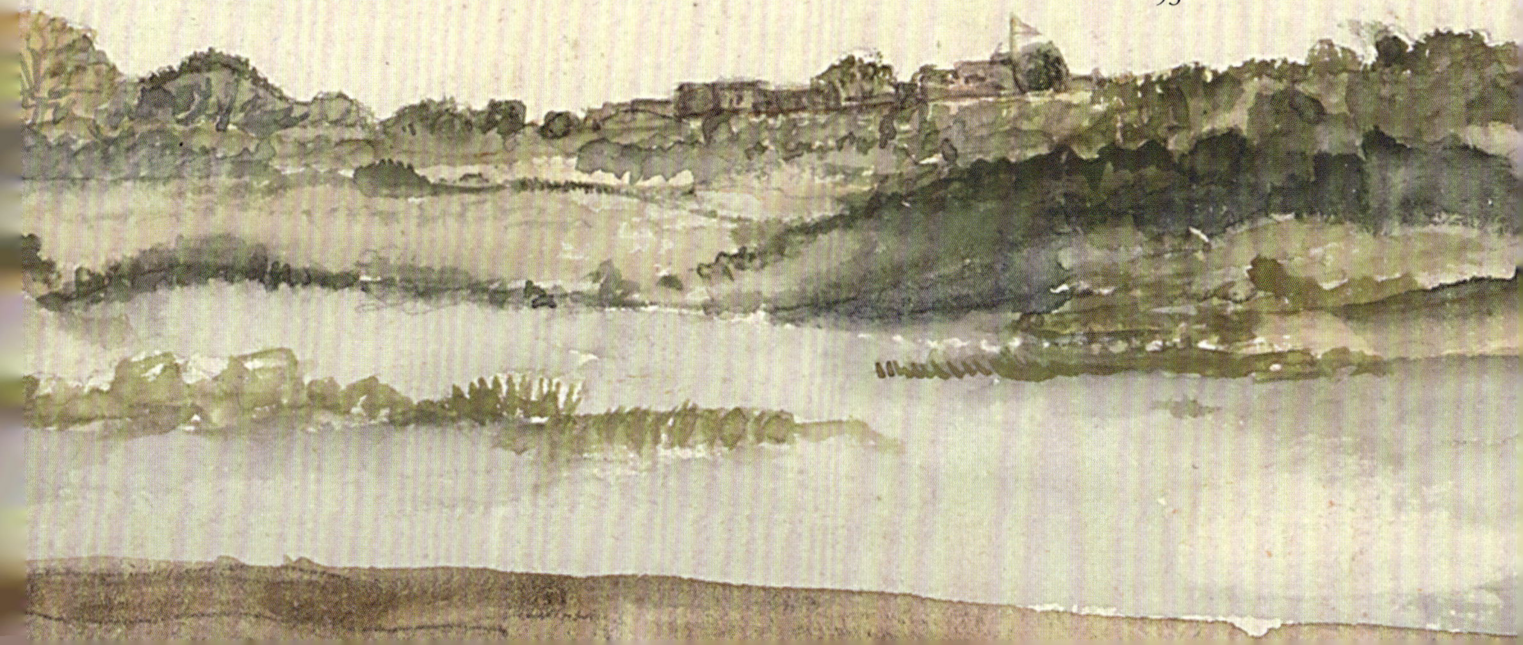

Acknowledgments

This book foregrounds relationships that drew together a range of people; here I extend that notion to thank wholeheartedly the many individuals who helped me create this book and the institutions that supported its research and writing. This project started in an archive at the Yale Center for British Art while I was a graduate student in the History of Art department at Yale University. I am grateful to my advisors Tim Barringer and Tamara Sears, and my committee members Molly Aitken and Gillian Forrester for trusting me to follow the artists and objects in that archive wherever they led, and for their guidance at each juncture since. The dissertation was nurtured into a book at Dartmouth College while I was on a Mellon postdoctoral fellowship, and it came into its own in my position as an assistant professor at Brown University. I thank my departmental colleagues Sheila Bonde, Lindsay Caplan, Evie Lincoln, Jeff Moser, Jeff Muller, Dietrich Neumann, Doug Nickel, Itohan Osayimwese, and Gretel Rodriguez at Brown; and Mary Coffey, Ada Cohen, Chad Elias, Allen Hockley, Christie Harner, Doug Haynes, Katie Hornstein, and Sunglim Kim at Dartmouth, for their insights and encouragement as I reconceptualized the materials and developed the framework of graft.

Some people have been touchstones for this project, as readers and interlocutors. I thank Shahzad Bashir, Esther Chadwick, Ned Cooke, Chanchal Dadlani, Debra Diamond, Meredith Gamer, Shailka Mishra, Suzy Newberry, Henry Noltie, Alex Seggerman, Samira Sheikh, and Emma Stein for their careful reading and insights in conversations that propelled the project forward and refined its arguments; I extend special thanks to Douglas Fordham for his generous comments on this material and our spirited discussions over many years. I am also grateful for other colleagues, including Anna Arabindan-Kesson, Susan Bean, Prasad Boradkar, Crispin Branfoot, Rebecca Brown, Ainsley Cameron, Robert J. Del Bontà, Harold Cook, Natasha Eaton, Anne Feldhaus, Margot Finn, Kate Fitzpatrick, Cécile Fromont, Finnian Moore Gerety, Tapati Guha-Thakurta, Navina Najat Haidar, Sylvia Houghteling, Aaron Hyman, Dipti Khera, Sonal Khullar, Nisha Kommattam, Dian Kriz, Risha Lee, Dana Leibsohn, Simon MacDonald, Rosalind O'Hanlon, Laurel Peterson, Christopher Pinney, Andrei Pop, Ami Potter, Fatima Quraishi, Ayesha Ramachandran, Adrian Randolph, Romita Ray, Yael Rice, Kishwar Rizvi, Cynthia Roman, Angela Rosenthal, Malini Roy, John Seyller, Yuthika Sharma, Heeryoon Shin, Catherine Shteynberg, Allie Stielau, Sarah Victoria Turner, Narmada Upadhyaya, Peter Van Dommelen, Dominic

Page i Gangaram Tambat, *A Model of a Lion* (see fig. 37)

Frontispiece Shivram Chitari, *A British Hunter in a Maratha Landscape* (detail of fig. 38)

Pages iv–v Gangaram Tambat, attrib., *View on the River Bhima at Deval Gaun, 28 Miles E of Poona* (detail of fig. 43)

Vendell, Chris Wood, Vazira Zamindar, and Karin Zitzewitz. Thank you for your thoughtful guidance and the pleasure of our conversations.

I am grateful to those who invited me to present my work in connection to this project and to the respective audiences for their helpful feedback. These included talks at the Bhau Daji Lad Museum, Mumbai; at "Curious outside of Europe" at Yale University; "The East India Company at Home" conference at University College London; "Global Encounters and the Archive" at the Lewis Walpole Library; "The Global 19th-Century Workshop" at University of California at Riverside; "Peripatetic Empires" at Rutgers University; "Photography and Britishness" at the Yale Center for British Art; "Recent Studies in Indian Painting" at the Jagdish and Kamla Mittal Museum of Art, Hyderabad; a lecture at the Sigur Center for Asian Studies at George Washington University; and panels at conferences hosted by the American Council of Southern Asian Art, the American Society for Eighteenth-Century Studies, the College Art Association, and especially productive ones on "Producing India" at the South Asia Conference at the University of Wisconsin-Madison and on "Uncommon Knowledge" at the Association for Asian Studies.

Research for this book was mainly carried out in India, Britain, and America. I am indebted to the curators, librarians, scholars, collectors, and journalists who supported my research and provided new paths of inquiry.

In India, I am grateful to Dr. Bhave and staff at the Bharat Itihas Sanshodhak Mandal for aiding my research and linking me to numerous scholars throughout western India. I thank scholars and librarians at Deccan College for their aid as well as the teachers at the American Institute of Indian Studies Marathi language program. I thank the directors and curators at all of the institutions that hosted me, including (but not limited to) the Bhandarkar Oriental Research Institute, Pune; the Bhau Daji Lad Museum, Mumbai; the Chhatrapati Shivaji Maharaj Vastu Sangrahalaya, Mumbai; the Historical Museum and Research Centre, Ahmednagar; the History Museum at Dr. Babasaheb Ambedkar Marathwada University, Aurangabad; the Oriental Institute of Baroda; the Raja Dinkar Kelkar Museum, Pune; the Maharaja Sawai Man Singh II Museum, Jaipur; and the Scindia Oriental Research Institute, Ujjain. I am also grateful to collectors who allowed me to access their materials, including Sanjay Godbole, Pheroza Godrej, Mansingh Kumthekar, Jagdish Mittal, the Patwardhan family, Anil and Manan Relia, and Prashant and Rashmi Tapadia, as well as to friends who made this research all the more fun, including Rachel Ball-Phillips, Dr. and Mrs. Bhave, Saili Datar, Meera Kosambi, Rucha Kulkarni, Anita Joshi, Mircea Raianu, Varunika Saraf, Pushkar Sohoni, and Rachel Sturman. I owe especially warm thanks to Ashok Phadnis and his family who welcomed me into their home over many years to delve into the history of their ancestor Nana Fadnavis.

In Britain, I was able to work closely with the Moor Collection at the British Museum thanks to Richard Blurton and Michael Willis; I thank them also for their support and guidance. Malini Roy, Cam Sharpe Jones, J. P. Losty, and Jennifer Howes aided my research at the British Library, as Nick Barnard did at the Victoria and Albert Museum; thank you for your help as well as your comradery. Thanks are due to Deborah Swallow at the Courtauld Institute; David Jones at the Ipswich Museum; Ed Weech at the Royal Asiatic Society of Great Britain and Ireland; and librarians at the Wellcome Collection, and the Flaxman Collection and Warburg Library at University College London. I thank Charles Dobree and Charles and Henrietta Malet who allowed me to study their ancestors and provided me with unparalleled assistance and guidance.

In America, I am indebted to the curators, librarians, and scholars at the Beinecke Library; the Brown University Library, with particular thanks to Karen Bouchard and Peter Harrington; the Metropolitan Museum of Art; the Sackler Archives at the Smithsonian Institution; the Yale Center for British Art, whose James Wales Archive inspired this book, with special thanks to Mark Aronson, Martina Droth, Elisabeth Fairman, and Gillian Forrester; and to the Yale University Art Gallery.

Multiple fellowships and institutions supported the research and writing for this book, including the American Institute of Indian Studies, Brown University, Dartmouth College, the Getty-ACLS, the Metropolitan Museum of Art, the Paul Mellon Centre for Studies in British Art, and Yale University – thank you. This includes the publication division of the Paul Mellon Centre; I sincerely thank the editor Emily Lees, the editorial assistant Tom Powell, and the copy-editor Katharine Ridler for producing this beautiful book.

There are longstanding friendships that sustain work, which ceases to be work after a while. To Dayanita Singh and Nomi Stone, your prompts have catalyzed much thought in this book and your insights thread through the pages; thank you for our joyful meandering conversations. To Laura Grey and Alex Kendall, who brought their skills in graphic design as well as their wisdom to this project, I give my heartfelt thanks.

My family by birth and by marriage has supported the drive to create this book, from graduate school to research journeys serious and whimsical. I am beyond grateful to my mother and father, Arline and Norman, as well as to my siblings, Lauren and Chip, and their spouses, Scott and May; to my mother- and father-in-law, Elizabeth and Randy, and brother-in-law Tim and his fiancée Anthea; to my grandmother Saundra, and my cousins Andy, Gisella, Liz, Ryan, and Vicky – thank you.

This book is dedicated to Andrew, my husband, who spiritedly talked through all of the ideas within it and patiently edited every single page, and to our son, Hugh, whose gestation inspired its completion.

Note on Translation and Transliteration

When referencing materials in languages other than English, I have italicized the words and included an English translation in the first citation and references to a published English translation of the work if available. All subsequent citations of the title are given in the English translation. Unless otherwise noted, the translations in this book are my own.

I have transliterated words from South Asian languages without diacritics in accordance with bibliographic conventions. In some cases, proper names have had different spellings in different periods, which I have indicated in the notes. In general, I have used the most common historical spellings.

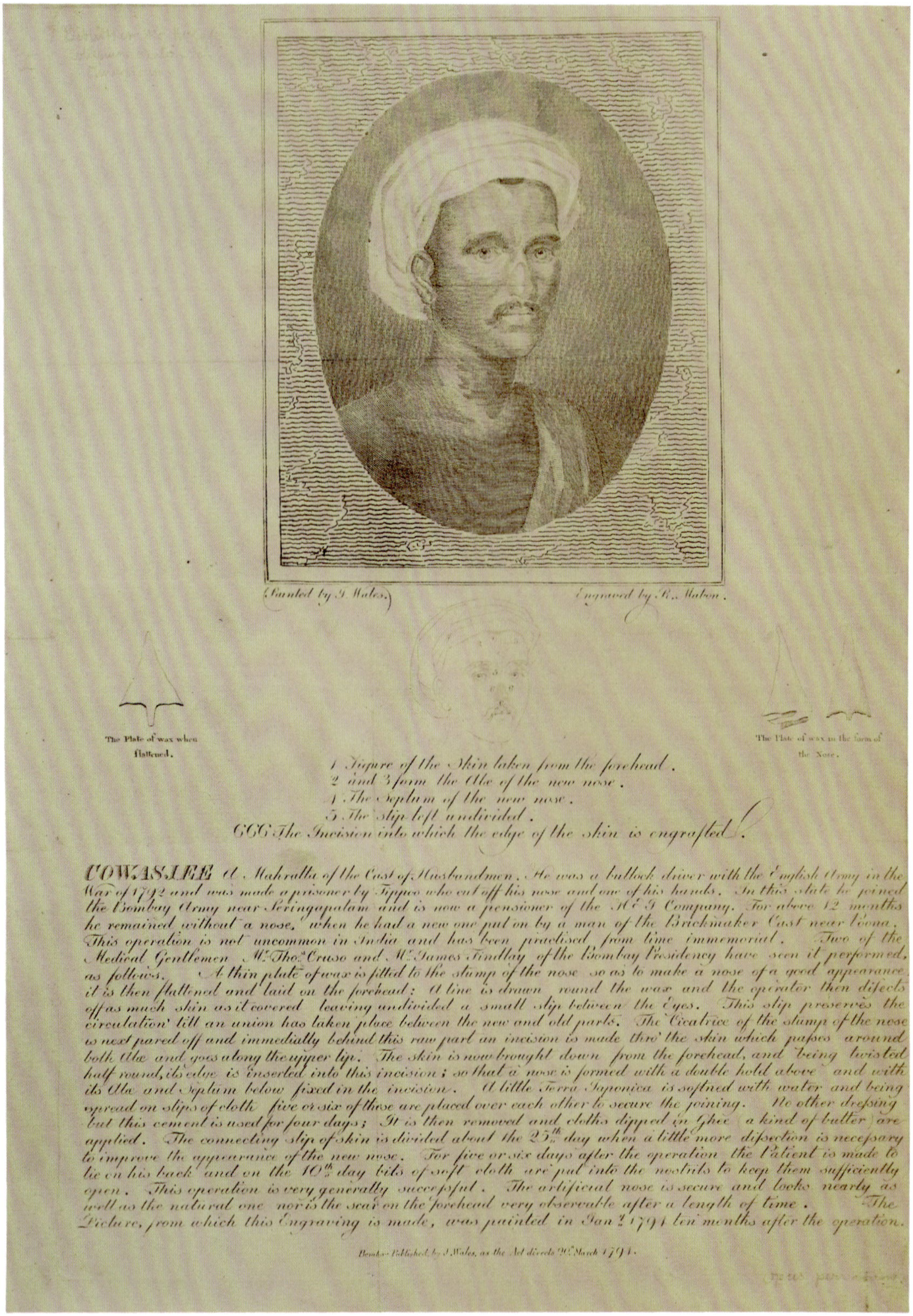

1 Robert Mabon after James Wales, *Cowasjee*, March 1794. Etching. Printed in Bombay by James Wales. Göttingen State and University Library, Göttingen

Introduction

In the 1790s, a Maratha bullock driver named Cowasjee who worked in the British East India Company Army in western India was captured by an enemy of the British, Tipu Sultan, the ruling "Tiger" of Mysore. Tipu's soldiers cut off his nose and one of his hands as a message of defeat. A Company soldier and draftsman Robert Mabon etched a portrait of this man after a painting, since lost, by his employer, the artist James Wales (fig. 1). It shows the violence that ensued from these wars, the information garnered from the alliance between the East India Company and the ruling Marathas of western India, and a remarkable procedure of repair. A Maratha surgeon sculpted a new nose out of wax, cut a triangle of skin from Cowasjee's forehead, twisted it down and over the modeled nose, and grafted it to his face.

Mabon was as skilled with an etching needle as he was with a pen: the portrait manages to show the sorrow and pride in Cowasjee's eyes as it does the shadow of the scar left on his forehead to the bridge of his new nose. In Marathi, one word for chopping off body parts is *kalam*, which also means a painter's brush, pen, or pencil, and the grafting of one thing onto another, like a bud to a tree or new skin to cover a wound.[1] The multiple parts of this definition should give us pause; they connect the means of bringing a picture into being with the forceful processes of excision and suture.

That the process of making art consists of layers and additions, some of which show the seams of accretions while others smooth them over, seems intuitive. In courtly artistry for the Marathas, artists built a drawing from lines or by copying another's design, added color, burnished the paint, adorned it with liquid gold or silver, punctured patterns or inlaid the iridescent wings of beetles to ornament. British artists working in the same region integrated preparatory drawings – sometimes made by a range of artists – to make a plan, adding another and another until it was ready to be sketched on canvas, brushed and layered with oil paint, dried, and then varnished. These artists depended on a pen, brush, or pencil, but also on sources and relationships. They learned models and techniques and developed collaborations, but in western India in the eighteenth century that often meant violently: through the stitching together of Maratha and British artistries, the plunder of forts or palaces for images or their purchase via other means of gain, or even by way of the platform of a person's face like that of Cowasjee.

To graft is a method of creation as much as it is one of taking. It is a process of production and collection as well as a relationship between a foreign body and a host that illuminates the political and artistic circumstances in western India in this period. As the Mughal empire fragmented in the eighteenth century, two regional powers – the Marathas and the British – fought for control of the subcontinent. The Marathas were military chiefs who rose to power in the seventeenth century and expanded their territories and revenues across west, central and north India, even into Mughal Delhi, in the eighteenth century. The English East India Company had also arrived in the 1600s; originally in India to trade, over the course of the eighteenth century it worked more like a semi-autonomous state. Beginning as mercenaries, bankers, and businessmen, the British became conquerors of the northeastern state of Bengal and from there, and outposts in Bombay (present-day Mumbai) and Madras (present-day Chennai), they sought rights, revenue, and territories across India in the second half of the eighteenth century.

The relationship between the Marathas and the British was forged in the crucible of this territorial contest, and it is in this period that the materials of this book are set. At times deadly foes and at others allies, the Marathas and the British chose to collaborate in the 1790s against their common enemy to the south, Tipu Sultan, who had stymied trade, and for the British at least, raised fear by courting the French.[2] Their brief alliance united transcultural diplomacy with the realities of combat. According to the treaty, the Marathas and the British would both send troops to attack, but they would also embed personnel like Cowasjee, artists like Robert Mabon and James Wales, and soldiers in each other's armies to aid communication, increase intelligence about the other, and of course to wage war.[3]

For instance, similar to the way that Cowasjee was a Maratha bullock driver in the Company army and became the medium of production for a surgeon and artists, the British soldier Edward Moor was a lieutenant in a Company regiment that fought from within the Maratha army and reported to its generals. From this vantage point, Moor became a collector of goods and data about Maratha devotion. Via loot, gift, or sale, he gathered a variety of iconic representations to satisfy his interest in the Hindu gods, but these objects were often damaged by age and war. "Not one subject is perfect," Moor wrote in one of his subsequent publications, "in some particular, sometimes trifling, there is a defect or fracture."[4] He gathered some of the hundreds of thousands of objects that were flushed out in the wars that consumed India in the eighteenth century. Many were damaged as a result, such as a statuette of the Hindu god Shiva and his consort Parvati, which has normal wear from devotees rubbing the reddish copper of the bronze (fig. 2), but also an abnormal

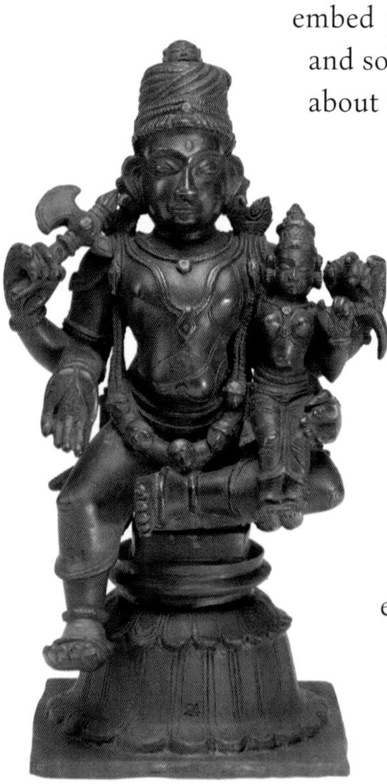

2 *Shiva and Parvati*, Maharashtra, 18th century. Bronze, h. 37.8 cm. British Museum, London, Edward Moor Collection, 1940,0716.23

separation from its base that marks a disturbance. Sieges, marches, and raids provided opportunities for a British official like Moor to plunder or purchase this bronze as well as to add to it. He had a tiered brass base cast in the shape of a lotus to complete the image; the two parts can be identified where the metal alloys meet.[5] This portable sculpture makes visible the damage and modifications that could result to itinerant objects, but it should remind us of injuries that also changed people, like those experienced by the bullock driver Cowasjee.

A THEORY, METHOD, AND HISTORY OF GRAFT

Much art in this region and period was produced in circumstances of war and diplomacy, which drew a wide array of people and objects together. This book conceptualizes these processes as ones of "graft": artists and collectors joined materials from diverse sources and groups – including those violently plundered as well as creatively sutured – to speak to diverse audiences as well as their own particular interests. By tracing grafted arts from multiple perspectives – Maratha and British, artist and patron, soldier and collector – this book charts the methods of empire-building that transformed artistic production and collection in western India and from there across India and in Britain.

Graft in English and *kalam* in Marathi are historical terms used by figures discussed in this book. James Wales described Cowasjee's surgery in medical terms, as skin "engrafted" onto the face, and Maratha writers used *kalam* to describe manners of painting, which demonstrates the word's artistic roots. Yet they did not use these terms explicitly to define their practices of making art, nor did they use another one to summarize their approach to artistry, even though they left ample visual and textual materials that illustrate their motivations to make and collect art. Methodologically, these materials can be brought together to reckon with the arts made by the Marathas and the British in western India, but they can also be productively theorized through a consideration of graft and *kalam*.

Graft is rooted in the Latin *graphium* (via *graff*), meaning to write (with a stylus); *kalam* (कलम) derives from the Persian and Arabic *qalam* (قلم), in turn descended from the Ethiopic, Aramaic, and Greek *kalamos*, or reed, including those reeds used for pens.[6] The material cutting of the pen or brush to write or paint aligns with the botanical quality of the term and extends to the medical. A young branch (scion) is grafted onto a stock (host) to produce a new plant, flower, or fruit, just as skin or a limb can be grafted to a receiving body to heal a wound.[7] The relationship between host and graft is therefore asymmetric. There are, however, aspects of these terms that are distinct in the different languages. In Marathi, *kalam* is identified with writing and painting, and in its botanical and medical definition, it extends to the removal of body parts. In English, "graft" came to mean corruption in the mid-nineteenth century, including the dishonest or illicit acquisition of goods, which I shall use in my application of the term, especially in Chapter Three.[8]

The themes that rest within these terms – an attention to processes of artistry, their connection to injury and innovative repair, problematic methods of acquisition, and the imbalance between graft and host – elucidate those that run through this book. One theme is artistic mixture. The protagonists of this project purposely joined different sources and materials and worked with others from a range of cultures and skill sets to promote artistic fusions. They created and collected arts in this manner to speak to diverse audiences, religious and political programs, and to satisfy individual concerns.

These processes of artistic grafting, however, were dependent on the penchant of both the Maratha rulers and the British East India Company for war, which is a second theme. In this period, Maratha and British diplomacy and the battles that ensued enabled lucrative trade, and became an additional source of profit by way of mercenary armies supplied to those paying or the reward reaped from conquered territories. This method of sucking the wealth from other domains to feed one's own has been termed a "vampire economy" by Kaushik Roy, a historian of the Marathas, or simply "anarchy" by William Dalrymple, a scholar of the British East India Company.[9]

Gain marks a third theme, which is inevitably paired with loss.[10] Graft simultaneously acknowledges the coercive means of gain, such as by loot or collection, while it also points to botanical, bodily, or even cultural additions. A foreign substance like wax or a bullet can become part of one's own self, but so can the people or lands that one encounters, perhaps even more so following separation, as with the loss of a limb. As words, graft and *kalam* in the form of the composite noun *nirvamshi kalam* reckon with the scars that form between loss and gain.[11]

The intersection of the Marathas and the British in western India offers an opportunity to trace why, and how, art was created, collected, and disseminated to be interpreted in myriad ways through visual and material mixtures. A Maratha painting layered over a British print emblematizes this process of grafting (fig. 3). An artist embellished the linear design of a British soldier on horseback with indigos, greens, pinks, yellows, and gold, and also made additions. The foreign soldier now dashes through a local terrain of flowering trees, birds, leaping antelope, and villages. The conditions that brought this print into the orbit of this artist were brutal – indeed its subject has his sword raised – but nevertheless the artist domesticated the content and rendered it charming.

Such artistic mixtures vary widely in their construction and references, but they were all created in an unrestrained context of empire-building whose conclusion had yet to be determined. Unlike north India, where the British had seized control of Bengal and annexed Awadh by the late eighteenth century, in western India the Marathas negotiated

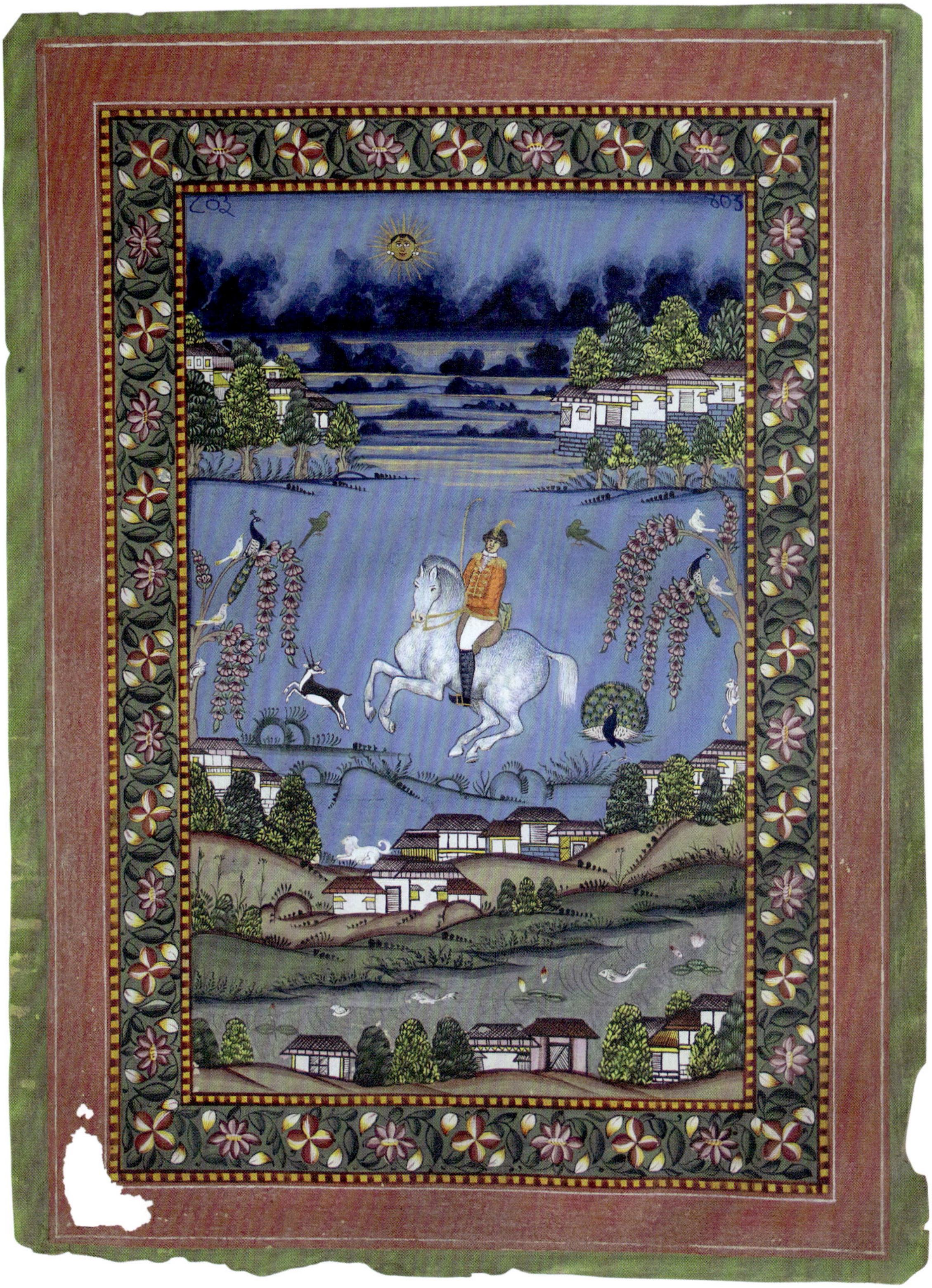

3 *British Soldier in an Indian Landscape*, Britain and Maharashtra, late 18th or early 19th century. Ink and opaque watercolor on printed paper, approx. 18 × 24 cm. Bharat Itihas Sanshodhak Mandal, Pune

with the British, whom they considered subservient to them, or repulsed them as adversaries. In this period, the Marathas and the British engaged in wary, but supplicative communications that spanned relationships among artists and patrons, ministers and generals, and circles of collectors, writers, and artists, who also ranged across Maratha, wider Indian, and British territories. By engaging the perspectives of different types of Maratha and Company actors as their tense dynamics shifted, I find the joints that connect art with empire.

Graft in its botanical and medical sense is a useful concept here as well. We might think of these relationships, and the artistic and collecting practices that ensued, as encompassing the surprising twining together of Maratha and British practices, along with the asymmetric connection of graft and host as when a branch is grafted onto a tree or a new limb onto a body. Maratha and British artists and patrons converged in their dialogues, but the Marathas also grafted British arts into theirs for distinct purposes, just as the British did with Maratha arts toward their own ends. Some of the branches fused and developed great charm while others rejected the joining or never took, were pruned, or sown entirely anew. A Maratha painting of a glimmering, upside-down tree visualizes this metaphor (fig. 4). It illustrates a passage in the Hindu epic, the Bhagavad Gita, in which the god Krishna discusses the need to chop away the illusions of the sensory world, which a devotee proceeds to do in the picture.[12] However, here I use the painting metaphorically to visualize how Maratha and Company artists, soldiers, deities, and artworks were grafted together in this period. This was a world turned topsy-turvy and dependent on uncertain alliances; a person must choose whether to be seduced by the tree's golden beauty, to remove a branch or develop a new bud, or whether to chop the whole tree down.

This book is organized around relationships among artists, patrons, and objects; it is through these that the means of art making and collecting become clear. Decades ago, Edward Said lamented in *Culture and Imperialism* (1994) that "little time is spent . . . studying the map of interactions, the actual and often productive traffic occurring on a day-by-day, and even minute-by-minute basis among states, societies, groups, identities."[13] In the field of art historical study, this provocation to create an imperial or colonial "map of interactions" has largely gone unheeded. Parul Dave Mukherji has proposed that if global art history "abandons its overarching story of progress and canonization and turns its gaze on the non-Western and postcolonial archive and its overlooked sites, it will have much to gain from a local and regional focus, which can best be conducted as case studies."[14]

Scholarship has addressed how arts produced within imperial contexts remade those in the metropole;[15] this project reconfigures western India, and its multiple vantage points, as a center from which to rethink artistic production and collection across India and Britain writ large. It identifies the actors who created, collected, entwined, sepa-

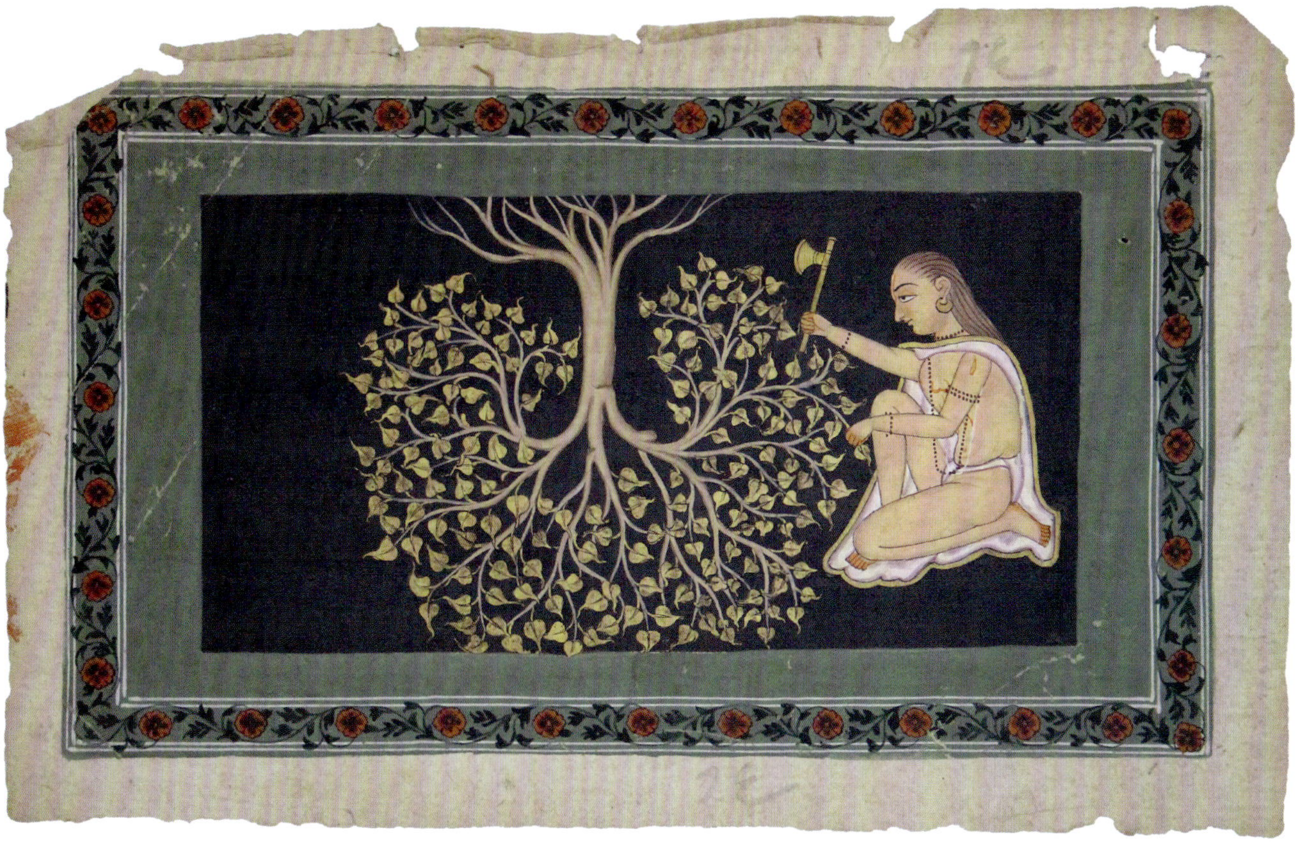

rated, and reproduced arts to build visual and material worlds that crossed hierarchies, cultures, and skills. It situates their artistic processes within the militaristic ones that undergirded their aspirations for empire.

I chart British and Maratha artists, patrons, and soldiers' methods and means of graft to propose that their mercenary, predatory, yet unboundedly clever model of mixed artistries counters court and academic ones of making identifiable, even branded, arts. Their arts, however, are often camouflaged by their mixtures, and thus they have remained indecipherable to scholars, or have been dismissed for the very fusions that make them fascinating. Maratha art has long puzzled art historians because of its unclassifiable "hybridity," while British art made in colonial contexts similarly has been written off as neither properly British nor Indian, or simply derivative.[16] These are critiques of Maratha and Company artistry, which from the earliest art historical commentary to today have been assessed negatively as "eclectic," agglomerations of too many disparate forms to be distinct, in contrast to an ideal of style identified in a renowned workshop or individual genius.[17] The colonial assessments of stylistic mixture were often underwritten by fears of

4 *The Upside-Down Tree from the Bhagavad Gita*, Maharashtra, 18th century. Opaque watercolor and gold on paper, approx. 16.5 × 25.5 cm. Bharat Itihas Sanshodhak Mandal, Pune

sexual or cultural mixtures, which postcolonial theorists also consider in their formulations of hybridity.[18] According to Homi Bhabha, a "third space" opens in the relationship between colonizer and colonized in which cultural subjectivity becomes mutually combined and constituted.[19] Although many of the arts in this book were produced during a period of fluctuating power between the Marathas and the British, and therefore before colonial control was established in western India, these earlier analyses raise the question of how the eclectic, working practices of artists – whose methods depend on the selection and mixture of materials – relate to spaces of cultural encounter.

This book identifies the artistic and military procedures behind these charges of eclecticism and hybridity against Maratha and Company arts; it details why, and how, people from widely different backgrounds purposely combined arts and created their contents anew. Through a framework of graft – and its suturing together of arts and wars, gains and losses – I conceptualize processes of cultural mixture as forceful, strategic, and specific to the field of artistic production and collection in which the dynamics between actors could shift, and combinatory techniques of art making were standard.[20] I also expand the term and methods of eclecticism beyond the realm of European aesthetic theory and academic discourse by locating a site of its artistic practice in the entanglement of Maratha and Company arts in western India.[21] The Marathas and the British both realized – though in different ways – that an eclectic method of artistic selection and combination was particularly well suited to the multivalent arts that the politics of empire required. This flips the script on nineteenth- and twentieth-century critics of eclecticism who contemptuously dismissed, on so-called aesthetic grounds, the very model that helped fuel their vast imperial and colonial economies and challenged the foundation of their arts.[22]

To reckon with these arts' multiplicity, I have collated a range of texts and images that remain from eighteenth-century western India. The fact that many records and objects have been destroyed or are dispersed across regional, national, and international collections has contributed to this region's status as an overlooked site.[23] The figures and objects that I draw together are those whom Marathi- and English-writing record-keepers and curators deemed relevant enough to maintain in papers and objects in archives, museums, historical societies, and collections. This means that some of the figures are well-known, and from middle to high rank, while others appear only once (like Cowasjee) or enter the story through their or others' drawings and notes, such as the artist Gangaram Tambat.[24] Gangaram worked for James Wales and Charles Warre Malet, the Company ambassador to the Marathas, but he also depicted himself, as in a striking self-portrait as a devotee (fig. 5; see also Chapter Two). Objects in turn survived for specific reasons, as with Edward Moor's attention to the Hindu gods, regardless of whether the representations he accessed were fragmentary (see fig. 2). Meanwhile, other histories become

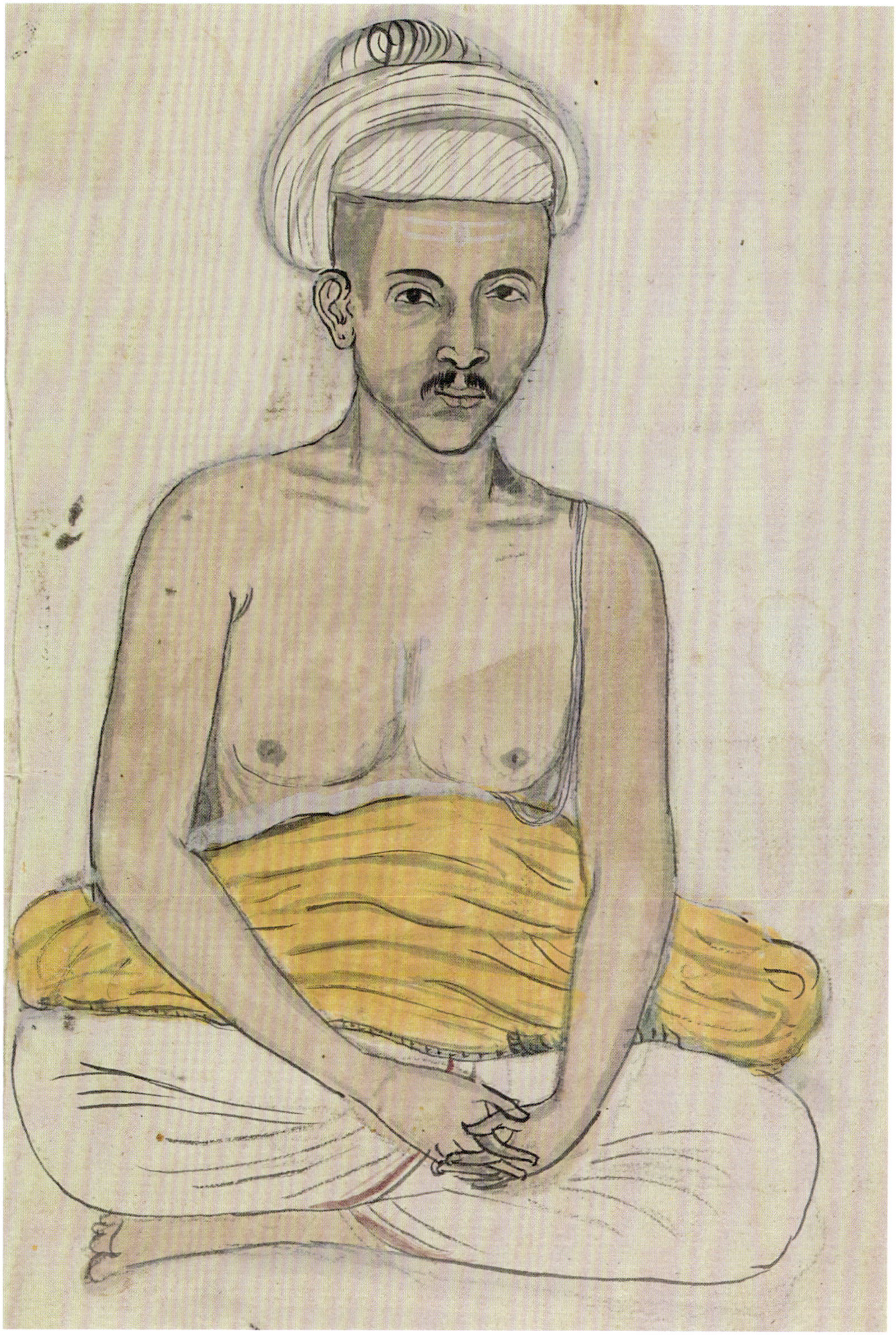

5 Gangaram Tambat, attrib., *Self-Portrait of Gangaram as a Devotee*, Poona, ca. 1790. Watercolor, gouache, and graphite with pen and black ink on paper, 22.9 × 15.2 cm. Yale Center for British Art, New Haven, Connecticut, Paul Mellon Collection, B1977.14.22417

evident through only a single line, like Robert Mabon's statement in one of his journals that it was "disagreeable circumstances" that brought him to India.[25]

These broken sculptures, single-line biographies, scrappy self-portraits, and etchings of wax-formed noses, which are ephemeral, marginal, and interstitial materials in a conventional account, are vital evidence for a history of art that gains shape through assembly and juxtaposition, and an attention to processes of graft. By joining the details of artistic practice with a range of private and public conditions of diplomacy and combat, this book identifies a mercenary method of artistry, and the resultant mixed and fractured arts, that thrived in western India in the eighteenth century. These arts emblematize how forms can transform by way of a different artist, patron, viewer, or troubling circumstance. Indeed, they continued to iterate across India and Britain over the nineteenth century either to consolidate empire or revolt against it entirely, and still remain instigators of nationalist agitation today.

ASSERTING ARTISTRIES

My focus on the political and material practices of making arts across cultures places this project within the broader "global" and "material" turn in the field of art history. Nebahat Avcioğlu and Barry Flood have articulated the relationships among "mobility, mercantile imperialism, and eclecticism" that changed the arts in the "globalizing eighteenth century."[26] Meredith Martin and Daniela Bleichmar, in turn, have emphasized the importance of "objects in motion," including the ingenuity of artists' craft and adaptation of "local idioms, traditions, genres and forms for distant audiences."[27] Their scholarship and that which they have gathered in edited journals, alongside incisive work on the British empire, such as by Douglas Fordham on aquatint, Natasha Eaton on color, and Mary Roberts on collecting, unite the global and material in studies of European artists working in Mughal India, Ottoman Turkey, imperial China or Indigenous artists working in Europe.[28] Yet few studies work from different points of view.

My project asserts a history of art in western India that integrates multiple perspectives and is materially granular. By drawing together conversations among British, Maratha, and other Indian artists, and assembling a diverse array of works across media, this book aims to understand how arts are mixed, fused, and grafted onto one another in a step-by-step, dialogic manner through relationships. In this sense, it seeks a "connected history" in the framework of Sanjay Subrahmanyam, but also a "disconnected history" in that of Zoltán Biedermann.[29] The Marathas and the British overlapped in their artistic productions, but they also diverged in their independent imperial and personal goals, particularly in terms of religion.

While this project participates in theoretical concerns across the discipline, it is also engaged with the history of eighteenth-century art in South Asia and the British empire. Although the Marathas rose to control much of India in the eighteenth century, their critics from that period till today have contrasted their military prowess with their supposed lack of artistry; their arts remain virtually unexplored by modern scholars.[30] My project addresses this lacuna in the study of South Asian art at the same time as it intervenes in the history of British art by focusing on western India as its center of inquiry with Britain a node in its network. Tim Barringer, Geoff Quilley, and Douglas Fordham have insisted that British art historians place empire "at the centre, rather than in the margins" of the field.[31] They, and others, have emphasized that the identification of a British "nation" is interdependent with artists working throughout the maritime "empire" and the range of arts that traveled home with Company officials.[32]

I build on these concepts of multidirectional flows, or "mimesis in flux" in Natasha Eaton's terminology, by unpacking the practices of Maratha and British artists and patrons in western India and the movement of objects to Britain.[33] In this, I also rethink the longstanding postcolonial question about the collaborative relationship between Indigenous and British colonial knowledge production in India, which in the history of art has specifically been identified with the Indian "Company" artist who worked for the British.[34] Through the workshop practices of the artists I discuss in this book, I redefine the Company term as a manner or style of making art (rather than the identity of a person) in which Indian artists grafted European artistic practices onto regional ones, just as British artists did with western Indian techniques onto their own methods of working.

My focus on transcultural artistic production complements innovative scholarship on other Indian regions. Scholars have traced the interactions between a variety of Indian and British figures and works, which provide a foil to the Marathas in terms of history, rank, patronage, and purpose. As Chanchal Dadlani has argued, the Mughals historicized their illustrious lineage to substantiate their legitimacy, and employed artists and architects to do so.[35] Rajput rulers in Rajasthan boasted genealogies, and invested in court workshops to support the arts, which invited new approaches to sensuality, emotion, and landscape in the eighteenth century.[36] Even rulers with short lineages, such as in Mysore, were capable of "visually asserting a notion of kingship and authority," according to Janaki Nair.[37] In contrast, Maratha and British officials in western India did not invest in a visually consistent formula to mark their respective and overlapping rules. Instead, these figures adjusted to opportunities and used the arts to negotiate vast, complicated, and often unstable relationships and terrains. This is a mercenary mode of art rather than a masterful one, but its program should be taken no less seriously.

THE MARATHAS AND THE BRITISH IN EIGHTEENTH-CENTURY INDIA

In focusing on the interactions of the Marathas and the British in western India, this book opens up a geography to study as well as a mercenary approach to politics, religion, and art. As the Mughal empire fragmented in the eighteenth century, the Marathas and the British rose to become two of the most significant military forces in India, as seen on a map showing the subcontinent in 1790 (fig. 6). "Maratha" most broadly defines the residents of the region where Marathi is primarily spoken, mostly in present-day Maharashtra. However, following the establishment of the Sultanates in the Deccan from the fourteenth century, "Maratha" came to signify a new martial elite drawn from the farming, craftworking, and shepherd communities who served the new kingdoms.[38] In the seventeenth century, while the Bijapur Sultanate was distracted by Mughal invasions, the Maratha military leader Shivaji Bhonsle took advantage; he founded an independent Maratha polity and was crowned Chhatrapati Maharaj in 1674, an event that gave a historical and dynastic specificity to the term "Maratha."[39]

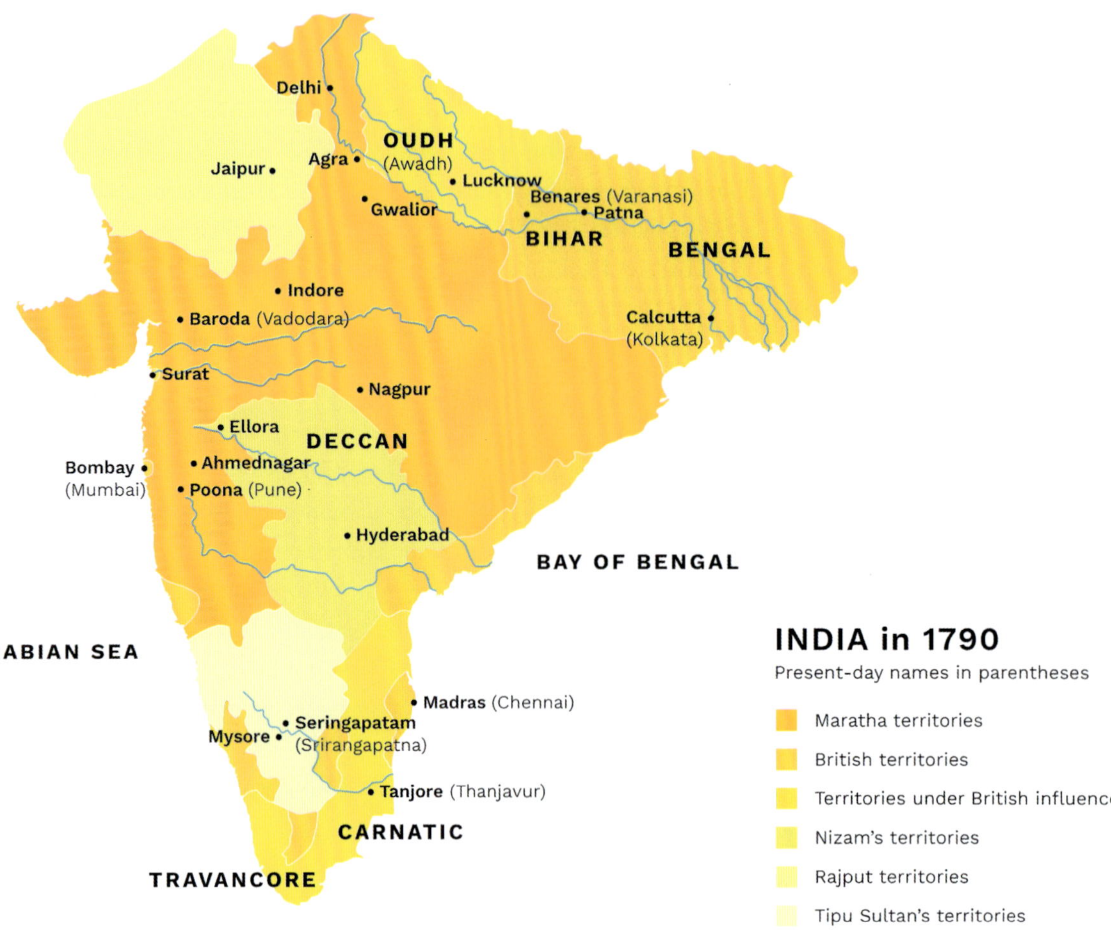

6 Map of India in 1790

In the eighteenth century, due to a series of succession crises, Maratha rule passed from the kings to their ministers, the Peshwas, who moved the capital to Poona (present-day Pune) in 1730, and Maratha generals who governed the lands the Marathas had conquered in western and central India. In this period, the Maratha empire was thus politically tied together by a confederacy of the Peshwa and Maratha generals who oversaw shifting mercenary armies.[40] These included Maratha, Arab, European, and Indian Muslim warriors, and an equally mixed group known as Pindaris who were, in Margot Finn's resonant phrase, "highly mobile freebooters," feared especially for their skills as light horsemen, armed with spears and matchlock guns.[41] The makeup of a mercenary army of entrepreneurial soldiers ready to change sides for an advantage parallels that of mercenary artists. Itinerant artists, as the modern artist K. G. Subramanyan insightfully wrote, are like "lightly armed soldiers" who can "graft motifs and styles" and "cross borders and change tactics without much effort."[42]

Religion was equally, and strategically, put toward imperial and populist ends. The Marathas encouraged a cultural and religious Hindu identity in literary, artistic, and administrative contexts.[43] In artistic spheres, the Marathas from Shivaji to the Peshwas aligned their rule with specific local gods and heroic narratives (see Chapter One). These intersected with other regional religious movements (see Chapter Three), including those of personal devotion (*bhakti*) to a god, such as forms of Vishnu, Shiva, or Devi, as well as pilgrimage routes to regional gods.[44] In the Peshwa period, which saw the ascendance of Brahmin rulers, Brahmin interpretations of religion were favored. These factors together fed an "emerging sense of a corporate Hindu identity," which, as scholars have argued, strictly adjudicated social interactions among castes and different religions, while also allowing for religious pluralism in general, since it supported political purposes.[45]

The Marathas were one of many regional powers who used religious differentiations alongside artistic and military ones in their bid for sovereignty during what scholars have called the "gentrification" and "localization" of the Mughal and Deccan empires in the seventeenth and eighteenth centuries.[46] As these empires fractured, those who had been in their service returned or succeeded to power (see fig. 6), such as the Marathas in western, central, and southeastern India, the Rajputs in Rajasthan, and the Mughal governors, or *nawabs*, in the northern Indian regions of Awadh and Bengal, while the Mughals retained control of Delhi. In the southwest, Haidar Ali, followed by his son, Tipu Sultan, fought to gain control of Mysore. In the eastern Deccan, Afghan rulers who had formerly worked for the Mughals established sovereignty as the Nizams of Hyderabad. These regimes primarily perpetuated a Mughal format of administration, while differentiating themselves through architecture and religion, and by promoting new technologies of warfare, banking systems, and agrarian management.[47]

Thus, how I define the Marathas as an "empire" in this book must be qualified. While they ruled "over a complex territorial polity," which as Krishan Kumar has recently summarized, is part of the basic definition of an "empire,"[48] they did not obtain the second part of the definition – "absolute sovereignty" – in this period in India.[49] Rather, they were an aspiring empire. They participated in a dispersed, often contested, system of government founded on the organization of disparate soldiers to control western and central India.

The same qualified definition of empire can also be applied to the East India Company in this period. Their realm stretched "over a complex territorial polity" from the British Isles, to parts of India, America, and the South Pacific. But in India the British, like the Marathas, certainly did not have absolute sovereignty.[50] Composed of multiple figures in its charter, the Company had initially been incorporated through joint-stock investments in 1600. By the eighteenth century, it ran as a semi-autonomous state under the board of directors in London and a network in India unified by the governor-general in Calcutta (present-day Kolkata) in the northeast region of Bengal.[51] He oversaw governors at trading depots on the coasts such as in Bombay and Madras and diplomats, known as Residents, installed at key Indian courts. Initially in India to secure trade, over the course of the eighteenth century the Company also gained territorial revenue in Bengal and political power in Awadh and the Carnatic by lending money and running an army that was not only made up of British soldiers and Indian and European mercenaries as diverse as the Maratha army (in fact many like the Pindaris shifted sides), but was also hired by other rulers to serve as their mercenary army.[52]

In western and southern India, the Company fought with some rulers, such as Tipu Sultan, the Marathas, and the Nizams, and strategically allied with others, including those same Marathas and Nizams, to solidify British interests across India. While the Company initially sought to keep religion out of politics, by the nineteenth century Christian policies, including missionary permission to proselytize in India and political and disciplinary ones that classified peoples according to religion, increased as colonial control was established.[53] However, in the eighteenth century, Company officials, like the Marathas, participated in a dispersed system of government that hinged on the organization of disparate soldiers in mercenary troops, in parallel with an accumulative style of artistic production and collection.

In fact, the relationship between the Marathas and the British began with a Maratha request for British mercenary troops and proceeded from there. As their interactions were complex, I will briefly detail internecine Maratha politics in order to approach the question of their arts.[54] In the second quarter of the eighteenth century, the Peshwas had become the de facto rulers of a confederacy of Maratha generals and governors. Then in 1761, the Marathas suffered a major defeat at the Battle of Panipat, outside of Delhi.

Soon after, the Peshwa Nana Saheb died, and his seventeen-year old son, Madhavrao, succeeded him. However, Nana Saheb's brother Raghunathrao, who had initially served as the principal adviser to the young Peshwa, decided to raise his own army after Madhavrao began to assert his authority. Eventually, the Peshwa had his uncle imprisoned, but Madhavrao died in 1773, and Raghunathrao instigated the assassination of the Peshwa's son, Narayanrao, and became Peshwa himself. However, the powerful minister Nana Fadnavis successfully deposed him in favor of Narayanrao's as yet unborn child, Savai Madhavrao.

This succession shows the fluctuations within the regime in the second half of the eighteenth century, but also one primary way the Marathas became involved with the British. In exchange for 2,500 troops to fight other Maratha factions, Raghunathrao ceded tracts of Gujarat as well as the islands of Salsette and Bassein (home to the famed rock-carved temples of the region discussed in Chapter Two) to the Company. The British alliance with Raghunathrao began a seven-year dispute with the government in Poona, led by Nana Fadnavis and the child Peshwa Savai Madhavrao, which became known as the First Anglo-Maratha War (1775–82). Nana Fadnavis and the Peshwa won and signed the Treaty of Salbai in 1782, which inaugurated peace between the two Maratha factions as well as the British for twenty years, until the Second Anglo-Maratha War of 1803–5, and the last of 1817–18 that resulted in British control of the subcontinent.

However, in precisely the same period, the Marathas and the British also became allies. The Company fought the First Anglo-Mysore war against Haidar Ali from 1767 to 1769, in which the Marathas, the Nizam of Hyderabad, and the British continually changed sides; the Second followed just over a decade later, from 1780 to 1784, but resulted in a draw. The historical background for this book is the Third Anglo-Mysore war (1790–92), which saw the British establish more solid alliances with the Marathas and the Nizam, though I will focus on the former. While the British troops were led by Charles Cornwallis, the Governor-General of India (who had recently suffered defeat in the American Revolutionary War), the Company also sought Indian allies. To negotiate a treaty with the Marathas against Tipu Sultan, the Company requested that a Resident be posted to the Poona court, with which the court complied.

The British appointed Charles Warre Malet who took up his post in 1785, serving until 1797. His residence at the court prompted the artistic dialogues and exchanges that are at the core of this book, particularly in relation to the Maratha minister Nana Fadnavis, his regent, Peshwa Savai Madhavrao, the British artist James Wales, the soldier-draftsman Robert Mabon, and the local Poona artist Gangaram Tambat, whom Malet and Wales employed. While Nana Fadnavis and Malet were in charge of diplomacy in Poona, bullock drivers like Cowasjee and soldiers like Edward Moor took to the field. Moor especially provided a perspective from the military side as compared to that of diplomacy in Poona, and opened up the market for objects and their reuse, in contrast with dialogues among artists and patrons.

All of these interactions, from those that flourished within diplomatic conditions to those of battle, were not only aspirational but also transactional. Each participant sought to gain something from the other, and thus the perspective of the agent of each of the relationships that I discuss can be shifted from the inside to branch in multiple directions. This is part of the project of graft – which branch hosts the sapling can switch. I parse these changing relationships, alongside the multivalent creation and collection of arts, in the individual chapters of this book.

CHAPTER STRUCTURE

The book is organized to begin with the formulation of Maratha arts at the Poona court, including their grafting of British arts, to the joint constitution of Maratha and British arts, to the British grafting of Maratha arts in India and use of Maratha arts to reconceive those in Britain. Each of the five chapters also has a particular focus, from patrons to artists, objects, and their reformulation and regeneration. Therefore, through different perspectives and processes of graft, the book attends to both Maratha and British arts separately, and as they overlapped and informed one another, to recognize the complex procedures of these arts.

Chapter One is concerned with patronage. It begins in the latter half of the eighteenth century with the Marathas, and Nana Fadnavis's diverse collection of art from regions with which he was politically engaged. After discussing the development of an eclectic Maratha aesthetic tied to conquest and diplomacy as well as religion through Nana Fadnavis's patronage, I home in on the artistry of the arts produced. I focus on the Marathas' employment of James Wales to paint academic-style oil portraits that asserted Mughal-invested honors as well as Hindu devotional status.

Chapter Two turns from the patron to the artist, specifically Gangaram Tambat, who worked for Malet to draw the life and scenery of western India, including animals in Maratha grounds, bouts of wrestlers at court, and the extraordinary rock-cut temples of the region. Gangaram's watercolors, drawings, and sculptures substantiated Malet's political projects and Wales's antiquarian ones in the service of acquiring colonial knowledge about western India. However, at the same time that this artist participated in European forms of representation, he also altered how his British patrons deciphered and published aspects of Indian art and culture through his experience and artistry. In current terminology, Gangaram would be called a "Company" painter; I use this opportunity to redefine the term and the artistic production related to the British in India.

Chapter Three expands from the attention to patrons and artists to objects. It is concerned with the complexity of collecting and plundering practices in a marketplace of "men and gods, and things," in the words of Edward Moor. As a result of the Anglo-Maratha alliance, Moor's military movements converged with routes of pilgrims and the transfer of booty. He began to collect, evaluate, and sell jewelry, manuscripts, coins, and Hindu devotional arts. His collection preserves the objects and transactions of a little-understood but remarkably diverse market for arts in eighteenth-century India, while it also points toward his colonial engagement with Hindu "mythology."

Chapter Four traces the process of how this soldier's collection of western Indian objects came to illustrate *The Hindu Pantheon* (1810) in London. It therefore focuses on reformulation. Using western Indian materials, Moor's book transformed the monist Hindu philosophy that Company orientalists had discussed in text into the neoclassical design promoted by artists in the circle of his publisher Joseph Johnson, like Henry Fuseli and William Blake. Indeed, the book inspired Blake to imagine an anti-tyrannical British history through other mythologies, but it was also used by Christian missionaries bent on converting Hindus. Thus, Maratha arts were remade to take two divergent paths toward a propagation of religious difference or as a means of regeneration and the recognition of similitudes between east and west.

The book is structured to explore the Maratha and Britain's East India Company collection and patronage of arts, as well as the practices of artists, as they developed independently and overlapped through patrons, artists, objects, and their reformulation. Chapter Five draws all of the chapters together through the late nineteenth-century regeneration of these earlier materials. In this period, western Indian nationalists collected many of the eighteenth-century materials that I discuss throughout the book but put them toward a distinctly anti-colonial purpose. They founded the Chitrashala Press (Art School/Gallery) to educate a western Indian population through chromolithographs whose aesthetic diversity, they believed, would enable the unity necessary among varied groups to resist the British colonial project.

These nationalists and printers used these arts to foment discord as well as revolution, but I also use their reinterpretations to conclude the book. By conceptualizing graft and *kalam*, my goal is to draw attention to the rich varied arts that formed in western India, and were plundered from there, as well as to the artistic and military procedures that stitched them together. That these processes were mercenary is uncomfortable, that they kept changing according to the graft or the host is too, but they present a way to make visible the roots and branches from which they were sutured, and therefore also of their subsequent graftings, which can provide an art historical model for thinking about mixture as well as regeneration.

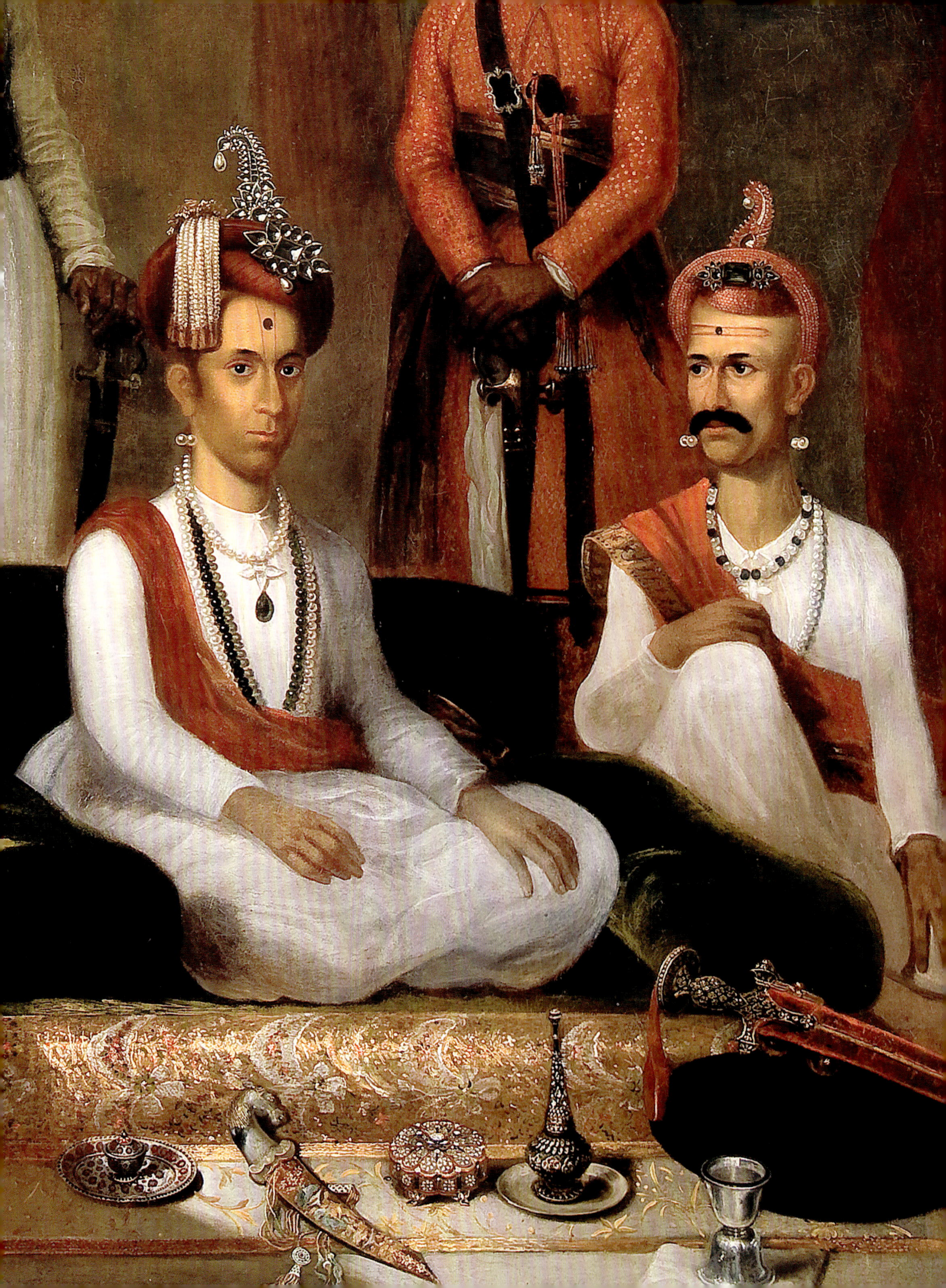

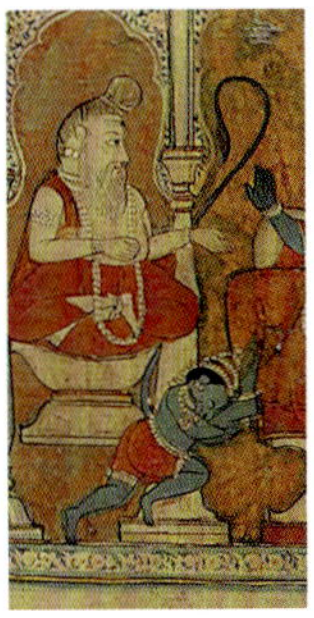

CHAPTER ONE

"Take all of them": A Patron at the Poona Court

"I was early disposed to worship the deity," wrote Nana Fadnavis, a nineteen-year-old administrator at the Maratha court in Poona in western India, in his 1761 autobiography. His piety attracted him to art. As a child, he recalled, he possessed "the habit of forming lumps of clay into the shapes which are commonly ... in the temples." Dissatisfied with these results, he was led to pilfer and "often stole the household images of the family ... and carried them away to some secret place.[1]

As the Marathas conquered territories across India in the eighteenth century, and Fadnavis's authority increased, this early engagement with art objects – the making and taking of religious representations – evolved into an impressive program of commissions and acquisitions, encompassing not only the divine realm of the Hindu gods but also more worldly spheres. His desire for art was profoundly felt and of considerable sophistication, but it could also be ruthless. In 1786, for instance, he discovered that a neighboring family owned a fine series of paintings. He ordered his officials to ask surreptitiously about the pictures, and when the family was away, to search the house and "take all of them."[2]

Nana Fadnavis's command is a succinct expression of his appetite for works of art, but the phrase suggests something greater about his sensibility that can elucidate the arts produced for the Marathas in this period and the role of the patron and collector within them. To "take all of them" suggests a practice of collection that depended on

Details of fig. 25 (opposite) and fig. 19 (above)

modes of acquisition connected to military force and diplomatic negotiation as well as artistic production. Fadnavis, and others at the Poona court, not only collected varied arts but they also hired artists from across India and Britain to "take all" portraits, both of men and of gods, in a range of representations.

The collection of practitioners alongside artistic models served as a catalyst for Maratha artistic endeavors. Artists played a key role in negotiating the diverse needs of their employers through combining sources, mixing styles, and engaging in a workshop type of manufacture. In the first part of this chapter, I focus on patrons at the Poona court, specifically Nana Fadnavis, to identify their motives for artistic production. In the second, I turn to the practices of the artists that they hired, including those at the court, like Sabaji Anant, and those at the British Residency, like James Wales. These artists were encouraged to engage in an artistic dialogue with one another, but Wales also hired Indian and British artists with varied skills to anticipate what his patrons desired. The penchant for patrons to graft works of art as well as the techniques of artists together – and for artists to do the same – informed a transcultural agenda of collecting and patronage at the Poona court. This program was not only conversant with sacred and profane spheres, as Fadnavis's writings signal, but also deliberately eschewed strict stylistic categories to inaugurate an aesthetic of the eclectic rather than the unique.

A STRATEGY OF ACQUISITION AND PATRONAGE

In the middle of the eighteenth century, at the peak of Maratha power, Nana Fadnavis showed himself to have a passion for art, which he exercised through acquisitions during his and his fellow administrators' travels. In Persian, *fadnavis* means "maker of lists," indicating an accountant and financial administrator, and Nana Fadnavis, born Ballaji Janardan Bhanu in 1742, had a gift for this role.[3] He became one of the most powerful ministers of the Maratha polity. In his autobiography, one of the earliest in Marathi, he narrates his life, from his childhood experiments with making and pilfering images to his journey north with the Maratha army to confront the threat of the Afghans in 1760. His route began at a temple in Toka, in the central Indian region of Maharashtra, where he sought to suppress a teenage boy's "propensity to the society of loose females" with acts of veneration.[4] He then continued with his young wife and his mother to Mathura and Vrindavan, two villages "thickly studded with branches and leaves," where the Hindu god Krishna spent his childhood in playful mischief, fought demons, and sported with the cow-herding girls known as *gopis*. Nana Fadnavis "bathed in the very pool where the divine [K]rishna crushed the serpent Kalya ... visited several temples ... [and] rolled in the soft sand-hills ... which still remain[ed] as in the time of the god." Having atoned for his desire and performed his devotions, he continued to Delhi, where he "purchased a number of pictures," and, in line with his earlier efforts took "care to make a selection free from all immodest and indecent representation."[5]

Noting (remarkably in such a short text) these purchases, he says nothing about their form and little about their content. Yet by examining the pictures that he bought at this, or a later, date, it becomes clear that Fadnavis sought Mughal paintings of the finest quality that he could obtain, particularly those that portrayed religious subjects rather than "indecent" ones.[6] Fadnavis's collection is dispersed, but parts of it can be traced in extant images and texts, including sixteen Mughal paintings that remain from one of his albums that is now held in the Chhatrapati Shivaji Maharaj Vastu Sangrahalaya (CSMVS), Mumbai.[7] Drawn in the seventeenth and eighteenth centuries, they appear to have been collected and set in densely floriated golden borders by Fadnavis or his agents in the latter half of the eighteenth century.[8]

The subjects of the paintings relate to devotion in multiple religious practices and royal piety. For two pictures, the artists creatively adapted European prints of the Christian Holy Family; one shows the Virgin Mary draped in pearls and with an Indian *bindi* on her forehead (fig. 7).[9] Groups of Sufis in meditation or chanting prayer, yoginis playing music, and one dervish tipped over from too much drink are represented in five images. The Mughal emperor Jahangir (r. 1605–27) is displayed at the Sufi shrine at Ajmer at three stages of life: distributing alms, feeding the slow-baked rice and meat dish *biryani* to the poor, and, in old age, on pilgrimage there. An attention to royal genealogy is apparent in the album. Besides the narratives of Jahangir, it includes portraits of the Mughal emperors, from Babur (r. 1526–30) and his son Humayun (r. 1530–40; 1555–6) to Shah Jahan (r. 1628–58), and another fine equestrian portrait of Muhammad Shah, who ruled during Fadnavis's childhood.[10] The paintings that remain from this album match Fadnavis's preference for avoiding "immodest" pictures, and confirm that he sought to emulate elite Mughal practices of collecting, rearranging, and reframing exquisite paintings in albums, known as *muraqqa'*, from an early age.[11] He could realize these projects because of his and other officials' mobility, and the strong Maratha military presence in Delhi.

Nana Fadnavis's journey with his fellow Marathas from Maharashtra to Delhi ended in disaster. The general Sadashivrao Bhau, "though wise, valiant and experienced, had latterly become proud and arrogant," according to Fadnavis's account.[12] He had not anticipated the forces under the Afghan ruler Ahmad Shah Abdali, who had organized an alliance with the Nawab of Awadh to take Delhi, which the Marathas had recently occupied. On January 15, 1761, Afghan troops "dismounted from their horses, and stormed the camp on all sides" at the Maratha encampment at Panipat. A confused cyclone of a Mughal painting exhibits the blurred smoke of the cannons as the Afghan and Nawab armies

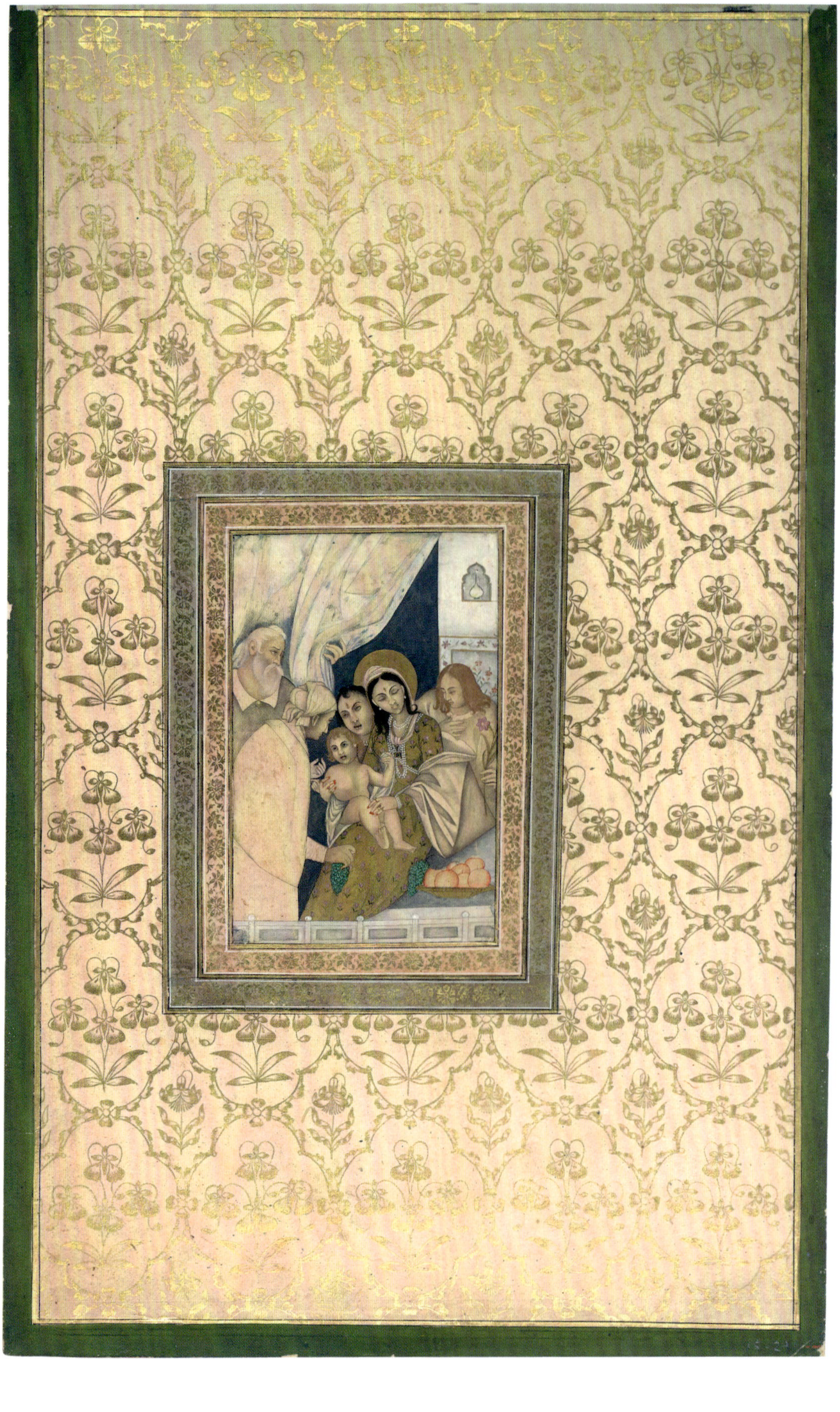

breach the curved lines of the Maratha camp (fig. 8).[13] The two spots of color consist of the blue-green foliage just outside the high turreted walls of Delhi on the verge of pillage, the women inside already victim to rape, and the pink-clad figure of Ahmad Shah, poised on his beautiful brown stallion. A chalky white pigment has been smeared over a dying Sadashivrao Bhau. His eyes are closed and his body slipping, as if his spirit has paled and fled from the wound in his chest. "The battle was now brought to cuts and slashes," Fadnavis wrote, and everyone still alive fled.[14] In a single battle, the Marathas' territory was drastically reduced and their prestige destroyed. Fadnavis stripped to a loincloth and disguised himself as an ascetic, hiding in the tall grasses. Taking a circuitous route, he was able to return to Poona.

Over the next few decades, Fadnavis rose through the ranks. He became the confidant and minister to the new Peshwa, Madhavrao (r. 1761–72) – who strove to regain the territories that the Marathas had lost after the defeat at Panipat – and subsequently the regent to the newborn son of Madhavrao's successor, Narayanrao, Savai Madhavrao (r. 1774–95), who succeeded his father after a series of crises. Madhavrao was also a patron of the arts; in 1764, for example, he constructed a special hall for musical performances that he had decorated with thirty-six paintings of music known as a *ragamala*.[15] He also leaned on Fadnavis to carry out his commissions of adornment. In 1767, when the Peshwa constructed a new home in Poona, Hira Bagh, he instructed Fadnavis to "have the female apartments over the terrace of the new pleasure house prettily painted . . . so that they may be worth looking at." Further, he left this "entirely" to Fadnavis's "own taste."[16] Indeed, a portrait of the Peshwa by one Bhojraj, a painter from Jaipur who was hired during this period, remains extant as a testament to the arts that were patronized under Madhavrao's reign, and moved through the channels presided over by Fadnavis.[17]

The story of Fadnavis's own collecting and patronage practice resurfaces after Panipat primarily in letters to Mahadji Scindia, a prominent Maratha general.[18] Scindia had also escaped from Panipat, and after recovering from the rout managed to regain much of North India with his impeccably trained troops.[19] He defeated the Afghans and the Jats between 1770 and 1772, and reinstated the Mughal emperor Shah Alam II on the throne in Delhi.[20] In 1784, Shah Alam II again summoned Scindia to protect the Mughals. After these successes, Scindia was awarded, under the Peshwa's aegis, the title of *vakil al-mutlaq* (regent of the Mughals), which included the right to collect tribute in Awadh and in Rajput states such as Jaipur.[21]

Maratha officials seeking to purchase or plunder objects found in newly accessible locations documented the movements of generals like Mahadji Scindia in letters – and so did artists. Works made in Delhi and Jaipur, for instance, attest to Scindia's presence in these places. Ramjidas Chitara, an artist at the Jaipur court, drew Scindia confidently

7 *Madonna and Child*, *Mughal*, 1620–30. Opaque watercolor and gold on paper, with border, 55.5 × 34.9 cm; without border, 16.6 × 11.2 cm. Courtesy of the Trustees of the Chhatrapati Shivaji Maharaj Vastu Sangrahalaya formerly Prince of Wales Museum of Western Mumbai

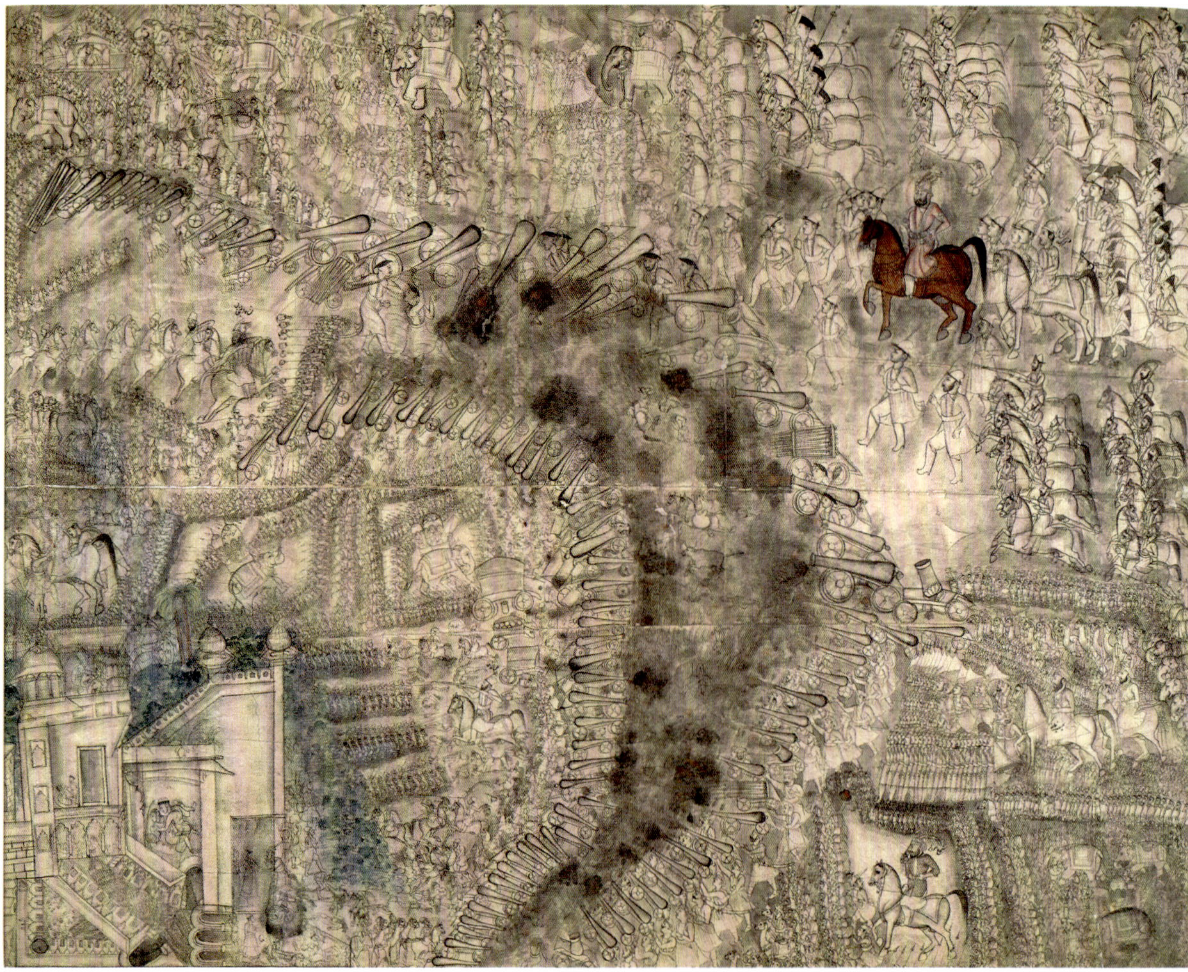

astride a horse, his right hand parallel to the picture plane, holding a falcon (fig. 9).[22] Yet we might imagine Scindia clutching a portfolio of paintings: taking advantage of Scindia's position and influence, Fadnavis regularly requested that the general acquire paintings and hire artists in his domains.

Jaipur, for instance, was renowned for its arts, and Fadnavis sought Scindia's aid in wooing artists and purchasing works from that city, often through surreptitious means. For example, Scindia arranged for Bhojraj Minegar, an artist skilled in enamel work, to travel south from Jaipur to Poona and then to return; two hundred rupees were given to him for his expenses.[23] Surely for selling his trade to rivals, Bhojraj was arrested when he reached Jaipur and was ordered to pay a fee. Scindia was able to negotiate his release, but Bhojraj does not seem to have been able to travel again to Poona. "Without the Maharaja's permission no

8 *Battle of Panipat, January 13, 1761*, Faizabad, ca. 1761. Drawing with some colour on paper backed with cloth, 51 × 66 cm. British Library, London, Johnson Album 66,3

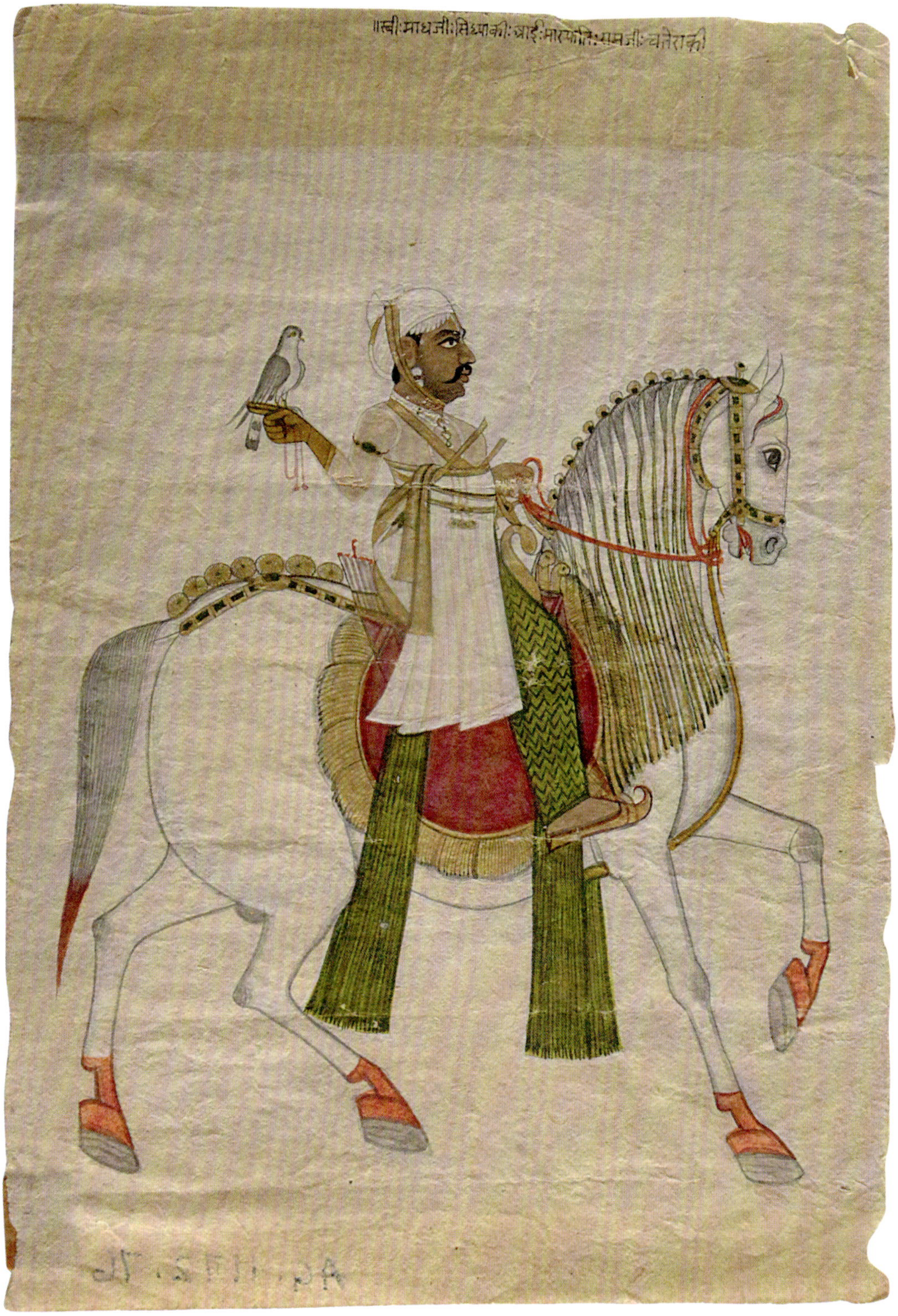

9 Ramjidas Chitara, *Mahadji Scindia*, Jaipur, late 18th century. Ink and watercolor on paper, 19.2 × 13.8 cm. Maharaja Sawai Man Singh II Museum Trust, The City Palace, Jaipur

one can leave or go outside the city," one of Scindia's agents lamented, but he did not give up hope: "Bhojraj cleverly should be brought. We are busy with this work."[24]

In addition to cultivating artists, Scindia also tried to procure paintings in accordance with Fadnavis's orders. This followed a precedent of Maratha rulers seeking paintings from Jaipur from the early eighteenth century. Records in Jaipur show Shahu Maharaj Bhonsle purchasing "pictures of paper . . . with color" from the painting workshop in 1716.[25] By the late eighteenth century, Scindia was pursuing the acquisition of the Jaipur Maharaja Pratap Singh's heavily illustrated manuscript of the *Bhagavata Purana*, the tales of Krishna's childhood and adolescence set in the landscape that Fadnavis had visited on his way to Delhi. One letter between Scindia and Fadnavis's agents admitted that the "taking of the *pothi* [manuscript] . . . will happen secretly"; however, it is unknown whether Fadnavis was successful.[26] The agents also shrewdly sought to obtain paintings in Delhi, with the aim of gaining those from the Jaipur collection.[27] Wary of fraud, Fadnavis's agent discussed this process with Scindia's: "We have sent to Delhi skillful examiners to see whether the paintings are authentic or not." Deception must have been a worry, for he concluded, "We will not delay the affairs or be lazy."[28]

Further correspondence between Fadnavis and his assistants reveals a desire to secure religious images, a task that proved remarkably difficult. "We need to get the album of the paintings of gods," Fadnavis wrote to his assistant Sankaraja Satyadeva in 1783. "For this get the really good pictures of Shri Krishna done by old painters like Nidhamal who painted in Delhi. Buy them, have the golden borders made, make an album . . . carefully . . . whatever price it is."[29] Satyadeva discovered that Nidhamal had left Delhi for Lucknow after the Battle of Panipat and had died there; his sons remained but were not as talented as their father. He had searched for images (*tasvir*) that could be used for meditative devotion (*dhyana*), like those of the Hindu god Krishna that one Devrao Tatya had given to Nana Fadnavis. Unfortunately, Satyadeva wrote in response to Fadnavis's request, he had not been able to find such images in Delhi. The type of meditative picture he mentions, though, offers a tantalizing clue as to what Fadnavis might have required in a devotional painting. Muslim artists, he noted, were painting such works, but they did so in the style of the time and he did not approve.[30] "Agra has become a really barren city," Scindia's administrator Sadashiv Dinkar wrote in correspondence with Nana Fadnavis in this period. "The painters . . . don't have the power to do artistic things . . . Delhi is better . . . but these ornaments still aren't found."[31]

We know, then, that Nana Fadnavis hunted for the finest Mughal and Jaipur paintings, especially those that depicted deities or devotional scenes.[32] Yet only a single large-scale work of the Hindu gods that relates to late Mughal painting is extant from Fadnavis's collection (fig. 10). The palatial complex is depicted in sharp perspective in a palette of

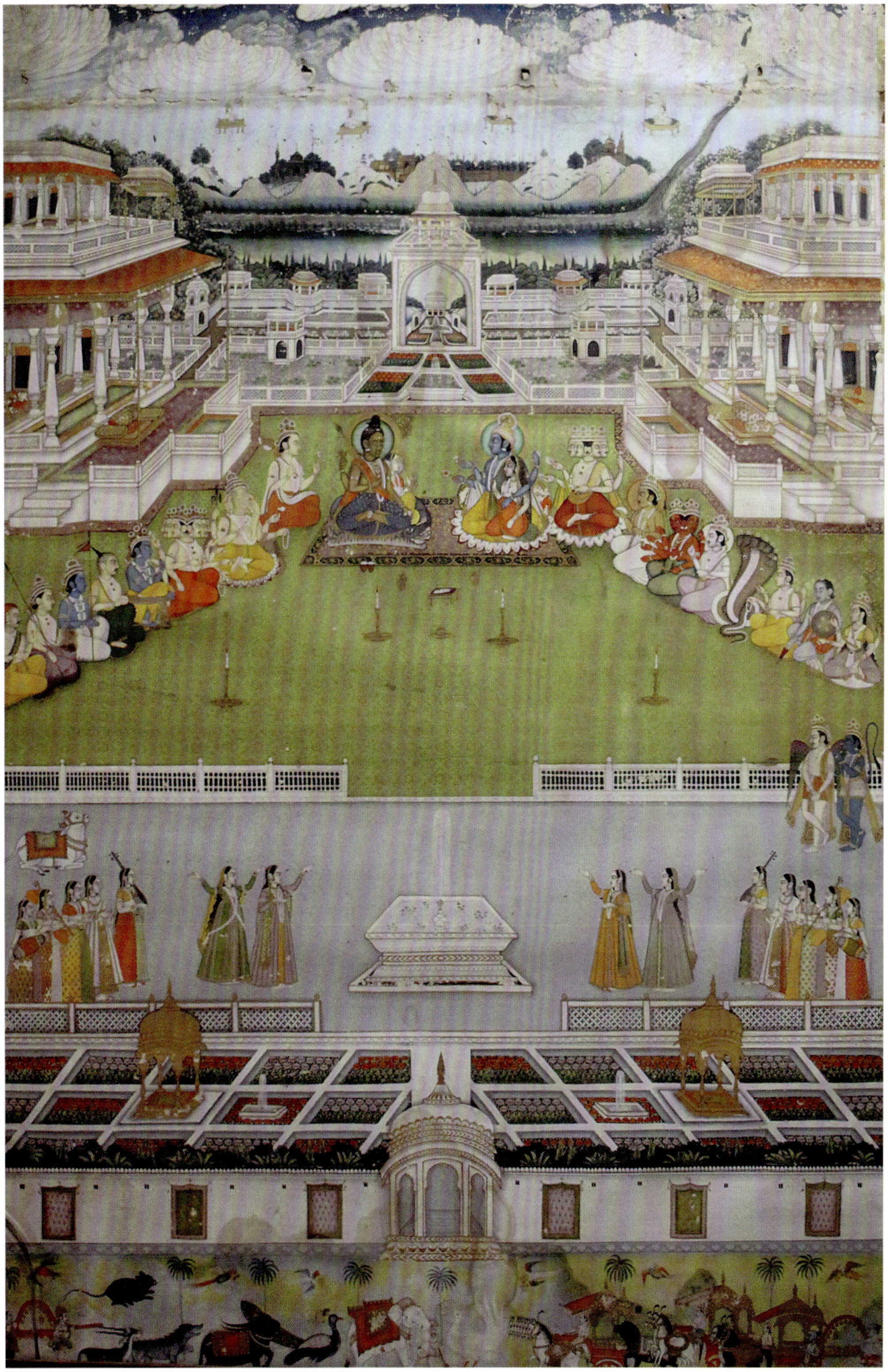

10 *A Meeting of the Gods,* Maharashtra, late 18th century. Shrub and organic colors and gold on handmade paper, 76.2 × 106.7 cm. Phadnis Family Collection

white and pastel tones, with puffy clouds floating over a mountainous landscape. The work mirrors the composition of late Mughal paintings produced in Delhi and Awadh in the 1770s, such as a setting of a palatial garden in which a woman entertains a princess by balancing a bottle on her head (Chester Beatty Library, Dublin).[33] Yet the scene in Fadnavis's picture is not one of entertainment. Rather, it is a conference of the gods, with Shiva and Parvati, Vishnu and Lakshmi at the center, and other regional gods, heroes, and sages in attendance.[34] Prayer books rest on a central platform inscribed with "Shri Rama, Shri Rama," as if the meeting had been called to invoke Rama, Vishnu's incarnation as ideal king and statesman and analogue to Fadnavis's desired role at the Poona court, and invite him to the court's counterpart, the celestial palace.

Painters in North India were capable of doing such work;[35] but perhaps these types of icons did not satisfy Fadnavis's standards (as Satyadeva wrote about those depicting Krishna from this region[36]). The deities in Fadnavis's painting are inconsistent with the background. They wear crowns typical of Maharashtra, tiered and adorned with pearls. On the far right, the goddess's dress is pulled up at the ankles, indicating local female dress, the nine-yard sari. Some garments are outlined in a deeper color, a quality typical of local depictions, and seen strikingly in the figure of the red-skinned, fire-breathing god Agni. Deities are, moreover, drawn in a local manner. Ganesha, for example, has arms that radiate out from the elbow and his skin is of a single color, unlike in many paintings made further north, where he is shown as having two-toned skin.[37] These features of the painting are puzzling. The most likely explanation is that north Indian artists working for the Poona court created the background while those locally trained depicted the gem-colored gods. Another possibility is that the background of this painting was made by late Mughal artists in north India, purchased by Maratha agents, and completed by local artists in western India.

Such a picture is a remarkable example of invention in the face of competing desires. Fadnavis wanted, on the one hand, late Mughal paintings and, on the other, paintings of specific Hindu gods holding court. In the absence of an acceptable late Mughal painting of the Hindu gods, the artists in his employment grafted significant regional deities who invite just rule to a court with a late Mughal composition of a pleasure palace. This painting exemplifies Nana Fadnavis's eclectic practices of artistic collection and production. Maratha routes of conquest opened up collections for plunder or purchase, and provided opportunities to hire artists from a range of locales. As one patron, Nana Fadnavis took advantage of these circumstances to build albums of exceptional paintings for his personal collection, but he also grafted together diverse works to formulate a political iconography for the Poona court and his position within it.

A WORLDLY AND DEVOTIONAL PROGRAM OF WALL PAINTING

The wall paintings in one of Nana Fadnavis's homes further emblematize the diverse types of artistic mixtures favored by patrons at the Poona court and deepen our understanding of their symbolism. Murals of gods were deemed auspicious and meritorious throughout India and prescribed by religious leaders in Maharashtra, but they could also serve a political purpose.[38] Those in Fadnavis's home connect the arts of Indian courts with which Fadnavis and the Marathas were engaged militarily to the nascent political and religious iconography of the Poona court's rule. Their tendency to project power through a blend of courtly and divine representations aligned with that of other rulers across India in this period, but their method of plucking and combining diverse styles and subjects – as well as the specificity of the iconography – was particular to the Maratha realm.

Fadnavis built his two-story mansion (*wada*) along with two temples, one dedicated to Vishnu and the other to Shiva – in accordance with the minister's heritage and his family's devotion – on the banks of the river Krishna in the village of Menavali in the Satara district of Maharashtra in the 1770s.[39] Constructed of teakwood, with long, flat brick-and-mud walls and packed dirt floors, the home contains a series of rooms arranged around open courtyards, three of which are painted. Early twentieth-century drawings of the house, made by the modernist architect D. R. Chowdhari as a student at the Sir J. J. College of Architecture in Mumbai to document prominent homes in Maharashtra, offer cross and longitudinal sections of the house and a floor plan of the rooms (figs. 11 and 12).[40] A rectangular room in the upper right-hand quarters that Chowdhari labeled "Ladies Room" (see fig. 12), situated on the second story, above the family's home shrine, is painted with gods, including Vishnu, Shiva, Ganesha, Surya, and Durga who are worshipped together as five deities, or a *panchayatan*, by the Chitpavan community of Brahmins, to which Nana Fadnavis and the Peshwa belonged.[41]

From the northern entrance, directly across the room and above the door, the sun god Surya, the origin of Fadnavis's genealogy, or *suryavamsha*, instructs a sage in the Vedas (fig. 13).[42] Surya's golden chariot rides through coconut palm trees along the Konkan coast, the homeland of his family, the Bhanus. On the left, Krishna and his eight wives, giving visual form to pleasure, balance the image on the right of Rama in court, an emblem of statecraft – as if mythologizing the sexual proclivities that Fadnavis's autobiography claims he had sought to control with the self-discipline most evident in his administrative abilities. Across from Surya is another expression of council; Krishna drives Arjuna's chariot to the epic battle in the *Mahabharata* and offers him advice. They traverse a pink and turquoise mountain, which encloses the warrior goddess Durga (whom the Fadnavis family worship as a family deity, or *kuladevata*) and the ascetic god Dattatreya.[43] During a conversation

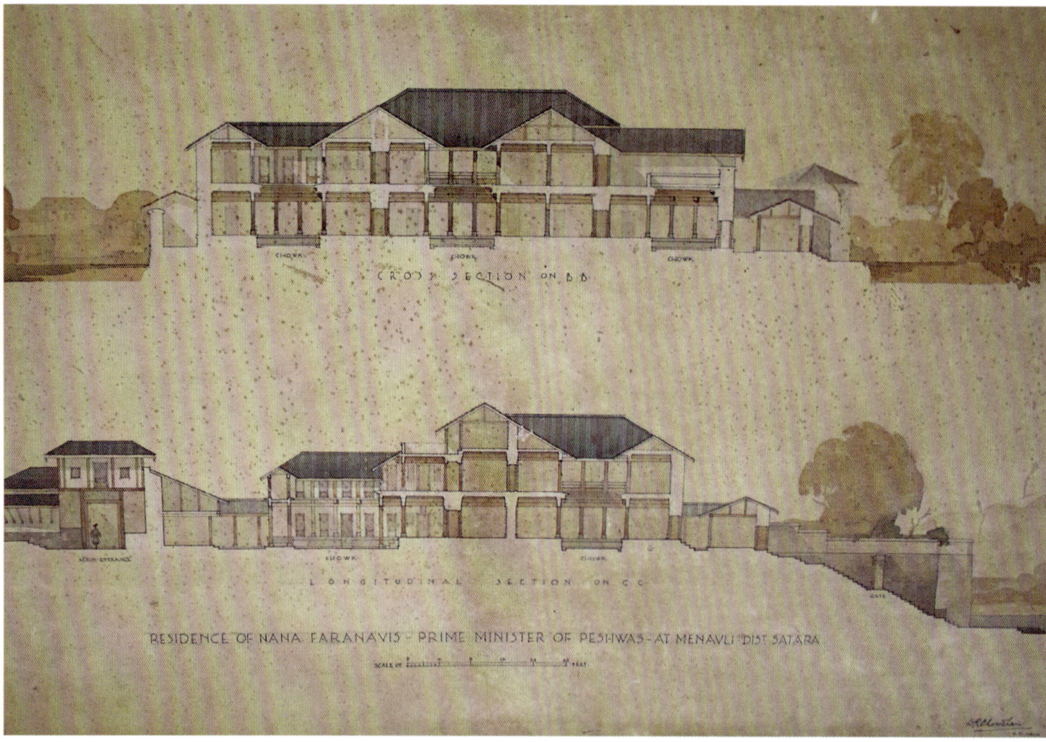

with Arjuna, Krishna narrates his incarnations as Vishnu. In this room, Vishnu's avatars start from the left, on the wall facing the Krishna River flowing outside the window.

Significantly, Vishnu's sixth avatar, the Brahmin Parashurama, is in the center, as if a manifestation of the patron, Nana Fadnavis and his community of Chitpavan Brahmins (fig. 14). The Chitpavan trace their origins to Parashurama, who, like many of the figures and artworks I have discussed, has varied characteristics. An incarnation of Vishnu, Parashurama is also a great devotee of Shiva; a Brahmin from the caste of priests, he also has the qualities of a warrior.[44] Vishnu was incarnated as Parashurama to defeat the caste of warriors and kings (*Kshatriya*). In the aftermath of their defeat, he gave the world to the sage Kashyapa and created the Konkan coast of western India for himself, populating it with the Chitpavan who became warriors and administrators, like Nana Fadnavis.

On the opposite wall, two groups of deities inhabit the neighborhood. On the left, Shiva sits with his wife Parvati and their elephant-headed child, Ganesha, above an ascetic's retreat, possibly the nearby hermitage of Dhom.[45] Behind rise the temple towers of the town of Wai, such as the conical Ganesha temple built in 1762, which is next to Menavali.[46] Above the window onto the courtyard, Vishnu rests atop the serpent Shesha (fig. 15);

11 D. R. Chowdhari, *Cross and Longitudinal Section of the Residence of Nana Faranavis – Prime Minister of Peshwas – at Menavli, District Satara*, 1929–46. Pen, graphite, and watercolor on paper, approx. 63.5 × 89 cm. Sir J. J. College of Architecture, Mumbai

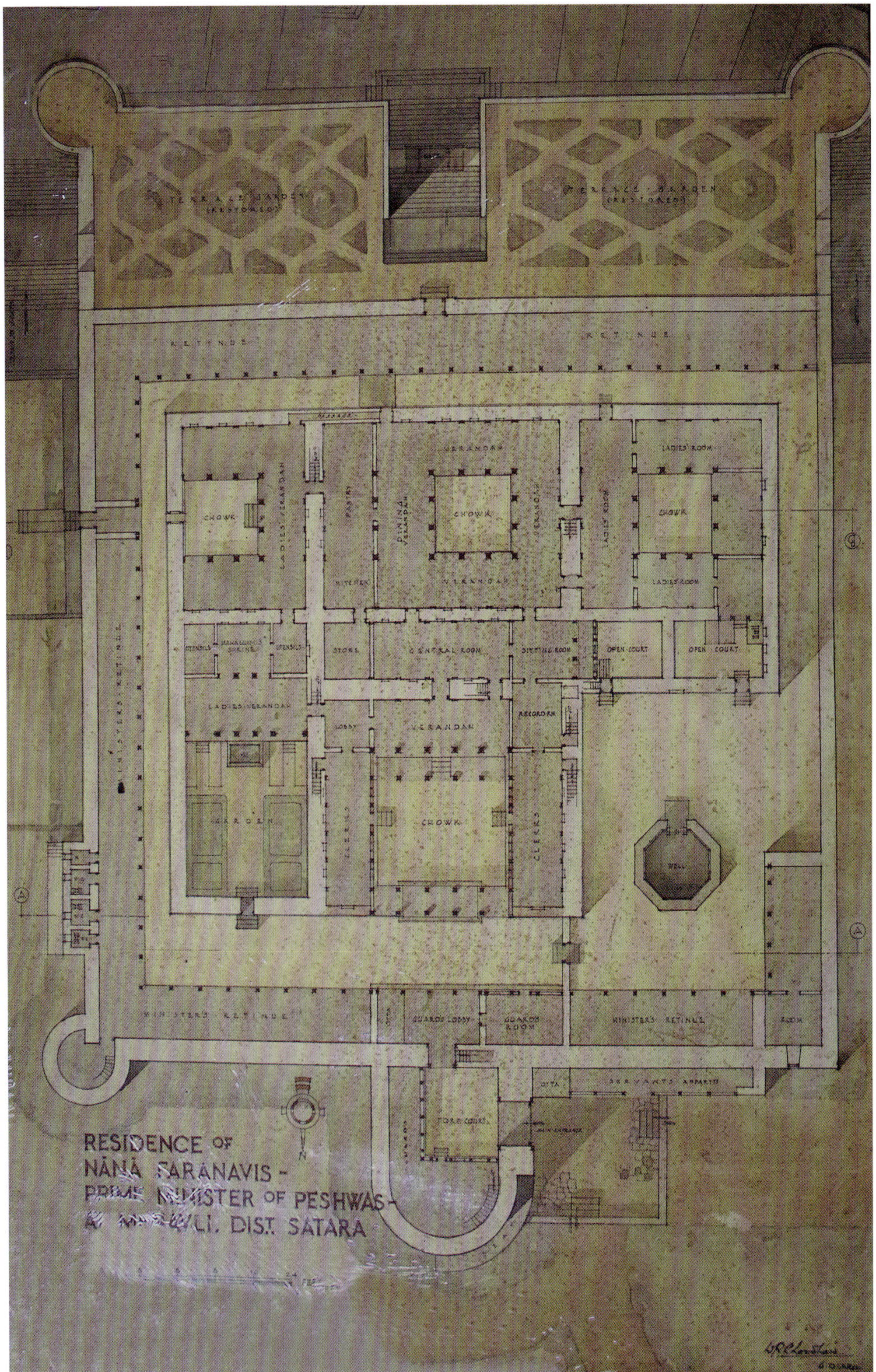

12 D. R. Chowdhari, *Floor Plan of the Residence of Nana Faranavis – Prime Minister of Peshwas – at Menavli, District Satara*, 1929–46. Pen, graphite, and watercolor on paper, approx. 63.5 × 89 cm. Sir J. J. College of Architecture, Mumbai

13 (Overleaf) Wall paintings of Krishna Ashtanayika (left), Surya (center), and Rama and Sita in Durbar (right), ca. 1770–1800. Nana Fadnavis Wada, Menavali, Maharashtra

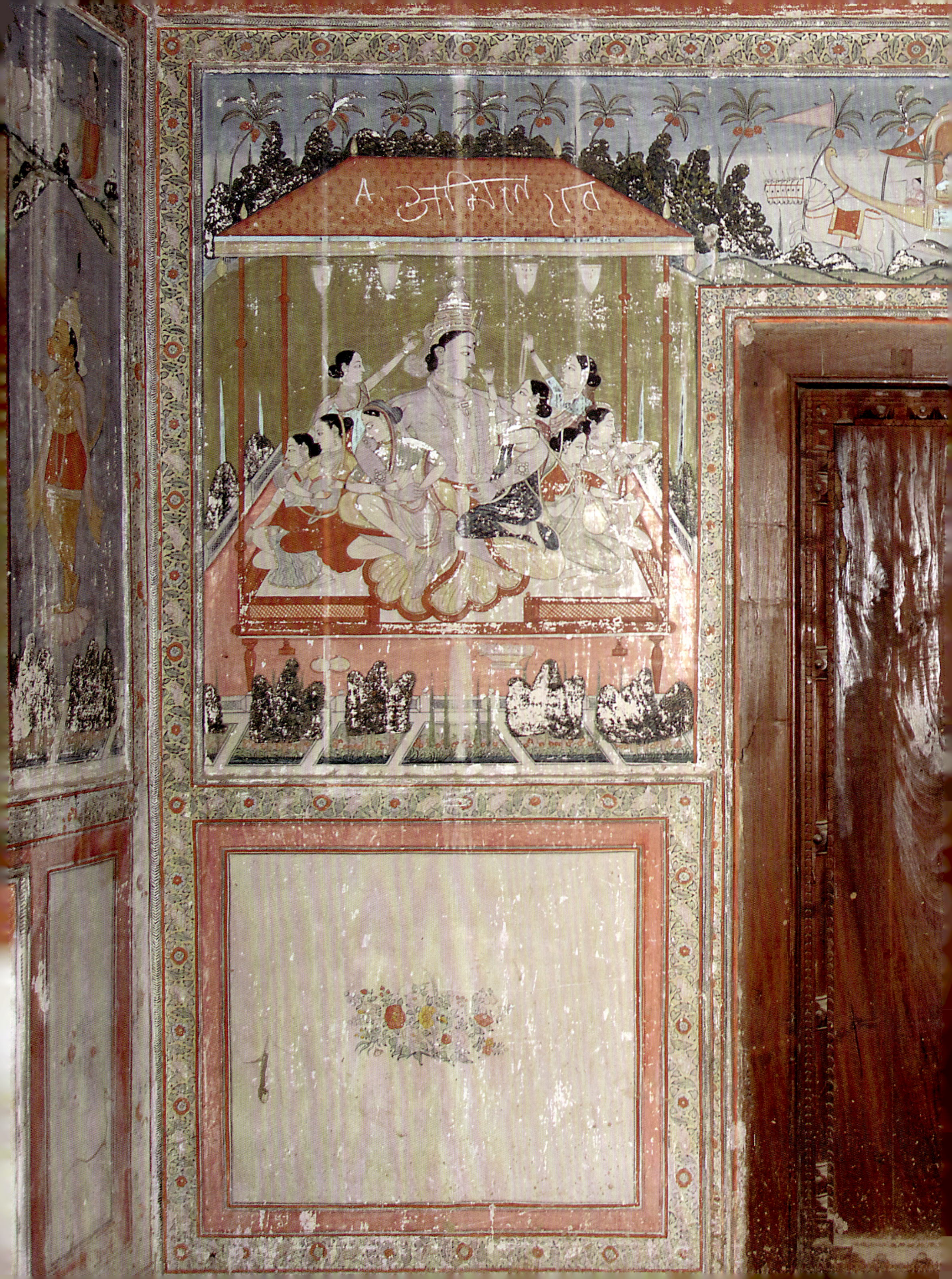

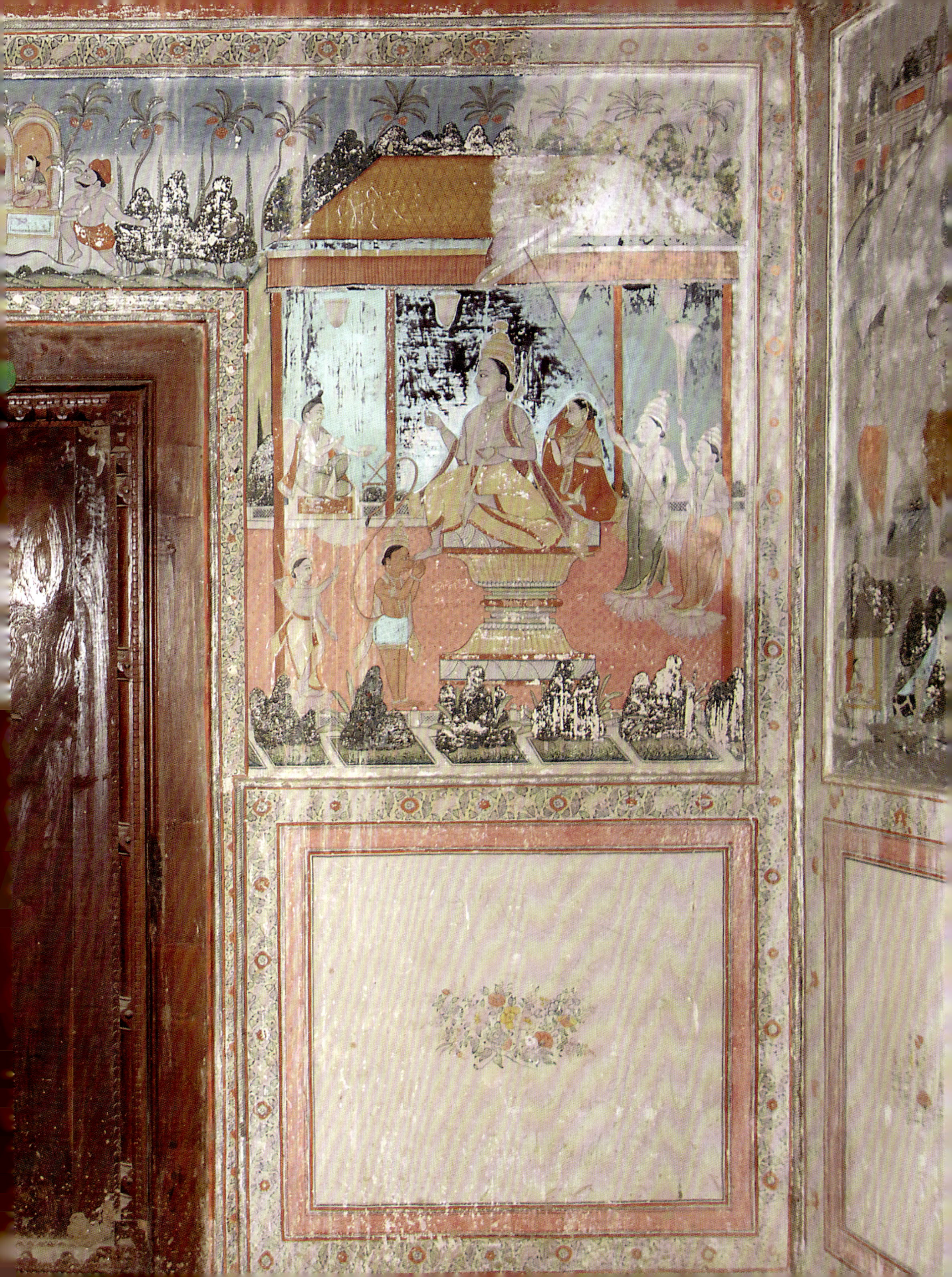

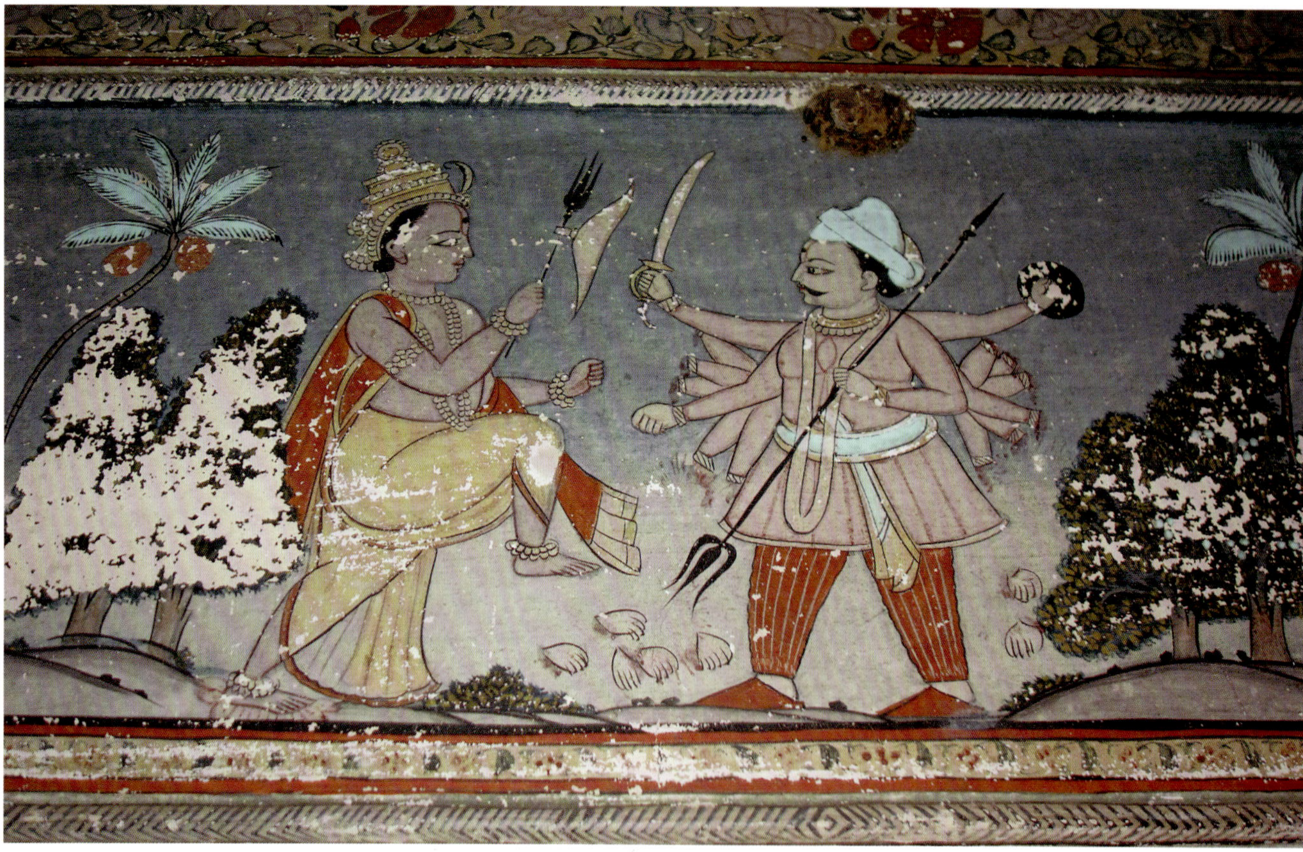

he is the origin of the regeneration of each age by means of the incarnations depicted on the opposite wall. On the right, Ganesha is enthroned in front of Fadnavis's own home – where the viewers are located – its windows flung open (fig. 16).

The painted landscape represents the divine and the worldly; the deities held in reverence by Nana Fadnavis (see fig. 10) inhabit the same terrains that he and his ancestors do on the walls, just as they do in his home and the adjacent temples he constructed on the riverbanks. The mural balances domestic scenes of sensual pleasure, play, and fecundity with ones that also bear political import. There are overt references to advisers such as Krishna and Surya – who align with Fadnavis in his role as adviser to the Peshwa – and to a ruler's balance of Krishna's sensual play with Rama's representation of statecraft of the sort sought by Fadnavis. Further, the deity who inhabits the most intimate landscape here is Ganesha, remover of obstacles and household god of the Peshwas, who rose in prominence under their rule.[47] Earthly, devotional, and political prospects mingle just as they do in Fadnavis's autobiography, his art collection, and his home.[48]

14 Wall painting of the Dasavatara (ten incarnations of Vishnu), ca. 1770–1800. Nana Fadnavis Wada, Menavali, Maharashtra

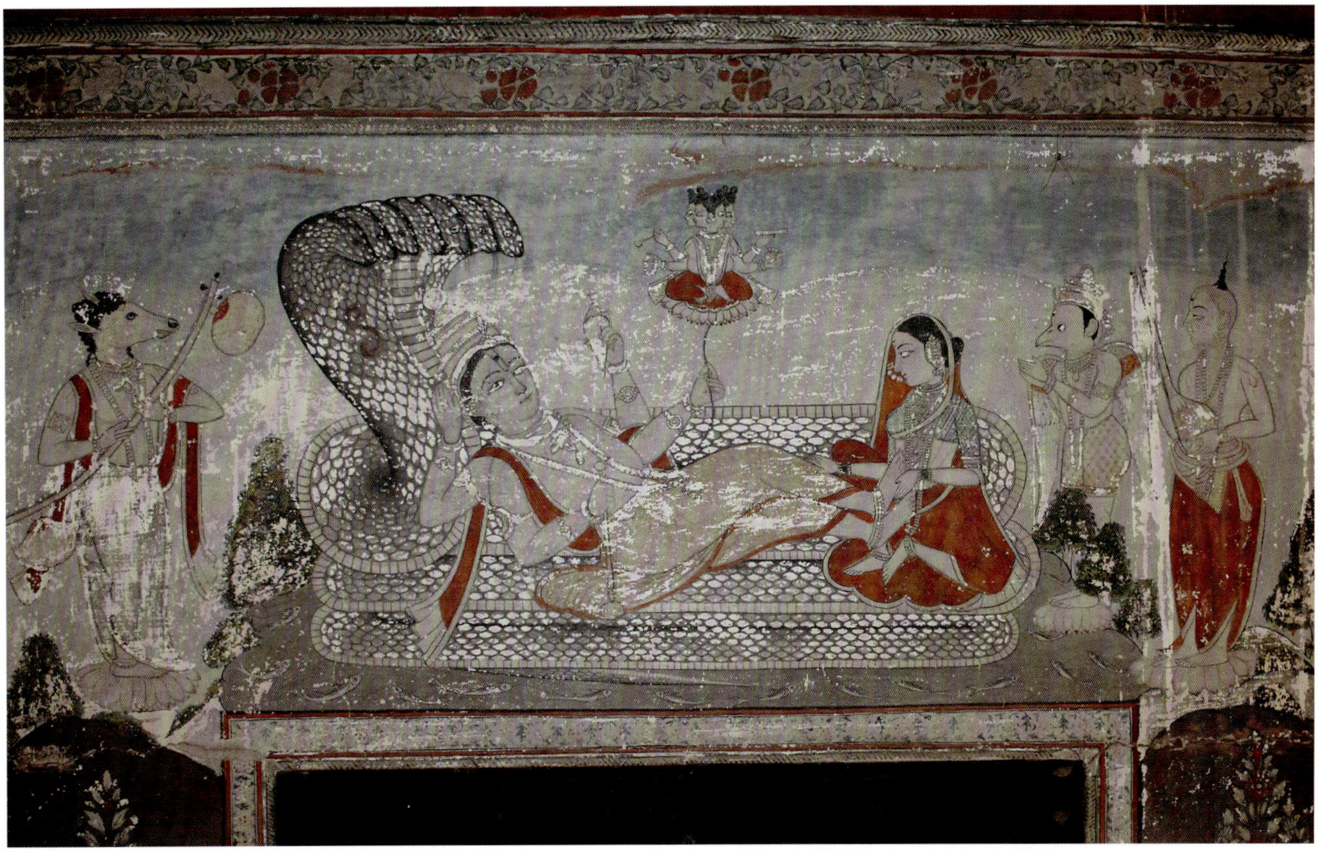

These paintings emphasize piety, sensuality, and the administration in which Nana Fadnavis participated on a symbolic level, but they also show artists blending local and transregional styles in their production. The murals exhibit a mix of Mughal, Deccan, and Rajput courtly qualities in the ashy pastel palette, twisting postures, and robust forms that fuse with popular local examples, indicating that the artists – who are not known by name – were familiar with traditions in the Poona region, in Mughal territories in the north, and in ones to the east and south in the Deccan.[49] The clothing and ornamentation, for instance, are local – the women wear nine-yard saris and wrap their braids into a bun known as a *kopa*, while crowns are three-tiered and adorned with pearls – as are certain iconographic choices.[50] The painters may have been from Maharashtra and received training elsewhere, or they could have migrated to the region and became familiar with its customs.

Fadnavis patronized artists from multiple localities. A second rectangular room in the lower left area of his home, a verandah that opens onto a garden, has traces of paintings in an idiom popular in Maharashtra (see fig. 12; the room is labeled "Ladies Verandah").

15 Wall painting of Vishnu resting on the serpent Shesha, ca. 1770–1800. Nana Fadnavis Wada, Menavali, Maharashtra

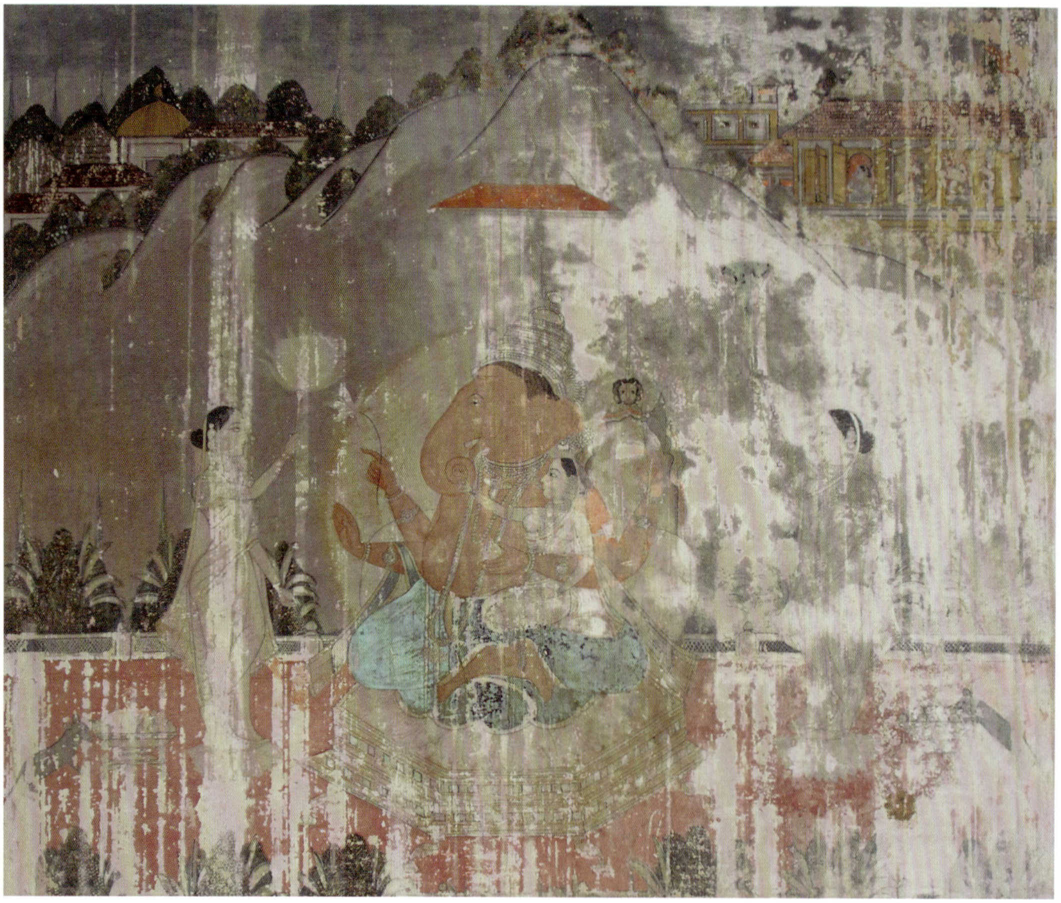

In this space for women, the guardians Jay and Vijay visually flank the entrance, and the murals evoke seasonal celebrations such as *haldi kumkum*, when women honor goddesses, including Jivati, who protects children.[51] Although damaged, a flowing black outline of Jivati in a coral-toned sari rocking a child's crib is still visible (fig. 17).

Fadnavis and other officials employed painters for *haldi kumkum* and other celebrations, and thus would have supported a local painting tradition attached to a ritual calendar. On March 18, 1826, for example, Ramji Chitari from Poona was contracted to paint the walls of the Tulshibagh temple complex for sixteen rupees on the occasion of the festival devoted to Shri Rama. The contract noted that the work was to be completed by the first half of Chaitra (March–April), and that the four sides of the temple, the area outside the door, and the surrounding walls were to be painted. The older, damaged pictures on the three walls immediately preceding the shrine were to be whitewashed and redrawn with color, including red *hindol*, and framed with twisting vines.[52]

16 Wall painting of Ganesha, ca. 1770–1800. Nana Fadnavis Wada, Menavali, Maharashtra

A third room in Fadnavis's *wada* in Menavali is painted in yet another style (fig. 18; see fig. 12 for the central "Sitting Room"). It is ornamented with flowering potted cypress trees, parrots, and blooming interlocked borders, and shows the artist taking advantage of a different palette: reds, greens, and golds that appear lacquered or oiled. This is probably the type of painting known as *rogani ranga*, or oil colors. Jiwaji Ganesha Khasgivale discussed this method along with others in the artists' repertoire in a letter written around 1790 to the Peshwa Savai Madhavrao concerning his order for a painting of Ganesha and Parvati.[53] He told the Peshwa that if he liked the picture, then a series of gods could be completed. The letter recommended the artists' employment and detailed their different skills, which included working with golden dust or ash (*bhasma*), with varnished colors (*rogani ranga*), a scented yellow (*argaja*), and making pictures (*chitra*) on buildings.[54] This suggests that artists painted on multiple media, including walls and paper, and used various techniques. It is likely that these artists came north from Karnataka, as their paintings bear a striking affinity with those from the Vijayanagara period, such as at Lepakshi, and with paintings from Mysore.[55] As in the first painted room, prominent deities include Vishnu, Shiva, and Ganesha.

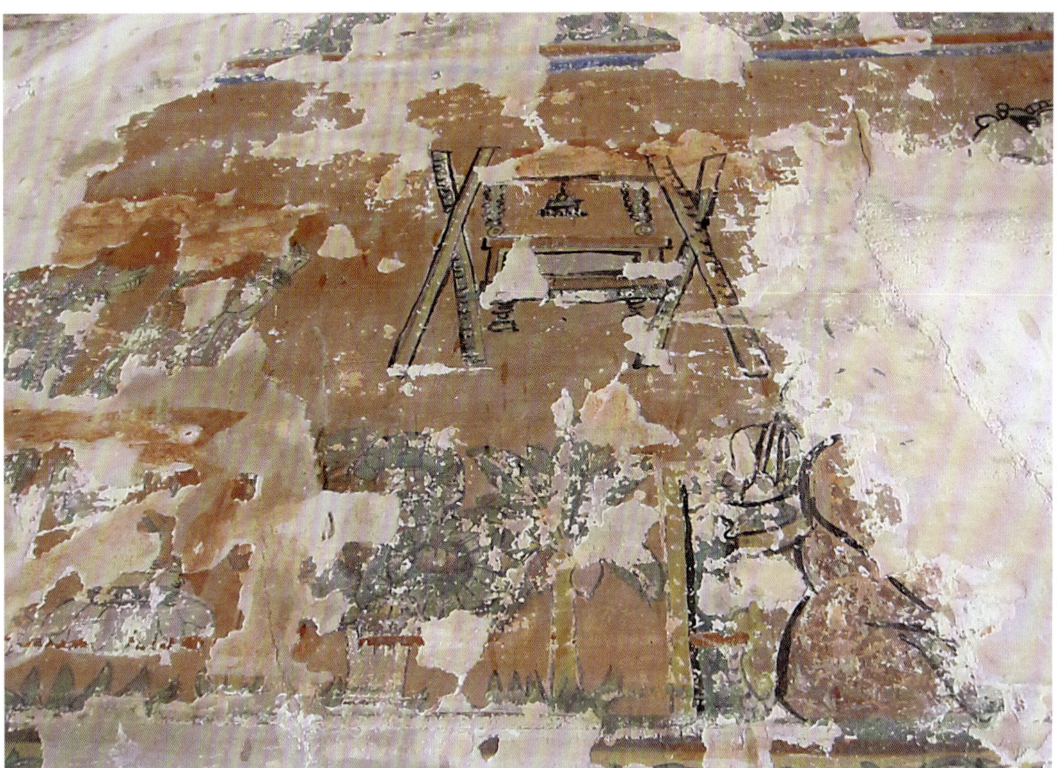

17 Wall painting on the verandah, ca. 1770–1800. Nana Fadnavis Wada, Menavali, Maharashtra

The paintings Fadnavis owned or commissioned offer material evidence of political relationships. Under his patronage, regional painters – not only from Maharashtra and further south into Karnataka, but also from the northern and eastern parts of the Deccan – covered the walls of his home in Menavali with gods revered by both his family and the broader Chitpavan community in Poona. Fadnavis also sought to hire artisans and painters from Jaipur, to commission works in Delhi, and to collect, through sleuthing or force, the highest-quality Mughal and Jaipur court paintings from the same region. His connoisseur's impulse toward northern India was probably informed by his early experiences in this region and its accessibility when Mahadji Scindia came to control the Mughal throne. Each of these regions negotiated with Fadnavis and the administration at the Poona court, and the works produced by the artists they employed were dependent on routes of conquest and often in dialogue with one another. Taken together, they support a cosmopolitan and devotional culture of collecting at the Poona court that was enabled by opportunities opened up by military developments.

AN ICONOGRAPHY OF RULE

This culture of collection, however, was also geared toward the production of a Maratha aesthetic that visualized devotional and political aims in iconic representations of deities to exemplify the Poona court's rule. The diverse mural program painted in Fadnavis's home in Menavali, for example, connects to other works by Poona-based artists that share its subjects, compositions, and techniques. While its patron is unknown, a composition just short of two meters in length of a palace of gods painted by Poona artists in *rogani ranga* (oil colors) on a textile support draws together the themes from Nana Fadnavis's mansion with those depicted at the court (fig. 19).[56] This painting is divided into three sections: at the center, Vishnu lies on the serpent Shesha beneath an icon of Ganesha; he is flanked by Krishna playing the flute on the left and Rama in court on the right. Vishnu's incarnations appear above and warriors ride on horseback in Peshwa-style peaked turbans below. The relationships among these gods, and their method of depiction, parallel those of the paintings in Fadnavis's home in Menavali, where the first room shows these gods displayed in a similar fashion (see figs. 13–16), and in the same method of *rogani ranga* oil painting that was applied in the third room (see fig. 18). Further, the gods are framed within vast royal complexes akin to the design of another of Fadnavis's mansions, in Poona, and the neighboring palace of the Peshwa, the Shanivarwada.

It is significant that representations of Vishnu asleep, and of his incarnations awake, hovered above Fadnavis and the rulers of the Poona court in the spaces under their

18 Wall painting of Shiva and Parvati with family, ca. 1770–1800.
Nana Fadnavis Wada, Menavali, Maharashtra

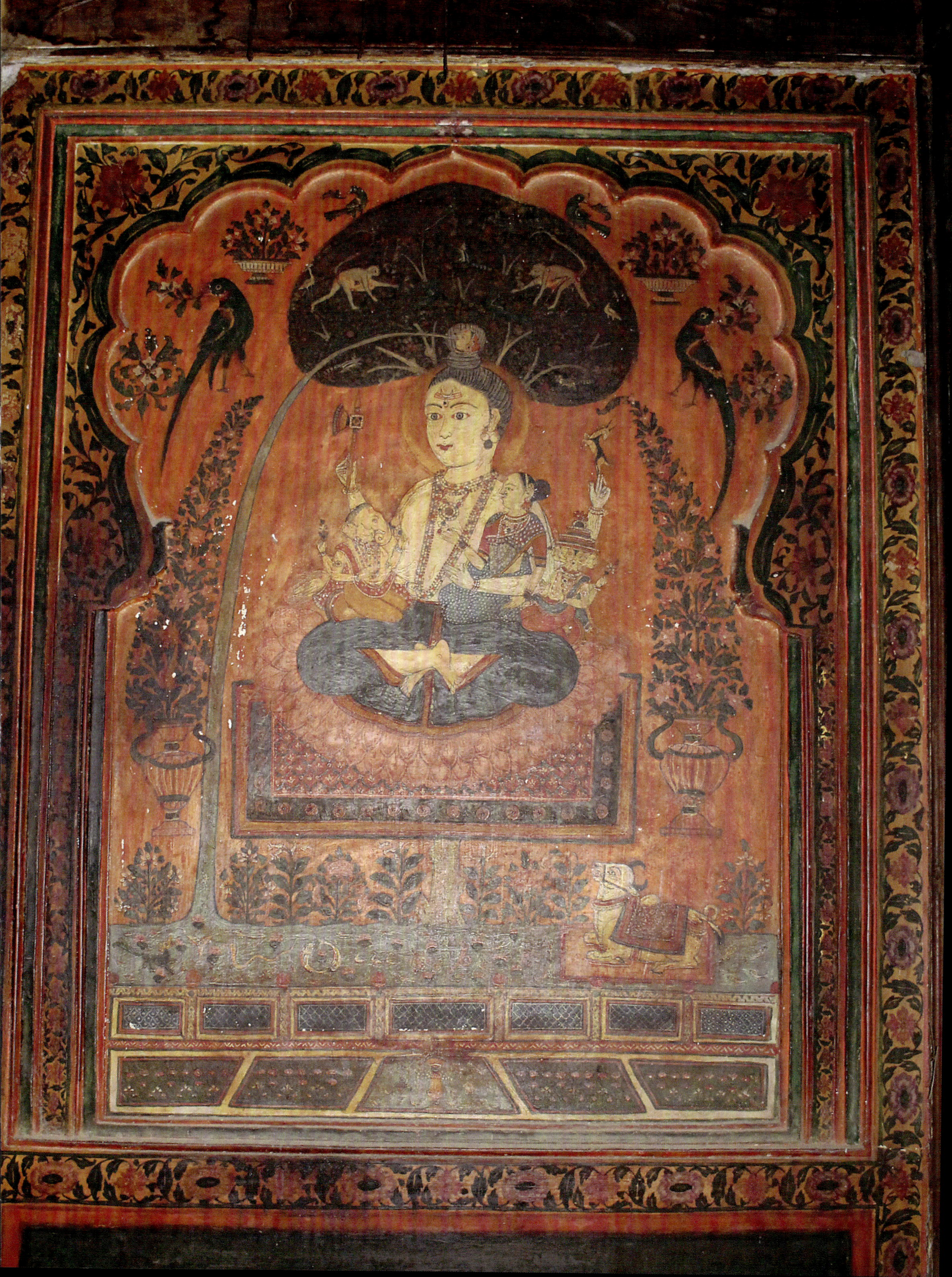

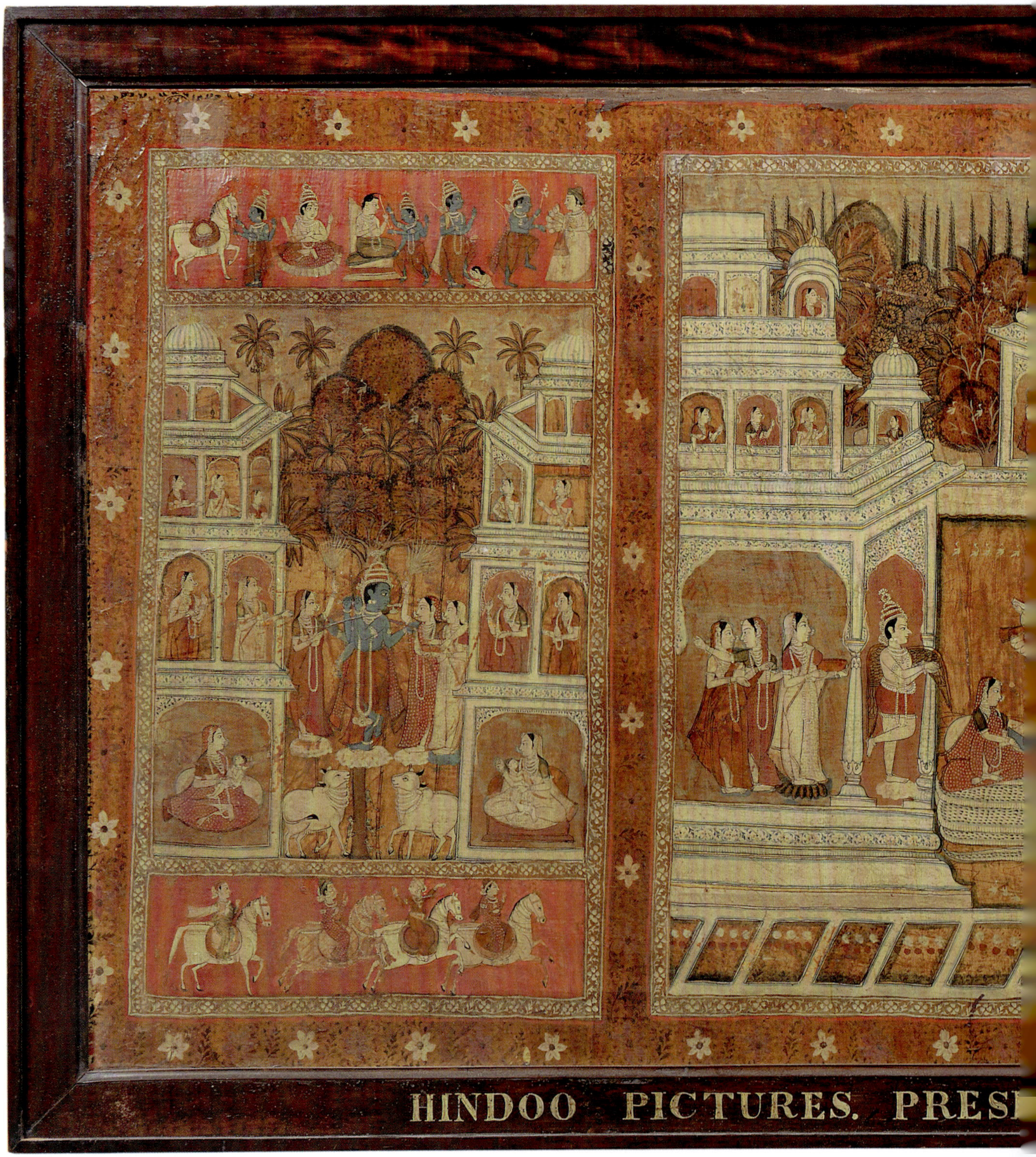

19 *Vishnu on the Serpent Shesha, Flanked by Rama and Krishna,* Poona, ca. 1800. Paint and varnish on cloth, approx. 80 × 180 cm. Ipswich Museum, Ipswich

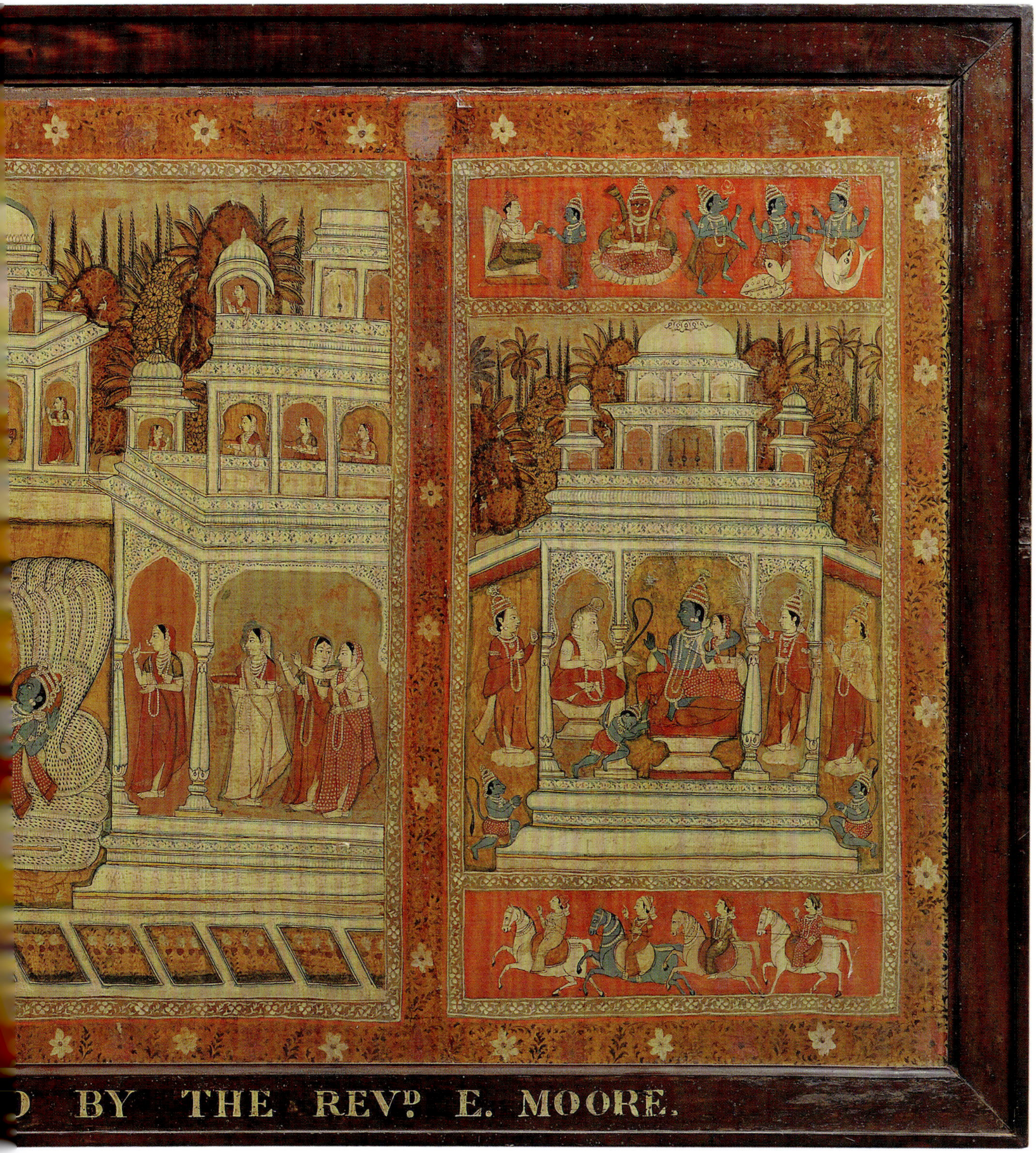
D BY THE REVD E. MOORE.

command. Vishnu resting on the serpent Shesha is portrayed in the tripartite painting of gods, in Fadnavis's home in Menavali (see fig. 15), and, in Major Edward Moor's words, "in glaring colours, of colossal proportions," on the outer gateway of the Peshwa's palace, and his incarnations adorned a main hall inside (seen in fig. 20).[57]

Paintings of deities are auspicious; but in this context, those honored by Fadnavis and others at the Poona court mirrored and supported their rule. They even suggest that a deity could be incarnated as the ruler. The repeated representation of Vishnu asleep on the serpent indicates his rise to augur a new age through the Poona court (as in the invocation to his incarnation Rama to the court in fig. 10). In seventeenth- and eighteenth-century Marathi texts, "epoch making heroes," as N. K. Wagle explains, "appear on earth periodically to protect and restore *dharma* in peril."[58] The court in Poona was in peril in the late eighteenth century. Besides the disaster at Panipat in 1761, the Peshwas had undergone a series of succession crises in the second half of the eighteenth century. In 1773 the ruling Peshwa, Narayanrao, had been assassinated by his uncle Raghunathrao. Only the birth of a child to Narayanrao's widow and a coalition of ministers who supported his succession, including Fadnavis, maintained the rule in his line.

Perhaps this political instability is one reason why the populace looked on the new child Peshwa, Savai Madhavrao, like a god incarnated to defeat their enemies, akin to the Hindu god Krishna's incarnation as a child of cow-herders to kill his demon-uncle Kamsa in disguise.[59] Poets affirmed such an alignment; in the 1790s, Prabhakar compared the Peshwa with Krishna, and Poona with the realm of Krishna's childhood, which Fadnavis had traversed as a young man.[60] The youthful Peshwa's patience in court was praised as "like a god only."[61] Although this Peshwa too succumbed to misfortune, dying unexpectedly in 1795, he was still eulogized in divine terms: "In all the human beings Savai Madhavrao Peshwa / Was like Surya [the sun god]."[62]

Gods were likened to the Peshwa in a similar manner to how the Peshwa was associated with gods. The portrayals of Vishnu (including Rama and Krishna), Surya, Shiva, Ganesha, and Durga in the *rogani ranga* painting (see fig. 19), in the court depicted in the late Mughal painting (see fig. 10), and within the landscape of the wall paintings (see figs. 13–16) chart a religious iconography that blurs the divine and the worldly. Around Poona, the Peshwas had contributed to transforming the region into a sacred center. They instituted the *panchayatan* of deities in temples on Parvati Hill in Poona, increased donations to eight temples to Ganesha that encircle the city (known collectively as the *ashtavinayak*), and instituted an annual festival (*utsava*) to Ganesha.[63] In fact, in one of the few extant representations from the Poona court of military action, it is Ganesha, rather than the Peshwa, who traverses the landscape as a warrior leading troops into battle.[64] Through the institution of the festivals of Dasara and Holi in the city, the Peshwa and generals like Mahadji Scindia aligned Poona with Rama and his symbolism of peaceful rule as well as with Krishna and his symbolism of prosperity.[65] As these gods recurred across media and technique, across palace and landscape, and across poetry and epic, they became the divine rulers in parallel to the earthly ones at the Poona court, if not explicitly incarnate.

While possessing its own specificities, the Poona court's pursuit of divine and courtly symbolism corresponds with the efforts of other rulers across India to affirm their leadership through sacred geography and iconography, including a branch of the Marathas who ruled in Tanjore (present-day Thanjavur) and the Kachwaha Rajputs in Jaipur.[66] In her study of the Tanjore Marathas, Indira Peterson has discussed how Serfoji II asserted his political legitimacy, ritual sovereignty, and dharmic piety by performing a two-month pilgrimage to sacred sites after his accession to a contested throne in 1798, and by adorning and renovating temples and courts with portraiture of men and gods.[67] The Maharaja of Jaipur, Sawai Pratap Singh, had similarly constructed his capital city in 1727 on sacred shastraic terms, as Vibhuti Sachdev and Giles Tillotson have argued. Planned as a Hindu symbol of the universe, or mandala, the city surrounded the palace, which was placed at the center of a triangle of Vaishnava temples to instantiate formally the "role of the god [Krishna] in the management of the state."[68]

Nana Fadnavis and other members of the court in Poona were eager to project their power through a blend of courtly and divine representations, as did rulers across India, but their method of grafting a variety of styles together to visualize their subjects created a specific eclectic aesthetic and iconography of rule. This depended on the acquisition of art and artists from contentious regions across India, as I have discussed in the previous sections, but also drew on those from Britain.[69] For instance, artists made the tripartite painting (see fig. 19) using oil paints (*rogani ranga*), but their application of a South Indian technique on this long horizontal textile also connects to British history painting. Indeed, Edward Moor purchased this work in Poona around 1800 and had it stretched and framed after he returned to England.

The British presence at the Poona court was established in 1786 with the arrival of Charles Warre Malet as the first British ambassador, known as a Resident. Malet's brief was to broker an alliance between the Marathas and the British against their common enemy to the south, Tipu Sultan of Mysore. The treaty was signed in 1790 and Tipu surrendered in 1792 (but only conclusively defeated and killed in 1799). Directly afterward, Malet commissioned an ambitious oil painting from James Wales to commemorate the treaty, which Wales and his assistant Robert Mabon produced based on sketches made at the court. After Wales's death in 1795, Thomas Daniell completed the picture in London in 1805 (fig. 20).[70]

This British painting adds another layer to the analysis of the artistic mixtures pursued by patrons at the Poona court. In its depiction of a diplomatic pact between men set in a

20 (Overleaf) Thomas Daniell after James Wales, *Sir Charles Warre Malet, Concluding a Treaty in 1790 in Durbar with the Peshwa of the Maratha Empire*, 1805. Oil on canvas, 182.3 × 278.5 cm. Tate, London, T12511

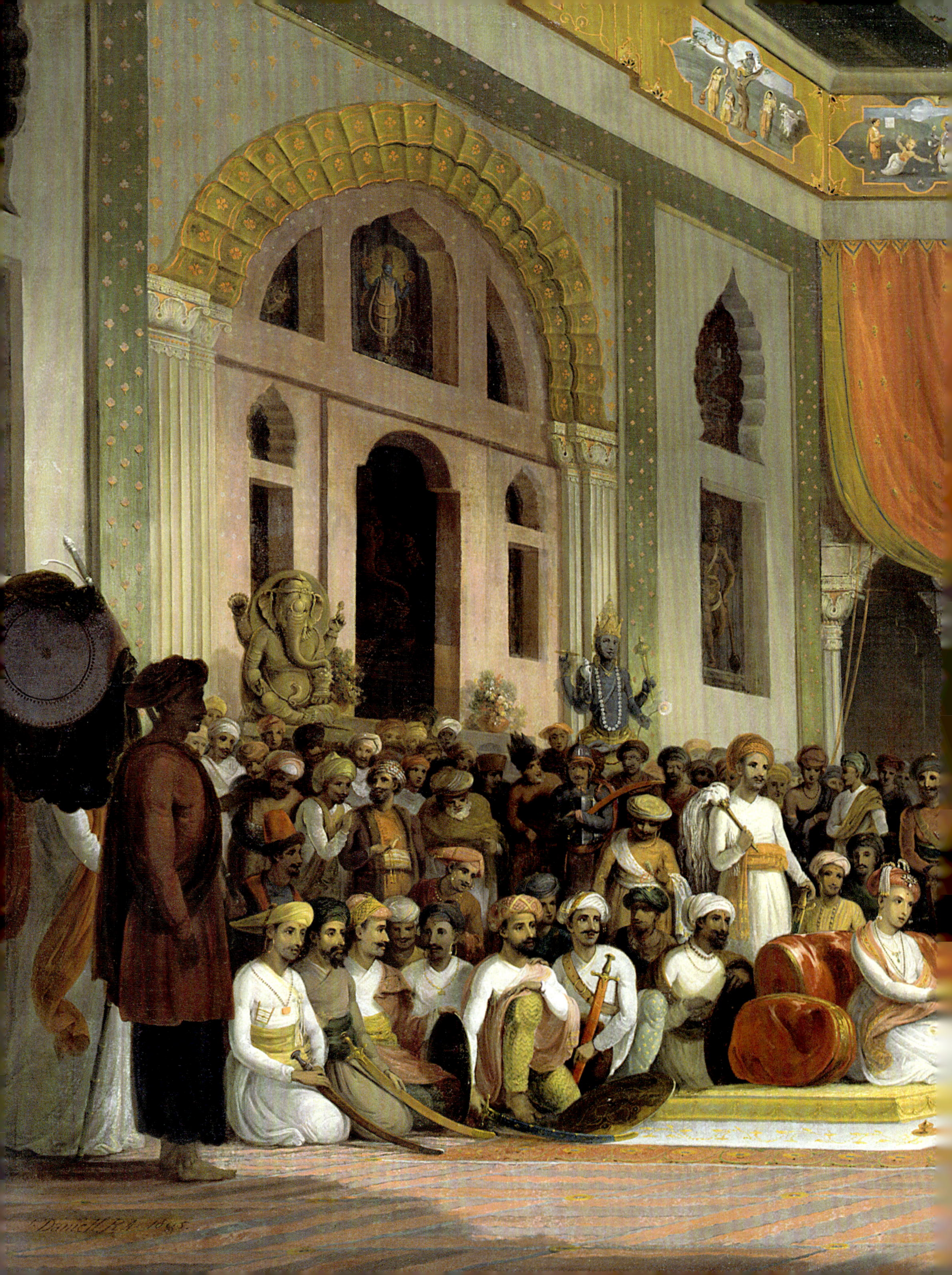

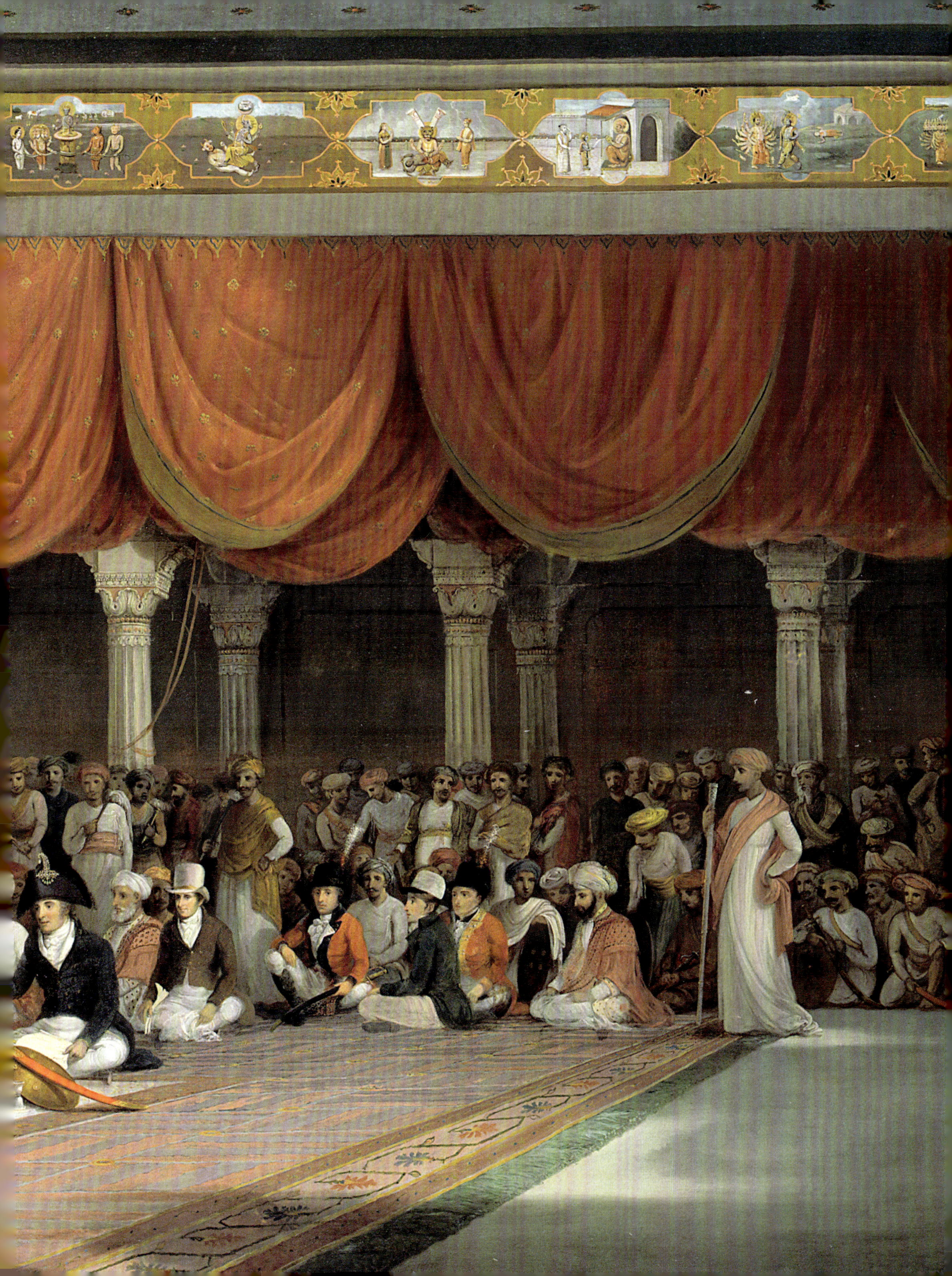

room adorned with gods, it seems to sit comfortably in the British genre of contemporary history painting. Yet when it is placed in conversation with the lacquered portrait of the Hindu gods ruling from a palatial analogue to the Poona court (see fig. 19) – which was also painted at large scale and in oils – it can be understood as that painting's inverse. In Wales and Daniell's painting the official men are watched over by a frieze of Vishnu's incarnations and sculptures of Ganesha and Vishnu with attendant deities placed in niches behind, while in the Poona artist's painting it is the gods who replace the men in the palace.[71]

Nana Fadnavis worked with artists to graft different traditions of painting together to reach his desired theme, as seen in the painting of regional gods set in a late Mughal palace garden (see fig. 10). This lacquered painting is probably another of his painted experiments, but this time related to British rather than to Mughal art (see fig. 19). Both the British and Maratha paintings blur the line between portraits of men and icons of gods, between politics and worship, and between the Mughals and the British as worthy visual models. They offer a frame for how the Marathas merged men and gods to produce an iconography of rule at the court.

PORTRAITURE BY A BRITISH PAINTER FROM BOMBAY

Nana Fadnavis acquired paintings and patronized artists from the region as well as from Britain and across India to visualize political and sacral rule, yet the results depended on the approaches of artists. By selecting sources and combining styles, artists who worked for the Poona court – from Sabaji Anant to James Wales – pursued a method of artistry as eclectic as their sponsors' practices of collection and patronage. In this section, I turn specifically to the history of James Wales to explore how artists worked with patrons at the Poona court and established their professional success. I focus on Wales because his drawings, paintings, and journals remain extant, alongside those of the artists who worked for him. Together they offer a picture of an artist who dutifully responded to court officials' commissions and anticipated their wishes through a workshop manner of production. For Wales employed Indian and British artists with diverse skills – from a Goan painter named Jossi adept in oils to the Company soldier Robert Mabon who excelled in draftsmanship and a sculptor from the Poona region named Gangaram Tambat who was skilled in depicting three dimensions – to generate portraits that would be legible across cultures and reproducible to support multiple buyers. An investigation of Wales, his workshop, and his dialogues with artists at the Poona court therefore opens up the processes of artistry that sit within the question of patronage.

Wales was invited to Poona, "by desire of the court," through Charles Warre Malet, who described him in his memoranda simply as "a Painter . . . from B[om]bay."[72] Nana Fadnavis and Malet both had a passion for art, and it is likely that the invitation arose from Fadnavis's wish, and that of other figures at the Poona court, to be portrayed in a novel fashion, but they also used the painter to gain insight into the British.[73] Nana Fadnavis, in particular, was renowned and feared for his personal intelligence service and had assigned one of his officials, Mahadji Chintaman, to report on Malet's activities, which included those of Wales.[74] Wales also served as Malet's diplomatic agent to gain entry to the court, as Douglas Fordham has eloquently discussed.[75] He was his own agent as well, working as hard to succeed at the business of being an artist in India as he had in Britain.

Within a week of Wales's arrival at the court in July 1792, he wrote to his wife, Margaret Wallace (1759–1795), that he had been "employed by the Prince at Poona" and had met and sketched the ministers and "chiefs of this great Empire." These included the young "Prince," Peshwa Savai Madhavrao; the Maratha "Chief," the general Mahadji Scindia; and, of course, the Peshwa's regent and minister, Nana Fadnavis. Wales concluded his letter with the confident statement that "[m]atters are in a prosperous Strain for me," though his words belie the unsettled circumstance of the rulers among whom he shuttled.[76] After a striking absence of twelve years, Scindia had returned to Poona and was encamped just outside the city with a massive army, barely veiling a threat of revolt. He claimed to have traveled to confer on the young Peshwa the honor of *vakil al-mutlaq*, the Mughal regent of Delhi affairs, yet he also demanded resolutions to various disputes, chief among them remuneration for reconquering most of the territory that the Marathas had lost in the battle of Panipat in 1761, including lands under Mughal rule.[77]

Fadnavis was apprehensive about Scindia's visit and attendant strength. On notice of his approach to Poona, the minister requested that the British dispatch the Bombay regiments to Poona for protection.[78] Malet, for his part, hoped that the British could serve as a "check on the dangerous genius of this [Maratha] empire" by rending apart its "great members."[79] Meanwhile, the young Peshwa flirted with all parties involved; a Deccan artist he employed, Sabaji Anant, documented an animated conversation with Scindia, for instance (fig. 21).[80] A heavy curtain swells against the cords that bind it, as if to emphasize the hushed secrecy of the scene and the potential of imminent exclusion.

Alongside such Indian artists who traveled to Poona, Wales accompanied Malet as the new British artist-in-residence as he moved between Fadnavis's home, the Poona court, and Scindia's camp. He was complicit in Malet's diplomatic machinations as well as the court's. On July 2, 1792 he met and sketched Scindia, whom he described as a "chief of great force" but of "mean appearance and rather low of stature." Scindia was attended by a startling six or seven hundred people for his three o'clock meeting at Malet's bungalow. On July 6, Wales visited Fadnavis, whom he described as "a man of great business" and "an ally" with "a sound head," which he thought to be "express'd strongly in his countenance."

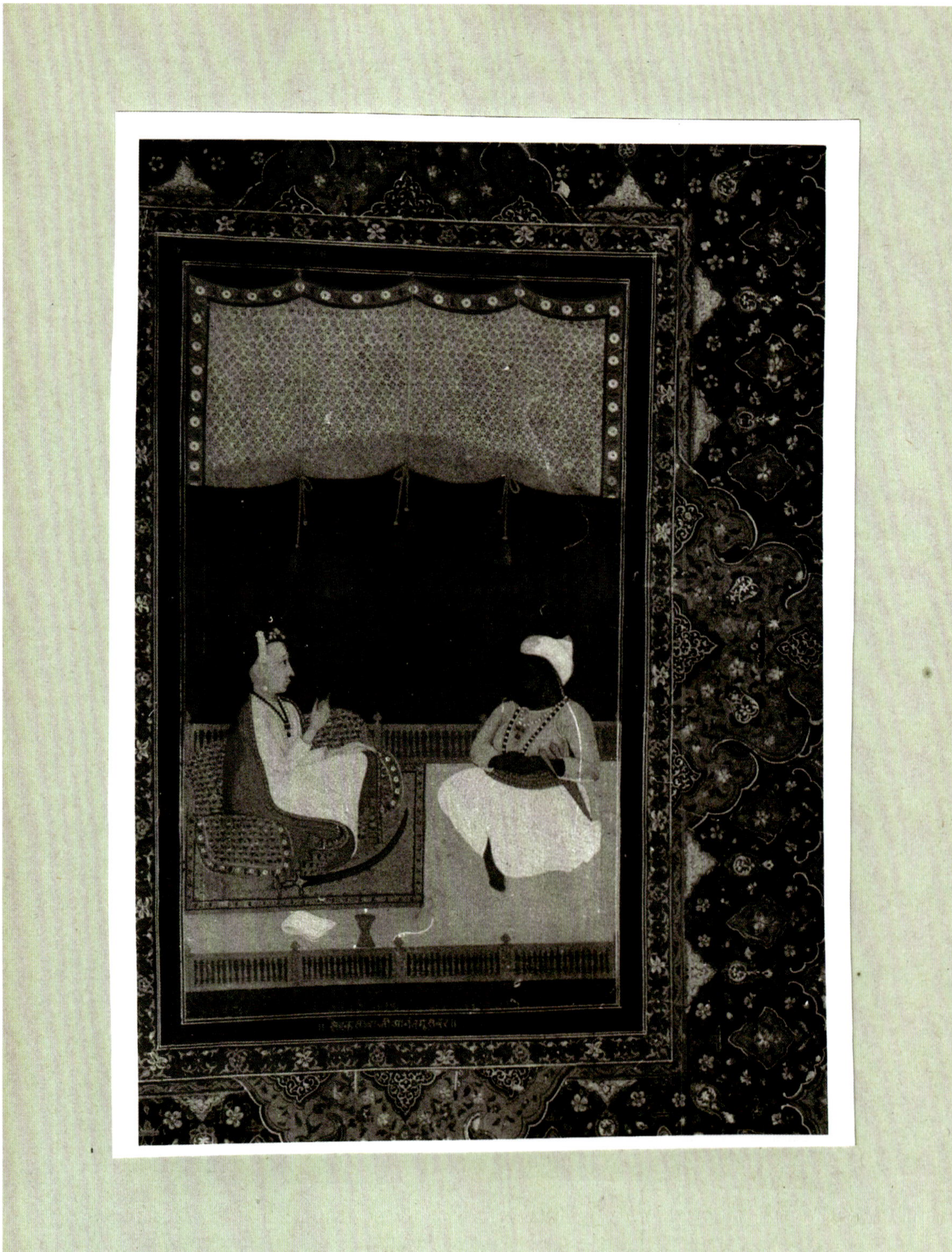

21 Sabaji Anant, *Peshwa Savai Madhavrao with Mahadji Scindia*, Poona, ca. 1790. Opaque watercolor with gold on paper. Location unknown, formerly in the Sir Cowasji Jehangir Collection

Indeed, Wales's assistant Robert Mabon sketched Fadnavis with purposeful eyes and a square jaw; his jewels are prominent, and a scarf is draped to display its shimmering gold thread (fig. 22). Subsequently, Wales met the Peshwa Savai Madhavrao, who, he wrote, was "about eighteen years of age." Despite "his gravity of character," he noted, the Peshwa was "very agreeable and pleasant."[81]

Such candid character sketches do not suggest the stress that Fadnavis revealed elsewhere, for Wales was more interested in gaining commissions than in the fate of the Marathas. His journal is full of notes regarding supplies, which he purchased from as close by as Poona and as far away as China. He put in an order with a Captain Smith to bring canvas and more than a hundred frames of various sizes from China and Calcutta.[82] Later in July, he turned to pigments, noting those that he had discovered for sale in Poona, including ultramarine ("call'd by the natives 'lausi verd'"), "another curious color viz a green stone," a "native cinnabar," a "black made from coca nut shell," "Indian Red," "Gold Red," wood oil, poppy oil, and "Rogan [oil]," which was surely that used in *rogani ranga*.[83]

These provisions would be necessary. By July 19, about three weeks after his arrival, Wales had already begun to paint more than ten pictures, even though his bungalow, which must have included a studio, was still being prepared in Malet's garden on the Peshwa's orders.[84] In three of these early "specimens," as he called the paintings, Wales tested different media, formats, and scales to offer options to his patrons. One was a "miniature" of Malet that is no longer extant. If standard, it might have been a pocket or necklace-sized oval of about four or six centimeters in height. The second was of James Findlay, one of the doctors in the British Residency, in an intermediate size, 32 by 27 centimeters, on an oval board; perhaps canvas had yet to arrive.[85] Wales drew Findlay using loose brushstrokes to create the soft, romantic effect typical of many British portraits. The doctor's intelligence is conveyed through the eyes, sharp nose, and pursed lips, but the likeness gives little indication of his profession or habits.

The third painting was a half-length, and therefore the largest in scale, an oil portrait of "the Mogul Con Saib" (fig. 23), Malet's translator and employee Nur al-Din Hussein Khan (known with the honorific Saheb).[86] Wales identified him as a Mughal from Delhi

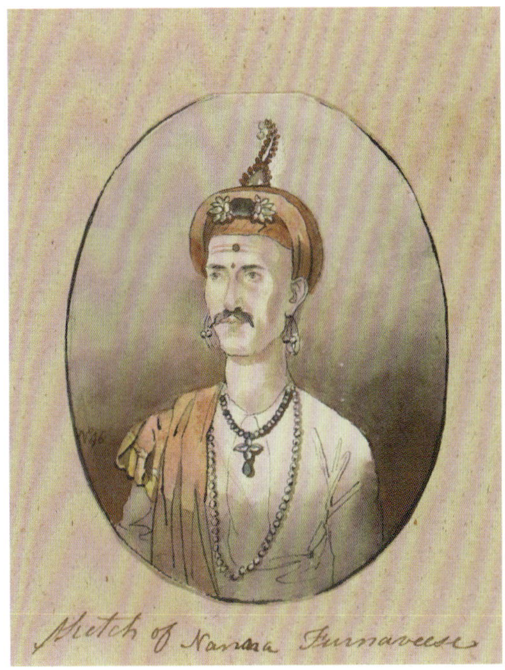

22 Robert Mabon, "Sketch of Nana Fadnavis," Poona, 1792–5. Watercolor and graphite with pen and black ink on wove paper, 11.4 × 8.9 cm. Yale Center for British Art, New Haven, Connecticut, Paul Mellon Collection, B1977.14.22273

and sought to paint him in a Mughal manner. In his journal, Wales wrote on July 23: "Worked all day upon Con Saibs picture – this picture I am finishing in a very uncommon style in compliance with Sir Charles' desires, as the natives are very fond of high finished pictures and this is to be shown as a specimen."[87] Khan Saheb is seen in profile, kneeling and fingering prayer beads in a typical Mughal portrait pose. Wales presented him as stately, with a crisp white turban and manicured beard, richly garbed in patterned textiles and diaphanous muslin folded in a play of shadow and cloth.

In his portrait of Khan Saheb, Wales seems to have approximated the composition of Mughal paintings and turned his British training in oils toward a "high finish," which probably refers to the Mughal technique of burnishing layers of opaque watercolor to render a fine and smooth surface. He portrayed Khan Saheb with legs tucked under his body, rather than seated on a chair, standing, or in a head-and-shoulder pose, as seen in James Findlay's portrait. The British termed this method "miniature" painting because the scale and precision was commensurate with their own handheld miniatures, such as Wales's miniature of Malet.[88]

Wales was being instructed in the aesthetics of Indian painting. In an undated Marathi record, Mahadji Chintaman, the intelligence officer whom Nana Fadnavis assigned to report on Malet, discussed the exchange of paintings among Fadnavis, Wales, and Malet, as well as Fadnavis's aesthetic pedagogy. "Yesterday," Chintaman wrote, "the [Nana] Swami's picture had been given to him," probably one of the portraits drawn by Wales or Mabon (see fig. 22). Chintaman asked "if I should have him draw another like this, or if he should be shown how to draw it," implying a process of editing. That this might have included overt guidance is indicated in the next part of the letter: "Other of these [types of] pictures should be shown. If we get the time, then please put them aside. We should show him good and bad Indian pictures so that he knows what types of pictures are good. For him this study of pictures is new, therefore we should instruct. . . ."[89] As a result of a similar exchange, Wales may have emulated the technique of finely burnished Mughal paintings, such as those in Malet's collection, or of the kneeling, bearded figures in Fadnavis's collection whose poses resemble that of Khan Saheb.[90] Wales must have spent enough time with such images to copy them, as he translated a Mughal composition of a dance, or *nautch*, into the pale washes of a watercolor sketch (fig. 24).

By grafting together disparate models, Wales's practice accorded with the Poona court's requirements; it also followed the pedagogy of the Royal Academy in London. The president, Sir Joshua Reynolds, promoted an eclectic model of selection and imitation, or "borrowing" in his terms, which proved particularly apt for a royal academy that trained students to work across Britain and the British empire.[91] By selecting "both from what is great, and what is little," the student in Reynolds's concept, could bring "home knowledge

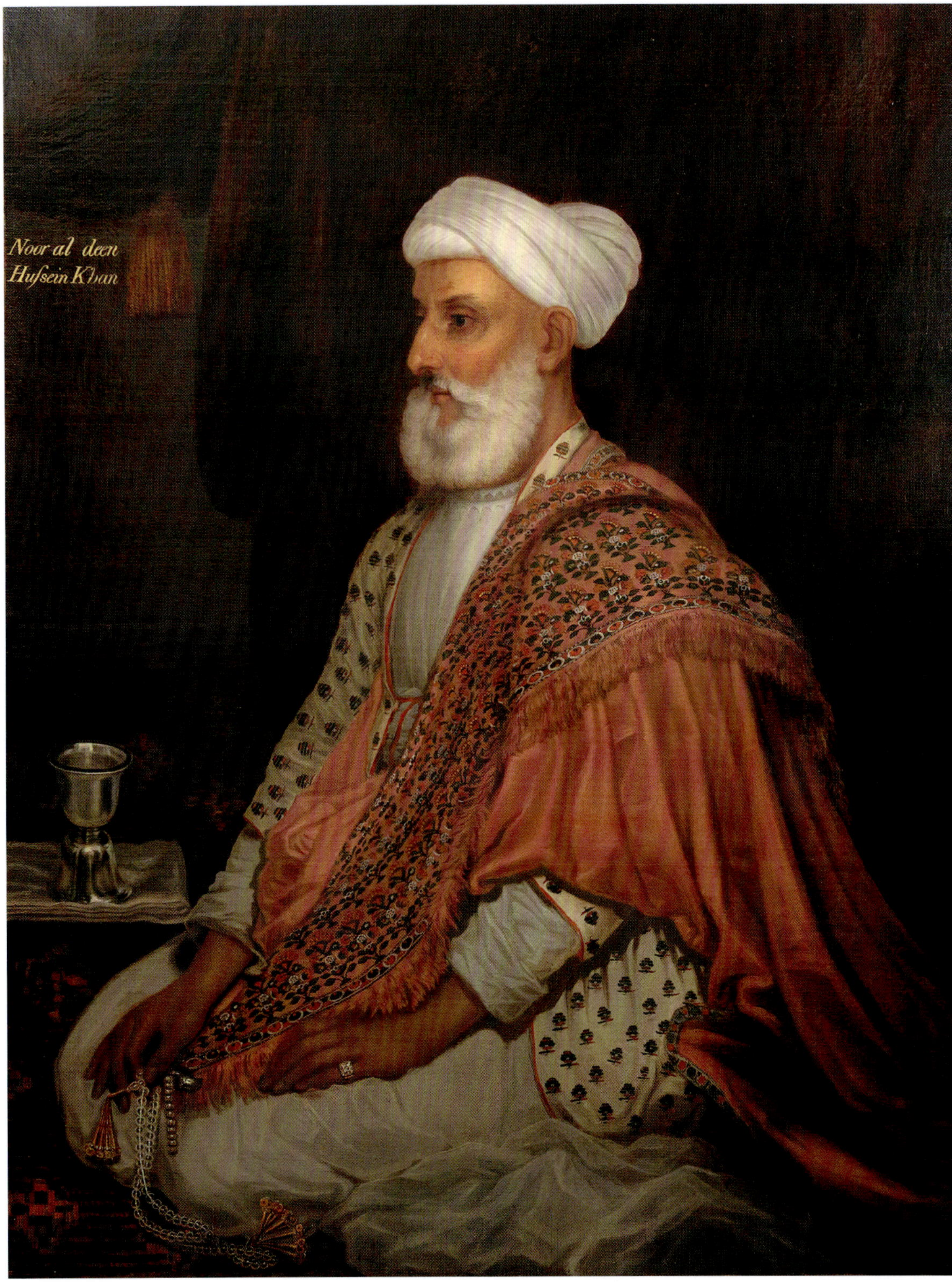

23 James Wales, *Nur al-Din Hussein Khan, the Residency Vakil*, Poona, 1792–3. Oil on canvas, 122 × 95.5 cm. Islamic Arts Museum, Kuala Lumpur, Malaysia

from the East and from the West; making the universe tributary towards furnishing his mind and enriching his works with originality, and variety of inventions."[92]

Wales was primarily self-taught but may have absorbed the teachings of the Royal Academy after moving from Aberdeen to London in 1783. He exhibited paintings there in 1788 and 1789, and at the Society of Artists in 1791, the year he went to India.[93] Although Reynolds maintained a hierarchical model of art in his *Discourses*, which the Royal Academy reinforced, his expansive method of imitation encouraged artists engaged with empire to remake that order according to the demands of new markets.[94] Indeed, Wales applied Reynolds's method of extraction and recombination, but instead of picking and choosing from ancient or Renaissance models, he looked to Mughal, Hindu, and British examples to guide his method. He portrayed Khan Saheb, for example, in a typically Mughal rather than British pose and in the "high finish" of a Mughal painting, but he did so in oils on a large scale to graft an Anglo-Mughal portrait.[95]

On August 10, Wales wrote that he had exhibited his three "specimens," which were received with "great satisfaction" at the court.[96] He also noted that he was presented with shawls; a reference in the court records, or daftar, also recorded the gift by its monetary value, precisely 342 rupees.[97] It turned out that Wales had pleased not only those at the Poona court but also Malet. Wales wrote, "Sir Charles came home with me in the evening confessing great pleasure at our success."[98] Malet clearly considered the artist, and the act of portrait painting, as benefiting his diplomacy, offering access to court and credit through representation. The young Peshwa also found the portrait intriguing; a month later, he "sent to ask a sight of Con Saibs picture," and Wales complied.[99]

In late October, Wales began a grand portrait of Nana Fadnavis, the Peshwa, and two servants (fig. 25). The composition, accoutrements, and "high finish" tell us why the Peshwa might have sought to see Khan Saheb's portrait a second time. The Peshwa is garbed in a Mughal mantle. He sits with hands on lap, and a shawl with a gold and flower border is draped elegantly over his fine white muslin dress, as if modeled on the "Mughal" Khan Saheb whom Wales had portrayed (see fig. 23). The Peshwa's turban is adorned with strings of pearls (*tura*), a diamond ornament (*kalgi*), and a jewel-studded aigrette (*sarpech*). These types of objects were listed among the gifts that Mahadji Scindia presented to the Peshwa from the Mughal emperor,[100] and were also carefully documented by Mabon alongside Scindia's own gifts to the Peshwa, including a jewel-studded sword.[101]

In this portrait Wales highlights the Mughal honor Scindia had secured (and its attendant monetary gains) in the form of valuable gifts, yet the Peshwa's allegiance adheres to Nana Fadnavis, who sits beside him in the manner of earlier portraits of the Peshwas and their ministers (see fig. 75).[102] It was, in fact, Fadnavis who controlled the throne. The Peshwa and the minister thus form a visual political bloc that accepts Scindia's prestige

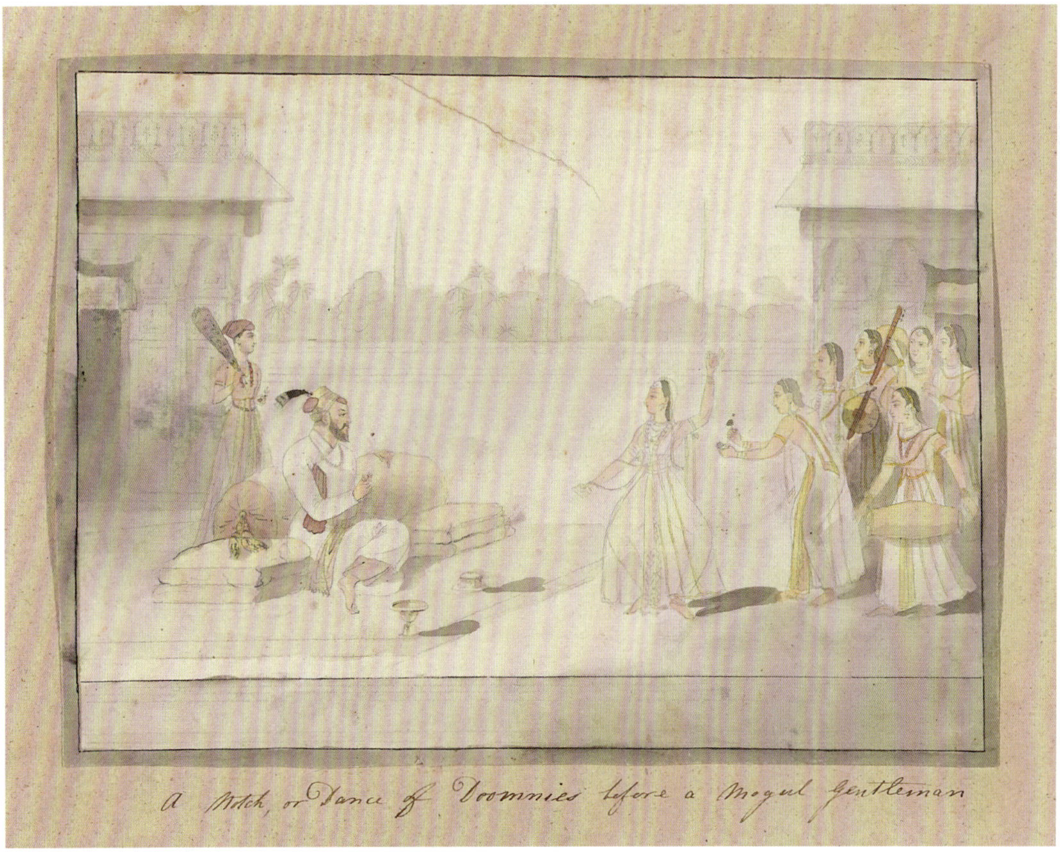

while refusing his admission to the court; in this way, the painting signals a triumvirate of ruler, administrator, and warrior at the same time as it shows these same "great members" of the court cleaved apart, just as Malet and Fadnavis must have wished. Other paintings produced in the same period – for example, of the Peshwa and the general (see fig. 21) – of course offer a competing story of the young Peshwa's affiliations; a year later, when Wales was on a trip to Bombay, the Peshwa managed to reconcile the differences between Fadnavis and Scindia.[103]

By requesting to see the "Mughal" model of Khan during the making of Wales's portrait in 1792, the Peshwa acknowledged the Mughal aspiration of the portrait but also his acceptance of Wales's British training as a painter (see figs. 23 and 25). In particular, the Peshwa, Fadnavis, and others connected to the Poona court, lauded portraiture that was *hubehub* – identical, exactly similar, or closely resembling – which accorded with Wales's ability to produce a naturalistic likeness. When Mahadji Scindia asked about the portrait of Nana Fadnavis, for example, it was described as drawn in an identical or exactly

24 James Wales, attrib., *A Nautch or Dance*, Poona, ca. 1792. Watercolor and graphite with pen and black ink on paper, 29.8 × 36.5 cm. Yale Center for British Art, New Haven, Connecticut, Paul Mellon Collection, B1977.14.22430

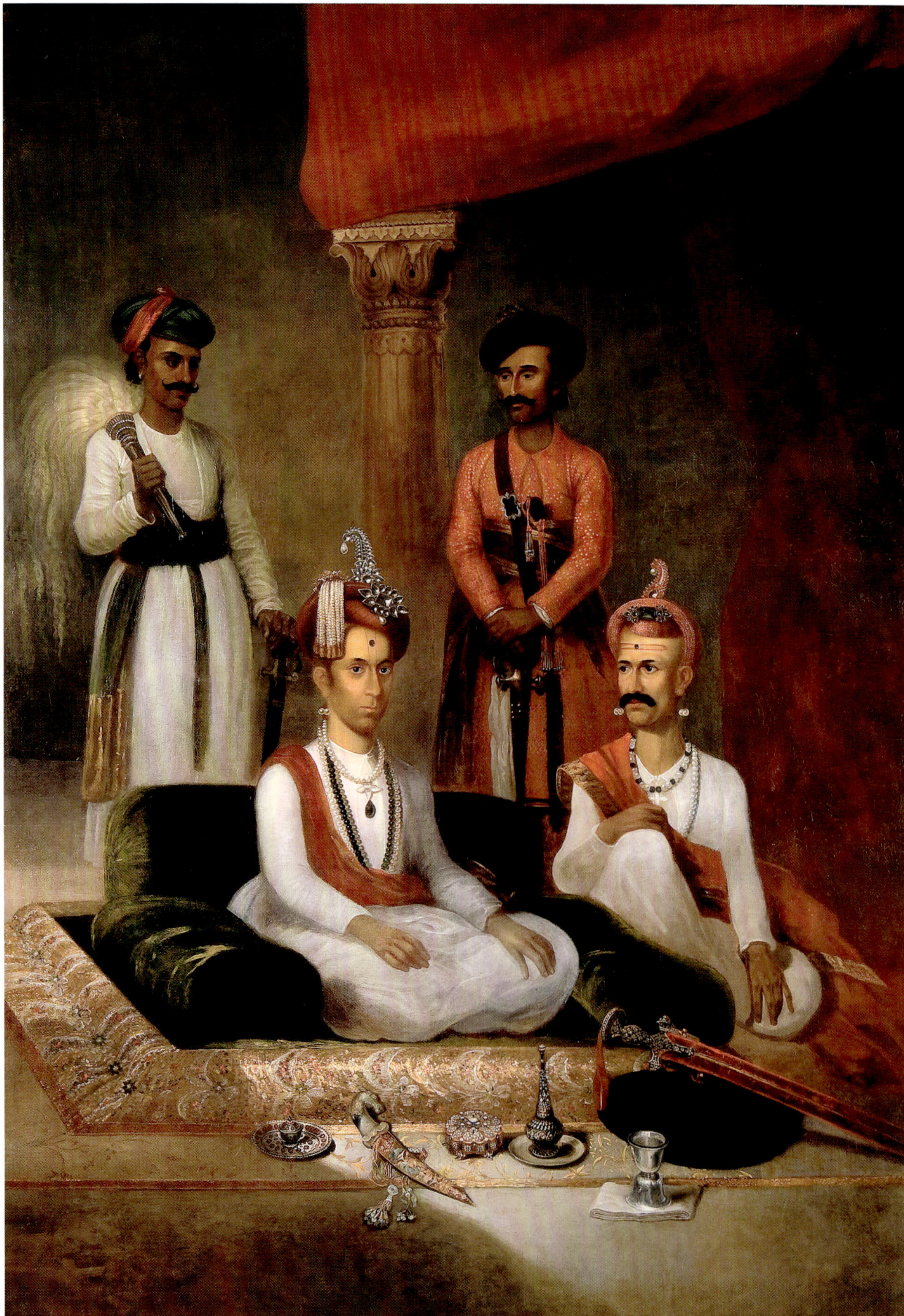

similar (*hubehub*) manner to his person; likewise, the Peshwa's portrait was recognized as a close resemblance.[104] That Wales's talent in likeness was recognized at the court could have been connected to his use and sale of optical technologies, including camera obscuras, a telescope, a "day and night glass," and a "gold miniature lens," which would have satisfied and supported the court's interests.[105]

The Peshwa and Nana Fadnavis recognized that Wales could graft multiple representational qualities together – a Mughal pose and regalia with a Maratha composition of a ruler and his minister with a British attention to resemblance at a large scale – but they further sought another factor: religion. They edited the model and the preparatory drawings to permit devotional modes of reception to coexist with the worldly, thus emblematizing the specific mixtures practiced by the Poona court. In the portrait, the Peshwa's eyes are not cast downward, as Khan's are in his portrait, nor is he in three-quarter view like Khan or in the profile view of works by Mughal and Deccan artists such as Sabaji Anant (see fig. 21). Furthermore, in sketches for the painting, both Mabon and Wales drew attendants in front of the Peshwa with their backs to the viewer, but these figures do not appear in the final oil portrait.[106] The primary attendant at court thus would have been the intended viewer of the picture, looking at it from outside the frame. This alteration would allow the Peshwa to face forward, as Natasha Eaton has persuasively suggested, so that his viewing audience could behold him in *darshan* (the reciprocal viewing between god, ruler, or guru and devotee), and receive his gaze and blessings in return.[107]

Commissioning the portrait of the Peshwa and Nana Fadnavis involved a negotiation between Wales and his patrons. The painter gave three options as to scale, technique, and composition, and the Peshwa and Nana Fadnavis manipulated the results to balance a historical and political event with a spiritual and worldly presence, which accorded with texts and the public perception of the Peshwa as like a divinity incarnate. By encouraging Wales to join Mughal, British, and Hindu modes, they placed their portraits within longstanding traditions of the ruler, minister, and audience at court, for instance, while also updating their aesthetics by combining them with new modes.

That Wales was successful is supported by the fact that he continued to receive commissions. The circumstances that surrounded Mahadji Scindia's portrait, for instance, further reinforce what the Marathas desired from portraiture at this time. Scindia not only sought a veritable resemblance in his picture but also to be represented as a powerful warrior on horseback, in the manner of his portrait by a Jaipur artist (see fig. 9). Malet describes Scindia's sitting for Wales in his letter book: "Visited Mahajee Scindia and introduced him to Mr. Wales a portrait painter.... He expressed a desire that his picture may be drawn on horseback, observing that everyman's character and way of life should be painted in his picture and that his whole life had been present in the fields."[108]

25 James Wales, *Savai Madhavrao and Nana Fadnavis in Durbar*, Poona, 1792–5. Oil on canvas, 228 × 186 cm. Royal Asiatic Society of Great Britain and Ireland, London, RAS 01.014

Malet's interpretation of Scindia's desire for his portrait as a window into his character recalls the treatise on painting by the eighteenth-century English artist Jonathan Richardson, who wrote that "to sit for one's picture is to have an abstract of one's life written, and published."[109] Although equally attentive to useful information, Chintaman's Marathi report of the same event focuses on the immediate stages of production. "Wales *musavir*" (the painter) began to draw Scindia's picture, for which he sat over the course of a few hours. The initial picture was "from the face until the waist," but he later drew Scindia's horse, and subsequently his gun was displayed for sketching.[110] Unfortunately, only a portrait "from the face until the waist," rather than the entire equestrian picture, remains extant (fig. 26).

Together, these British and Marathi reports reveal that the identification of a specific person and his associated objects was to be balanced with an archetype, such as the warrior or the minister.[111] They record that Wales's paintings of Scindia, and of the Peshwa and Fadnavis, emphasized an amalgamation that drew on mimetic recognition (being *hubehub*), while also parlaying a traditional visual genealogy and a composition in which the sitter is placed in a setting characteristic of his prototype – the hero dashing across the terrain, for example, or the ruler and minister depicted in court. Yet Wales was just one of many painters who conjured the rivalry between the bureaucrat Fadnavis and the general Mahadji Scindia in portraiture, as seen in Sabaji Anant's painting (see fig. 21).[112] Fadnavis and other members of the court sought a diversity of representation, not only to collect a range of images but also to gather information from various artists.

The competition that these artists documented concluded in 1793, and Mahadji Scindia died soon after. His passing showed that Wales's portraits had articulated professional and political rivalry in life while containing the seeds of deification after death. Marathi sources support Eaton's argument that Scindia's portrait gained potency after he died, just as the picture of the Peshwa and Fadnavis was probably composed to embrace *darshan*.[113] In one of Mahadji Chintaman's reports to Nana Fadnavis, one Bhivajipant Scindia is described as paying a visit to the Peshwa to meet Wales and see the portrait of his relation Mahadji Scindia. On arrival, the visitor asked whether the painter had come to the court and was told to sit in the room adorned with mirrors (*arasemahal*) – a rich metaphor for the reflection and duplication of images.[114] In the interval that Wales fetched the painting, the Peshwa told Bhivajipant that the painter had reduced his visits to the court and had become afflicted with sadness since the general's death.[115] The Peshwa then praised Mahadji and told Bhivajipant that the deceased had appreciated merit in others, including Wales, and was irreplaceable.[116] From this conversation it seems that Mahadji's qualities had greatly affected the painter. The two men had developed a bond through the production of the general's image.

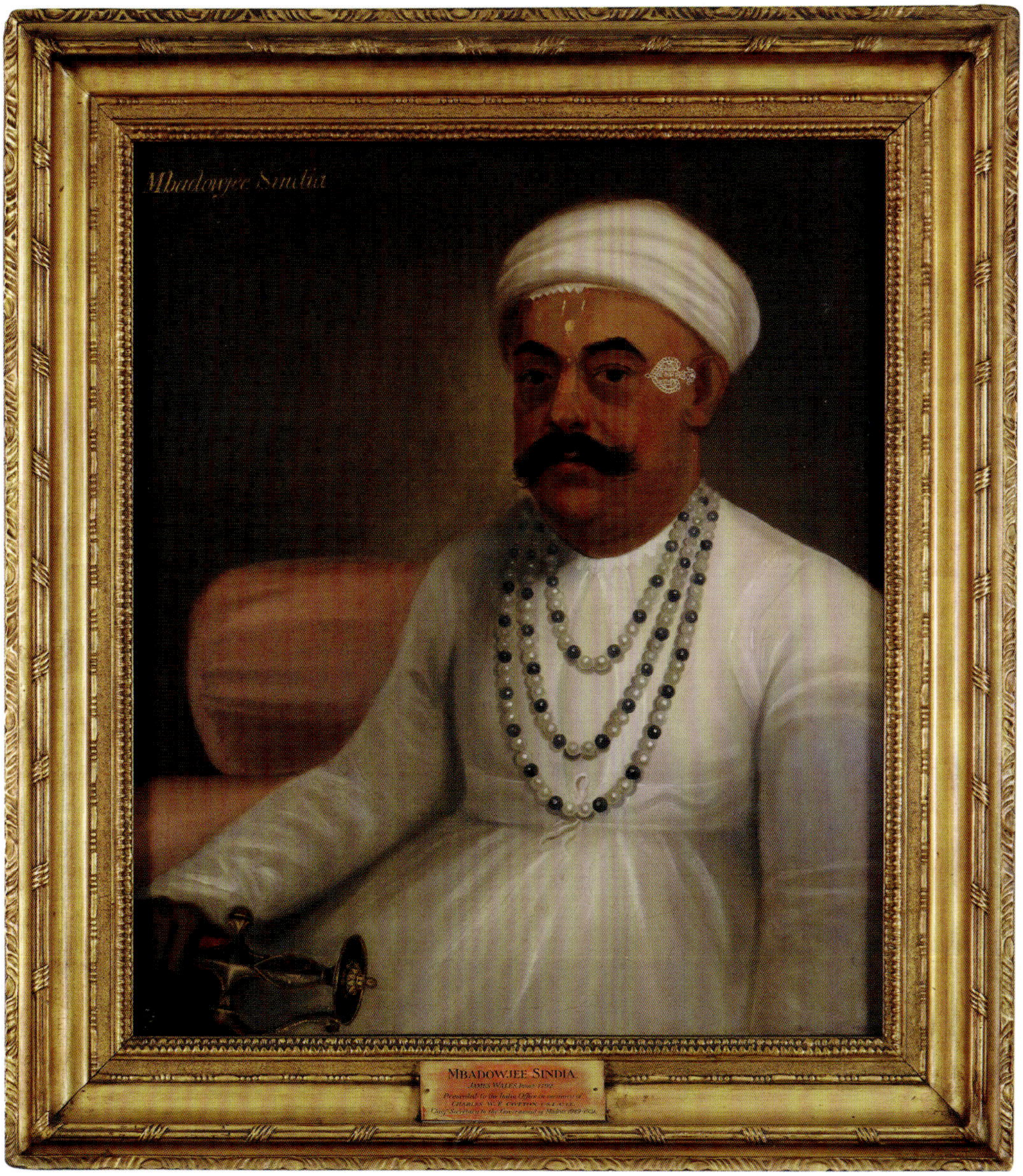

Scindia's portrait therefore recalled his presence and positive qualities. But it also forged a relationship between artist and subject, as if the very act of making an image or *murti* – an embodiment, manifestation, incarnation, or personification – established a type of sanctification.[117] Wales's portrait of Scindia became an object of veneration after his death. On a visit to Poona in 1805, the recorder and judge in Bombay James Mackintosh reported that a picture of Scindia had been installed "in the usual place of

26 James Wales, *Mahadji Scindia*, Poona, 1792–5. Oil on canvas, 76.5 × 63.8 cm. British Library, London, Malet Collection, Foster 826

the principal deity" in a temple in his recently constructed Hindu funerary memorial or cenotaph, known as a *chhatri*. "Before the picture, a light is kept constantly burning and offerings daily made by an old servant of the Maharajah."[118]

In Maratha territories, the consecration of people and their representation after death has a substantial history. A king or warrior could be memorialized in a stone pillar; in a *chhatri*, which was popularized by the Rajputs and emulated by the Marathas; or, more rarely, sculpted as an icon in a temple.[119] Regarding later, nineteenth-century *chhatris* of the Scindia family in Gwalior, Melia Belli has argued that the architecture was organized to imbue the deceased ruler, presented in a hyper-realistic depiction modeled on a photographic portrait, with the status of the divine.[120] Wales's instantiation of Scindia's image and its reception after death was similarly iconic. Indeed, it is possible that Wales's patrons at the Poona court turned the quality of being *hubehub* into a local form of Hindu iconicity, with Wales's artistry molded to conform to such a devotional paradigm.

In western India, a hero or heroine could be revered like a god, or slip into a god's form, which parallels practices throughout early modern India. In Mughal and Rajput courts, artists elevated rulers to semidivine status through motifs such as golden halos, the sheer size of the work, and by displaying them enshrined in a window known as a *jharoka*, or on a sparkling mount.[121] While the identification of a ruler was key to portrayal in Rajput court workshops, similarly to Mughal ones, mimetic exactitude was not an imperative for the creation of likeness; in fact, under the Rajputs, illusionism was usually rejected prior to photography.[122]

Similarly, South India had a medieval tradition of royal portraits bearing the resemblance of gods or taking the form of a sculpted intermediary between devotee and god.[123] During the rule of the Nayakas in the seventeenth century, the Marathas in Tanjore in the eighteenth century, and the Wodeyars in Mysore in the nineteenth century, the production and display of sculpted portraits of kings as well as their instantiation as icons increased.[124] In the contexts of Tanjore and Mysore, Indira Peterson and Janaki Nair have regarded the new value placed on frontality in royal portraiture as a compromise between the divine and the human figure that may have resulted from Indian engagements with European portraiture.[125]

Wales's portraits of Peshwa Madhavrao, Nana Fadnavis, and Mahadji Scindia mark this transition. They do not show the sitters in the South Indian pose of devotee or in the Mughal royal profile. Their faces turn for a three-quarter view or have the frontality of an icon, as if negotiating with Wales's eclectic technique and the vision of Fadnavis and his other patrons in Poona. For in this period, under Fadnavis's patronage, human representation moved toward divine representation and vice versa. These modes mixed in a shared landscape or were fused within iconic portraits heightened by naturalistic representation.

A WORKSHOP PRACTICE OF PAINTING

James Wales never mentioned the potential for iconicity in the portraits he produced for the Peshwa, Nana Fadnavis or Mahadji Scindia, nor whether his patrons desired such a status or had conceived it through their interaction with his compositions; rather, he complained about their requests for details. Douglas Fordham has demonstrated that Wales struggled to achieve an aesthetic balance between the Poona court's demands for specificity and Joshua Reynolds's prerogative for general pictorial cohesion, which was expected by his London audience. For the picture of the Peshwa and Fadnavis, Wales longed to produce "a Noble Simplicity and grand Powerful Harmonized effect of the whole before any part of the detail is introduced." Yet he felt that he had to sacrifice the "best principles of his art" to please his patrons in India, "people of distinction" who were "fond of... rather rich dresses with watches, snuff boxes, rings &c &c introduced" in their commissions.[126]

Indeed, Wales consistently adjusted his works – even through the employment of artists with skills complementary to his own – to please his patrons at the Poona court and to imbue their bodies and objects with symbolism. He did so, in part, through a workshop method of production as diverse as his employer Fadnavis's patronage and collection practices. To overcome his weaknesses in detail and to increase production, Wales hired artists from different cultural and artistic backgrounds – most significantly, the British soldier Robert Mabon and the Goan artist Jossi. Their contributions substantially altered the resulting products.

Wales hired Mabon for intricate sketches of objects and scenes. Mabon made sketches for Wales of figures, weapons, and jewels at the Poona court, and also planned out entire compositions, "to make out more particularly the design."[127] Wales must have valued Mabon highly, since he bought out his commission in the Company army for two hundred rupees.[128] By incorporating Mabon's precise drawings into his final paintings, Wales might have been able to overcome his distaste for "all singular forms, local customs, particularities, and details of every kind."[129]

In 1794, for example, Fadnavis commissioned Wales to paint his "household god" Krishna with his beloved Radha.[130] The dialogue that ensued between patron and artist offers an example of their working method, and it affirms that Fadnavis commissioned Wales to portray together figures of gods and of men and women, just as local, Mughal, and South Indian artists had done under his patronage. Although no longer extant, this work would have been an early example of a British oil painting of Hindu deities.[131]

A tonal sketch for the prospective painting softly outlines the movements of Radha and Krishna: the musculature of their raised arms as each plays a flute, the stress on their stiff and bent legs, and the sharp foreshortening of their feet (fig. 27). This classi-

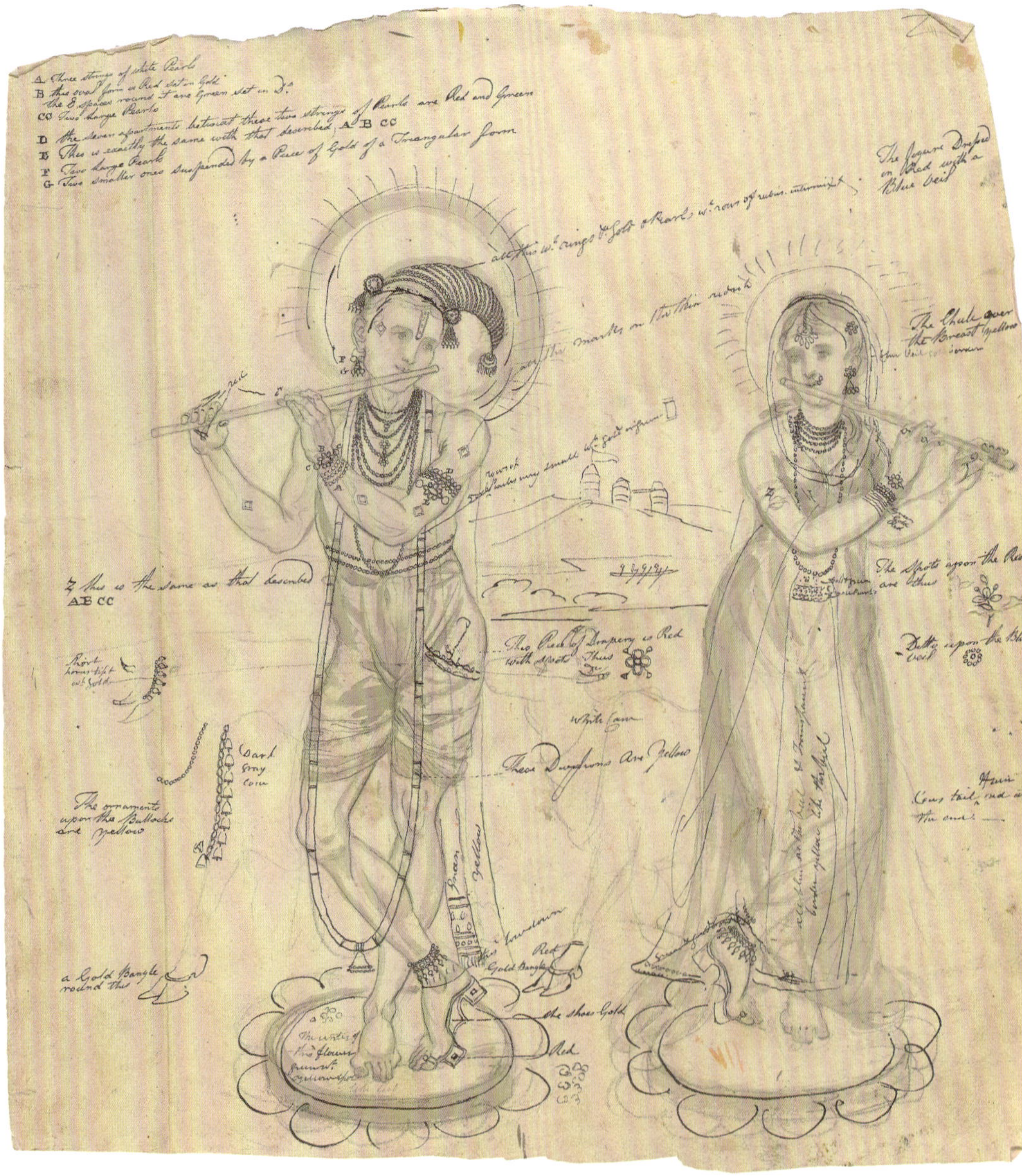

cal drawing seems to be in Wales's hand, but the modifications in sharp black ink are clearly Mabon's. Besides his attention to the coloring of the figures, Mabon seemed most concerned with the details: pearls and rubies, gold and emeralds, the length and size of the jewels and fabrics. Fadnavis must have recognized the contrasting qualities from the two hands in the work as unsatisfactory. When he met Wales to discuss the preliminary painting, Wales recorded the need to recalibrate the detail and character: "the god should

27 James Wales and Robert Mabon, attrib., *Krishna and Radha*, Poona, 1792–5. Gray wash and graphite with pen and black ink on paper, 37.5 × 34.3 cm. Yale Center for British Art, Paul Mellon Collection, New Haven, Connecticut, B1977.14.22431

not be quite so red and only fifteen years old, his feet shorter and his hands not so fat... The lady twelve years old and as delicate and as beautiful as can be made."[132]

The timeline and mingled hands in the ink-and-wash sketch cannot be verified, yet the work fuses the academic style that Wales promoted with Mabon's meticulous articulation, reflecting the combination that would have resulted in the final oil painting. It is tempting to see this integration as a grafting of oil painting at the Royal Academy with that of military draftsmanship, or an Anglo-Company painting akin to the Anglo-Mughal one discussed earlier. Yet we know little about Mabon's background except that it was troubled. A single enigmatic sentence in his journal is suggestive: "Awaked in the morning with a violent headach [*sic*] – felt uneasy and restless fearing the disagreeable circumstance which brought me to India."[133]

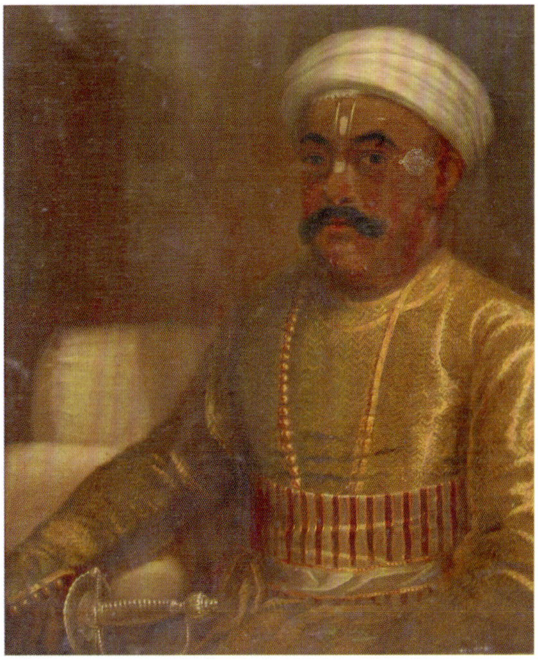

Whereas Wales employed Mabon for particularities in design, he hired an artist named Jossi in Bombay to aid in finishing his oil paintings, in making smaller copies, and in drafting. "Jossi," whose name Wales also spelled "Josi" and "Josir," is identified only as a "young Goa painter," implying that he was from Goa, a Portuguese colony from 1510 until 1961.[134] He could have been Portuguese, Indo-Portuguese, simply from Goa, or trained in a Goan manner.

Jossi seems to have made both large and small copies of Wales's paintings, including single portraits of Fadnavis, the Peshwa, and Mahadji Scindia.[135] In one painting of Scindia, for instance, the subject, shown gripping a sword, appears in precisely the same pose as in Wales's portrait (see fig. 26), but here his costume is a rich gold and green shimmering garment adorned with gold buttons, with a striped sash tied at his waist (fig. 28).[136] The year after Scindia's death in 1793, Wales recorded in his journal in December 1794 that he had "painted as well as my light would admit at a picture of the late M. Scindia having got his dress to finish it by."[137] However, this painting has qualities that differentiate it from Wales's autograph works. Its finish is matte and the sitter's head is not haloed in diffuse light. In his writings, Wales signaled that luminescence was integral to his portraits: "the manner in which the portraits of the Marhatta chiefs are to be painted is first a grand effect of broad light – understood and produced thro each picture."[138] Jossi, in comparison, chose a matte brown background that aligns with portraits made of Portuguese governors by other Goan artists. Such a style must have been suffi-

28 James Wales and/or Jossi, attrib., *Mahadji Scindia*, Poona, ca. 1795. Oil on canvas, approx. 76.5 × 63.8 cm. Central Museum, Nagpur

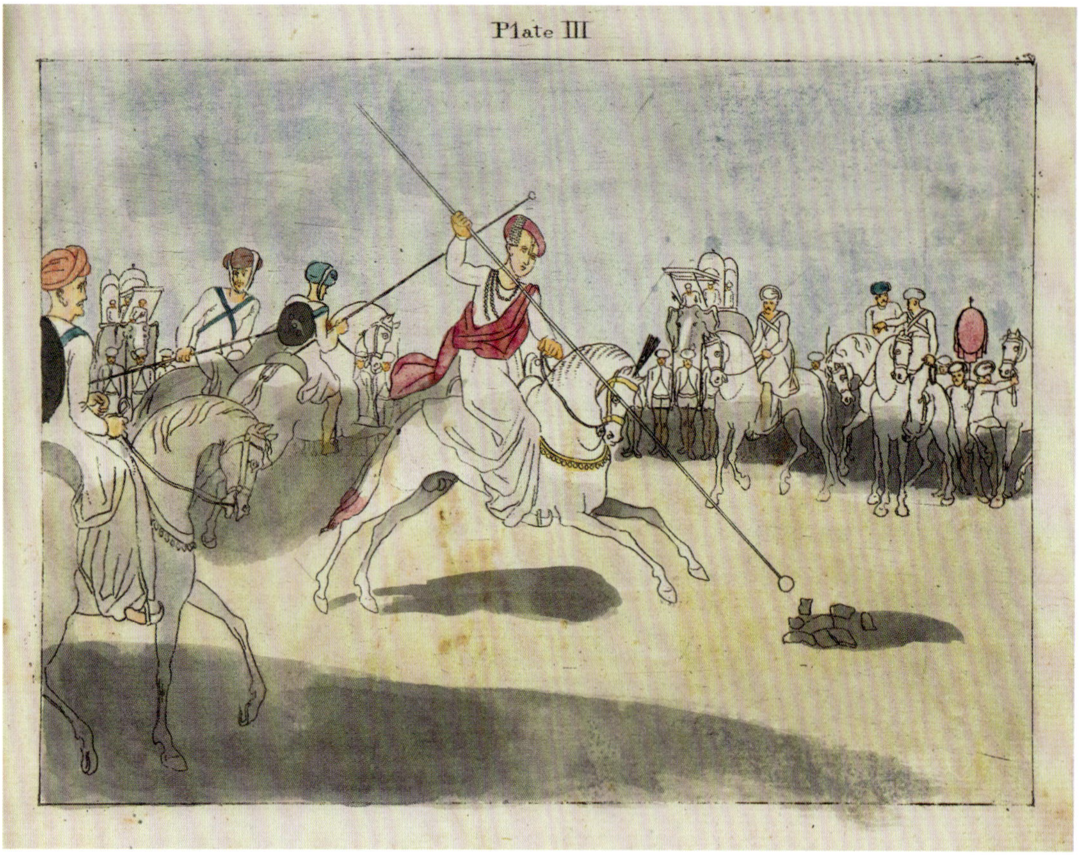

cient for his role in completing Wales's paintings and generating replicas at different scales in order to expand production.[139]

Wales and Jossi's coproduced works fuse a Goan style with a British academic one into a type of Anglo-Goan portrait, just as those with Mabon could be Anglo-Company, and Wales's adaptation of Mughal compositions and techniques Anglo-Mughal. But this parlance obscures the emphasis behind Wales's workshop production. To meet the demands of his commissions, he assigned his assistants to work in the medium in which they were skilled and grafted the results together. In sum, he reformatted British academic and military aesthetics within the context of empire, and he diligently responded to Maratha ones.

Wales was also in dialogue with Poona court artists, which adds another facet to the cultural interactions that ensued among Wales, his assistants, and Fadnavis and his other patrons. One artistic conversation revolved around an equestrian portrait that the Peshwa commissioned from Wales in October 1794, in which the Peshwa, followed by several attendants, rides a running horse. Wales must have completed this work, as it was

29 Robert Mabon, "Savoy Mahadowrow, late Peshwa of the Mahratta Empire, exercising the Long Spear, with other Bramin Chiefs, near Parbuttee, at Poona" from *Sketches Illustrative of Oriental Manners and Customs* (Calcutta? 1797?), pl. III. Etching with hand coloring on paper, 18 × 23 cm. British Library, London, T 39881(3)

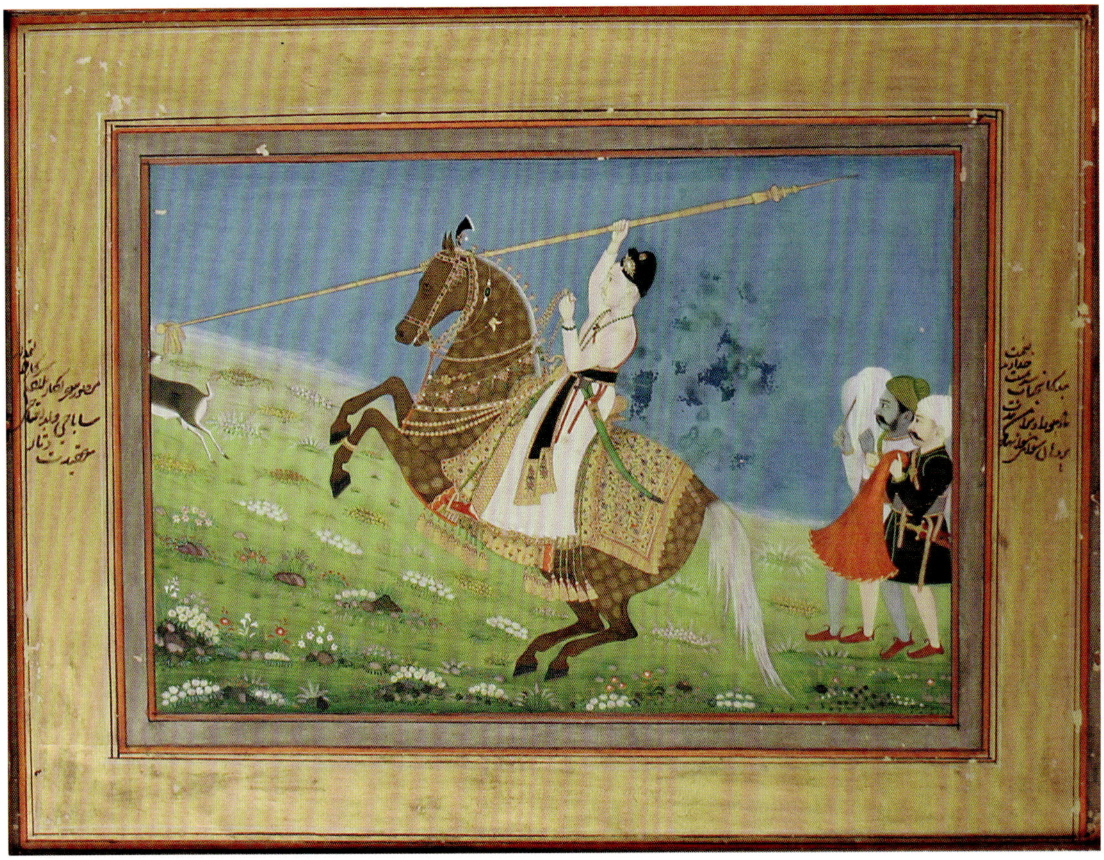

recorded as being in Malet's collection, although its present whereabouts, as with many others, are unknown.[140] The basic appearance of Wales's oil painting may be imagined by consulting the journals Wales wrote and the sketches that Mabon made. In one sketch that Mabon later etched and colored (fig. 29), the Peshwa rides a horse while he wields a long spear. The spear is tipped with a sphere that he aims at a pile of rocks, as if at a mock deer. He wears a bright red scarf, and the horse has an ornament on his forelock that tips forward as his head bows toward the intended goal.

Another painting in brilliant blue and parrot green remains from this period in which the Peshwa is engaged in an exercise (fig. 30). Drawn by the artist Sabaji (probably Sabaji Anant who painted the Peshwa and Mahadji Scindia; see fig. 21) who worked for the court, it may be related to Wales's lost portrait of the Peshwa on horseback.[141] The horse has accoutrements similar to those that Mabon sketched in preparation for Wales's portrait, including a horse and its feather ornament.[142] Wales's journal further records that he completed a preparatory study for an equestrian portrait. The study was apparently

30 Sabaji Anant, attrib., *Peshwa Savai Madhavrao Exercising with a Long Spear*, Poona, ca. 1795. Opaque watercolor and gold on paper, approx. 25.4 × 35.5 cm. Raja Dinkar Kelkar Museum, Pune

successful in garnering him the Peshwa's commission, but with a number of "alterations," notably that "the lower man should carry their scarves . . . ."[143] Linking Wales's oil painting with this watercolor, a brilliant red scarf – like the Peshwa's in Mabon's sketch (see fig. 29) – fans out from the hands of the lower man in the extant watercolor.

Both James Wales and Sabaji Anant would have been familiar with the genre of the equestrian portrait. In Europe, this imagery could range from a grand-scale oil portrait by Joshua Reynolds to a print of royalty. In fact, as his diaries reveal, Wales was in the business of selling these kinds of engraved reproductions to the Poona court.[144] The equestrian portrait also had an equally long tradition among the aristocracy in India (see fig. 9). Wales regularly consulted and reproduced other paintings, such as those sent by Fadnavis, which makes it likely that he had viewed other Indian equestrian portraits of hunting deer as models for his own, just as Sabaji probably did for his rendition.[145]

Yet Sabaji's equestrian portrait differs from both traditions in significant aspects, as one imagines Wales's must have, and these differences may have emerged through the engagement between Wales and artists at the court. The composition of the ruler astride a horse in which both are in strict profile and two attendant figures are placed behind conveys a typical equestrian pose that was intentionally made to refer to earlier traditions and seem timeless. Yet here a specific experience is also captured. The Peshwa is engaged in a routine where his spear is tipped with a small ball, which Wales observed and Mabon recorded in sketches (see fig. 29) and in writing.[146] While the horse's head does not turn toward the action, as Mabon relayed in his rendition, the hill does tilt up asymmetrically, with the flowers following in upward movement, and the deer is sliced in half by the frame, as if the horse's movements were made manifest in the landscape. Thus, the convention of the equestrian pose is maintained, but disrupted by the specificity of a witnessed event.[147] In this watercolor, Sabaji seems to unite British documentation with an Indian equestrian model in gouache. Even as he maintained the scale, bright palette, and static profile of the latter, he added the evidence and temporality of the event from the former. Sabaji and Wales were both at the Poona court. In the watercolor that remains, the artists together forged a new type of image by interpreting, and perhaps also misinterpreting, multiple traditions.

Wales consistently lamented that his patrons at the Poona court demanded a close attention to specific details. However, he longed to achieve for his paintings what he called "a Noble Simplicity and grand Powerful Harmonized effect of the whole" in the tradition of Reynolds. This picture may have harmony and noble simplicity, but I have suggested that Wales achieved these qualities by working with Indian art and artists, copying Indian paintings, and grafting his techniques with those of the artists in his workshop. Sabaji likewise attained the status of a painter of "magical forms," as written in a Persian inscription on the golden frame of the work.[148] In Indo-Islamic tradition, the rhetoric of the painter's "magical" ability to conjure life in an illusion was standard.[149] In the context of Fadnavis and the eclecticism at the Poona court, Sabaji's ability to evoke historical time alongside visual continuity must have been lauded.

Although Wales's equestrian painting of the Peshwa is lost, it is clear that Sabaji's watercolor was the result of a complex of cultural interactions in which the stages of artistic production altered how it might be received. The bright watercolor acknowledges the traditions of painting already flowing at the Poona court before Wales arrived, as well as what he offered and gained. On the surface, Wales's portraits are similar to other oil paintings produced by the British in India during the same period. Yet when considered within the context of their production, his paintings and those with which they were in dialogue appear decidedly experimental in their mixtures of different traditions and therefore unique.

James Wales, his assistants, and artists at the Poona court adopted a method of production that uprooted and recombined styles and subjects for varied audiences. The results were often legible across cultures, though it is unclear if the artists always expressed them consciously. Yet, when aligned with the North and South Indian artists whom Fadnavis patronized, and the paintings he acquired by coin and by force, Wales and his interactions with the artists in the workshop he inaugurated and with those employed by the court become only one facet of a broader aesthetic articulation of graft in which artistic mixtures that crossed cultures and regions were the source of innovation. Together, these patrons and artists cultivated a worldly art conversant with motifs and techniques from across India and the globe, but they also constituted a political and devotional imagery that legitimated, if not divinely activated, the Poona court's rule through this layered application in paint.

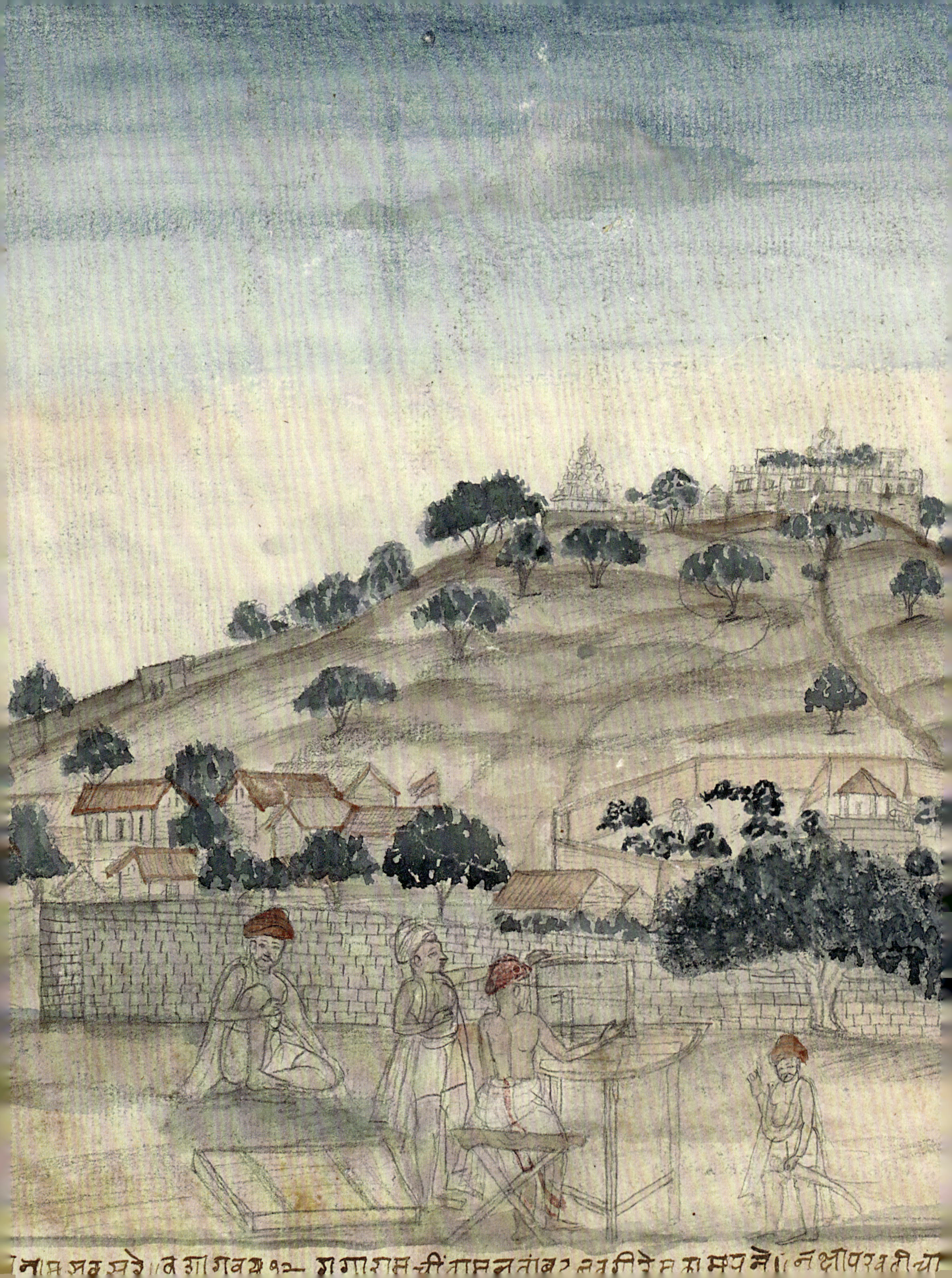
।नाम सकसके। व आगवय १२ गगागम-चीं ताम न तांब र लवणिरे म का मपमे। नश्रीपरवतीचा

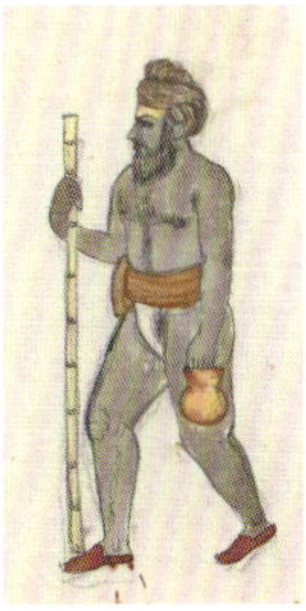

CHAPTER TWO

A Poona Artist at the British Residency

In a watercolor sketch, an artist sits at a drawing table at the bottom of Parvati Hill in Poona (fig. 31).[1] The sky is pale and cloudless, the hill uneven and studded with trees. Aided by an assistant, he uses a viewing frame to draw the Peshwas' temples that are depicted in the distance. Nevertheless, the artists are included within the ostensible subject of the hill, unlike a drawing from the opposite side that is populated with pastoral figures (fig. 32). Here, herdsmen graze their cattle and women carry waterpots on their heads. The sky has become a mass of indigo water blots. Dense at the edges, they pull down the slender register of cloud streaks typical in paintings from western India to cover the sky like a Constable. The artists have disappeared, and their absence makes the landscape picturesque, rather than documentary. Are the subjects the makers of the depictions or the scenes depicted in these sketches? It must be both, as the artist, Gangaram Chintaman Tambat Navgire, signed his full name, gave each a title, "Plan (*naqsha*) of Parvati," a Poona location, and a 1795 date.[2]

As an artist from Poona working for the British East India Company, Gangaram was new to these genres of landscape and architecture. Visual techniques formulaic in Britain – the distant, perspectival view of a scene framed with trees, the ratio of sky and earth, and the use of shadows and pale earth-toned colors to model forms – here he rendered deliberately. In his care with the composition and the depiction of artists within it, Gangaram not only drew attention to the manner of the pictures' construction but also to his signature below.

Details of fig. 31 (opposite) and fig. 51 (above)

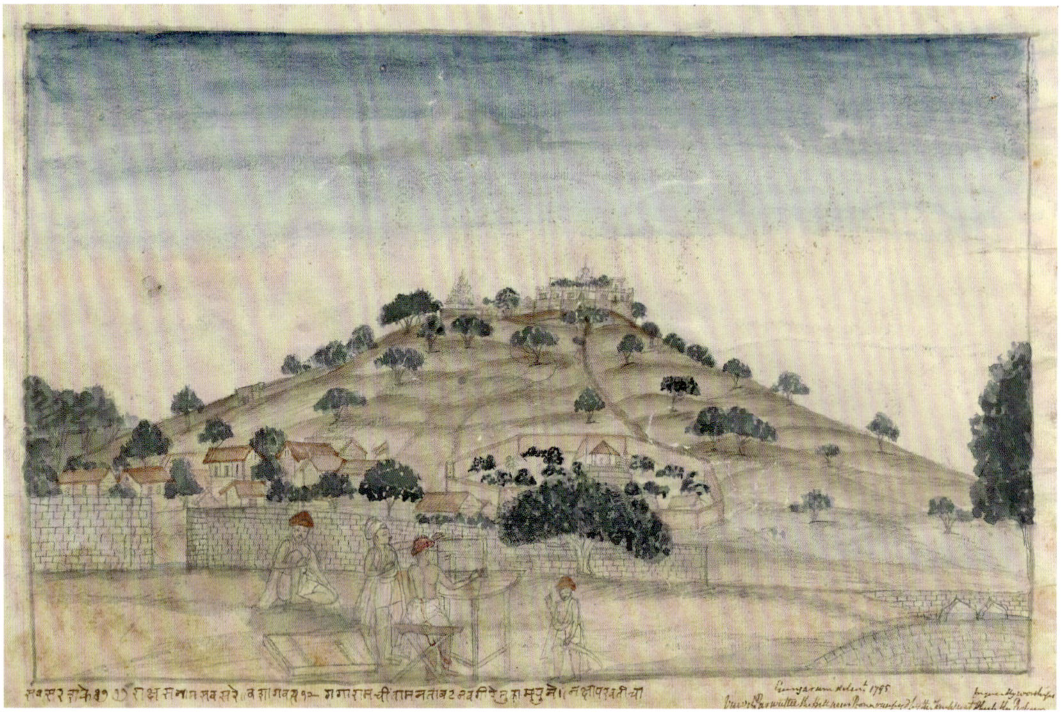

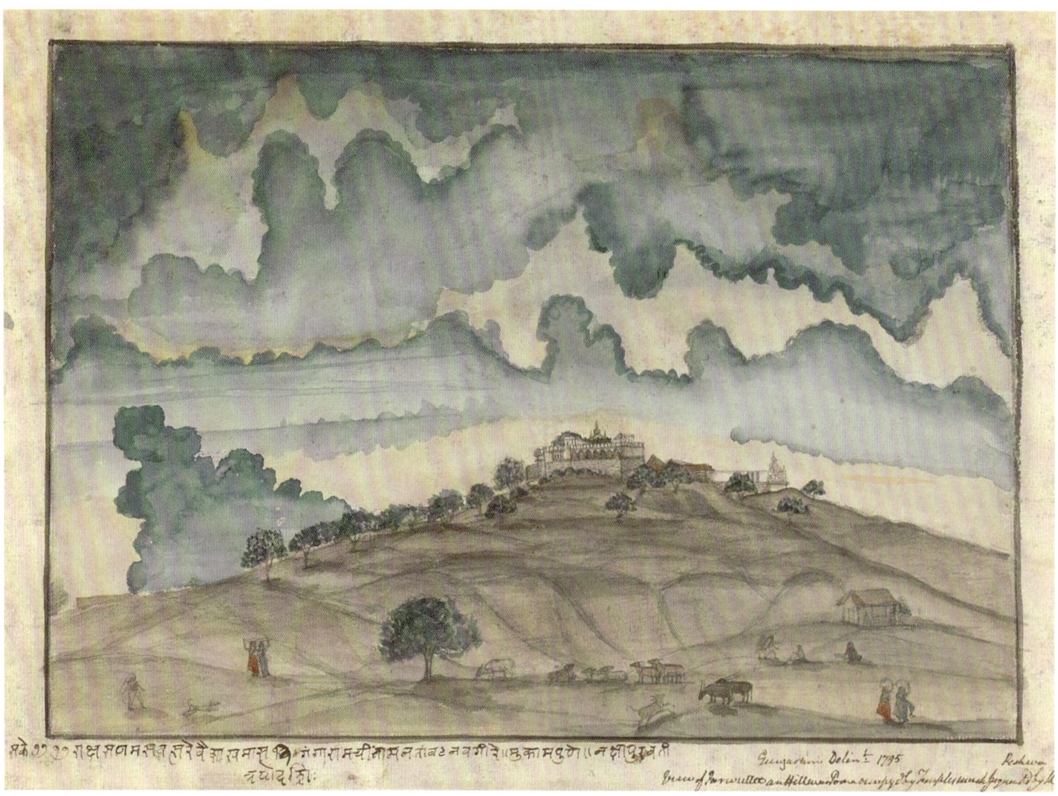

31 Gangaram Tambat, *View of Parbati, a Hill near Poona Occupied by the Temples at Which the Peshwa Frequently Worships*, Poona, 1795. Watercolor and graphite on paper, 27.9 × 42.5 cm. Yale Center for British Art, New Haven, Connecticut, Paul Mellon Collection, B1977.14.22364

32 Gangaram Tambat, *View of Parbati, a Hill near Poona Occupied by Temples Frequented by the Peshwa*, Poona, 1795. Watercolor, graphite and pen and brown ink on paper, 29.8 × 50.2 cm. Yale Center for British Art, New Haven, Connecticut, Paul Mellon Collection, B1977.14.22368

The Company Resident, Charles Warre Malet, and the artist James Wales employed Gangaram to assist their intellectual and professional pursuits.[3] He was responsible for sculpting animals in the Maratha ruler's menagerie at the base of this hill as well as drawing the renowned rock-carved temples of the region, wrestlers in training, and other scenes of life around Poona. As an Indian artist conforming to the aesthetics of British patrons, Gangaram came to be called a "Company" painter in scholarly terminology.[4] He not only worked within a British rubric of perspective and naturalism with a subtle palette, but he also attended to subjects like landscape, architecture, manners and customs, and natural history that were part of the "history, science, and art" that William Jones noted in the journal *Asiatick Researches* would advance understanding of the subcontinent and therefore the prowess of the East India Company.[5]

Yet Gangaram drew a surprising number of self-portraits that point to a life outside of his work for the Company. He depicted himself as a devotee, face in profile and body three-quarters to the viewer, with his hands folded in the respectful gesture of *anjali mudra* (fig. 33). He rotated himself to face forward and lock eyes with the viewer in another self-portrait (see fig. 5). A sprightly asymmetry in his mouth, moustache, and eyes determines a lilt of the head, and a bright yellow cloth is draped across his lap. Others also depicted him. An unknown artist showed him in similar garb, but with his body hunched and smeared with ash in a third picture (fig. 34). He is labeled as "a Fool," and his face, rendered with scruffs of facial hair and wrinkles around the eye, registers as different from the others. In yet another portrait, Gangaram is shown as an artist with one knee up, balancing a drawing board, his reed pen marking the page with a fluid line (fig. 35).

Gangaram's portraits, drawn by his and other hands in different modes, gesture to a biography as multifaceted as the artist's portrayal. They, along with his extant drawings, annotations, and sculptures, offer an opportunity to understand more about eighteenth-century artists in India, especially those trained outside of court contexts or family lineages

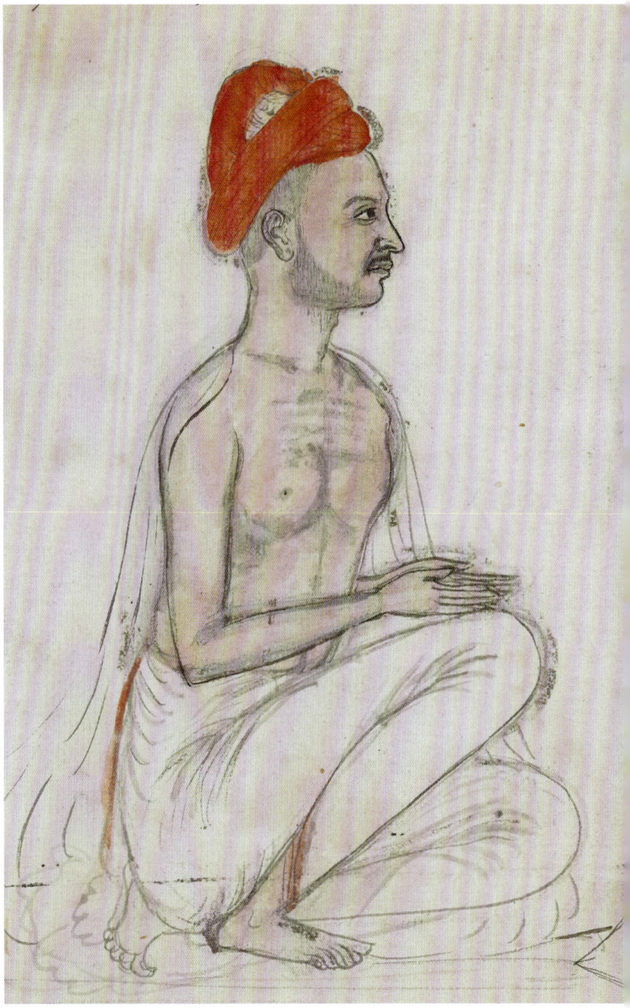

33 Gangaram Tambat, *Self-Portrait of the Artist Gangaram with his Guru*, Maharashtra, ca. 1790 (detail of fig. 72)

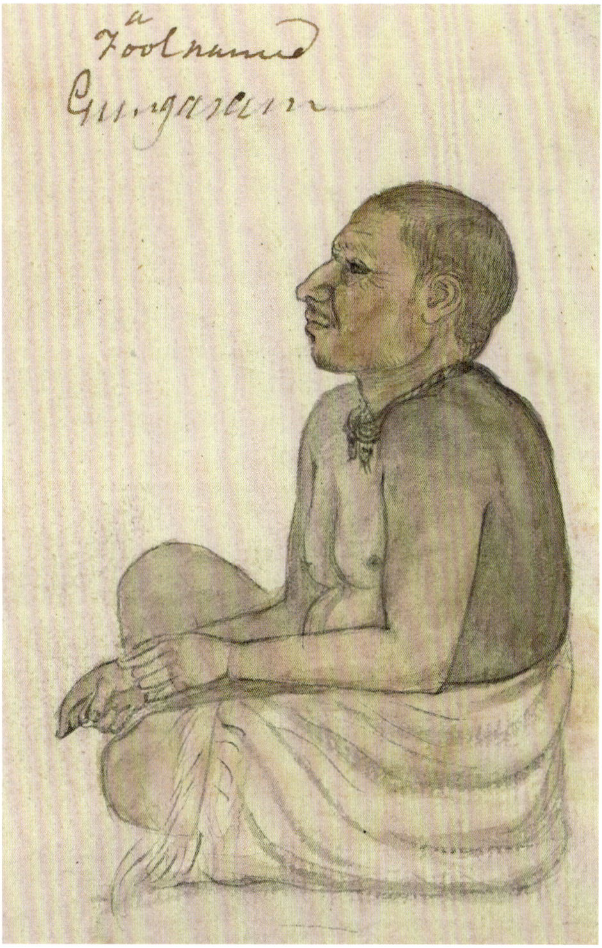

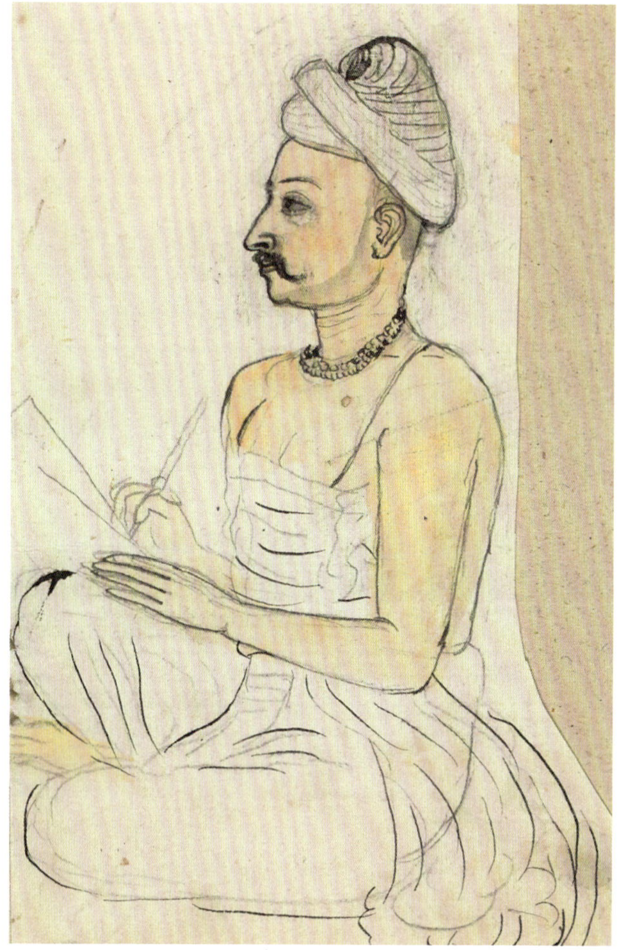

who remain little known.[6] They also aid in rethinking the term "Company" painter. Gangaram worked in a vernacular sphere of artistic production as well as for the British Residency. He also experimented with copying styles of painting from other areas of India. By grafting these different approaches to art into his practice, he created his own particular manner of making images. Further, in his work for Malet and Wales he encouraged them to approach artistry from different perspectives, much as they informed his practice.

Gangaram's adaptive approach to style (*kalam* in Marathi) redefines the term "Company" painter as one of manner rather than identity. An Indian or a British artist could work according to the rubric of a "Company" mode and also a "Mughal" or a "Poona" one. In this chapter, I thus focus on Gangaram as an artist from Poona who both enabled and altered the course of his British employers' projects, but I also emphasize his role simply as an artist.

34 *A Fool Named Gungaram* [Gangaram], Poona, ca. 1790. Watercolor and graphite with pen and black ink on paper, 17.1 × 13 cm. Yale Center for British Art, New Haven, Connecticut, Paul Mellon Collection, B1977.14.22249

35 *Portrait of Gangaram as an Artist*, Poona, ca. 1790. Watercolor and graphite with pen and black ink on paper, 20.3 × 13.7 cm. Yale Center for British Art, New Haven, Connecticut, Paul Mellon Collection, B1977.14.22416

"FROM THE LIFE": ANIMALS IN POONA

Gangaram's first extant commission from Malet was to draw and sculpt animals in the Peshwa's menagerie. Malet had been appointed the first Company diplomat, or Resident, at the Poona court in 1786. However, he only gained consistent access to the Peshwa a few years later when he began to negotiate with the Marathas to forge an Anglo-Maratha alliance against Tipu Sultan. In November 1790, Gangaram delineated the Peshwa's rhinoceros "with great fidelity," as Malet inscribed on the drawing (fig. 36). He detailed the rhinoceros's spotted, plated body and large ears, and measured its length in Devanagari script, which Malet transcribed into English from "outside of the tail to the foremost wrinkle." As it was "taken from the Life" in the Peshwa's menagerie, the rhinoceros bears specificity. The horn is small, though it would grow with the animal, according to the keeper, and the "genital parts" curved back to identify it as "retromingent." Gangaram subsequently prepared a "Wax Figure" on a wooden base whose color, Malet noted, was "excellently conveyed."[7] While "taken from the Life," the rhinoceros also suggests the "Life" that Malet employed Gangaram to capture – his own. Gangaram produced ani-

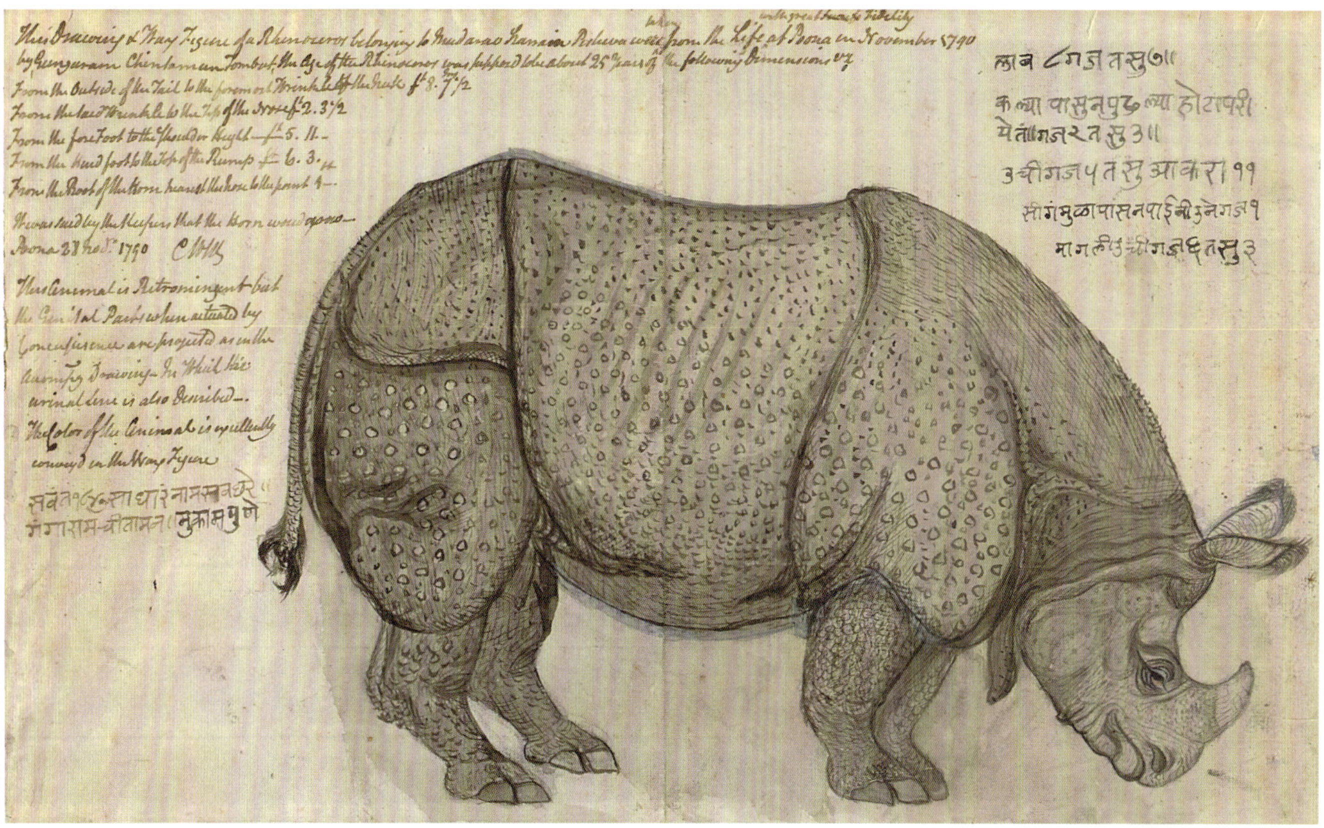

36 Gangaram Tambat, *A Rhinoceros in the Peshwa's Menagerie at Poona*, Poona, 1790. Pen and black ink, brown ink, gray wash, gouache, and graphite on paper, 22.5 × 37.1 cm. Yale Center for British Art, New Haven, Connecticut, Paul Mellon Collection, B2006.14.33

mal figurines for Malet as part of his mission to build a relationship with the Peshwa through an exchange of gifts and entertainment. They were also part of his intellectual engagement with Company officials who sought to contribute to the study of Indian natural history, as well as a more intimate, personal document of the Residency in Poona and his own rising status.

Malet had arrived at the court in 1786 with a rare bird (though it died en route), and those at the court reciprocated when they learned of his appreciation of horses.[8] In November 1789, Nana Fadnavis presented Malet with a "mare of the Deccan breed" that the Marathas "preferred to all others" having heard that he was "fond of horses and had very fine ones of most other countries." She "proved to be a very beautiful animal" to Malet. Soon after, the Peshwa visited the Residency. Malet presented him with animals, luxury goods, and art: "Figures of Plaster of Paris" that the Company had sent for the occasion, "elegant table linens, a Gold Time Piece and chain, 12 Trays of cloth . . . an elephant and an Arab horse."[9]

The exchange of gifts was part of the protocol of Anglo-Maratha negotiations, and Gangaram's documentation of them confirms their success. On August 6, 1790, the Peshwa signed the treaty in a grand ceremony in his palace, which included additional gifts to Malet and the men of his party of textiles, jewels, and another horse.[10] James Wales recorded this in paint the next year at Malet's behest (see fig. 20). In the months after the alliance, Malet was in frequent communication with Nana Fadnavis and the Peshwa, which included trips to the Peshwa's palace and must have afforded entry to the artist in his employment.[11] It is in this period that Gangaram drew and sculpted the series of animals in the Peshwa's menagerie and hunting grounds with which I began, as well as animals that Malet owned, including a model of the Peshwa's lion whose head is raised with uncommon pathos (fig. 37). While the Marathas and the British prepared for battle, Gangaram made at least two sketches of the Peshwa's animals: the rhinoceros in November and in December, an elephant named Ally Burh, along with the "seat of the prince," his attendant, the saddle, and dimensions. Sketches of the Peshwa's leopard, lion, lynx, tiger, and two-humped Bactrian camel followed.[12]

The Peshwa's collection continued a Maratha tradition of keeping rare and exotic animals that emulated a Mughal practice of cultivating plants and animals and skill in the

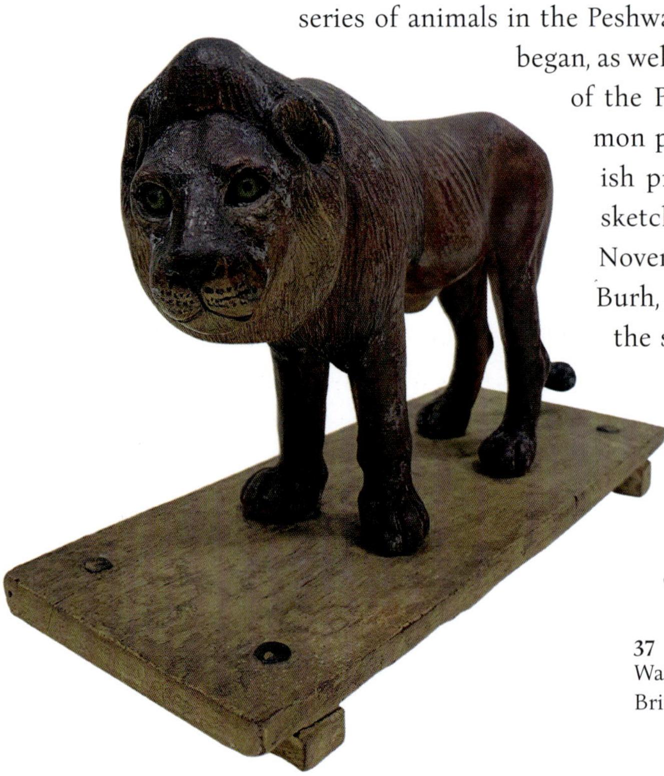

37 Gangaram Tambat, *A Model of a Lion*, Poona, ca. 1790. Wax, painted. Wooden base 20.5 × 9.75 × 2 cm; animal h. 12.5 cm. British Library, London, F872

hunt in order to model just and cultivated rule.[13] Accordingly, the Peshwa's records indicate purchases for the menagerie with gifts accruing in the time of the young Peshwa Savai Madhavrao (1774–1795) for his education and pleasure.[14] The Peshwa visited Parvati Hill almost daily to exercise on horseback as part of his military training (see figs. 29 and 30).[15] Nana Fadnavis and others procured myna birds and parrots, ducks, peacocks, hundreds of deer, black buck, and hares, ten to twenty tigers, leopards, and crocodiles.[16] Mahadji Scindia sent the rhinoceros and Bactrian camel, and Malet presented the Peshwa with rare birds and two tigers.[17] These animals were put to use as entertainment. The Peshwa trained antelopes to crouch "in the most graceful attitude" on a swing while music played, according to Malet.[18] At other times, the court organized fights between tigers and elephants, tigers and antelopes, and among different kinds of deer.[19]

Malet recognized the significance of the animal park for the Marathas, and the Marathas also identified their joint interest in painting as well as in gifts. Shivram Chitari, an artist who worked for the Marathas, painted a British hunter at the center of a novel composition: a parrot-green field teeming with animals, each on a lime green tuft: black bears and an elephant, foxes chasing birds, monkeys munching fruit, horses, boar and deer, puffs of rabbits and squirrels (fig. 38). At any moment the hunter could lift his gun and slay the animals, yet the animals do not appear threatened by him. Rather, it is the hunter, set against a deep green bush, who is equally observed by the viewer of the work. There is evidence that the figure is Malet, which places this painting in dialogue with Gangaram's equally perceptive sculptures of the Peshwa's fauna (see fig. 37).[20] When placed side by side, Shivram's courtly cosmopolitan painting and Gangaram's vernacular, western Indian sculptures, reveal two aspects of an artistic and diplomatic conversation that depended on agile practices of mutual Maratha and British curiosity as well as surveillance.[21] Indeed, similar to Gangaram's travels to the Peshwa's hunting grounds and menagerie to study his animals, Shivram appears to have depicted Malet among his collection of animals at the Residency. In the early twentieth century, D. B. Parasnis even suggested that Shivram showed him among Gangaram's sculptures rather than the living animals, which implies that the court studiously observed Malet's observation of their customs.[22]

Shivram's and Gangaram's depictions of animals correlate with diplomatic and social circumstances, but they also refer to varied artistic practices. Shivram Chitari drew on circulating compositions of courtly hunts and Sufi epics of lovers lost in the wilderness searching for their beloveds; it is likely that he also turned to British prints of hunting parks that were locally available.[23] Gangaram's work registers different visual sources. Although the details were based on observation "from the Life," they also relate to contemporary compendia. Malet owned a "dictionary of arts and sciences," according to his friend James Forbes.[24] Gangaram's rhinoceros with its head dipped low has an affin-

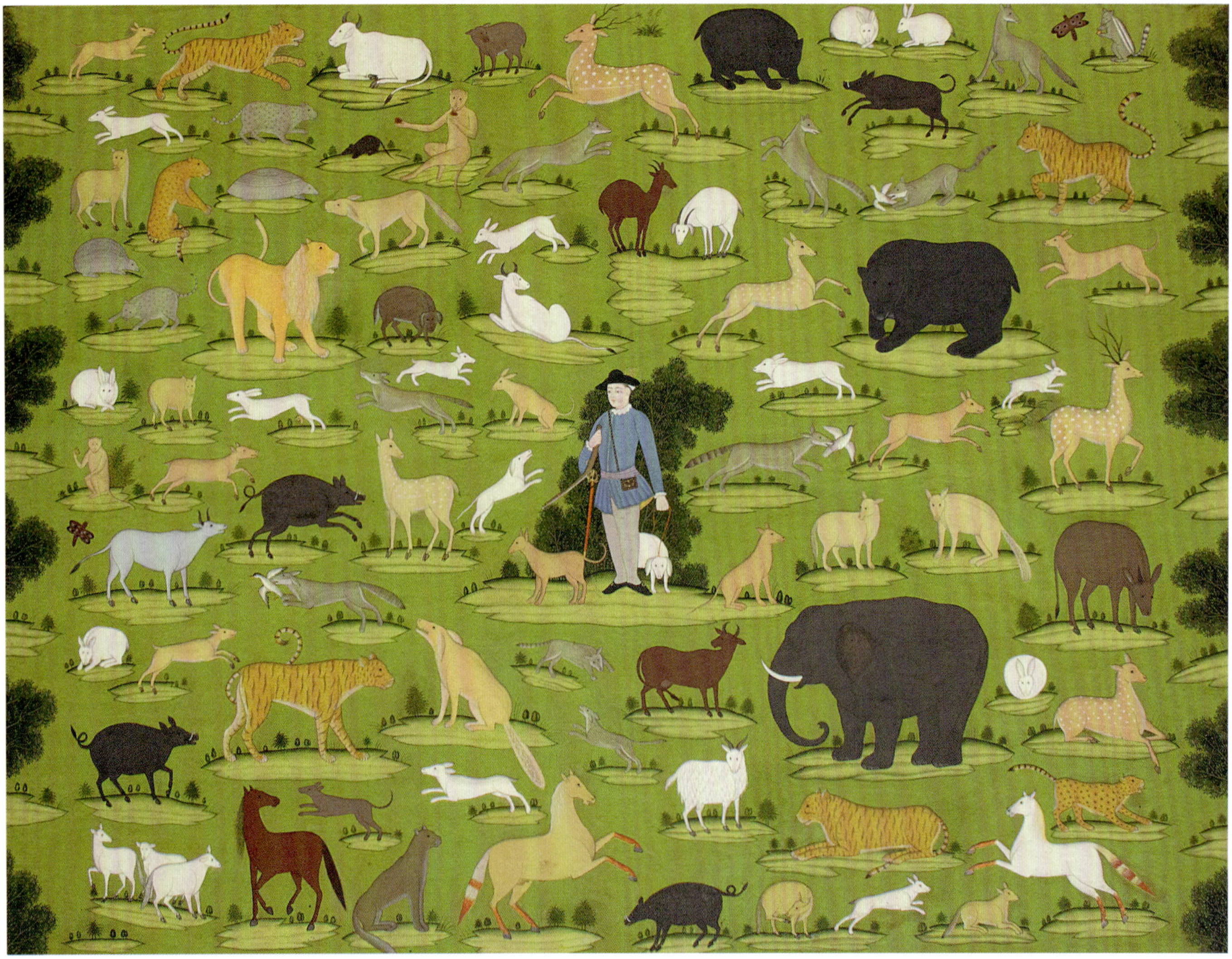

ity to the illustration in the fourth volume of *A New and Complete Dictionary of Arts and Sciences . . . engraved by Mr. Jefferys* (1764), though which dictionary Malet owned is unknown.[25] Beyond diplomacy, Malet might have wanted Gangaram to document the animals to provide additional information or update and correct such compendia (see fig. 36).[26]

These books offered a mode of observing scientifically from life and encyclopedic conventions of illustration, which Gangaram surely consulted. However, the techniques he used, and even the subjects he depicted, equally relate to vernacular traditions of sculpture and metalwork. Gangaram's two final names are Navgire and Tambat.[27] According to the 1885 Bombay *Gazetteer*, in the "Poona district" craftsmen with the surname

38 Shivram Chitari, *A British Hunter in a Maratha Landscape*, Poona, late 18th century. Opaque watercolor on handmade paper, 34 × 44 cm. History Museum, Dr. Babasaheb Ambedkar Marathwada University, Aurangabad

Navgire followed a variety of callings including "casting metal, carving stones, painting, making figures of clay and cloth, carving wood, and repairing boxes, padlocks, and watches."[28] Tambat specifically indicated a coppersmith, a group that became upwardly mobile in the early modern period through their craft.[29] In his portraits, Gangaram is portrayed with Brahminical attributes such as sacred threads worn across the body, and Moor described Gangaram as of a higher caste, a "Brahmin," as did Malet and Wales. The British sought to justify their sources through status – and the assertion of "Brahmin" knowledge punctuates their writings in this regard – but it also shows flexibility in caste claims in the Peshwa period, which is generally known for increasing rigidity around these categories.[30]

From a foundation in metalworking, Gangaram was able to see new opportunities for patronage and adapt new modes. For instance, he drew pages of "Utensils" (fig. 39). The organization of the tools on the page is rooted in an encyclopedic format, as was the rhinoceros described earlier.[31] Yet the tools that Gangaram depicted were local. Those on the right relate to coppersmithing, such as the slender hammer used to chase copper vessels at the top of the page, and the thicker, central hammer for raising and shaping vessels against the stakes depicted alongside.[32] Gangaram also sculpted the animal figurines from wax or resin, such as *dhuna*, an aromatic gum of the *sal* tree, *Shorea robusta*. These are substances that would have been familiar to metalworkers: wax or pitch is poured into a vessel or against the backside of a plate to support the surface while chasing decoration.[33]

Gangaram's drawings, figures, and knowledge of tools identify his ability in regional styles of sculpting and draftsmanship. Moor wrote in *The Hindu Pantheon* (1810) that he saw a "well modelled group" of Krishna plaiting Radha's hair by Gangaram that substantiates the claim that he sculpted in a local manner, and other drawings indicate that he painted in one too.[34] Although unsigned, a drawing of Krishna riding a horse composed of women remains in Malet's archive and appears to be in Gangaram's hand (fig. 40). The sure but sketchy lines, eyes dashed in with two strokes at a thirty-degree angle, with pupils mismatched, blank background, light watercolor washes, and articulation of muscles with darker shades of wash (as in the horse's neck) are also seen in his signed drawings of athletes (see figs. 44 and 45). These conform to a regional idiom of western Indian painting: figures are drawn by thick continuous lines to define the forms and filled with flat planes of color, crowns are tiered and rimmed with pearls, and women wear their saris pulled up between the legs in the local style.

Such works indicate that Gangaram was well-versed in a range of arts from drawing and painting to *tambat* metalwork to modeling figures of wax and clay. This range of material not only points to a wider sphere of production, but also to the fact that designs

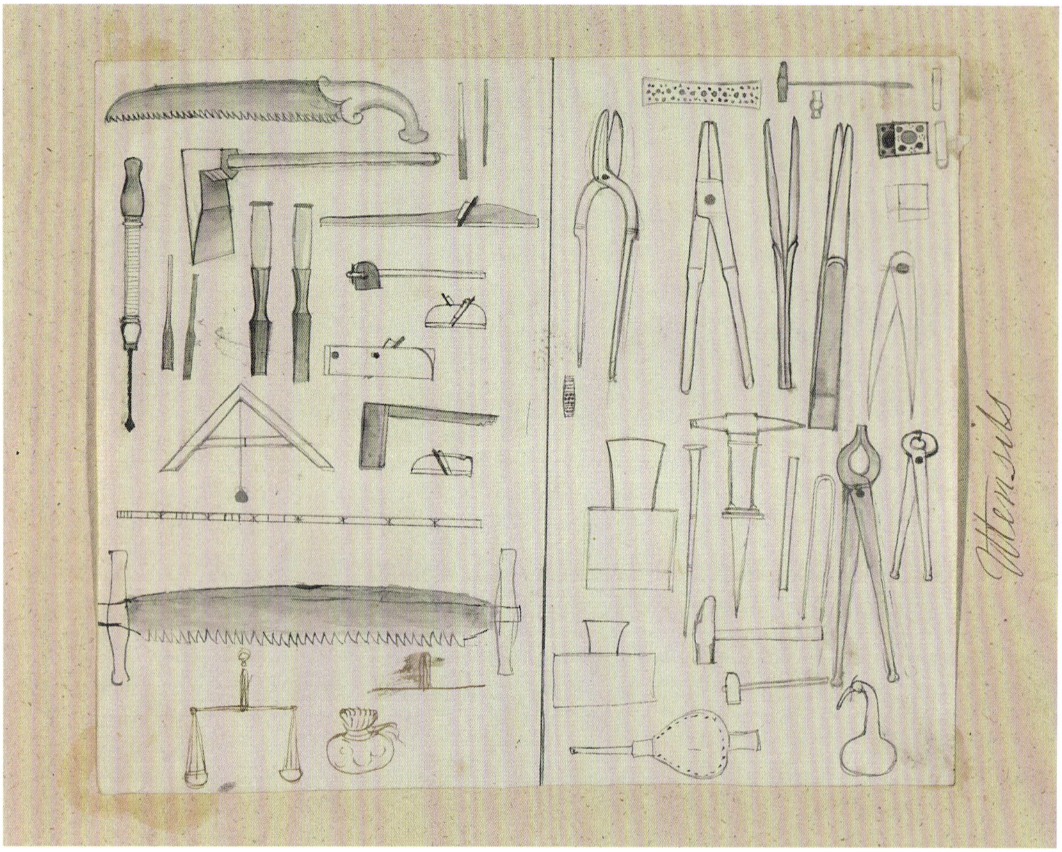

could move across media. Wax, clay, and bronze sculptures were popular in western India. Similar to Gangaram's drawing of Krishna on a horse, Moor purchased "models in wax and clay" of Krishna riding an elephant composed of nine women (*navanari kunjara*).[35] Although the sculpture is not extant in his collection, there is an elegant black and white drawing of the subject by an artist from Poona in Moor's employment (see fig. 122), which supports the connection between local drawings and sculptures.

These types of arts were widely available in the markets. Artists formed representations of Ganesha and other deities from clay for processions in festivals, as they did whole armies and forts, which included elephants and other animals.[36] Popular deities, such as Khandoba astride a horse, attest to bronzes made at this time (see fig. 81). By the middle of the nineteenth century, the region had become well known for its "Poonah" figures that were often sold from specialty shops and included, as one Mrs. Hervey wrote in 1853, "little figures . . . representative of the . . . various classes of the natives . . . servants, tradesmen and fakirs, also of different animals, idols and other varieties . . . ."[37] These

39 Gangaram Tambat, attrib., *Utensils*, Poona, ca. 1790. Gray wash and graphite with pen and black and brown ink on paper, 21.9 × 29.2 cm. Yale Center for British Art, New Haven, Connecticut, Paul Mellon Collection, B1977.14.22311

figures, primarily molded in clay, were displayed at international exhibitions to classify animals, such as a sacred bull, laden bullock, and dancing bear, and to identify Indian peoples and their productivity in the empire.[38] Gangaram's animal sculptures thus pivot between figures produced for regional festivals and worship, and those that came to signify colonial systems of control.

Gangaram worked within a local system of popular artistic production and one of Company officials interested in hiring local artists to make models pertaining to their colonial and antiquarian projects. Adam Blackader, a British surgeon stationed at Madurai, for instance, had eighteen models cast in a copper alloy of a temple's freestanding pillared hall, often known as Tirumala Nayak's *choultry*. Along with 143 related drawings, he sent the models in July 1789 to the Society of Antiquaries in London.[39] In the same

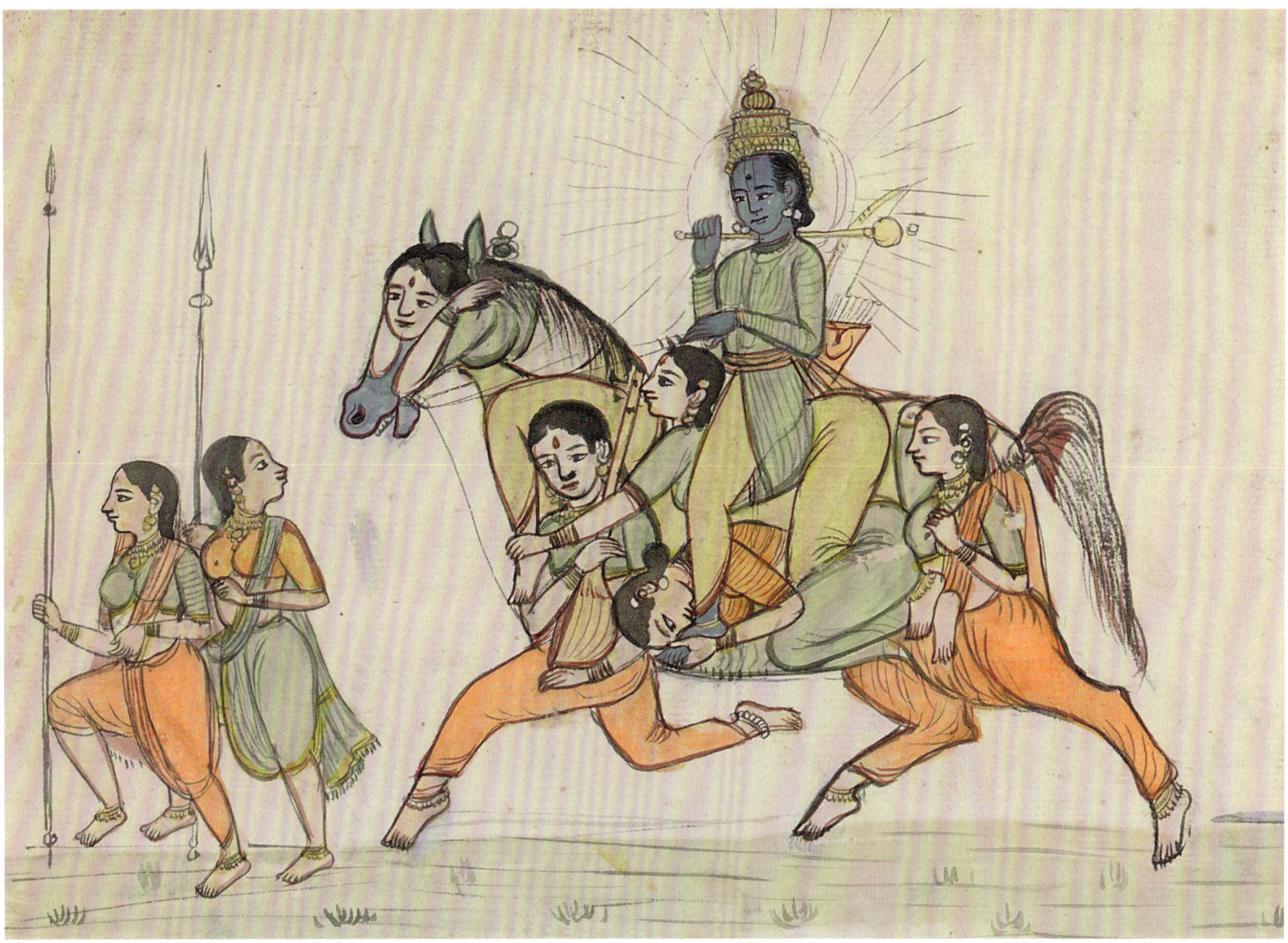

40 Gangaram Tambat, attrib., *Krishna Riding a Horse Composed of Women*, Poona, ca. 1790. Watercolor, gouache, and graphite on laid paper, 18.4 × 27.3 cm. Yale Center for British Art, New Haven, Connecticut, Paul Mellon Collection, B1977.14.22304

period, the Sanskritist Charles Wilkins had zinc models cast in Benares of the incarnations of Vishnu, probably because these could not be readily found on the market, which Moor reproduced in *The Hindu Pantheon* (see fig. 114).[40] Yet we know little about the artists who produced works for these projects.

In comparison, Gangaram grafted regional and Company traditions, as well as those of natural history, to make his animal figures respond to his patron's requirements. In this, they reveal another quality of Malet's commission: these were intimate documents of his access to the Peshwa and of his Residency in Poona. They exemplify diplomatic exchange, but also a shared love of the hunt and keeping animals. For, besides sculptures of the animals in the Peshwa's menagerie, Malet also had animals sculpted that were important to him, including his favorite camel, a horse given to him by the Peshwa, and his hunting cheetah.[41] Malet kept numerous camels, elephants, and horses at the Residency. "After dinner" one evening James Wales wrote that he went and "met Sir Charles' elephants, he has three, and his camels, of which he has about twenty, his shed of horses."[42] The horse that the Peshwa had given to Malet must have been kept in this "shed," and the "common" camel that Gangaram sculpted paraded the grounds. While Malet was the Resident in Cambay (1774–86), a local ruler had given him two cheetahs. Gangaram sculpted one of these, along with a lynx (*siyah-gosh*), both excellent for hunting antelopes.[43]

In Poona, animals inhabited vast parklands and were kept in private grounds by those of high status; Malet's social aspirations followed the Peshwa, as well as the British aristocracy, in his taste for hunting, displaying trophies, and keeping exotic animals. Indeed, as noted earlier, Shivram's painting of a British hunter in a field may depict Malet in the grounds of the Residency (see fig. 38) just as the artists who worked for Malet sought to depict the Peshwa and his animals on Parvati Hill.

There are an ample number of descriptions of the animals that roamed the Residency grounds. Wales wrote that he "went out with Sir Charles . . . at 4 o clock to take a ride . . . there was a park of grey hounds upon the ground before us – we saw several fine Views – and also many hares . . . quails and flocks of sheep with wool like those of Britain."[44] Many of those birds and hares, and antelope and boar, were hunted and shot, as sketches in Wales's journal, and the teeth and tusks that stud the length of Malet's silver horse harness (fig. 41), attest.[45] Such hunts and retinues of animals were "requisite at Eastern Courts," as Moor wrote, "where there is always considerable pomp, and it is necessary for ambassadors to assume an appearance of ceremonious dignity."[46]

Malet clearly adopted such an "appearance of . . . dignity" in India, just as he did when he returned to England at the higher status of baronet, and with far greater wealth. In Poona, Malet owned forty or fifty horses of a variety of breeds.[47] A similar stud is seen in an oil painting of Malet's new estate, Wilbury House, in Wiltshire, England. Malet employed

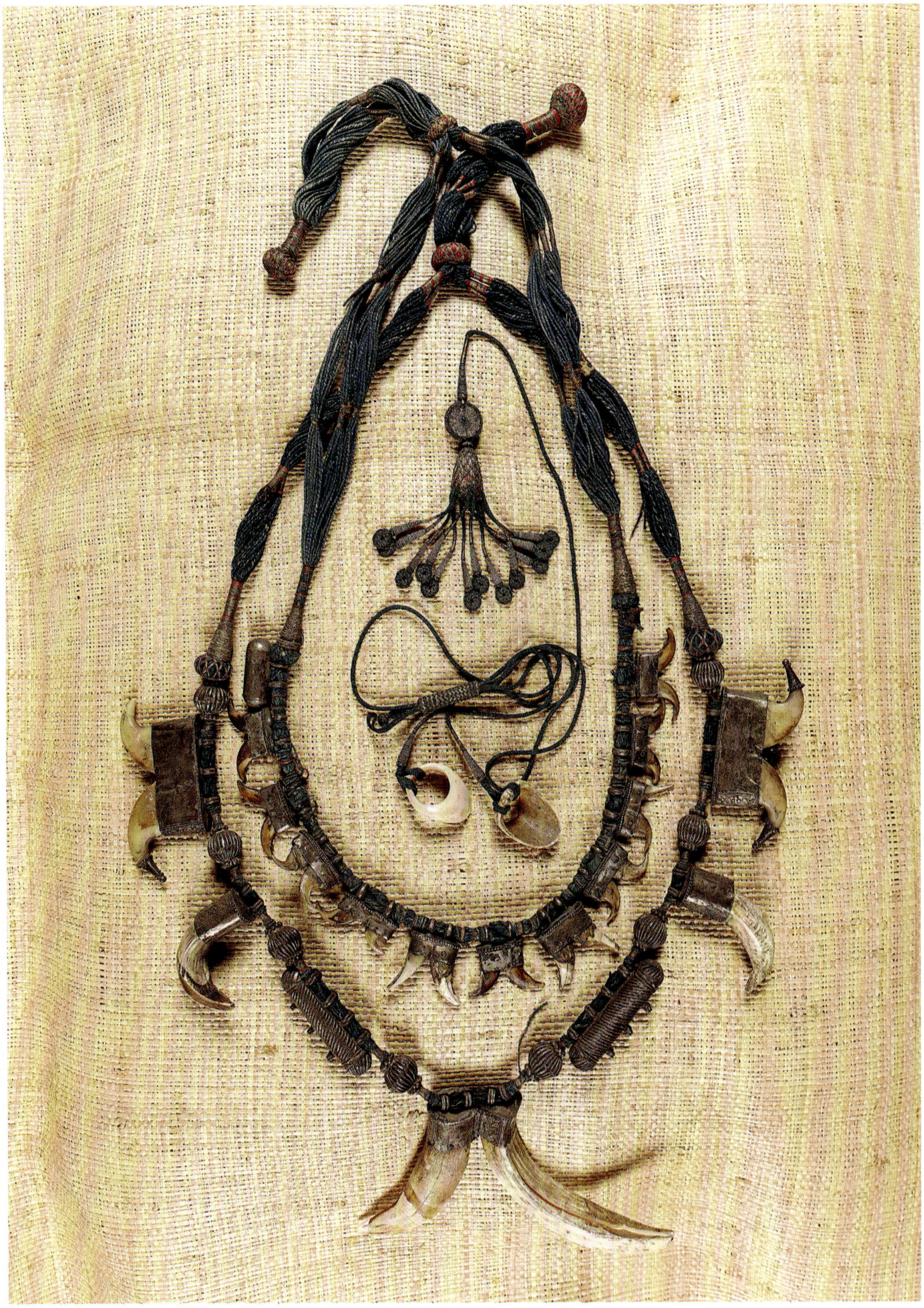

41 Charles Warre Malet's horse ornaments with boar tusks and teeth and ivory archer's rings, late 18th century. Niall Hobhouse Collection

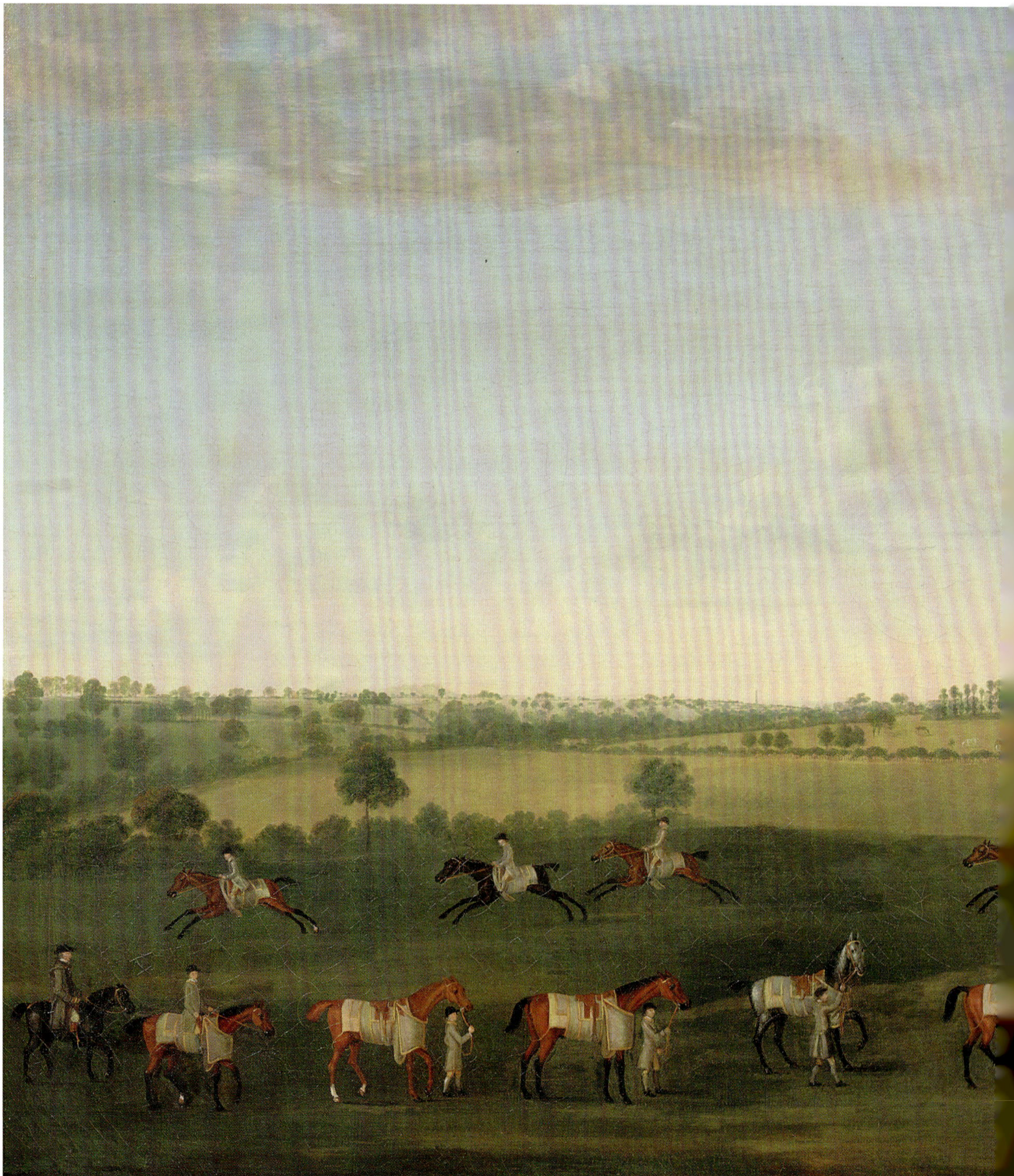

42 Francis Sartorius and James Wales, attrib., *Sir Charles Warre Malet's String of Racehorses at Exercise*, probably Poona and Newton Tony, Wiltshire, 1800. Oil on canvas, 57.2 × 75.6 cm. Yale Center for British Art, New Haven, Connecticut, Paul Mellon Collection, B2001.2.282

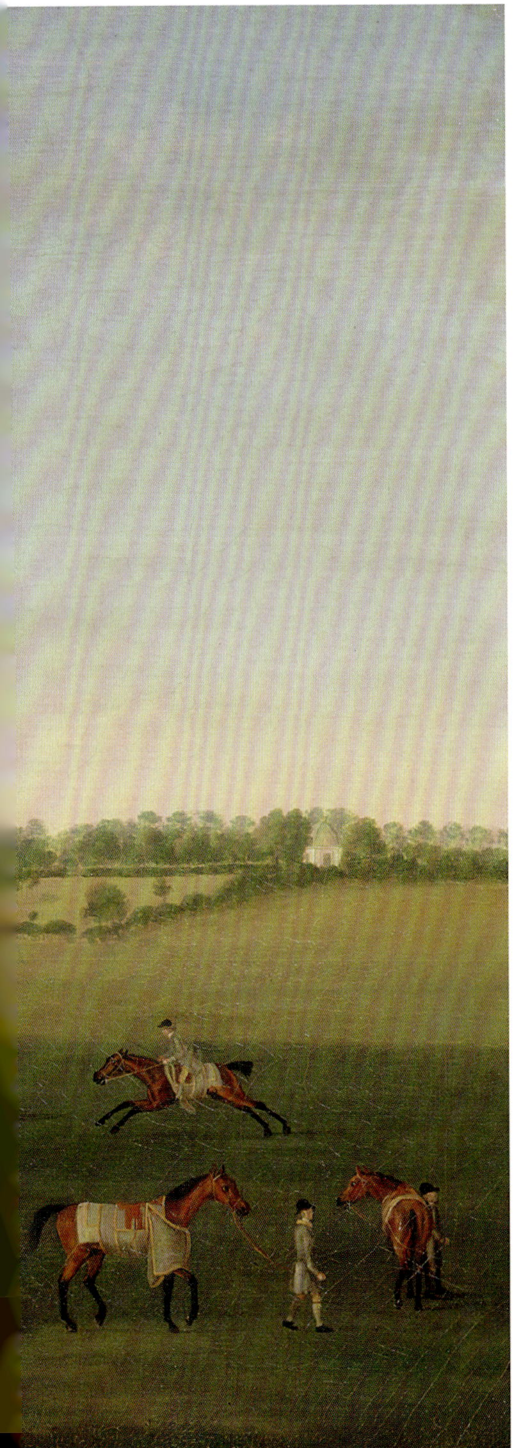

the artist Francis Sartorius to depict the horses parading and galloping on a deep green ground (fig. 42). This appears to be a typical British painting. Yet the painted landscape looks surprisingly like that near Poona: indeed, William Lyons, a British historian of Wiltshire, asserted that Malet had purchased this property for that precise reason.[48] There are a series of rolling hills dotted with small trees and familiar, albeit more muted, greens, and the low composition is comparable to a watercolor of a landscape near Poona in Malet's archive (fig. 43). Features in the oil painting point to a circuitous avenue of production. Although Malet could have instructed Sartorius to amalgamate two of the highly important landscapes of his life, it is more likely that Sartorius completed a painting that Wales had started in Poona but needed to be finished in Britain after his death, much like Wales's painting of the Treaty that Thomas Daniell finished at Malet's request (see fig. 20). Wales wrote in his journals that he was painting a landscape for Malet,[49] and a landscape is recorded (but not identified as extant) in Malet's collection.[50] A Marathi letter further documented that Indian artists had worked on at least one of Wales's landscapes in Poona.[51] While an octagonal summerhouse to the north of the mansion and a temple to the southwest are recorded as being in the gardens of Wilbury, it is curious that an additional, faint building that looks like a Mughal mausoleum is included in the British countryside of Sartorius's painting, hinting at the Poona hills that lay beneath.[52]

Charles Warre Malet, the son of a rector of Combe Florey, Somerset, became princely in India, a "Nabob" in the terms of the time.[53] He took on the habits of the ruling Peshwa and the hunting traditions that would have been familiar to him from England, but out of reach from the station in which he was born. The British landscape in Sartorius's painting not only appears to overlay the Indian one, but also emerges from the Indian wealth that

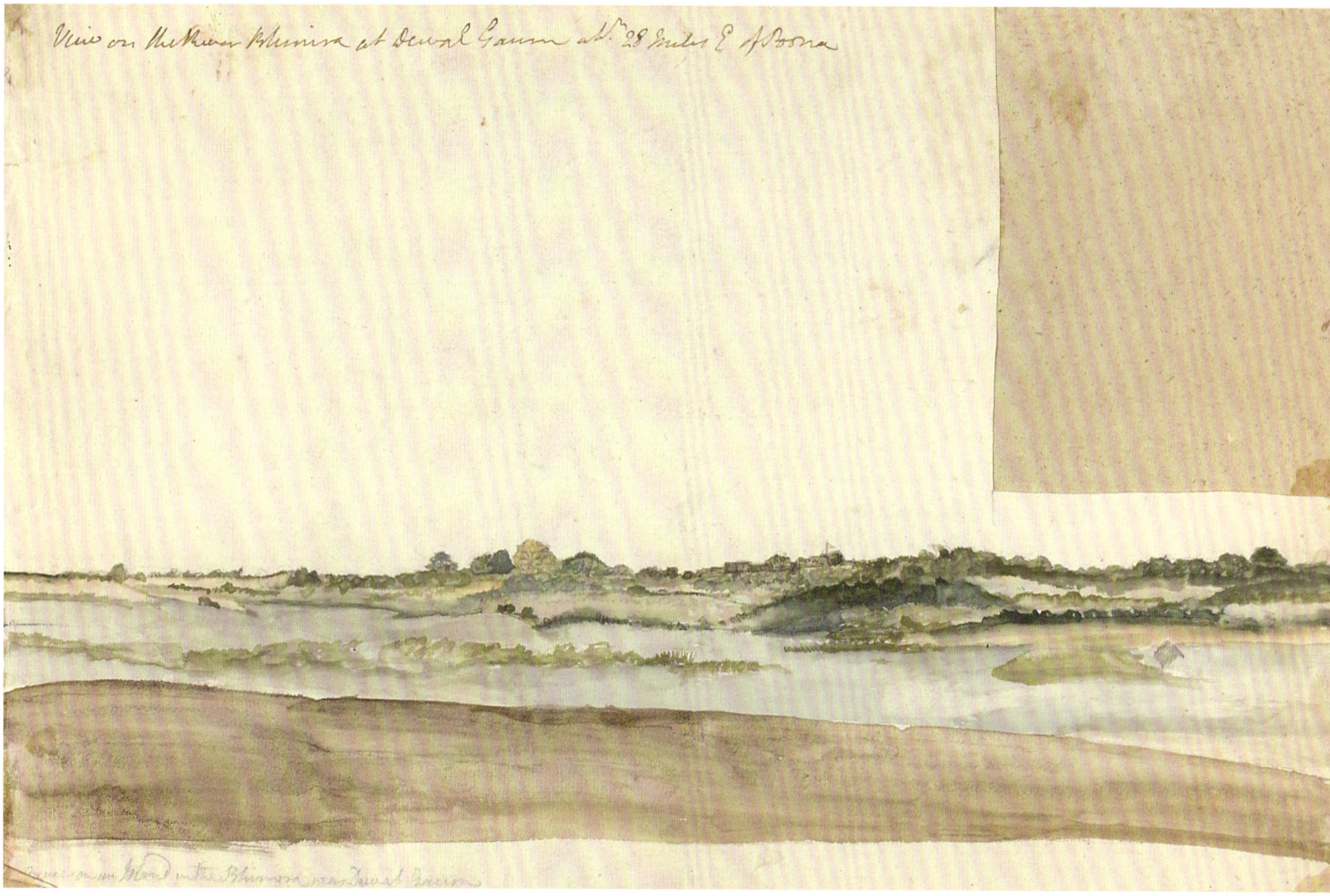

allowed its purchase. The construction of Malet's status is also marked in how Gangaram's sculptures of the Peshwa's animals are set to graze in Malet's collection alongside those that he owned. The production of these animals participated in his building a relationship with the Peshwa; they were an extension of his mission. They also enabled him to participate in a network of Company officials who were keen to add knowledge of Indian animals to the broader effort of European naturalists, and in rare cases, even transferred animals they owned in India to Britain.[54] But primarily they seem to have been a personal memento of the "wild animals" of Poona and Malet's efforts to mimic the status of the Peshwa, one that would register in Poona and transfer to Britain, which Gangaram matched in his sculptures by nimbly fusing multiple modes of artistry.

43 Gangaram Tambat, attrib., *View on the River Bhima at Deval Gaun, 28 Miles E of Poona*, 1792–4. Watercolor, graphite and pen and brown ink on paper, 29.8 × 48.6 cm. Yale Center for British Art, New Haven, Connecticut, Paul Mellon Collection, B1977.14.22361

A HISTORY OF THE MARATHAS

Gangaram documented at least two histories of the Marathas: one which focused on Malet and his interactions with the Peshwa and the Poona court, and another for Malet which ostensibly focused on the Maratha past. His drawings can be read as a timeline of Malet's personal history with the Marathas. If he depicted animals related to diplomacy and nobility in the first series, then in the second he focused on wrestlers, which related to Malet's study of Maratha history and culture to inform his work as an ambassador, and to connect to an East India Company network of knowledge acquisition.

In September 1791 the Peshwa invited Malet, as he wrote, to an "exhibition of Pugilists and Wrestlers," known as *jethi* or *jetti*. Under "a very large tent pitched for the Purpose," the contestants sparred in the "Square of one of his troop's stable yards."[55] The Company official David Price, who was in Malet's party that day, also described the event:

> There is . . . a circular pit . . . about 7 feet deep, and perhaps 30 feet in diameter, the bottom well covered with sand. The jetties are naked, with the exception of a pair of very short drawers. Their hands are armed with a kind of cestus, made of horn, shaped into knuckles, and drawn on the fingers . . . [they] had evidently been well and carefully trained. The young Peshwa appeared to be delighted . . . not the less so when the pugilists . . . saluted him as "Dekhan ki Badshah" – Emperor of the Dekhan.[56]

Noting the scene, the tools, and the skill of the performers, Price also commented on their flattery of the young Peshwa and his empire. Malet's study moved beyond the circular pit and the Marathas to that of the world. In his memoranda, he wrote that the "Pugillators were much worthy the Observation of those who are fond of comparing the Manners of men in different Countries and ages these seeming exactly to resemble those of the same Profession Who used to exhibit at the Games of Greece and Rome."[57]

A few months later, in January 1792, Gangaram drew eleven sketches of wrestlers in the middle of exercise or combat. The spare style and annotations are a mix of Price's historical documentation and Malet's comparative ethnography of the match, but they focus on the preparation. In one drawing, two muscular men, thick in build, twist up and down wrestling pillars with their faces hidden from view (fig. 44). They wear pale orange fabric knotted into shorts, are bare-chested, and their heads are shaved except for a knot of hair. The scene is simple, with red-orange earth as the land and blank page as the sky. Another drawing shows a series of tumbling exercises, while others depict athletes lifting a round circular weight known as a *nal* or straining to swing bottle-shaped clubs called *gada* or *mugdar*.[58] Of the latter, Malet even returned to England with a burnished and painted pair.[59]

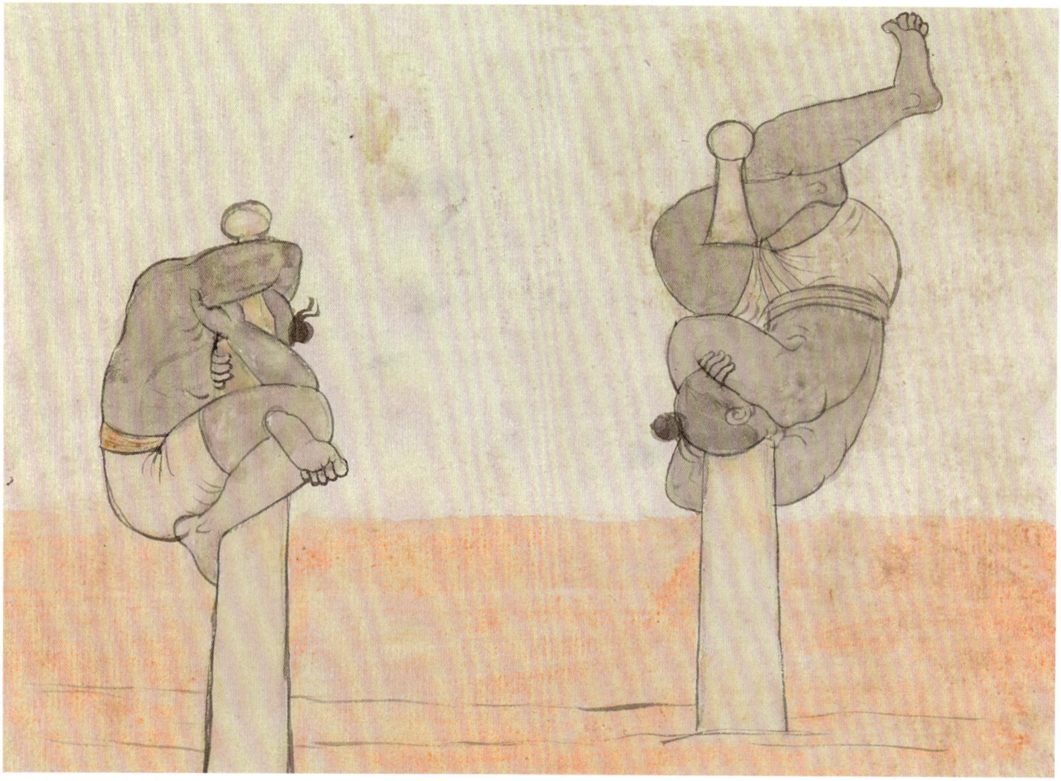

On a watercolor of men sparring, Gangaram captioned them as "brave rivals (*virodhi*) with the tiger claw" weapon and gave the date and his signature (fig. 45). Below, Malet wrote:

> A Representation of the style of fighting of the Jeyties or Indian Pugilists – this style of fighting seems peculiar to the upper Carnatic... from whence the practitioners go to different parts of India and are entertained by different rajas and princes before whom these contests are exhibited with great show and apparatus.

Malet's description suggests that these athletes were trained in Karnataka (in Tarapur), south of the Deccan, but employed beyond the region. An early eighteenth-century painting of the Udaipur palace in Rajasthan, for example, portrays such wrestlers in combat before Maharana Sangram Singh II.[60]

Training in wrestling and boxing, and its spectatorship, was part of the principle of Maratha military leadership; in the eighteenth century the minister Ramchandra Amatya wrote that "professional wrestlers and other experts... should be engaged" as royal teachers.[61] The Peshwa Savai Madhavrao employed *jethi* in pairs who excelled in a particular

44 Gangaram Tambat, *Two Jeyties*, Poona, ca. 1792. Watercolor and graphite on paper, 17.8 × 23.8 cm. Yale Center for British Art, New Haven, Connecticut, Paul Mellon Collection, B1977.14.22293

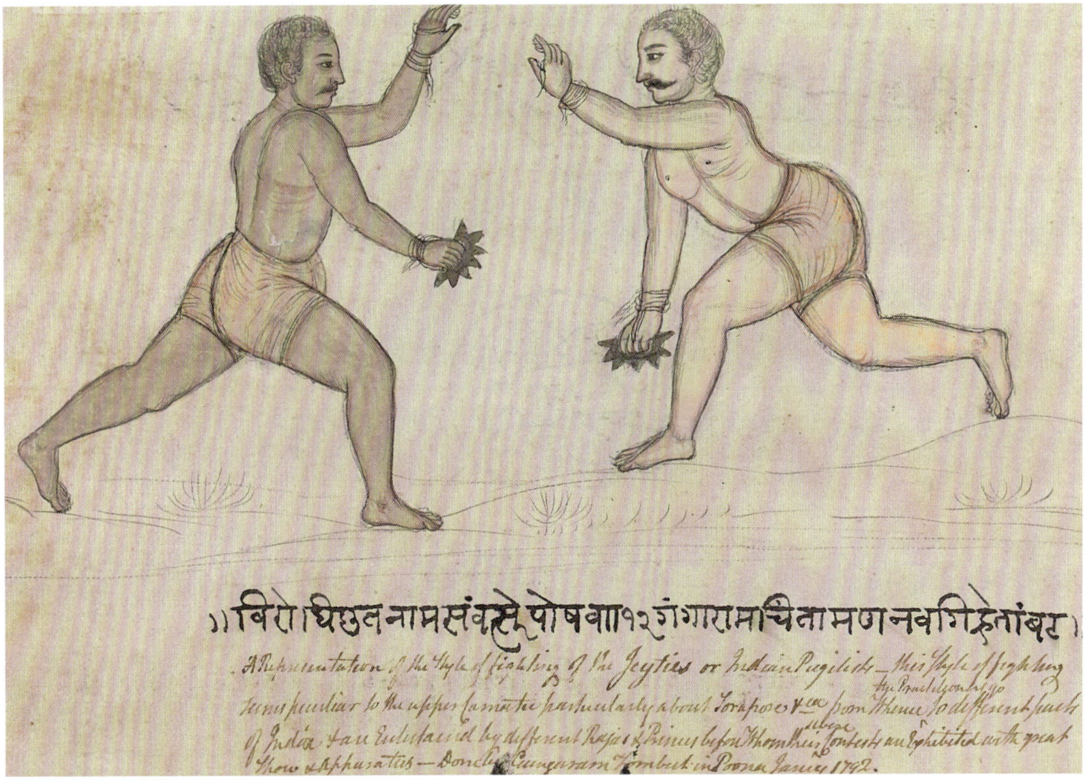

blend of boxing and wrestling known as *vajra mushti*.[62] They instructed him and he took pleasure in watching their bloody bouts that often ended in death.[63]

Gangaram's series of drawings focuses on athletic training in a nearby neighborhood called Narayan Peth rather than such palace matches that Price and Malet had described and those depicted in the Udaipur painting.[64] He must have sought out the wrestlers and boxers when they were not explicitly on show, when he, and they, were away from their patrons.[65] They are displayed in sequences of exercise and combat, with various weapons and poses. The bodies are rendered robust yet fluid by Gangaram's use of outline to define and delineate the forms, much like other regional representations, such as of the monkey god Hanuman wrestling with Garuda, the divine bird (fig. 46). While both create stark and provocative images, Gangaram's drawings leave the sphere of the mythic to enter that of the instruction manual.

Traditions of village and urban sport also co-existed with soldiering. The artist Deen Ali captured a similar group of wrestlers exercising in a Maratha military camp; he drew them in a "Company" mode for the official Thomas Duer Broughton's 1813 publication *Letters written in a Mahratta camp* (fig. 47). The accompanying letter describes the day on

45 Gangaram Tambat, *Two Jeyties Fighting*, Poona, ca. 1792.
Watercolor and graphite with pen and brown ink on paper,
17.1 × 25.4 cm. Yale Center for British Art, New Haven, Connecticut,
Paul Mellon Collection, B1977.14.22294

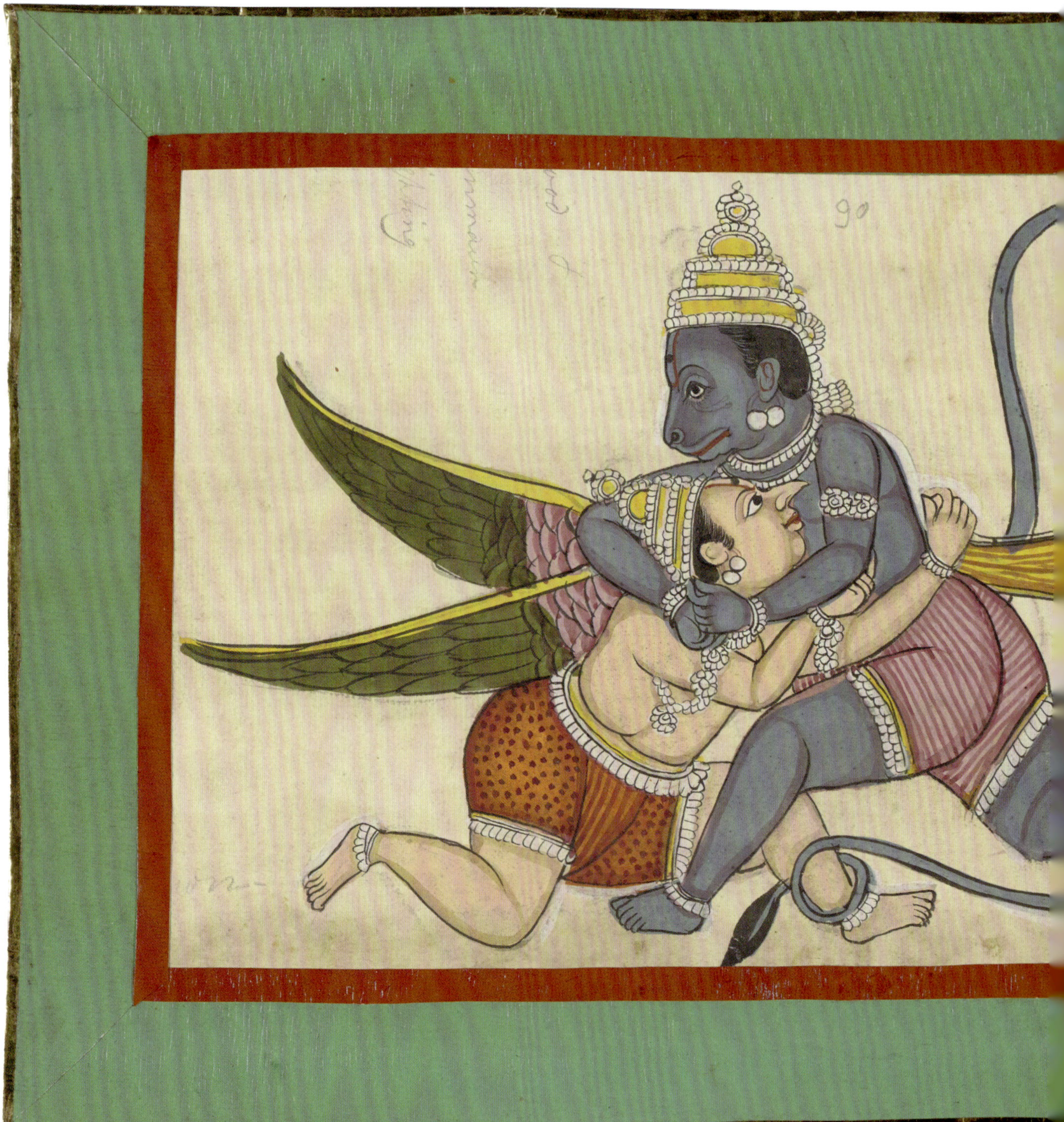

46 *Hanuman Wrestling with Garuda*, Poona, 1800–05. Opaque watercolor on paper, 23.25 × 32.4 cm. British Museum, London, Edward Moor Collection, 1940,0713,0.214

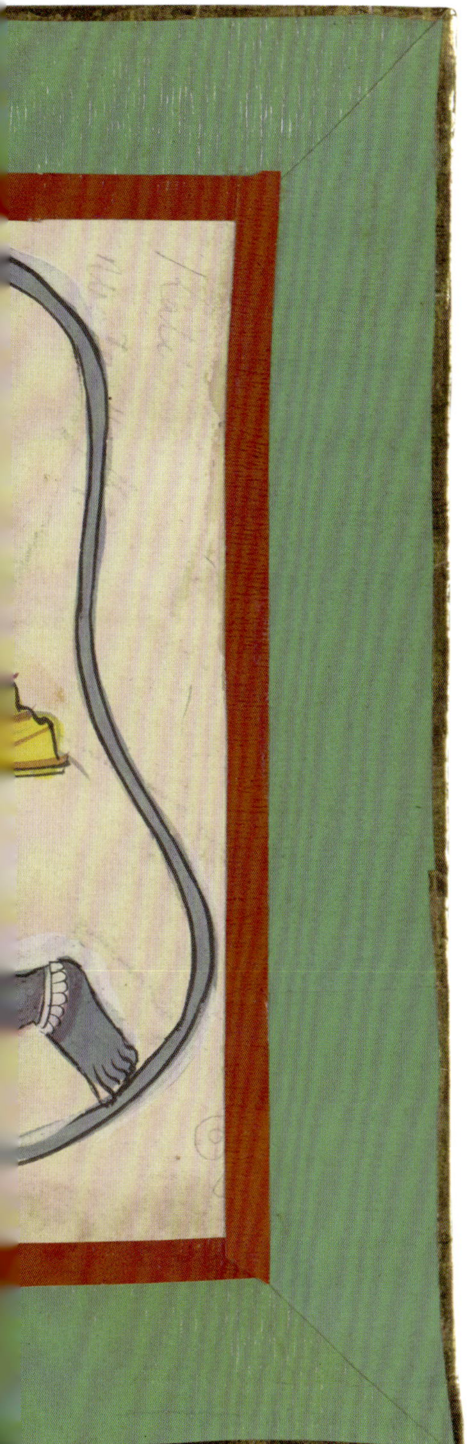

which sepoys (Indian soldiers in the Company army) began their springtime exercises. While Broughton describes those athletes paid by the British, such *jethi* were equally a part of the Maratha general Daulatrao Scindia's camp, to which Broughton was attached as part of the British Residency.[66] In fact, peasants and ascetics took up arms as mercenaries in the political struggles between the Mughals, the Marathas, and the British in the eighteenth century.[67] Like the mixture of diplomacy, natural history, and pleasure emblematized by the role animals played in Poona, wrestling and boxing highlight the diversity of the army alongside entertainment.

Unlike Deen Ali's book illustrations, the circumstances of Malet's commission for wrestlers and boxers from Gangaram, as with many of his drawings, are unknown. The works themselves, the inscriptions, and the consistent payments registered in Malet's ledger book afford the evidence for Gangaram's practice.[68] The watercolors clearly collect information on the Peshwa's activities, locations, and entertainments at which Malet was present. In this, Gangaram seems to play a role in Company documentation similar to the artist Sita Ram, who was employed in Calcutta in the early nineteenth century by the Governor General of Bengal, Francis Rawdon (1754–1826), the Marquis of Hastings, and his wife Lady Flora. The first governmental tour on which Sita Ram accompanied them, from Calcutta to the Punjab (1814–15), resulted in more than two hundred paintings. J. P. Losty has correlated these watercolors with Hastings's journals, and they chart the cities and architectural sites that the governor and his wife saw, and the people whom they met on their journey.[69]

As a record of colonial duties, Gangaram's drawings relate to Malet's desire to document the Peshwa's animals and athletes, and his interactions with the court in Poona, but they are not as systematic or consistent as those for Lord Hastings. While they pertain to Malet's official work, they also relate to his scholarly and artistic endeavors. Like other Company officials, Malet was engaged in projects that

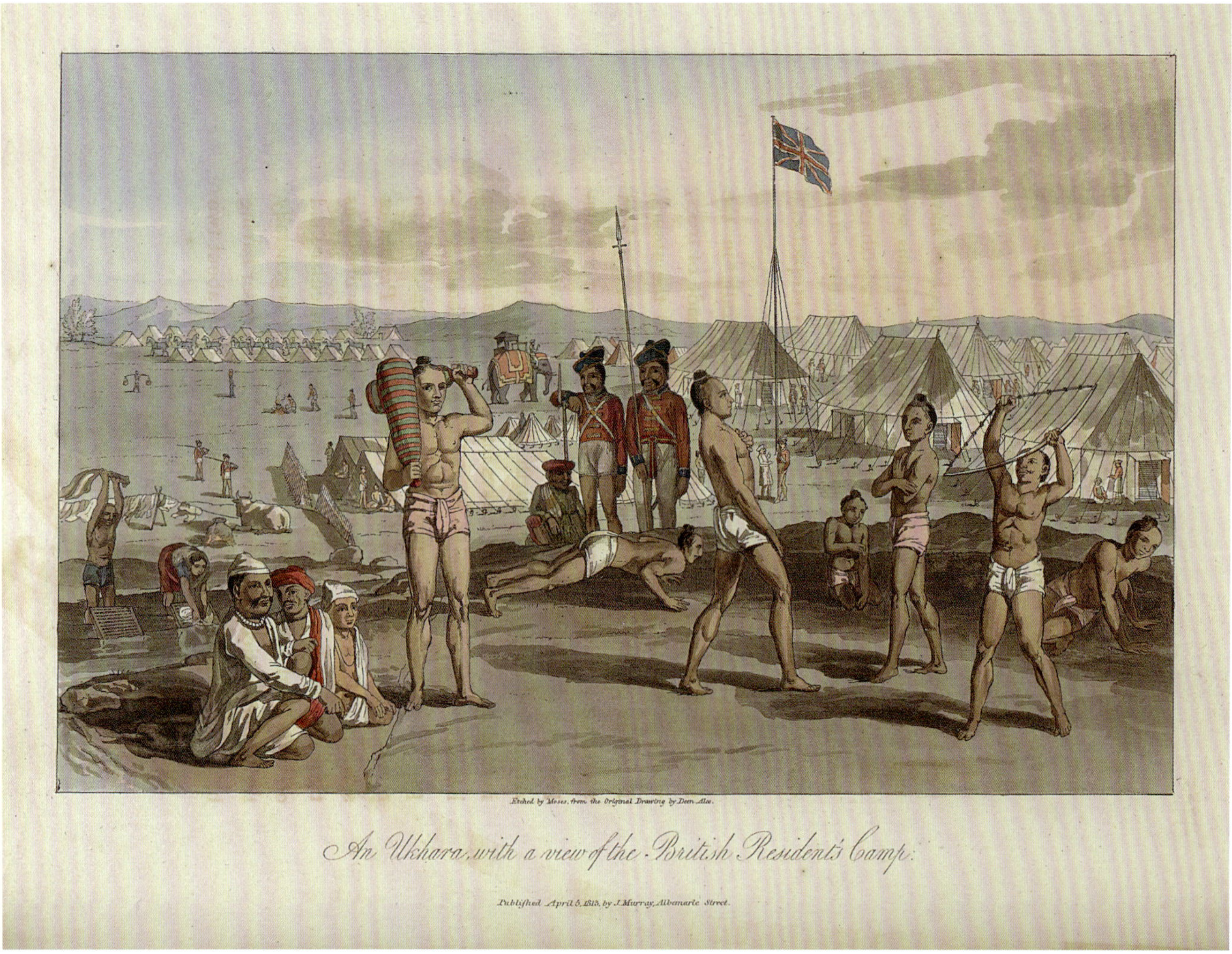

supported his political, economic, and military purpose. For instance, Gangaram's drawings of athletes, as well as those of animals, are connected to Malet's research for his proposed "History of the Marathas."

During his residency in western India, first in Cambay (1774–86) and then in Poona (1786–98), Malet read, collected, and commissioned documents and pictures related to the history of India and specifically the Marathas. Although he was supported by the Governor of Bombay, R. H. Boddam (1784–8) in this project, it was never realized perhaps because works by Henry William Tone (1799) and Edward Scott-Waring (1810) preceded his manuscript's completion.[70] Yet copious notes for this project remain in his memoranda in the British Library. In a "Sketch of a Maratta," he defined the Marathas by geography, lan-

47 Henry Moses after Deen Ali, "An Ukhara with a View of the British Resident's Camp," from Thomas Duer Broughton, *Letters written in a Mahratta camp during the year 1809* (London: John Murray, 1813), after p. 218. Etching and aquatint with hand coloring, 28 cm. Yale Center for British Art, New Haven, Connecticut, Paul Mellon Collection

guage, festivals, and military divisions.[71] He also offered detailed accounts of the "ancient" Maratha "chieftains," and the rise to power of their ministers, the Peshwas, Poona court ministers like Nana Fadnavis, and Maratha generals, such as Mahadji Scindia.[72]

Malet sought to engage – and correct – previous historians' accounts of the Marathas alongside collating materials. In a letter to Edward Orme, who discussed the Marathas in his *Historical Fragments* (1782), Malet wrote that he was "sanguine" in his "expectation of being able to collect a particular and authentick account" of the Bhonsle family "of which Sewajee [Shivaji] was undoubtedly the most illustrious character." He relayed that "the Governor's Agent at Poona, a well-informed Mahommadan," had been "directed to collect and is employed in translating into Persian the Hindoo manuscripts on this subject."[73] Malet worked to edit and amend published information by collecting sources (texts and images) and having them translated, probably by Nur al-Din Hussein Khan, whose portrait Wales painted (see fig. 23).

To write such a "history" was part of a general Company initiative to learn about the country the British wished to control, as William Jones outlined in his introduction to *Asiatick Researches* discussed earlier; indeed, the writing of history was intimately tied to the present and linked to British imperial aims. Many of the figures Malet commented on in his notes were the ones with whom he was in constant negotiation. We might consider Gangaram's visualization of the events connected to Malet's tenure as part and parcel of a Company iconography of rule.

Drawings that Malet had commissioned when he was the Resident in Cambay provide an antecedent and comparison to Gangaram's in their colonial context. They served as a visual dictionary to identify Indian groups or persons whom Malet perceived as potential threats, including bandits and ascetics who played transformative mercenary roles in the political struggles between the Marathas and the British in this period. This series includes figures of warriors, ascetics, and bureaucrats whom Malet identified in handwritten titles, such as "*A Sewra or Juttee [Jain] – A Kind of Hindu Monk*."[74] At times, these pictures also accord with his memoranda, such as on the "numerous and various tribes of sectaries amongst the Hindoos as Joguies [yogis] . . . Jutties . . . Gosaines."[75] These rough sketches have been cut and pasted onto rag paper, possibly by Malet or his descendants, perhaps to compile in an album. The drawings are similar to regional works. For example, the warrior defined as a "Banditti" from "Cottyawar [Kathiawar]" in Malet's collection (fig. 48) in another context could figure as a Maratha nobleman soaring across a quickly brushed sky, honored by attendants one of whom holds regalia reminiscent of a gargantuan spear (fig. 49).

Malet's image, however, reframes the warrior as a military threat against blank paper, a "Banditti." The Company official James Forbes, who was Malet's friend and stationed

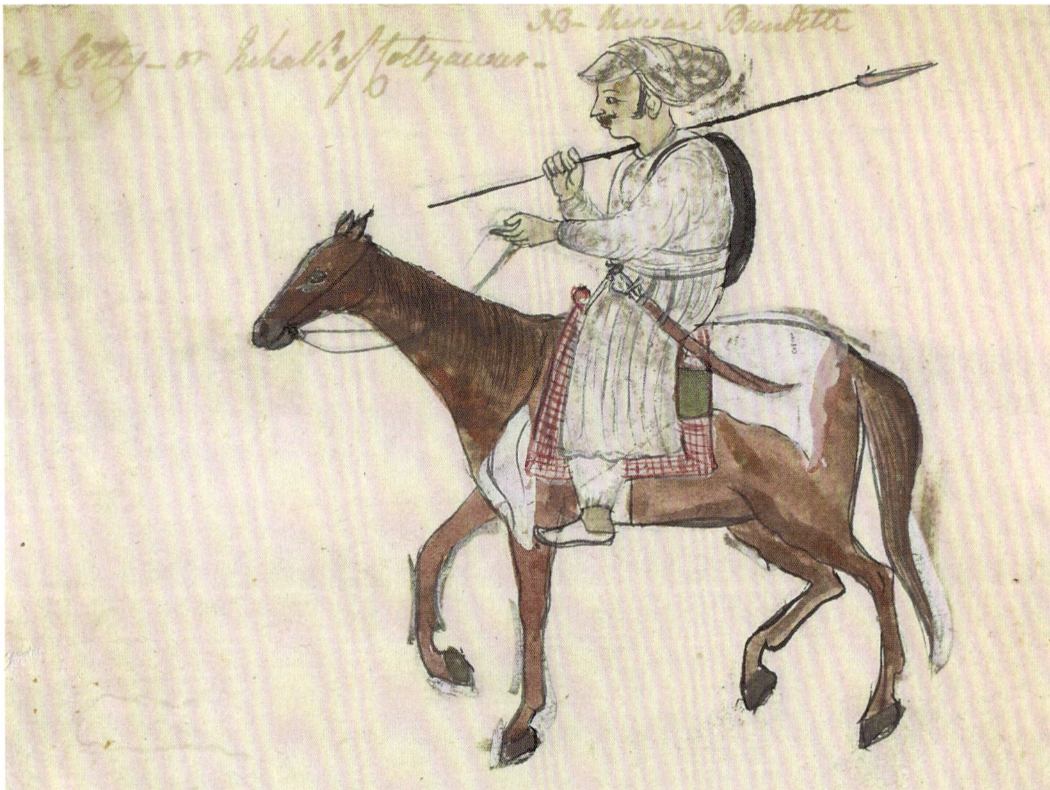

in Gujarat, defined this group as "another tribe of freebooters inhabiting the country of Cottyawar.... They are always well mounted and roam in troops, to lay travellers under contribution, rob villages, and drive off the cattle." Forbes did not go as far as to admit that the British initiated a parallel practice of plunder, legally named as prize, through their own roaming troops, which I will discuss in the next chapter, but he did acknowledge a system. While he feared such "robbery and plunder," he recognized that the Gujarati "districts [were] under excellent cultivation," which pushes the bandit horse-rider back to the image of a nobleman.[76]

According to Forbes, "a Brahmin who was intimate with Sir Charles Malet" in Cambay was responsible for these drawings.[77] The historian Samira Sheikh has identified this man as the learned astronomer and cartographer named Sadanand Vyas, who combined regional knowledge with methods of classification that he acquired by consulting books in Malet's library, including the dictionary of arts and sciences mentioned earlier.[78] Forbes described fifty portraits "of different tribes and religions, in their various costume and distinct character of countenance" that this man made for him and that pertain

48 Sadanand Vyas, attrib., *A Bandit from Kathiawar*, Gujarat, late 18th century. Watercolor, gouache, and graphite with pen and black ink on paper, 14 × 18.7 cm. Yale Center for British Art, Paul Mellon Collection, New Haven, Connecticut, B1977.14.22390

to Malet's drawings.[79] They included a representation of "A Brahmin" (perhaps akin to the "Brahmin at Cambay" that Forbes used to describe the artist who drew him) and a "Gosannee" (Gossain), and were pasted into one of Forbes's albums (fig. 50), just as similar ones remain loose in Malet's collection (fig. 51).[80]

Sadanand's drawings thus served as a visual dictionary for at least two Company officials to identify Indian groups or persons perceived as informants, threats, or combatants. Forbes's figures are even named in three languages to decipher the population of western India, just as Malet titled his pictures. A Cambay scholar created figural types for Malet similar to how Gangaram documented animals and athletes that Malet accessed through the Peshwa in Poona. These forms of knowledge parsed and defined western Indian culture; they would have informed Malet and supported his negotiations with local rulers. Gangaram's surveys of the Peshwa's temples, series of animals, and his

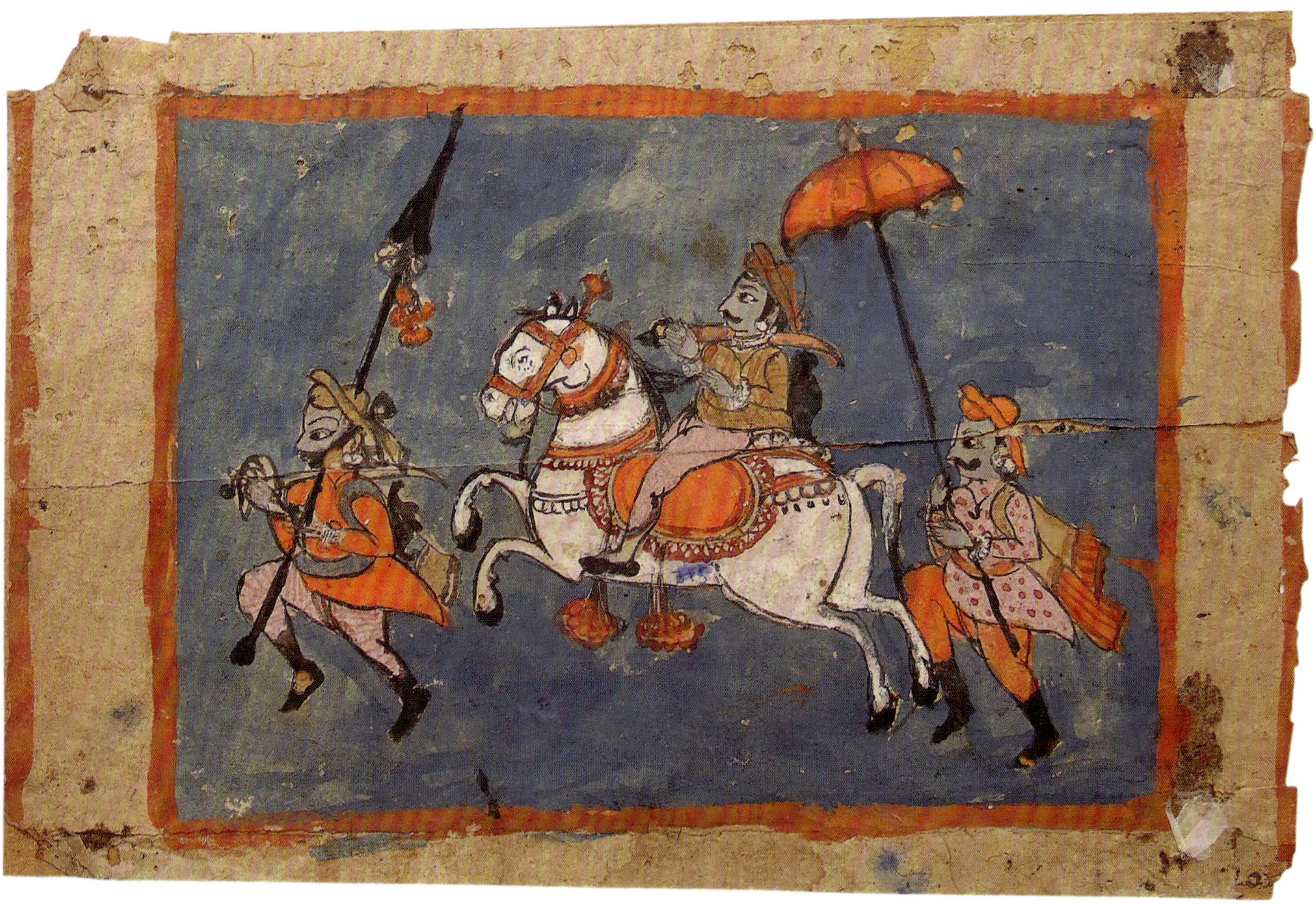

49 *A Maratha Sardar (Commander)*, Deccan or Malwa, 18th or 19th century. Opaque watercolor on paper. Raja Dinkar Kelkar Museum, Pune

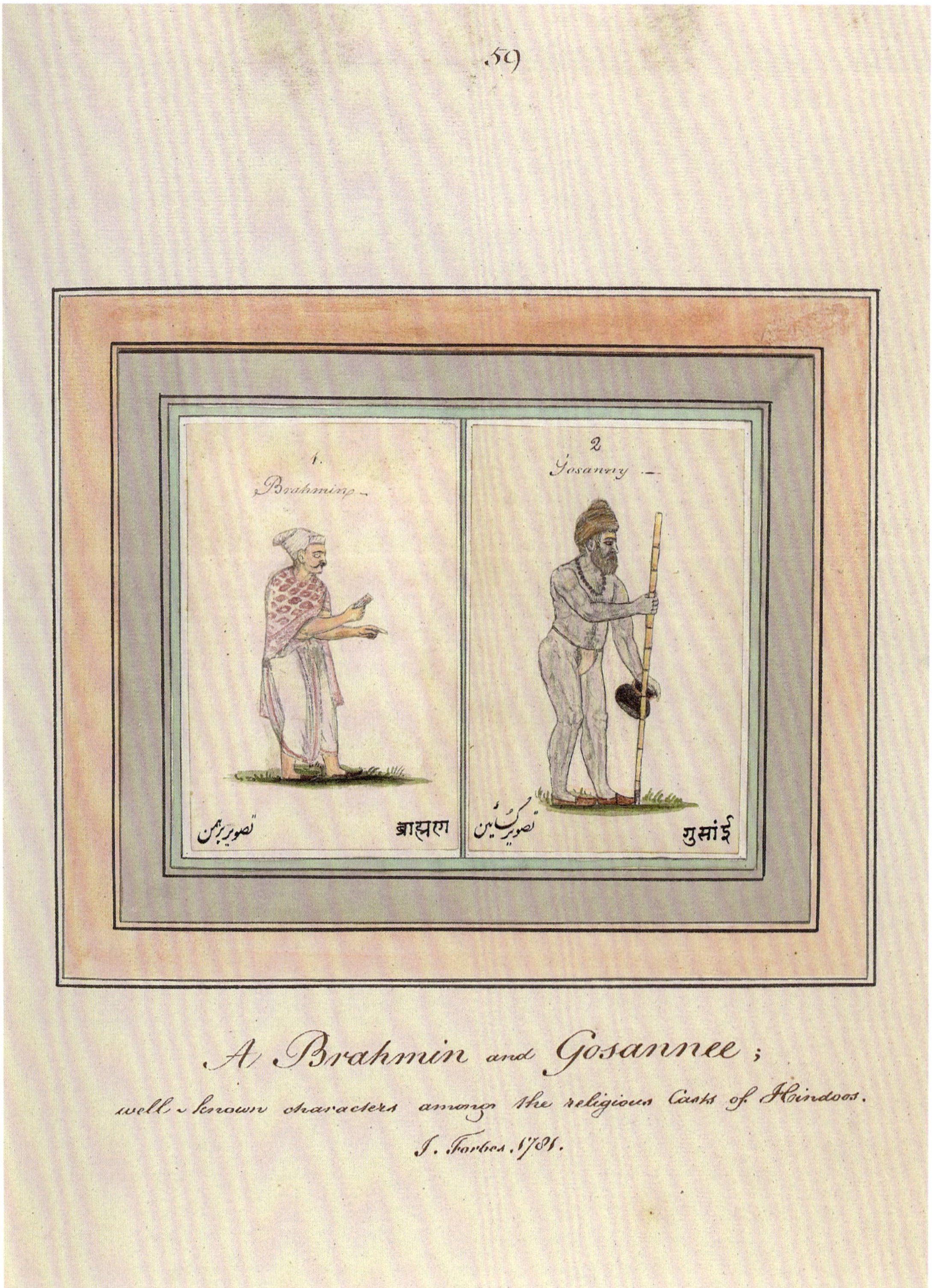

50 Sadanand Vyas, attrib., "A Brahmin and Gosannee" (1781), in James Forbes, *A Voyage from England to Bombay, with Descriptions in Asia, Africa, and South America, 1776–1784*, vol. 12 of his *Descriptive Letters and Drawings, Presented to Elizabeth Forbes*, 1800, 59. Pen, ink, watercolor, and gouache on paper, drawing 12.2 × 20 cm. Yale Center for British Art, Paul Mellon Collection, New Haven, Connecticut, MSS 66

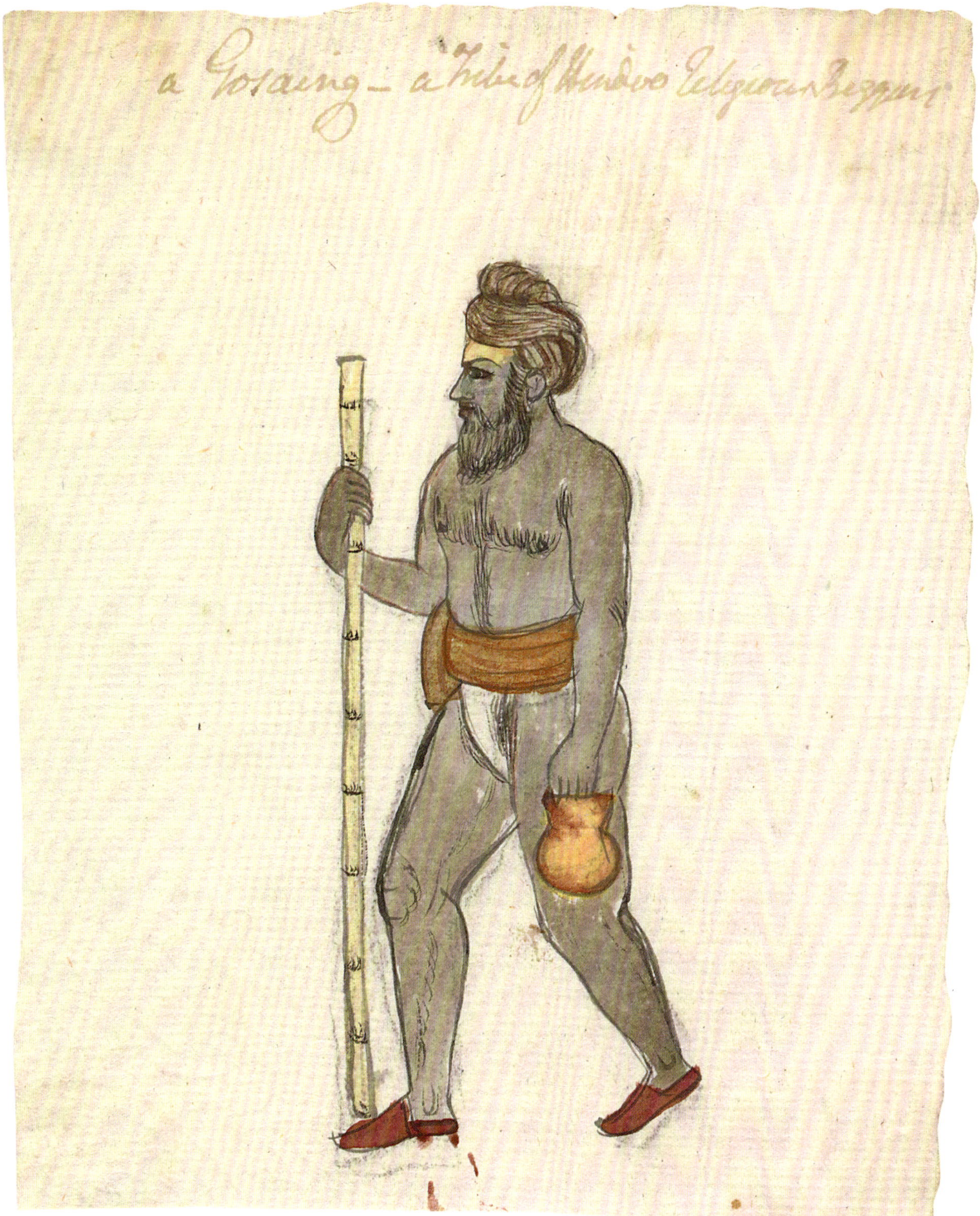

51 Sadanand Vyas, attrib., *A Gosain – A Tribe of Hindu Religious Beggars*, Cambay, Gujarat, 18th century. Watercolor and graphite with pen and black ink on paper, 14.3 × 15.2 cm. Yale Center for British Art, New Haven, Connecticut, Paul Mellon Collection, B1977.14.22399

sketches of wrestlers and boxers are part of the materials that Malet gathered on the Marathas even as they stand as personal memorabilia. These projects simultaneously documented Malet's elevation in status and wealth, and his participation in an East India Company network that gathered information on the people and country it sought to control. As is well known, military action, including the "material loot, booty and prize" that boosted British military officers' standing in the world, became "entangled" with "archival and history writing practices" developed by the same officers, as Margot Finn has articulated.[81]

"INDIAN ANTIQUITIES": PRINTING INDIAN ARCHITECTURE

Malet's engagement with multiple histories did not stop with animals and wrestlers; he, along with Wales, sought to document and understand the rock-carved temples of western India in the 1790s. This project, like the last two, was realized through diplomatic access but more distinctly driven by art historical goals. In the series of drawings that map Malet and Wales's architectural investigations, I trace how Gangaram upset conventional British modes of draftsmanship by grafting his own aesthetic interventions.

In 1799, Malet published an article on the rock-carved temples at Ellora, which had been excavated between the sixth and ninth centuries, illustrated with engravings after Gangaram's drawings in *Asiatick Researches*, the journal of the Asiatic Society of Bengal. This essay responded to earlier studies that travelers published after they gained access to these temples following the Portuguese invasion of Goa and Bombay in 1510.[82] In the early seventeenth century, for example, Jean Thévenot was struck with "wonder to see so great Mass in the Air"; he could "hardly forbear to shiver at first entering into it."[83] Malet echoed the overwhelming nature of these excavations, while also humbly acknowledging his, and Gangaram's, deficiency in their record.[84]

Malet's scholarship was a link in a chain of European history of Indian architecture, and its interpretation through the aesthetics of the sublime and the picturesque.[85] He looked back, but also forward, hoping to awaken through his own account "curiosity" in James Wales's prospective luxury print publication, *Indian Antiquities*.[86] Malet determined that while his essay would offer illustrated information to Company scholars in the Asiatic Society in which he participated, Wales's would add his "laudable pencil" to the antiquarian skills of researching, drawing, and measuring to reach a commercial market that sought new information within familiar frames of delineation.[87]

Wales's death, however, led Malet to request Thomas Daniell to complete and publish this project, which resulted in *Antiquities of India* and "Hindoo Excavations in the Mountain of Ellora near Aurangabad," both published in 1803. The latter became the fifth volume of Thomas and William Daniells's opus devoted to the landscape, architecture, and customs of India, *Oriental Scenery* (1795–1808).[88] Therefore Malet's article and Daniell's publications after Wales's works not only contributed to the study of rock-hewn temples, but also, as Douglas Fordham has vividly articulated, determined their status as worthy examples of "Hindoo architecture" that could compare with other "wonders" in the world through the medium of aquatint.[89]

It is likely that Malet and Wales were introduced to the temples through their friend Forbes's previous inquiries, but military circumstance also determined their access.[90] The East India Company controlled most of the islands of Bombay by the 1660s, including Elephanta. However, it occupied the islands of Salsette and Kanheri only in 1774, and formally acquired them in 1782 in the Treaty of Salbai that concluded the First Anglo-Maratha War.[91] In 1774, Forbes traveled to these "new conquests," as he described the islands, to sketch and contemplate the myriad "wonderful productions" of rock-hewn temples.[92]

Malet and Forbes had begun their friendship in 1775, and Forbes's dedication of his *Oriental Memoirs* (1813) to Malet attests to their closeness.[93] After Forbes returned to England in 1784, he also became acquainted with Wales and employed him to adapt two of his drawings from India into oil paintings. *The Temple of Elephanta* was exhibited in 1785 at the Summer Exhibition of the Royal Academy and *The Great Banyan Tree* two years later in 1787. In June 1790, James Phillips made deeply cut, velvety engravings after the paintings, which visually enclose the viewer in the dark depths of the temple and the banyan tree respectively.[94] It is probably through this exchange that Wales was inspired to go to India, and specifically to Bombay, with which Forbes was familiar and where he had connections to officials like Malet.[95]

Since coming to the region, Malet had developed an interest in the rock-carved temples of western India, particularly at Ellora. To help decipher the inscriptions there, he called on a network of antiquarians affiliated with the Asiatic Society in Calcutta, as well as a "very learned Bramin at Bombay."[96] But in February 1793, he sought his own documentation and employed Gangaram to travel to Ellora to delineate the temples. Gangaram drew the façade of "Biskurma" or Vishvakarma, for example, within a thick black watercolor frame (fig. 52). In the drawing, the temple stands symmetrically but unsteadily against a faintly limned grid, probably produced with a viewing frame. Thick seams parallel the lines of the façade, drawing attention to the paper wings that were grafted to the central sheet. Folded forward, these additions create a three-dimensional diorama of the site, as if Gangaram had fused his sculptural sense with the viewing frame's transcription. These wings mark the façade as sculpted from the rock with projecting arms, while also signaling the sunlight, conveyed through lighter and darker gray washes, as seen at the actual site (fig. 53).

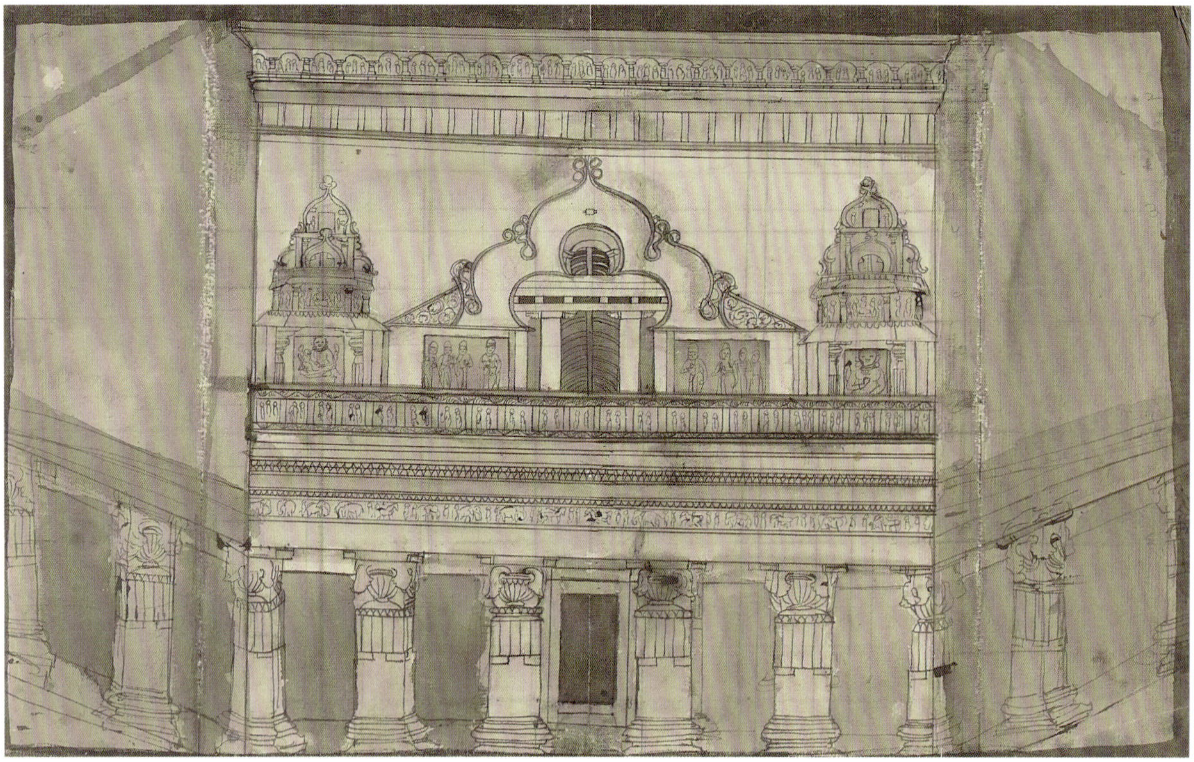

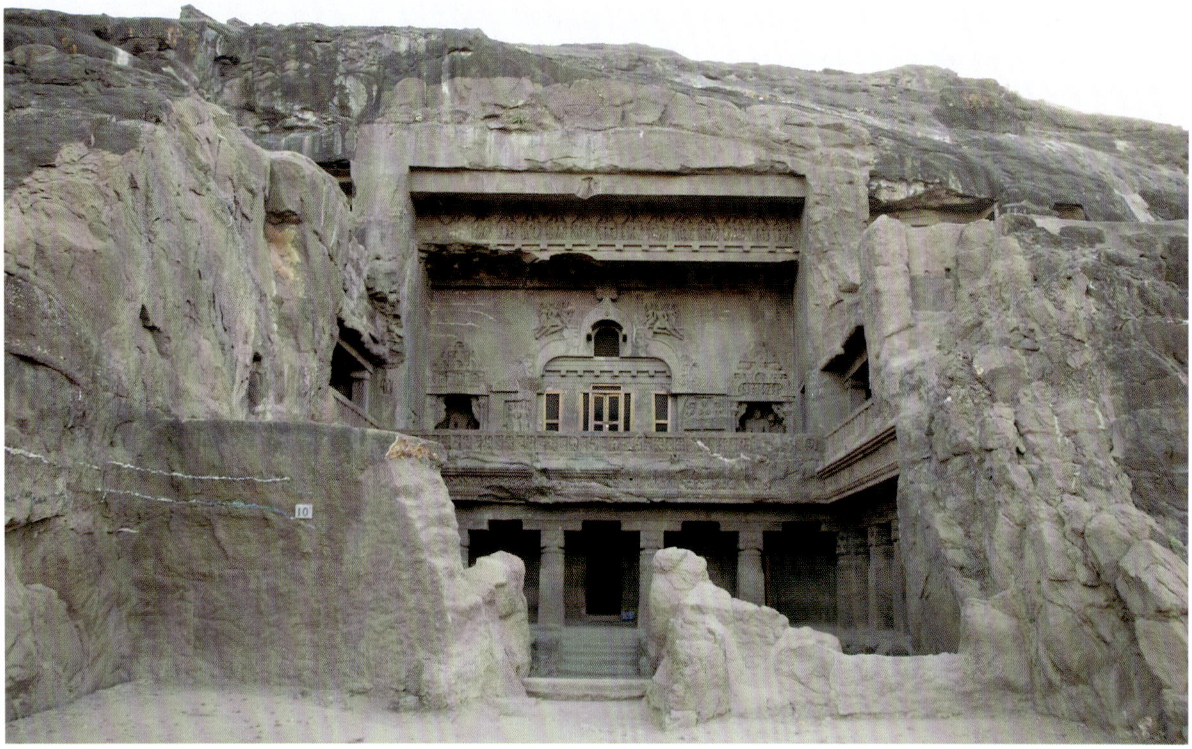

52 Gangaram Tambat, *Outside View of Biskurma ka Joompree (Vishvakarma)*, Ellora, 1793. Gray wash and graphite with pen and black ink on paper, 30.2 × 48.6 cm. Yale Center for British Art, New Haven, Connecticut, Paul Mellon Collection, B1977.14.22333

53 The entrance hall and interior *chaitya* hall of Vishvakarma, the tenth Buddhist Temple excavated at Ellora, constructed ca. 700 CE

Gangaram used such gray and black washes to depict the actual color of the rock, but they also map onto the subsequent print, as if already en route to the engraver. When Malet traveled to Ellora a year later, in June and July of 1794, the temples carved from deep black basalt must have made a striking contrast to the lush greens sprouting over the Deccan plateau during the monsoon rains. He published his account in the sixth volume of *Asiatick Researches* (1799), which was illustrated with engravings made after Gangaram's drawings.[97] However, much of Gangaram's original vision was lost in its transmission to print. The engraver recognized Gangaram's signals for three dimensions, but not necessarily their essence (fig. 54). Pulling back from the tight frontal access, the engraver included the rock from which it was cut as well as floating clouds, grasses, and trees to render the image picturesque. Gangaram's diagonals of space, light, and three-dimensionality were interpreted to the extreme. Their projectile linearity became a trapezoidal courtyard unrelated to the rectangularity of the site and the seams became blunt edges. The façade floats in the center like an independent graphic page.

Malet apologized for what he perceived as the "numerous errors and imperfections" of Gangaram's drawings (as viewed through their engravings) in the preceding letter

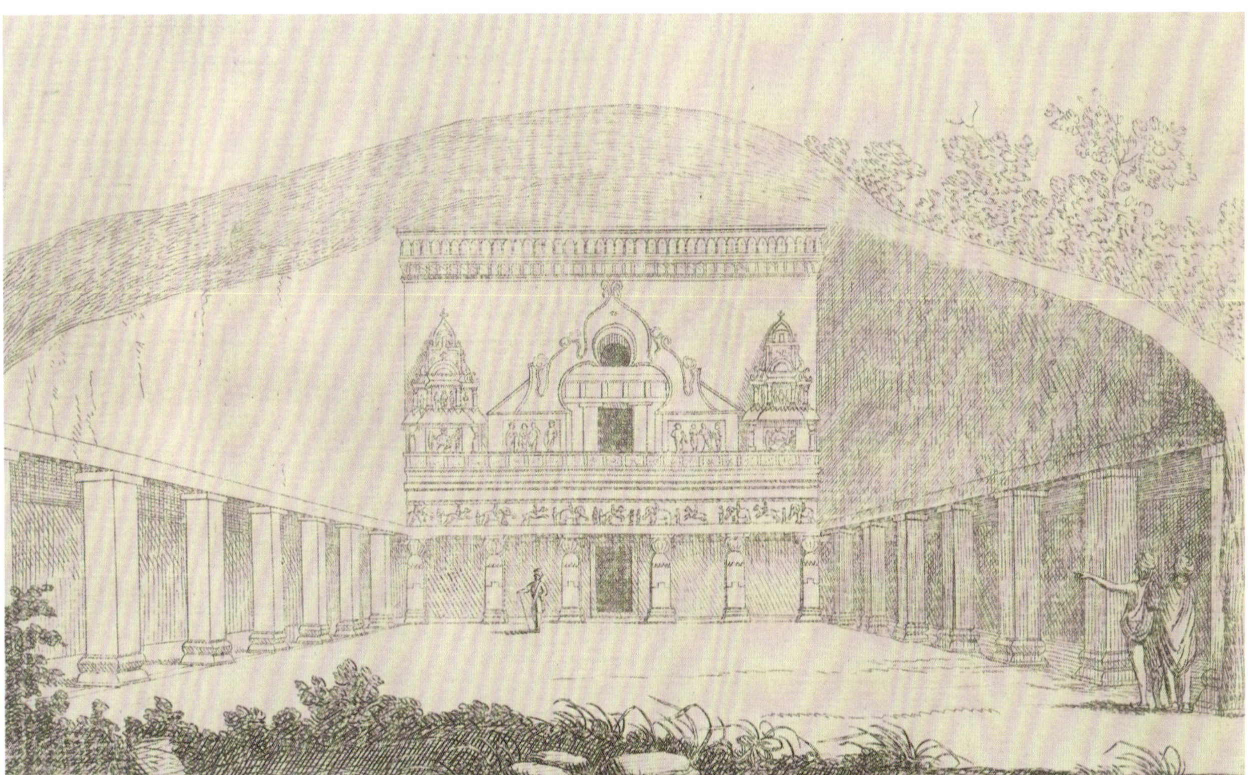

54 J. Basire after Gangaram Tambat, "Biskurma or Viswakurma ka Joompree," in Charles Warre Malet, "Description of the Caves or Excavation, on the Mountain, about a Mile to the Eastward of the Town of Ellora," *Asiatick Researches* 6 (Calcutta: The Society, 1799), pl. H. Beinecke Rare Book and Manuscript Library, Yale University, New Haven, Connecticut

to his "Description" written in 1794 to Sir John Shore, President of the Asiatic Society. Indeed, Gangaram's spare hypnotic drawing of the interior of the temple exhibits a marked difference from Malet's awed prose:

> According to legend, Biskurma [Creator of the world...] was the artist, who fabricated the whole of these wonderful works in... six months; but the cock crowing before they were finished, they remained imperfect, and he retired, having wounded his finger, to this his hovel, in which the state of the figure in front of the entrance of this beautiful excavation is said to be a representation of him holding the wounded finger; but I rather think, with all due respect to the legend, that the figure is in the act of devout meditation, as many fingers, with similar positions of the hands, occur. But quitting the fable for the fact, this excavation is, in beauty, inferior to none.... This singular form of cave, wherever I have met with it, has conveyed the same impression of its being a place of congregation and adoration, rather than of residence or habitation, and has given rise to an idea in my mind... that it may be meant to represent the Almighty, meditating the creation of the world, under the arch or canopy of unlimited space.[98]

Gangaram's drawings strove to transcribe the architecture's symmetry, attending to recession, light, and depth that accorded with the site. He must not have understood the precise mix of fable, fact, and supposition that Malet sought to convey alongside the architectural documentation, which the engraver did glean. In the print, the barrel-vaulted hall that Gangaram drew was transformed into a gothic "arch," and the sculpted figure scaled down, as if aligning the architecture of a "chapel" with the "rise" of "unlimited space" in Malet's mind. For Malet, the figure of "Vishvakarma" was a legendary craftsman ("fable"), a repeating iconographic type of a meditating figure ("fact"), and in his own interpretation a fusion into "the Almighty."[99] Although unsatisfied with the drawings, Malet did not "hesitate to submit" them to the Asiatic Society since he reckoned Gangaram would attend Wales on his journey to Ellora for Wales's prospective publication, *Indian Antiquities*. Gangaram would therefore "be enabled, by the liberal instructions of that gentleman, to correct his errors of delineation and perspective."[100]

In 1794, Wales first wrote about this vast publication that he at times called "Oriental Antiquities" and at others "Indian Antiquities."[101] The prospectus advertised that it would contain a large portfolio of prints and a folio volume of letterpress to be purchased by subscription and cut by "Capital Engravers" in London. Wales assured his subscribers that he would oversee such "eminent Artists" to produce the plates "in a stile which he thinks most proper for producing the truest representations." The volumes would include "Perspective views, internal and external, groups of Figures, obelisks, pillars, inscriptions, measurements, ground plans etc, with full and accurate description of the following stupendous work of antiquity... on the West side of India."[102]

On October 15, 1794, Wales discussed his prospectus with Malet to whom he wanted to dedicate the publication. Malet "thankfully accepted" and "proffer'd giving every assistance in his power" to the project.[103] Both Malet and the Poona court aided Wales in his pursuit, which happened to coincide with growing tensions between the court and the Nizams of Hyderabad (which was decided in the Marathas' favor at the Battle of Kharda in March 1795). After the Nizam refused Wales a "passport" to travel to Ellora some months earlier, in February 1795, Malet brokered one for Wales with the Maratha general Daulatrao Scindia (Mahadji's successor), and offered his own letters in case of "accidents."[104] In fact, Wales accompanied Malet, alongside the Peshwa and Scindia, for two and a half weeks on the campaign against the Nizam before diverting to the caves in mid-February.[105]

The Anglo-Maratha alliance, and proceeding war, enabled Wales's research; he highlighted the Poona court's support of his project in a 1794 letter to Sir Joseph Banks: "There is not one groupe or even a single figure in all the wonderful performances here mentioned, but what is well known to the intelligent Bramins. It is principally to the knowledge of those enlightened men and the indulgence of the Court of Poona, that the publisher owes the most valuable part of his materials."[106] He claimed "assistance" from "several Brahmins," who resided in the temples that he drew and measured to "elucidate" the works, as well as those of "gentlemen" who had long resided in India, to substantiate the validity of his project for prospective subscribers.[107]

Such an extensive work demanded employees to aid in the research and production. To prepare for the journey, Gangaram made "tracings" of his 1793 drawings of Ellora at Malet's request for Wales to "put up as memoranda."[108] Two of these drawings remain in Moor's albums on thin tracing paper as directives to the sites and sources of identification. Gangaram copied the details of his original drawing (see fig. 52 for instance) in fine black wash to emphasize the columns, arched balcony, and bands of ornament.[109] In addition to these tracings, Gangaram informed Wales about temples along the road to Ellora and supplied him with an account of when the excavations had been made.[110] He also introduced Wales to religious figures who provided information. These included the practical – an "intelligent Bramin to write down the names of each group or figure" while they sketched at Ellora – and the curious.[111] Wales sketched a "Manbhou Gossang," probably a follower of the Mahanubhav sect numerous in western India, through Gangaram's initiative.[112]

Gangaram was one of twenty people who accompanied Wales to Ellora; Wales wrote in January 1795 that his "people" included "W. Mabon – a draftsman, Gangaram – a native sculptor, Josir (Jossi) – a young Goa painter, my servant, a carpenter, 15 bearers...."[113] At the site, Wales divided the labor between himself and the other artists. He described the process in a journal entry:

> Gongram [Gangaram] to trace the Rauven internal view and the internal view of Ramishwar. Josir to draw groups of figures. Mr Mabon to be at Doomarlena. Myself at the Kylas and another one... Josir to attend trace on paper as fast as I draw. Gongram to trace groups of figures the same way. Both on glass and paper. To draw my Views on drawing paper by candle light. It will take two days work.[114]

He boasted to Malet that his system of employing "several people upon one subject and each upon the parts that he was capable of" was a cost-saving one.[115]

Whether Wales grafted his artist assistants' preparatory works into his own drawings or used them directly for the prints remains unknown since he died in late October 1795. According to Captain George Millett, who had accompanied him to draw the caves at Kanheri on Salsette, he "fell a victim to the putrid air... inhaled at the caves in an unhealthy season of the year."[116]

Malet was dedicated to seeing Wales's project through. After he returned to England, he hired Thomas Daniell to adapt Wales's views of Indian architecture. In the introduction to "Hindoo Excavations, in the Mountain of Ellora, near Aurungabad, in the Decan, in Twenty-Four Views" (1803–4), sometimes labeled the fifth and sometimes the sixth volume in the series *Oriental Scenery*, Daniell traced Wales's work, through Malet's hands, into his own:

> The drawings from which this series of views is engraved were presented to the publisher by Sir Charles Warre Malet, Bart., many years resident at the Durbar, or court of Poonah, who, on the death of Mr. Wales, became possessed of all his drawings. Sir Charles has given a full account of these excavations in the sixth vol. of the Asiatic Researches, from which are extracted many parts of these descriptions; but as the plates accompanying it were etched from the sketches of an Indian artist, they will be found to differ in many respects from the drawings of Mr. Wales's collection; to make which as correct as possible, no labour or expense has been spared. These views were taken in the years 1792 and 1793.[117]

In this passage, Daniell clearly separated "the drawings in Wales's collection" from the "Indian artist" Gangaram's, as "differ[ing] in many respects."

It is not likely that Daniell copied Gangaram's 1793 drawings, or the engravings made after them for Malet's publication, yet he surely encountered his 1795 drawings because they were integrated with Wales's collection and workshop practice described earlier.

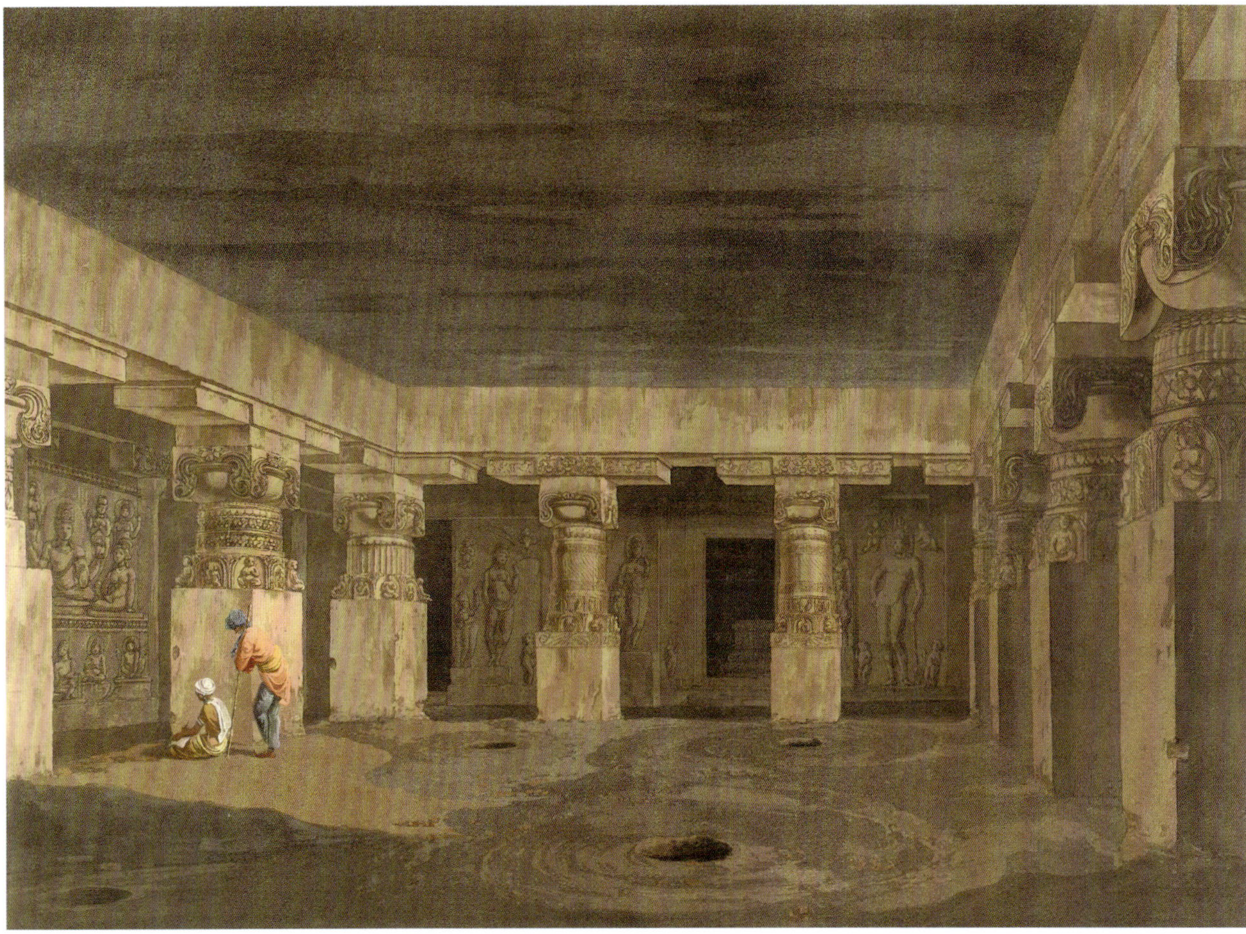

This is visible in one of Daniell's prints when it is correlated with Wales's journal entries. Wales mentioned, for instance, that Gangaram drew the "Rauven internal view," which refers to the cave temple called Ravana-ki Khai or the Ashes of Ravana, and traced "groups of figures." This temple dates from the seventh century and includes figural panels of scenes connected to Shiva and Vishnu. In Daniell's plate, the massy enclosure and its pillared expansion is the point of focus, rather than the main deity (fig. 55). The view is oriented toward the left, where a small figure intently draws a sculptural frieze.[118] This is probably Gangaram drawing "groups of figures," such as Shiva and Parvati perhaps playing a cruciform board game of *chaupar*, akin to *pachisi*. A sketch of this scene remains in Malet's archive.[119] Wales must have combined such drafts of Gangaram's with his own to produce finished ones, perhaps "by candlelight."[120]

That Daniell preserved an Indian artist at work in this aquatint is an acknowledgment that Wales's method of co-production was integral to his project. Indeed, Wales strategically used a collaborative method of production in his work. As I argued in Chapter One, he did so not only to make more pictures for the Marathas and for those at the British

55 Thomas Daniell after James Wales, "The Ashes of Ravana, Interior View," in *Oriental Scenery*, vol. 5: *Hindoo Excavations in the Mountain of Ellora, near Aurangabad* (London, 1803), pl. 19. Aquatint with hand coloring, 54 × 73.8 cm. British Library, London, X432/6(19)

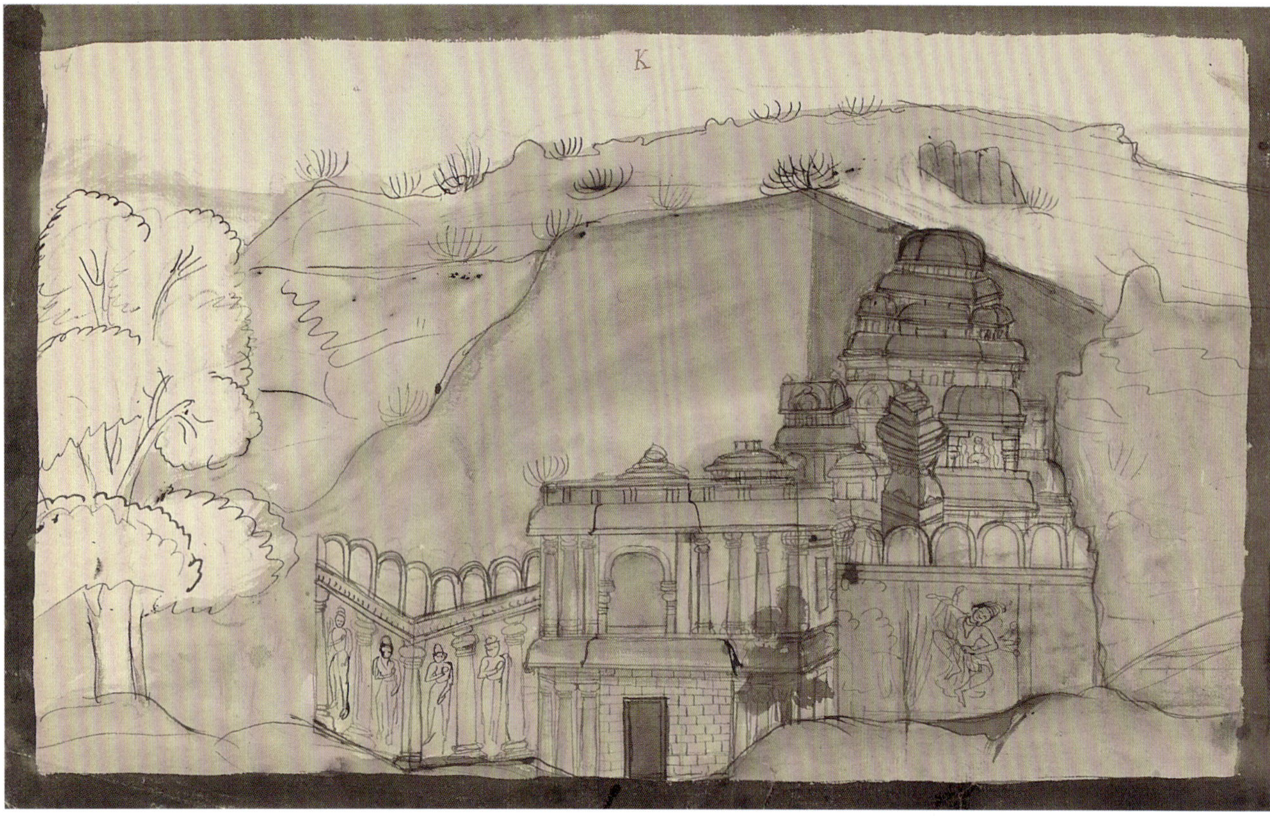

Residency, but also to lean on the complementary skills of his assistants. If Mabon was a gifted draftsman and Jossi adept at European oil painting, what did Gangaram bring to the drafting table? Wales described him as a "sculptor," and it is his sense of three-dimensional space that Wales seems to have prized. Nonetheless, Daniell's remark that Gangaram's drawings "differ[ed] in many respects" from those in Wales's collection gives one pause. There is a difference between Gangaram's initial drawings of Ellora for Malet in 1793 and those that he did for Wales in 1795, but both were integrated with Wales's whether he or Daniell acknowledged it or not. The question then is about the overarching aesthetic of the works; Daniell's comment thus seems to allude to Gangaram's inferior style of drawing, his approach to the material rather than the content.

Two views of the rock-cut temple of Kailasha display how Gangaram's studies changed over time and adjusted to the requirements of his British patrons. The first drawing is probably from his first trip to Ellora for Malet, in 1793 (fig. 56), and the second from his trip with Wales in 1795 (fig. 57). In the first, Gangaram approached the temple from its entrance, making its excavation from the rock clear. However, the angles of the temple are

56 Gangaram Tambat, *Exterior View of Keylas* (Kailasanatha), Ellora, ca. 1793. Gray wash and graphite with pen and black ink on paper, 28.3 × 38.7 cm. Yale Center for British Art, New Haven, Connecticut, Paul Mellon Collection, B1977.14.22330

confusing. Aspects of the building appear from different directions, creating a stacking, tiered effect rather than a single perspectival view. The actual site, though, is just as confounding (fig. 58): the temple was carved out of the rock as a sculpture rather than constructed as built architecture. It was not made for European perspective, and neither was Gangaram's first, accurate drawing of the site. Yet this approach did not adhere to Malet and Wales's aesthetic framework. They clearly sought to correct his work: ruler-drawn lines remain on some of Gangaram's drawings, such as those meant to revise his rendering of the perspectival recession of columns in Indra Sabha, another temple at Ellora.[121]

The second watercolor of Kailasha (see fig. 57) bears witness to such training. It is remarkably different from the first. Here, Gangaram approached Kailasha from "one Side," at an "Oblique" angle, so as to capture the full length and breadth of the temple.[122] The various depths of the building are portrayed through one-point perspective and shading, emphasizing recession. It is unlike the first image (see fig. 56), but primarily in that it is an impossible view. The temple was constructed for ritual circumambulation rather than for distant panoramic contemplation. Its sculpted form limits visual access; columns puncture the surrounding portico and the corridor around the temple is narrow. Gangaram must have moved positions multiple times within the complex, as well as going along the rock edge to view it from above, in order to achieve the unimpeded breadth of this drawing.

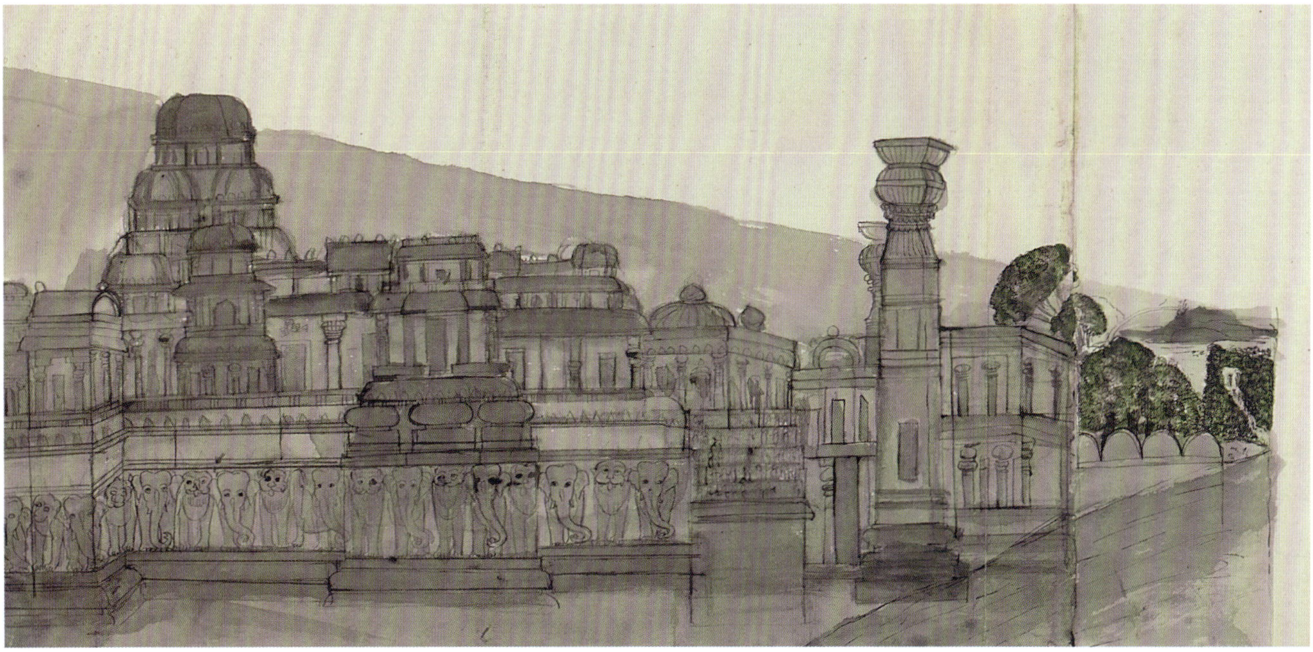

57 Gangaram Tambat, *Exterior View of Keylas* (Kailasanatha), Ellora, ca. 1795. Pen and black ink, gray wash and watercolor on two joined sheets of paper, 30.5 × 67.3 cm. Yale Center for British Art, New Haven, Connecticut, Paul Mellon Collection, B1977.14.22329

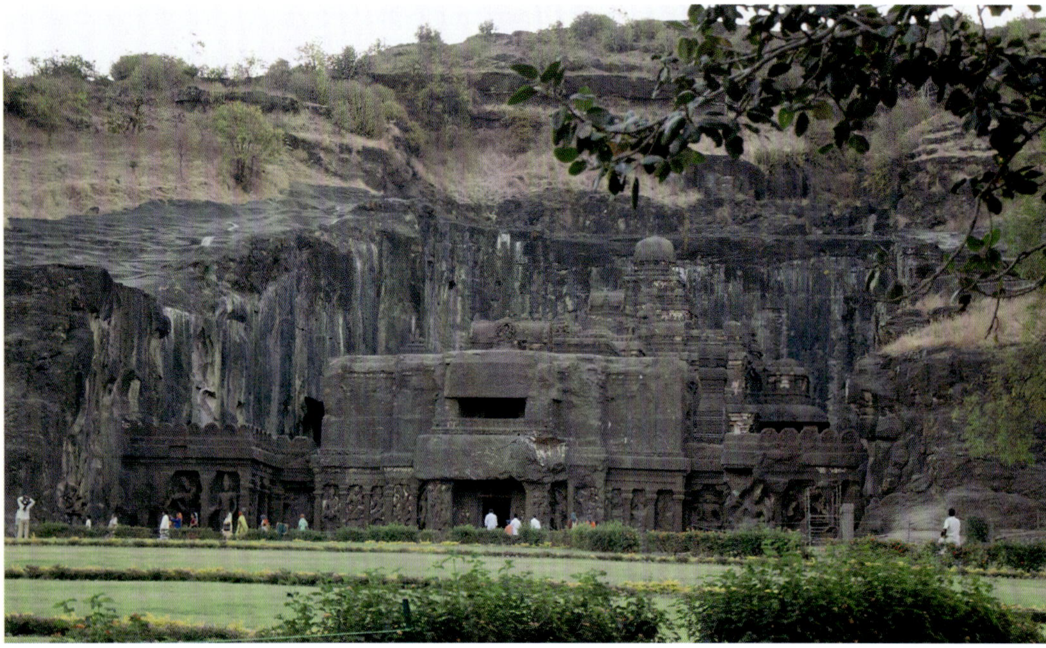

This composite nature is striking, because a sharp diagonal crosses the page and stops a number of centimeters before the frame's edge. The abruptness of the stop leads the eye to a second stop, a seam, which indicates that Gangaram joined a second piece of paper to the first to fit the entirety of the temple he was drawing. This diagonal "Line joining the Sky describes the Slope of the Mountain in which this Wonderful place is Excavated," according to the inscription on the back of the final version of this work (see fig. 59). Its precision and angle, and the sharp stop in painting before the edge, however, equally points to the use of a viewing device, which either frames the structure into squares for easier drawing or, if a camera obscura, projects the outline of what is being viewed onto glass to be traced. Clearly, the viewing frame's picture extended beyond the width of the original paper, but not far enough to fill the additional section. This drawing reveals Gangaram's process of production, including how he adjusted to European visual technologies.

In his journal, Wales described Gangaram, Jossi, and Mabon as outlining, tracing, and drawing different parts of the temples, alone or together, while at Ellora.[123] Gangaram used these devices, but he must have done so with considerable thought. He strategically confronted and upset the temple's own demarcation of architectural space, which he had previously drawn, and subsumed it into what his British patrons desired, to create an unimpeded – but impossible – view of Ellora. His final presentation draft of this view

58 Exterior View of Kailasanatha Temple, Ellora

barely references the rock enclosure, and the temple has shrunk to fit onto a smaller swatch of page (fig. 59).

Malet's comment on Gangaram's "errors in delineation and perspective" was a critique of how Gangaram first approached and delineated architecture. His articulation of the antiquities "differ[ed]" from Wales's, as Daniell published. To Malet or Wales this must have proved the limit of European training, but to Gangaram it seems like a choice. He does not seem to have been constrained by British artistic approaches, even as he adapted them into his artistry. In the same way that he extended paper via a seam to lengthen the sheet, Gangaram joined certain European techniques with his own. But as a tree might refuse a grafted branch, he did not accept all equally. A series of his watercolors from 1793 depict the rock-cut Buddhist temple at Karle; they show his attention to different aspects of architecture, and his acceptance and rejection of British techniques.[124] In a rough sketch (fig. 60), Gangaram depicted a distant view, which included a diagonal road into the site, a lion-topped monumental pillar, and adjacent structures that partially obscured

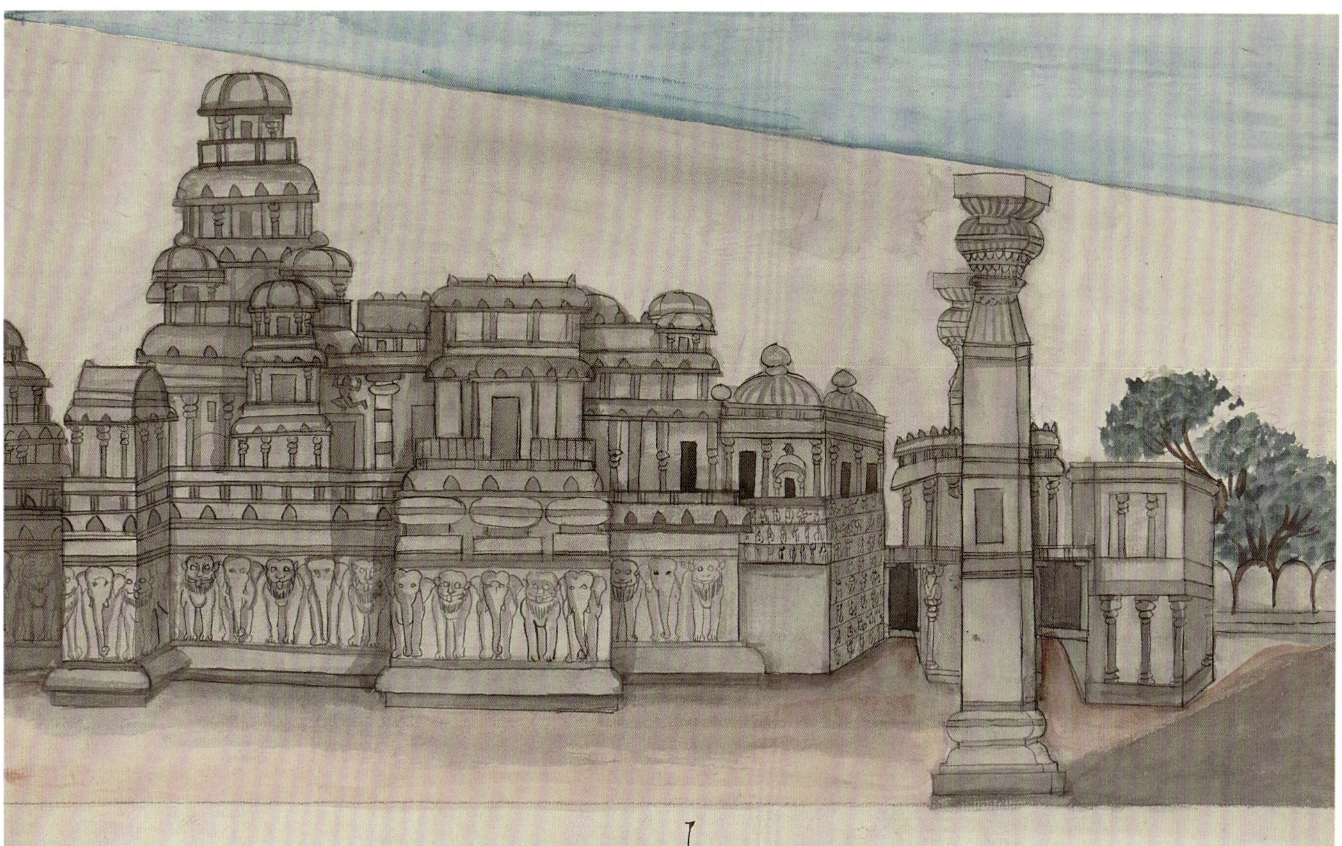

59 Gangaram Tambat, *Exterior View of Keylas* (Kailasanatha), Ellora, ca. 1795. Watercolor and graphite with pen and black ink on paper, 28.3 × 42.9 cm. Yale Center for British Art, New Haven, Connecticut, Paul Mellon Collection, B1977.14.22337

the façade. Another study zooms into the barrel-vaulted hall itself (fig. 61) and its receding ornamental pillars, which become the central focus of another detailed study.[125]

Although these works seem to focus on parts of the building in progressive stages, Gangaram gives the most attention and largesse to the façade (fig. 62). Stretching boldly across more than eighty centimeters of paper, the sculptural design is graphically displayed. The bulbous onion curve of the central arch is emphasized as utilitarian by opening into the hall and also as material, the red wash indicating wood rather than the gray stone. However, the arch is also understood as the formal origin of the miniaturized replication of prayer halls (*chaityas*) banding the façade. The play of material and ornamentation is stressed. Horizontal stripes of latticework are reminiscent of the bumpy texture of weaving or woodwork, while the base sculptures of lovers (*mithuna*) and elephants pop out via their loose energetic brushwork. Although now flattened, this drawing seems to have been intended by Gangaram to be folded. Seams at each end, a quarter way in, and the slightly darker tone of grey wash, indicate that when flipped forward, the watercolor would transform into a three-dimensional paper replica of the site.

As perceived through this watercolor, Gangaram's graphic yet sculptural, multidimensional approach stands in contrast with an aquatint by Daniell adapted from Wales's collection of drawings. In one of four views, he depicts the rock-cut temple from a distance (fig. 63). Cut out of the shaggy hillside, the façade and its prominent arch are partially obscured by the ruins of the gate, an adjacent modern temple, and the lion pillar. Similar to the rough sketch by Gangaram (see fig. 60), this aquatint differs in key additions familiar from its picturesque framing. The subtle focus on time affects the mood of the image. Besides the crumbling columns and mossy overgrowth, the inner portion of the arch is in ruins. The rectangular door, black from the shadow of the interior, becomes a modern asymmetrical introduction, cut into the fill of the older door that might have been added at the same

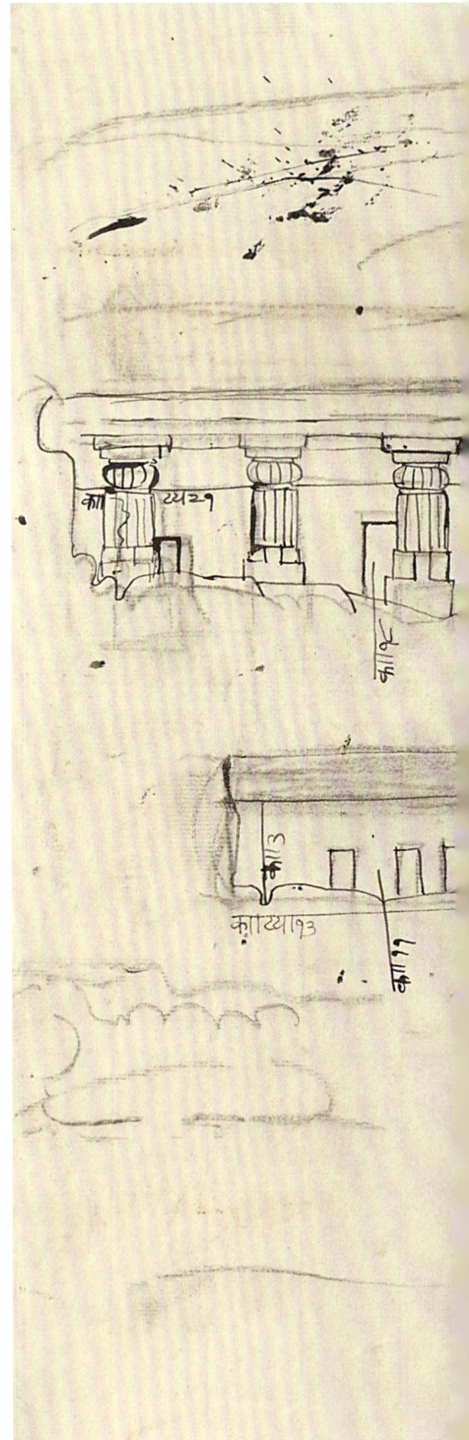

60 Gangaram Tambat, *Exterior View of the Temple at Ekvera* (Karle), Maharashtra, ca. 1793. Pen and black ink, black chalk and gray wash over graphite on paper, 41.6 × 54 cm. Yale Center for British Art, New Haven, Connecticut, Paul Mellon Collection, B1977.14.22341

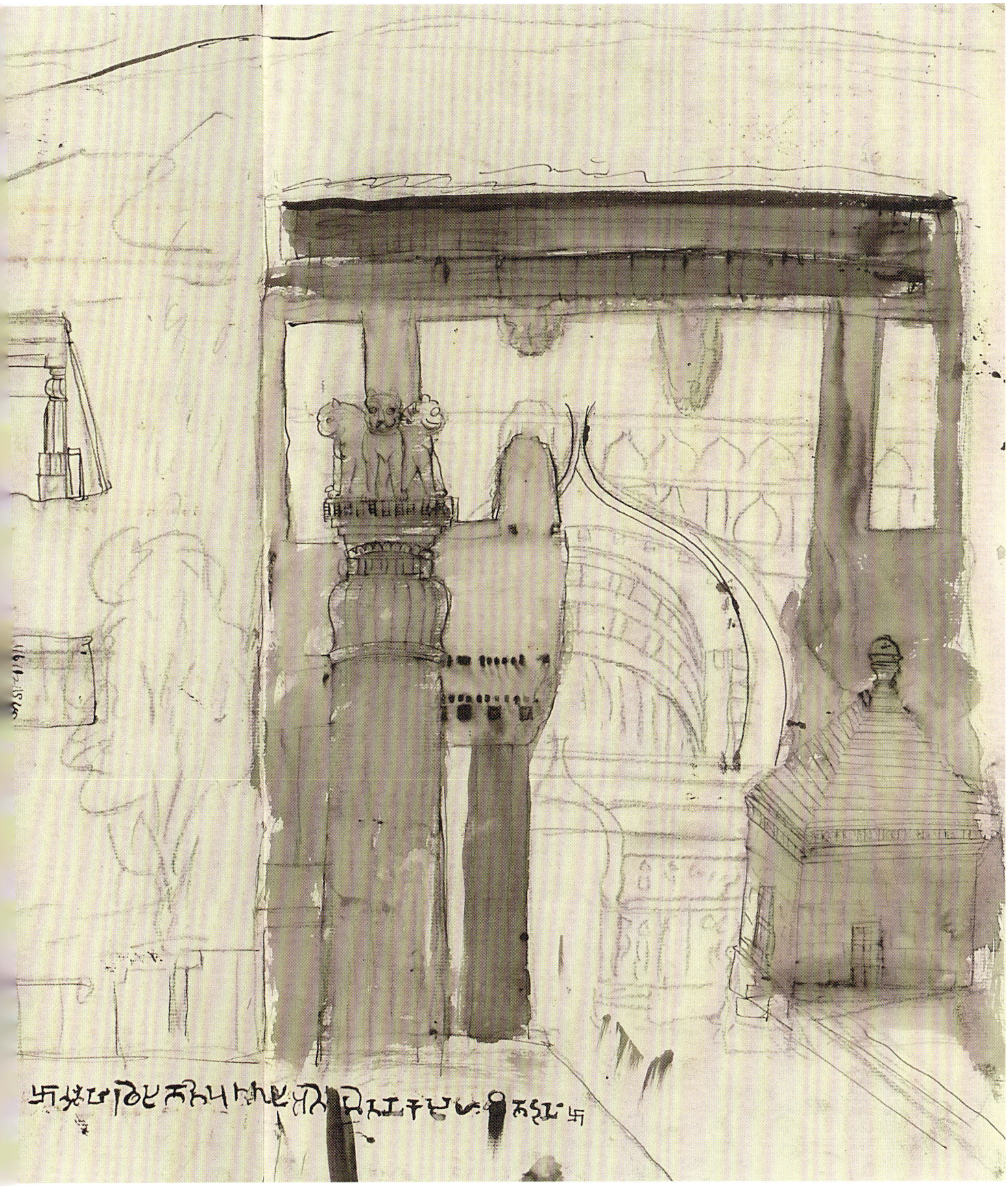

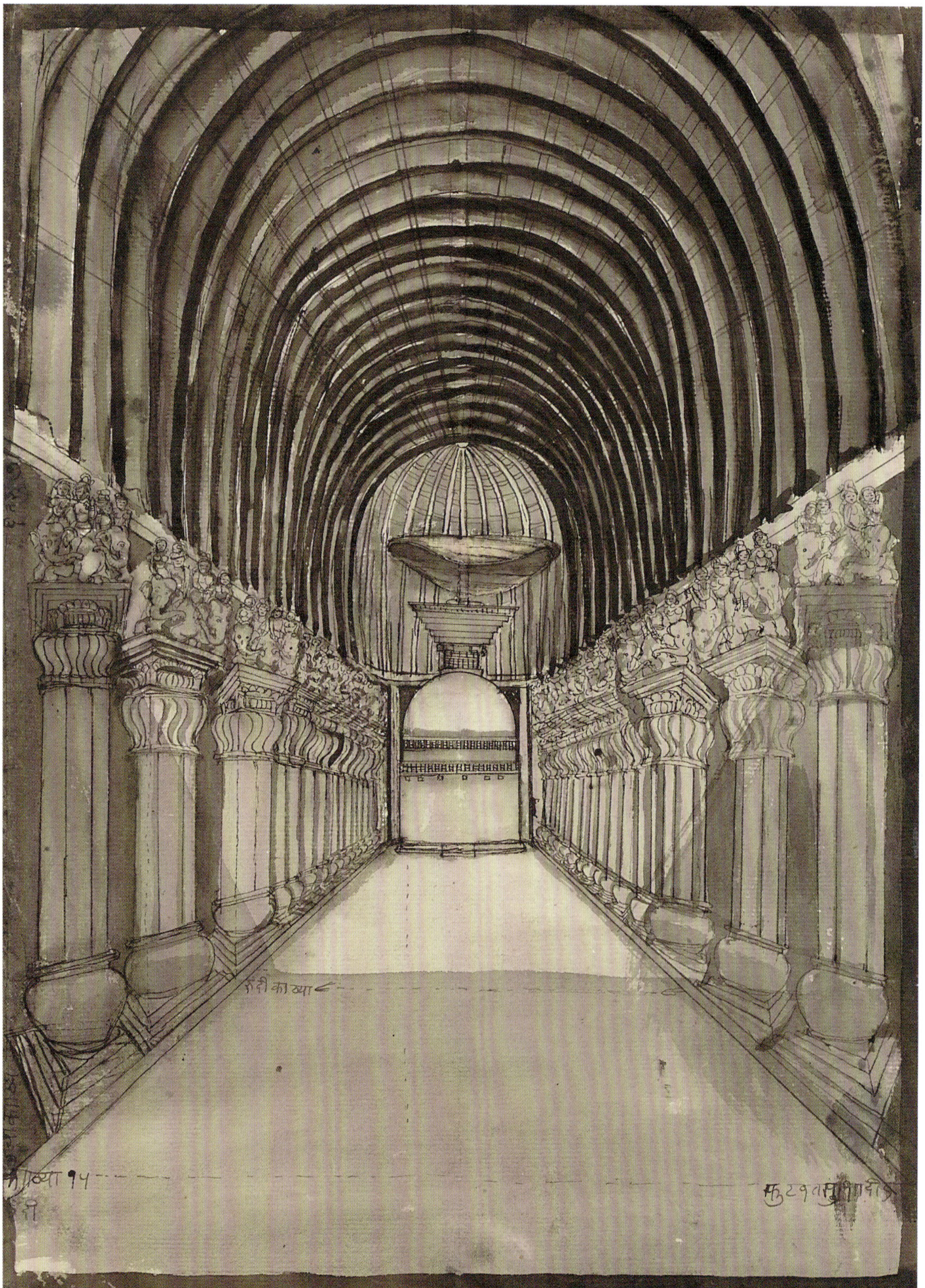

61 Gangaram Tambat, *Interior View of the Temple at Ekvera* (Karle), Maharashtra, ca. 1793. Gray wash and graphite with pen and black ink on paper, 38.7 × 28.3 cm. Yale Center for British Art, New Haven, Connecticut, Paul Mellon Collection, B1977.14.22320

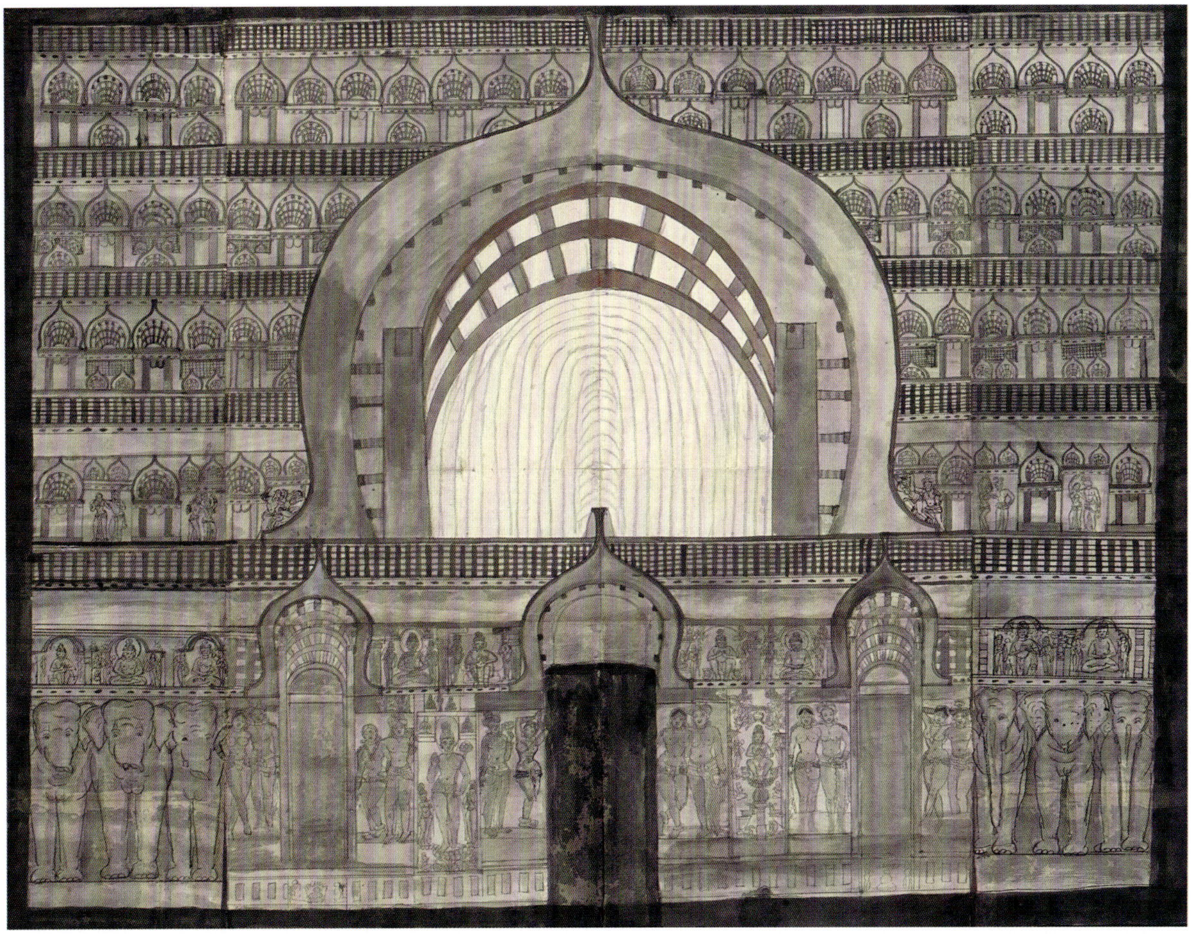

time as the square temple to the Hindu goddess Ekvera, after which Wales named the site, rather than after the Karle *chaitya* hall, which he did not recognize as Buddhist. Thus Gangaram's "errors" in "perspective and delineation" were really "errors" in the production of a specific British visual format.

Daniell published three other views of the site of Karle, but it is the distant view that held other British artists' imaginations. Many artists repeated it, stultifying it into the prime view of Karle. Tapati Guha-Thakurta has emphasized British artists' ingestion of the picturesque frame regarding their delineation of Indian architecture, in *Monuments, Objects, Histories* (2004): "As the Daniell landscapes became synonymous with the early colonial vision of the wilds and ruins of India, the 'picturesque' naturalized its presence as an innate ingredient of the terrain. From a filter, it grew into a frame, inscribing itself onto the body of the physical space and its structures."[126] Such a naturalization of the picturesque is proven in the repetition of this view of Karle. It is possible, of course, that the British artist Henry Salt saw Daniell's 1803 image since he visited the temple a year later with Viscount Valentia. But his choice of view had already been standardized, even

62 Gangaram Tambat, *The Temple at Ekvera* (Karle), Maharashtra, ca. 1793. Gray wash, watercolor, pen and black ink, and black chalk on paper, 64.1 × 84.5 cm. Yale Center for British Art, New Haven, Connecticut, Paul Mellon Center, B1977.14.22324

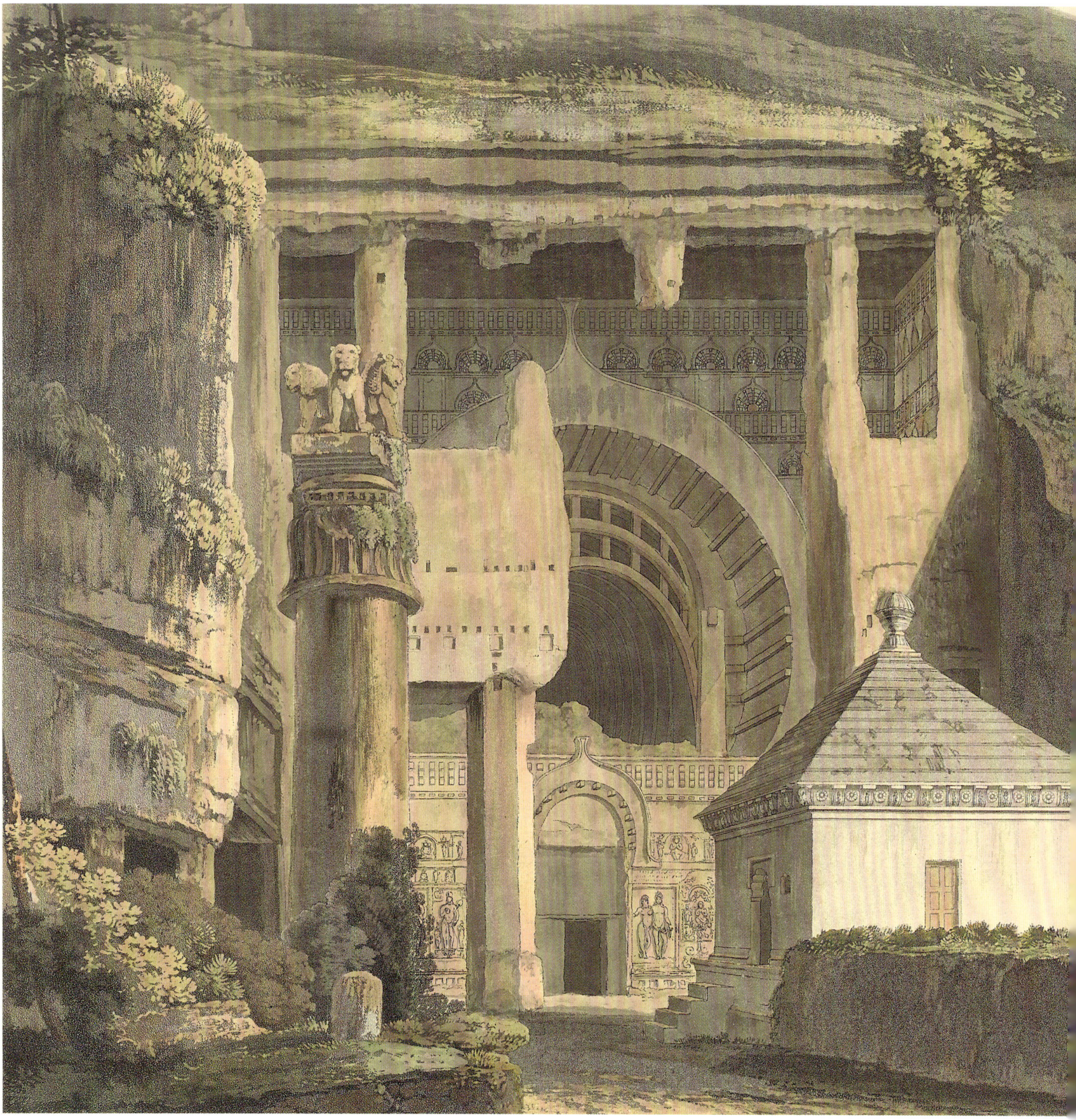

63 Thomas Daniell after James Wales, "Ekvera," in *Antiquities of India* (London, 1803), pl. 5. Aquatint with hand coloring, 54 × 74.2 cm. British Library, London, P178

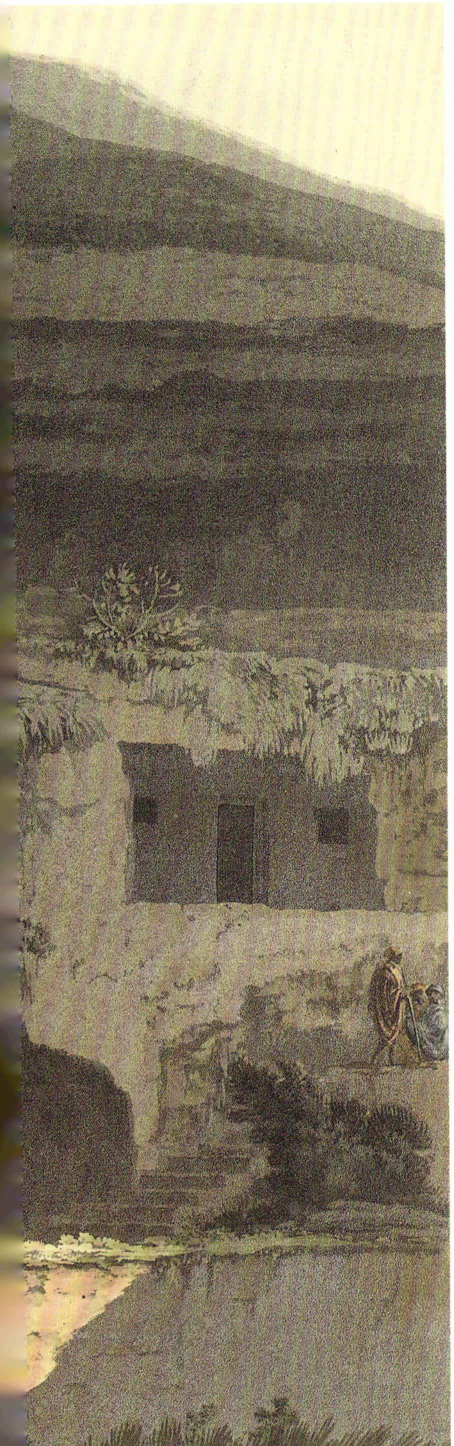

though it obscured the façade and its intricate detail.[127] If we think of Salt's print as an iteration of Daniell's, James Fergusson took it one further; he used Salt's plate in his *Illustrations of the Rock-Cut Temples of India* (1845). This is surprising since Fergusson, as Guha-Thakurta notes, had an "obsessive preoccupation" with "information and instruction" supported by his use of a camera lucida rather than "pleasing artistic compositions." Fergusson argued that Salt's plate was "so unusually correct, as to supply all the details that are required for comparison." Fergusson's reuse of the plate indicates that even he could not "adequately transcend the European 'picturesque' eye."[128] These three nearly identical prints of Ekvera fuse a romantic approach to the site with a topographical one to create a highly constructed mediation, which Giles Tillotson termed the "Indian picturesque."[129]

Yet this mesh of viewing methods ran counter to Gangaram's own. Although Gangaram sketched the approach to the temple at Karle, it was manifestly not his chosen view. He was interested in representing the surface of the façade, which he depicted frontally (see fig. 62), not at an angle, in order to provide the most information about the three-dimensional architectural structure, material, inscriptions, and the elaboration and play of design.

Furthermore, Wales's drawings, even viewed through Daniell's adaptations, have a different tenor from Thomas and William Daniell's other work in *Oriental Scenery*, in particular their third volume on Indian antiquities published in two parts (1800, 1808). The Daniells, though they claimed an unmediated transcription of architecture from building to page via the camera obscura, regularly took the distant sidelong, picturesque view for that delineation.[130] In 1792 before the Daniells met Wales, for instance, Thomas drew the rock-cut temple at "Mavalipuram" (Mamallapuram) under the guidance of Robert Home (fig. 64).[131] His chosen view is an approach from a distance, with the sharp diagonal of the road offering an equally slanted view of the temple, its rocky enclosure, and a wide swathe of curving cloudy sky balanced by a leafy tree on the

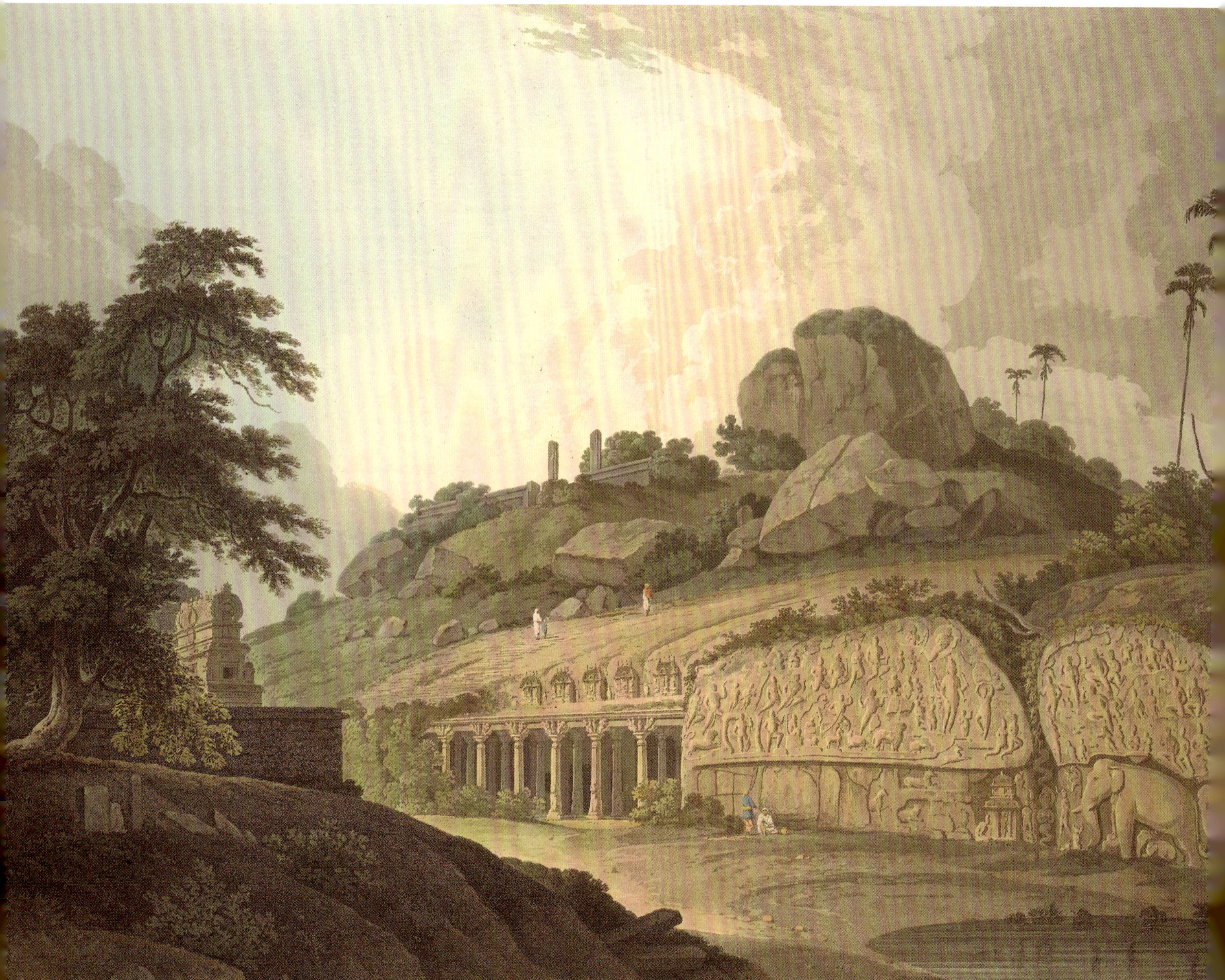

64 Thomas Daniell, "The Entrance of an Excavated Hindoo Temple, at Mavalipuram, on the Coast of Coromandel," 1799, in *Oriental Scenery*, vol. 3: *Twenty-Four Views in Hindoostan* (London, 1808), part II, pl. 2. Aquatint with hand coloring on paper, 54 × 73.7 cm. British Library, London, X432/5(2)

left. Wales's images, in contrast, offer different points of departure. Some emerge from the deep recesses of the temple, giving an embodied, if not ghostly experience (fig. 65), whereas Daniell's interiors are symmetrically and neatly delineated and bathed in light (fig. 66).

Of course, physical attributes of rock-carved temples offered a certain sublime terror that artists explicitly sought. Wales regularly commented on their "dark apartments" and even singled them out as worthy of notice, alongside the number of pillars, and the height of the roof, in organizing his documentation.[132] Such recesses housed danger like "Batts who . . . fly at the . . . face of the intruders" or threat in the "innumerable footsteps of the leopard."[133] In a slender journal, Robert Mabon evoked his feelings that the cave temples inspired, such as his second night in Candali, when he thought himself "as disagreeably situate as in Hell." To make it worse, on his eleventh night he was arrested for being a "spy!"[134] To Europeans educated in the picturesque and especially the sublime, this architecture evoked Edmund Burke's "vastness," "infinity," "succession and uniformity," and "magnitude in building" that could make a viewer shiver with terror and pleasure.[135]

In spite of three more views of Karle that Thomas Daniell published after works in Wales's collection, these were not repeated by other artists, perhaps because of their unusual viewpoints. They not only evoked the darkness and overwhelming nature of the temples, but also sliced the structures at odd junctures, unsettling the compositions. Wales's drafts for the descriptions in his prospected publication offered dry facts more than a meditative or a comparative approach, which leaves his choice of view and its inherent moodiness unexplained. He simply described the hall at Karle as having a "fine appearance" with a "durable" structure of "beams of wood" that supported the roof.[136]

This attention to the "length" and "loftiness" of the roof is reflected in one of Wales's rare hypnotic drawings (fig. 67), which is repeated in Daniell's colored proof and final print (fig. 68), confirming that Daniell based at least some of his prints on Wales's drafts. There is a leap, however, from Wales's spare tracing to Daniell's print. Could this be found in Gangaram's draft in grey washes (see fig. 61)? Gangaram attended to the play of light and shadow, the repetition of the banded ceiling and the infinite columned hall that Wales simply adjusted to view from the side rather than straight on. Together, Wales and Gangaram's drafts created the setting for Malet's meditative, awestruck description of the *chaitya* hall of Vishvakarma as the abode of the "Almighty," quoted earlier, that Daniell acknowledged in this temple dedicated to the "artist of the [Hindu] gods" in the text of *Oriental Scenery*.[137]

Other prints that Daniell published based on Wales's have a visual affinity with Gangaram's, particularly when they cut the view at a disjuncture and approach a structure as three-dimensional in space. One print situates the viewer extremely close to the building,

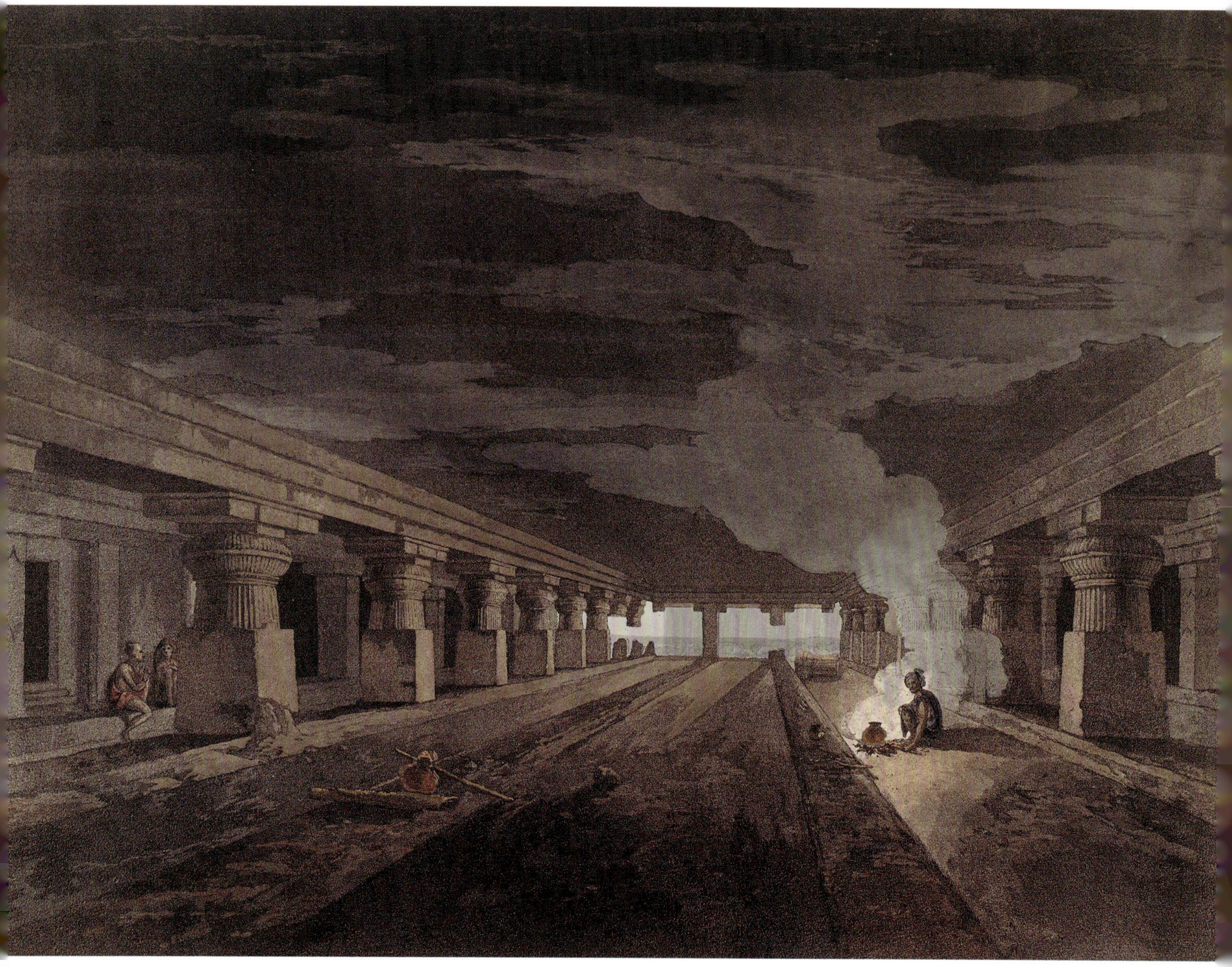

65 Thomas Daniell after James Wales, "Dehr Warra," in *Oriental Scenery*, vol. 5: *Hindoo Excavations in the Mountain of Ellora near Aurangabad* (London, 1803), pl. 24. Aquatint with hand coloring, 53.8 × 74 cm. British Library, London, X432/6(24)

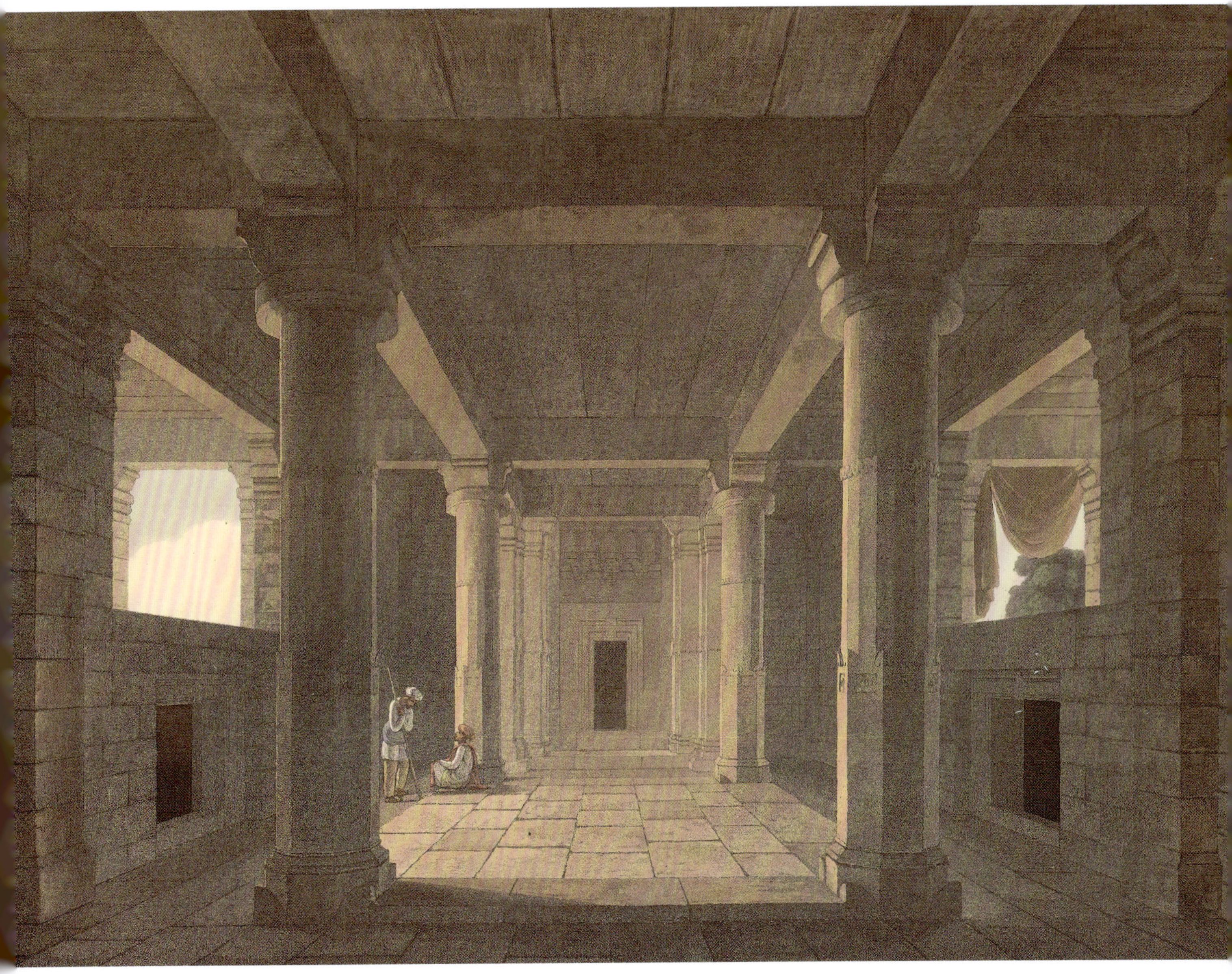

66 Thomas Daniell, "Interior of a Temple near Muddunpore," 1808, in *Oriental Scenery*, vol. 3: *Twenty-Four Views in Hindoostan* (London, 1808), part II, pl. 16. Aquatint with hand coloring, 54.4 × 74 cm. British Library, London, X432/5(16)

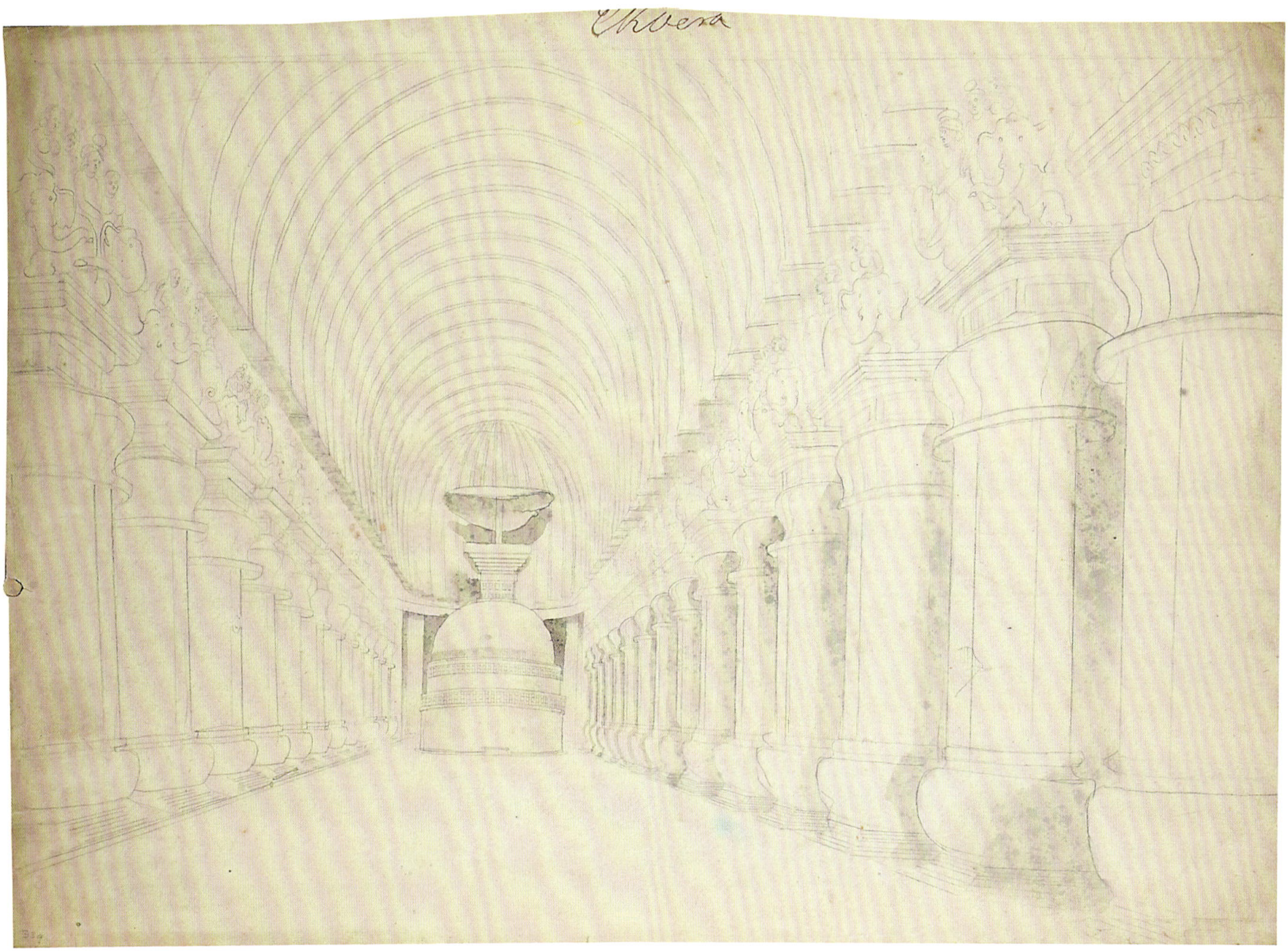

67 James Wales, *Interior of the Chaitya Cave at Karle*, Maharashtra, 1793 or 1795. Pencil and gray wash on paper, 47 × 66 cm. Photograph courtesy Christie's, London, Sale 6807, "Arts of India," lot 52

68 Thomas Daniell after James Wales, "Ekvera," in *Antiquities of India* (London, 1803), pl. 8. Aquatint with hand coloring, 55 × 75 cm. British Library, London, P181

69 Thomas Daniell after James Wales, "Ekvera," in *Antiquities of India* (London, 1803), pl. 7. Aquatint with hand coloring, 54 × 75 cm. British Library, London, P180

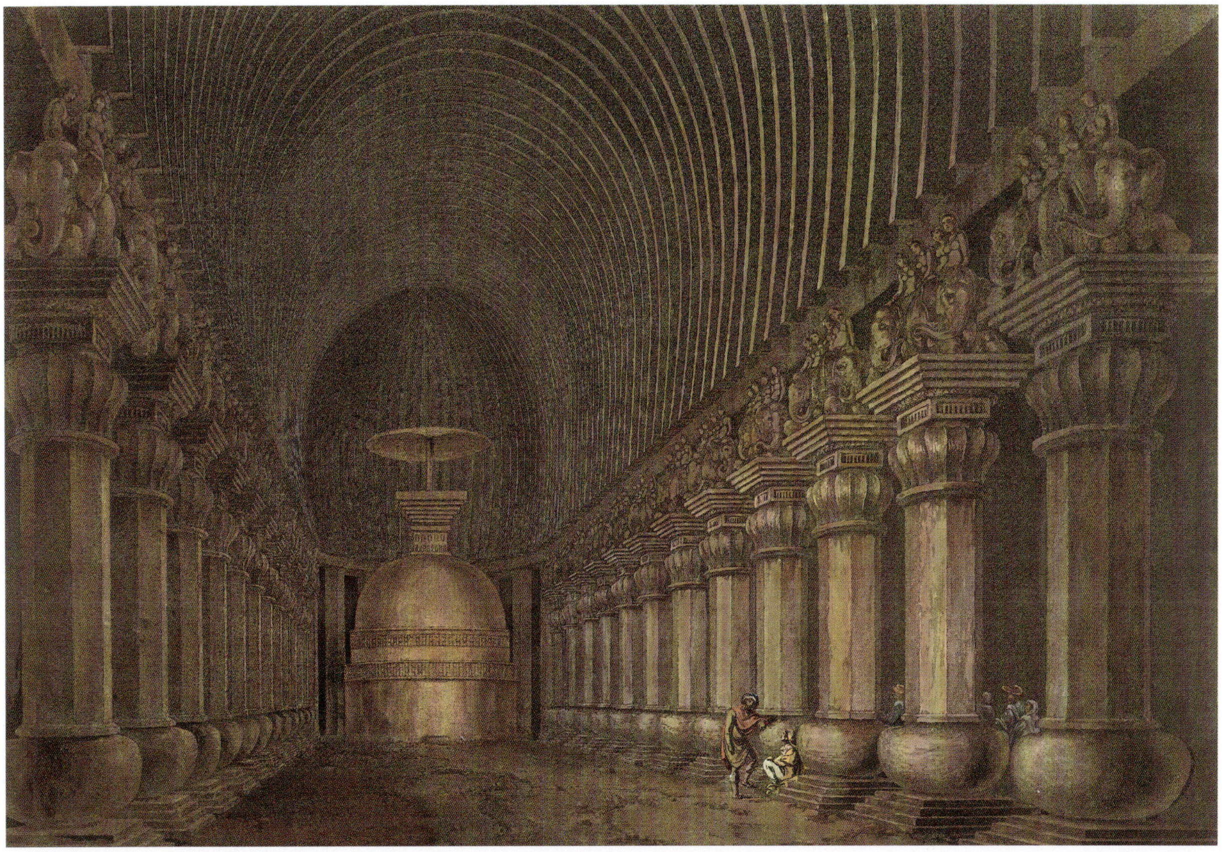
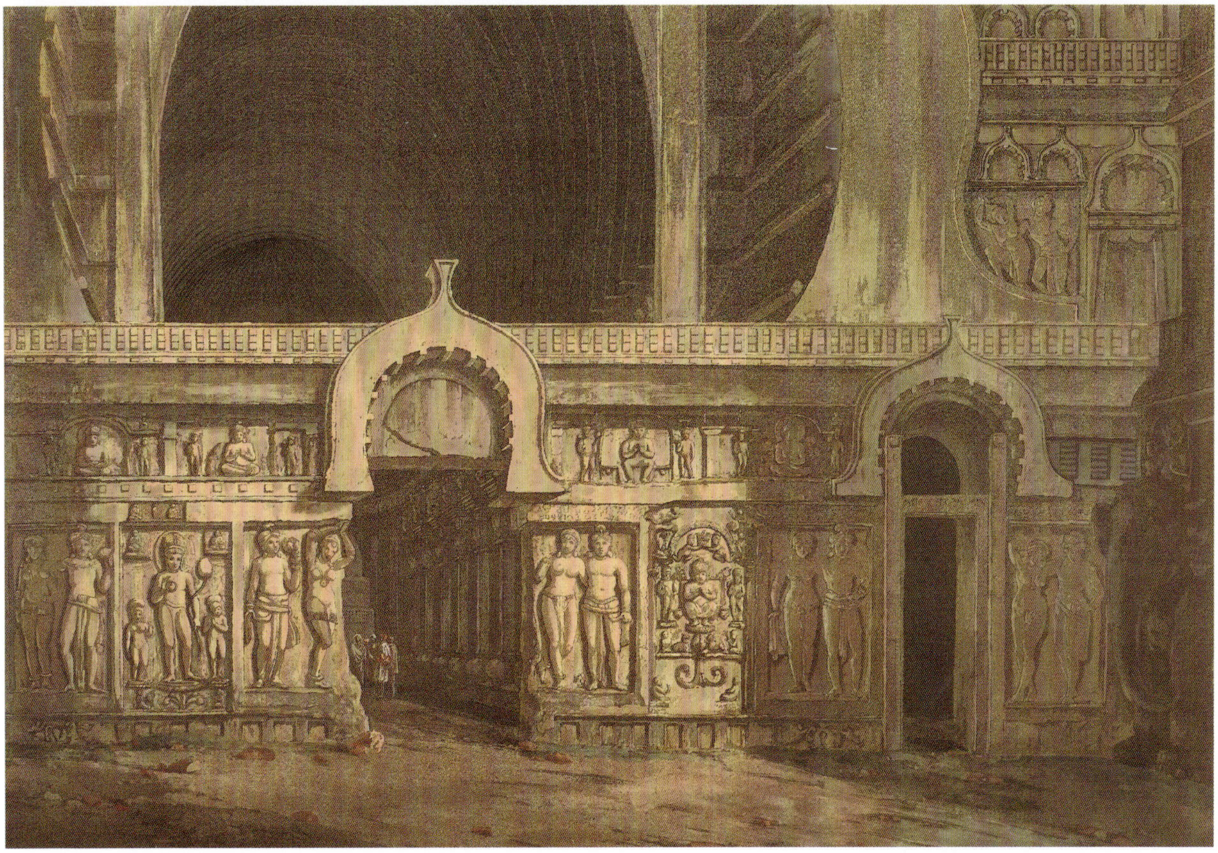

at the base of the temple with a view of the rock it was carved from, like Gangaram's view of Kailasa nestled in the mountain (see fig. 56).[138] The sculptural detail of the side of the portico is faced frontally, as Gangaram was wont to do. Another view essentially crops Gangaram's large presentation work of Karle (see fig. 62) and angles it slightly (fig. 69).

There are other affinities. Gangaram's representation of an unfinished temple at Ellora encloses the artist, as well as the temple, in between panels of rock (fig. 70). This watercolor is from Gangaram's first trip to Ellora, thus one of those traced for Wales. Similar to other works from that time, it shows a stacked approach rather than a perspectival view, with the rock at the base merging with the temple in the middle ground that in turn is placed before the exterior rock in the background. It forcefully portrays the building as emerging from rock, the power of that materiality, and of the artist hemmed in by the enclosure. In a like view (fig. 71), though of a different temple (Indra Sabha), Wales too chose to draw from within, as if attracted to the weightiness of the rock and the cropping of the frame. He has placed himself, the artist, looking out.

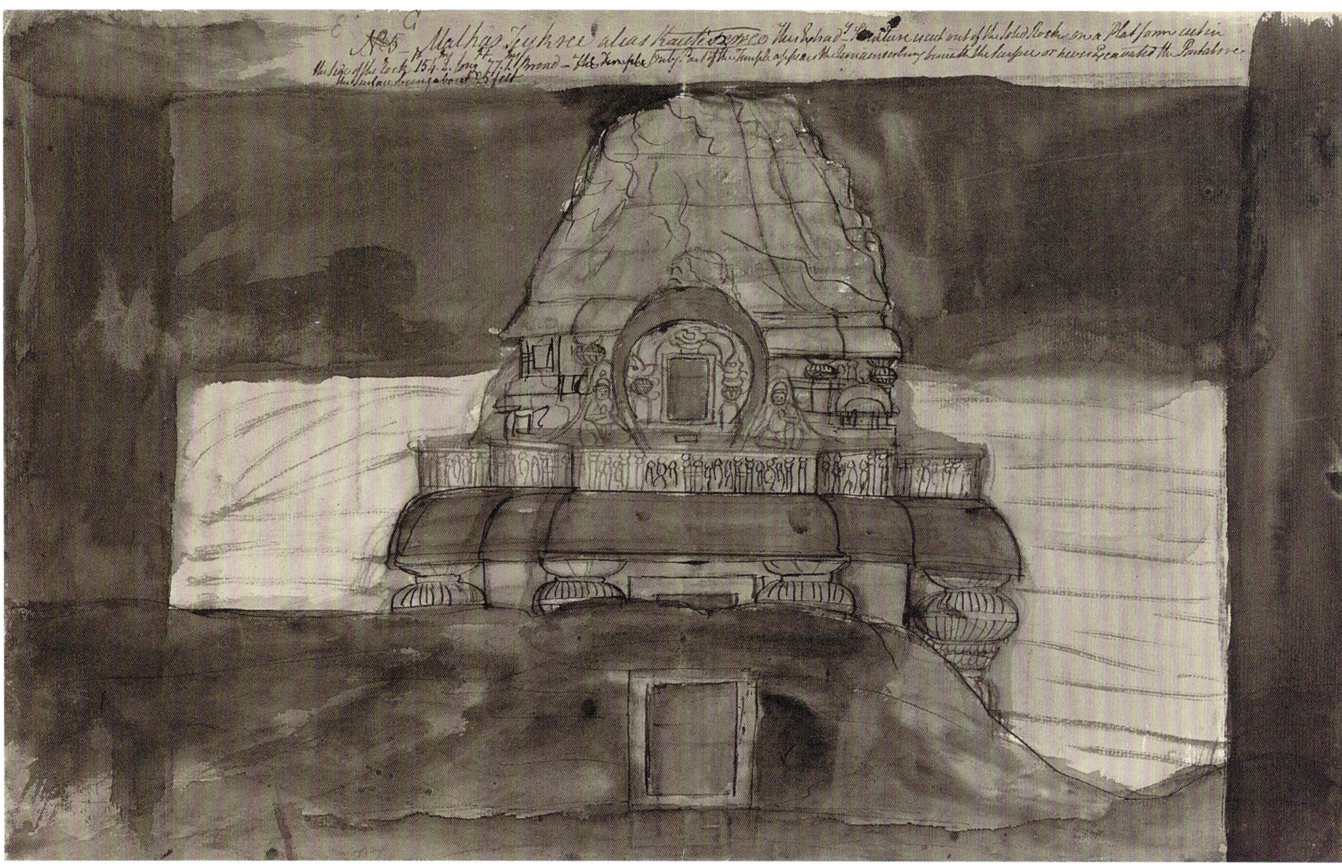

70 Gangaram Tambat, *View of a Rock-Carved Temple*, Ellora, 1793 or 1795. Gray wash and graphite with pen and black ink on paper, 30.5 × 48.6 cm. Yale Center for British Art, New Haven, Connecticut, Paul Mellon Collection, B1977.14.22336

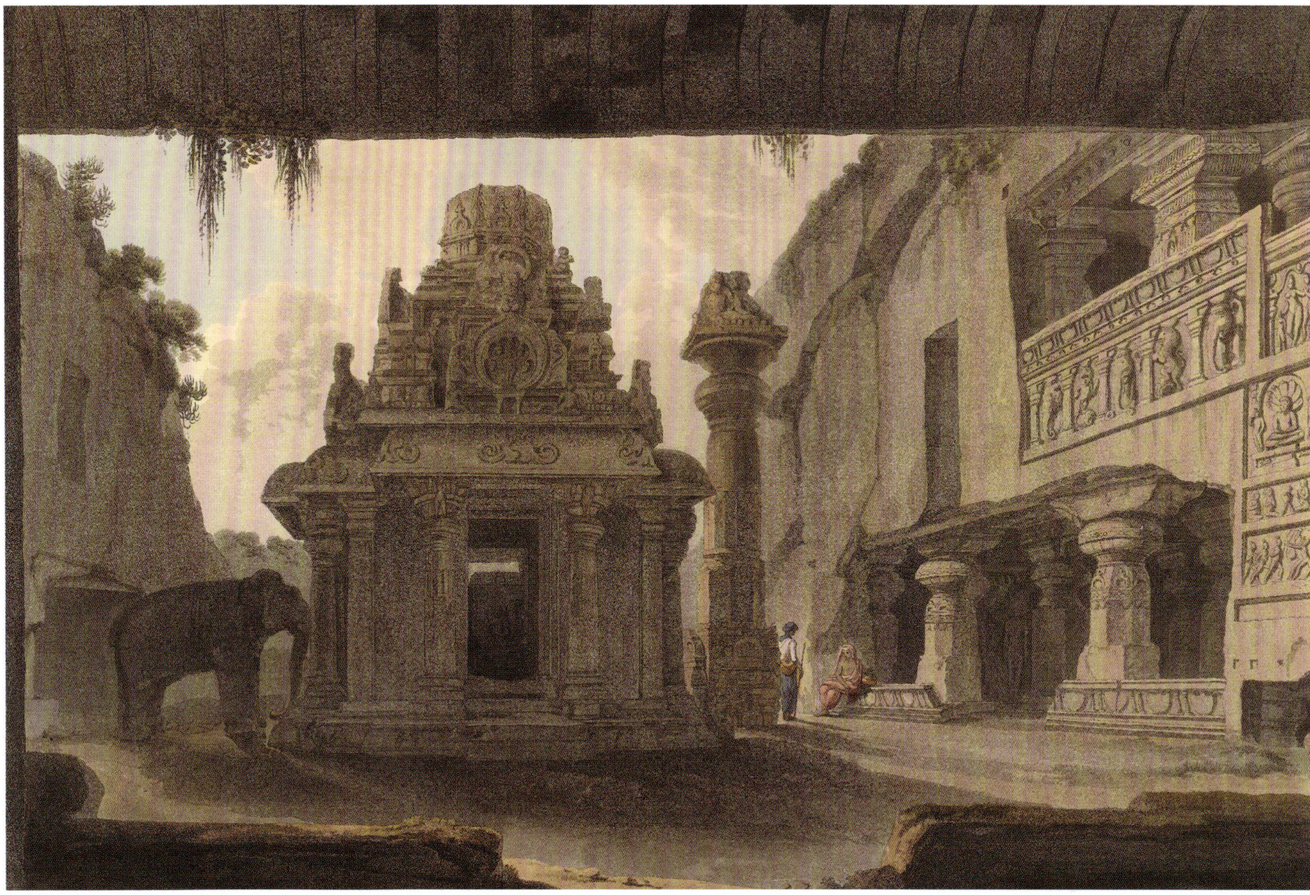

It is not a simple matter of Wales copying Gangaram's work. Rather, it seems that Gangaram's watercolors and distinctive manipulation of space and dimension might have offered Wales a new visual access to rock-cut architecture's articulation, a way to break out of the picturesque frame, and to use the camera obscura's direction in unconventional, striking ways. Unfortunately, the majority of Wales's drawings and those produced by Mabon and Jossi, are lost. Perhaps Wales's use of perspective or other qualities of their work were also absorbed into Wales's. However, it is clear that Gangaram affected Wales's approach to Ellora and Karle, and his production of drawings and plans of the site inflected Wales's work.

Daniell's published aquatints defined Indian architecture for generations and remain a touchstone for this period, yet they are not Daniell's alone. He acknowledged that they were based on Wales's drawings, but what of Gangaram's, Jossi's, and Mabon's? It is well-established that Indian artists played a distinct role in the colonial production

71 Thomas Daniell after James Wales, "View of Indra Sabha looking outward," 1803, in *Oriental Scenery*, vol. 5: *Hindoo Excavations in the Mountain of Ellora near Aurangabad* (London, 1803), pl. 7. Aquatint with hand coloring, 53.8 × 73.5 cm. British Library, London, X432/6 (7)

of knowledge about India. As I stated at the outset of this chapter, Mildred Archer pioneered the term "Company" painter to define Indian artists who used European artistic techniques to visualize subjects of interest to their British patrons and the tourist trade. These often included works on natural history, manners and customs, and portraiture in India. Albeit often "asymmetric" in their power dynamics, these relationships, as Kapil Raj has demonstrated, produced "certified knowledges which would not have come into being but for the encounter between South Asian and European intellectual and material practices that took place" in India.[139]

Yet Tambat did not become subsumed in British visual practices, just as Wales did not blindly adopt Maratha ones in his work for the Poona court or in relation to the artists he hired. Wales used Gangaram's regional approach to a frontal close access, a sculptural means to define space, and a placement from within rather than a distant view, just as Gangaram used perspective, architectural drafting, shading, and framing devices in the "Company" mode. Wales, in turn, was clearly competent in a "Company" manner of delineation, just as Gangaram used a "Poona" one. "Company" should be recognized as a style of making, rather than as a classification of a singular method of making art, a style that both Indian and British artists used in the period, among others.

This is true for other artists who worked for the British in this period. In Delhi, artists such as Ghulam Ali Khan simultaneously worked for the Mughal emperor Shah 'Alam II and for the Company official William Fraser to produce illustrated Persian poems and Mughal court portraits for the former, and topographical paintings of Delhi and ethnographic portraits of its inhabitants for the latter. As Yuthika Sharma has written, "his artistic trajectory reinforced conventions and stylistic norms but, more importantly, conflated them too."[140] In Udaipur, the practice of an artist named Ghasi similarly "refracts . . . his embodied experience of multiple political interests and his learning from multiple aesthetic and knowledge traditions," in Dipti Khera's words.[141] Employed by the Company agent Colonel James Tod to draft architecture in Udaipur's domains, Ghasi also drew processions of the Maharana in the manner of Udaipur court painting, just as he would to portray Tod in his encounters with the court.[142] Ghulam Ali Khan and Ghasi were court-trained artists who worked for well-established courts and Company agents. Artists worked in a wide manner of styles, including that of the Company, even if they were not specifically in Company employment. For example, Shailka Mishra has shown that Deepa Chatera, an artist at the Amber court in Rajasthan, drew devotional paintings of Krishna, a European-style map of Ayodha, and courtly portraits of the king.[143]

Style of course is linked to process. Wales amalgamated the work of multiple artists, across cultures and artistic training. He promoted an eclectic manner of working in his own practice, and as a fruitful, cost-effective, and time-efficient method of co-production in a workshop. He was aware of mixture, and Gangaram was too. Gangaram worked in a regional idiom of sculpting wax and clay as well as that of popular painting. He was also skilled in European modes, and copied European prints, and, as I shall discuss in the next section, Indian court paintings as well. These works of his are not simply hybrids; rather, they evince conscientious artistic graftings that pushed toward something new.[144]

British artists in India adapted Indian techniques just as Indian artists adapted British ones, and their work was transformed as a result. If Wales's individual flourish was located in the mystery of the sublime or the cropping of the camera obscura, when joined with Gangaram's rubric it gained eeriness and confrontation, an emptiness laden with threat. Gangaram's arts also changed. When joined with Malet and Wales's attention to the people and animals in western India, he applied their urge to classify to portray himself and those whom he knew.

A PORTRAIT OF GANGARAM TAMBAT

In a double portrait, Gangaram depicts himself wearing a bright red turban; he listens to his teacher, hands folded in the gesture of *anjali mudra*, indicating attention, respect, and honor (fig. 72).[145] His guru in turn teaches, with one hand resting in his lap and his other raised holding prayer beads. According to Malet's inscription, this is "Gangaram by Himself, very like + a very ingenious Person at Poona in the service of CWM, by whom the subsequent native sketches were drawn chiefly from life + His G'roo a celebrated holy Hermit near Poona."[146] The thirteen additional "native sketches" are drawings of individual devotees, who must also have been participants in this religious group (fig. 73). Most of the men are shown cross-legged, in profile, with bodies turned three-quarters to the viewer. They are relaxed. One man leans on his hand, shoulder pushed up, while another hunches over. Others have folded their hands in their laps or count prayer beads, possibly listening to their guru. One man, however, turns forward, boldly staring straight out – he also appears to be Gangaram (see fig. 5).

"Gangaram," Wales wrote, "is the Chapl[a]in of our company." Devoted to a "spiritual Director," he also knew a range of religious practitioners.[147] On their journey to Ellora in 1795, Gangaram introduced Wales to a Mahanubhava priest "of liberal mind" on January 30, whom I mentioned earlier, and a week later on February 7, a *marabout* (holy man), whom Wales described as having "much sweetness of temper and intelligence."[148] Gangaram also seems to have had a particular character. Wales wrote in his journal:

> Gangaram a native artist who accompanied me [to Ellora], having heard of an old pagod about one coss off ... told me his fear of being ... beaten by [robbers]

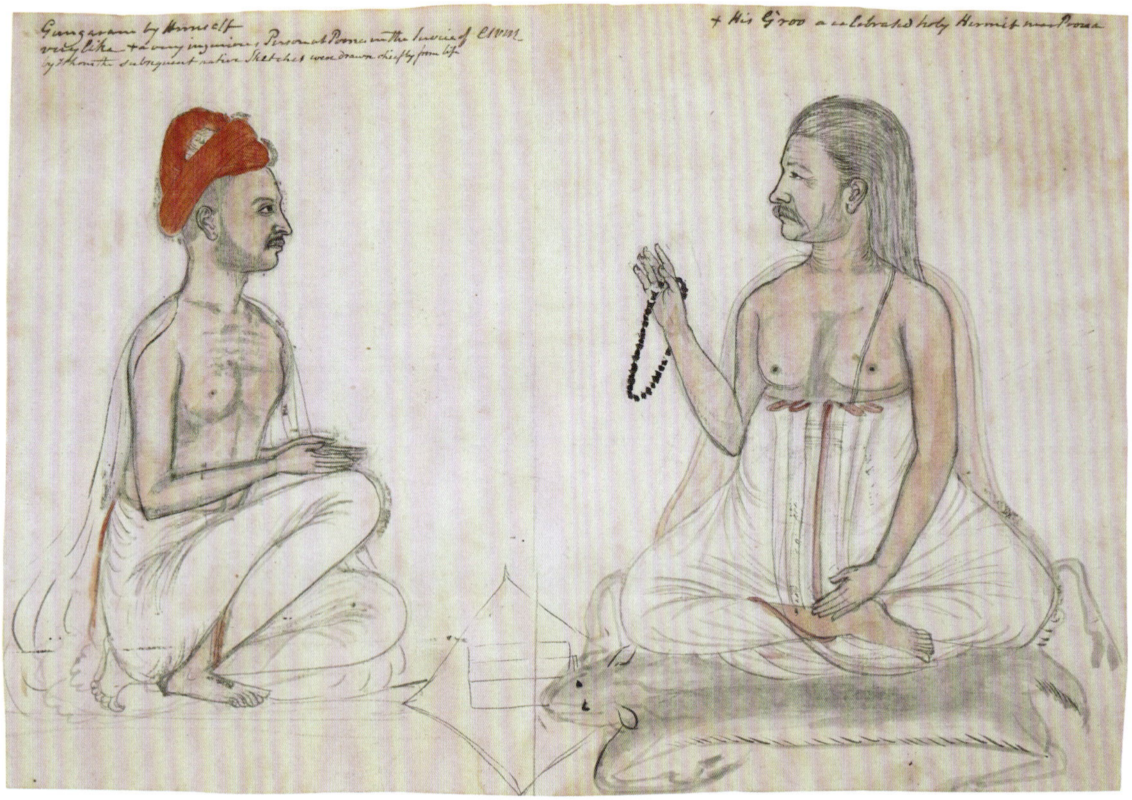

> who lay in wait near the Pagoda. After various consultations he [was] to borrow a musket to defend himself but it being suggested that a musket being the kind of booty which would be more acceptable to robbers and he never having fired a musket . . . he resolved [that] to prevent his being robbed of his clothes, he should strip and go naked and in this manner he accomplished his journey in perfect safety.[149]

This anecdote is incredulous, but also respectful. It illuminates the annotation of "A Fool named Gungaram" on one of his portraits (see fig. 34). Gangaram was one to play the "Fool" – void of common sense – only to prove his acumen.

The composition of the portrait of Gangaram and his guru is also worldly. Numerous paintings from the Poona region depict noblemen as disciples of a spiritual leader or god. In one painting, a sage offers the blue-skinned god Krishna knowledge in an illustration to the Sanskrit philosophical treatise the Bhagavad Gita (fig. 74).[150] A comparison of the poses is instructive. The sage is seated just like Gangaram's guru: cross-legged with his torso toward the viewer, head in profile. Krishna has one leg bent just like Gangaram.

72 Gangaram Tambat, *Self-Portrait of the Artist Gangaram with his Guru*, Maharashtra, ca. 1790. Watercolor on paper, 25 × 36.2 cm. British Library, London, Add. Or. 4145

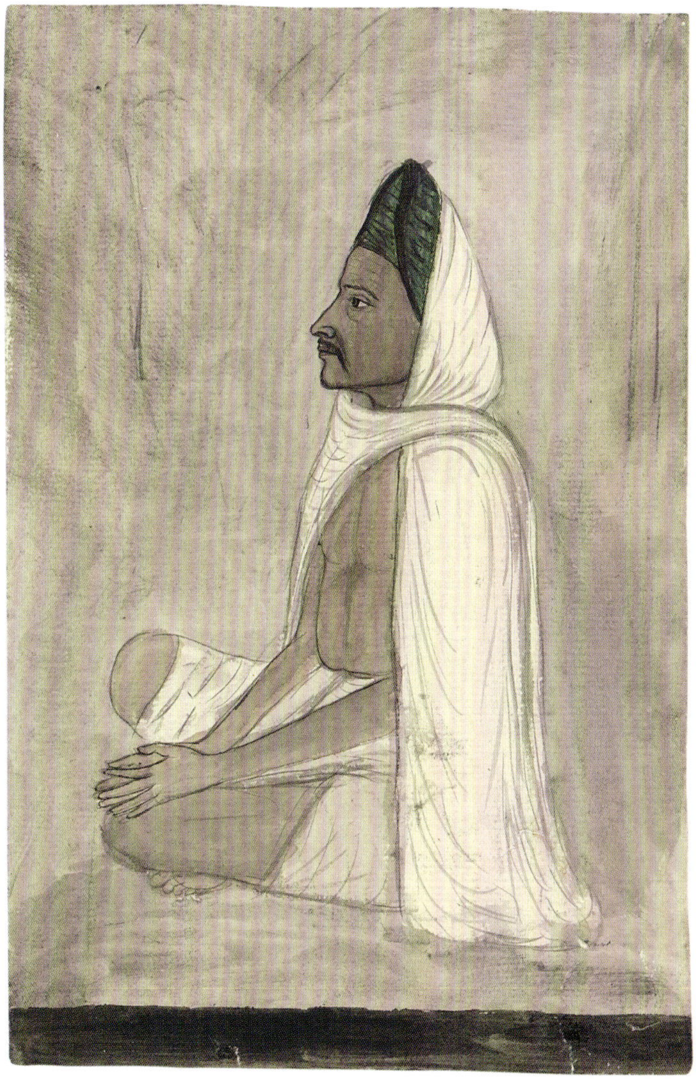

Another painting, however, could also have served as a model. Shivram Chitari, who painted the British hunter in the parrot-green field of animals (see fig. 38), also depicted the Maratha king Shahu Maharaj attended by his prime minister, Peshwa Narayanrao (fig. 75). These two figures are situated within a similar parrot-green landscape to the sage and Krishna in the Bhagavad Gita image, which was familiar throughout the region. The poses are nearly identical, though here there is aspiration for elevation. Gangaram becomes the minister and his guru becomes the king.

This portrait of Gangaram and his guru invokes the compositional format of regional paintings, which Gangaram probably accessed, just as he did European prints (see figs. 36

73 Gangaram Tambat, *Devotee in a Green Turban*, Poona, ca. 1790. Watercolor and graphite with pen and black ink on paper, 22.9 × 15.2 cm. Yale Center for British Art, New Haven, Connecticut, Paul Mellon Collection, B1977.14.22394

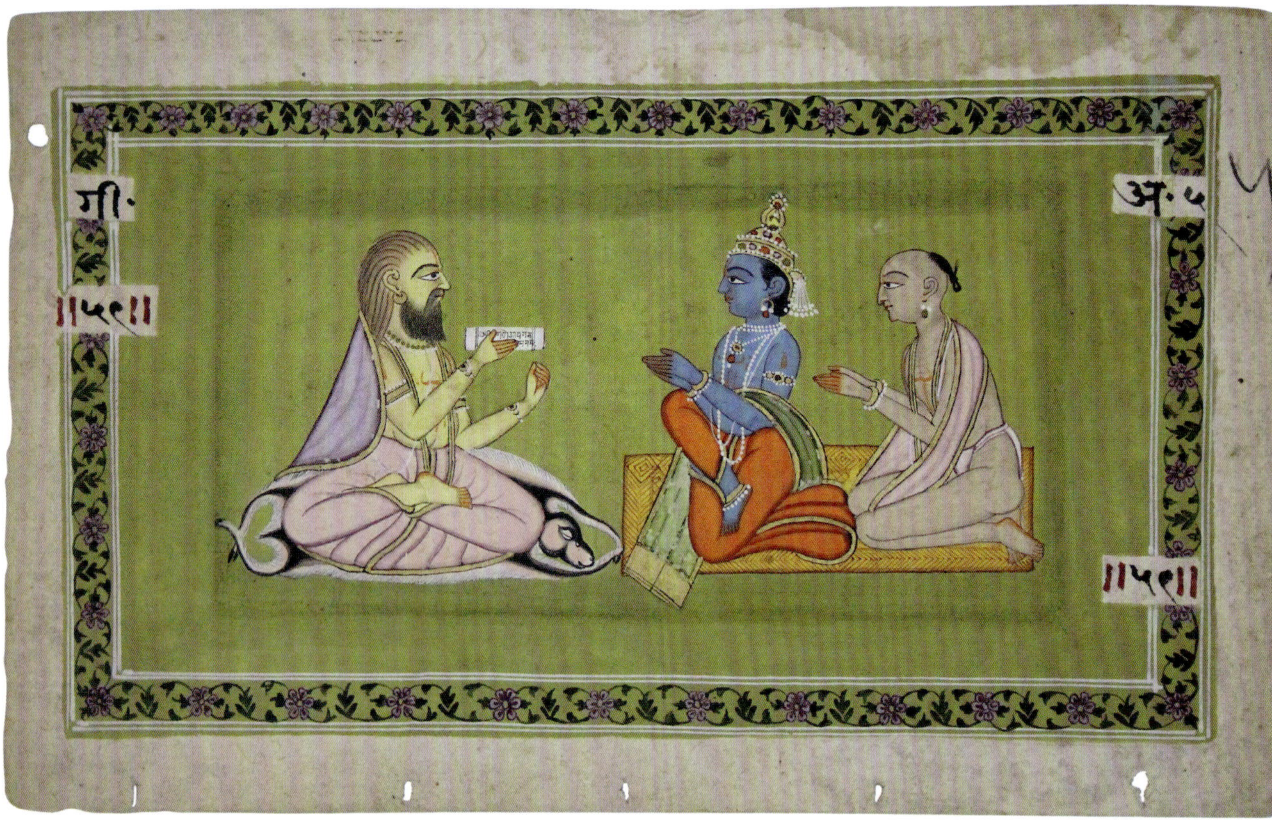

and 39). At least one of his drawings after an Indian painting remains in Malet's archive. Gangaram drew a priest of the Bohras named "Manpuri Baba" (fig. 76), which appears to be based on a Mughal type prevalent in Jaipur.[151] This attribution is registered in the inscription; he termed this painting a *tasvir* (picture), rather than a *naqsha* (sketch) as he did on his architectural drawings (see figs. 31 and 32 for *naqsha* in the inscriptions). In light of his devotion, it might be significant that Gangaram chose to copy a painting of a holy man, especially as he could probably access a range of works. Malet owned Mughal paintings and Nana Fadnavis sent paintings to the Residency from his collection, as noted earlier.[152] Indeed, this holy man's profile and seated three-quarter pose is shared

74 *A Sage Offering his Knowledge of Devotion to Krishna and a Devotee*, Maharashtra, 18th century. In an illustrated manuscript of the Bhagavad Gita. Opaque watercolor and gold on paper, approx. 16.5 × 22.5 cm. Bharat Itihas Sanshodhak Mandal, Pune

75 Shivram Chitari, *Shahu Maharaj with Nanasaheb Peshwa on a Hunt*, Maharashtra, mid- to late 18th century. Opaque watercolor and gold on paper, 47 × 30.5 cm. History Museum, Dr. Babasaheb Ambedkar Marathwada University, Aurangabad

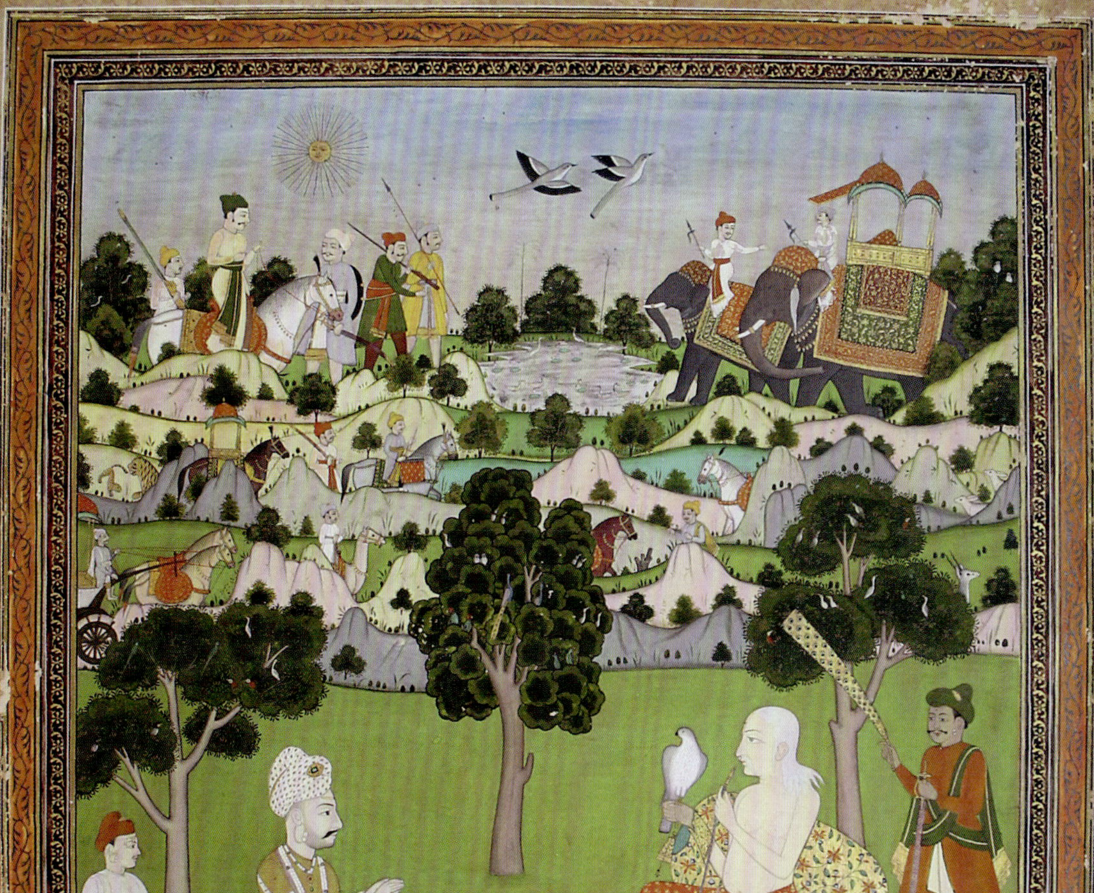

Shahu with his prime minister.

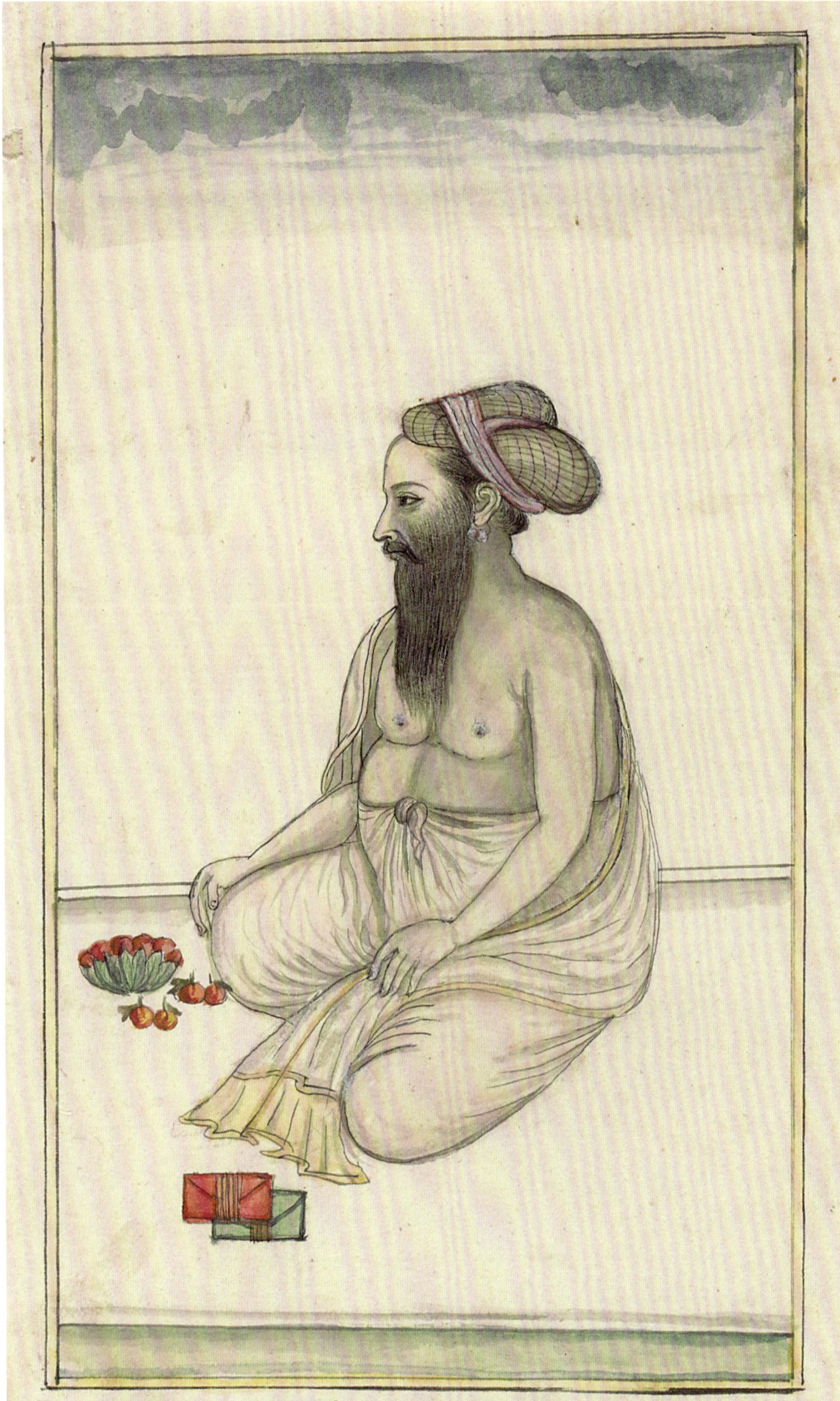
Portrait of a priest of the Borahs
Gungaram
1794

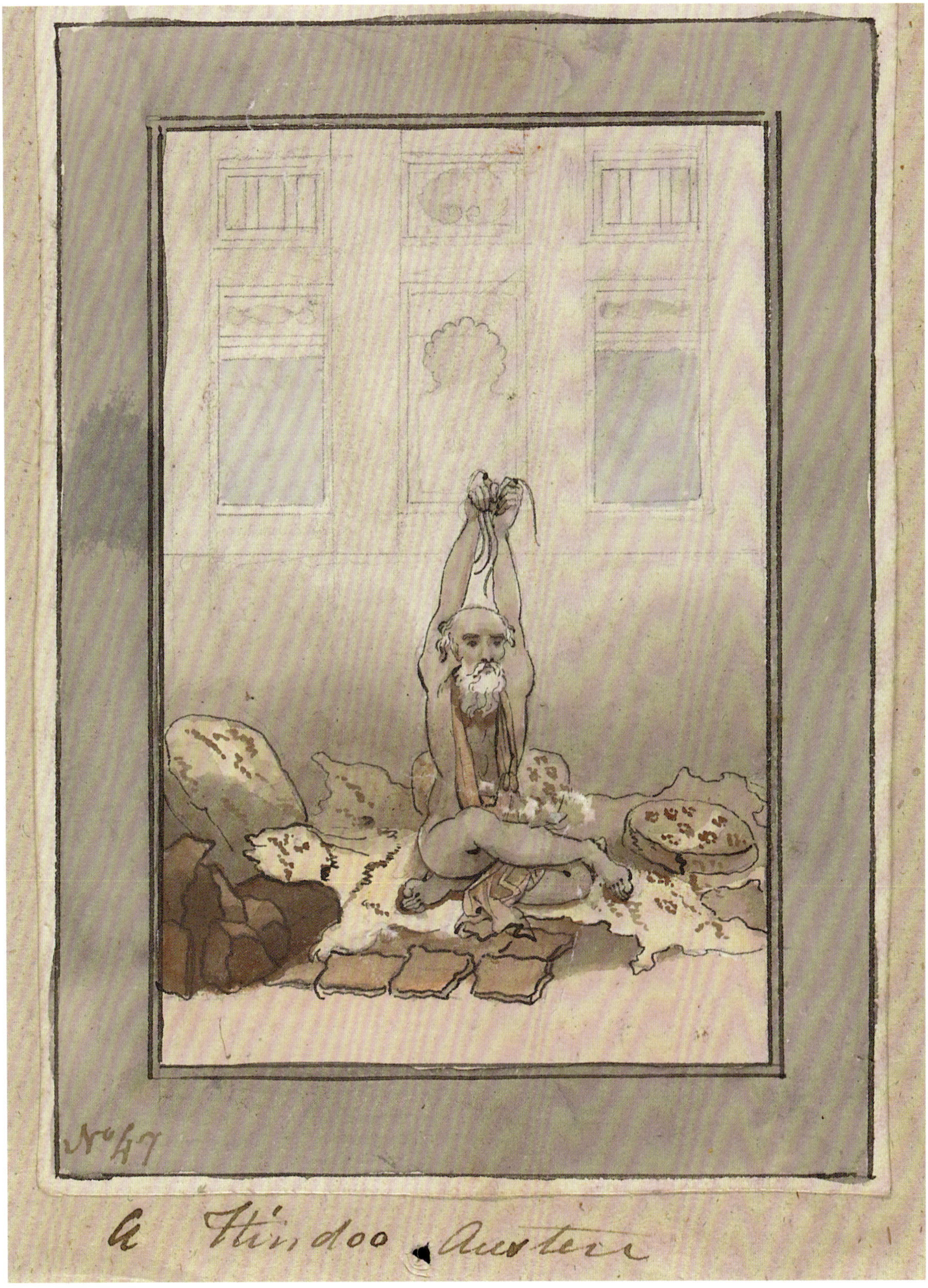

76 Gangaram Tambat, *Portrait of a Priest of the Borahs* [Bohras], Poona, 1794. Watercolor and gouache with pen and ink on paper, 24.4 × 16.5 cm. Yale Center for British Art, New Haven, Connecticut, Paul Mellon Collection, B1977.14.22418

77 Robert Mabon, *A Hindu Austere*, Poona, ca. 1792. Watercolor and graphite with pen and black ink on paper, 18.1 × 13.3 cm. Yale Center for British Art, New Haven, Connecticut, Paul Mellon Collection, B1977.14.22283

with other devotees that Gangaram limned (see fig. 73). Yet, while Gangaram clearly considered the varied techniques of composition and draftsmanship in other regional Indian paintings, his works also differ from them. Rather than the densely applied colorful gouache, Gangaram's portraits are simple, sketch-like, and seem to be for personal if not devotional use.

Other series in Malet's archive complicate Gangaram's. Mabon, who also assisted Wales, deftly outlined and colored what appear to be ethnographic types of ascetics rather than portraits. He subsequently etched some of his drawings to illustrate his *Sketches of Oriental Manners* (Calcutta?, 1797?) and provided a judgmental assessment of the Muslim "Fakers [Fakirs]" and Hindu "Jogees [Yogis]" depicted in plate XIX who "pretend to great austerity, and devotion; in order to procure alms . . . ." In Mabon's drawings as well as the related prints, the men are identifiable by their attributes of deprivation. One man is captioned as a "Hindoo Austere" (fig. 77). He is one of a type that at: "a very youthful period, clinch their fists very hard, and extend their arms in an erect posture; at the same time making a vow never to alter it – the nails of the fingers in course of time, grow into the palms, and appear through the back of their hands, hanging like so many icicles." Mabon's representation defines "austerity" within the trope of the fanatic that had been repeated for centuries in European publications about Indian ascetics, rather than as a description of an individual.[153] His drawings stereotype ascetics and cater to a market for Company officials and for wider European audiences attuned to the exotic.

Gangaram's series of devotees suddenly may be related to any series of "fakirs," "yogis," and "austeres," while also resolving to be a series of known people, a series of portraits. These drawings register a fault line. In an aesthetic analysis that line marks a gap between different types and methods of depiction. By delineating "people of a certain group" on separate sheets of blank paper Gangaram followed a European way of depicting types, such as those by a "Brahmin" in Cambay, likely Sadanand Vyas, and by Mabon.[154] However, in both contexts, the figures are not portraits but types meant to delineate and identify separate members of a certain, often feared, group in India. In comparison to these, Gangaram's drawings register as divergent. They are of devotees, but they are not defined by attribute. Rather they have physiognomies that indicate individual identities well known to the artist.

Gangaram also could have been following a regional style of depiction, where scenes of noblemen and religious figures set in a landscape were common, or a Mughal or Rajput one, where portraits of noblemen in the position of devotees, or simply of devotees or other regional figures, are well known.[155] Yet Gangaram presented a series of informally sketched, ordinary devotees who appear to be specific individuals. Such a series of ordinary disciples and their guru rather than a noble or iconic figure is equally compelling and equally strange. Gangaram was a sculptor and painter who worked for the public rather than the court; he was trained by Malet and Wales, and by the works that he copied in their collections. Yet his series of individual devotees seems to be a graft of his own volition. In the spaces left among methods of depiction, Gangaram lit upon something familiar and unfamiliar to them all.

Thus, the ingenuity of the "ingenious artist" Gangaram, as Malet described him, lay precisely in his ability to innovate. Gangaram altered how Malet and Wales saw and interpreted India, but he also took the skills that he learned in unintended directions. While drawing on his training in the regional arts of the Poona region and his particular metalworking communities, he was also able to accommodate the techniques and subjects that his British patrons required. Gangaram's artworks display a distinctive aesthetic that emerged from an artistic practice that was hinged between India and Britain (and the nuances within each), and among the popular traditions he knew, the courtly ones that he studied, and the British ones that he gained.

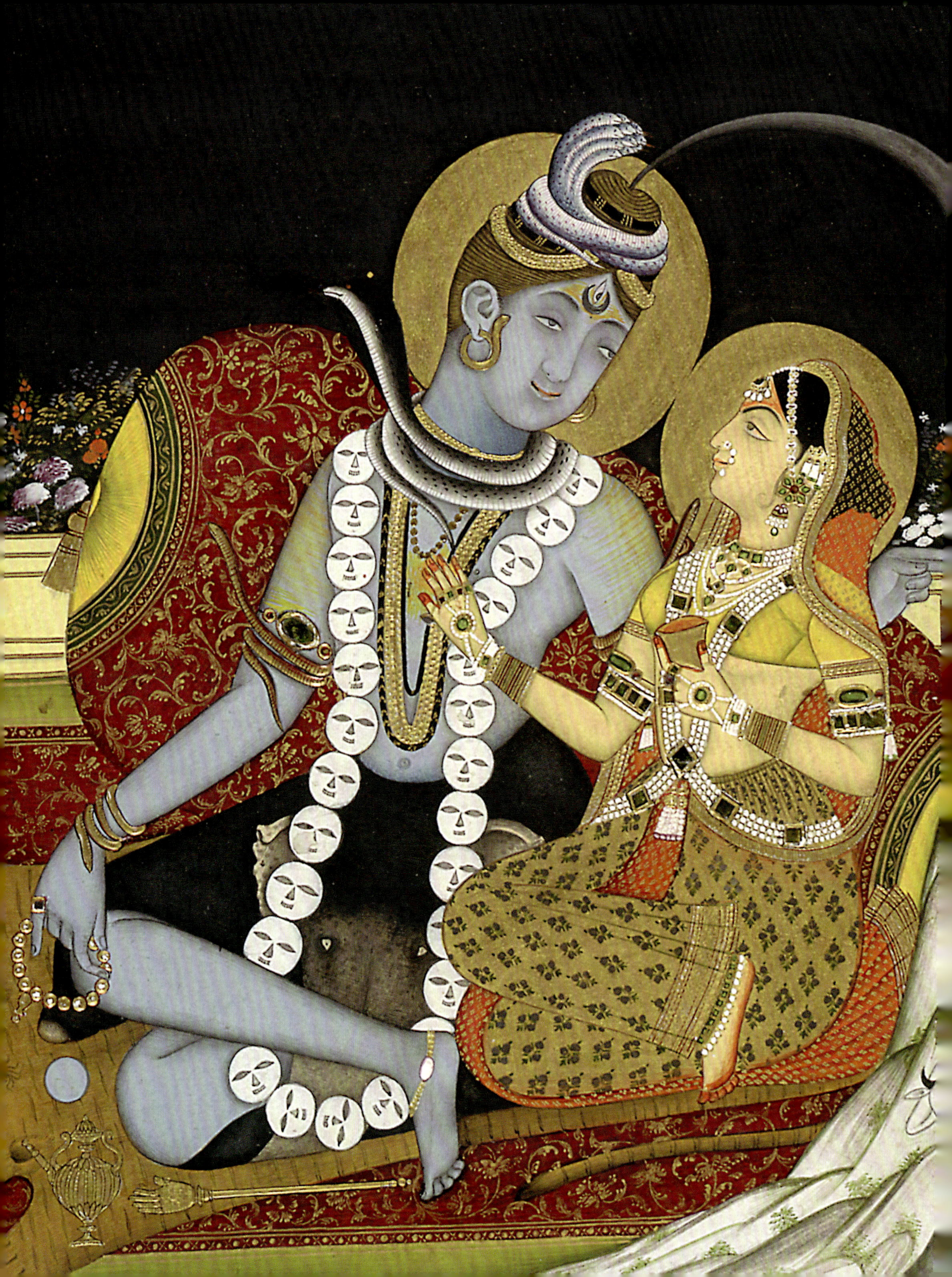

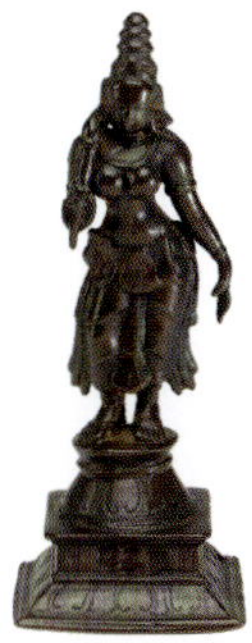

CHAPTER THREE

"Men and Gods, and Things": Objects in an Indian Art Market

A bronze cast of Lakshmi, the goddess of wealth, her arm paralleling her hip in a sinuous curve, was once in the home shrine of Nana Fadnavis (fig. 78; see fig. 22).[1] In 1797, the figure was plundered from his home when a Maratha general sacked the city and imprisoned Nana Fadnavis during the succession crisis that followed the death of the Peshwa Savai Madhavrao in 1795.[2] A symbol of bounty, here Lakshmi also allegorizes the wealth derived from the booty that fueled the Maratha military and political economy, as it did that of Britain's East India Company. Satirists in London identified the motivation behind the Company wars in western India with the "millions" of gold coins that ideally would be "secured" (fig. 79). This traffic of sculptures and currency shifts our attention from the diplomatic circumstances in which Maratha patrons and artists commissioned and made art in Poona to the collection of objects in the military circumstances that the Marathas and the Company pursued across India, and to their dissemination. By focusing on goods gained through graft and the disruptions of war, this chapter considers different markets for religious arts in eighteenth-century western India and the ones that emerged for British patrons.

Four markets in particular intersected with British and Maratha soldiers on their routes of conquest during war and at their military posts during peace. The first consists of bronze sculptures of deities and those made of precious materials associated with pilgrimage sites that were located on the same roads that soldiers took. The plunder, relocation, and even

Detail of fig. 91 (opposite) and fig. 78 (above)

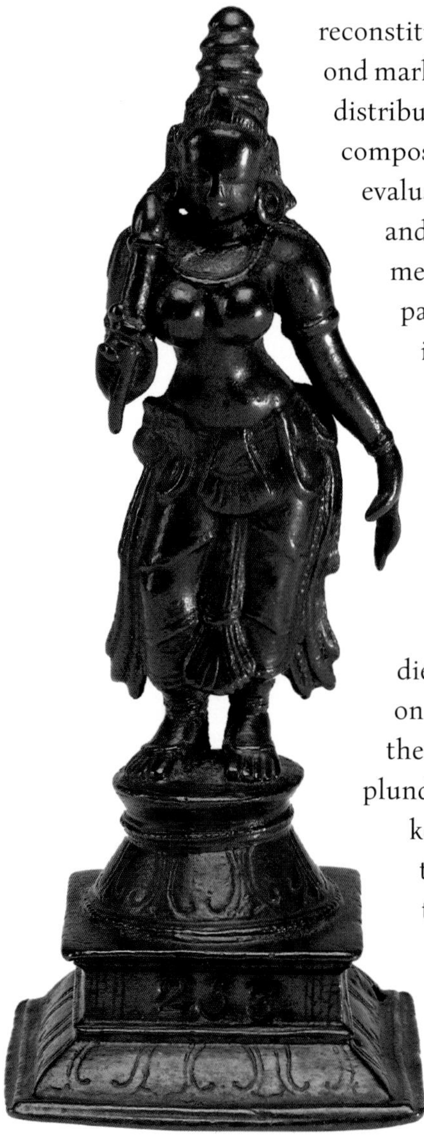

reconstitution of these and other items at forts and palaces attest to a second market for spoils (known as "prize" to the British), which were officially distributed after a war's conclusion. A transregional trade in paintings composes a third market. Collected in north India, these paintings were evaluated according to Mughal and Rajput systems of connoisseurship and sold by merchants to buyers in western India. Alongside commerce in these three trades in iconic sculptures, plunder, and fine paintings, there was also a fourth, local market for devotional paintings on walls and paper that were connected to a ritual calendar. While many of these economies were founded in well-established patterns of exchange, their intersection created opportunities for Maratha and Company patrons to collect, evaluate, and also commission art in new modes.

I focus on Edward Moor, who is the source of the materials that I will discuss. In accordance with the Anglo-Maratha treaty, Moor was embedded in the Maratha army as a British soldier in the wars against Tipu Sultan from 1790 to 1792. He marched on roads that passed forts, temples, bazaars, and palaces along with the devotees, merchants, and artists who bought, sold, made, and plundered various arts. This mobility enabled, in his words, a marketplace of "men and gods, and things" to flourish.[3] Moor was tenured in western India from 1782 to 1805; in 1792 he returned to England to heal war wounds for four years, then in 1797–8 was stationed in Poona and from 1799 in Bombay.[4] During this period, he witnessed the relationship between the Marathas and the British shift. From the British entreaties to the Marathas to engage Tipu Sultan in the early 1790s, the Marathas turned to seeking their help in the late 1790s or waging war against them. The Marathas lost to the British in the Second Anglo-Maratha War, 1803–5, the year Moor left India. In 1818, the Marathas were definitively defeated by the British, which led to their colonial control of the subcontinent.

Over the course of these military alliances, defeats, and changing Anglo-Maratha dynamics, Moor collected more than 360 sculptures and 250 paintings in western India, of which he had commissioned around 100 from a Poona artist.[5] Moor's collection is rare in that it includes a range of eighteenth-century popular Maratha arts and documents them in relation to British and Maratha military and collecting practices.[6] In art his-

78 *Lakshmi in the Form of Bhudevi ?*, Deccan, 16th–17th century. Cast bronze, h. 12.3 cm. British Museum, London, Edward Moor Collection, 1940,0716.250

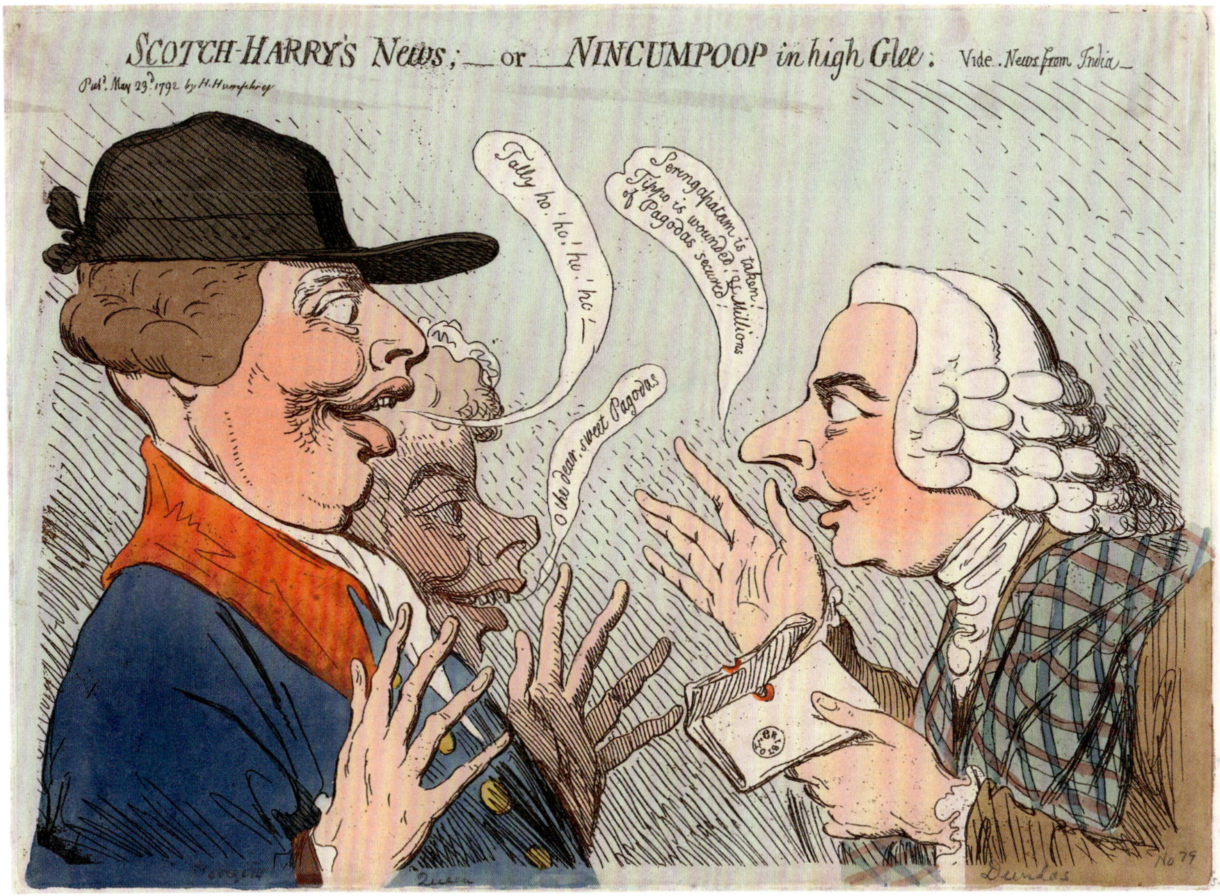

torical terms, this means that his objects have a provenance. Therefore, they provide an opportunity to study a little-known material culture of Hindu devotion in western India, particularly when placed in relation to western Indian arts dispersed in other locations. At the same time, they are a window into the turbulent circumstances of their collection by a Company soldier engaged in Anglo-Maratha affairs, as well as invested in understanding the religion of Hindus through iconic representations. In Chapter Four, I turn to how these objects informed his best-known book, *The Hindu Pantheon* (1810); here I consider their acquisition and the damage that marked people, gods, and things as a result.

The circulation of these arts in religious, monetary, and military contexts changed their histories and informed official and unofficial British policy on the accession and evaluation of another culture's arts that inevitably became part of British culture. While I am alert to the histories of the Maratha objects on their own terms, the circumstances of their circulation demonstrate increasing British power in Maratha territories. Rather

79 James Gillray, *Scotch-Harry's News, or, Nincumpoop in high Glee* (London: H. Humphrey, May 23, 1792). Etching with hand coloring, 26 × 36 cm. Lewis Walpole Library, Yale University, New Haven, Connecticut

than Maratha patrons or artists grafting the arts of the British, or their joint constitution, as I discussed earlier, here the relationship between the Marathas and the British shifts to a British host, Edward Moor, and his accumulation of Hindu objects in Maratha territories. My use of the term "graft" also takes on one of its subsidiary definitions – of corruption and illicit gain – more forcefully.

THE ROUTES OF SOLDIERS, PILGRIMS, AND SCULPTURES

Moor arrived in India in 1782 as a cadet in the Bombay establishment of the Company, and by 1788, at the age of seventeen, he had gained the rank of lieutenant; a certificate documented his "very great proficiency" in the country language.[7] In 1790, as a result of the Anglo-Maratha treaty brokered by Malet, Moor joined the brigade under Captain John Little that was embedded in the Maratha army led by its general, Parshuram Bhau Patwardhan.[8] One can chart their path on the map that Moor published in his first book, *A Narrative of the Operations of Captain Little's Detachment . . .* (1794; fig. 80).[9]

From Bombay, Moor and his detachment sailed down the coast and disembarked at "Jaighur" (Jaigad) to march inland via the Amba pass to meet the Maratha general in his territories near "Meritch" (Miraj). Following the road, and crossing two rivers to the south, they marched from fort to fort, with one long-lasting siege of "Darwar" (Dharwad), and continued on to "Hurry Hall" (Harihar), which became a base for operations as it lay at the convergence of roads and a river. At the assault on the hill fort of "Dooridroog" (Devarayanadurga), Moor was shot through the right shoulder. He managed to continue fighting, however, looping back toward the northwest to storm and capture "Hooly Honore" (Holehonnur). At the following battle of "Gadjnoor" (Gajanur) Moor penetrated the enemy's camp but received a wound in his right knee and a musket ball through his left elbow that would bother him for life.[10] In 1792, the allied armies were victorious: they roundly defeated Tipu Sultan and took his sons hostage.[11] The troops returned to Harihar, but, starved for grain, Captain Little's detachment split from the Maratha forces, their aims complete. Rather than returning to Bombay by sea, they took the overland route of four hundred miles to Poona.[12]

Moor's map shows only a few main roads and rivers that directed traffic. The names of the towns are listed according to their size, status, and fortification. However, both Marathi maps and Moor's descriptions of the routes that he traveled relay proximate orientations to historical, geological, and religious destinations. For example, one early nineteenth-century Maratha map mentions the shrine of Trimbakeshwar.[13] Probably because Moor was embedded with the Maratha army, he became aware of these religious orientations. He noted the placement of temple towns and, even in the middle of war, paused

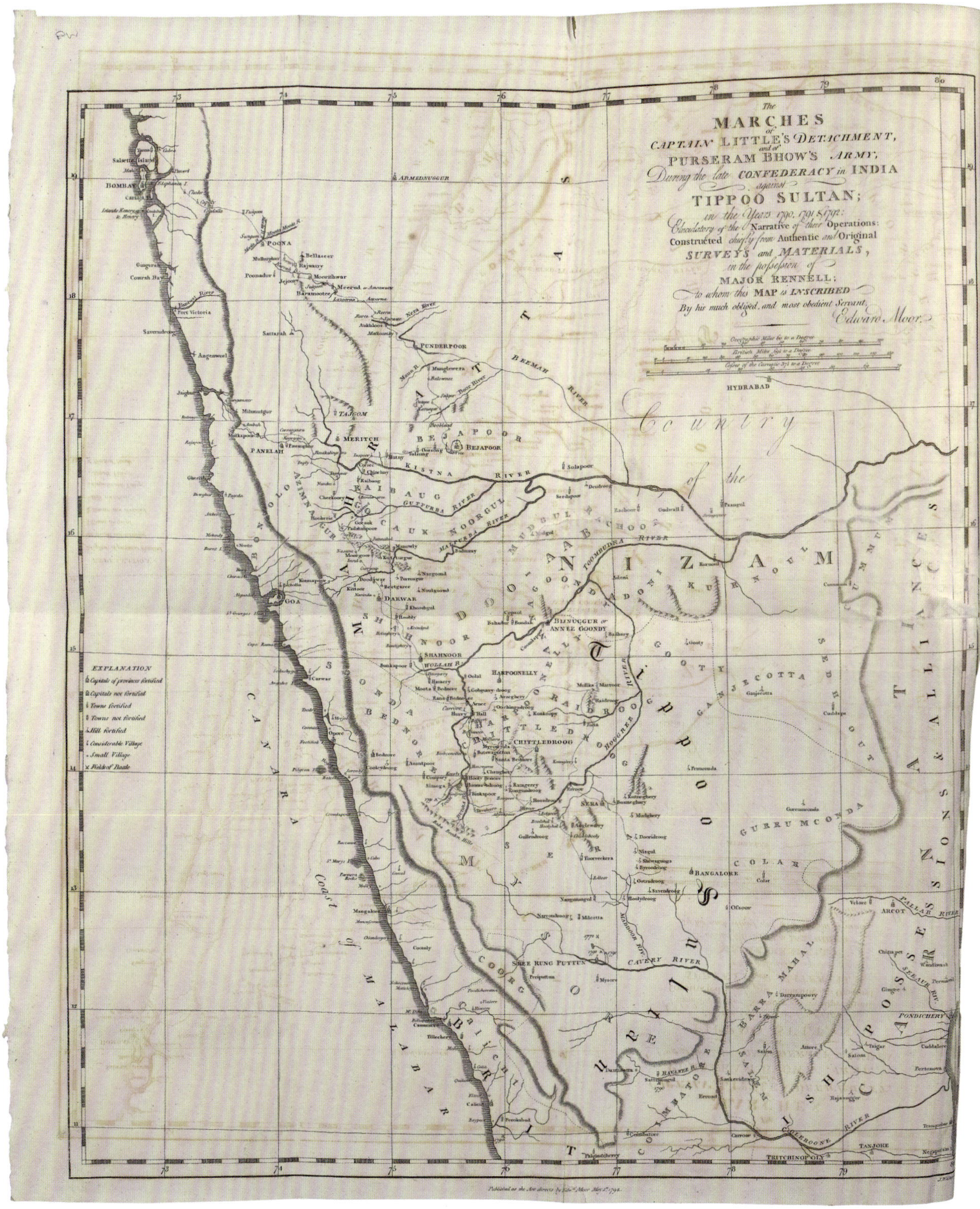

80 "The Marches of Captain Little's Detachment," in Edward Moor, *A Narrative of the Operations of Captain Little's Detachment and of the Mahratta Army* (London: J. Johnson, 1794). Hanna Holborn Gray Special Collections Research Center, University of Chicago Library

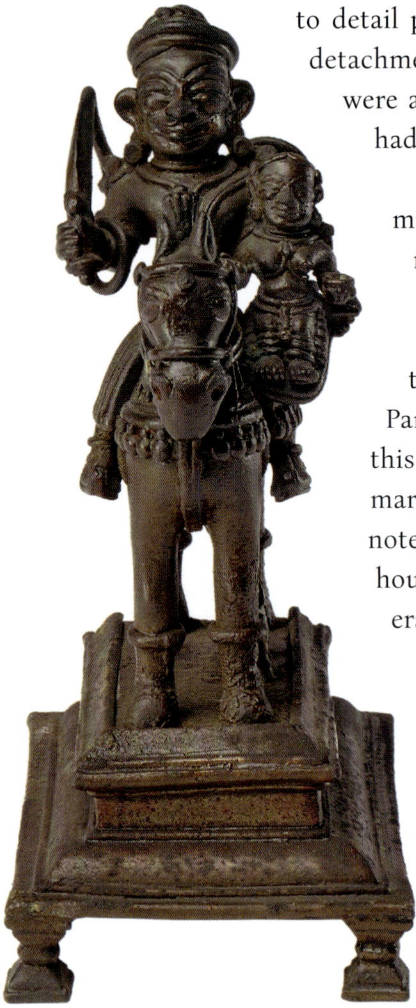

to detail processions of icons.[14] After Tipu's surrender in 1792, the British detachment diverged from the Maratha army and Moor and his company were able to visit sites – from forts to mosques to temples – that they had determined from the Marathas to be worthy of interest.[15]

This impulse to see sites in more depth, or explore new ones, must have pushed them to take a road "far eastward" to visit the mosques and palaces of the renowned city of the Deccan Sultanate at Bijapur, "being to Europeans unknown." From there, as seen on the map (see fig. 80), they stopped at renowned temple towns along the route to the Peshwa's capital of Poona, such as Pandharpur where they were "very agreeably entertained examining this beautiful city," including the "very handsome" temples, "extensive" markets, and the "noble stream," the river Bhima. Pandharpur, Moor noted, "was daily increasing in populousness and splendour;" "noble houses" of the Peshwa, Nana Fadnavis . . . the Scindias," and the general for whom he had just fought, Parshuram Bhau, "adorned" the "broad and very well paved" streets. A week later, they reached Jejuri. They climbed the hill to the temple of "great celebrity" that is dedicated to the god Khandoba; they claimed to be pestered by beggars and enthralled by the hundreds of dancing girls devoted to the temple before they rode to the next town.[16]

Moor traveled out along Maratha routes as a soldier on military marches and on his return; in both cases his paths intersected with Hindu pilgrimage and commerce, which came to inform his collection.[17] Numerous sculptures connected to Pandharpur and Jejuri remain in his assembly (figs. 81 and 82).[18] It is possible that he bought some representations at that time and others later in his career as he described in *The Hindu Pantheon*: Khandoba, who is instated at Jejuri, is represented around twenty times, often with his wife Malsara, while Vithoba and his wife Rukmini, worshipped at Pandharpur, find form in six pairs.[19] These sculptures are portable and intimate; they connect to pilgrimage sites and to the consecration of a deity worshipped there as a *kuladevata* (family god for a home shrine).

Khandoba is worshipped by warriors, merchants, and other groups belonging to the forest and pasture regions as he protects the community, cattle, and agricultural lands; many Marathas include him among their family gods. Records suggest that he could have been a historical figure who underwent apotheosis, perhaps even a king of the Yadava dynasty (12th–14th century).[20] However, over time, worshippers associated Khandoba

81 *Khandoba and Malsara*, Maharashtra, 18th century. Bronze, h. 12 cm. British Museum, London, Edward Moor Collection, 1940,0716.140.ab

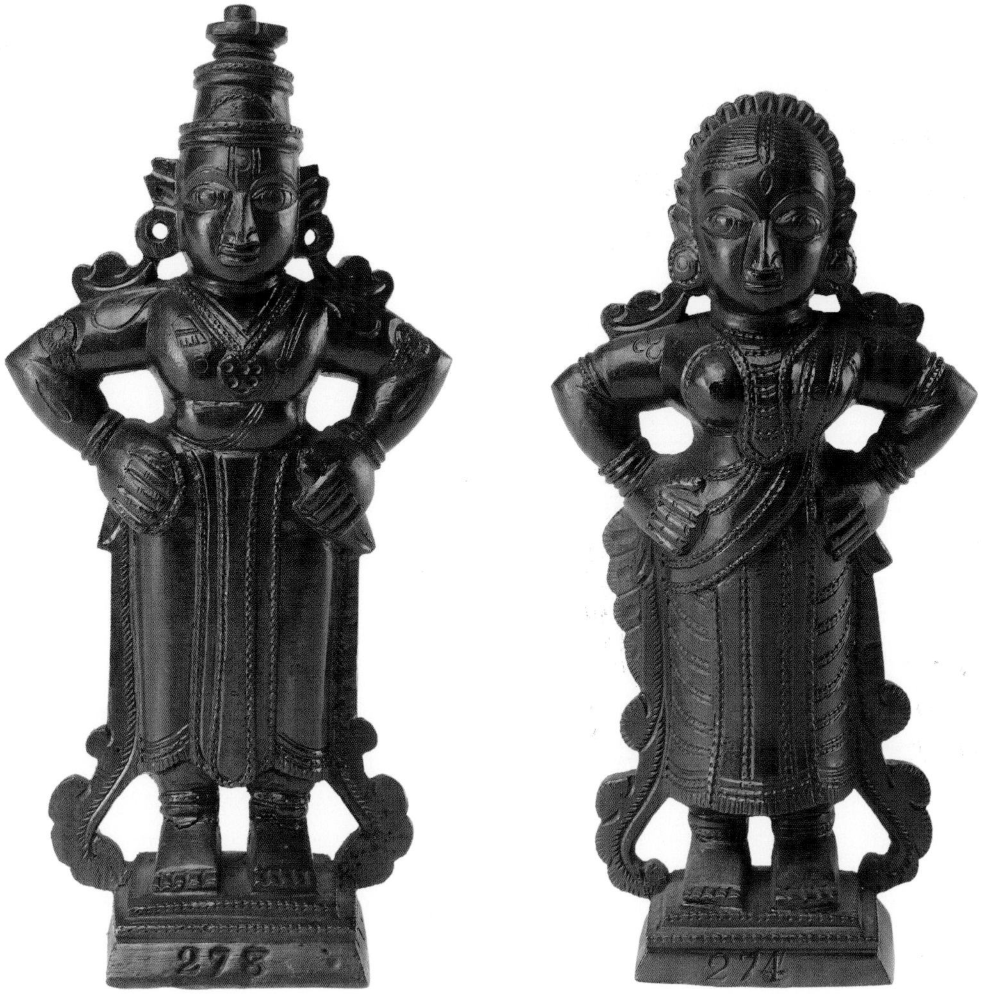

with the pan-Indic god Shiva, especially in the form of Martanda Bhairava to fight two demons named Mani and Malla.[21] Sculptures depict Khandoba as a warrior, back straight with sword and shield in hand, riding a horse with his wife Malsara on his lap, a dog at their feet (fig. 81). In some of their images, the heads of the demons roll defeated under the hooves of their horse.[22] But in most, Khandoba and Malsara are depicted as deities with multiple arms astride a horse in small bronze sculptures or on silver or copper plaques (*tak*) for a home shrine, on charms worn around the neck, or as masks worn in processions or pilgrimages, or used to adorn Shiva's abstract form, a *linga*.[23]

The deities Vithoba and Rukmini worshipped at Pandharpur are also prevalent in Moor's collection (fig. 82a and b). They stand with arms akimbo, waiting, first for each other, and then for their devotee Pundalik.[24] According to common narratives, which

82 a and b *Vithoba* and *Rukmini*, Maharashtra, 18th century. Bronze, h. Vithoba 14.3 cm; Rukmini 11.4 cm. British Museum, London, Edward Moor Collection, 1940,0716.270 and 1940,0716.271

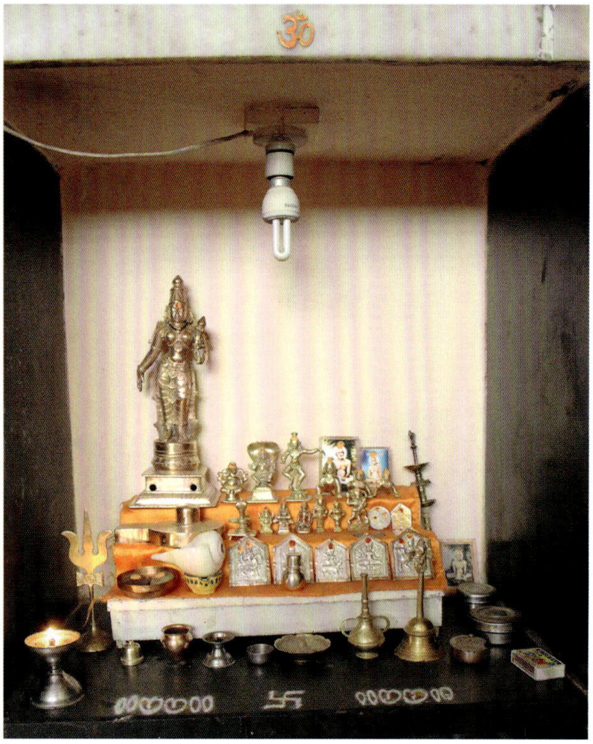

Moor relayed in the *Hindu Pantheon* as he did tales of Khandoba, while Pundalik was on pilgrimage to Pandharpur, he recognized his lapses in filial duty and humbly turned his devotion to his parents while Vithoba, understood as a form of the pan-Indic god Vishnu, remained waiting.[25] Although modern, a home shrine of the Navgires, descendants of Gangaram, provides a context for how such deities could have been honored (fig. 83). A cast of Lakshmi similar to that plundered from Nana Fadnavis's home shrine is on the left (see fig. 78), Khandoba and Malsara are represented on silver plaques (*tak*), and Vithoba and Rukmini stand in metal casts on one of the tiered shelves among other deities.

Worship of these deities extends back to the medieval era, at least, but Moor encountered the temple towns in a period of burgeoning Maratha patronage in the eighteenth century. Pandharpur, for example, was probably founded by King Vishnuvardhan of the Hoysala dynasty in the Karnatak in the twelfth century. However, the Marathas gave donations and grants to the temple and erected palaces and rest-houses along the banks of the Bhima river. Similarly, the temple at Jejuri dates to the fourteenth century, but the Marathas commenced large-scale renovations to the temple in the eighteenth century, which increased its profile.[26]

Moor visited Pandharpur and Jejuri because they were on the route back to Poona from the Mysore wars, but the Marathas endowed pilgrimage centers throughout western India, as seen on a 1987 map of Maharashtra (fig. 84). Although Moor did not visit all of these sites, he collected the deities worshipped at them and in domestic shrines as *kuladevata*, such as the goddess Durga in her manifestation as slayer of the buffalo demon (*mahishasuramardini*; fig. 85).[27] Durga is worshipped across India, but regionally she takes on forms that connect to specific places, like Bhavani of Tuljapur, the family deity of the first Maratha king Shivaji Bhonsle; Saptashringi who is housed at Vani; or Yogeshvari of Ambajogai.[28]

In addition to figures of these deities associated with pilgrimage sites, there are about eighty sculptures in Moor's collection that depict different subjects – portable shrines and household gods of tribal communities – which offer an opportunity to understand

83 Home shrine (*devghar*) of the Navgire family, descendants of the family of Gangaram Chintaman Navgire Tambat, Ahmednagar, 2014

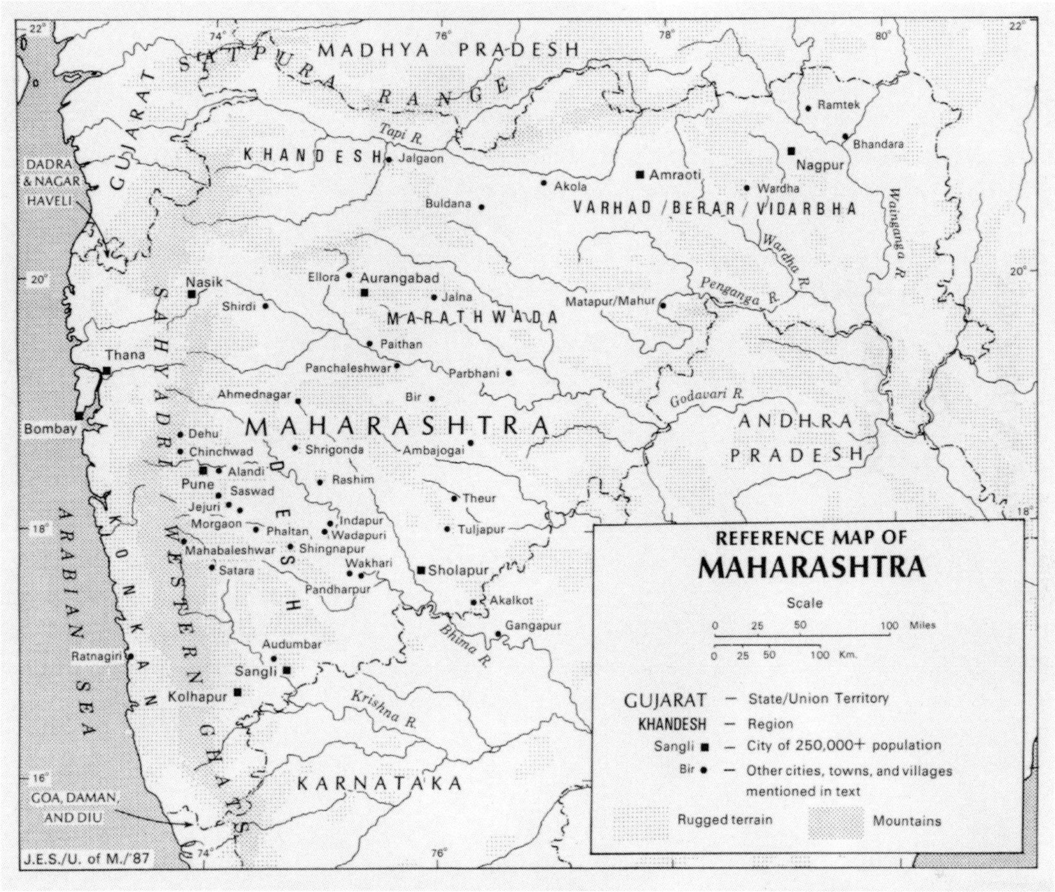

their manufacture (fig. 86).[29] While Moor's collection maps onto regional centers of worship and local practices, it can only be surmised where the sculptures were made. For instance, there were centers of production, such as Nasik, Poona, Ahmednagar, and Satara. According to late nineteenth- and early twentieth-century authors, these workshops produced bronze, brass, and copperware in lost-wax and sand-casting techniques and through molds and sheet-work, both for sale in town and for distribution through merchants, including to pilgrimage centers.[30] A workshop at Nasik, for example, is associated with the small shrines in Moor's collection that show a *linga* at the center with deities in attendance.[31] Artisans, such as metalcasters and smiths (*sonar*) based in the market, also worked with families to make and repair their family's gods over generations.[32]

Thus far I have situated Moor's variegated iconic sculptures in relation to the routes he traveled for war and pleasure as well as at their places of production, devotion in domestic shrines, and in relation to pilgrimage centers that the Marathas endowed. But

84 "Reference Map of Maharashtra," from *The Experience of Hinduism: Essays on Religion in Maharashtra*, ed. Eleanor Zelliot and Maxine Berntsen (State University of New York Press, 1988)

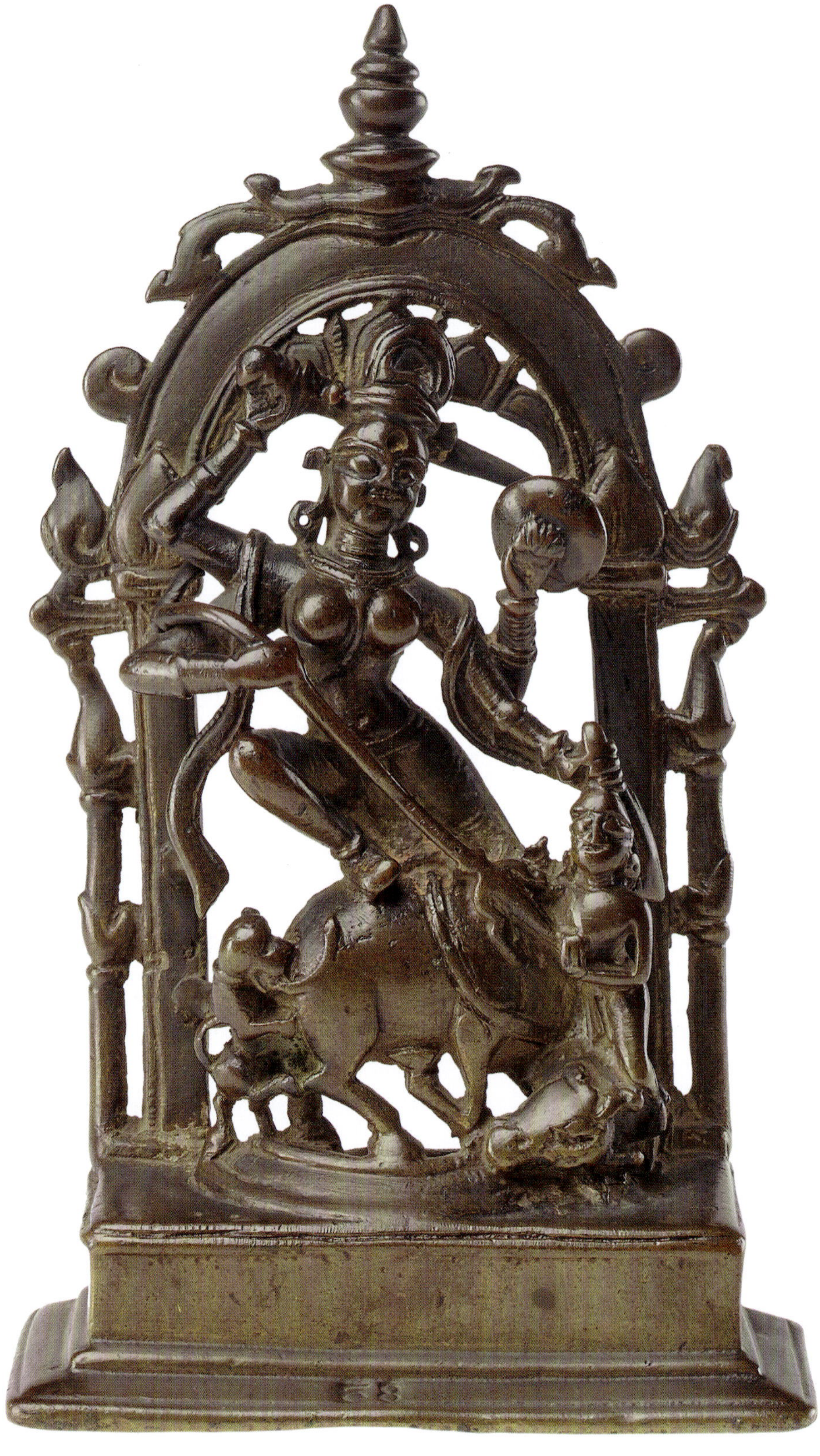

85 *Durga Mahishasuramardini and/or a Local Goddess*, Maharashtra, 16th–18th century. Bronze, h. 16.5 cm. British Museum, London, Edward Moor Collection, 1940,0716.36

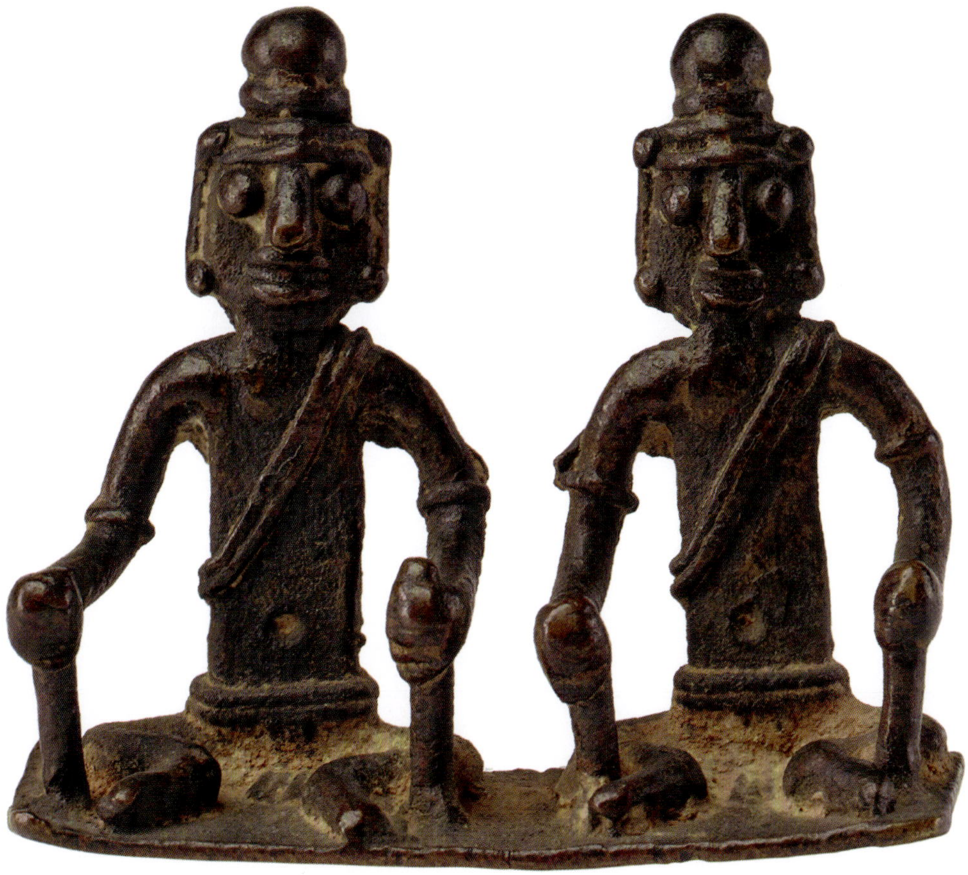

in the late eighteenth century, these items were taken out of their places of worship or manufacture and entered a British soldier's collection. A watercolor in an album compiled by Moor's son raises the question of how Moor accessed materials (fig. 87). The central small sculpture depicts two of the household gods of tribal communities just discussed (see fig. 86): two devotees, Yehu and Kansarya, pay homage to the corn goddess Kansari. This type of deity would probably not have been in consistent worship by a family, but kept enclosed in a basket or clay jar and taken out and assembled in a house shrine, only if, as Cornelia Mallebrein writes, "a deity has expressed such a wish to the family by creating some kind of trouble."[33] Moor must have gained this figure outside of such ritual contexts; it is no longer connected to other figures in a home shrine or to the ceremonies that would have animated its form.

Moor's interest in the Hindu gods was piqued by his experiences, but he obtained many of his objects after he returned to India from healing his wounds in Britain in 1796. He accrued many through transactions – "the means of correspondents on the continent:

86 *Yehu and Kansarya, Devotees of Kansari*, Konkan coast?, Maharashtra, 18th century. Bronze, h. 4.5 cm. British Museum, London, Edward Moor Collection, 1940,0716.222

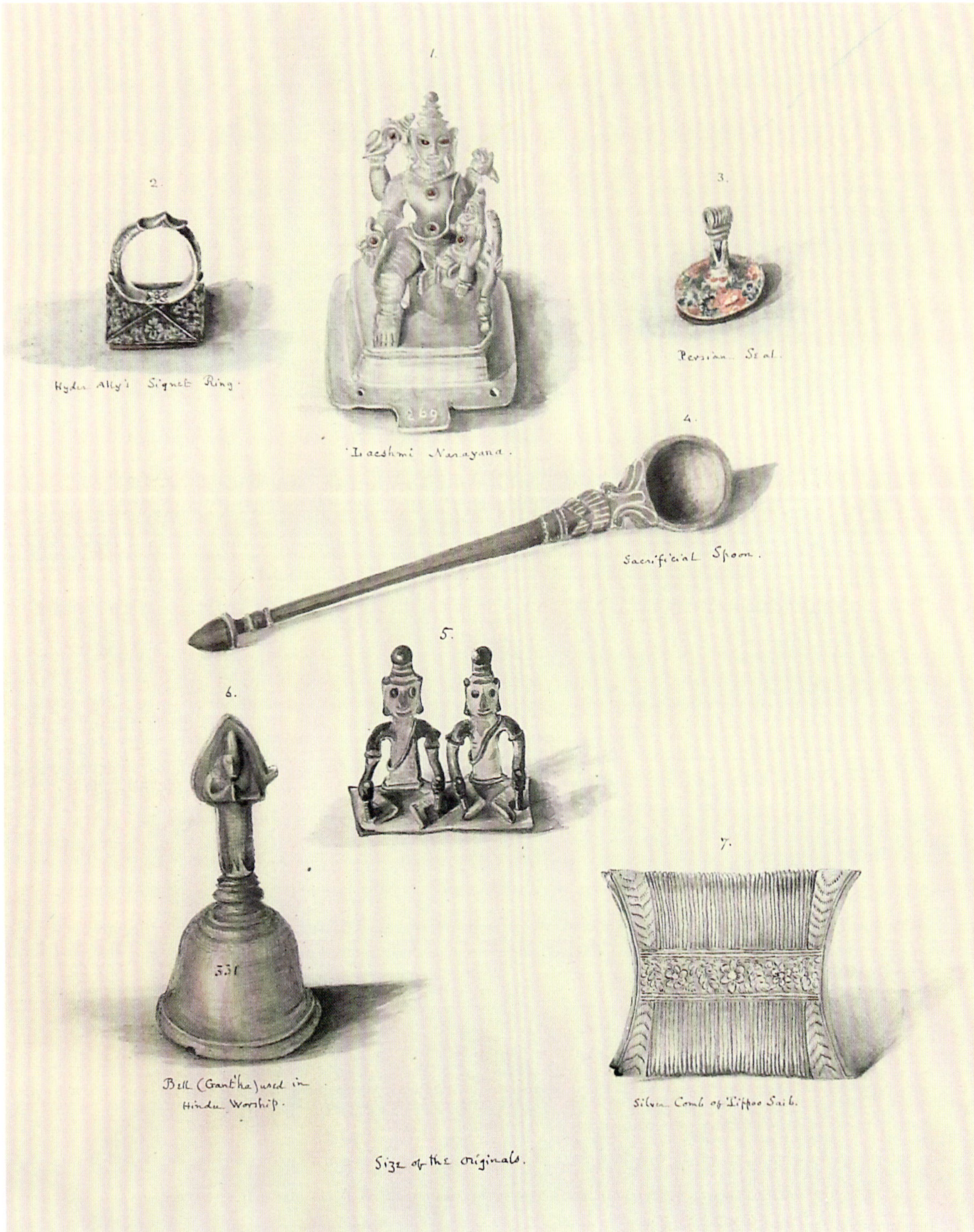

87 Henry Davy, *Specimens from Major Moor's Oriental Collection*, 19th century. Watercolor and ink on paper, 65 × 50 cm. Private collection

a native or two, with the expectation of profit, sent people into the interior to purchase such things" – as well as from "travelling friends." However, he and his friends and correspondents were able to purchase items because of "the unhappy state of the Mahrata country, during the last years of [his] residence in India."[34] Moor had commanded the honorary escort of two companies for the Resident, Charles Warre Malet, in Poona from 1787 to 1788, and Tipu Sultan was defeated in Mysore in 1799, but different Maratha factions also fought against each other. In 1802 the Peshwa signed a treaty with the British to maintain subsidiary forces against some Maratha chiefs, like the Holkars, but other Maratha generals, including the Bhonsles and Scindias, protested, which led to fighting in 1803 that lasted until 1805.[35] It is this "unhappy state" that sent many objects as well as people into flux.

OBJECTS OF PLUNDER TURNED INTO PRIZE

The watercolor in Moor's album aids in understanding this flux (see fig. 87). Besides the humble representation of family devotion, it also includes precious objects that he seems to have bought, including a gilt brass sculpture of Vishnu and Lakshmi inset with rubies.[36] It also exhibits booty. Moor's friend, David Price, a prize agent appointed after Tipu Sultan's 1799 defeat, purchased a silver comb that is drawn on the page; Moor also received the signet ring of Tipu's father, Haidar Ali, displayed upper left, from one of these caches.[37] While valuable, these two objects pale in comparison to other items that exited the coffers of Tipu to enter those of the British, as well as those that moved between different Maratha factions.

From 1754, British and Indian troops in the East India Company army were subject to the British army's Mutiny Act and the Articles of War, which prohibited the unorganized looting of enemy territories ("pillage"), the items of which were often quickly sold, and regulated the plunder that was legally organized after conquest and distributed in ranked shares to British troops ("prize").[38] But parliamentary laws that instituted the details, like the appointment of a prize agent, the auction of plundered goods, and a prize roll to record the amount of money awarded to military personnel and its distribution in London only started to be instituted from 1811, after soldiers in the Indian and European peninsular wars advocated for reform.[39]

Moor participated in the procedures that came to regulate prize in the crucial years of their formation during the Anglo-Mysore wars in the last decade of the eighteenth century. In 1801, he compiled the orders and regulations of the Bombay army for the government that included soldiers' letters concerning prize in the wars against Tipu Sultan. In 1790, on the eve of the third Anglo-Mysore war (in which Moor fought), writers recorded in the compilation were surprised at the handling of prize in the previous war (the captors received all), and recommended increased supervision, including that prize agents should be appointed by different detachments and required to prepare and submit an account of prize distribution between the Company and the captors "in any manner" they "think proper."[40] In his unofficial *Narrative* after the war, Alexander Dirom, a compatriot of Moor's, expanded on the manner. He believed that the troops should receive the "advantage" of prize to reward their "reduction of so many forts and countries," but that there should be a just system. He advised that prize be equitably distributed by five agents who would "lodge all money received for the captured property with the paymaster of the army," as was later instituted.[41]

These records emphasize the distribution of prize, but not the challenges of evaluating foreign treasuries, libraries, furniture, and wardrobes.[42] After Colonel Arthur Wellesley, the future Duke of Wellington, defeated Tipu Sultan at Seringapatam in 1799, he published his *Despatches and Memoranda* with tables that proudly show the organized means by which "prize" shares were accorded to ranked military personnel in the currency of pounds.[43] Yet, as David Price outlined in his *Memoirs*, the task of appraising the "complicated masses which filled" Tipu's "depot" was vast and resulted in error, even with the aid of a "Hindu goldsmith, or jeweller."[44] Angry shareholders returned with gems that had turned out to be flawed, tarnished, or little more than colored glass.[45] Moor had encouraged Price to canvass for the position of prize agent, but neither realized the magnitude of the charge to turn "things" such as the silver comb carefully outlined in watercolor in Moor's album into Indian coins or English pounds. Even beyond the unknown of comparative prices, this was not a simple assessment. Markets proliferated beyond official spheres as the result of the looting and trophy "frenzy" that occurred after Tipu's defeat, as Susan Stronge and Richard Davis have described. In 1799, Tipu's mustache was snipped off and his throne, plated in gold and bejeweled tigers, sundered.[46] In a saturated market, there was also a continuous recalibration of values as new owners sought to exchange their prize for recognizable currency or to cohere with particular antiquarian or memorabilia interests.

Moor not only recorded these types of exchanges but also illustrated many of the goods in his publications. This reaction was distinct from other soldiers and artists who wrote only sparely about, and decidedly did not depict, plunder within their extensive documentation of the Mysore wars against Tipu Sultan. For instance, after the 1790–92 Mysore war, Alexander Allan, Robert Colebrooke, and Robert Home published luxury editions of prints. In the texts, they mention the plunder of grain, cattle, and weapons as a matter of course – and the boon of Tipu's defeat in the amount of bullion he paid the victors – but the texts dwell on other factors, such as how many soldiers died and where.[47] In Colebrooke's "East View of Bangalore," the conflict is memorialized simply by the tiny British flag raised over the fort (fig. 88). The ruined mausoleum on the left implies change, but through the trope of the decline of Indian civilization and the rise of British rule in India. This picturesque mode of landscape obscures the actual discord that occurred or the exchange of goods to create "distance" from the military reality, as Mary Favret and Rosie Dias have discussed, and provides a comfortable access into the scene for viewers at home.[48]

In contrast, Moor detailed the mechanisms of war, especially those related to the exchange of goods, and participated in their sales. He relayed the play by play of battle, the resultant objects plundered, and their fluctuations in value; he also connected the

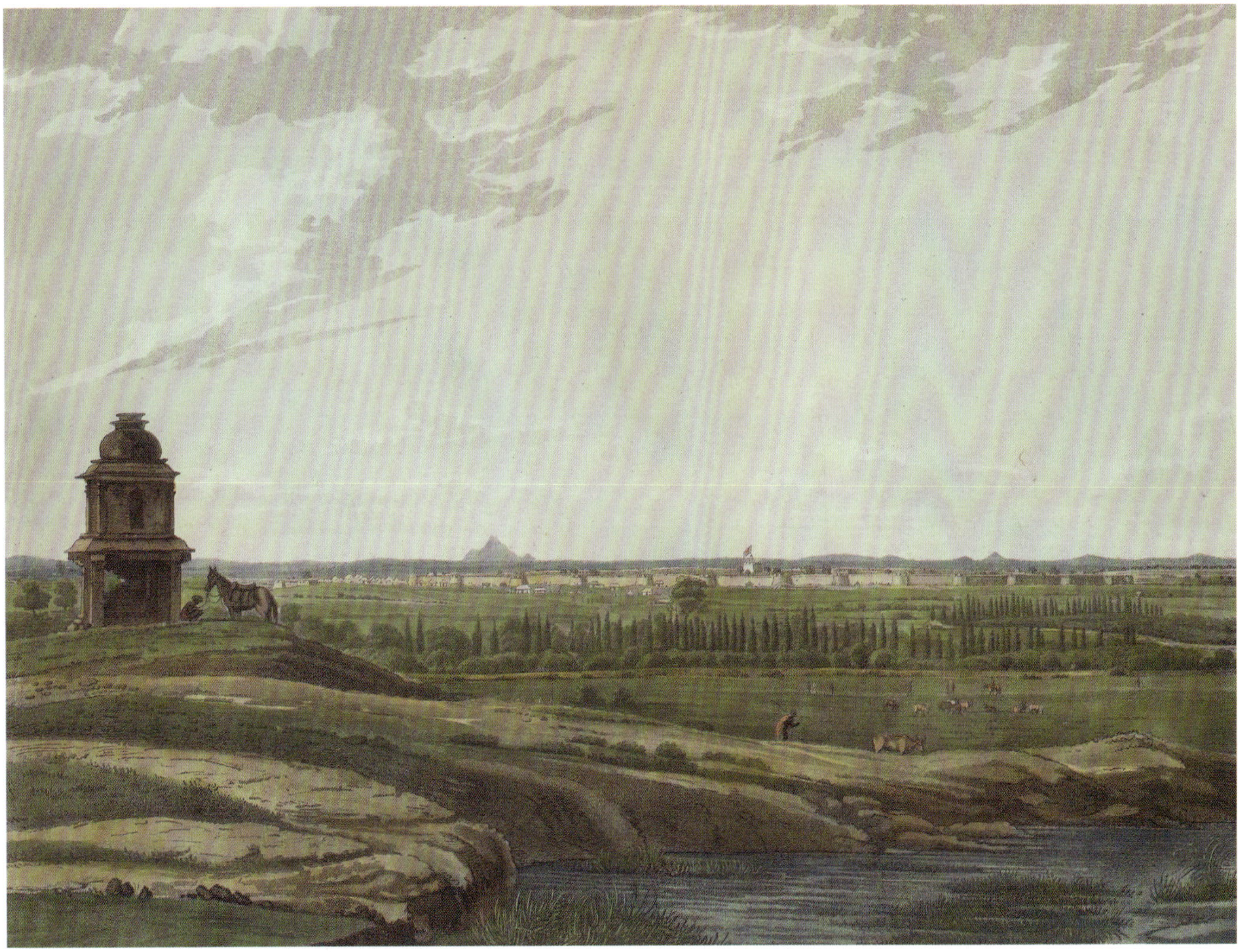

88 "East View of Bangalore," in Robert H. Colebrooke, *Twelve Views of Places in the Kingdom of Mysore, Country of Tippoo Sultan, from drawings taken on the spot* (London: Thomson, 1793), pl. 1. Etching and aquatint with hand coloring, 52 × 71 cm. Anne S. K. Brown Military Collection, Brown University Library, Providence, R.I.

records to the objects themselves. In his first book, *A Narrative of the Operations* (1794), Moor paid particular attention to the coins and seals of Tipu Sultan, which he had obtained or borrowed from other British officials after Tipu's 1792 defeat.[49] Indeed, Moor saw an opportunity for gain in the relationship between the plunder garnered through war and the evaluation necessary to quantify the price of art. Besides his profession as a soldier, he became an appraiser, dealer, and mediator for the sale and resale of goods on the ground.[50] For someone had to convert the prize plundered from Indian treasuries to British currency, not to mention the goods that were pillaged before their bureaucratic assembly and apportionment.[51] Unofficial agents like Moor, as well as official ones like Price at Seringapatam in 1799, rose to this task. They were the "intermediaries, art dealers, commercial agents, carriers, as well as diplomats, soldiers, and other military staff, and private collectors" who created the categories of value that came to inform auction, museum, and army records, and "contributed locally to the shaping of global markets and to the massive relocation of objects to the western world," as the art historians Charlotte Guichard and Bénédicte Savoy have stressed.[52]

Moor translated finely wrought jewelry, manuscripts, paintings, gem-encrusted thrones, and gold and silver coins into British values. For instance, he had friends "among the sharers in the Seringapatam booty" after 1799 who sent to him "their allotment of jewels" in Bombay "to keep or sell for them," and he became "somewhat skilled in gems and *orfévrerie* [gold and silver]."[53] After the prize sales in Poona following the defeat of Daulatrao Scindia in 1803 by the Peshwa and the British, Moor sold "a great collection of paintings and coloured drawings" that had been taken from Scindia and others, including Nana Fadnavis, which included "mythological, some historical, some portraits, &c." as well as erotic imagery.[54] In addition to his own appraisals, Moor also reported on others' profit (or dupe). One of his friends, Captain Hugh Massey Fitz-Gerald, purchased "a very splendid, large-paper copy of the Koran" for 5 rupees after Tipu's defeat in 1799, for instance, but made a huge profit in a later sale to N. H. Smith of the Bombay Civil Service when he sold it for around 2,000 rupees or £250.[55]

Besides noting the jewels and works on paper that passed through his or others' hands, Moor attended to the movement of iconic Hindu representations. Some were plundered again and again in British and Maratha routes of conquest (as both depended on booty for government revenue) and taken as prize.[56] A small silver shrine that represented the god Ballaji and his two wives was originally in the care of a Maratha general, Raghoji Bhonsle, taken by another one, and again taken by Wellesley in the wars fought by the Peshwa and the British against the Bhonsles and Scindias in 1803–5.[57] Moor bought it from one of his "correspondents," for which he believed he paid "something more than their weight in rupees."[58] He describes each attribute of the deity, even though only the back-plate (*prabhavali*) remains (fig. 89) since Moor noted it was again taken – "illegally and insolently" – by the "*King's* custom-house officers" upon his arrival in Britain and never returned to him.[59]

He discussed (and bought) others whose qualities of material value or political association could either prompt their pillaging or aid their survival. In the same fort of Raghoji Bhonsle, the British took a silver shrine that had, according to Moor, "niches and places for a great many deities, male and female, of all sorts and sizes," and brought it to Poona as "public prize" in 1803. While the British considered having it coined, the Peshwa offered "to preserve it" by paying "its weight [20,000 oz.] in silver," which equaled "40,000 rupees, worth intrinsically, 5,000 pounds sterling." Communities sought to protect sacred objects during times of war. The cast of the goddess Lakshmi, with which I opened the chapter, had once been in the home shrine of Nana Fadnavis (see fig. 78), and had been plundered by Daulatrao Scindia while Moor was resident in Poona in 1797–8, though he wrote that it "did not come into my hands until some years afterwards."[60] He determined that it had "apparently been buried," probably to prevent it from falling into the wrong hands.[61]

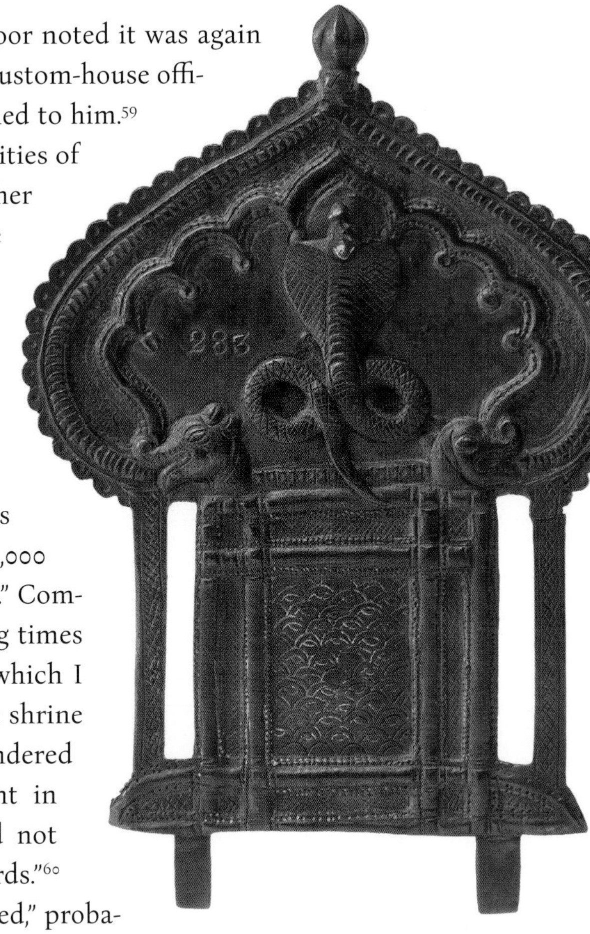

The circumstances of plunder led to injury; many sculptures in Moor's collection arrived worn or fragmentary, which parallels the wounds borne by soldiers.[62] Moor himself gained a portion of metal in India; in the 1790–92 war against Tipu Sultan, a lead musket ball lodged near his left elbow, which altered the angle of his arm and inaugurated relentless pain.[63] Others had limbs amputated, as with Moor's friend Price, or "lost their noses," as did the bullock driver Cowasjee, captured and mutilated by Tipu's army, as discussed in the Introduction (see fig. 1).[64] Mabon documented Cowasjee's repair in an etching of the Maratha surgeon's "singular operation" to reconstruct his nose, from the excision of skin from the forehead to twist and graft the newly modeled wax nose to his face.[65]

Moor sought to mend sculptures that came into his collection either physically or through reproduction. "A much valued friend, a Poona Brahmin," for instance, gave him "an uncommonly well cast image in bronze, representing Mahadeva with Parvati on his

89 Part of a backplate from a group representing Ballaji with his two wives, now missing, found in Gavilgarh Fort, near Berar, Maharashtra, 18th century. Bronze, silver, and gold, h. 15.2 cm. British Museum, London, Edward Moor Collection, 1940,0716.280

knee" (see fig. 2). Here Shiva as an ascetic, his dreadlocks piled high on his head and his necklace of skulls swinging low, proffers his bottom right hand, palm out in the *varada mudra* to offer a boon. Both bodies, especially the bellies and breasts, have been rubbed in devotion, releasing the reddish copper of the bronze. Yet Moor recognized that this sculpture was missing parts and had a brass base affixed to complete the image.[66] He also repaired objects through reproduction as engravings in his publication. For example, in his description of a bronze figure of Shiva dancing on a demon, in his form commonly known as *Nataraja*, Moor noted that the left leg had been broken off at the knee. But for the engraving in Plate 14 of *The Hindu Pantheon*, the artist "very abl[y] restored" it. Likewise, a "fine statue in black marble, of the size of an ordinary man" of a Jain saint (*Jina*) probably had its nose lopped off, according to Moor, by an iconoclastic "Portuguese zealot"; his draftsman, however, was able to reconstruct it "skillfully" in the engraving (Plate 68), much like the Maratha surgeon did Cowasjee's face.[67] Objects can be reconstituted like people, whether their scars remain or register as invisible.

"Not one subject is perfect," Moor noted, "in some particular, sometimes trifling, there is a defect or fracture." While some of the objects in his collection were circulated as plunder, many were worn from use, or inauspicious due to damage, which relates to his sources. He accrued images through dealers, "correspondents," and "travelling friends, who, aware of [his] idle propensity, procured for [him] what they deemed curious."[68] It is possible that Moor's "friends" and "correspondents" were able to purchase such images because they had already been discarded. In the twentieth century, the folklorist Günther Sontheimer regularly encountered devotees "trading in used or damaged" images "for new with the scrap metal dealer" in the old metal bazaar in Poona.[69] These images either had never been consecrated, or were no longer so.[70] Indeed, Moor's "Pandit and others" were surprised, as he wrote, at his expenditure "on such useless articles as defaced images, coins, &c.," which implies that these types of items would not traditionally have been for sale.[71]

These sculptures left pilgrimage sites, forts, or home shrines by force as plundered "treasure" or were reduced to "detritus" in the wear of time. Yet Moor re-evaluated those that he admired solely as "treasure" and once again displayed them in a home shrine.[72] When Moor returned to England in 1805, he purchased a country home in Great Bealings, Suffolk, close to where he had been raised as the sixth son of a steward of a local estate. In 1840, he hired a local artist, Henry Davy, to paint the house; on the left wall of the breakfast room, the shelves are stacked with books and many-limbed bronze sculptures neatly arranged in rows (fig. 90). "'Gods' were the Major's weakness," according to Thomas Wright, the biographer of Edward Fitzgerald who translated the famed *Rubaiyat of Omar Khayyam* (1859) and looked up to this "glorious man" as a boy. He recognized that

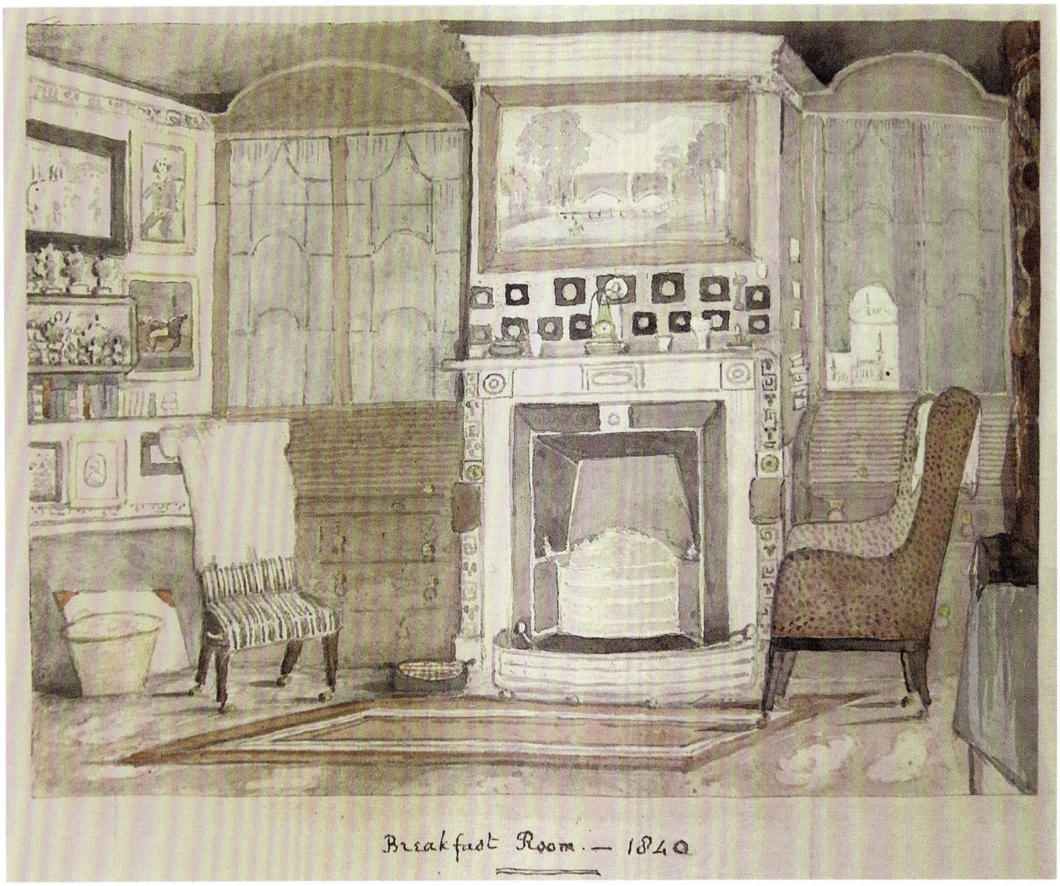

Moor offered these deities "a sort of reverence as the objects of other men's worship," but that respect for Hindu materials was also an addition, a part of India that he grafted onto his own life.[73]

A CONNOISSEUR'S MARKET FOR PAINTINGS

Moor obtained his mixture of metal objects – from popular bronze deities to Tipu Sultan's silver comb – due to the cross-section of conquest and religion in western India. As a soldier and dealer interested in the Hindu gods, he took advantage of the sudden availability of these objects in times of war, but the paintings that he collected demand a different rubric. The paintings offer evidence of Indic methods of attribution and of their circulation and sale through merchants in the public realm rather than in court contexts. Unlike Moor's acquisition of relatively humble statues, and the paintings of

90 Henry Davy, *Edward Moor's Breakfast Room, Bealings House, Great Bealings, Suffolk*, 1840. Watercolor on paper, page 65 × 50 cm. Private collection

devotional narratives that he later commissioned from a Poona artist (discussed in the next section), here his purchases intersected with well-established Indian art markets, especially between Jaipur and Poona, and dealers conversant with Mughal and Rajput modes of artistic connoisseurship. Moor was attuned to the quality of all of the works that he collected, but with these paintings he explicitly placed them within Indian aesthetic systems alongside those of religious identification.

When it came to certain paintings, Moor engaged with them through their quoted price, location of production, technical and compositional merit, and materials – all qualities of aesthetic evaluation rather than devotional value. A painting of Shiva and Parvati, was, according to Moor, "the most beautiful and highest finished thing" he "ever saw" (fig. 91). Considering the length of time it would have taken to complete ("considerable") and the "consummate skill" of the artist to produce such "excellence," he paid forty rupees (£5) for the work, though the seller had asked for a hundred. Time, skill, and material (the use of "liquid shining gold," silver leaf, azure, crimson among other colors, and shimmering beetle wings) generated the value of the painting for Moor alongside his remarks on the subject, specifically the "impassioned manner" in which Shiva looks on Parvati. He applied similar criteria to another painting of these deities (fig. 92). Commenting on the copper colors and the "style not usually met with," he surmised that the work was "painted in a very northern country; Tibet or Kashmir perhaps."[74] The snow-capped mountains of the abode of Shiva, called Kailasha, might have directed his guess at the painting's place of production (which was closer to Poona), but it is likely that the seller provided this information.

From the sixteenth century, artists and archivists developed systems of evaluation at Mughal and Rajput courts. Records of court painting workshops (*suratkhana*) identify the purchase prices of paintings (*ruqam*) and their inspection at inventory (*kimat*) that often included a re-evaluation of worth.[75] Imperial and scribal notations on the works themselves also designated quality. At the Mughal library, value correlated to the type of text, the presence and number of illustrations and illuminations, and the status of the calligrapher. John Seyller has identified a grading system at the Mughal atelier that descended from first class/first grade (*awwal, awwal*) and that was disseminated to other courts, such as to Rajput courts in Rajasthan.[76] Shailka Mishra has deciphered inscriptions on paintings in the Amber-Jaipur court workshop that note they are excellent (*uttam*) or good (*achhya*); the cataloguers also recognized particularly fine features within the overall work.[77] At Rajput courts, value included the use of expensive materials (such as gold and silver), the number of figures limned, the time labored, and the subject. Holy men often held high valuations in the Mewar court records as did paintings in the Delhi manner (*Dilli kalam*), for instance.[78]

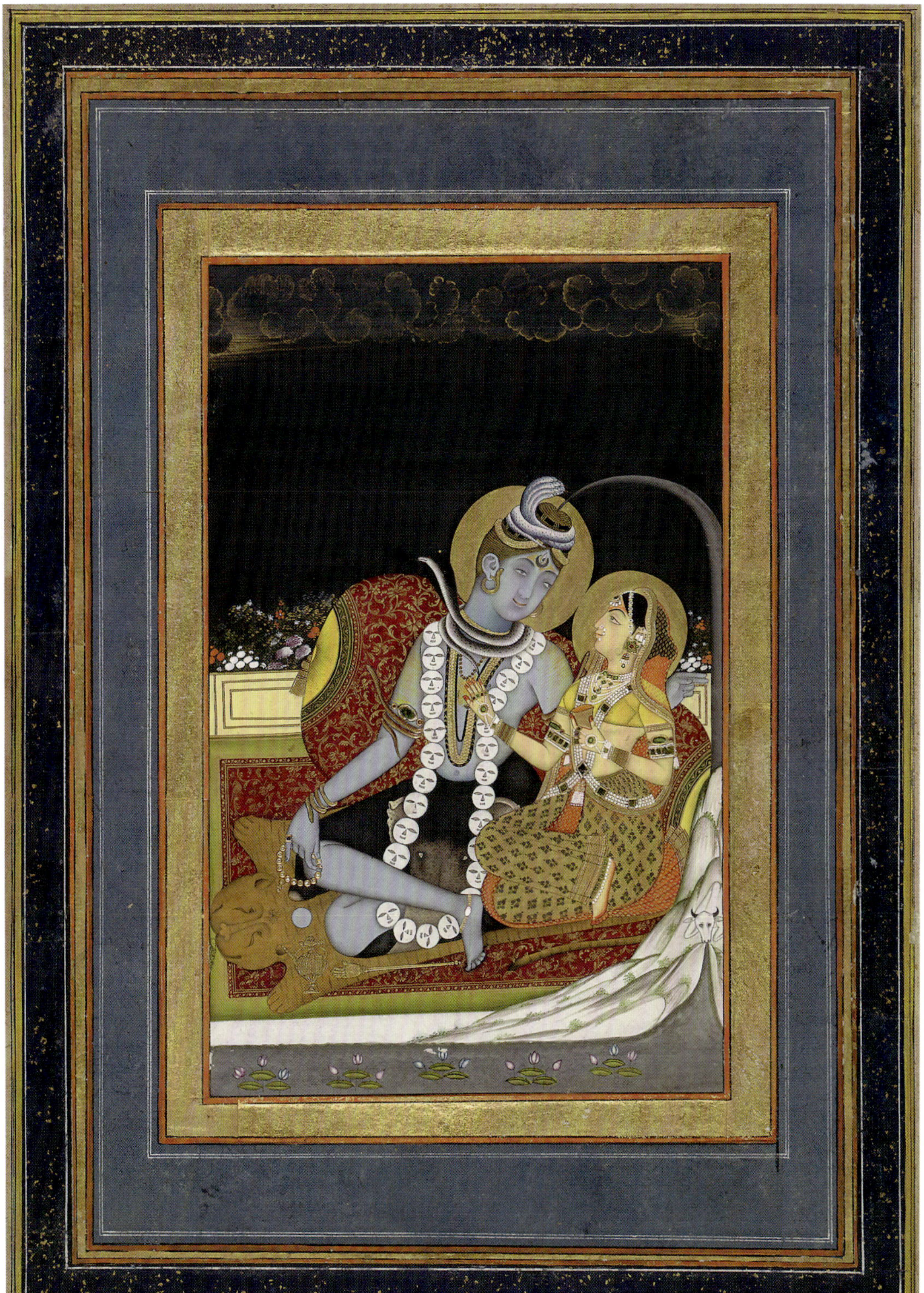

91 *Shiva and Parvati*, Jaipur, ca. 1800. Opaque watercolor and gold on paper, 56.9 × 40.6 cm. British Museum, London, Edward Moor Collection, 1940,0713,0.51

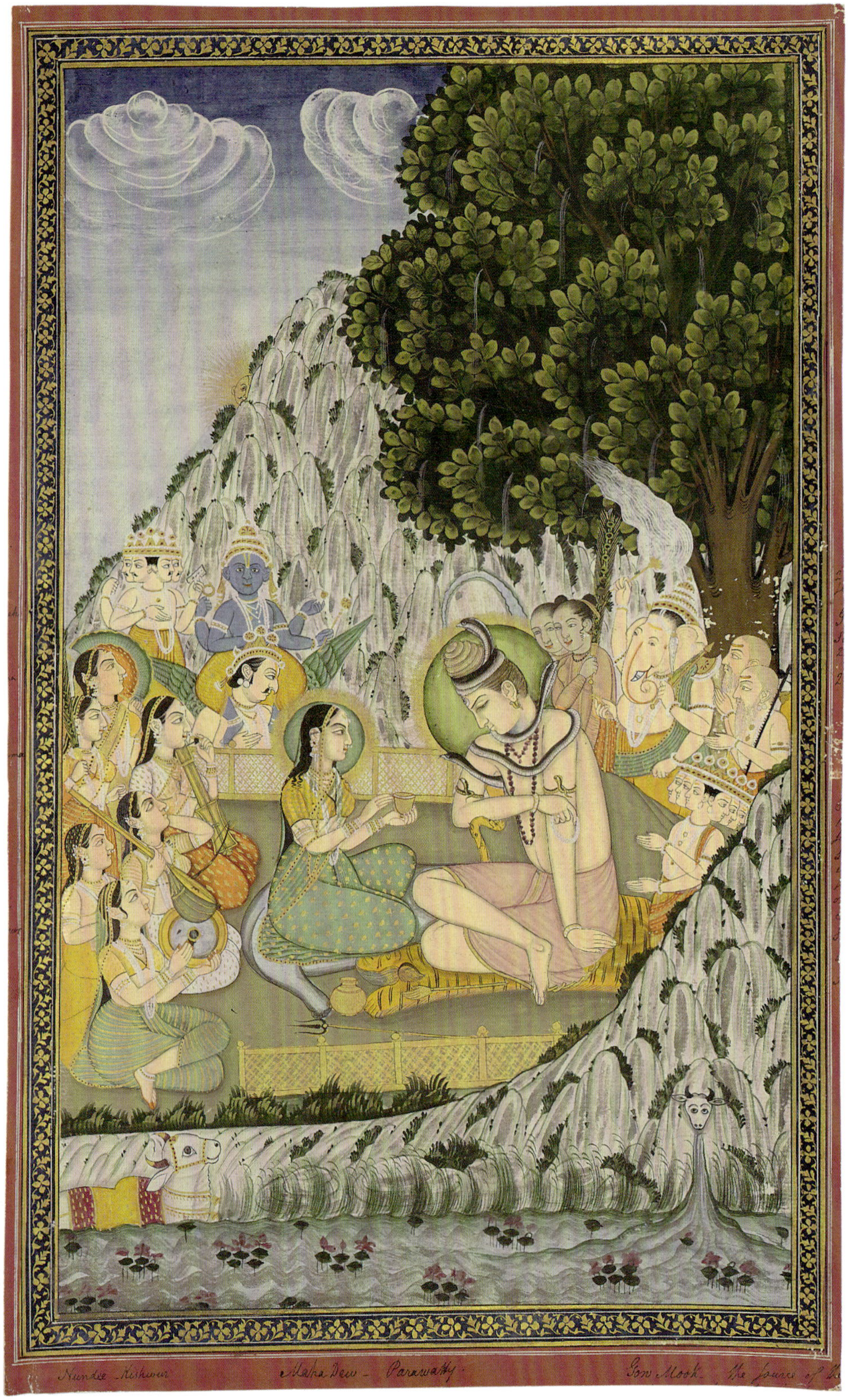

92 *Shiva and Parvati*, Poona, Lucknow or Jaipur, ca. 1800. Opaque watercolor and gold on paper, 40.2 × 25.4 cm. British Museum, London, Edward Moor Collection, 1940,0713,0.74

The person who sold the paintings of Shiva and Parvati to Moor must have framed their values accordingly, in contrast to the dealers of iconic sculptures who valued them by the type and quality of metal and undamaged state. Moor's descriptions of the paintings promote the location of production, the application and quantity of gold, and the skill and extent of labor in a manner different from others in his text, which point to a merchant's, rather than his own, evaluation. These qualities of appraisal would have resulted in the judgment of a work as "excellent," as well as a price of at least forty rupees. By comparing this price to those of similar paintings in Amber/Jaipur, it seems likely that Moor's painting was priced by materials and labor, and was of a high, but not a superior, quality.[79] Curiously, that was the advertised price for one copy of *The Hindu Pantheon* in India in 1810.[80]

Moor noted this intermediary simply as a "seller," but there are court and artist records that detail the types of merchants who acted as agents for artists or as dealers to sell older collections. For example, one Vyas Fakirdas sold paintings of music (*ragamala*), an album of portraits, and a *dasavatara* series of Vishnu's incarnations to the Jaipur court through the minister Raja Ayamal from 1721 to 1725.[81] Other intermediaries named over the course of the eighteenth century who came to Jaipur and Lucknow include a Hakim (doctor of Islamic medicine), a Qazi (an Islamic judge), a Sayyid (a descendant of the prophet) from Lahore, and a Brahmin from the Himachal Pradesh region, among others, which indicate that the role was established by a professional, mobile class of people who could sell paintings from distant locales.[82] Similar to how ministers for the Jaipur court sought paintings from elsewhere, the Peshwa and his ministers in Poona had agents who coordinated the purchase of "beautiful" paintings from Jaipur, Delhi, and Lucknow (see Chapter One).[83] The same could be said for agents who were hired by Europeans; the Swiss-French military entrepreneur Antoine Polier worked with a network of Indian agents. According to his letters, two from Calcutta sent him "batches of pictures" and reconnaissance on others available nearby in Murshidabad.[84] The sellers who sold Moor his fine single folios of deities, such as of Shiva and Parvati, must have similarly accessed certain types of work based on their locations, connections, and the price.

Besides serving as brokers for valuable paintings, merchants also coordinated the sale of artists' works for general public consumption. Shailka Mishra has identified merchants who sold paintings that would be popular and easily disseminated, including copies after Mughal paintings and portraits of noblemen and beauties.[85] It is likely that these figures had shops in the market where a visitor could stop and purchase paintings, comparable to those that Yuthika Sharma has identified in nineteenth-century Delhi, such as the studio and warehouse of Lala Faqir Chand in Dariba Bazaar that specialized in ivory. Chand employed artists to reproduce portraits, landscapes, and architecture,

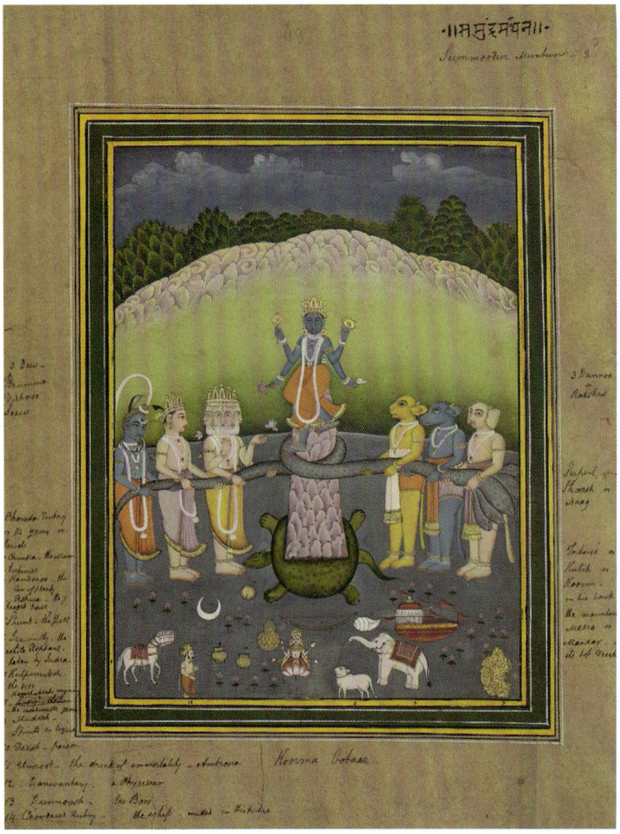

and contracted artisans across India to make goods for his store.[86]

The artists who made Moor's paintings must have been from diverse backgrounds: some were employed by the court, others were not but had received some instruction there, still others were trained through regional, professional castes. For example, Moor bought a series of incarnations of Vishnu (*dasavatara*) in Poona (fig. 93), but he noted that they were like others of this series that were "commonly offered for sale in different parts of India" and had been reproduced in European publications since the seventeenth century.[87] It is likely that these paintings were made by an artist trained at a court who had expanded his consumer base, since Moor also owned portraits of a Peshwa and a military chief by the same or a similar hand.[88] He owned another rendition of the *dasavatara* that was probably produced in Jaipur (fig. 94). The image of Kurma, the turtle who stabilizes the churning of the ocean, for example, closely resembles the one in the Poona *dasavatara*, but the former was painted more quickly and in a manner associated with artists in Jaipur, for example, with reds rather than the hot greens used in the Deccan. In comparison to the Poona series, the one from Jaipur was probably made by a professional caste of artists based in the bazaar, for example, the *chitaris* or *chateras* of North India.[89] These artists produced paintings for popular or devotional consumption, according to commission, or were employed by patrons on a long-term basis.

The possibility for artists to work for multiple patrons or for the public increased in the seventeenth and eighteenth century; those who painted for Moor fit within these broader employment trends. Research continues to reveal that artists who worked for the Mughal court could leave and work for other courts, take commissions from patrons, or be based in the bazaar and intermittently work for the court depending on their specialty and skill.[90] Many of the portrait albums that were purchased by Europeans, for example, seem to have been made by Mughal or Deccan court-trained artists who worked on commission or for a workshop in the market.[91] Another stream of production was located in families of painters who made devotional works, such as those in Nathadwara who

93 "Kurma Avatar," from a series of the *Dasavatara*, Jaipur?, ca. 1800. Opaque watercolor and gold on paper, 34.7 × 26.3 cm. British Museum, London, Edward Moor Collection, 1940,0713,0.26

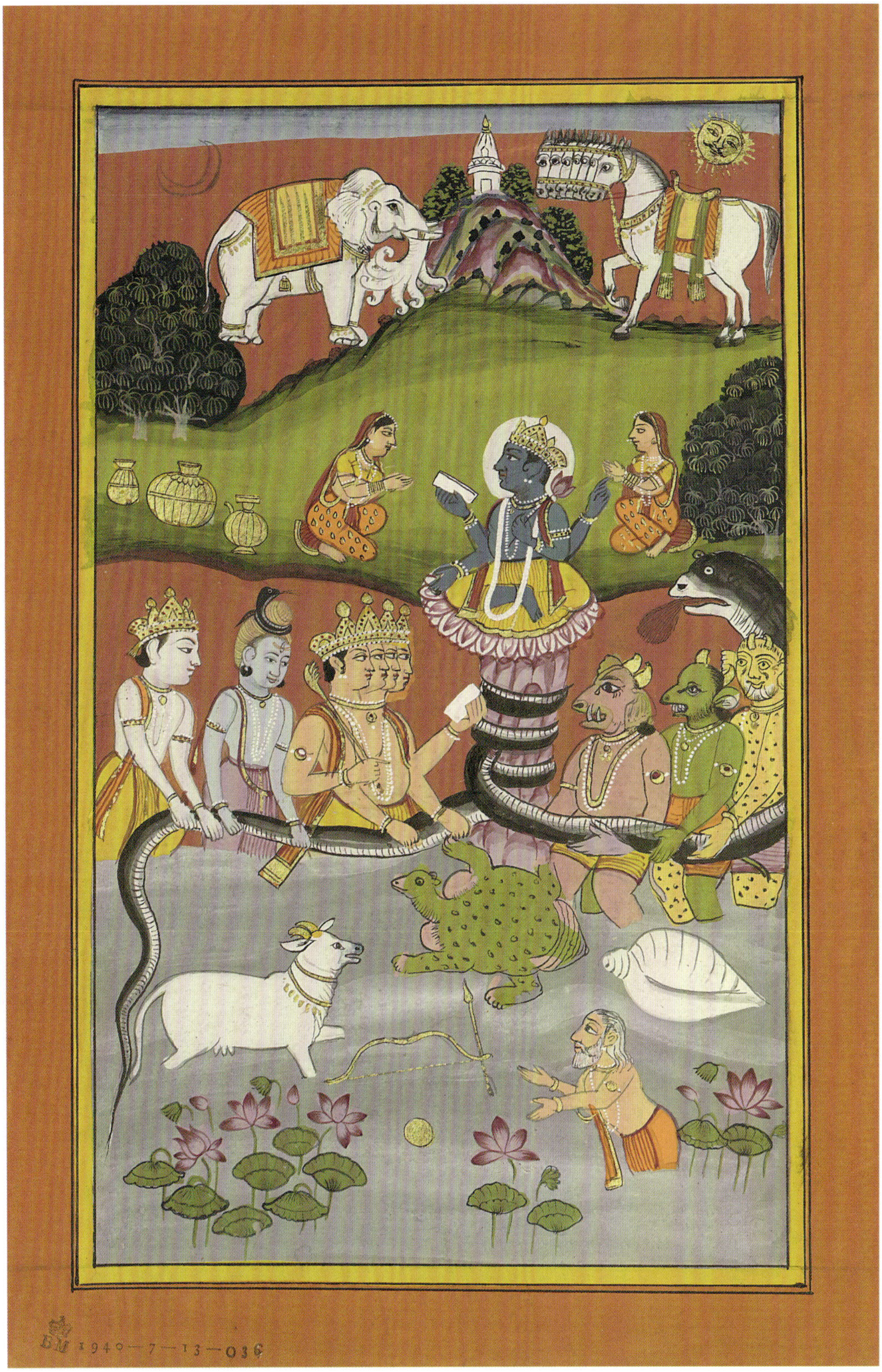

94 "Kurma Avatar" from a series of the *Dasavatara*, Jaipur?, ca. 1800. Opaque watercolor on paper, 26.2 × 16.6 cm. British Museum, London, Edward Moor Collection, 1940,0713,0.36

worked for the shrine of Shri Nathji, royal courts such as at Udaipur, and for merchants who hired them for the adornment of walls for special occasions.[92]

The paintings that Moor collected appear to be part of a common repertoire in Jaipur in particular. Jaipur artists regularly produced series of paintings that idealized women, men, and gods as lovers, and organized romantic types and moods to align with the months, as in *baramasa*, or music, as in *ragamala*, or in the eighteenth century with Krishna's adventures.[93] Moor owned such series as did numerous Maratha families, indicating a wide base of circulation and consumption.[94] While a few paintings in Moor's cache came from other regions, such as of Jagannatha, a form of Krishna worshipped in Puri, the majority seem to have traveled on the routes from Jaipur to Poona or Bombay.[95] As I discussed in Chapter One, the art and artists of Jaipur were admired at the Poona court. Peshwa Madhavrao I hired the artist Bhojraj to paint the walls of the Shanivarwada palace with scenes of Krishna's life and the incarnations of Vishnu; Nana Fadnavis particularly requested artists from Jaipur and paintings from that region. The Jaipur court also recognized the Poona court's admiration for paintings of the Hindu gods, and they sent albums of deities to them specifically.[96] Either the merchants with whom Moor transacted had access to Jaipur collectors and/or artists, or Jaipur artists recognized a market and distributed their paintings from Jaipur to be sold in Bombay and Poona, among other locales, as Jaipur paintings were admired and recognized as special in the period.[97]

There are numerous works in Moor's collection that parallel those in the Jaipur palace collection. They indicate that artists worked with a consumer base that ranged from the public to the palace, and that they flourished in a market for arts both within and outside of the court. Moor owned a painting (fig. 95) similar to one that the artist Harji Chatera offered to the Jaipur Palace that remains in their collection. Both schematically depict Krishna's adopted mother, Yashoda, churning cream. While his brother climbs up her dress, tugging and waving to distract her, baby blue Krishna reaches into the pot to steal freshly whipped butter. Harji Chatera could have given this picture of Krishna to the Jaipur court to celebrate one of Krishna's festivals, as artists often gave pictures of auspicious gods to the ruler according to a ceremonial calendar as *nazar* (a gift), as well as to signal their eligibility for future commissions.[98]

Moor owned other evocative scenes of Krishna as a child and in his love-play with Radha that align with those in the Jaipur Palace Collection and offer clues to the circumstances of their production and patronage. The Jaipur queen Maji Shri Rathor owned a series of paintings of the months (*baramasa*) that entered the Jaipur library with the rest of her collection in 1802.[99] Moor owned nearly identical paintings of Krishna and Radha's dalliances, such as Radha pulling Krishna to view the rains in the month of *Ashada* (June) (fig. 96). Moor could have bought a queen's group of paintings, or those based on one.

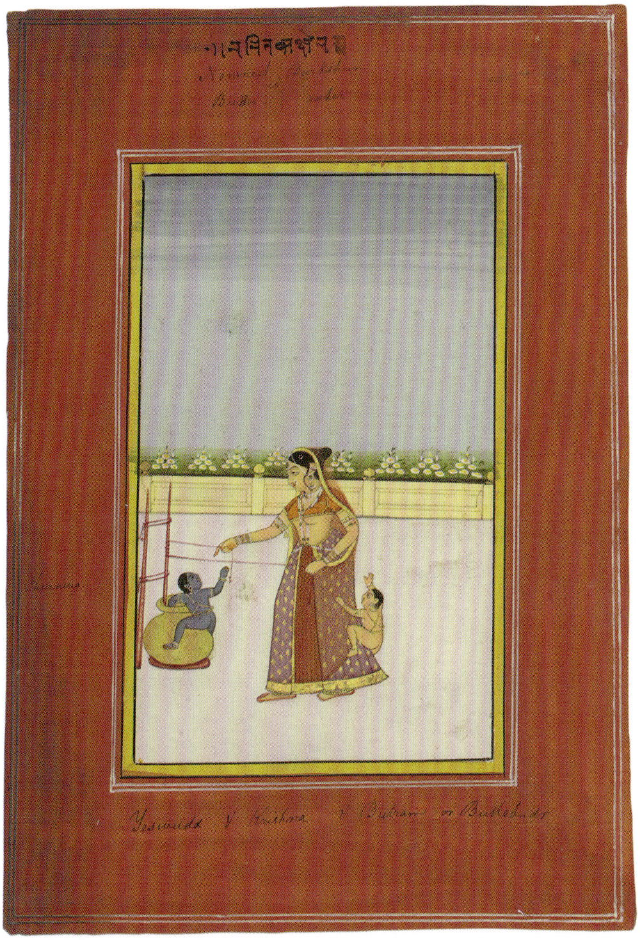

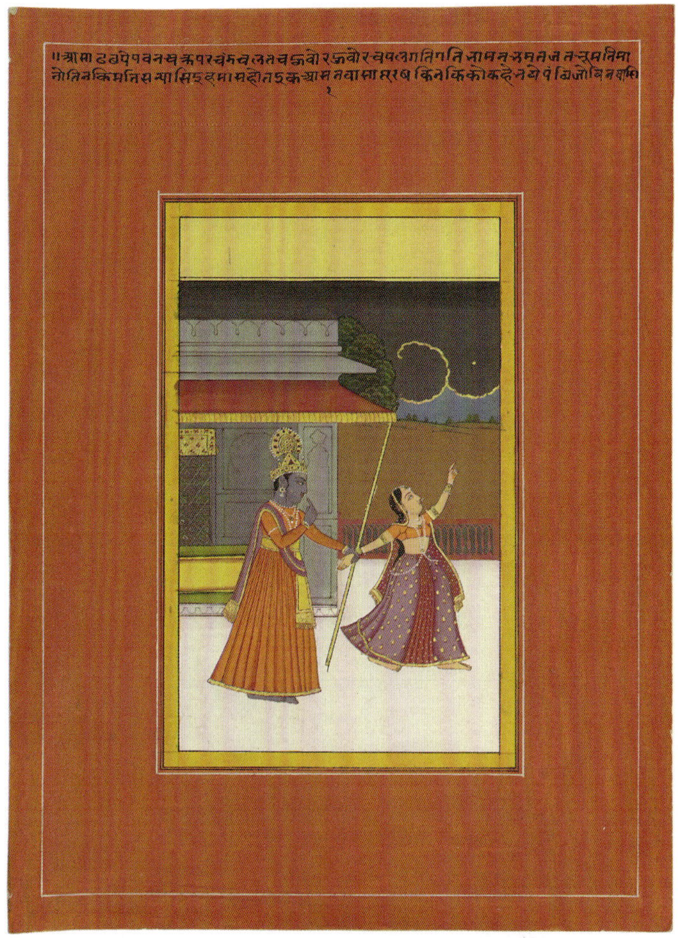

The ninety-three paintings in Maji Shri Rathor's collection include representations of deities, ascetic figures, and *baramasa*,[100] which precisely parallel those in Moor's group.[101] Yet, series regularly found in collections of the same period, caliber, and production, such as of *ragamala*, are scarce in both Rathor's and Moor's groups, which supports the idea that Moor purchased a specific person's assembly of paintings.[102] Collections could be dispersed after death, if a family fell on hard times, or if a fort or palace was plundered, as noted in Chapter One in relation to Nana Fadnavis's collection of paintings. Artists could also copy works if they recognized a demand in the market, as Varunika Saraf has deciphered for twentieth-century miniature painters in Rajasthan.[103] A Jaipur artist could have painted one set for a noble patron and others for public sale, which compels us to think about the chain of intermediaries, from artist to merchant to patron, and from Jaipur to Poona, that swept Moor into its orbit.

95 *Krishna Stealing Butter*, Jaipur, ca. 1800. Opaque watercolor on paper, 30.1 × 21 cm. British Museum, London, Edward Moor Collection, 1940,0713,0.143

96 "The Month of Ashada (June)" in a *baramasa*, Jaipur, ca. 1800. Opaque watercolor on paper, 27.1 × 20.1 cm. British Museum, London, Edward Moor Collection, 1940,0713,0.16

Moor was not alone in western India in his appreciation for paintings from Jaipur. Wealthy bankers and officials in the Poona region, such as the Raste and Khasgivale families, owned Jaipur paintings. Yet their interests varied; the Khasgivales, for instance were drawn to personifications of music visualized in *ragamala* paintings.[104] Other families collected works from regions that are not represented in Moor's collection.[105] The Raste family owned a striking painting of Narasimha (fig. 97), Vishnu's incarnation as a man-lion, fiercely untangling the intestines of the demon supine on his lap, as part of a *dasavatara* series from the eastern Deccan, for instance, that does not have a match in Moor's assembly.

Like Moor's collection of iconic metal sculptures that related to specific pilgrimage routes and local worship, his aggregation of paintings is particular. It encapsulates the trade between Jaipur and Poona, and the sale of certain types of paintings, such as pop-

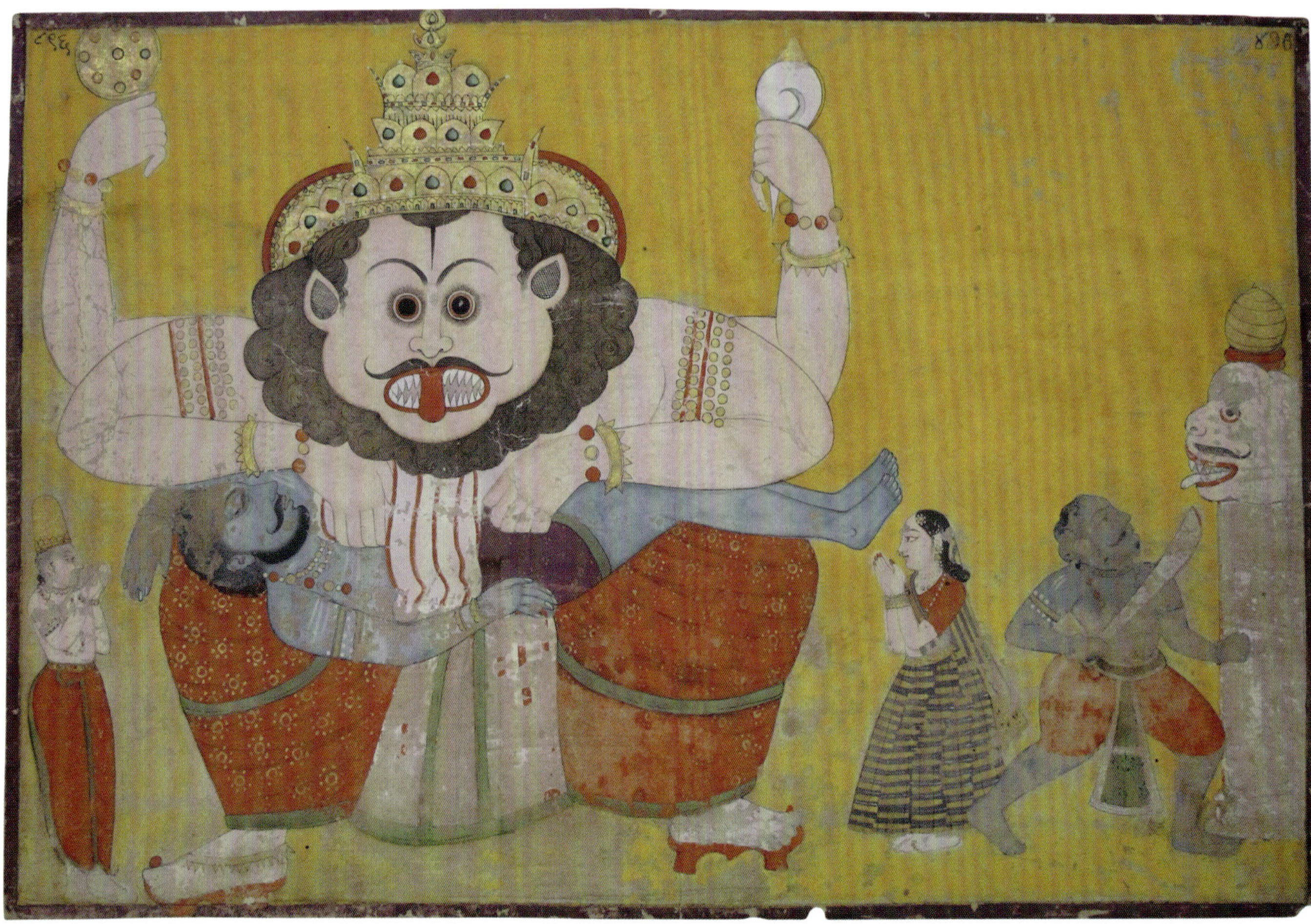

97 *Narasimha*, South India, 18th century. From the collection of Goshale Raste, Wai, Maharashtra. Opaque watercolor and gold on paper. Bharat Itihas Sanshodhak Mandal, Pune

ular and affordable series of gods, and the artists and merchants who made and sold them. His works allow insights into the means of circulation for paintings in the late eighteenth century, but only gleanings of their previous owners and purpose outside of the question of connoisseurship.

PAINTED STORIES ACROSS MEDIA

A fourth market proposes another realm of art making distinct from the plunder and pilgrimage of the bronzes and from the transregional circuits of the paintings just discussed. This is the local economy of popular devotional painting in western India, in which Moor also participated. For example, he hired an artist from Poona, whom he called a "man of some genius," to paint stories that were not otherwise illustrated in his collection.[106] These paintings include vernacular iterations of popular devotional narratives that adorned manuscripts and walls in the region, and those used by storytellers to illustrate their tales. As with the other objects discussed in this chapter, the paintings that Moor commissioned serve as a means to understand local commerce at the same time as they illustrate his own interest in the materials. These "pictures and visible objects," as he termed them, aided Moor in understanding the "Mythology" of the "extraordinary people" with whom he lived in India. But they also demonstrate a regional trade in Marathi manuscripts and the commissioning of Hindu narratives and iconic representations on paper to which Moor's artist turned in order to define compositions for his Company patron.

The name of the artist employed by Moor is unknown, but like others discussed in this book he was probably a *chitari*, a professional-caste painter; I will refer to him as the Poona painter. Other artists who worked as painters of popular, religious material on the basis of commissions are discussed in the records and help to situate the Poona painter in the market. In a letter to the Peshwa, an agent identified three artists named Anuprao, Ragho, and Tanhaji Chitari who could paint series of gods in a variety of media and manners.[107] Other records highlight the devotional occasions for which painters' services were required, like Ramji Chitari's commission to paint the walls of a temple in time for a festival to Rama, or Dhanaji and Bapu Chitari's employment to paint murals for a child's religious thread ceremony.[108] Akin to these *chitaris*, the Poona painter probably dealt in a local market and was employed according to a ritual calendar and for the painted series of deities or illustrated manuscript a customer required. It is probable that he could paint on multiple supports, including walls and paper, and in various media and techniques. However, for Moor he drew in opaque watercolor on European laid paper and was instructed to compose scenes to certain specifications.

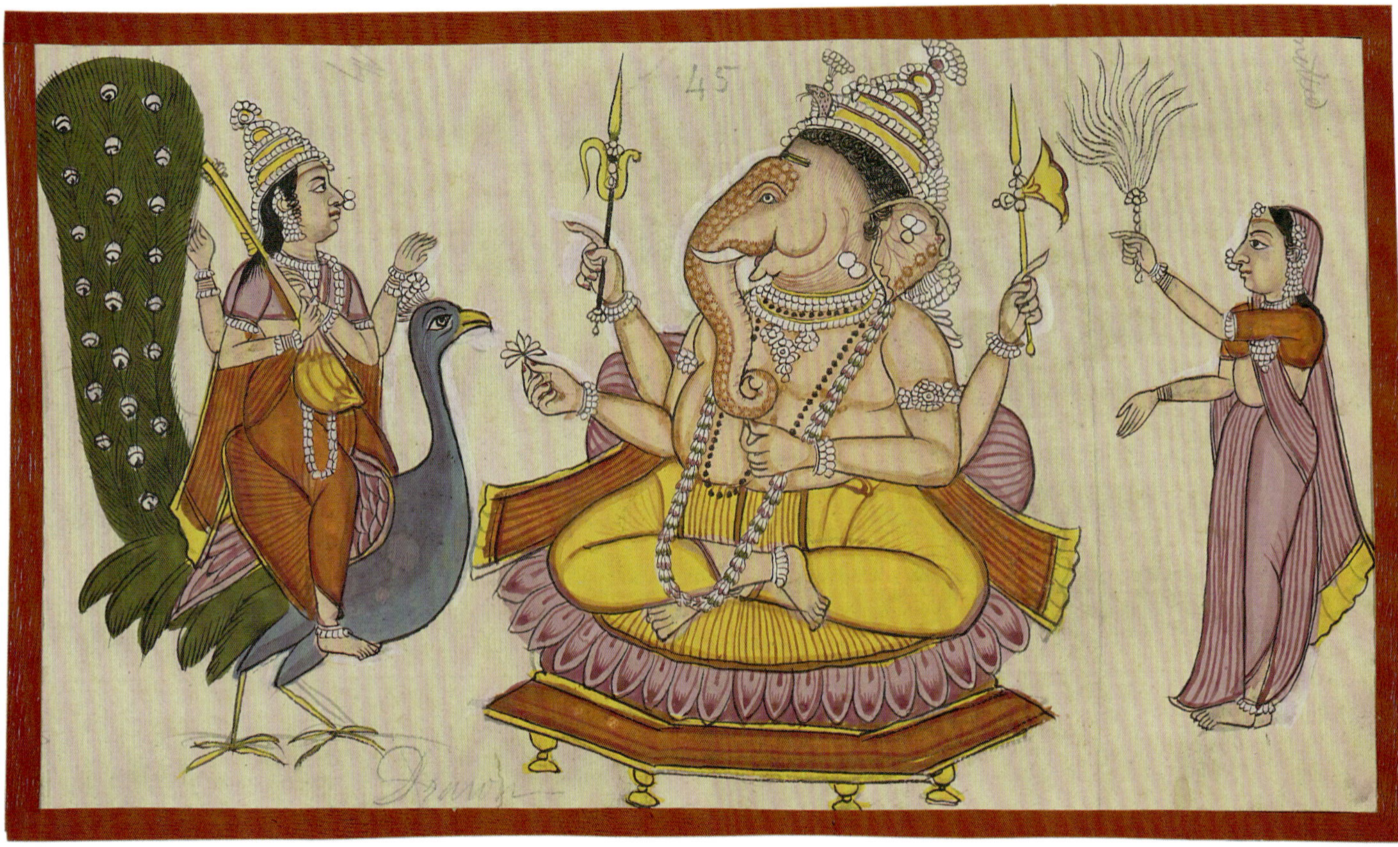

Moor employed a religious teacher (a "Pandit") to enforce the artist's rule-bound productions. He wrote that the artist "would ... have improved himself, if let alone; but as I wanted from him accuracy, rather than invention, his performances were scrutinized by my Pandit: and if, at any time the painter's imagination was too prurient, the Brahman ... immediately restored him to orthodox sobriety."[109] Regardless of the overbearing presence of this purported expert, it is clear that the Poona painter was versatile. He seems to have consulted a range of sources for Moor's projects – including manuscripts for certain compositions and painted series of gods for others – but edited them from their narrative programs to stand as iconic images scaled to the dimensions of European laid paper.

The relationship between the Poona painter's works and local manuscripts, series of painted deities, and murals provides insight into an economy for painting on paper and walls in the region. For instance, the Poona artist drew Saraswati, goddess of wisdom and learning, and Ganesha, the remover of obstacles, for Moor in bright gem-toned colors on paper (fig. 98).[110] These two deities often auspiciously meet at the beginning of narrative

98 *Ganesha and Saraswati*, Poona, ca. 1800. Opaque watercolor on paper, 23.1 × 35.75 cm. British Museum, London, Edward Moor Collection, 1940,0713,0.232

manuscripts (*pothi*) in western India, and it is from such a stock that this artist probably drew. The composition bears a striking similarity to a frontispiece of the Marathi poet Shridhar's early eighteenth-century popular poetic narrative, *Shivlilamrut* (The Nectar of Shiva's Play; fig. 99), which was produced in eighteenth-century Nagpur, the seat of the Maratha Bhonsle family.[111] Set in a midnight sky framed by leafy trees, the painting depicts the opening salutation of the poem: "Shri Ganesha, I pray to you; Shri Saraswati, I pray to you" (*Shri Ganeshaya nama, Shri Saraswatya nama*). Both deities raise manuscripts in their hands as if proffering their own blessings to the poetic effort. While the Poona painter's rendition of the deities differs subtly in style – compare the three-tiered crowns adorned with pearls, Saraswati's peacock, and Ganesha's peachy coloring in the Poona painting (see fig. 98) to the representation of those features in the Nagpur one – the subject matter speaks to a robust trade in vernacular religious texts illustrated in western India.[112]

Many of the Poona artist's pictures appear to have been clipped out of such narrative programs. In the thirteenth century, the saint-poet Jnaneshvar wrote and annotated the

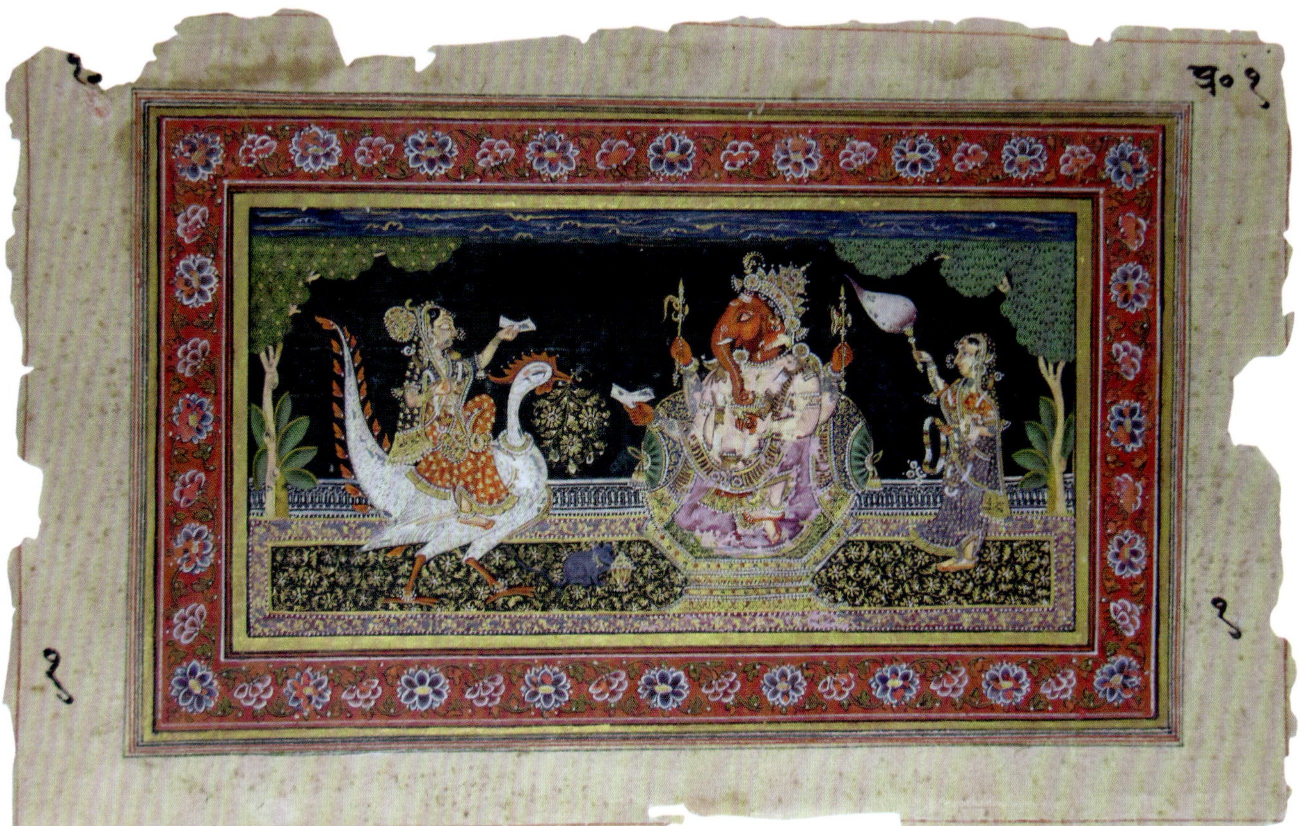

99 "Ganesha and Saraswati." from the *Shivlilamrut* (The Nectar of Shiva's Play), Nagpur, 18th century. Opaque watercolor and gold on paper. Bhandarkar Oriental Research Institute, Pune

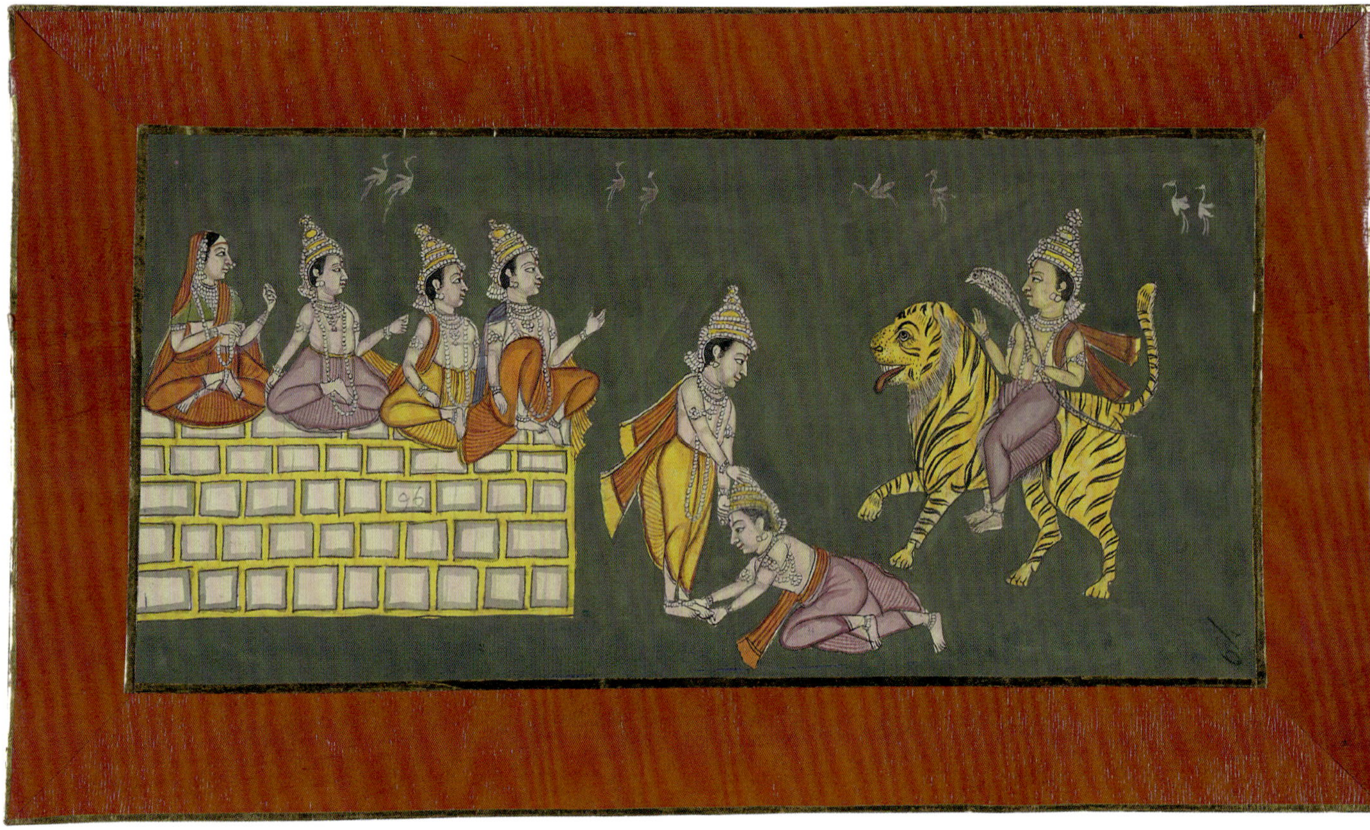

Bhagavad Gita in Marathi. Known as the *Jnaneshvari*, it was reprised by later poets such as Mahipati in his eighteenth-century *Bhakta Vijaya* (Lives of saint-devotees).[113] The Poona painter depicted Jnaneshvar miraculously moving a high yellow and cream brick wall to greet the visiting sage Changdev in one continuous narration (fig. 100). Changdev first approaches on a tiger, and then is repeated bowing to touch his feet in awe of Jnaneshvar's power to move the wall. An illustrated version of the *Bhakta Vijaya* also renders the miracle, though here the wall has shrunk to two bricks high and is ridden by Jnaneshvar through the cornflower-blue sky (fig. 101).[114] Moor's painting is clearly in dialogue with other eighteenth-century illustrated texts, but there is a difference: the scene in the *Bhakta Vijaya* is one of many illustrations to an accompanying written narrative, while Moor's is singular and not tied to the written word.

Series of paintings on separate sheets of paper suggest common iconographies of regional gods with which the Poona painter engaged, similar to how narrative manuscript paintings point to the range of Marathi literature illustrated in the eighteenth century. One series of thirty deities implies the diversity of gods depicted in recognizable iconic

100 *Jnaneshvar Performs a Miracle at Alandi*, Poona, circa 1800.
Opaque watercolor on paper, 22.8 × 40 cm. British Museum, London,
Edward Moor Collection, 1940,0713,0.200

formats in western India, including Ganesha (fig. 102) and deities discussed earlier like Khandoba and Malsara astride a horse, Vithoba and Rukmini with arms akimbo (fig. 103), and Vishnu's ten incarnations. The Poona painter drew these gods in the same compositions for Moor along with others in the series like Yama, the dark-skinned "regent of the south," and Indra, the eye-splashed king of the gods.[115] The similarity between these series indicates that the Poona painter, like other *chitaris* whom I described earlier, was capable of producing a set for a general market as well as a specific patron. In this case, that patron was a Company official.

The Poona painter was flexible; he seems to have referred to manuscripts, painted series of gods, and murals for different compositions, or simply to have worked across these multiple formats. With murals, though, as with manuscripts, the Poona painter edited episodes from a larger program to fit the size of individual sheets of paper. Murals of gods were deemed auspicious and meritorious in the region, and they appear on the walls of local mansions, such as Patwardhan Wada in Wai.[116] On one wall of this home Ganesha is displayed in a niche, surrounded by episodes from the life of Krishna and the epic *Mahabharata* (fig. 104). These scenes flow into one another on the wall, like the river full of fish that runs across the surface, but the Poona artist separated these types of images onto discrete sheets of paper for Moor. Ganesha, for instance, is displayed on the wall in

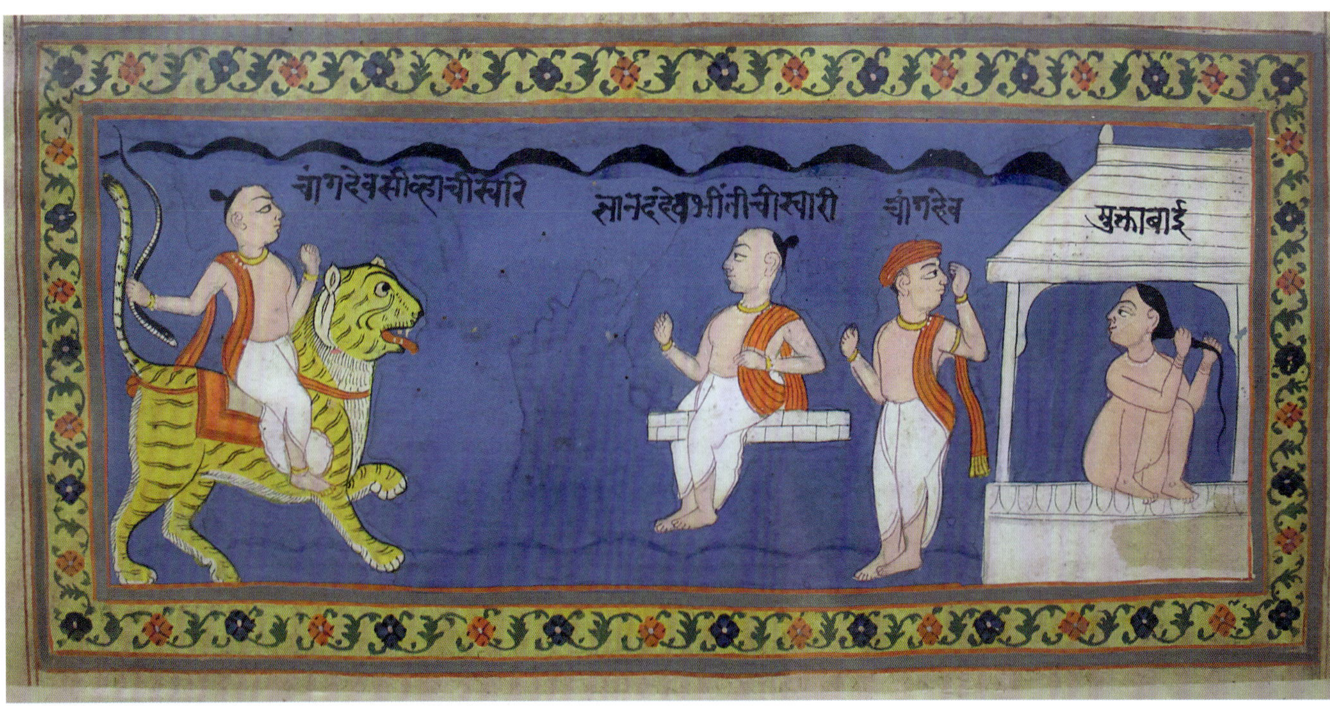

101 "Jnaneshvar," from the *Bhakta Vijaya* (Lives of the saint-devotees), Maharashtra or Madhya Pradesh, 18th century. Opaque watercolor on paper. Scindia Oriental Research Institute, Ujjain

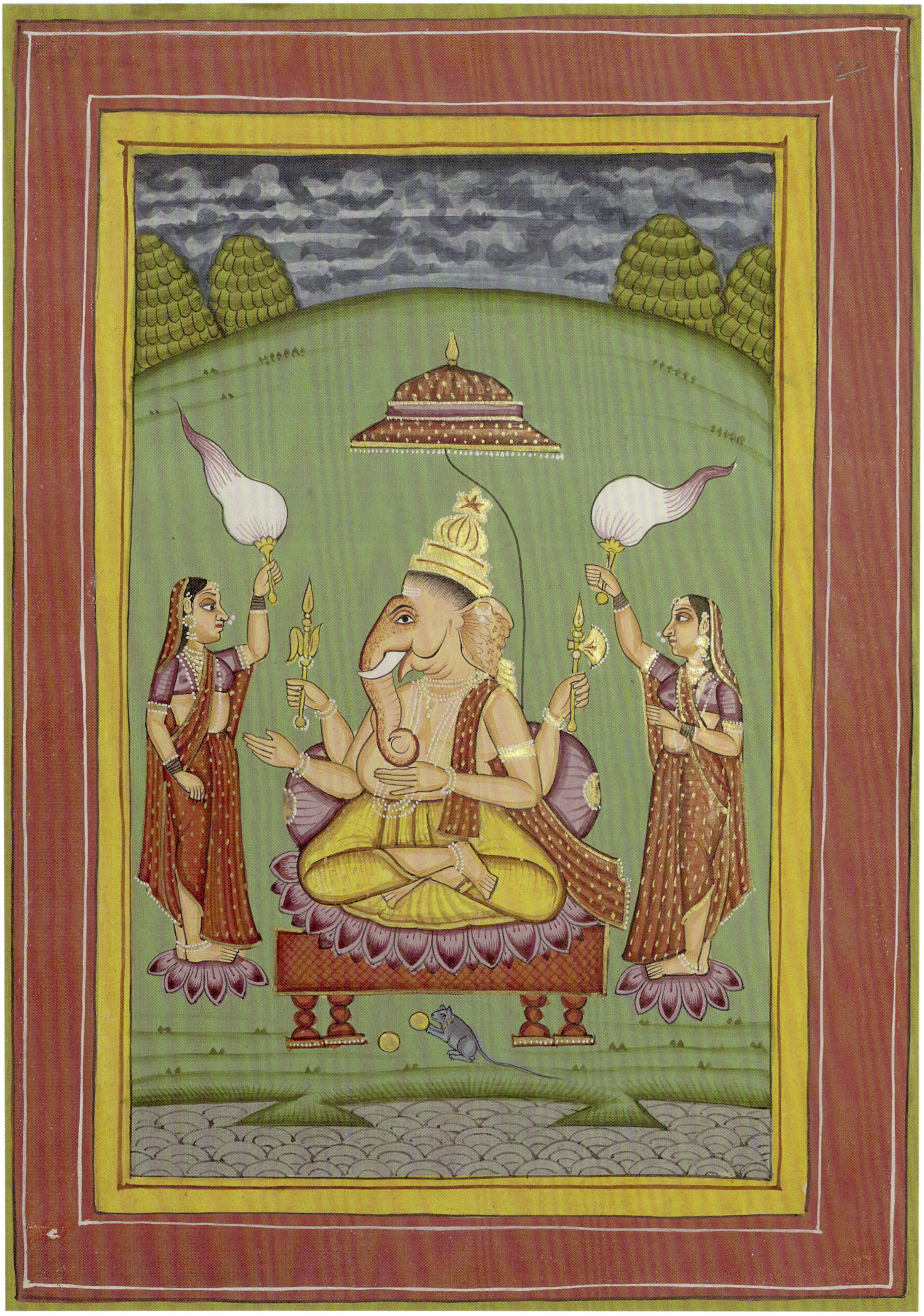

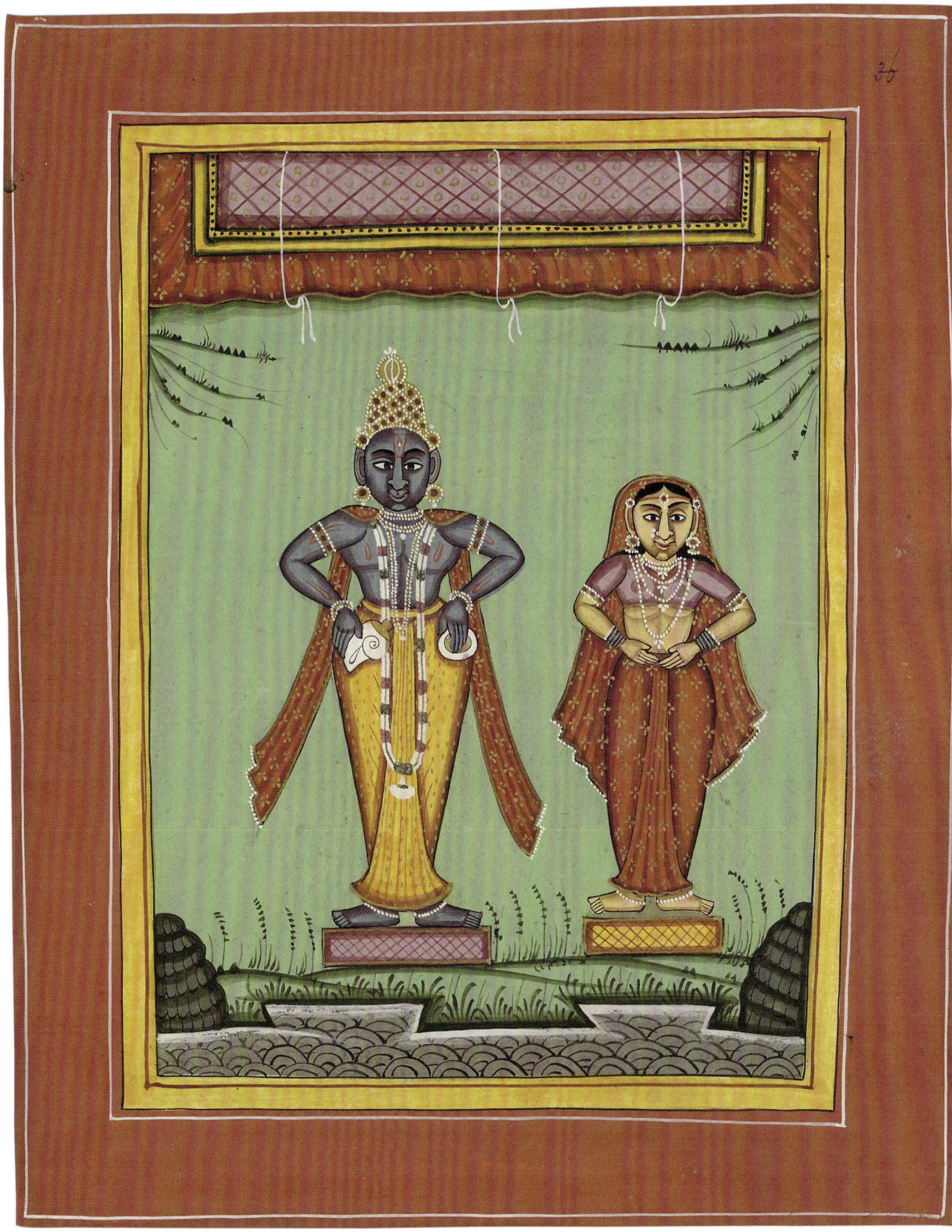

102 *Ganesha*, Maharashtra, ca. 1800. Opaque watercolor on paper, approx. 18 × 24 cm. British Museum, London, 1974,0617,0.14.15

103 *Vithoba and Rukmini*, Maharashtra, ca. 1800. Opaque watercolor on paper, approx. 18 × 24 cm. British Museum, London, 1974,0617,0.14.28

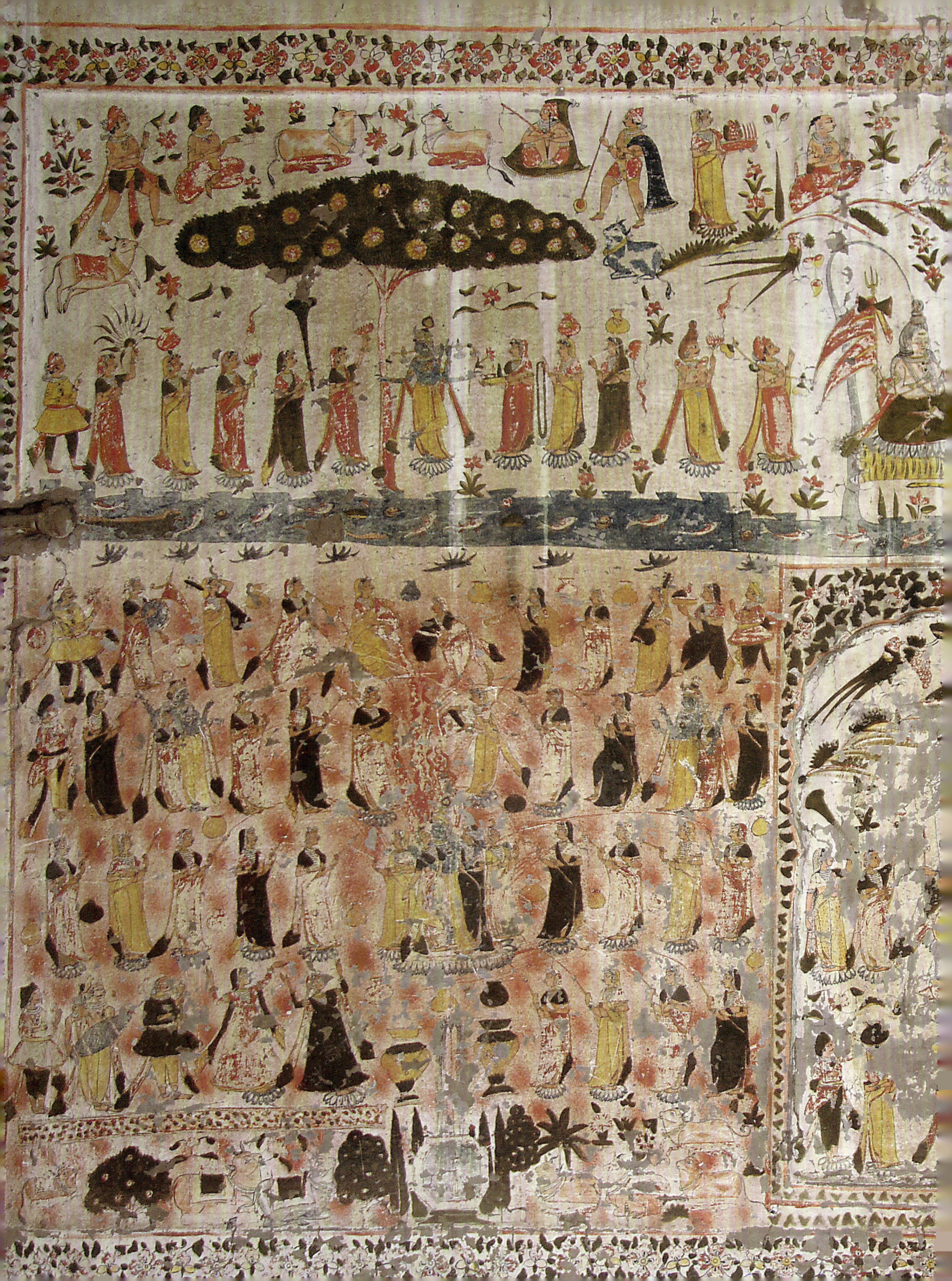

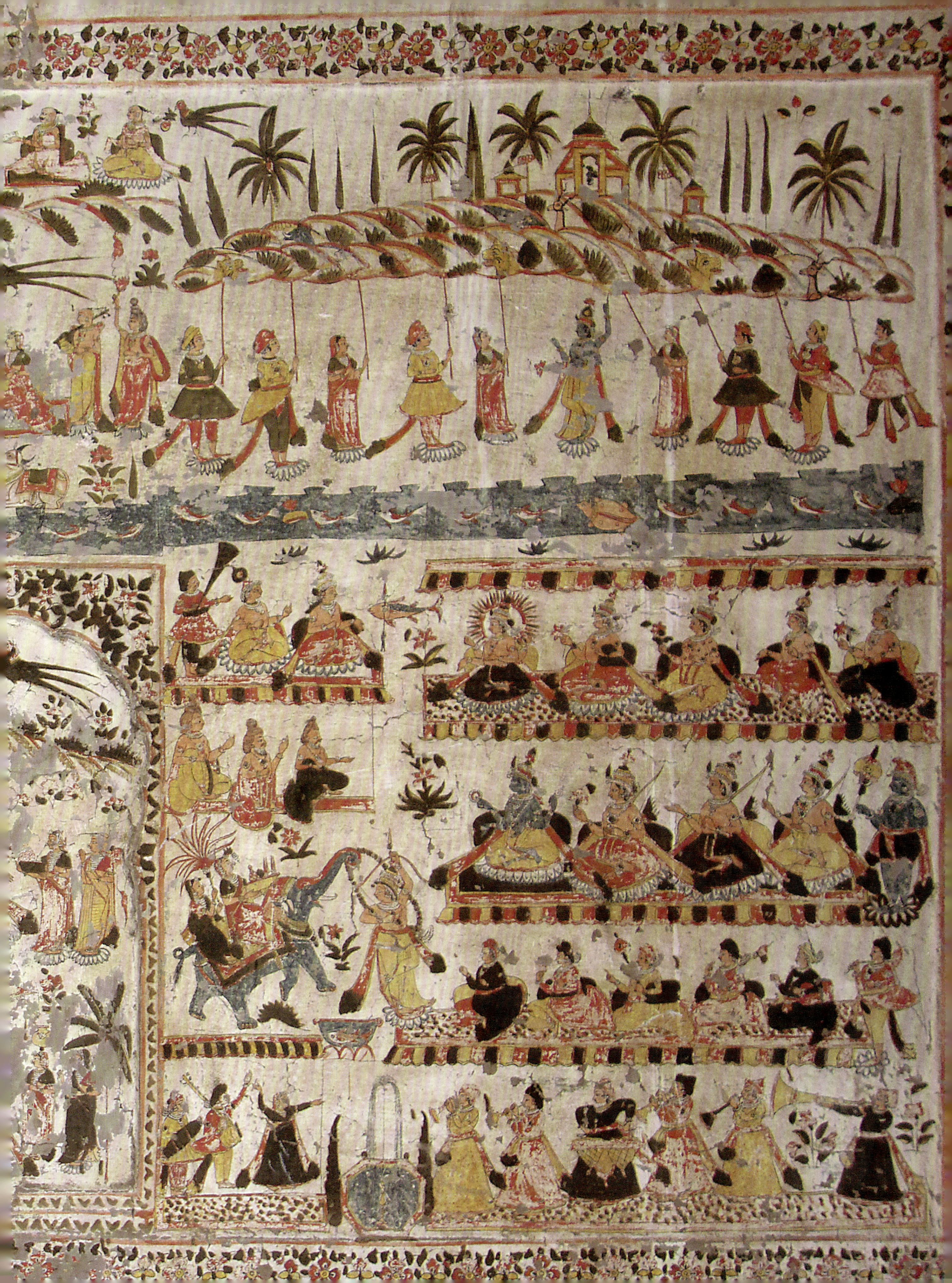

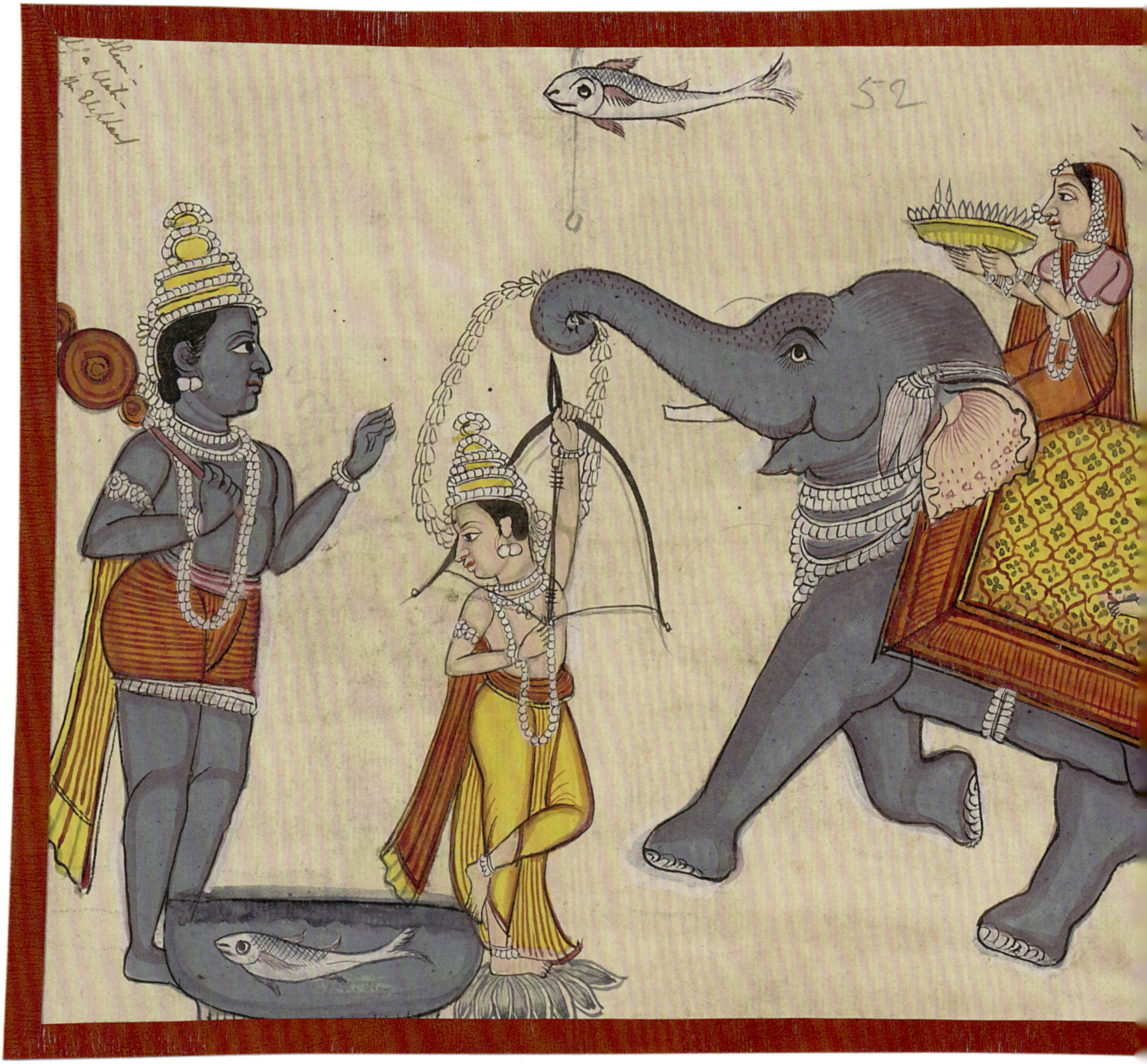

104 (Previous pages) Wall painting in Patwardhan Wada, Wai, early 19th century

105 (This page) *Draupadi Swayamvara*, Poona, ca. 1800. Opaque watercolor on paper, 26.1 × 27.8 cm. British Museum, London, Edward Moor Collection, 1940,0713,0.154

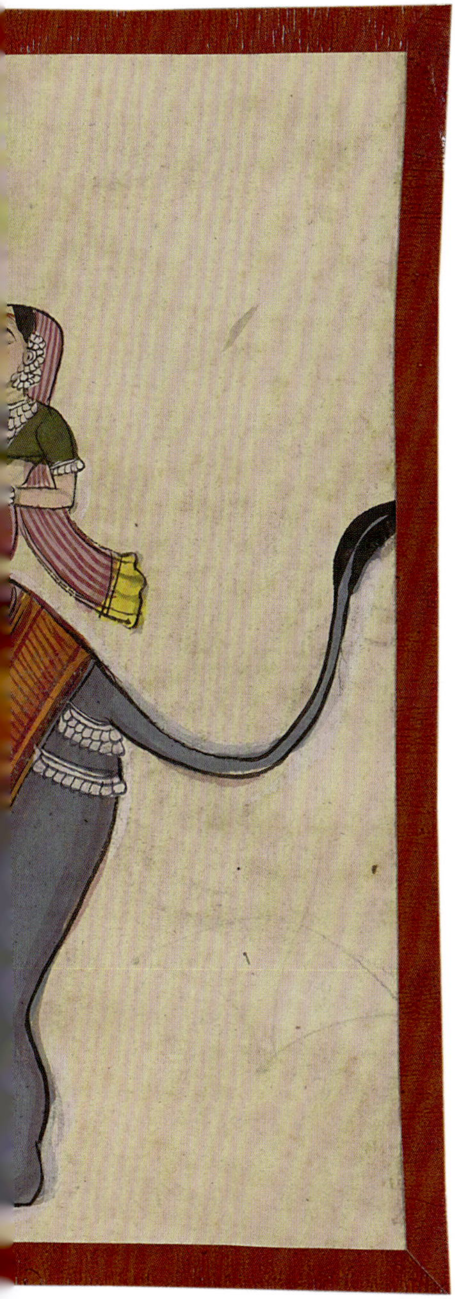

a format familiar from the Poona artist's rendition as well as others locally made (see figs. 16, 98, 99, 102). In the upper right, Krishna balances the mountain Govardhan on one finger, which the Poona artist also drew as an individual painting.[117] In the bottom right, in a scene from the *Mahabharata*, Arjuna wins Draupadi's hand in marriage in a contest (*swayamvara*); he lifts the heavy bow and spears the fish target with an arrow by looking at its reflection in the pool, which again the Poona artist singled out for depiction (fig. 105).[118]

These images work differently, though, in their different formats. Paintings strung together in a manuscript follow a narrative, whereas these iconic episodes have been selected and juxtaposed in the Patwardhan wall painting like a garland at the discretion of the artist and the patron. Seventeenth- and eighteenth-century Marathi poets, for instance, arrayed prayers (*stotra*) in poetic garlands (*mala*) to interweave themes nimbly in meditative couplets, much as these images have been patchworked. The poet Devadas, for example, strung "one hundred verses" into a *mala* to offer Vishnu in the form of Vyankatesh (also known as Ballaji), in his *Vyankatesh Stotra*. One by one, Devadas praises deities, first with "obeisance to thee Heramba [Ganesha]" and to she "who ridest the swan" (Saraswati), to Lakshmi envisioned "ever at Thy feet," and "Kuber . . . Thy treasurer." Devadas invokes scenes through pictorial epithets: Draupadi, her garments unfurled by the Kaurava brothers, the tortoise Kurma who "took on itself the whole weight of the earth, and has not ceased to bear that enormous burden," or Shiva, who "held the poison in his throat, whereby it became dark blue in color." Each god is pictured in a single prayer, just as the deities are portrayed in iconic fashion in the Patwardhan wall painting one next to the other, until the main deity (Vyankatesh, in the case of this prayer, or Ganesha on the wall) could be constructed prayer-limb by image-episode into a complete vision, "exceedingly beautiful."[119] These representations depend on one another; through association, they are grafted together in the eye and mind to form a whole.

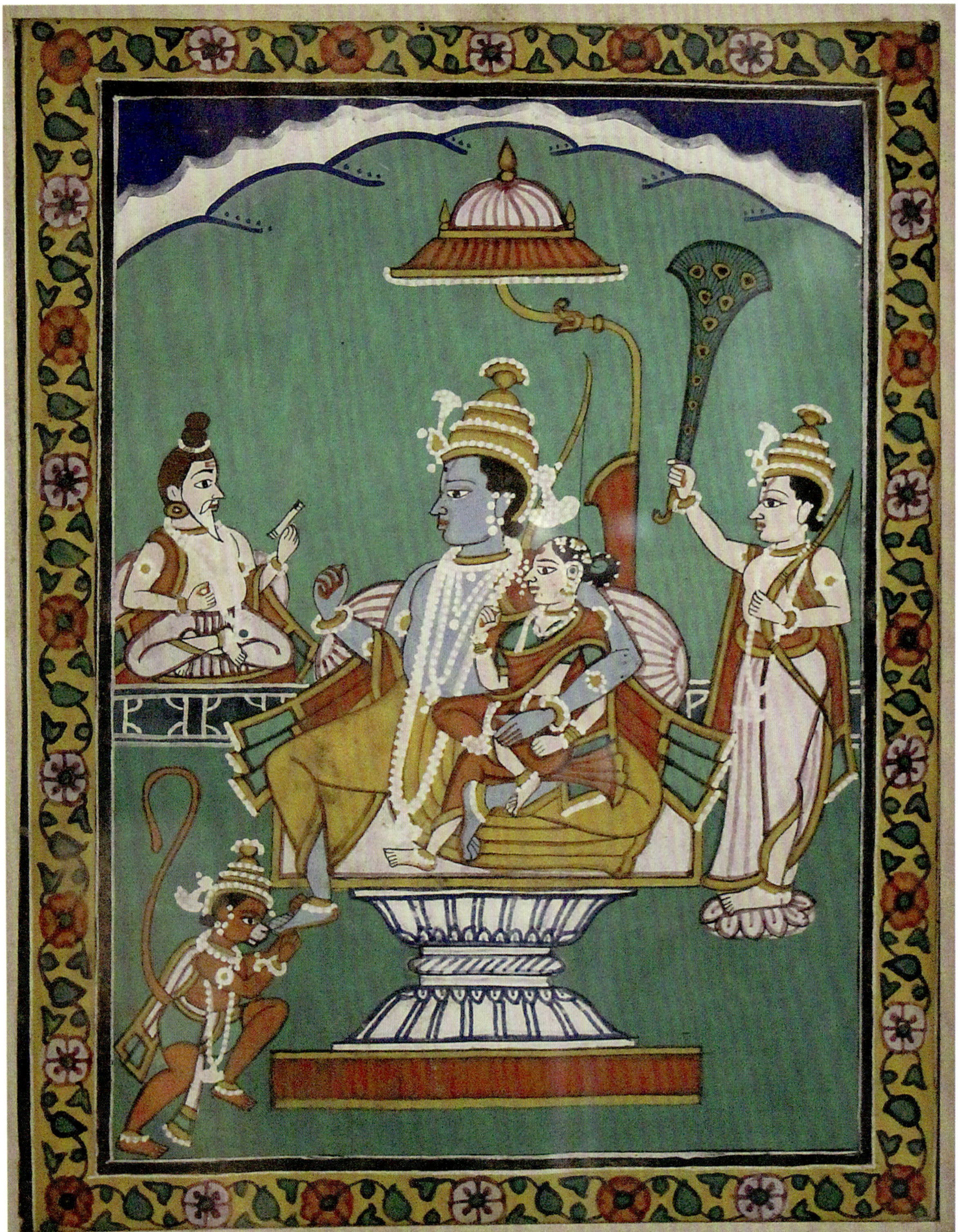

106 *Rama Enthroned with Sita*, Mate Ram Mandir, Satara, late 19th or 20th century. Opaque watercolor on paper. Chhatrapati Shivaji Museum, Satara

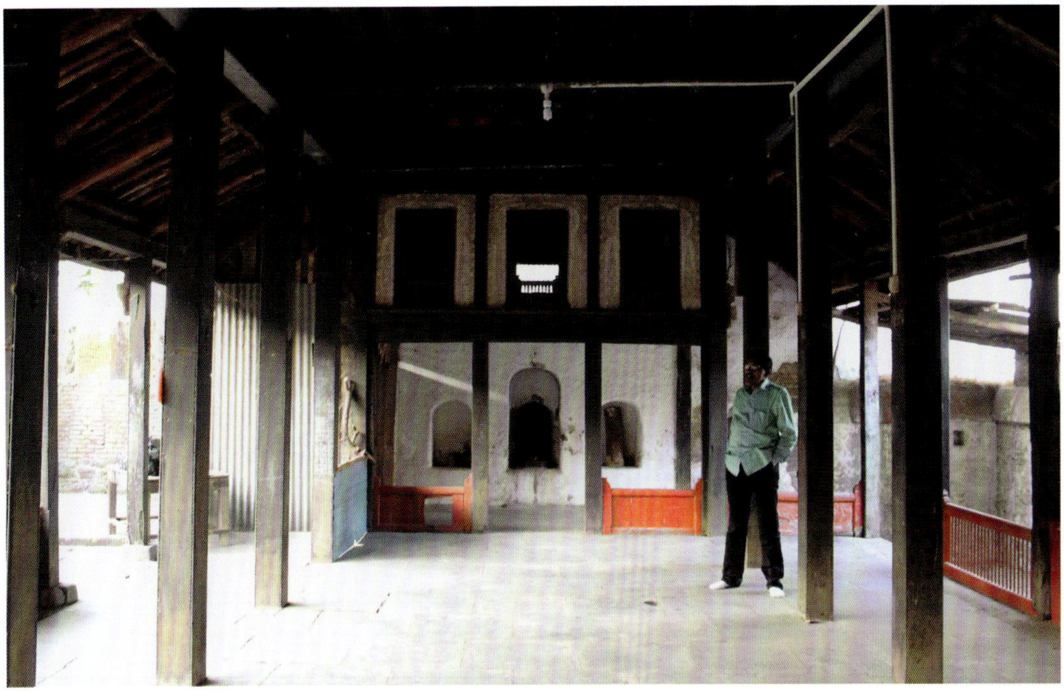

The Poona painter either worked in manuscript, single-folio painting, and mural formats or consulted common designs with the aid of Moor's "Pandit." However, there is another genre of production with which his work for Moor intersects: ritual and performance. His paintings, like those on paper in the region (see figs. 102 and 103), are similar to those that hang in temples or were used in dramatization. Moor noted that the incarnation of Vishnu as a tortoise (Matsya) was "one of the most popular, both in recitation and painting," which Marathi records confirm.[120] In 1785–6, "rewards were paid to actors who acted the ten incarnations in the Royal Palace during the *Shimga* [Holi] festival."[121] Indeed, the *dasavatara* and Krishna's adventures adorned the walls of the Peshwa's palace in Poona (see fig. 14). "Semi-religious prototypes for rudimentary dramatic performances had existed for centuries," the scholar Meera Kosambi has written, "elaborating upon widely known mythological episodes ... a variety of night-time, torch-lit performances ... included impersonations of Vishnu's ten incarnations (in *dashavatar*), of deities and their miracles (in *lalits*), or of secular characters (by *bahurupis*)."[122] In 2014, Mr. Mate described how a late nineteenth-century painted series of gods, many of which are extant, such as one of Rama and Sita enthroned (fig. 106), were hung from the columns in his family's temple, known as the Mate Ram Mandir, in Satara (fig. 107).[123] These paintings were a dynamic part of the temple, changed according to ceremonies, similar to the way

107 Mate Ram Mandir, Satara, Maharashtra, 2014

murals were painted fresh for a specific deity's festival, and animated through recitation and performance.

These manuscripts, paintings, and murals in the Poona region were part of a "picture practice," in the words of Woodman Taylor, which included "the performative uses of paintings as well as the artistic practices of producing paintings in many formats within varying physical spaces, from manuscript pages to palace walls."[124] Many of Moor's pictures can be understood to have functioned within such a visual economy or "picture practice." The series of incarnations of Vishnu on a parrot-green ground that Moor purchased in Poona (see fig. 93) could be copies of those destined for a temple, hung according to the deity being celebrated, and then switched as the calendar turned, as in the Mate Ram Mandir. At the same time as the Poona artist painted compositions for Moor, he could have drawn deities on the walls of another patron's home, to illustrate a manuscript, or to paint on single sheets of paper for storytellers to illustrate their tales.

Moor patronized storytellers who used pictures, as he recounted at length:

> In almost every part of India is met a description of persons who publicly narrate, to admiring audiences, stories or legends from the heroic and amatory histories . . . the extreme beauty of the moon-light nights in India peculiarly invites to this species of recreation . . . the tales recited on these occasions are as varied as the tastes, or as the imagination and ingenuity of man: portions of heroic history from the Mahabarat or Ramayan, or other similar works, are oftenest the subjects of public declaimers; who sometimes read, but more commonly recite from memory. In large towns they fix themselves in some open room, or, in fine weather, in the open air, the neighbours knowing where and when to seek them: in the country they travel from town to town, attended frequently by women, who play on some instrument as a kind of accompaniment to the drawling sort of nasal recitative of the principal performer, *who sometimes exhibits in succession a series of pictures illustrating the history he recites.* [my emphasis]

One such "composer" attended Moor's family almost every night in his recollection, to "the great edification and delight of the children and servants, who would listen to him for an hour with attentive pleasure."[125] The Poona painter's pictures could have provided the illustrations to such itinerant storytellers, or they could have been modeled on them.

With the support of the Poona artist, Moor created new renditions of stories, or "tellings," in the language of the literary scholar A. K. Ramanujan, in which stories are continuously "translated, transplanted, transposed."[126] Moor proposed a translation of the epic Ramayana, which the Poona artist illustrated with episodes drawn from vernacular sources.[127] One painting visualizes a haunting scene in the tale when the ghost-hand of

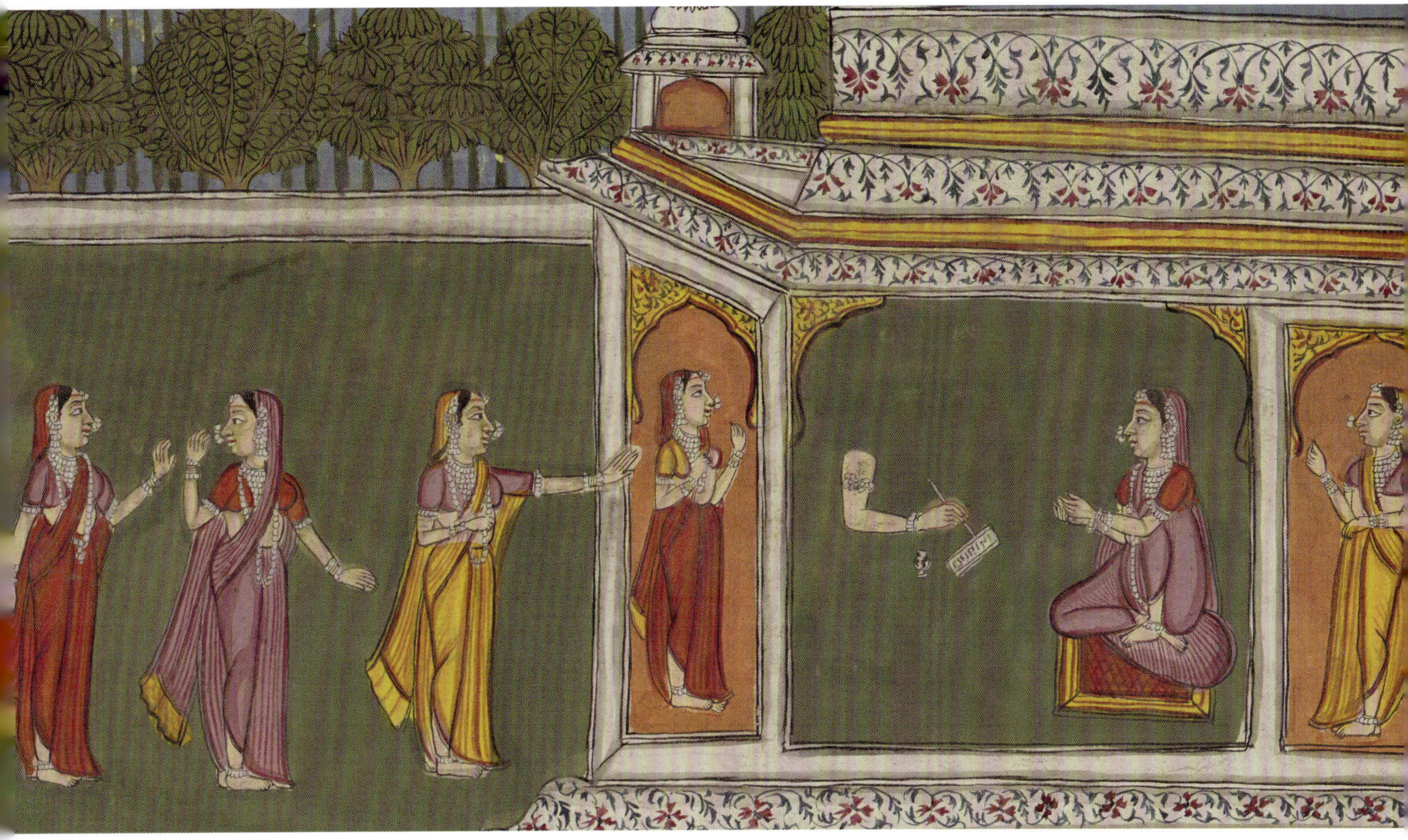

Indrajit writes to his wife of his death in battle (fig. 108), which is rarely included in other versions.[128] Others introduced novel, at times visually arresting, forms like the Poona painter's representation of the snake-demon Ugrasura (fig. 109). His fanged mouth opens wide to swallow Krishna and the cow-herding girls (*gopis*), while his pink and black-dotted body curls decoratively around the page. The Poona painter's interpretation of one of Krishna's adventures seems drawn for an audience sitting on the terrace, eyes glued to a picture as the evolution of the tale unfolded.[129]

Moor accessed a cross-section of such "tellings" during his tenure in India through "travelling friends," "correspondents," and "Brahmin[s]" in the same manner as he invented his own with the aid of the Poona painter, a "Pandit," and perhaps the "composer" who entertained his children. He engaged with these modes of worship and entertainment just as he did with markets that ranged from iconic metal sculptures circulating through pilgrimage and plunder, to a well-established transregional trade in Mughal and Raj-

108 "The Ghost-hand of Indrajit" from the *Ramayana*, Poona, ca. 1800. Opaque watercolor on paper, 22.1 × 36.15 cm. British Museum, London, Edward Moor Collection, 1940,0713,0.199

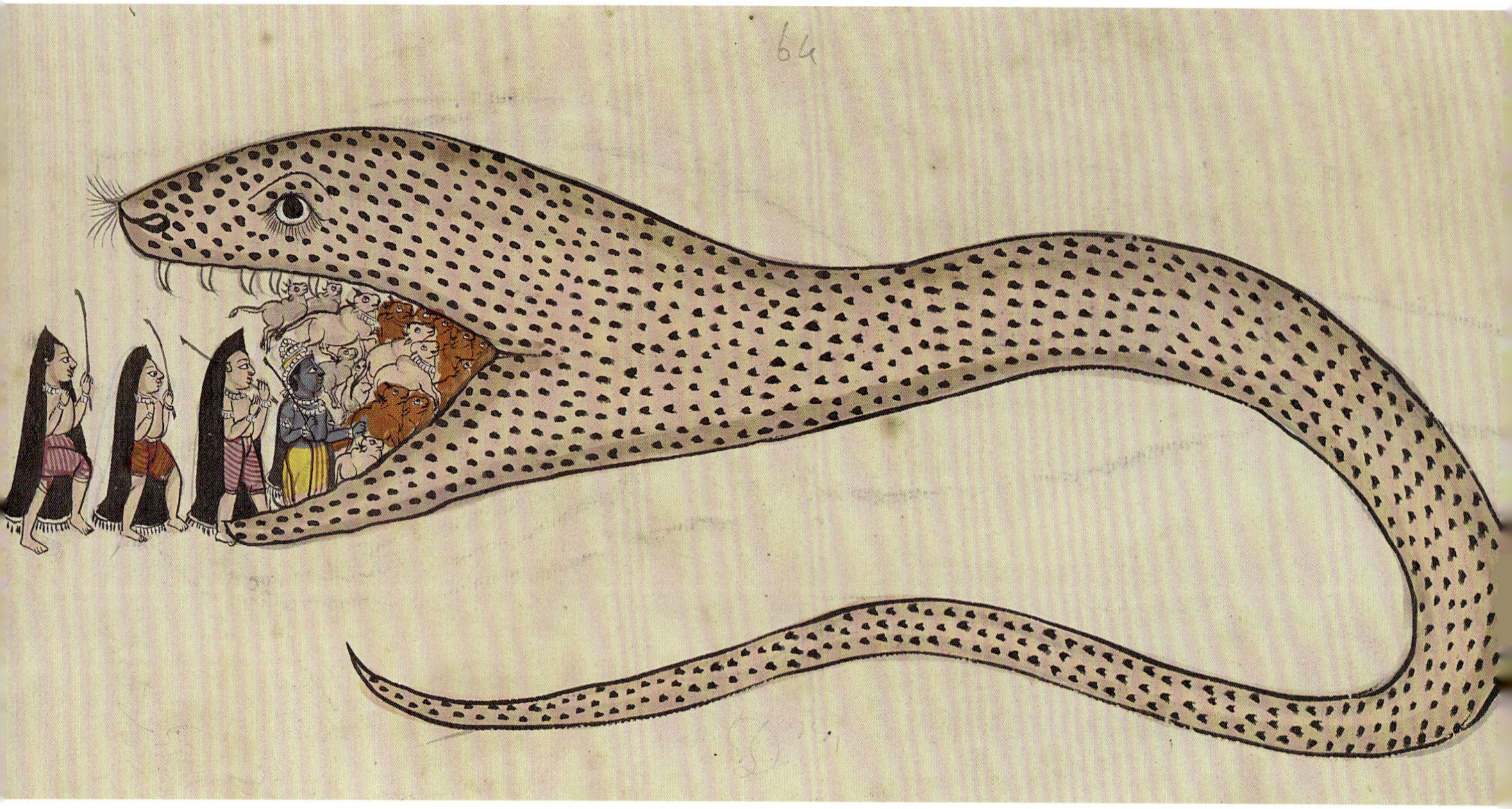

put paintings. Moor also participated in a local system of artisanship by employing the Poona painter who was well-versed in popular narratives and iconic representations of deities on walls and on paper. Yet, it is important to remember that the works Moor commissioned were not made for storytellers, as Paithan paintings were made in southern Maharashtra, or as illustrations of the Ramayana were produced in Orissa, or as Patua paintings were made in Bengal, nor were they made for manuscripts, wall paintings, or series of gods to be hung in a temple.[130] Rather, they were created for a Company soldier who would have them engraved and distributed to a transnational audience.

Moor's collection nevertheless elucidates the production and circulation of objects as well as the fluctuations that can occur in the evaluation of things when situated within the wide-ranging art economies of eighteenth-century India. Within a context of plunder, values can dip and soar according to the availability of materials or simply be misplaced due to a lack of knowledge about them, but they can also stabilize around certain factors like precious metals or the number of faces and quality of paint in a picture. However, when it comes to the judgment of values connected to cultural considerations, or

109 *Krishna and Ugrasura*, Poona, ca. 1800. Opaque watercolor on paper, 22.8 × 38.4 cm. British Museum, London, Edward Moor Collection, 1940,0713,0.209

when the desperation on the part of the seller is taken into account, evaluation becomes more complicated.

Moor grafted these arts – the narratives, murals, and manuscripts from which the Poona painter snipped, the paintings that dealers sold, and the choice items soldiers looted – into his collection, but he also transformed them into a book, *The Hindu Pantheon*, which attempted to classify the Hindu gods for a European audience. In the next chapter, I will assess this book's production, purpose, and impact, but here I have traced the varied markets through which Moor's objects passed to consider a sparsely documented material culture of religion in western India and how the wars that ravaged the region created modes of evaluation and sent works traveling to new domains. Moor's collection forces us to ask how "men and gods, and things" can be made and remade through processes of graft, and to what end.

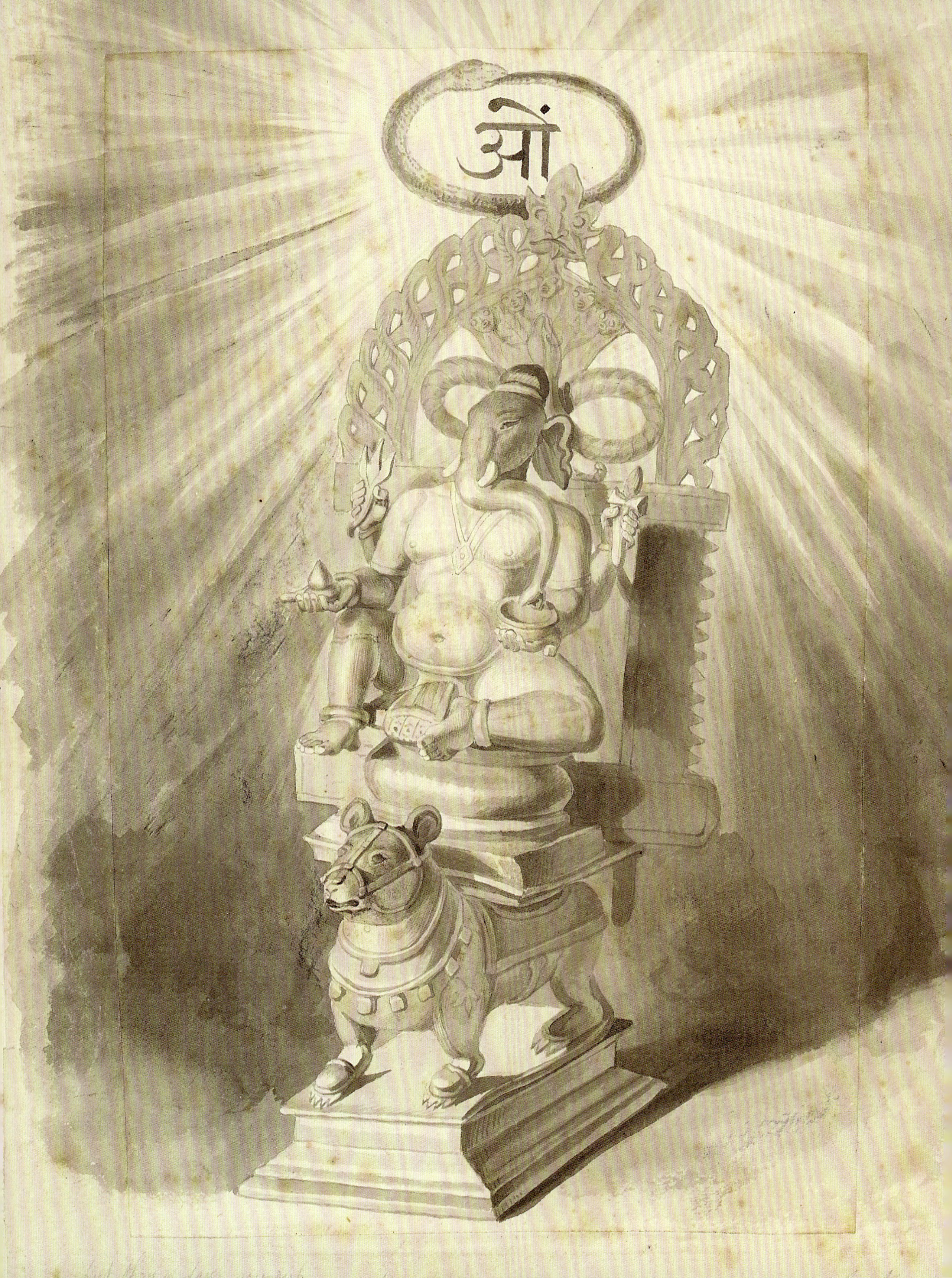
ओं

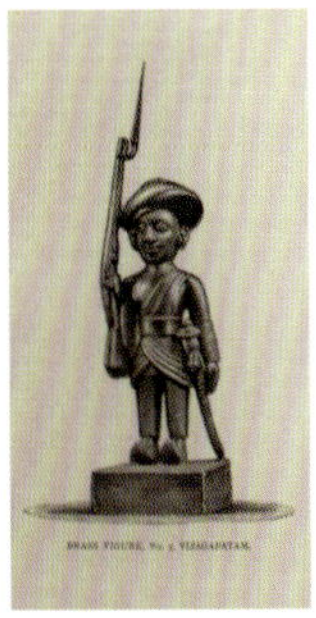

CHAPTER FOUR

The Hindu Pantheon and the Reformulation of Maratha Arts

In 1810, Edward Moor published *The Hindu Pantheon* in London, an early attempt in English to classify the Hindu gods (fig. 110).[1] A tome of 451 pages, it also included 105 plates engraved after the iconic sculptures and bright paintings of deities and devotional narratives that Moor and his East India Company colleagues had collected in India. An advertisement claimed that "nearly Two Thousand Mythological Subjects" had been reproduced "in exact imitation of the original Images, Pictures, Excavations, Medals . . . ."[2] Although hyperbolic, the advertisement pointed to the breadth, and worth, of information housed within the book. *The Hindu Pantheon* outstripped existing publications in its number and variety of illustrations. Whereas Pierre Sonnerat's *Voyage aux Indes Orientales* (1782) had thirty images of deities, for example, *The Hindu Pantheon* had more than three hundred.[3]

Moor further reformulated his "original Images" in ways that differed markedly from the iconographic summaries of earlier books about the Hindu gods. First, he emphasized the relationship between images and the theological texts published by the Asiatic Society of Bengal to engage a network of scholars and raise his status in the Company. Second, in collaboration with his publisher Joseph Johnson in London, and artists in his circle like Henry Fuseli, Moor transformed his collection of Hindu materials into one relatable to the Greco-Roman pantheon of antiquity through line engravings in neoclassical style, which formatted the publication into a model for other artists including John

Details of fig. 116 (opposite) and fig. 135 (above)

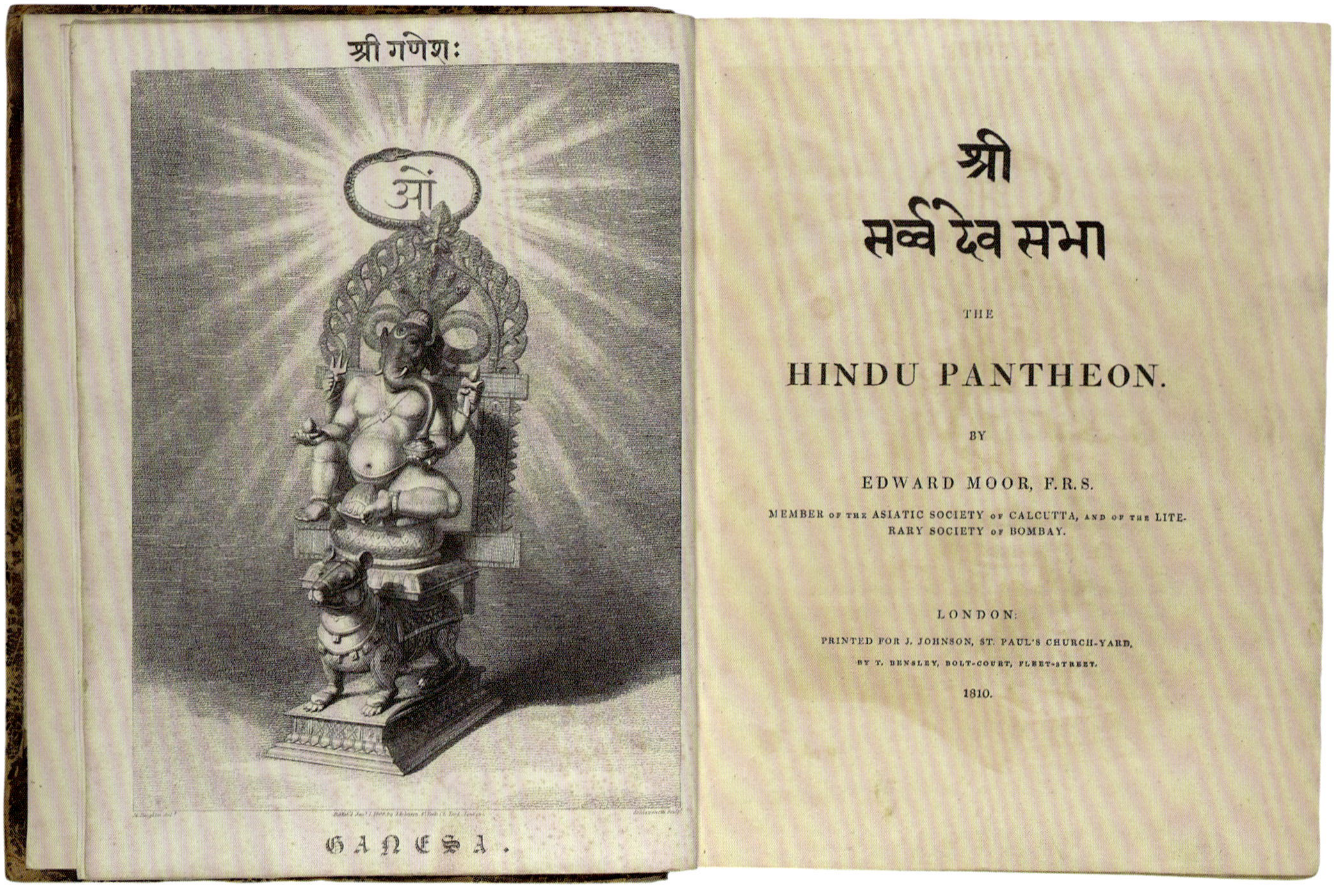

Flaxman and William Blake. The combination of these two factors resulted in illustrations of the Hindu gods that situated the book within debates about how religion, art, and empire should interact in this period.

The collection of *The Hindu Pantheon*'s materials in India and its production in Britain extended from the eighteenth to the nineteenth century when the Company's policy about governmental intervention in Indian religious matters changed. Moor was in India in the late eighteenth century, and his approach to Hindu objects was connected to the adaptive imperialism promoted by Warren Hastings and William Jones at the Asiatic Society. They sought to understand Hindu and Muslim legal, religious, literary, and artistic codes in Persian and Indian languages in order to facilitate British rule and to engage longstanding intellectual debates about the origins of, and relationships between, art and religion. The publication of Moor's book marked the second decade of the nineteenth century, when the British defeated the Marathas and renewed the East India Company's

110 Edward Moor, *The Hindu Pantheon* (London: J. Johnson, 1810), frontispiece and title page. British Museum, London, Edward Moor Collection, 1940,0713,0.253

Charter in 1813. The new Act countered earlier accommodations of Indian religions; it permitted Christian missionary activity and sought to establish "civility" via a Western-oriented English-language system of education in India.[4]

In Britain, this period also encompassed a range of engagements with Indian religious arts, from artists who identified them as a vital source of fine art and philosophical inspiration, to missionaries who condemned them as false idols. The particular visual and textual formulation of *The Hindu Pantheon* allowed it to speak to both audiences, which I trace from Moor's reformulation of the western Indian objects that I discussed being collected in the last chapter through their engraving, publication, and dissemination in his book. I emphasize that Moor grafted Indian arts onto British ones, which served at once to aid the acquisition of colonial knowledge and the promotion of conversion, but also to support comparative philosophies of religion on art historical terms. This last factor offered a means to confound imperial constructs, which artists like Blake would plumb to imagine Britain without tyranny, anew.

AN ASIATIC SOCIETY

Edward Moor collected "pictures and visible objects" to understand the "Mythology" of the "extraordinary people" he met in western India as part of a colonial practice of knowledge acquisition, which also allowed him to participate in a fellowship of Company officials.[5] In 1784, William Jones, an East India Company judge at Fort William in Bengal, discussed these mutually beneficial qualities of the Asiatic Society of Bengal in its journal, *Asiatick Researches*. The society, bound together through the publication, would be a "collective" enterprise to "concentrate[e] all valuable knowledge . . . attained in Asia." Modeled on the society of the "man of letters" in Europe, in India the society would fall to the "man of business in the civil or military state" who would "promote or obstruct its growth" depending on whether they "commit their observations to writing and send them to" the society for publication.[6]

For Moor, the Asiatic Society provided a network of Company enthusiasts with whom to engage in a disquisition on the Hindu gods, and one that would help him to expand beyond western India to produce a "satisfactory" account.[7] He joined his regional resources with articles published in *Asiatick Researches* and the knowledge he gained from Company acquaintances to manifest a pan-Indic pantheon in his book. For example, he described a deity as "Vishnu reposing on Sheesh – meditating the creation on *Chir-samudra* – a sea of milk" with "Brama springing in a lotus" from his navel "to create the world," in a tidy script on the border of one of his paintings from Jaipur that he had purchased in Poona or Bombay (fig. 111). While he depended on his Brahmin teacher in west-

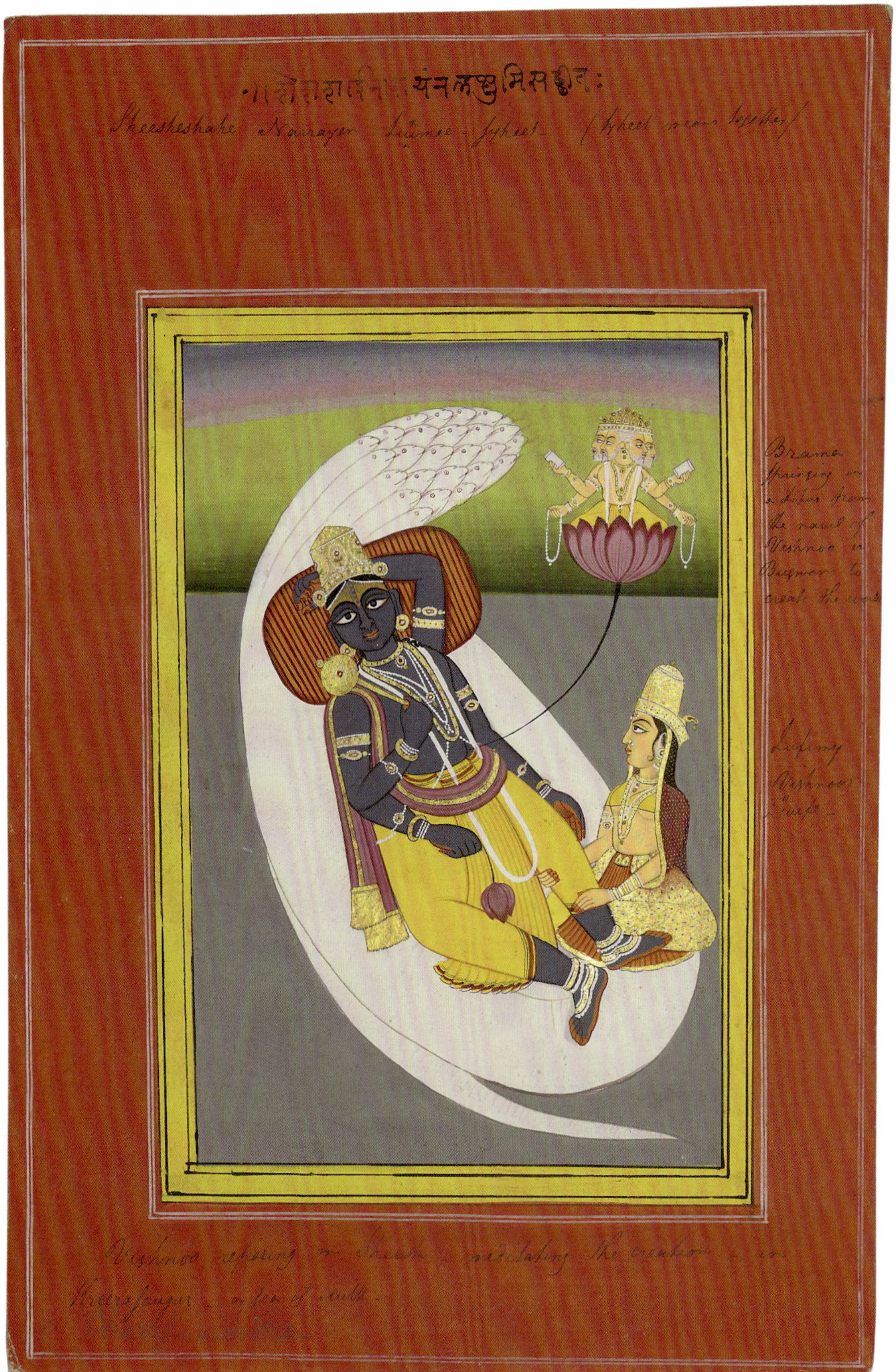

111 *Vishnu on the Cobra Ananta Shesha*, Jaipur, ca. 1800. Opaque watercolor on paper, 31 × 20.3 cm. British Museum, London, Edward Moor Collection, 1940,0713,0.110

ern India for the identification, he turned to Jones's translation of the "Bhagavata [Purana]" and other essays from *Asiatick Researches* to abstract the scene of the cyclical death and rebirth of the cosmos – the "spirit of god . . . imagined and personified . . . [by the] Hindu mythologist and metaphysician" into general terms in his text.[8]

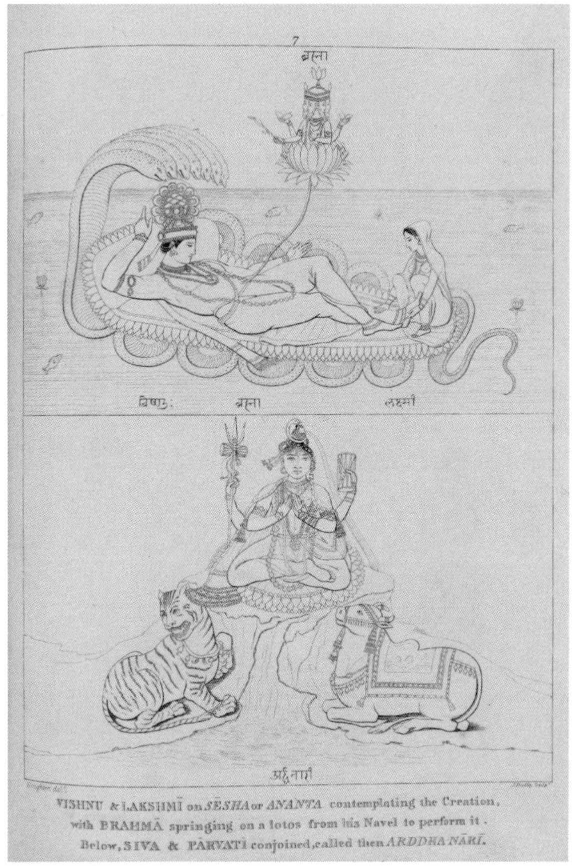

Moor also consulted Company colleagues to obtain complementary works of art and to debate their meanings. With Colonel Charles "Hindoo" Stuart, for instance, Moor discussed paintings (probably when Stuart was on furlough in London, after Moor had returned around 1805), including ones that were not extant in his collection like Brahma and "Maha Pralaya" or Fate.[9] He included such images in *The Hindu Pantheon* and compared representations of deities present in both of their collections, like Vishnu, but prioritized Stuart's representation rather than his own in the book (fig. 112).[10]

The incorporation of Stuart's materials added content to *The Hindu Pantheon*, but other works that Moor included served to enlarge his social network. The object-lenders read like a who's who of British power and interest in India. In addition to Stuart, Moor introduced another "noble" friend's contribution to the section on Vishnu, Lord Valentia, who "obligingly lent" him "a fine cast in bronze." As with Stuart's painting of Vishnu, Moor also owned a "cast of this subject," but he justified using Valentia's sculpture because of its finer execution.[11] For drawings of Jain monumental sculptures in Karnataka, he turned to Arthur Wellesley, the victor against Tipu Sultan in 1799 and later famed for his defeat of Napoleon in 1815, and included a sculpture of a liberated Jain teacher (*Jina*) that was located in the East India Company's museum.[12]

There were financial benefits alongside social and intellectual ones in Moor's publication practices. After Moor returned to England in 1792 to heal war wounds, he wrote letters to the Company, specifically to Marquis Cornwallis, under whom he had served in the wars against Tipu Sultan, to receive pay and to publish his first book, *A Narrative of the Operations . . . Against the Nawab Tippoo Sultan . . .* (1794).[13] Cornwallis facilitated an award of £400 from the Company to pay the *Narrative*'s publication expenses.[14] He also

112 Edward Moor, "Vishnu and Lakshmi on Shesha or Ananta . . . Below, Shiva and Parvati . . . From pictures in the collection of Colonel Stuart," in *The Hindu Pantheon* (London: J. Johnson, 1810), pl. 7. British Museum, London, Edward Moor Collection, 1940,0713,0.253

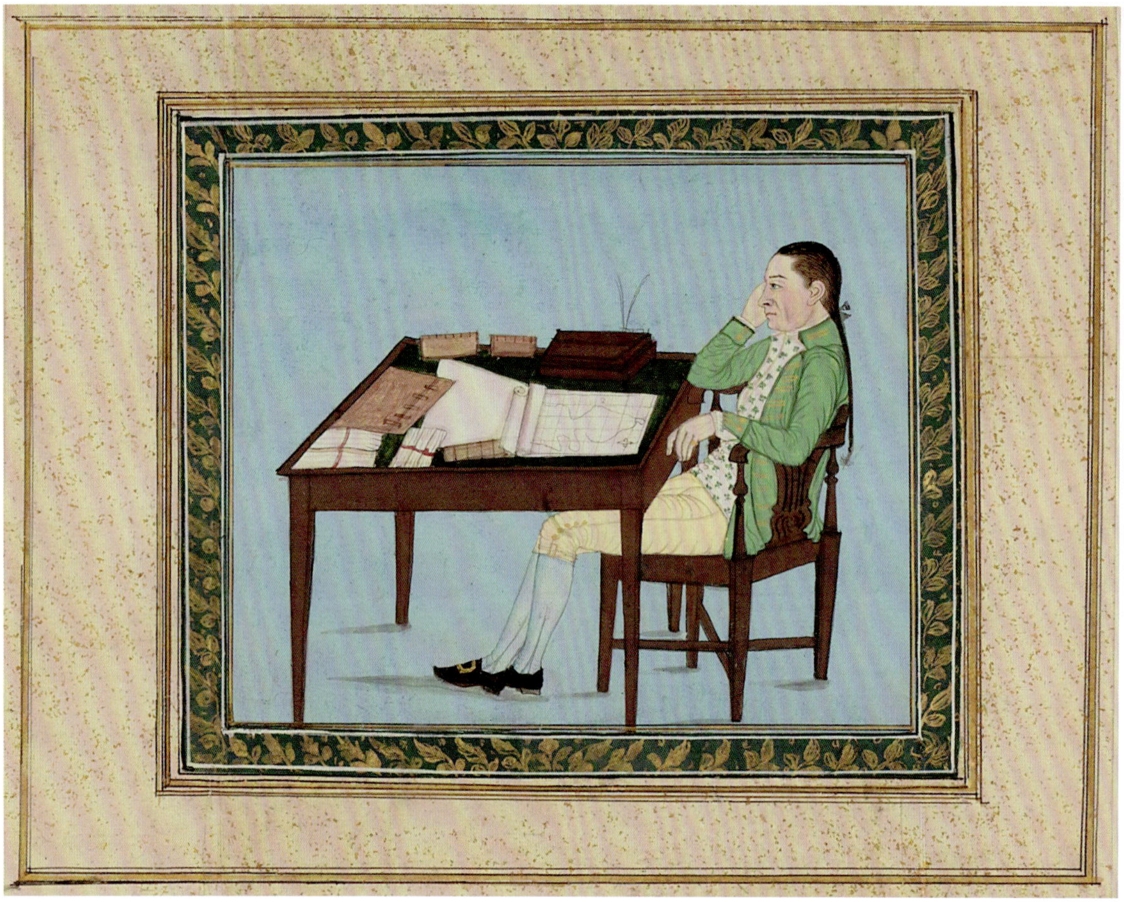

provided Moor with a letter of introduction to Jonathan Duncan, the Governor General of Bombay (1795–1811), which secured Moor a lucrative post as the garrison storekeeper (commissary general) from 1799, thus funding his ever-growing collection.[15] As an avowal of friendship and gratitude for his support, Moor dedicated *The Hindu Pantheon* to Duncan and included an engraving after one of Duncan's bronze sculptures from Kerala of the fearsome goddess Chamunda in the publication.[16]

A portrait of Jonathan Duncan that Moor owned further points to Moor's place as a collector and synthesizer within the hierarchy of the Company's production of knowledge in India (fig. 113). Shown studying materials acquired for political and commercial gain, the British governor is dependent on a descending chain of Company officials, like Moor, and Indian assistants, like the painter of the portrait, to graft together the maps and letters, paintings and records for colonial rule into a cohesive aesthetic. As discussed in Chapter Two, Indian artists working for Company officials grafted British techniques of perspec-

113 *Portrait of Jonathan Duncan, Governor of Bombay from 1795 to 1811*, Bombay, Maharashtra, ca. 1800. Opaque watercolor and gold on paper, 17 × 21 cm. British Museum, London, Edward Moor Collection, 2019,3010.1

tive and modeling to regional artistic idioms, which related arts produced across the subcontinent to one another. The Indian artist who drew this work selectively used European perspective and shading to mark out Duncan's aging face, and the table and chair's tilt, while conforming to the hot aquamarine ground typical of the region's paintings.

Moor included objects that other officials collected, but also ones that they commissioned according to such mixed Company aesthetics and categories. That these materials were some of the most often reproduced images from Moor's book speaks to the role that Asiatic Society members played in translating Indian arts for a British audience. Before his return to Britain in 1786, for example, the Sanskritist Charles Wilkins commissioned a series of zinc casts of the Hindu gods from artists in Benares, which he lent to Moor to reproduce in *The Hindu Pantheon*.[17] The artists he hired translated Hindu ritual and aesthetic formulas for sculpting deities into a simplified one for Wilkins, which clearly defined the attributes of the gods and modeled them with neoclassical touches.[18] Although many of the casts did not succeed in an Indian context – Brahma, for instance, lacks a base and needs a support (fig. 114) – they emblematize the process by which Hindu deities could be made legible to a British audience.

Wilkins was concerned with deciphering textual as well as visual languages, and it is the former for which he is most renowned. Besides translating literary works from Indian languages into English, he also produced typefaces, such as in Bengali, and designed others.[19] For instance, he provided Moor with the Sanskrit title and script of his book, *Shri Sarva Deva Sabha*, the Court of the Holy Gods. Wilkins's sculptures, forged from the same zinc alloys with which he experimented to make typefaces (zinc as a medium for sculpture was rarely used in India), can be understood as a typeface of gods or an iconographical alphabet. This dual interest in texts and images of the Hindu gods fits into a wider orientalist project on their universal origins. Scholars such as William Jones were particularly fascinated by language's genesis in symbolic forms or hieroglyphs that could be deciphered regardless of mutations that occurred over time.[20] In the next section, I will expand on this concept, particularly in connection to Moor's attention to the pictorial side of the equation.

While Moor participated in an Asiatic Society discourse about the Hindu gods, and an aesthetic process of translating the deities into a Company format understandable to the British, he was one of few officials who in

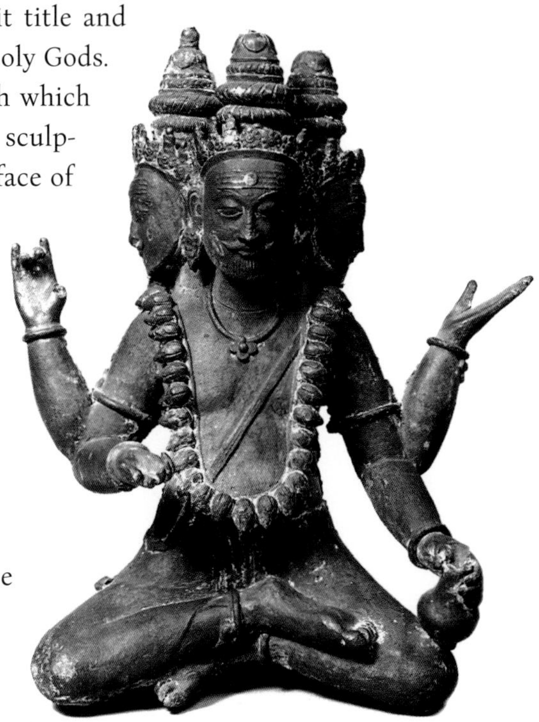

114 *Brahma*, Benares, late 18th century. Zinc alloy, 32 × 19.5 × 22 cm. Presented to the India Museum, London by Sir Charles Wilkins, Librarian of the East India Company. Victoria and Albert Museum, London, 912(IS)

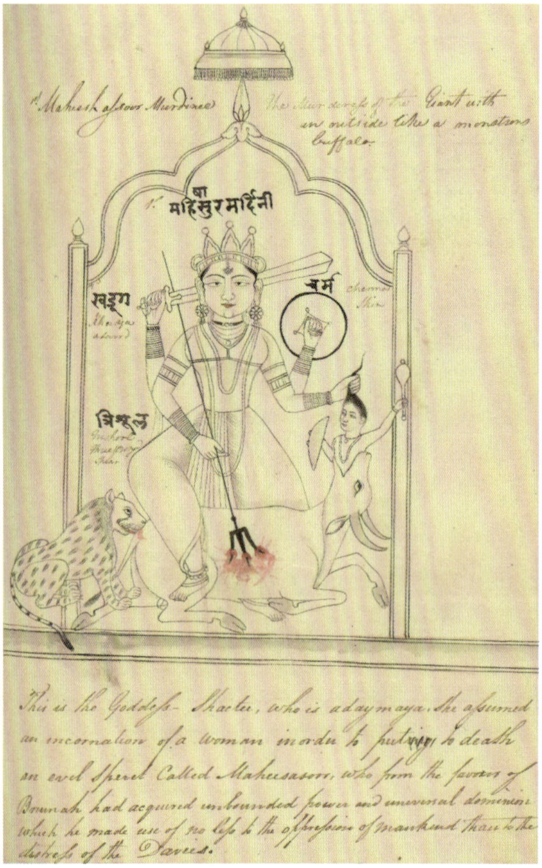

the decades around 1800 actually published his findings.[21] For example, Colonel Alexander Walker made an "Account of various Hindoo deities" in Gujarat in 1806 and employed an Indian artist to make illustrations and provide descriptions for thirty-six of the eighty-eight listed deities, such as of Durga (fig. 115).[22] Yet Walker's findings remained in manuscript form and Moor ended up being responsible for publishing aspects of his studies, specifically his outcry against "Hindu Infanticide."[23]

The same can be said for Company officials who compiled and illustrated information about Hindu gods beyond Moor's immediate network. In the north Indian region of Awadh, Colonel Jean-Baptiste Gentil and Colonel Antoine-Louis-Henri Polier hired Indian artists to depict Hindu gods, the former alongside ceremonies and practices of devotion and the latter in two volumes, one deity to a page.[24] In South India, Colonel Colin Mackenzie, as the Surveyor General first of Mysore and then of India, amassed information on religion for the colonial state with the aid of Indian assistants.[25] These projects ranged in their volume, method, and purpose, from antiquarian compilation to colonial domination, but they shared a desire to picture the Hindu gods. Nevertheless, they remained in manuscript rather than printed form and thus achieved only limited circulation.

In contrast, *The Hindu Pantheon* was disseminated to a wide market. Three hundred folio volumes were initially available for sale in London at three guineas each, and two hundred were shipped to India to sell at forty rupees, with a hundred additional sets of plates.[26] A further one hundred volumes were bound in calf by Joseph Bell of Oxford Street and embossed with gold deities.[27] In India, subscribers included Company officials, gentlemen, women, and prominent Indian businessmen and philanthropists who were based in Bombay, Baroda, Madras, and Goa.[28] Moor also gave copies to scholars including Baron Denon, the Duke of Wellington, and institutions like the Royal Academy, the Asiatic Society of Bombay, the Royal Society, and the Royal Asiatic Society.[29]

Moor's Company colleagues and Asiatic Society publications provided one of the networks that undergirded the publication of *The Hindu Pantheon* from its production to its

115 Drawing of Durga, in Alexander Walker, "An Account of Various Hindoo Deities," Gujarat, ca. 1806, p. 411. National Library of Scotland, Edinburgh, Walker of Bowlands Papers, MS. 13903

intellectual sources and visual illustrations, which expanded the book from a regional to a pan-Indic disquisition. Many of the objects Moor borrowed were also part of a Company aesthetic, in which officials commissioned Indian artists to transform representations of the gods into a format legible to a British audience, such as by perspective, modeling, and simplifying iconographies. In the next section, I will delve deeper into the question of aesthetics. For Moor's book makes an argument about picturing the Hindu gods in images, in comparison to earlier authors in the Asiatic Society who emphasized texts.

PICTURING A PHILOSOPHER'S PANTHEON

The Hindu Pantheon portrayed the religious philosophy of the emanation of many gods from one godhead that those in the Asiatic Society associated with pantheistic religions;[30] however, it did so in visual form. This began with the frontispiece, which dramatizes this Hindu religious philosophy across media (see fig. 110). Drawn by the "excellent engraver" Luigi Schiavonetti, the design was based on a gray wash drawing by the Royal Academy-trained artist Moses Haughton (fig. 116).[31] Haughton's drawing was, in turn, based on an eighteenth-century bronze sculpture of the Hindu god Ganesha that Moor had bought during his residence in western India (fig. 117).[32] Wilkins advised on the addition of the Sanskrit *aum*, which evoked eternity through the holy sound of the word. Adjoined to Ganesha's shrine, the word is encircled by a snake eating its tail in an ouroboros. Associated with Hindu, Egyptian, Greek, and Gnostic mythology, this snake also signaled the project's potential to be compared with other religious systems.[33]

For Moor, the word *aum* represented the unity of all gods in its sacred syllable. He quoted from Henry Thomas Colebrook that *aum* "intends every deity . . . is only One Deity," at times known as *Brahm* (the vast one), *Deva* (God), and *Adhyatma* (the superintending soul).[34] All-pervading, this Vedic incantation of sound could not be visualized – "Of Him . . . there is no image" – and Moor explicitly gave "no representation in the engraved portion" of his book to illustrate the "self-existing, incomprehensible Spirit" that he defined as a monotheistic god.[35] Nevertheless this spirit split into a pantheon of deities, like "the sun" into "rays or emanations from his own essence." Moor identified these emanations with Vedanta in India and related them to Platonism in Greece; Vedanta was also associated with, and to some considered the source of, other philosophies of monism, or oneness, in this period.[36]

Rays of light stream from the snake-encircled *aum* as if embodying the diversification of the all-encompassing spirit from the sun into many forms. One appears to be the formation of Ganesha himself; the apex of his shrine punctures the circle as if actualizing his creation from light firsthand. *Aum* and Ganesha are both invoked auspiciously at the

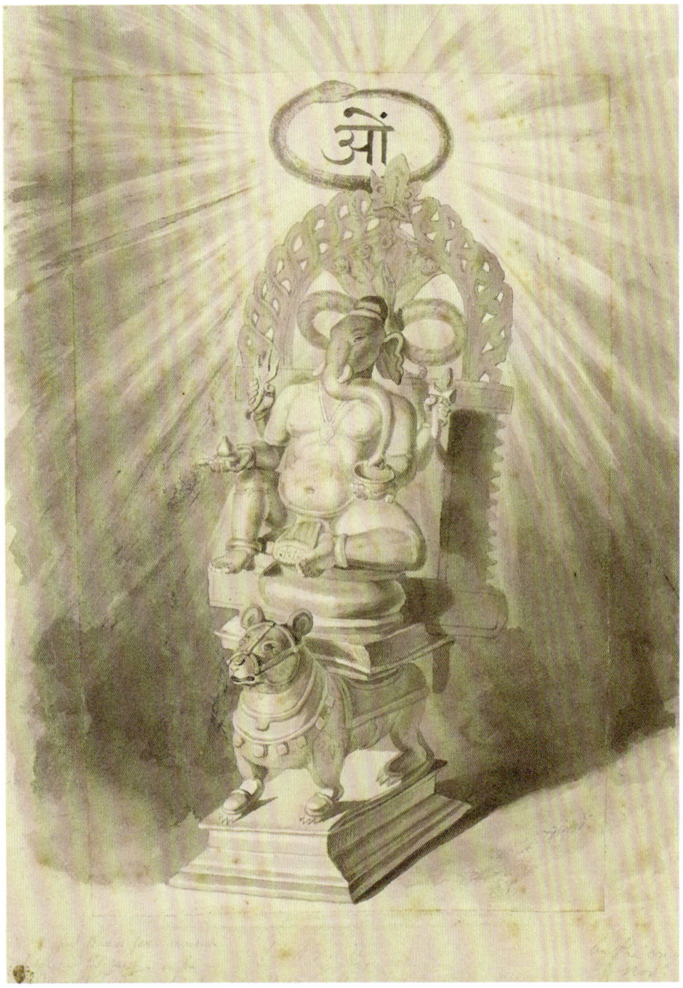

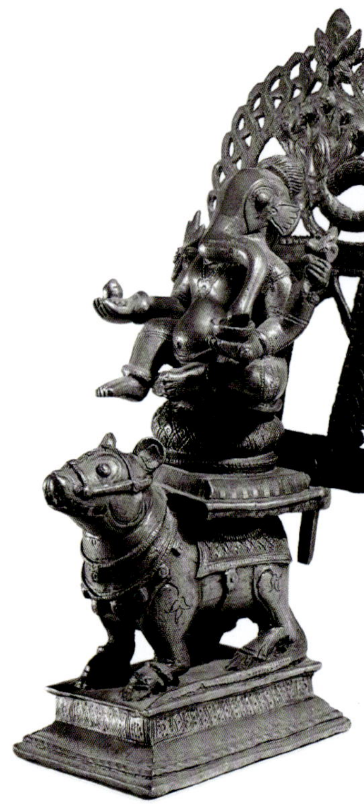

beginning of Sanskrit manuscripts, the latter in a text mantra as well as in a visual form (see fig. 99), but Moor uses Ganesha as a hinge between the unified world of a single aniconic spirit and its diversification into a panoply of iconic ones.[37] For Ganesha too was considered a summary figure.[38] As defined by William Jones, Ganesha was "a word composed of *esa*, the governor or leader, and *gana*, or a company of deities."[39] To his followers, the Ganipatyas, who notably worshipped the sun, Moor wrote that Ganesha united all of the attributes of the Deity in his person.[40] If Ganesha is an all-encompassing leader – hatched with shadow and light in the engraving – a container, his company of deities spills into hundreds of engraved outlines appended to the book.

The frontispiece thus stages a relationship between the formless and the formed, text and image, which is paralleled in the opening paragraphs of Moor's text:

116 Moses Haughton, drawings for *The Hindu Pantheon*, London, 1805–10, frontispiece. Gray wash, ink, and watercolor on paper, 43 × 30.5 × 4.2 cm. British Museum, London, Edward Moor Collection, 1940,0713,0.251(1)

117 *Ganesha*, Maharashtra, 18th century. Bronze, h. 29.2 cm. British Museum, London, Edward Moor Collection, 1940,0716.1.ab

> The religious doctrines of the Hindus may be divided into exoteric and esoteric; the first is preached to the vulgar, the second known only to a select number: and while the Brahmans are admitted to possess a considerable portion of unadulterated physical and moral truths, the exoteric religion of the Hindus, in general, consists in gross idolatry and irrational superstition.[41]

Moor staged Hinduism as divided between religion (esoteric, monotheistic, aniconic) and mythology (exoteric, pantheistic, iconic). While he condemned the "idolatry" of the latter, the religious doctrines that expound the esoteric or "incomprehensible Spirit" of the former are not in any way the focus of the book. Rather, it is the "amazing mass of mythology" and specifically artists' "rage for personification" that occupy the tome.[42]

This "amazing mass" takes the form of outline engravings, which fill 104 of the book's 105 plates. Each delineated a single deity's portion – and partialness via the blank interior – that came together into a single "Spirit," but individually they also served to personify myriad concepts and allegories. "The poet," Moor wrote, "at a loss for words to express so recondite a conception, has necessarily recourse to metaphor for illustration: the painter, at no loss, pursues the allegory, and fills up the ideal outline of the poet."[43] In this reading, the artist recognizes the outline of each god to embody a meaningful symbol or story.

Moor championed the "painter" and visual personification, which differed from those founders of the Asiatic Society absorbed in the "poet's" literary kind. The tenets of Jones's essay "On the Gods of Greece, Italy, and India," written in 1784 and published in 1788, a few decades earlier than *The Hindu Pantheon*, should sound familiar from Moor's locutions. Jones claimed that "numberless divinities have been created solely by the magick of poetry; whose essential business it is, to personify the most abstract notions" alongside "metaphors and allegories of moralists and metaphysicians."[44]

These gods, though dispersed visually and verbally across Greece, Italy, and India, according to Jones (like Moor's "rays") could be "melted" into each other to identify their common origin in the divinity of the sun.[45] As Moor wrote:

> The characters of all the Pagan Deities, male and female, melt into each other, and at last into one or two; for it seems a well-founded opinion, that the whole crowd of gods and goddesses in ancient Rome, and modern Varanes [Varanasi or Benares], mean only the powers of Nature, and principally those of the Sun, expressed in a variety of ways, and by a multitude of fancy names.[46]

Jones sought to understand society from its "symbolical representations" of deities, which could be read like language and tied to other mythologies, each in a process of metamorphosis away from an original universal.[47] He dismissed a hierarchical theory

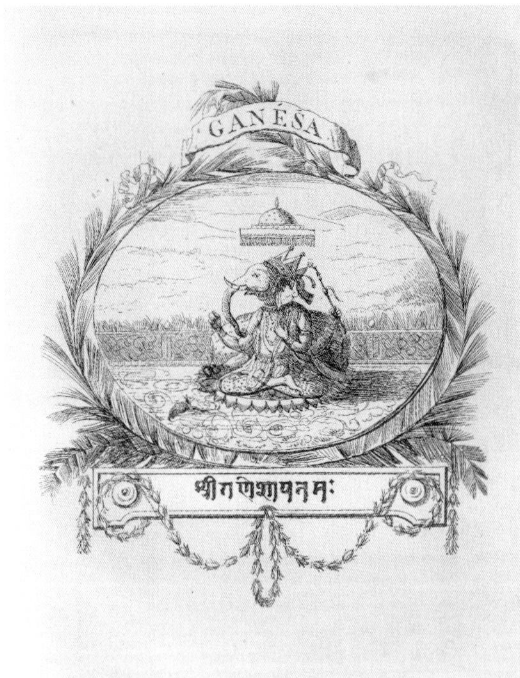

of gods and mythology evolving from one society to the next, and from the east to the west. In the process, he also established an antiquity that preceded Christian chronology and had the potential to threaten, in his words, the "truth of our national religion," to which I will return in the last section of this chapter.[48]

Jones recognized the possibility that representations of gods might be worshipped as gods, and the fear that icons could become idols is latent in his essay and in the research of the Asiatic Society. In 1785, Warren Hastings, then Governor General of Bengal, in his preface to Wilkins's translation of the Bhagavad Gita compared the sanctity of the text with the idolatrous representation of gods. The Gita, he noted, was the "single exception, among the known religions of mankind, of a theology accurately corresponding with that of the Christian dispensation." But this theology had one "blemish." The false note struck by the Gita was Indian philosophers' "attempt to describe spiritual existences by images which appertain to corporeal forms."[49] Jones, who had written his essay the year before, had included one iconic image per deity discussed, like Ganesha (see fig. 118); but his project did not pictorially witness the melting together of deities into one universal form or their dispersal into many that he described in his essay.

In contrast, Moor took the identification of the "corporeal forms" of Hindu spiritual existence as the subject, the very core, of his book. Parting with Jones's and Wilkins's focus on text, Moor sought to understand the society he encountered through "pictures and visual objects" and to foreground the visual melting and dispersal of deities. As early as his 1794 *Narrative*, he had confronted the worship of iconic images in one of his appended "Notes" through an infamous antiquarian text that included reference to Hindu devotion, Richard Payne Knight's *An Account of the Remains of the Worship of Priapus* (1786).[50] Knight's privately printed pamphlet had created havoc in British circles because of its attempt to understand the worship of the phallus across multiple cultures and religions through historical case studies and illustrations of explicit objects.[51] In parallel to Jones's study, the engravings allowed for comparison between fragments of erotic sculpture from classical as well as Indian antiquity, such as an eleventh-century relief displaying an orgiastic scene from Charles Townley's collection.[52]

118 "Ganesa," in Sir William Jones, "On the Gods of Greece, Italy, and India," *Asiatick Researches*, vol. 1 (Calcutta: The Society, 1788), after p. 226. Beinecke Rare Book and Manuscript Library, General Collection, Yale University, New Haven, Connecticut

Knight relished his illicit subject, but also emphasized a theory of art based on the evolution of "symbolic" forms through time, which simultaneously connected religions through form and archetype and argued for tolerance.[53] He regarded symbols, particularly those expressed in material form, as a significant force of culture to be understood in context, with tolerance, which Moor highlighted in his note: "The forms and ceremonials of a religion are not always to be understood in their direct and obvious sense; but are to be considered as symbolical representations of some hidden meaning, which may be extremely wise and just, though the symbols themselves, to those who know not their true signification, may appear in the highest degree absurd and extravagant."[54] While Knight discussed the phallic form in folk traditions, the "Dii Lares" (household gods) of the Romans, Moor was drawn to the "Dii Lares" of Hindus, the *kuladevata*, and tracked the relationship between their forms and identification.[55] These sculptures emblematize Moor's attention to "symbolic" forms transforming over time, "melt[ing] into each other" as Jones wrote about literature, but in material images, as Knight published.

Moor established that there was a relationship between the symbolism of a deity and its particular visual iterations. Numerous objects that he chose to engrave represented portable deities in western India that had been cast in bronze for distribution to pilgrims and home shrines (see fig. 86). He took pains to include multiple forms of a god's image and did not edit for clarity's sake. To Moor, the goddess Durga slaying the buffalo demon (*Mahishasuramardini*), for example, was first considered as a "symbolical representation," an emblem of Active Virtue (*Durga*) slaying Vice (*Mahishasura*), and then as "different characters" of the great goddess.[56] Moor considered each of her images as distinct, such as in his Plate 35 (fig. 119; see fig. 85): "Two brass casts, about seven inches high, of Durga in the act before described: that four-handed is old, and a very spirited composition.... The eight-handed subject is modern and clumsy.... Durga has no lion or tiger in the action; and this subject, may, perhaps, represent some other exploit of the goddess."[57] These images show a goddess in the act of destroying a buffalo demon, yet Moor attended to each as an individual representation to acknowledge that Durga, a pan-Indic goddess, could in fact be a local goddess, as discussed in Chapter Three, such as Bhavani of Tuljapur or Saptashringi of Vani. The single representation of Durga in Alexander Walker's compendium (see fig. 115) suddenly registers as an emblem rather than an individual, a letter rather than the sentence. Walker's sole image and short definition differs from Moor's capacious expansion. Moor included four images of Durga killing the buffalo demon in a section of at least thirty depictions of the great goddess in "different characters" (Plates 33–43) discussed over fifty pages.

Moor reveled in the extent of a deity's forms and he did not reduce their representation to those most prevalent or well-known. In fact, he did the opposite, as with

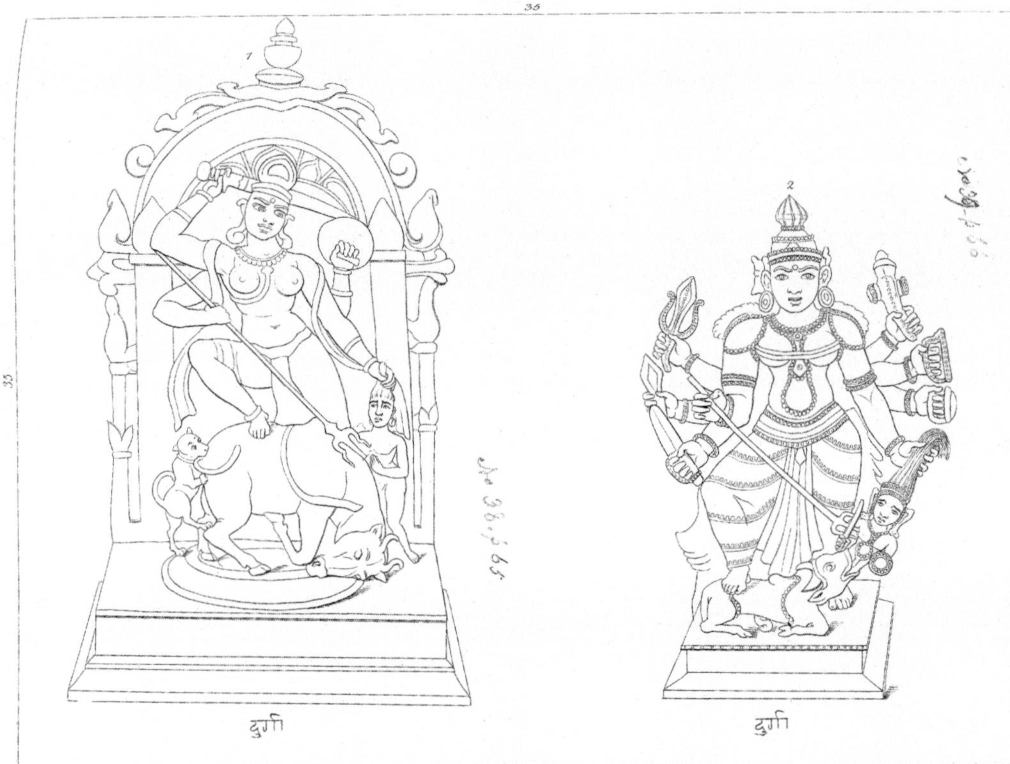

DURGĀ, or *ACTIVE VIRTUE*, slaying the monster MAHISHĀSURA, or *VICE* personified.

the example of Durga just discussed, which confused readers. A critic for the *Edinburgh Review* noted that "little attention . . . has been paid to keeping the subjects distinct." From this critic's perspective, Moor had prodigiously collected hundreds of paintings and sculptures – of which "the enchanting grace and elegant contour of the female form are well delineated" – but had failed to collate a standard iconography. According to him, Moor could have consulted, and even translated, pertinent resources like the "Matsya Purana," which "exhibits a very full code of laws for the guidance of the artist," in his book. Similarly, "a work in the Imperial Library at Paris," he wrote, included a paragraph of text explaining the iconography and the "character" of the deity that "follow the different proportions of his limbs and features" according to each form of the god.[58]

The *Edinburgh Review* critic was right; iconographies and descriptions of the Hindu gods were available in Europe and India. Numerous manuscripts from this period contained images of gods with attendant descriptions, primarily from South India. In the missionary text *Dieux des Indiens* (Gods of India), the blue-skinned "divinity and giant"

119 "Durga, or Active Virtue, slaying the monster Mahishasura, or Vice personified," in Edward Moor, *The Hindu Pantheon* (London: J. Johnson, 1810), pl. 35. British Museum, London, Edward Moor Collection, 1940,0713,0.253

Ravana is described as having ten heads and twenty arms, though this did not prevent his destruction by the Hindu god Rama.[59] Four-armed, weapon-toting Indra is named and compared to Jupiter in another manuscript from the Coromandel Coast.[60] Contemporaneous Marathi texts such as the *Shri Martanda Vijaya* also relayed instructions for making representations of deities such as Khandoba who could be created from "gold . . . silver, or copper . . . stone or clay" in "two types for meditation."[61]

While Moor does not refer to such manuscripts or treatises in Europe and India, he did cite readily available printed publications. Pierre Sonnerat's *Voyages aux Indes orientales . . .* (1782) and John Bell's *New Pantheon* (1790), for example, provided models for concise pictorial and written descriptions of gods in both Indic and classical contexts. Both displayed illustrations and texts in encyclopedic fashion to detail the iconography and mythology of each deity explained. Sonnerat, for example, described Vishnu's *Matsya* incarnation as a fish to save the world (fig. 120). Bell included descriptions of each deity ordered alphabetically and had them engraved as emblematic coins in outline on his

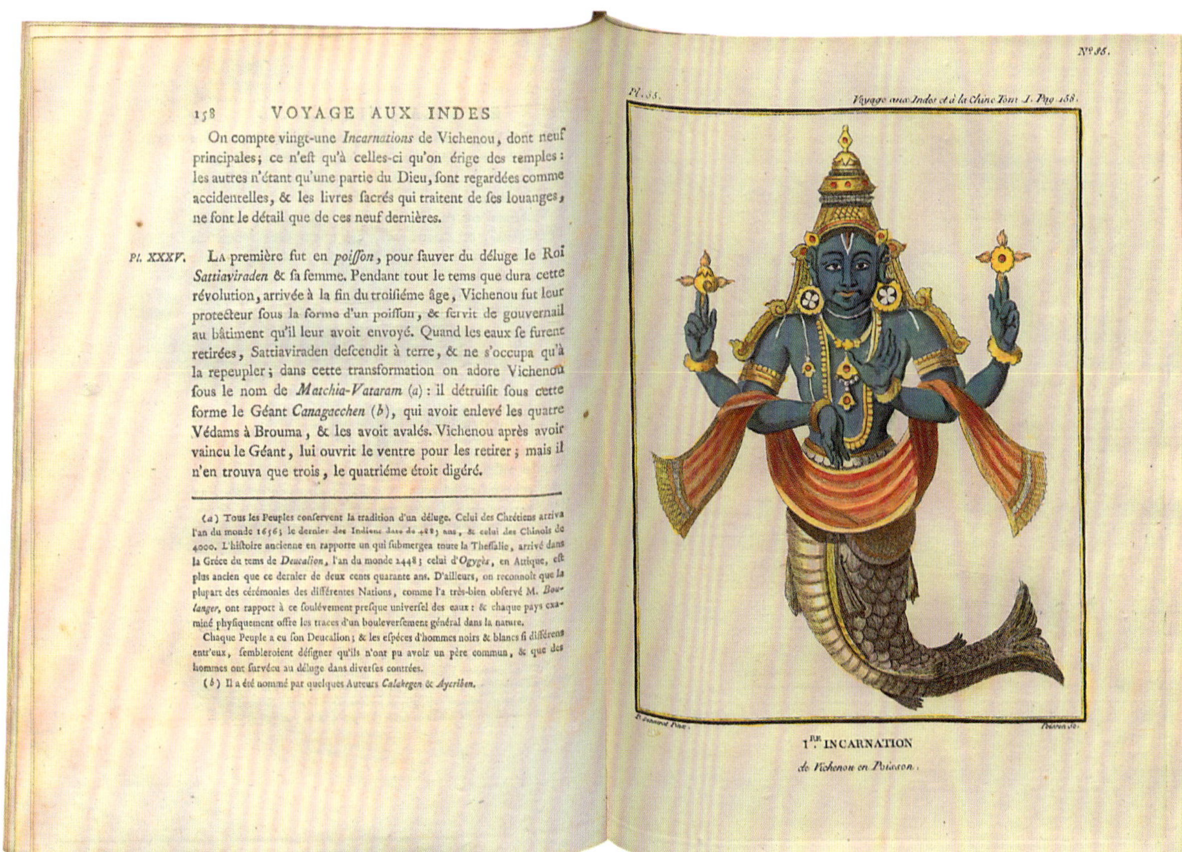
158 VOYAGE AUX INDES

On compte vingt-une *Incarnations* de Vichenou, dont neuf principales; ce n'eſt qu'à celles-ci qu'on érige des temples: les autres n'étant qu'une partie du Dieu, ſont regardées comme accidentelles, & les livres ſacrés qui traitent de ſes louanges, ne ſont le détail que de ces neuf dernières.

Pl. XXXV. La première fut en *poiſſon*, pour ſauver du déluge le Roi *Sattiaviraden* & ſa femme. Pendant tout le tems que dura cette révolution, arrivée à la fin du troiſiéme âge, Vichenou fut leur protecteur ſous la forme d'un poiſſon, & ſervit de gouvernail au bâtiment qu'il leur avoit envoyé. Quand les eaux ſe furent retirées, Sattiaviraden deſcendit à terre, & ne s'occupa qu'à la repeupler; dans cette transformation on adore Vichenou ſous le nom de *Matchia-Vataram* (*a*): il détruiſit ſous cette forme le Géant *Canagacchen* (*b*), qui avoit enlevé les quatre Védams à Brouma, & les avoit avalés. Vichenou après avoir vaincu le Géant, lui ouvrit le ventre pour les retirer; mais il n'en trouva que trois, le quatriéme étoit digéré.

(*a*) Tous les Peuples conſervent la tradition d'un déluge. Celui des Chrétiens arriva l'an du monde 1656; le dernier des Indiens date de [illegible] ans, & celui des Chinois de 4000. L'hiſtoire ancienne en rapporte un qui ſubmergea toute la Theſſalie, arrivé dans la Gréce du tems de *Deucalion*, l'an du monde 2448; celui d'*Ogygès*, en Attique, eſt plus ancien que ce dernier de deux cents quarante ans. D'ailleurs, on reconnoît que la plupart des cérémonies des différentes Nations, comme l'a très-bien obſervé M. *Boulanger*, ont rapport à ce ſoulévement preſque univerſel des eaux: & chaque pays examiné phyſiquement offre les traces d'un bouleverſement général dans la nature.

Chaque Peuple a eu ſon Deucalion; & les eſpéces d'hommes noirs & blancs ſi différens entr'eux, ſembleroient déſigner qu'ils n'ont pu avoir un père commun, & que des hommes ont ſurvécu au déluge dans diverſes contrées.

(*b*) Il a été nommé par quelques Auteurs *Calakegen* & *Ayeriben*.

120 "1st Incarnation of Vishnu as a Fish," in Pierre Sonnerat, *Voyages aux Indes Orientales et à la Chine . . .* (Paris, 1782), pl. 35. Engraving with hand coloring on paper, 26 cm. ETH-Bibliothek Zürich, Rar 7115 plates.[62] Moor cited these works; he could have followed their lead and collated a standard iconography.

However, Moor neither attended to European taxonomies of classical mythology nor their organization of Indian mythology in the presentation of text and images in *The Hindu Pantheon*. Neither did he yield to Indian textual proscriptions, nor to the craftsman's process for making correct, proportionate representations. Rather, he was motivated by other members of the Asiatic Society with whom he worked in the East India Company, the philosophical and antiquarian concepts he encountered in texts and images, and the "amazing" diversity of materials that he collected in western India. His book renders visible the fracturing of a single "spiritual existence" into the "corporeal forms" of the gods into outlines as they transformed over time, melted into one another as well as dispersed across India, and through him, to England.

A PANTHEISTIC BOOK OF NEOCLASSICAL OUTLINES

Moor intellectually engaged with a philosophical dialogue about the Hindu gods current in the Asiatic Society in late eighteenth-century India, but he made it material through his publisher Joseph Johnson after he returned to London in 1805.[63] The members of this "little Society," as Johnson called it in a letter of June 1796 to Moor, which included artists, writers, and radicals, held dissenting views that welcomed Moor's approach to the Hindu gods and impacted his publications in turn, especially regarding neoclassical design.[64]

How Moor befriended Johnson is unknown, but Johnson's firm published his first book, *A Narrative*, in 1794, and his second, *The Hindu Pantheon*, in 1810.[65] Johnson's catalogue lacks other books about India, but the journal that he published, *The Analytical Review* (1788–98), served as a forum for "free Enquirers," in the words of his obituarist John Aikin.[66] In its pages, authors evoked Hindu myth as an antidote to the strictures of the Church of England and the mores of government conservatism.[67] Garnered from a range of cultures, mythology could be a means to resist orthodoxy, to promote republicanism, and potentially to enable a new syncretic mythology to be imagined from diverse forms, which aligned with Moor's program.

Letters between Johnson and Moor indicate a friendship sustained by dining and selling books together. In the same letter from June 1796, after Moor had returned to India with his new wife Elizabeth Lynn, Johnson discussed the people whom they "used to meet" at his house and notified Moor that four trunks of books, mostly related to science, had been sent to him in India for commercial distribution.[68] They sustained a friendship; when Moor returned to England in 1805, he dined at Johnson's house along with Henry Fuseli and William Godwin, "the celebrated author."[69] This meeting, or a like one, could have inaugurated Moor's relationship with Fuseli, who promoted an expansive neoclassicism as the Professor of Painting and Keeper of the Schools at the Royal Academy. Through Fuseli, he probably met the draftsman Moses Haughton who resided in Fuseli's house from 1803 to 1819 and came to design the plates for *The Hindu Pantheon*, which were published by Johnson on January 1, 1809.[70]

Fuseli, like Johnson, had a capacious appetite for mythology that aligned with Moor's approach. For instance, Fuseli embraced Neoplatonism, which paralleled the oneness of monism and Vedanta that structured Moor's book. He translated the Greek Neoplatonic philosopher Proclus in Winckelmann's *Reflections on the Painting and Sculpture of the Greeks* (1765) as saying that arts are inspired not only by nature "but still more, something superior to nature; ideal beauties, brain-born images."[71] He was also attuned to the classical relationship between the arts of painting and poetry, and the role of personification in each, as Moor had identified in Hindu mythology and arts. In the first volume of Johnson's *Analytical Review* (1788), Fuseli translated the well-known Latin phrase that encapsulated the visual qualities of poetry and the textual aspects of pictures – *ut pictura poesis* – as "Painting is silent poetry / And Poetry is a speaking picture."[72] Similarly to Moor, alongside Neoplatonic philosophy Fuseli was as fascinated by vernacular devotion and its relationship to what he saw as the raw and base in culture. As discussed in connection with Payne Knight, the finds of classical Rome (particularly at Pompeii and Herculaneum) had disturbed the quality of "noble simplicity and quiet grandeur" by which Winckelmann had defined antique arts. The priapic Dii Lares of Knight's inquiry not only gave form to sensuality but also identified them as present in cultures across the globe. In Andrei Pop's terms, these finds forced Europeans to recognize that they "belonged to a series of cultures discontinuous in space and time: Ancient Greece and Rome were seemingly all of a sudden, as distant from Paris and London as Tibet and the Andes."[73]

In this period, the temporality and geography of antiquity expanded. Jones's essay "On the Gods of Greece, Italy, and India" proffered such a comparative philosophy of religions and united their antiquity. He spliced Neoplatonism, Vedanta, and vernacular devotion together in his juxtaposition of gods, which Fuseli appraised in *The Analytical Review* (1790):

> The design of this essay is, to point out the resemblance between the popular worship of the old Greeks and Italians, and that of the Hindus. – All mythology, our author observes, may be traced to four principle sources. 1st. Historical or natural truth, perverted into fable. 2d. A wild admiration of the heavenly bodies. 3d. The magic of poetry, "whose business it is to personify the most abstract notions, and to place a nymph or genius in every grove." 4th. The metaphors and

> allegories of moralists and metaphysicians; from which abundant fountain, "the richest and noblest stream" is . . . [the] tale of Psyche, or the progress of the soul.[74]

Fuseli would drink from such a fountain of "metaphors and allegories" to interpret deities from a range of antiquities in his sketches, including the Indian god Camadeva and the dog-headed Egyptian deity Anubis praying to the star Sirius for rain.[75]

Nevertheless, Fuseli united these novel subjects in an academic style rooted in neoclassical modeling and design, much as did another artist in their circle, John Flaxman. Flaxman became the Professor of Sculpture at the Royal Academy in 1810; he is credited with the popularity of "Outline" for delineating forms at the turn of the nineteenth century.[76] In dialogue with classical reliefs and vase painting, Flaxman reduced compositions to their essence in flowing lines on plain ground, but he applied this neoclassical aesthetic to works that ranged from illustrations of classical texts like Homer's *Odyssey* to modern designs for Wedgwood ceramics, which expanded the style's reach.

Flaxman applied his spare neoclassical mode to antiquities that paralleled – or preceded – the classical like the Indian and Egyptian, on which Fuseli also drew, but he explicitly connected neoclassicism with empire.[77] The rediscovery of classical antiquity coincided with British mercantile and colonial enterprises, which led to the discovery of antiquities across the globe.[78] Flaxman's practice pulled together the artistic study of Asia with its conquest.[79] He lectured on Indian, Persian, and Egyptian arts to students at the Royal Academy, and commemorated Company officials in marble throughout the Indian subcontinent and in Britain. His use of a neoclassical mode collapsed the distance between Britain's new empire and that of Rome's.[80]

Within this "little Society," which used neoclassical design to picture arts far outside of the classical world, Moor chose to depict the majority of his plates for *The Hindu Pantheon* in neoclassical outline. He hired Fuseli's draftsman, Moses Haughton, to design the illustrations, from the richly shaded frontispiece to the hundreds that followed in 104 plates.[81] While outline was less expensive than the twenty guineas Moor paid to Schiavonetti to engrave the frontispiece,[82] it was also a conscious choice. On the tracing paper that remains affixed to many of the paintings printed in the book, Moor wrote instructions such as "Outline" (fig. 121a and b). Such a command was often accompanied by specifics such as "outline in the manner of the original – reduced to four to a plate – handsome faces."[83] Haughton excerpted the deities from the landscape of the paintings, as in this image, which demonstrates that the outline outweighed the "original." The dark outlines that the Jaipur artists used to define forms must have stood out through tracing paper and eased the method of translation from painting to engraving, much like the manner of the Poona painter employed by Moor. That painter even made a series of draw-

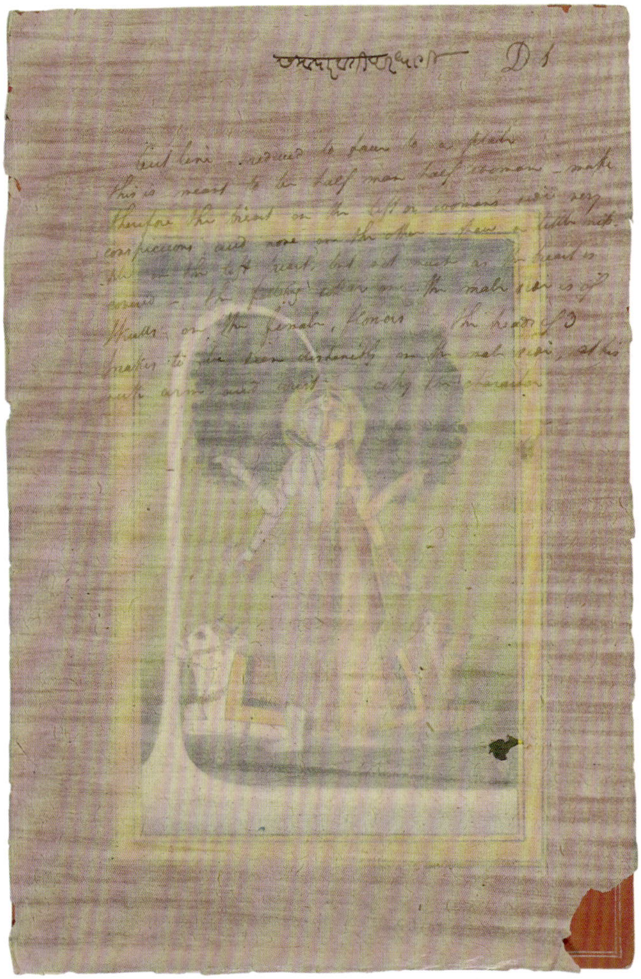

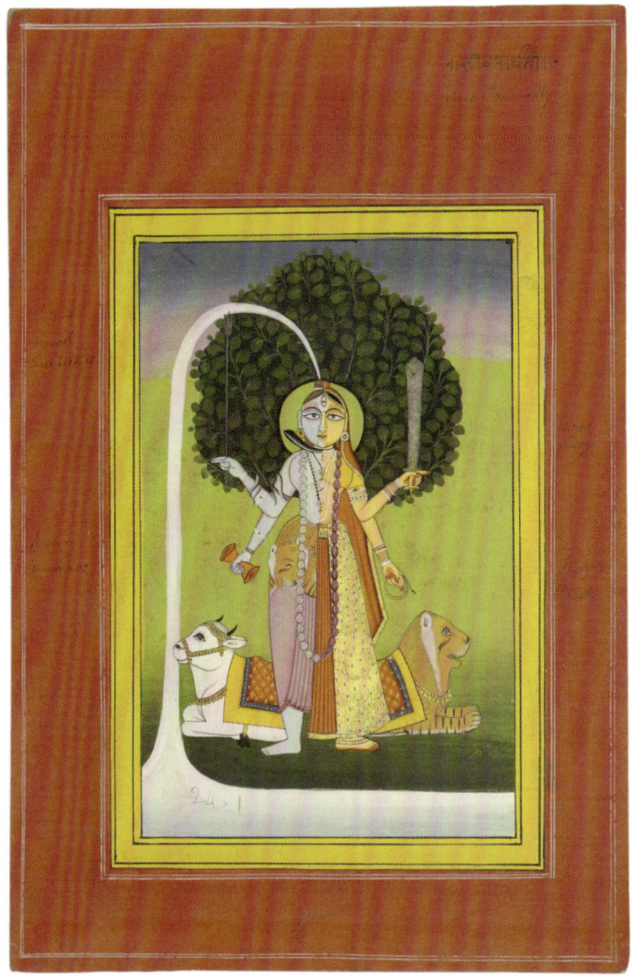

ings solely in black line as if to prepare them for transcription (fig. 122).[84] The same type of transparent paper that overlaid the Jaipur painting would have been used for tracing the image that lay underneath as well. There are tracings of Haughton's drawings, or the related prints, that Moor or someone else made to replace ones that had gone missing in one of Moor's personal copies of *The Hindu Pantheon*, such as of Plate 7 (see fig. 112).[85]

Haughton interpreted Moor's instructions and transformed the paintings and sculptures into gray wash drawings for the engravers, though he "threw in a little more taste and elegance than the originals chiefly warranted," in Moor's opinion.[86] He also experimented with techniques other than outline, especially for sculpture. With gray, ochre, and white wash to evoke three dimensions, Haughton modeled a striking bronze Bhadra Kali, weapons raised and linked, radiating power from hands to crown (fig. 123).[87] This

121 a and b *Ardhanarisvara* with instructions on attached tracing paper, Jaipur and London, ca. 1800. Opaque watercolor and gold on paper, 31 × 20.6 cm. British Museum, London, Edward Moor Collection, 1940,0713,0.79

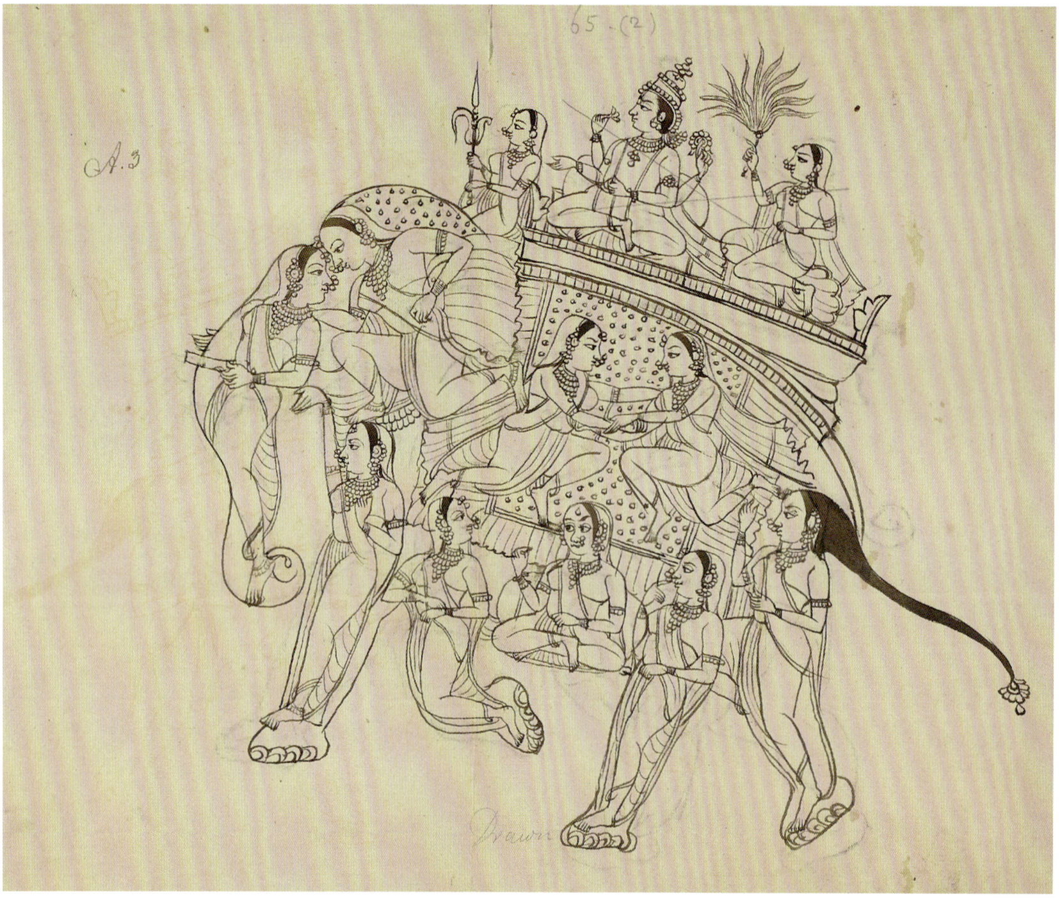

was not used in the book; as noted earlier, except for the frontispiece, all the plates were in outline, including the final rendition of this image in Plate 28.

There was a philosophical reason for Moor's use of outline, as I discussed in the preceding section, and an artistic one. Both situated Moor's book within a circle of artists in London invested in an expansive neoclassicism. However, outline also placed the publication in dialogue with a range of eighteenth-century publications related to the art, ethnography, and mythology of the classical world, such as Bell's *New Pantheon* (1790), mentioned earlier. A spare, even scientific, manner of outline for illustrations supported these authors' claim to veracity, which fused with the aesthetic revival of the classical world seen in Flaxman and Fuseli's art.[88]

However, antiquarians often took the outline a step further into naturalistic rendering. They translated two-dimensional sources into the appearance of three-dimensional shade, as we saw reversed in Moor's *Hindu Pantheon* (see fig. 110), with a fully hatched

122 *Krishna on an Elephant Composed of Women*, Poona, ca. 1800.
Black ink on paper, 37.5 × 49 cm. British Museum, London,
Edward Moor Collection, 1940,0713,0.244

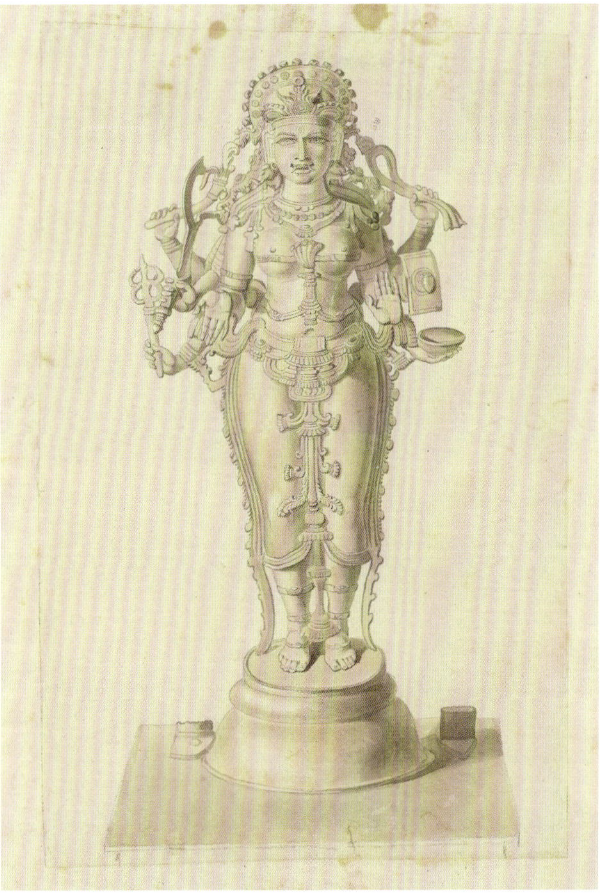

Ganesha in the frontispiece splitting into the multitude of outlined deities in the plates. In their *Pantheon* (1787), François Pomey and the translator Andrew Tooke described the god Jupiter according to his attributes and physical descriptions, which are synthesized in an engraving of a richly sculpted figure in a temple (fig. 124). However, the authors added information that would not have been visible in a temple. Jupiter's other guises and "fashions" are displayed in the coins and medals drawn at the bottom. These material resources are rendered in outline as if a guide to envision the "fabulous histories of the Heathen gods and most illustrious heroes" of antiquity in their myriad forms.[89]

The titling of *The Hindu Pantheon* suggests that if the Hindu "court of the holy gods" (*shri sarva deva sabha*) could be translated as a classical temple, a Pantheon, then so could the delineation of deities.[90] Neoclassical outline came to accommodate pantheons of gods far beyond the classical Mediterranean in an "international style," according to Robert Rosenblum, much as the picturesque aesthetic unified global landscape painting.[91]

123 Moses Haughton, drawings for *The Hindu Pantheon*, London, 1805–10, f. 27. Gray wash, ink, and watercolor on paper, 43 × 30.5 cm. British Museum, London, Edward Moor Collection, 1940,0713,0.251(27)

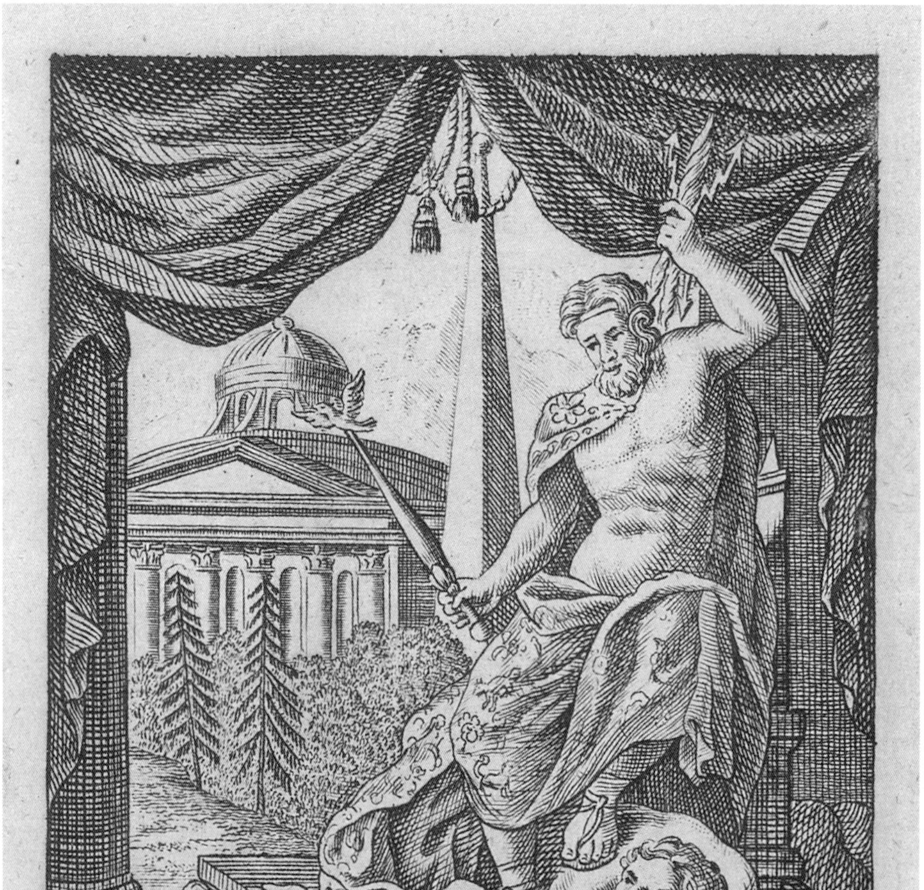

124 "Jupiter," in François Pomey, *The Pantheon: representing the fabulous histories of the heathen gods, and most illustrious heroes . . . translated by Andrew Tooke* (London: J. F. & C. Rivington et al., 1787), 10, pl. 2. Beinecke Rare Book and Manuscript Library, General Collection, Yale University, New Haven, Connecticut

Thus when S. Bartholomaeo Paulinus, for example, sought to illustrate his 1791 publication *Systema Brahmanicum*, his engraver turned to the spare outline manner to depict the god Brahma below and two Indian ascetics above (fig. 125), as Alexander Walker had similarly commissioned an Indian artist to render Durga in his manuscript on the Hindu gods (see fig. 115).[92] Other manners of engraving existed, such as Jones's illustration of Ganesha (see fig. 118), and Vishnu's incarnations included in Athanasius Kircher's *China Illustrata* (1667) were based on Indian artworks.[93] Moor knew these models, yet it is to the neoclassical one that he turned.

Moor had proximity to artists who promoted linear engraving and was cognizant of its association with classical mythology and arts, but there are additional, pedagogical, reasons why he might have chosen the medium of outline. Neoclassical outline helped artists decipher antiquities other than the Greek. By unifying diverse arts in line, it invited comparison among compositions – such as sculpture or deities – and was thus an ideal educational tool. In *Thoughts on Outline* (1796), George Cumberland identified the "inestimable value of chaste outline" with those "wrought by the Greeks and other ancient Artists," but he also acknowledged that even an "incorrect Outline" seen in Hindu pictures, as well as Etruscan and Egyptian works, could reveal "just action and composed dignity of attitude." Outline, like a graphic frame for a range of arts, could be a means for modern artists to see, and therefore to "create finer forms."[94]

The Hindu Pantheon was intended to be an accurate model for artists to copy. According to Moor, "Hindu artists" and "the amateur or artist of Europe" would find instruction in the "graceful models of outline" in his "plates." "Mr. Haughton," he wrote, paid "the greatest attention . . . in taking the portraits of the images and the drawings of the pictures." He insisted that they could "be relied on as faithful representations of the original subjects; and will, I hope, be deemed curious in themselves, as well as possessing, in many instances, a highly creditable portion of elegance in their execution."[95]

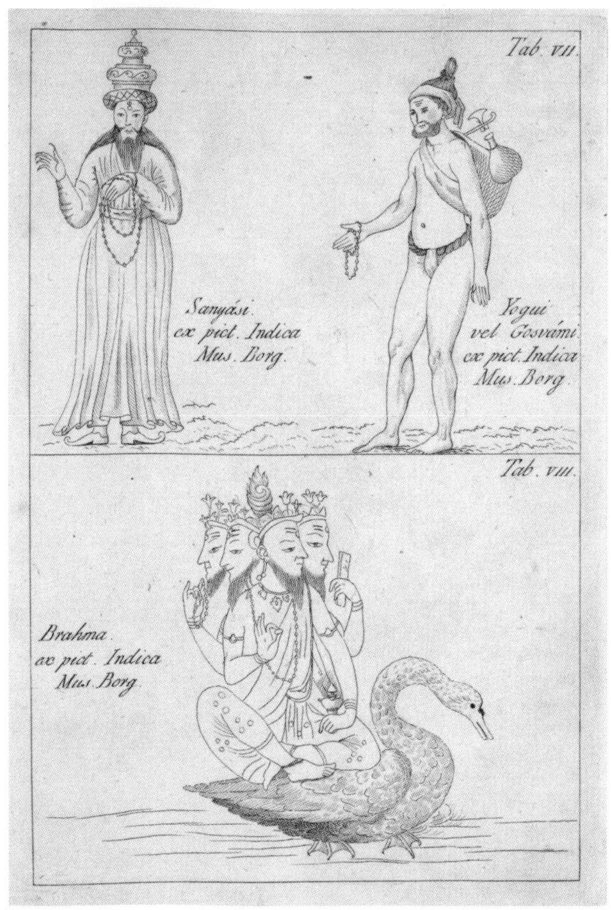

125 "Sanyasi; Yogui vel Gosvami; Brahma," in S. Bartholomaeo Paulinus, *Systema Brahmanicum Liturgicum, Mythologicum, Civile* (Romae: A. Fulgonium, 1791), Tab. VII and VIII. Engraving on paper, 26 cm. New York Public Library

Moor aligned the "gods" in a Hindu court or *sabha* with a Greco-Roman "pantheon" in the same manner that he gleaned the "mythology" of the Hindus from material and textual remains as scholars of antiquity had consistently published. The engravings make an argument, as Moor also punctuated his text, that Hindu mythology and art contained antiquity, an antiquity that had not only expanded far beyond the classical world but was also worthy of imitation. In this period, art historians identified a need for a source of outlines to establish the "principles of the ancients," as George Cumberland proclaimed, to give "stability to the fine Arts" in Britain and ensure the country's artistic "consequence" in Europe if not "over the whole world."[96] Winckelmann in *Reflections on the Painting and Sculpture of the Greeks* (as translated by Fuseli in 1765) also sought a book that collected every known image for artists to imitate in order to proceed to invention:

> The artist would require a work, containing every image with which any abstracted idea might be poetically invested: a work collected from all mythology, the best poets of all ages, the mysterious philosophy of different nations, the monuments of the ancients on gems, coins, utensils, &c. This magazine should be distributed into several classes, and, with proper applications to peculiar possible cases, adapted to the instruction of the artist. This would, at the same time, open a vast field for imitating the ancients, and participating of their sublime taste.[97]

One imagines that such a work would depend on multiple authors to provide the collections "of different nations." If such a book existed, Winckelmann and Cumberland would have contributed information on classical mythology while Moor would have provided knowledge of Hindu mythology in the language of neoclassical outline to which they also subscribed.

A "WORK COLLECTED FROM ALL MYTHOLOGY"

Such works "collected from all mythology" did come into existence on both academic and visionary terms, and Moor's *Hindu Pantheon* was a source for many, particularly those connected with the "little Society" in which Moor participated.[98] In the previous sections, I argued that Moor's engagement with members of the Asiatic Society and their publications in *Asiatick Researches* in India, and with Fuseli and Haughton as well as other proponents of the neoclassical outline style in England, shaped the final format of the book. In this portion, I turn to the book's reuse and how other artists in this circle, such as Flaxman and the radical poet and printmaker William Blake, engaged with the product as a source to understand, and reformulate, the history of art.

In the same year as the book's publication, 1810, Flaxman became the Professor of Sculpture at the Royal Academy. In his second lecture there, "On Egyptian Sculpture," he noted *The Hindu Pantheon*'s "upwards of 1500 outlines of Hindu painting and sculpture, faithfully copied from the originals." He included at least one of Moor's illustrations in his lectures; in their publication in 1829, Vishnu suckling his toe (Moor's Plate 20) was appended. In this lecture, Flaxman staged his discussion hierarchically beginning with the sculpture of the biblical era, the "Cherubim" above the Ark of the Covenant. While these had been destroyed, he provided the reference to prove that God's "command was not against the images themselves, but the abuse of them to impious and idolatrous purposes." He also suggested a means of accessing what they could have looked like by "analogy with Egyptian art," and from there to the Greek.[99]

Between his discussion of biblical and Egyptian sculpture, Flaxman paused on the Persian and Hindu. He noted a similarity between "Hindoo sculptures" and such "early productions," implying – much like William Jones had suggested in his essay "On the Gods of Greece, Italy, and India" (1788), and George Cumberland had stated in *Thoughts on Outline* (1796), as Moor did in *The Hindu Pantheon* (1810) – that India could be a source of Egyptian and therefore of Greek art.[100] Nevertheless, Flaxman placed the Hindu sculptures that he had seen in Moor's book and in the rock-carved temples depicted in Thomas and William Daniell's *Oriental Scenery* (1797–1808; discussed in Chapter Two) at a lower rung in the hierarchy. They had "some resemblance to the Egyptian," but Flaxman judged them "inferior both in science and likeness to nature."[101] Moor's book and Daniell's *Oriental Scenery* can be seen as two sources of Indian art that fed the Royal Academy's efforts to provide pedagogic materials for artists along with the Persian, Egyptian, and Greek – a rudimentary "work collected from all mythology" in Winckelmann's terms – and to decipher their expansive inquiry into the "origin of the arts."[102]

Encyclopedic projects worked toward similar pedagogic ends though across subjects. Flaxman and Moor both contributed to Rees's *Cyclopaedia* (1802–20), a "Universal Dictionary of Arts, Sciences, and Literature." Flaxman's entry on "Sculpture" reprised his Royal Academy Lectures, but he included more works from "different nations" in the engravings (fig. 126). Instead of Vishnu as a representation of Hindu sculpture in his teleology of the arts, he included the goddess Durga slaying the buffalo demon reproduced in Plate 35 of *The Hindu Pantheon* (see fig. 119), which was placed alongside an Egyptian monumental sculpture at Thebes, two Persian relief sculptures from Persepolis, a Chinese statue, and an Etruscan *patera* to illustrate those works that stood between biblical and Egyptian antiquity, before reaching the Greek.[103]

William Blake was employed to engrave this plate for Flaxman's "Sculpture" as well as the others that reproduced renowned works of classical antiquity such as the Lao-

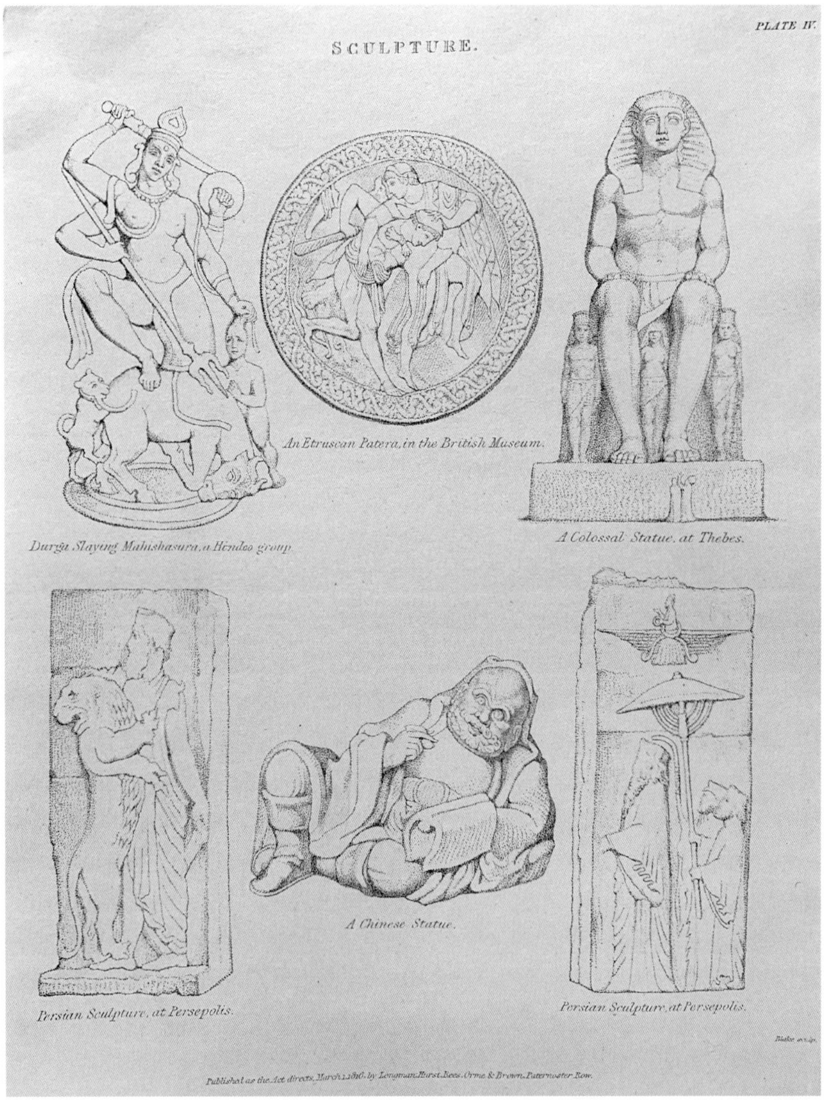

coön.[104] Blake was paid for the plates between 1815 and 1817, but he may have become involved in Rees's project as early as 1803. Moor's plates were published in the middle of this venture, on January 1, 1809; it is likely that Blake encountered them soon after.[105] While scholars have long surmised that Blake had access to Moor's *Hindu Pantheon*, this discovery confirms that he personally reproduced at least one image from the book.[106] For Flaxman's plate, Blake removed the shrine to focus on Durga's sculpted form; he gently shaded the flowing line of Haughton's design with stippling around the contours to emphasize the twist of the goddess's upper body and her limbs. This also translated

126 William Blake, "Sculpture," in John Flaxman, "Sculpture," in Abraham Rees, *The Cyclopaedia; or Universal Dictionary of Arts, Sciences, and Literature*, vol. 4 (London: Longman, Hurst, Rees, Orme & Browne, 1820), pl. IV

The Hindu Pantheon's linear print into Flaxman's preferred use of a stippled outline for the enterprise.[107] Her right arm is bent back and tensely holds a sword while the left grasps and pulls the demon's hair; the right leg pushes against the buffalo's back in equipoise to add counter-balance to the figure, which was based on a portable bronze icon that Moor had purchased in western India (see fig. 85).

While Blake was hired as a reproductive engraver to delineate the works on this plate, those works, along with Flaxman's text, seem to have encouraged him to think about artistry and temporality in his independent projects, including his illuminated manuscript *Jerusalem* (1804–20) and his *Descriptive Catalogue* (1809). The latter described the exhibition that he held in the rooms above his family's haberdashery store in 1809 to 1810. Flaxman had situated Moor's *Hindu Pantheon* within an academic, chronological evolution of arts from biblical antiquity to the Egyptian (by way of Indian and Persian) to the Greek. However, Blake reversed the progressive hierarchy that the professor of sculpture was proposing and worked backwards through his historical timeline. Morton D. Paley argued that Blake identified recently published antiquities from India, Persia, and Egypt as a means to access the biblical past in his *Descriptive Catalogue*.[108] To Blake, the "Apotheoses of Persian, Hindoo, and Egyptian Antiquities" that were still "preserved on rude monuments" in the early nineteenth century were clues – "copies from some stupendous originals" – to earlier arts "now lost or perhaps buried."[109] These antiquities (including Moor's) opened a path for him to travel in a "vision" to the biblical world and invert art history.[110] There, he viewed the "wonderful originals called in the Sacred Scriptures the Cherubim" (which Flaxman had discussed), noted their "very superior style," and recognized the "grand works" of Greek antiquity as their mere "copies," much as he had identified the Persian, Hindu, and Egyptian apotheoses as derived from earlier works.[111]

For Blake, this art historical inversion provided an opportunity to identify a path for artistic redemption in a debased present. This is clear from two of the paintings that resulted from the "vision" he described in his *Catalogue*, those of the "apotheoses" of the British statesmen William Pitt and naval hero Lord Nelson, as well as his now lost drawing of "The Bramins."[112] Claimed as apotheoses in the manner of "Persian, Hindoo, and Egyptian" shrines, the chaotic figures and roiling monsters that surround Pitt and Nelson allude to their status as false gods.[113] But we should be alert to the potential compressions in time that these works might hold. Their ancient composition could equally offer a prophetic means to see through the corrupt present, and the tyranny and war that these figures represented around 1810, to the attributes of their heroic predecessors, the Cherubim.[114]

In his drawing of "The Bramins" in the same exhibition, Blake represented Charles Wilkins, the translator of the Bhagavad Gita (1785), who had influenced his notions of time as cyclical and regenerative rather than linear and degraded; as discussed earlier, Wilkins's Gita was also key for Moor.[115] In the tenth entry of his *Catalogue*, Blake described "The Bramins":

> The subject is, Mr. Wilkin, translating the Geeta; an ideal design, suggested by the first publication of that part of the Hindoo Scriptures, translated by Mr. Wilkin. I understand that my Costume is incorrect, but in this I plead the authority of the ancients, who often deviated from the Habits, to preserve the Manners, as in the instance of Laocoon, who, though a priest, is represented naked.[116]

While this drawing is no longer extant, Blake offers clues to its form and meaning in his description. Even if "incorrect," he portrayed Wilkins in what he perceived to be a Brahmin's "Costume," and similarly he followed Greek sculptors of Laocoön in rendering the priest naked rather than in priestly garb. Through this comparison, Blake implies that he showed Wilkins in Brahmin dress to draw him closer to the "ancient language of the Brahmans" that Wilkins had translated, rather than in his East India Company garments.[117]

However, Blake's reference to the sculpture of Laocoön in his description of "The Bramins," which he first reproduced for Rees's *Cyclopaedia* in Flaxman's "Sculpture," and then in a separate plate in 1826, seems pointed. Blake considered the Laocoön as one of many Greek copies of the "cherubim on Solomon's temple," which implies that "The Bramins" too might go beyond a costume change to arrive at earlier models and a purer spirituality through a temporal collapse between the present and the antiquities of "Asia."[118] Scholars have held that Blake's drawing of "The Bramins" was modeled on Flaxman's of William Jones in Indian cap translating Hindu law with the aid of three Indian scholars.[119] However, Blake could have drawn Wilkins alone, as he mentions no others in his description. Wilkins would then have been the "copy" and conduit – the translator – of these earlier "Bramins" of the title, akin to how the "Apotheoses of Persian, Hindoo, and Egyptian antiquities" referred to earlier "stupendous originals." His Brahmin garments replicate those of the ancient Brahmins, even if "incorrect" or degraded: they serve as a link to connect the eras. This leap is supported by Wilkins's translation, which provides a cyclical model for the soul and time that accords with this interpretation of Blake's lost drawing. In the Gita, the soul is "ancient, constant, and eternal," as Krishna says to Arjuna, "as a man throweth away old garments, and putteth on new, even so the soul, having quitted its old mortal frames, entereth into others which are new."[120]

I have paused over the concept of temporal and pictorial compression in the 1809 *Descriptive Catalogue* and Blake's consideration of Indian arts because *The Hindu Pantheon* seems to have provided Blake with the visual source of Hindu deities that he needed for his culminating project, *Jerusalem*. Moor's plates mediated Hindu philosophical texts that Blake admired, like the Bhagavad Gita, and William Jones's "On the Gods of Greece, Italy, and India" through equally valid Hindu pictorial sources.

By focusing on Moor's figure of Durga that Blake reproduced for Flaxman, I argue that Blake reformulated the Hindu goddess as one of many mythical figures who defeats tyranny and reanimates Britain in a spiral of regenerative action and repose in *Jerusalem*. As I discussed earlier, Moor spent an inordinate amount of time discussing the many manifestations of the active form of the great goddess; he did not edit for clarity's sake. In one plate in *The Hindu Pantheon*, two outlines portray the great goddess seated resplendent as Devi on a lotus flower above in a position of repose, and below as Durga in her "active" form fighting "vice" (fig. 127). In the opening pages of chapter three of *Jerusalem*, to the Deists, Blake's illustration reflects Moor's plate: "In Great Eternity, every particular Form gives forth or Emanates / Its own particular Light & the Form is the Divine Vision" (54:1–2). This philosophy of the emanation of forms is given shape by Blake in the image of a crowned woman whose wings are the sky (fig. 128). Her seat on an open flower and her three-tiered crown formally echo that of Devi on the lotus flower in Moor's plate.[121] If she is Beulah, or "easeful repose," as David Weir proposed, Blake chose the design of this "goddess of the lotus" and "emblem of female beauty" in Moor's words, with purpose.[122] Indeed, it is as if Blake looked through the outline printed in *The Hindu Pantheon* to the bright painting from western India that informed it and replenished the copy (fig. 129). He seems to enact the Hindu philosophy of personification as described by Moor to fill "the ideal outline of the poet" with colors.[123]

In Moor's plate (see fig. 127), the reposing goddess is placed above a representation of another of her emanations, "Durga or Active Virtue Slaying Mahishasura, a personification of Vice," which was based on a painting rather than the bronze sculpture that Blake reproduced. In the text, Moor described Durga in relation to the city of Seringapatam in Mysore.

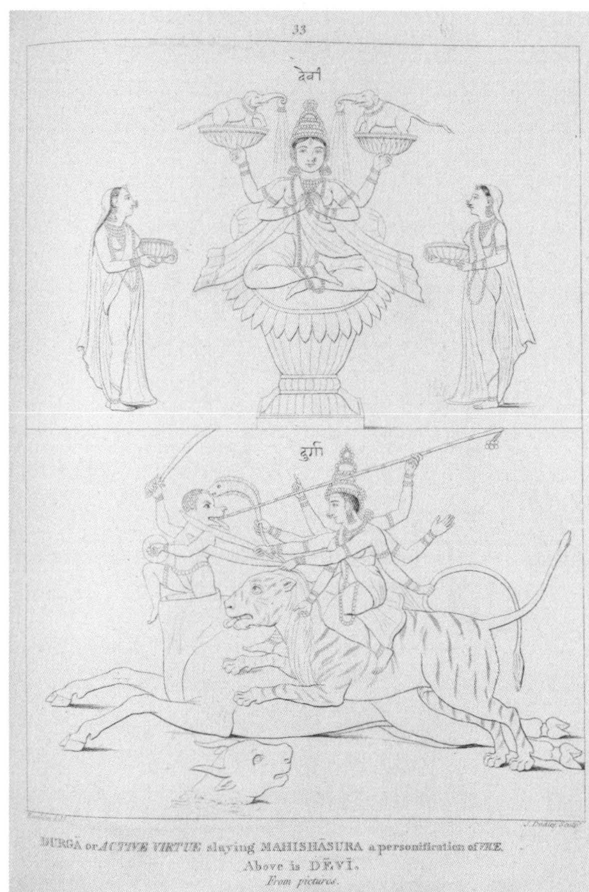

127 "Durga or Active Virtue slaying Mahishasura, a personification of Vice. Above is Devi. From pictures," in Edward Moor, *The Hindu Pantheon* (London: J. Johnson: 1810), pl. 33. British Museum, London, Edward Moor Collection, 1940,0713,0.253

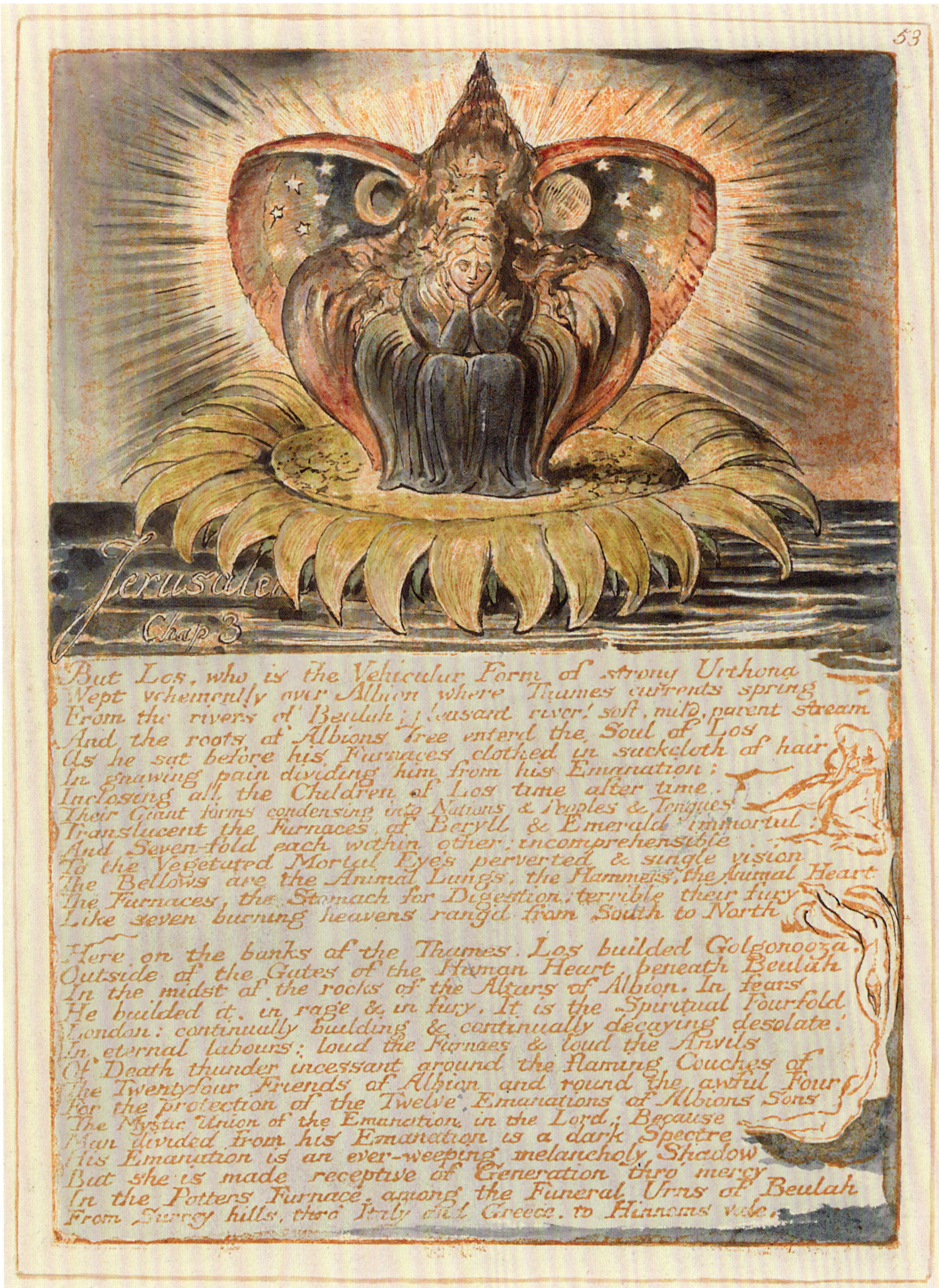

128 William Blake, "Jerusalem / Chap. 3," in *Jerusalem: The Emanation of the Giant Albion*, 1804–20, pl. 53. Relief etching printed in orange with pen and black ink, watercolor and gold on paper, 34.3 × 26.4 cm. Yale Center for British Art, New Haven, Connecticut, Paul Mellon Collection, B1992.8.1(53)

While this was the historical seat of Tipu Sultan (and a primary site of British colonial attention), Moor equally aligned it with myth: "This city is the capital of Mahishasur, the name of a demoniac giant, slain by the consort of Siva . . . [in a] contest between Vice, personified under the name of Mahishasur, and Active Virtue, under that of Durga."[124] The adjacency of Devi and Durga in Moor's book is important as Devi's transformation from one of ease to Durga's active virtue fighting vice to save a city re-emerges and connects Blake's third chapter to the fourth in *Jerusalem*.

In *Jerusalem* folio 53, underneath the image of the reposing butterfly-woman (see fig. 128), Blake focuses on Albion, the primeval man who founded Britain and serves as its personification in his mythology. While Albion slumbers throughout *Jerusalem*, he begins to rouse himself. But Albion's specter and "Reasoning Power" mocks Albion deigning to build "a World of Phantasy," a new Jerusalem in Britain, and criticizes it as "A World of Shapes in craving lust & devouring appetite" (54:23, 24).[125] Forty plates later, in the last sequence of plates in *Jerusalem*, Albion awakes as a "particular Form" and reiterates the possibility of a "World of Phantasy" in positive terms. He rises "speaking the Words of Eternity in Human Forms, in direful / Revolutions of Action & Passion" (95:9–10; fig. 130) to create a new Jerusalem in Britain.

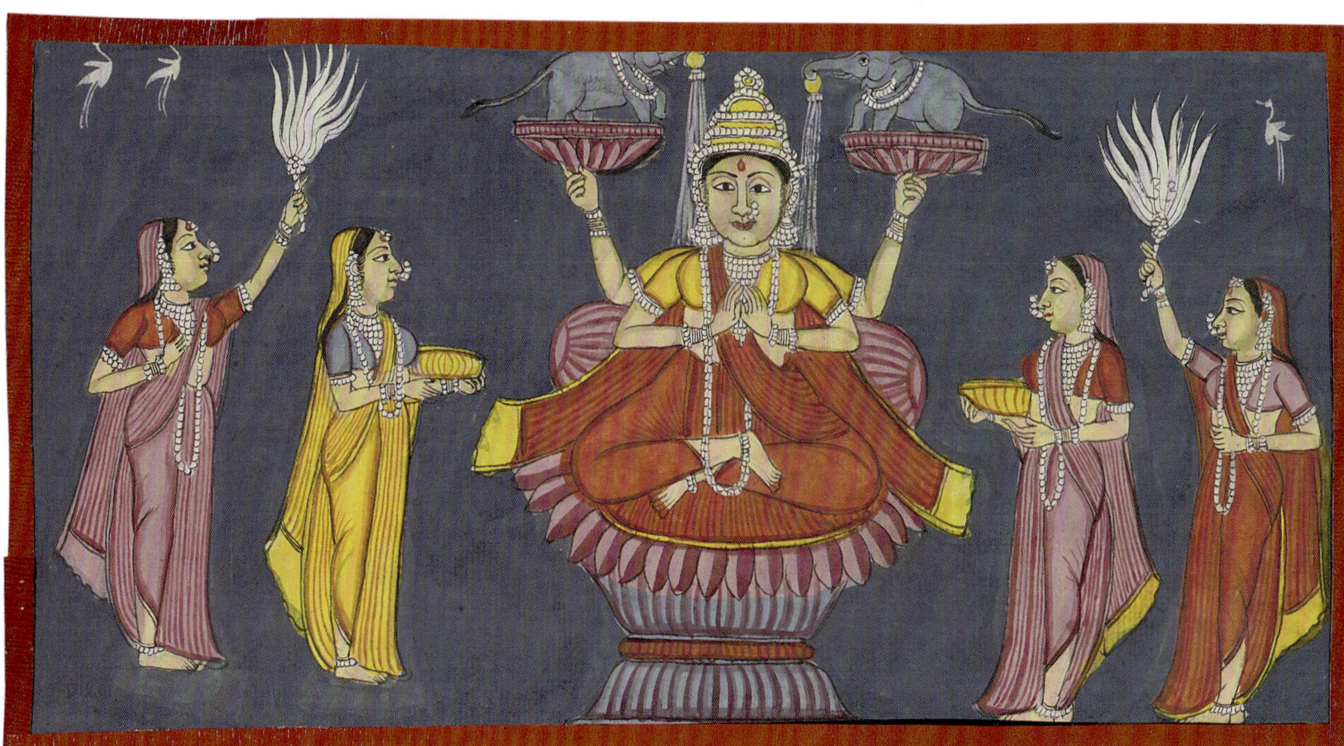

129 *Gaja Lakshmi*, Poona, ca. 1800. Opaque watercolor on paper, 20.55 × 34.8 cm. British Museum, London, Edward Moor Collection, 1940,0713,0.228

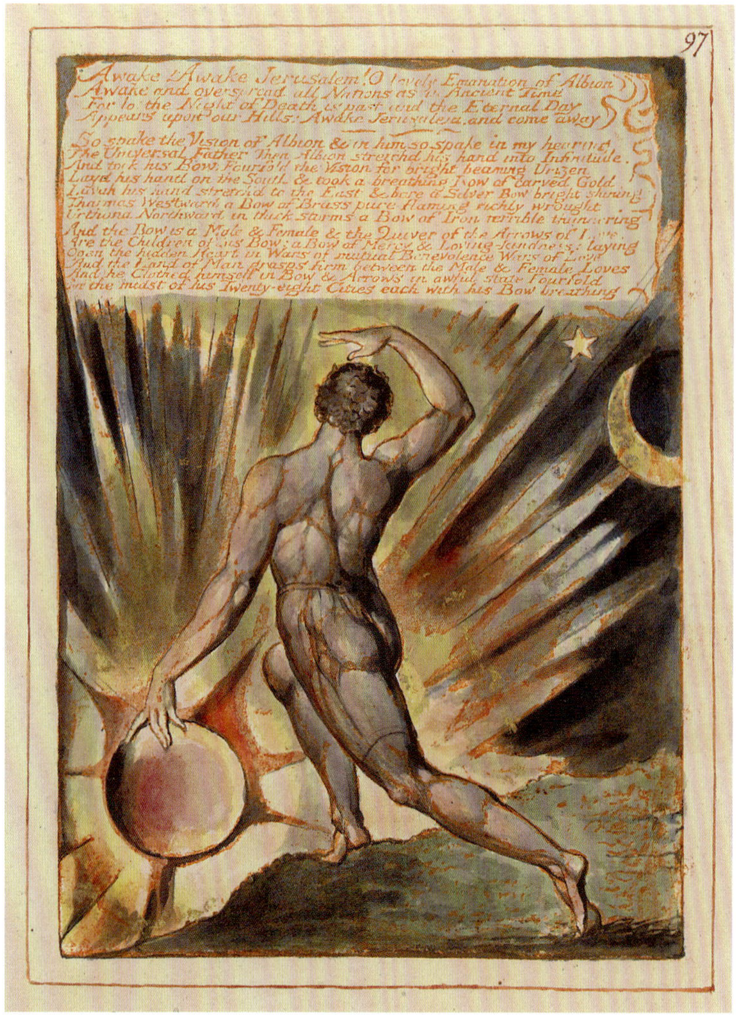

Blake used Hindu sculpture as well as texts like Wilkins's translation of the Bhagavad Gita as portals to see earlier arts in his *Descriptive Catalogue*. He also seems to compress ancient images within Albion's form, including Durga's "Active Virtue Slaying . . . Vice." In Plate 95 of *Jerusalem*, Albion is stretched formally like Durga if seen from behind (see figs. 85, 119, and 126). He reaches above his head, elbow bent as Durga's was to grasp her "golden lance,"[126] to choose "his arrows of flaming gold" (95:13). In Plate 97 (fig. 131), Albion lunges, like the goddess, to wrest the arrows of light, to pull them as Durga dragged the demon "Vice" by the hair, from that glowing orb (like rays from the sun), simultaneously to destroy in "Annihilation" (99:7) and create "Visionary forms dramatic" (99:28). The pathos of Devi or the butterfly-woman's form is transformed into sublime "Action &

130 William Blake, "Her voice pierc'd Albions clay cold ear," in *Jerusalem: The Emanation of the Giant Albion*, 1804–20, pl. 95. Relief etching printed in orange with pen and black ink and watercolor on paper, 34.3 × 26.4 cm. Yale Center for British Art, New Haven, Connecticut, Paul Mellon Collection, B1992.8.1(95)

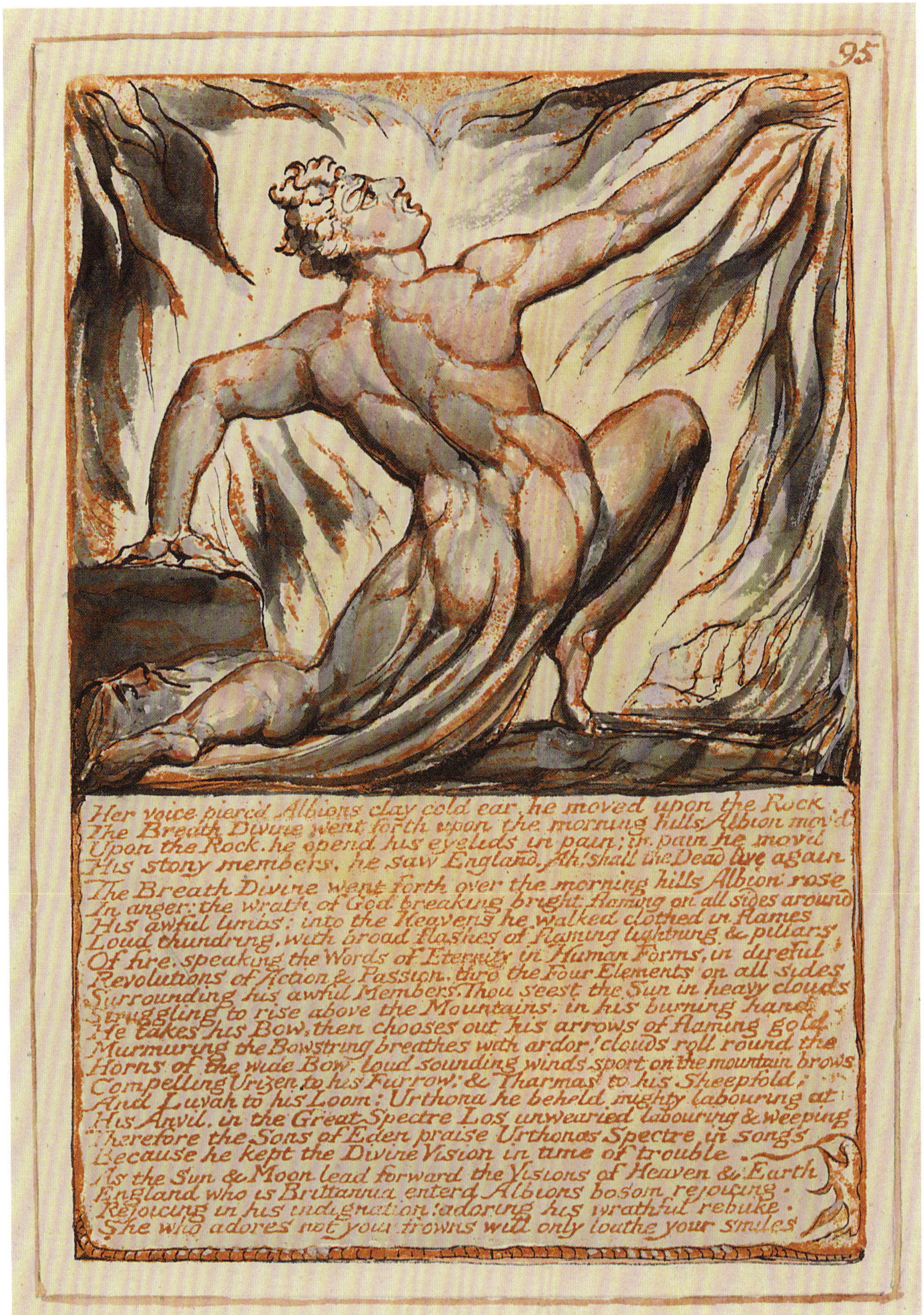

131 William Blake, "Awake! Awake Jerusalem," in *Jerusalem: The Emanation of the Giant Albion*, 1804–20, pl. 97. Relief etching printed in orange with pen and black ink, watercolor, and gold on paper, 34.3 × 26.4 cm. Yale Center for British Art, New Haven, Connecticut, Paul Mellon Collection, B1992.8.1(97)

Passion," Durga or Albion, who will regenerate the world and, in yet one more revolution, return to repose. Eternity and action, pathos and sublimity are linked in Blake as they are in their placement one on top of the other in Moor's book (see fig. 127).[127]

Blake not only consulted Hindu philosophy, and its personification, but he also grafted it with other materials, like the millenarian strand of thought and imagery that David Bindman and Esther Chadwick have discussed, to develop alternative, spiraling histories.[128] The last few lines of *Jerusalem* (99:1–4) evoke Hindu imagery and Christian revelation as part of a cycle:

> All Human Forms identified even Tree Metal Earth & Stone. all
> Human Forms identified. living going forth & returning wearied
> Into the Planetary lives of Years Months Days & Hours reposing
> And then Awaking into his Bosom in the Life of Immortality

The first two lines recall William Jones's "numberless divinities ... created solely by the magick of poetry; whose essential business it is to personify the most abstract notions, and to place a nymph or genius in every grove and every flower."[129] And the last two, as Paley identified, evoke the coming of the day of Brahma in Wilkins's translation of the Gita, when "all things proceed from invisibility to visibility ... the universe, even, having existed, is again dissolved; and now again on the approach of day, by divine necessity it is reproduced."[130]

The interpretation of a Hindu goddess sitting within the form of Albion in the last plates of *Jerusalem* can be pushed farther (see figs. 130 and 131). If Durga could exist inside Albion, other forms or emanations from earlier ages could awaken there as well.[131] Albion's stretched form is also reminiscent of the Laocoön. Durga saved the city Mahishasur from Vice by slaying the demon with a "golden lance," just as Laocoön with a spear struck the Trojan horse to save his city from destruction (though he failed), just as Albion with his "arrows of flaming gold" (95:13) needed to "Awake! Awake, Jerusalem" (97:1). Sequences of referents – male and female, successful and unsuccessful, the sublime and the pathetic – are compressed in Albion's form. Through them Blake transports us backwards, through the history of art, through Christian to Greek to Hindu to the arts of biblical revelation, as he did in the *Descriptive Catalogue* following Flaxman's "Sculpture" lecture and essay.

In the last plates of Jerusalem, Blake not only accesses the "wonderful originals" of Asia but he also resurrects "a lost common being," in the words of Saree Makdisi, "which might reunify humankind along with its differences" and mobilize them – in painting and poetry – to redeem the world, the nation, the city, the "Human form" from the forge in which the arts of war, tyranny, empire are produced to make a more virtuous world through those selfsame materials.[132] Albion would then be one form of many in a process of death and rebirth, a cycle of "Human Forms... reposing / And then Awaking" much like the Hindu reincarnation of ages and Christ's resurrection. While *Jerusalem*'s conclusion, as with the entire book, is polyvalent, the particularity of Moor's *Hindu Pantheon*, including its many representations of the great goddess and its visualization of abstract thought, seems to have encouraged Blake in his interpretation of history and its continual regeneration as a "work collected from all mythology."[133]

MISSIONARY AND COLONIAL DESIGNS

Moor's book was one source of mythology that Blake consulted to repair Britain, but other figures, especially missionaries and colonial designers, were also primed to consult it. Indeed, Moor's book seemed to open two contrasting paths for its use: empire and revolution. While Blake sought the latter – to free humanity from the bonds of tyranny and war through the arts – he was equally cognizant of their propensity to enable empire, as his annotation "Empire follows Art" on his copy of Reynolds's *Discourses to the Royal Academy of Art* implies.[134] W. J. T. Mitchell considered the conundrum that Blake's phrase presents. "If Joshua Reynolds is right",

> [T]he arts can do nothing but follow the train of empire, adorning the palaces of the new emperors. If Blake is right, the arts and the sciences are in a much more complex position. On the one hand, they are making possible all the techniques of domination and exploitation on which the new form of empire depends, and providing the ideological fantasies that make this process seem natural and inevitable. On the other hand, they provide the prophetic visions that let us see where we are going before we get there: like the idols of old, they "go before us" into possible and probable futures.[135]

In the *Hindu Pantheon*, Moor seems to propose that the "mythology" of the Hindus could offer the historical and living roots of a powerful system that had formulated, and could reformulate, the world as Blake did in his prophetic vision *Jerusalem*. Yet at the same time that Moor was inspired by Hindu icons as "art" for imperial, artistic, and philosophical purposes, he also disavowed them as "idols" on religious grounds.[136]

Moor's book had the capacity to encourage visionary arts, like Blake's, but it also supported Christian missionaries and British colonial educators in their "techniques of domination and exploitation on which... empire depends," as Mitchell analyzed. While Moor was amazed at the bounty of Hindu mythology, he also repeatedly admonished idolatry – the multiplicity of deities "forming links of that lengthened chain that binds in its superstitious and idolatrous folds so great a number of Hindus" – and pursued civic

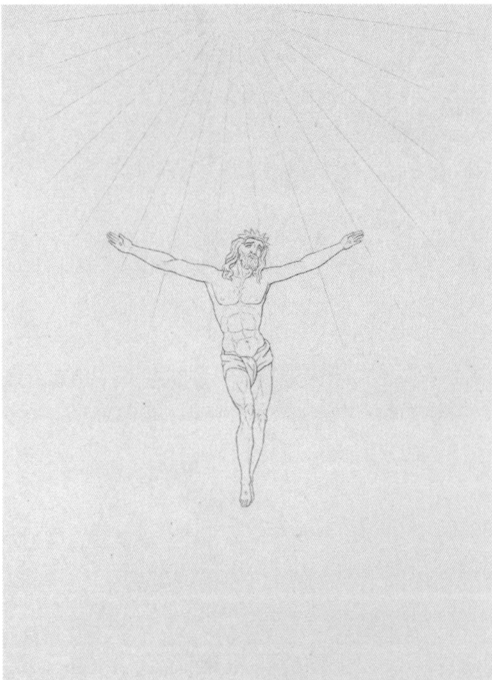

reform.[137] To support Jonathan Duncan's abolition of Hindu infanticide, Moor edited *Hindu Infanticide* (1811), which included Alexander Walker's account of the same name, the year after *The Hindu Pantheon*.[138] This publication sought to monitor Hindu practices, which resituates the collections of Moor and Walker and the information that they gathered on the Hindu gods.

Moor included a Christian image, the crucifix, on Plate 98 of *The Hindu Pantheon* (fig. 132). He wrote that a man "who was in the habit of bring[ing] me Hindu deities, pictures, &c." had presented him with two crucifixes. Moor asked him who the god represented, but he "professed his ignorance . . . but supposed, by the hole in the foot, that it might be Wittoba [see fig. 82a], adding that it was impossible to recollect the almost innumerable Avataras described in the Puranas."[139] Even if the Christian "pious might be hurt at seeing such a subject mixed with the apparent grossness of Hindu idolatry," Moor wrote, he included the plate because Christ had become one of the Hindu gods in India. This not only equated Christian, "Papish" in his terms, icons with Hindu "idolatry," but also the fallacy of "Christian missionaries" and their use of icons in conversion practices.[140]

The Hindu Pantheon stood at a juncture of East India Company policy in India. By 1813, a new Act in the Company's Charter included clauses to permit Christian missionary activity in India and to establish "civility" through a Western-oriented system of education for Indians.[141] But events preceding the charter did not bode well for the aftermath. In 1805, an evangelical chaplain, Claudius Buchanan, had written a pamphlet that sought *An Ecclesiastical Establishment for British India*; and in 1806, in Vellore, the *sepoys* reacted to Hindu and Muslim religious restrictions alongside perceived missionary actions in the army and rebelled. This publication and incident sparked a wide debate among the British regarding Christian intentions in India. Was conversion possible, desired, or disastrous for the Company's economic and political drives for colonial control? Many passionate responses ensued against missionary activity, including by Moor's friend, Charles "Hindoo" Stuart, who anonymously wrote a *Vindication of the Hindoos* (1808), in which he condemned any missionary imposition of religion on the Hindus and pleaded for religious tolerance.[142]

Moor's engraved crucifix stands as a printed footnote to the "pamphlet war" between the secular imperialists and the missionary ones. Like his friend "Hindoo" Stuart, Moor

132 Edward Moor, *The Hindu Pantheon* (London: J. Johnson, 1810), pl. 98. British Museum, London, Edward Moor Collection, 1940,0713,0.25

was against missionaries in India, and the unnamed figure in Plate 98 in *The Hindu Pantheon* was proof of the failure of the crucifix as an agent of conversion. Any enforced "coercion" to Christianity, Moor wrote, would lead to "disquietudes and tumults." Forcing "the Hindus at once to dismiss their Brahmans, and to renounce their religion," was, he considered, an "extravagant . . . proposition" and would deter the Company's imperial purpose.[143] But neither his comments nor those of his friends stopped the new "pious clause," which allowed Christian proselytization in India to move forward.[144]

In fact, Asiatic Society members' collection of information about Hindu deities and mythology was paralleled by a Baptist missionary one. As Partha Mitter articulated decades ago, the two sides of collecting pinpoint the tension Europeans felt between the fine material aspects of Indian arts as "art" on aesthetic grounds and their identification as monstrous and heathen "idols" on religious ones.[145] Around 1800, the writer Robert Southey (a friend of Moor's in Suffolk) wrote to Samuel Taylor Coleridge that he had encountered an "ugly brass epicene-looking God sitting cross-legged on a peacock" along with books in the Baptist Library in Bristol.[146] While Moor and other Company officials collected and commissioned Indian paintings and sculptures to contemplate their aesthetic forms, symbolic meanings, and relationship to other arts around the globe, missionaries packed such "idols" into boxes for display in the Baptist Society Museum in Bristol or the London Missionary Society as "trophies of Christianity."[147] They also printed and distributed Christian tracts with the aim of replacing "idols" in India. Missionary books similarly served to convert Indians and to convince the British of the necessity of conversion. In his book, also titled *The Hindoo Pantheon* (1849), Etienne Alexander Rodriguez wrote that he published images based on South Indian deities to "unveil" "the vast absurdity and horrors" of the "Hindoos" so that "it may lead them to renounce their superstitious vanities" and convert to Christianity.[148]

Moor's engravings became a source for missionary publications. They became loosened from their regional, artistic, historical, and devotional context of production as well as from Moor's attraction to them as both material and iconic objects. A clergyman, one D. T. Barry, used the engraving of Ganesha from the frontispiece of Moor's book (see fig. 110) to illustrate one of the playing cards of his *Travelling Game of India* (1858) for his "home circle" of missionaries. From a sign of auspiciousness and unity in Poona, the representation of Ganesha became an icon of "idolatry and blindness," the symbol of bestial murder in a temple in Benares.[149] The same image was included in *Books for the Children of India: A Paper for the Juvenile Friends of the Christian Vernacular Education Society for India* (London, 1865), to convince a different audience – the missionaries themselves – of the need to fund such publication projects.[150]

In the third edition of *The Hindu Pantheon* (1864), the Reverend W. O. Simpson explicitly reprinted the book in Madras as a missionary text:

> ...the polytheism of the pantheon is the religion of India. Every object in this museum of deities is here catalogued and the inquirer may trace its pedigree, watch the process of its apotheosis and in some measure creep into sympathy with the feelings with which it is regarded by the millions around him. Without such knowledge and such sympathy, there can be little hope of higher instruction becoming effective in the enlightenment and conversion of the people.[151]

Simpson edited Moor's book into a more rigid publication, supposedly eliminating its faults, but actually shifting its acknowledgment of religious pluralism toward a singular Hinduism.[152] He also removed any notion that Moor considered these sculptures and paintings as representative of fine art as well as a diverse aesthetic system. Simpson had the plates redrawn in lithography including only those "worthy of being called an *illustration*," such as one of Shiva and Parvati, which stands without the more than thirty figures of Parvati that Moor had included to stress iconographic variety (fig. 133).[153] Needless to say, Plate 98, the crucifixion, was excised.

All the editions of *The Hindu Pantheon* are symptomatic of the dialogic swings between religion, art, and revolution that haunted the period of its afterlife. Besides its reuse in missionary contexts, the publication also informed discourses on colonial art and design. Moor plainly wished his engravings to become "graceful models of outline" to improve the delineation of Indian and European forms.[154] The book's second edition augmented this purpose. Published in 1861 by a relative, the Reverend A. O. Moor, it contained a short catalogue and freshly printed images since A. O. Moor had "lately found that the ... finely engraved copper-plates ... had been preserved." Although he considered the text out of date, A. O. Moor determined that the plates were a "Gallery of Portraits ... by far the finest that have appeared in any work on this subject." However, he did not recognize the original organizational philosophy or geographic origin of the engravings, since he claimed that they illustrated "the most important form of the religions of Ancient India" rather than those arts primarily made in eighteenth-century western India under the Marathas.[155]

The re-publication of the plates sent an influx of Moor's engravings into the market, probably leading to increased circulation. One F. W. Emery, for instance, noted that he consulted "Moore's Hindoo Mythology" in order to describe the "popularly treated" "heathen deities illustrated on the silver *swami* tea service" that the Gaekwar of Baroda gave to the Prince of Wales on his visit to India in 1875.[156] His treatise offered short descriptions of the deities as well as multiple pages of advertisements for the company that

133 "Shiva and Parvati," in Edward Moor, *The Hindu Pantheon* (3rd edition, Madras: J. Higginbotham, 1864), pl. X. Lithograph with hand coloring on paper, 15.3 × 24 cm. Smithsonian Institution, Washington, D.C., Freer Gallery of Art and Arthur M. Sackler Archives, Robert J. Del Bontà Collection, FSA A2014.06

PLATE X.

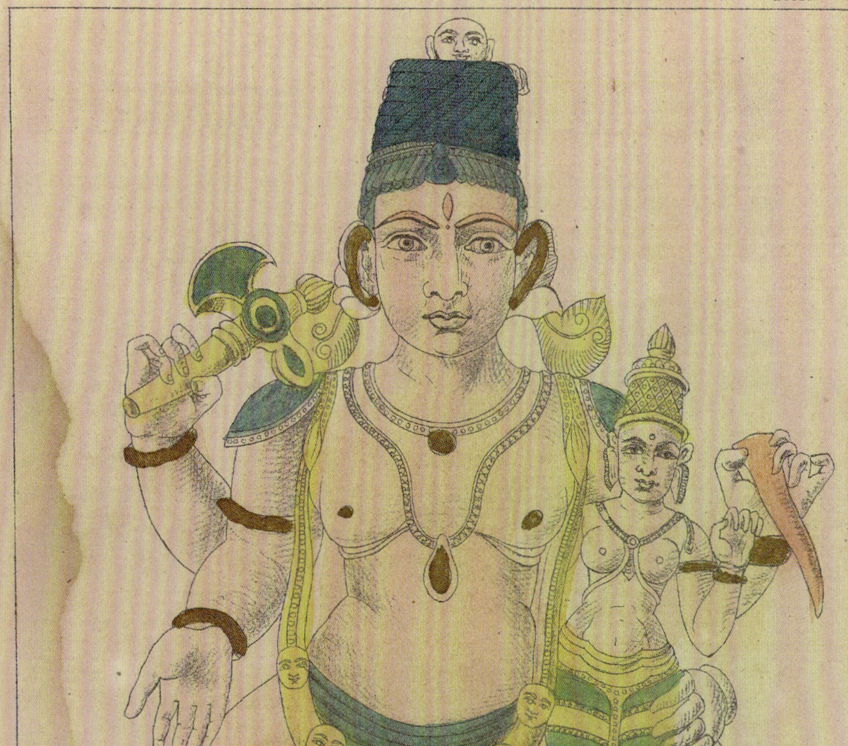

J. Higginbotham, Madras, 1864. A. Barren, Lithog.

MAHĀDEVA AND PARVATĪ.

PURANIC GODS.

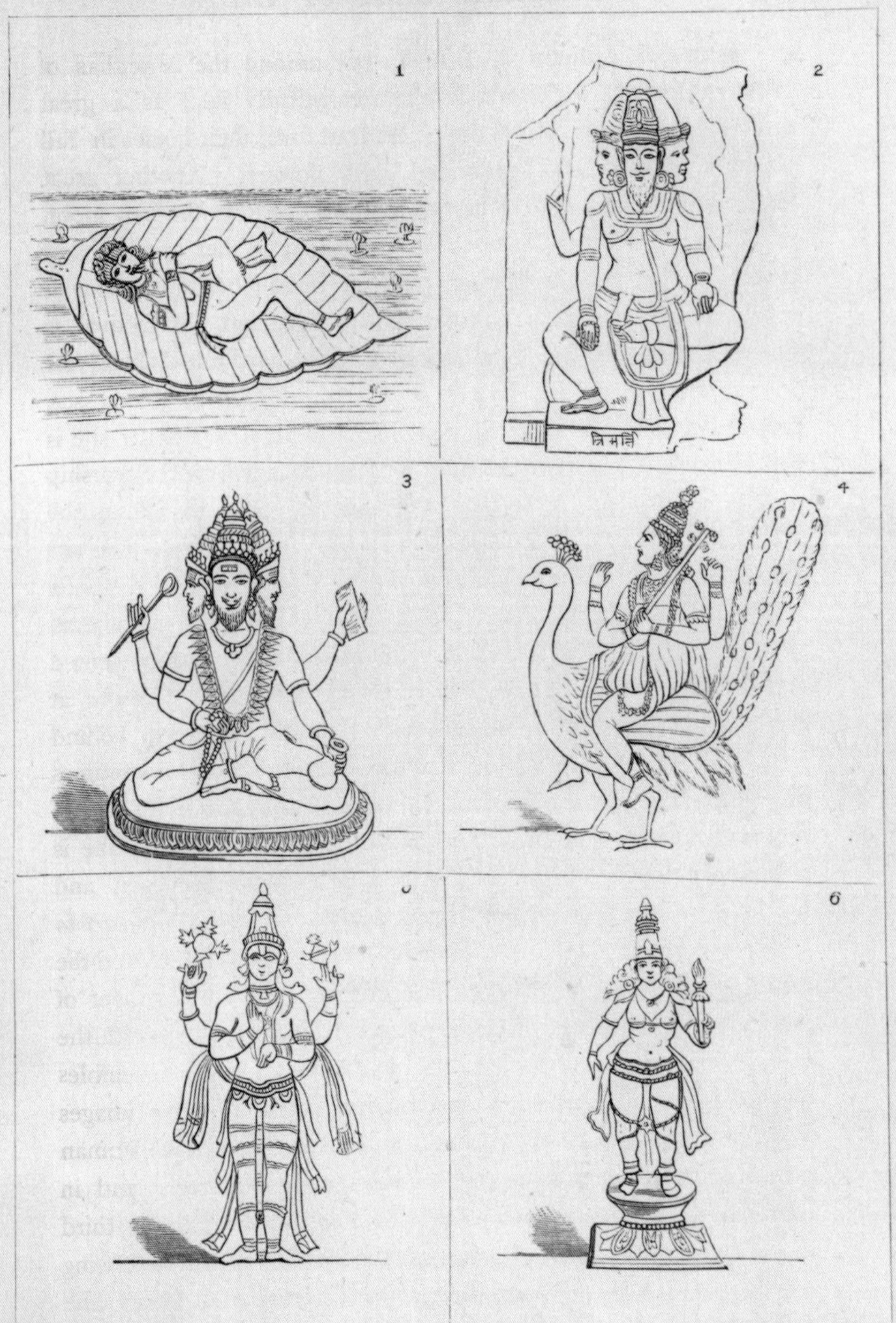

1. Narayana. 2. Trimurti. 3. Brahma.
4. Saraswati. 5. Vishnu. 6. Lakshmi.

manufactured the service, P. Orr & Sons. Emery's *Hindoo Mythology* lacked illustrations, but, as Dipti Khera has elegantly argued, subsequent Orr & Sons catalogues included outline engravings, though they were more closely related to South Indian paintings of the Hindu gods than to Moor's work.[157]

In 1880, Moor's engravings also supplemented George C. Birdwood's *Industrial Arts of India*, one of the most important Victorian publications about design in India. Moor's *Hindu Pantheon* engravings are the main, yet unidentified, source of Birdwood's illustrations for Part I, also titled "The Hindu Pantheon." A glance at one of Birdwood's plates (fig. 134) reveals one of the paradoxes of Moor's book. On the one hand, Birdwood announced the illustrations as a "universal symbolism of Indian art" as if a key or an alphabet to understanding the "manual arts" or crafts of India that Wilkins's sculptures, and Moor's reuse of them, had suggested. On the other, they reveal the local specificity and stylistic eclecticism of *The Hindu Pantheon* on which they were based. The top left picture is modeled on a painting from Jaipur that Flaxman used in his lectures on sculpture. Below is an engraving after one of Wilkins's zinc sculptures (see fig. 114). The Poona painter had depicted Saraswati on a peacock (on the right in Birdwood's plate), which was probably derived from a wall painting or manuscript frontispiece (see figs. 98 and 99). The bottom left image is after a drawing of a South Indian bronze. Meanwhile, the representation at bottom right was based on a sculpture probably looted from Nana Fadnavis's home shrine (see fig. 78).

Birdwood infamously despised "mythology," and he undoubtedly did not recognize the accumulation "of men and gods, and things" that Moor conjured through his reproductions. Decoration rooted in natural forms was preferred by Birdwood to "the monstrous shapes of the Puranic deities" that he considered "unsuitable for the higher forms of artistic representation," which reprises the tension between fine art and religious representation that Mitter highlighted.[158] Birdwood affected such a preference through the appended illustrations. The "Puranic gods" were abstracted in outline while the "master handicrafts" were pictured as physical objects of metalware, ceramics, and woodwork then on display, and on sale, in exhibitions worldwide.[159] The sculptures he illustrated in the second part of the book were not deities but small bronze soldiers, while gods only appeared when they were connected to objects of design, such as a "sacrificial vase" that was simply a ewer (fig. 135).[160]

Such objects were analyzed by Birdwood as sanitized handicrafts or utensils, objects of design rather than belief, similar to how missionaries had exhibited deities in their museums as Christian trophies emptied of content. Christopher Pinney has argued that Moor's *Hindu Pantheon* was an "early charter for some of the representational transformations the colonial state sought to effect." "Colonial art educators," he wrote, "sought to

134 "Puranic Gods," in George C. Birdwood, *Industrial Arts of India*, vol. 1, part I (London: Chapman and Hall, 1880), pl. C

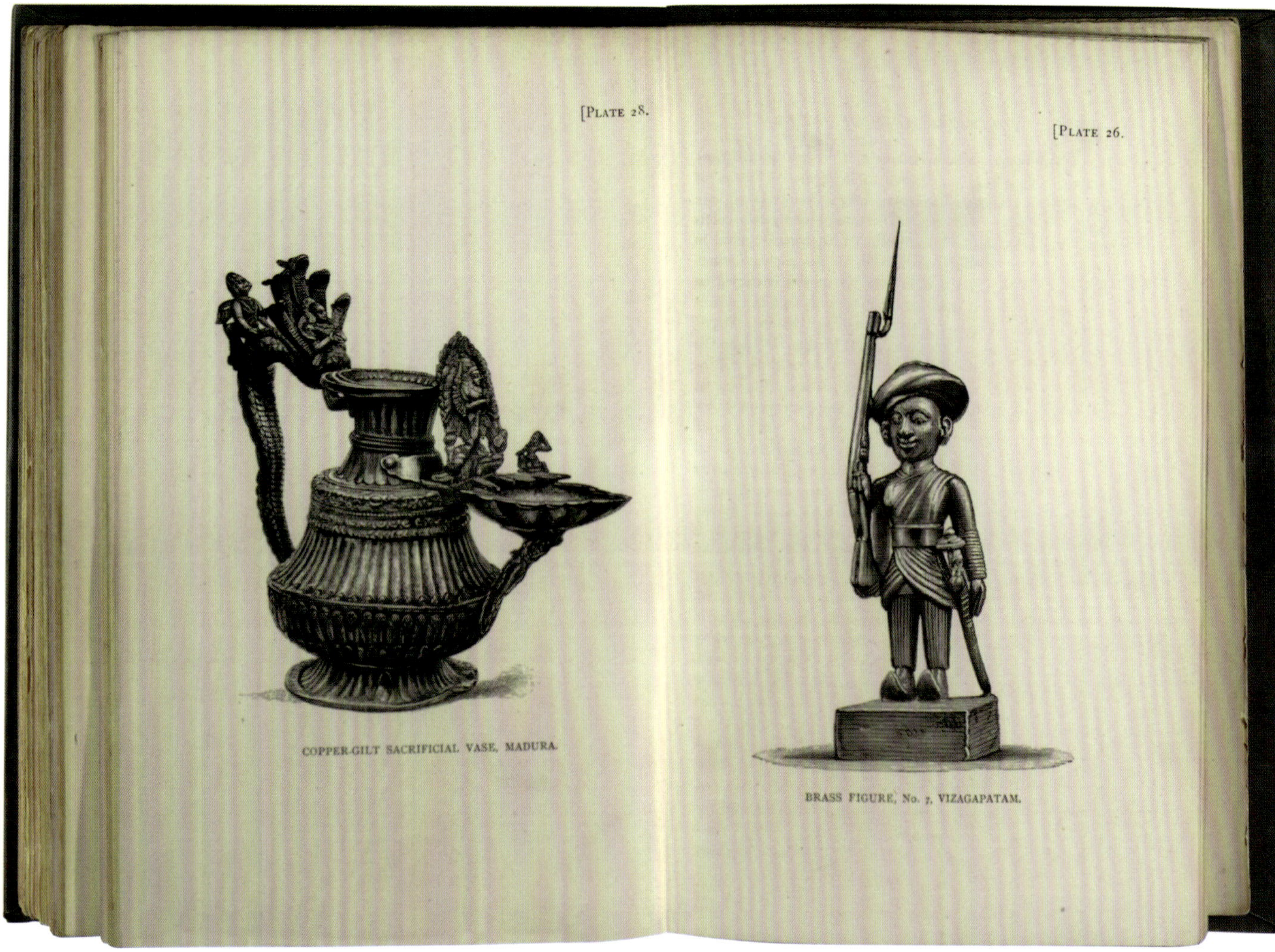

transform the intimate and interested engagement of the devotee into the disinterested and rationalized response of colonial political subjects to the image as 'art.'"[161] In this sense, those invested in colonial design were similar to those invested in proselytization; both saw in Moor's book icons emptied of meaning. Of course, this differed from artists like Fuseli, Flaxman, and Blake who identified *The Hindu Pantheon* as a revitalizing source of art and reformulated it toward their own ends.

Birdwood's *Industrial Arts of India* ends with an advertisement that reinforces the desacralization and subsequent classification of the Hindu gods as they were transferred from India to Britain. While the writer acknowledges the famine that led to the gods' sale, he does not identify the colonial state's failure to respond to its impact. Rather, the

135 "Brass Figure, No. 7, Vizagapatam" and "Copper-Gilt Sacrificial Vase, Madura," in George C. Birdwood, *The Industrial Arts of India*, vol. 1, part II (London: Chapman and Hall, 1880), pls. 26 and 28

advertisement reads as an opportunity to acquire plunder: "The Hindoo Pantheon" available at the Indian Art Gallery on 185 Oxford Street, London. "Messrs. Procter & Co. have in their possession nearly the whole of the Hindoo Gods as Illustrated in this Guide. The Famine, which devastated certain parts of India last year, having forced the Hindoos to part with even their family Gods."[162] This advertisement stands not only for the "Hindoo Pantheon" available at the Indian Art Gallery, but also for that illustrated in Birdwood's book, which was based on the engravings published in *The Hindu Pantheon*, which in turn were founded in the objects that had been taken or sold under duress in order to enter Moor's collection. Here, religious icons become icons of information, trophies, and plunder.

Moor's *Hindu Pantheon* is paradigmatic of the British grafting of Indian arts into their own artistic production at the turn of the nineteenth century. The book gathered individuals and networks, objects and artists, and evaluations into its pages. From the East India Company network in which Moor participated as a soldier to the orientalist and antiquarian philosophy and the radical publishers and artists with whom he engaged, Moor's book encompassed "men and gods, and things" between its covers. In the book's reformulation, some readers pushed *The Hindu Pantheon*'s materials in imperial and colonial directions, others in missionary or design ones, and still others identified it as a source of invigoration and repair. But the format of the Hindu gods that the book propagated took another turn in the late nineteenth century. Alongside the oil paintings, sculptures, and drawings I have discussed so far, *The Hindu Pantheon* and its iterations became a source for anticolonial resistance that was premised on the same terms of art, religion, and empire that it set forth but toward opposite ends.

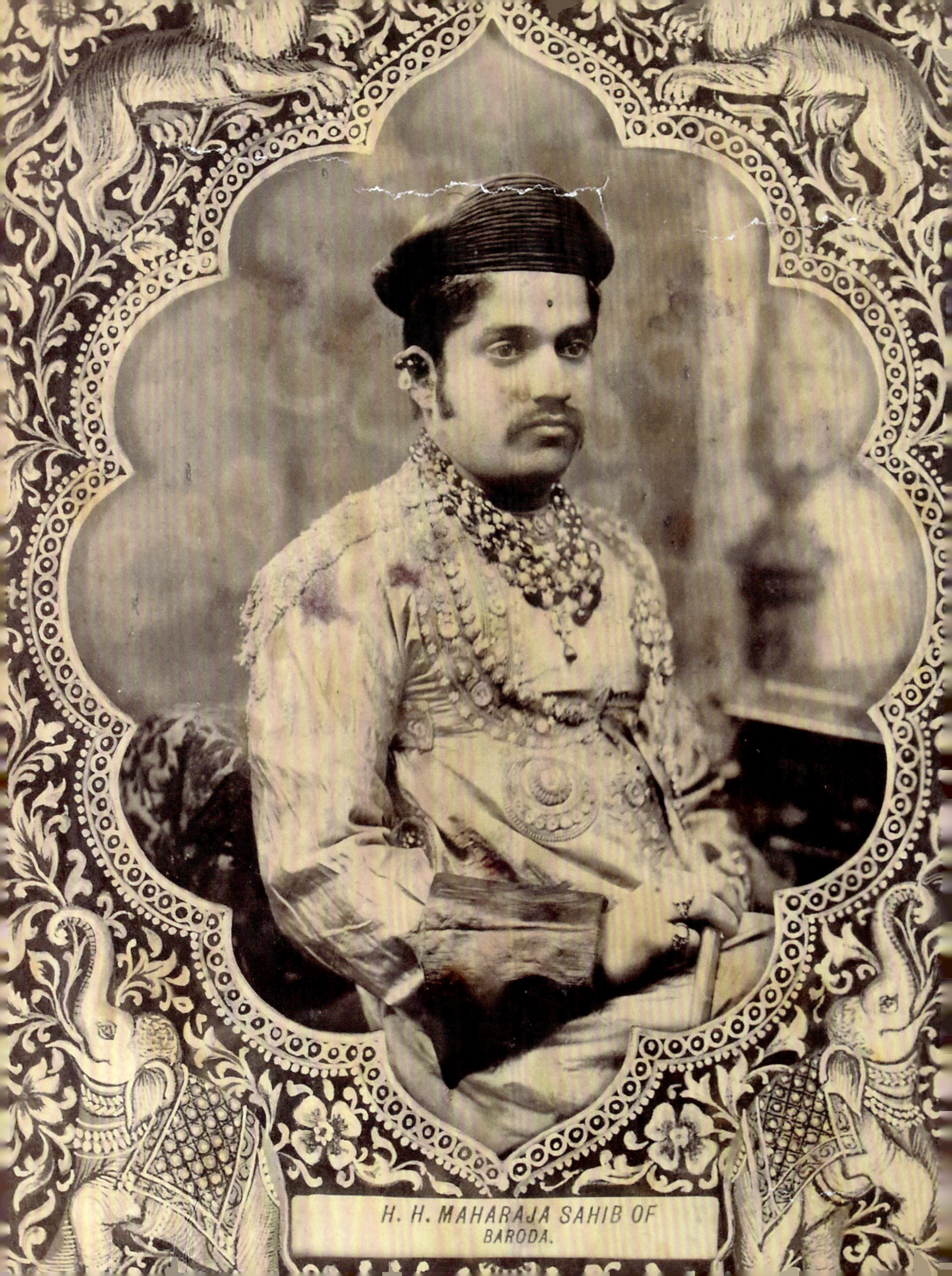

H. H. MAHARAJA SAHIB OF
BARODA.

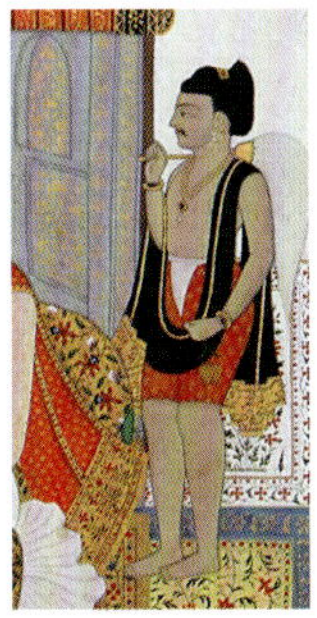

CHAPTER FIVE

A Maratha Press for Independence

In the late nineteenth century, western Indian nationalists founded the Chitrashala Press in Poona. The translation of the words that composed its name – *chitra* (picture) and *shala* (school or gallery) – reveal its purpose. The press was both didactic, a Picture School, and preservationist, a Picture Gallery. To inspire pride in the Maratha past and provide a model for India's future, the Chitrashala aimed to educate the public about their heritage through icon-like portraits of heroes as well as gods. This necessitated finding sources distinct from those under colonial supervision, to which they had limited access, and others that told alternative, positive histories. By scouring the region for family-owned collections and identifying locally available materials, these nationalists resuscitated the historical paintings, sculptures, and texts that I have discussed in this book for a new purpose: anticolonial resistance.

The scholars and printers associated with the Chitrashala Press, alongside others active in western India, compress the history of art that I have traced here. From the Maratha grafting of British arts to construct a visual ideology for their realm that drew on representations of regional Hindu gods and on Mughal courtly idioms and British techniques of portraiture (Chapter One), I turned to the British grafting of Maratha arts in their colonial acquisition of knowledge about India, which fused local objects with British aesthetics and civil and religious programs as exemplified in Edward Moor's *Hindu Pantheon* and its reuse (Chapter Four). In between, I delved into the convergence of

Details of fig. 142 (opposite) and fig. 146 (above)

Maratha and British arts through the production and flow of objects (Chapters Two and Three). This trajectory emphasized how art history shifts according to the perspective of the patron or artist, or by way of the circulation and reformulation of objects through artistic, military, and economic processes of graft.

Organized chronologically, this book's structure also marked the transition from Maratha power in the late eighteenth century to British dominance of western India in the early nineteenth. After *sepoys* revolted against Britain's East India Company army in 1857 in the Sepoy Rebellion (also known as the First War of Independence to Indians or the Mutiny to the British), the crown took over control of the subcontinent. From 1858 until 1947, the Raj consisted of direct British rule over former Company lands, including Maratha territories in western India colored pink on the map (fig. 136), as well as indirect power over those of Indian rulers, known as the "Princely states," which included Maratha territories in central India (colored yellow) that were subservient to the British yet governed autonomously.

By the end of the nineteenth century, the dynamics of power began to shift again. Western Indian writers, scholars, publishers, and educators grafted the grafts. They identified the mixed arts of the previous century as a means to incite change. By joining the Maratha incorporation of British arts with the British incorporation of Maratha arts, they instigated a revolution that envisioned a nation separate from the British empire. Yet this seemingly redemptive revivalism that established a path from empire to nation also consolidated a specific concept of an independent India as Hindu in orientation, which continued to develop over the twentieth century until today, with devastating communal effects.

The history I tell in this chapter thus honors the same ingenuity that marked the eclectic practices of the eighteenth-century artists whose works the Chitrashala came to reproduce, but it is also aware of the political and personal stakes of those who remade them, and those who continue to do so. While my primary aim is to explore western Indian nationalists' reuse of earlier arts, and, in the concluding section to reflect on my own archival methodology, I also remain alert to the arts in this book that did not proliferate – like Gangaram Tambat's experiments in drafting or William Blake's antidote to Britain's imperial tyranny – yet offer quieter, albeit no less radical, modes of regeneration.

THE CHITRASHALA PRESS: AN ART SCHOOL AND GALLERY OF RESISTANCE

In the late nineteenth century, the western Indian nationalist Vishnushastri Chiplunkar lamented in his writings that the British Museum housed hundreds of objects taken from India, including the first Maratha king Shivaji's famous weapon, the tiger-claw,

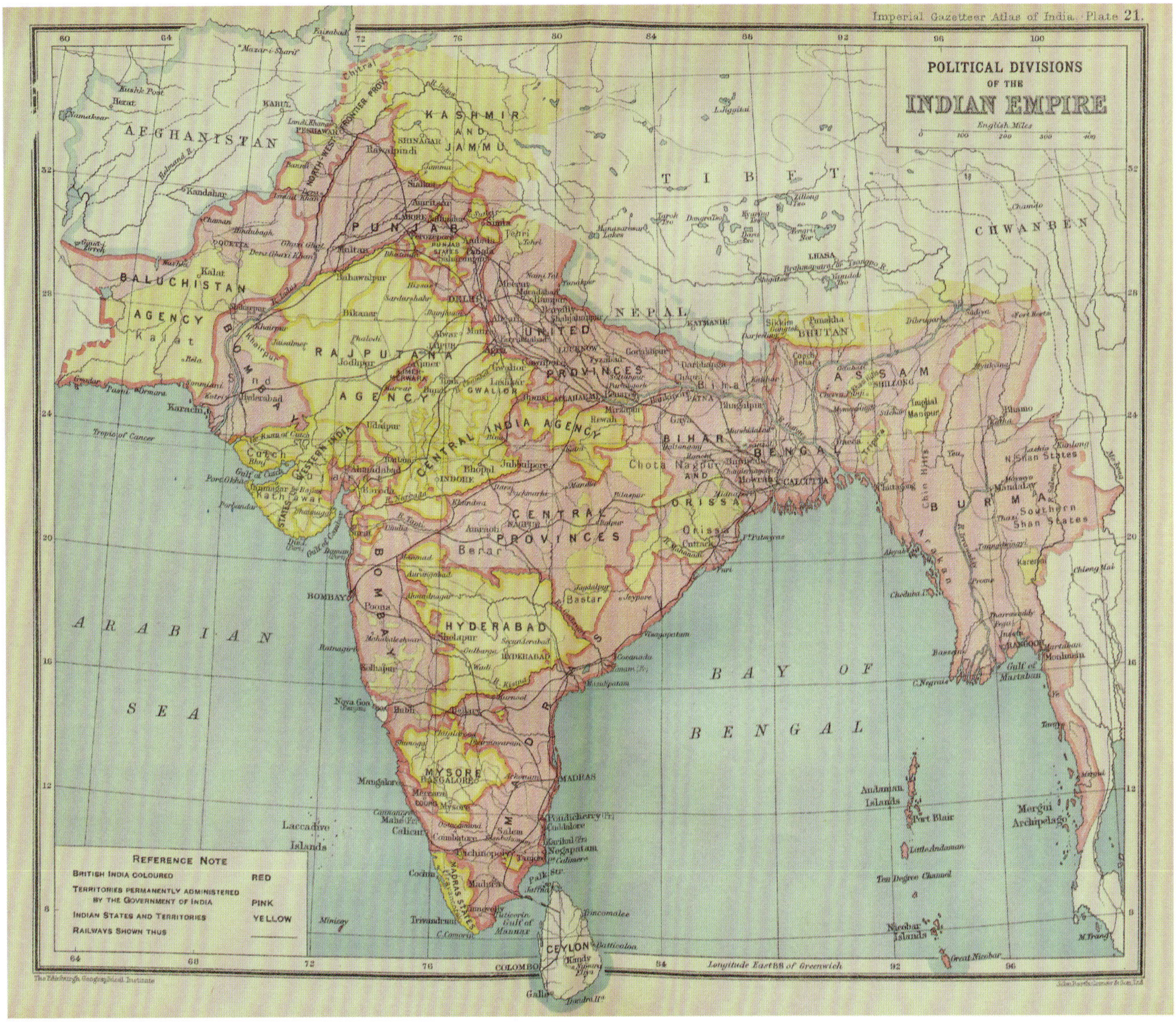

which in the seventeenth century had "pierced the [Mughal] enemy's heart," but now struck his with its loss to the British.[1] Such tiger-claws remain in British museums, for example that in the Victoria and Albert Museum, London (fig. 137). Hundreds of other items discussed in this book can be described in the same terms; they were removed from India by conquest, purchase, or under duress, transported to Britain, and housed in such museums. Chiplunkar sought to provide an alternative to British museums, which had not only taken significant objects to London, but also, according to him, did not

136 "Political Divisions of the Indian Empire," in William Stevenson Meyer et al., *The Imperial Gazetteer of India, Atlas*, vol. 26 (Oxford: Clarendon Press, 1909), pl. 20

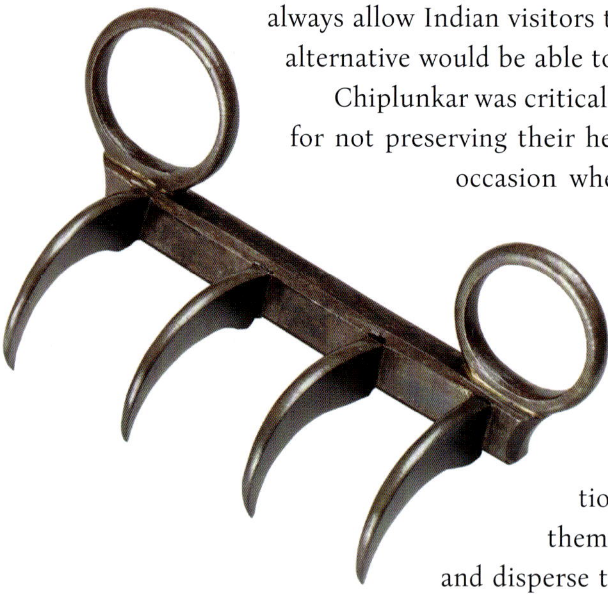

always allow Indian visitors to view them. By undermining British museums, this alternative would be able to "pierce" British hearts, but also Indian ones.[2]

Chiplunkar was critical of the British, but he also remonstrated with Indians for not preserving their heritage. In the old bazaar of Poona, he described an occasion when paintings of the late eighteenth-century Peshwa Savai Madhavrao and his wife were for sale. Rather than the pictures, customers were inquiring about their decorated frames. Appalled, he bought them, intending to create an accessible museum of figures important in Maratha history, as if fusing the British Museum with the National Portrait Gallery.[3] He had an innovative conception, though, for such "pictures." Rather than contain them in the walls of a museum, he sought to reproduce and disperse them in what we might call the nineteenth-century's mobile museum, the lithographic press. Chromolithography in particular enabled the mass-production of inexpensive colorful prints that owners could frame and display at will in their homes or institutions.[4] "Nowadays," Chiplunkar wrote, "these paintings are printed in our Chitrashala Press."[5]

This western Indian movement to reproduce such historical pictures and texts had begun in 1878 with the founding of the monthly magazine *Kavyetihas Sangraha* (Collection of Poetry and History), which sought to revive interest in Maratha history, and Sanskrit and Marathi poetry, while also preserving in print the content of the original fragile manuscripts. In the preface, the editors were explicit about their nationalist goals.[6] They aimed to create a printed archive of Marathi and Sanskrit materials in order to allow historians access to primary sources, and to preserve them from the deterioration of neglect, destruction, trade, or time. In the magazine's first few issues, for instance, they printed a recently discovered history (*bakhar*) of the Peshwa period (1728–1818) of Maratha dominance.[7] In this era, power was transposed from the Maratha king Shivaji's descendants to their Brahmin prime ministers, the Peshwas, and the capital moved from Satara to Poona. This history would have been particularly meaningful to the editors, printers, and their public in Poona, many of whom were descendants of the Peshwas or their administrators, and from a Brahmin, specifically Chitpavan, caste.[8]

Each Peshwa's reign received a detailed summary, akin to biography. The third issue, which focused on Peshwa Savai Madhavrao, included a novelty, a small brightly colored lithograph of his minister, Nana Fadnavis (fig. 138). This reproduced one of James Wales's oil portraits of Fadnavis, made around 1792 at the Peshwa's court, which still belonged to

137 *Wagnakh* (Tiger Claws), Maharashtra, ca. 17th century. Fitted case inscribed: "The 'Wagnuck' of Sivajee [Shivaji] With Which He Killed the Moghul General. This Relic was given to Mr. James Grant-Duff of Eden [1789–1858] When he was Resident at Satara by the Prime Minister of the Peshwa of the Marathas." Steel, 3.5 × 8.6 cm. Victoria and Albert Museum, London, IS.33-1971

Fadnavis's descendants in Poona (this portrait, though of a sole figure, is similar to that of Fadnavis included in fig. 25 and probably based on the same sketches).[9] This print was meant to be the first of a tri-monthly inclusion of "colorful dignified pictures of famous men" in the journal.[10] However, it spawned the independent press devoted to portraits, the Chitrashala. For Chiplunkar and other founders, this press emerged as the critical visual analogue to the historical, poetic, and biographical texts being published in their parallel venture *Kavyetihas Sangraha*. "One thing we especially want to tell our readers," Chiplunkar wrote, "is that we started our workshop [the Chitrashala] so the figures of men famous in history would remain for a long time."[11]

These publications, as Prachi Deshpande has analyzed, were reacting to the aftermath of the defeat of the Maratha Peshwa in 1818, the last dynasty to fall to the British, and the establishment of colonial control. Colonial pedagogy shifted from an Indian to a British-oriented education, which trained a Marathi-speaking intelligentsia in newly founded English-speaking institutes such as the Hindu College, later Elphinstone and then Deccan College in Poona (1821), and Bombay University (1857).[12] This program sought a new religious paradigm, as I discussed in Chapter Four, as well as a new historical one. British writers promoted socially conscious historical fiction and spirited biographies at the same time as they inaugurated particular historical discourses about the Maratha past. James Grant Duff's *History of the Mahrattas* (1826), for example, framed Maratha history as a negative one of political decline.[13] However, the editors of *Kavyetihas Sangraha* countered colonial analyses using the same pedagogical tools of historical practice and attention to culture as the British. They argued that Duff's *History* had actually failed to make use of all available primary documents, lacked an understanding of intuitive Indian qualities such as *dharma*, and concentrated on political history and not, for example, social conditions or biography.[14]

This newly educated elite, therefore, was steeped in English prose and history; however, they were excluded from the resources that would enable

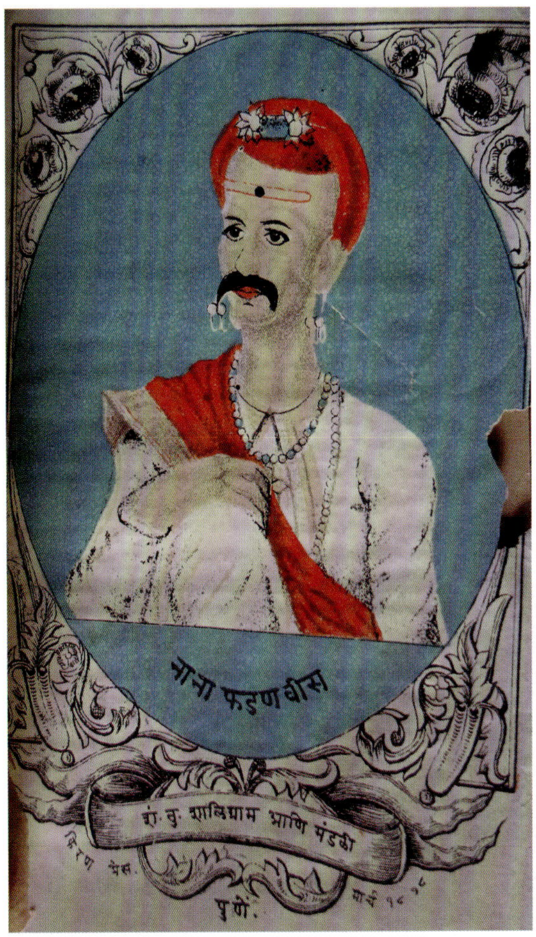

138 "Nana Fadnavis," *Kavyetihas Sangraha* 1, no. 3 (Fern Press, Poona, 1878). Lithograph with hand coloring on paper, 19 × 12 cm. Gokhale Hall Magazine Library, Pune

their own historical practice. For instance, Indian researchers were prohibited from consulting the primary Maratha archives for fear of sedition, much as Chiplunkar had noted them being refused access to Maratha arts in the British Museum.[15] The founders of *Kavyetihas Sangraha* and the Chitrashala were motivated by the inaccessibility of archives, and the prevalence of what they deemed inaccurate colonial histories, to find original materials in alternative locales and widely disseminate them.[16] These printed pictures and publications inspired precisely what the British hoped to repress: a burgeoning Indian nationalism.

Yet the Chitrashala and *Kavyetihas Sangraha* publishers were only one of many groups in western India that sought different pasts to regenerate. Rosalind O'Hanlon outlined three strands of nationalism that flourished in this region in the nineteenth century.[17] Mahatma Jotirao Phule advocated for lower castes and instigated the anti-Brahmin movement; he became the inspiration for Dr. Babasaheb Ambedkar's continued appeal for lower castes in the twentieth century. There were also reformists, like Justice M. G. Ranade, who identified a pluralist, confederate model in the Maratha past to unify diverse religious and political groups in the present. Finally, there were conservative Hindu nationalists, like Bal Gangadhar Tilak and Vinayak Savarkar, who promoted Maharashtrian culture including its religious traditions and Brahmin histories, often by way of contrast to Muslim ones and by de-emphasizing pre-colonial integration; they also advanced violence as a revolutionary strategy.

Chiplunkar's position, as well as that of the Chitrashala Press at the outset, sat in between the last two. His primary target was the British; he criticized the colonial system as flawed, especially the work of British missionaries, educators, and social reformers. The antidote, he believed, was in the past. By resuscitating Indian traditions and having pride in Indian – and specifically Maratha – history, Indians could seize control of their country's governance. However, Chiplunkar stressed a Hindu, specifically Brahmin, past as a source for that reform.[18] After his early death in 1882, the movements became fractured. Chiplunkar's successors, like Tilak, would press for Hindu communalism, which continued to narrow over the course of the twentieth and into the twenty-first century into religious fundamentalism.[19] To channel tradition and the revival of history, Chiplunkar emphasized the power of biography in his writings, which the Chitrashala paralleled in printed portraits.[20] In 1880, he wrote a review of *Kavyetihas Sangraha* that addressed what he anticipated would be its main criticism: a doubt that Marathi and Sanskrit literature and history were worthy of study. He called attention to the fact that although history told the story of people and things long gone, it was still a profound and potent resource for self-respect and national progress, echoing Carlyle's *Lectures on Heroes, Hero-Worship and the Heroic in History* (1841).[21]

Biography, in particular, was a conduit, such as James Boswell's *Life of Samuel Johnson* (1791), which taught how famous men's lives could help viewers absorb the "wisdom, bravery, or virtue" in historical places, and offered a virtuous model of intelligent, but determined and unceasing, work on the part of both Boswell as biographer and Johnson as subject.[22] In Chiplunkar's review he wrote about biography in a stirring Marathi adaptation of Victorian prose style:

> Far away from us . . . a group of stars with self-existent light . . . continually reaches our world; from the beginning their light guides us. Until today, all in countries who take the form of Shiva's incarnation, time after time, present themselves again . . . so also the biographies of people have been going towards progress. . . . By reading about a noble and intrepid man's importance, whose heart is not imprinted, whose mind's goodness is not subject, whose love is not drawn to the subject of the nation, who is not inspired?[23]

Using a comparative technique, he established that heroes were found throughout world history. Napoleon for instance brought Europe's states and Russia "under one umbrella" (of course, he was also a notorious British antagonist). Yet encountering one's own national heroes, their grandeur and conquest, was more advantageous. Shivaji, for instance, like Napoleon, unified "Maharashtra towards Delhi" under "Maratha flags raised on temple tops," which made him a king.[24] However, Chiplunkar stressed that Shivaji was just one of "Shiva's incarnation[s]" who "time after time, present themselves again," implying that the present was ripe for Maratha, and Hindu, leaders to revolt against their colonial British overlords and create their own nation.[25]

The first hero that these western Indian nationalists proposed was Nana Fadnavis. His portrait had been included in the third issue of *Kavyetihas Sangraha*, alongside a description of the Peshwa Savai Madhavrao's realm (see fig. 138). Probably based on the illustration in Captain A. Macdonald's *Memoir of . . . Nana Furnuwees* (1851), the reproduction was hasty and inexpensively produced.[26] The Chitrashala decided to recreate it six years later, in 1884 (fig. 139), along with a representation of the Peshwa, but on a much grander scale than the Fern Press could command. These printed portraits, as Macdonald's lithograph had been, were based on oils that James Wales made with his assistants, Jossi and Mabon, in the 1790s, which local artists copied for the task. Printers then translated the watercolors into chromolithographs over a meter high and half a meter wide, with an elaborate description, explanation, and five-rupee price tag.[27] They were prints that served as an advertisement for the Chitrashala's highly finished, densely saturated, multicolored products, which brilliantly used the technology of chromolithography to glorify and preserve Maratha, and specifically Peshwa, leaders.[28] By reproducing and dis-

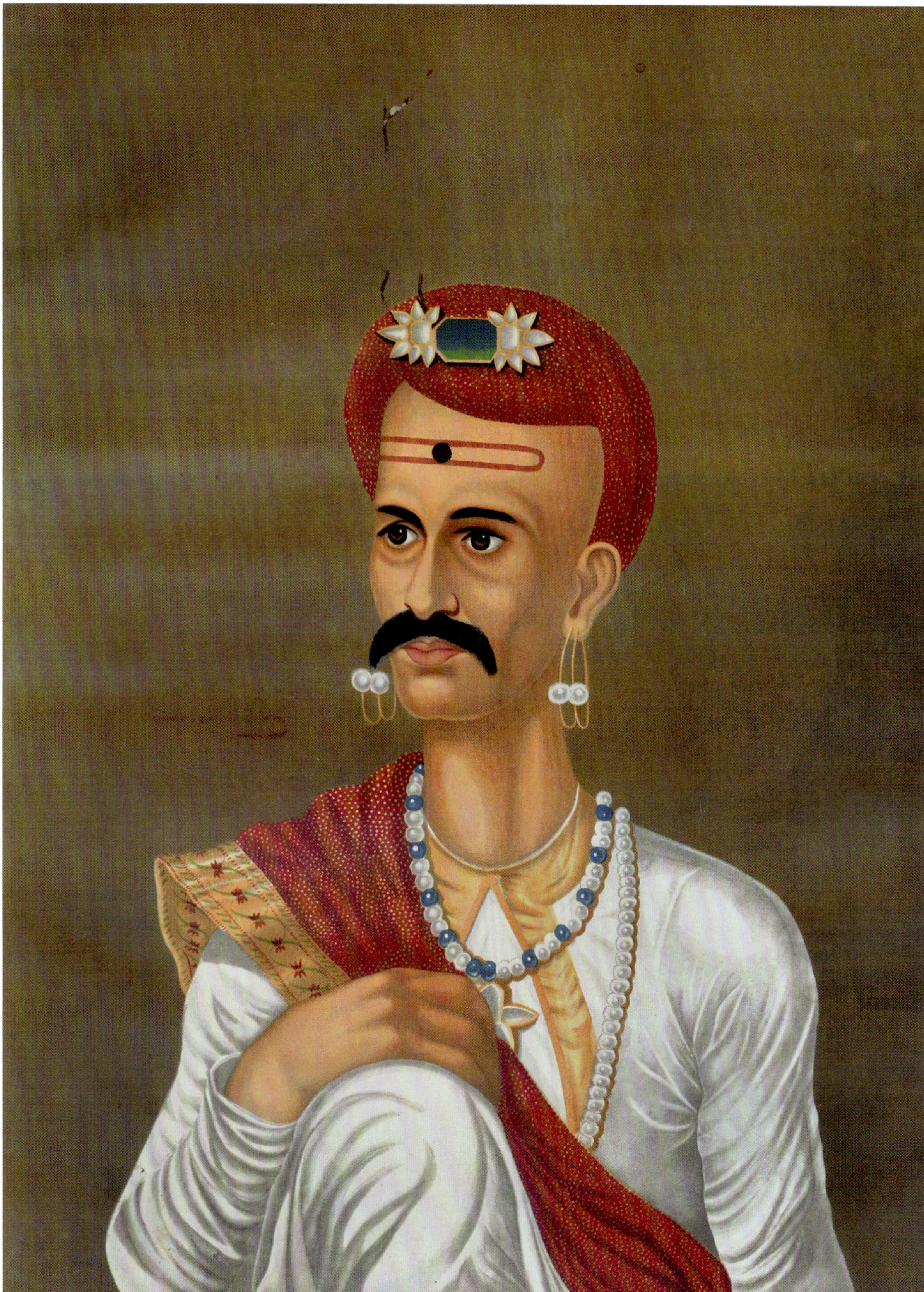

seminating these figures, they would encourage the public to purchase and display them to create personal museums in homes and institutions across western India.

To Chiplunkar and other western Indian nationalists, Nana Fadnavis was a perfect model. He had built an able Maratha administration while holding together a confederacy of the Peshwa and high-ranking Maratha officials over a tumultuous forty-year period (see the Introduction and Chapter One). The chromolithograph of Nana Fadnavis would not only memorialize his modernity in politics, but also promote his astute desire for the court to gain knowledge of British techniques of representation as well as other advances in science, medicine, map-making, and warfare. His invitation to James Wales and Wales's training of Indian artists, including Jossi and Gangaram Tambat, proved that Poona was at the vanguard of artistic pedagogy. Indeed, western Indian scholars identified Wales's workshop as the first art school in India.[29] The portrait itself – produced at large scale, in an academic manner, and in oils – also visualized Nana Fadnavis's recognition of British ways that he could wield as either their ally or enemy. To the Chitrashala printers and other western Indian nationalists, it was these aspects of Fadnavis's versatility, his strategic adoption of European technologies alongside his profound moral strength and sense of Maratha history, that could once again model Maratha, and Indian, ascendancy.[30]

As I argued in Chapter One, in the late eighteenth-century period of their composition, the portraits of Nana Fadnavis and Peshwa Savai Madhavrao hewed more to a British artist's submission to a Maratha visual paradigm inaugurated by the Poona court, which grafted other arts into their own, than it did to a late nineteenth-century interpretation of them as an example of studied mimicry. But in the course of more than sixty years of British colonial control, the potential in the variety of paintings, prints, drawings, and sculptures that I have discussed throughout this book generated a new anticolonial purpose.

THE MATERIALS AND POLITICS OF REUSE

The Chitrashala's visual program combined the past and the present, old and new technologies, and the East and the West in its pictorial reproductions. Nana Fadnavis and Savai Madhavrao were only two of the famous men in the Maratha history of the Deccan whose images the Chitrashala printed. In about 1885, the press published an innovative series of lightly colored prints that more explicitly sought to "pierce the enemy's heart" through lithography. This series aligned Maratha generals, the Brahmin Peshwas and ministers, and Hindu religious leaders with those starring in the contemporary nationalist movement, forging a link between past and present.[31] Maratha warriors, such as Malharrao Holkar (fig. 140), who governed the region the Marathas conquered around

139 *Nana Fadnavis*, Chitrashala Press, Poona, 1884. Chromolithograph on paper, 91.4 × 61 cm. Anil Relia Collection, Ahmedabad

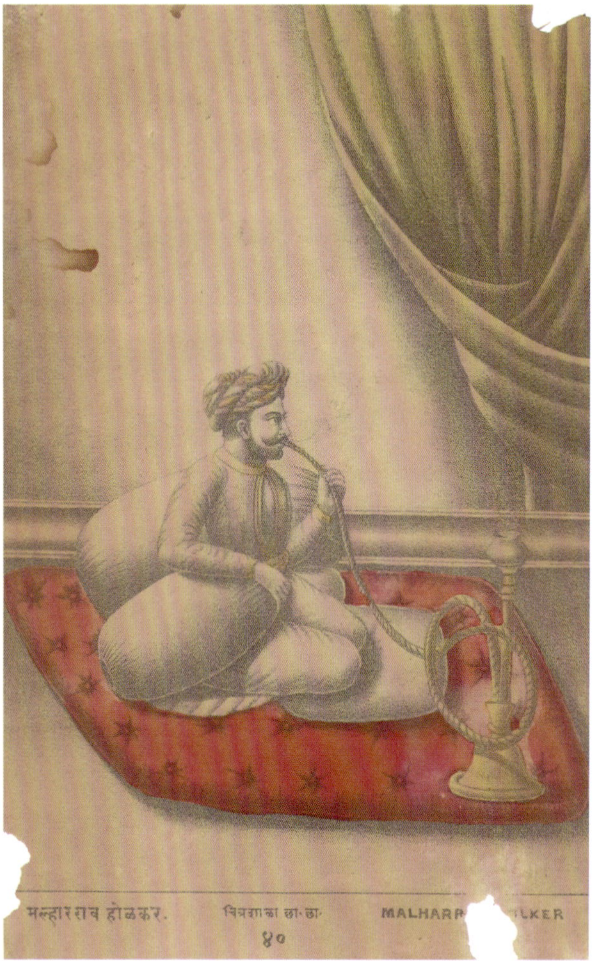

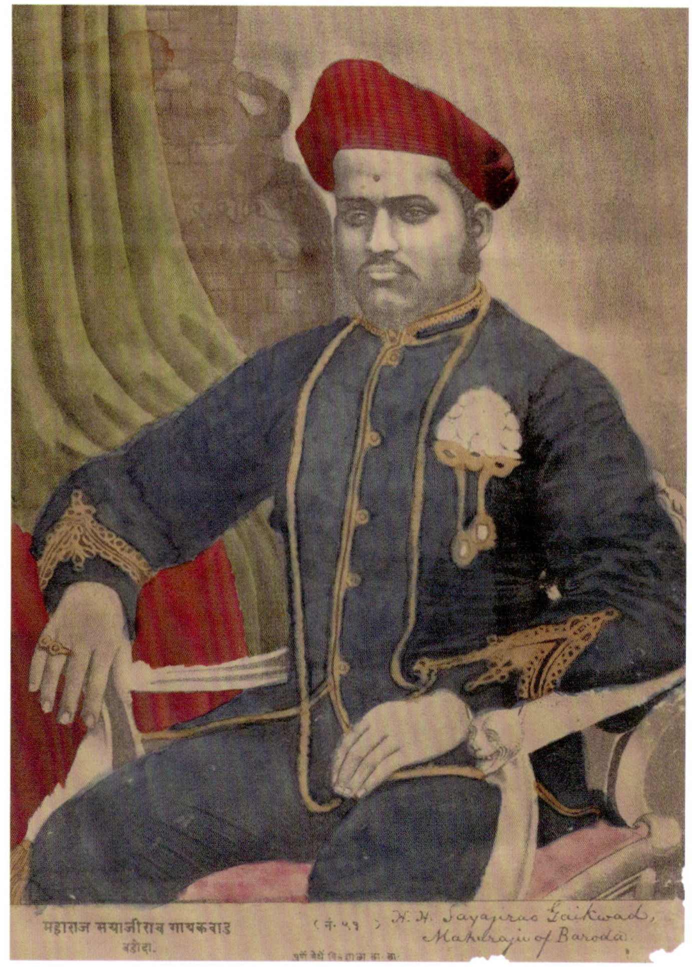

Indore, were portrayed alongside the late nineteenth-century inheritor-princes of those states, like the Maharaja of Baroda (fig. 141) who ruled as subservient governors and then "native princes" to the British after the fall of the Marathas in 1818.

Contemporary intellectuals were also included, like Justice Ranade whose portrait within the series seems to disseminate visually a paragraph of his reformist *Rise of the Maratha Power* (ca. 1900), which promoted the princely states as the precursor to an independent federated India:

> Even at the present day, though the British rulers of India occupy the place of the Peshwas and of the Moghul Emperors as suzerain power . . . the remnants of the Confederacy that are still in the enjoyment of subordinate independence at

140 *Malharrao Holkar*, Chitrashala Press, Poona, ca. 1885. Lithograph with hand coloring on paper, 22.7 × 16.5 cm. Dr. Prashant & Rashmi Tapadia Collection, Pune

141 *HH Maharaj Gaikwad Maharaj of Baroda*, Chitrashala Press, Poona, ca. 1885. Lithograph with hand coloring on paper, 22.7 × 16.5 cm. Dr. Prashant & Rashmi Tapadia Collection, Pune

> Gwalior, Indore, Baroda, Kolhapur . . . and the Maratha population of about thirty millions included in the Bombay Presidency and the Native States, as also in the Central Provinces, Berars, and the Nizam's country, represent a power which is second to none among the native communities and States. . . . This element of present influence cannot also fail to have a deep interest to those who can see far into the future of the possibilities open to a Federated India, distributed according to nationalities, and subjected to a common bond of connection with the Imperial Power of the Queen-Empress of India.[32]

The Chitrashala's sequence of prints offered a model of political unification. Yet the prints also proposed a material and stylistic model of unity through their varied visual sources and strategic reconfigurations. Similarly to the print of Nana Fadnavis, these lithographs achieve a careful balance among their claims to historical legitimacy, techniques of representation, and identification. For instance, the Maharaja of Baroda's likeness was based on one of his photographs as an Indian prince and a British subject, wearing gold-embroidered military dress and a simple Maratha-style turban (see fig. 141). The Maharaja sits confidently, back straight, on an armchair with a prominent bejeweled medal over his left breast, probably one of three bestowed on him by the British in the 1870s and 1880s.[33] This style of portraiture followed the standard set by Bourne and Shepherd during their 1875–7 tour of India to document the princes of India for Queen Victoria's accession as Empress of India. Although the Queen never came to the subcontinent, Indian princes' images passed to her via photographs, as hers did to them, to mediate their relationship.[34]

Such images and their subjects, however, could be repurposed. In one of their royal albums, the publishers at the Poona Photographic Company imaginatively reframed the photograph of the Maharaja of Baroda in a foliate border of elephants and lions akin to honorific wall paintings (fig. 142). In another, they grafted together images of Indian princes, Parsi industrialists, reformers, scholars, and nationalists like Justice Ranade around a photographic portrait of the Queen (fig. 143).[35] This image of Victoria ruling from the center of a diagram of subservience and loyalty seems to conform to the British colonial project, but the Poona Photographic Company's reuse of such images asserted their perspective from western India rather than Buckingham Palace.

The collage reveals a desire on the part of a regional population to participate in a network of empire that they imagined, including relationships that could produce political power akin to Justice Ranade's reformist model. Indeed, Ranade is pictured on the Poona Photographic Company's branching pictorial tree, which hints at another, subversive, interpretation of its contents. Even the portrait of the Maharaja of Baroda, which

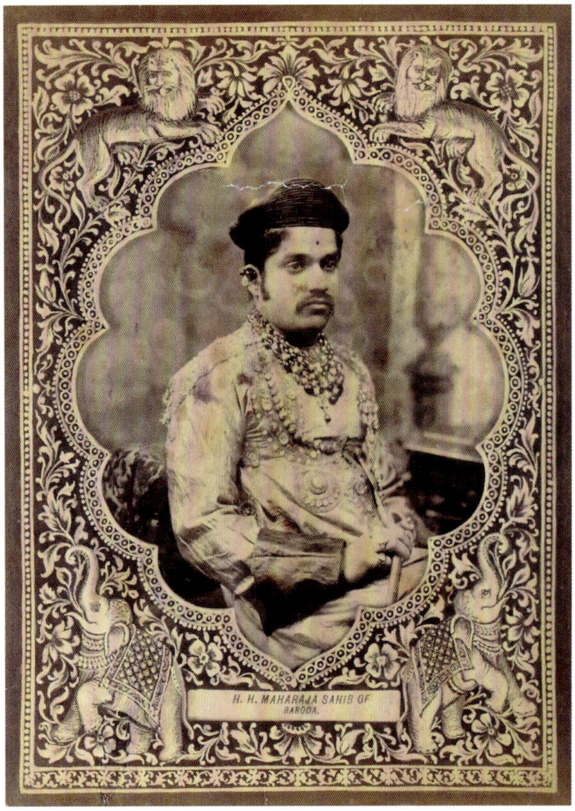

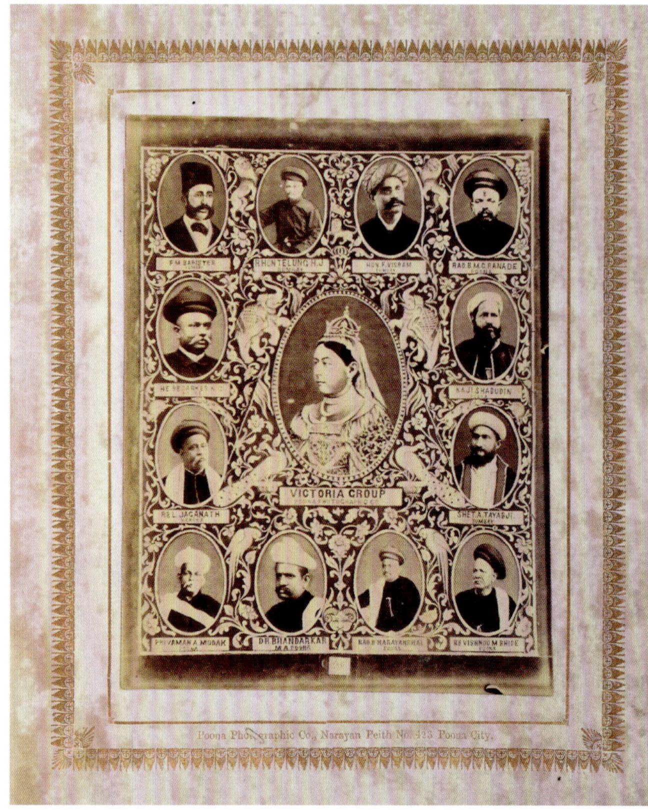

had initially been taken by British photographers for the Queen, by 1910 was identified as a nationalist symbol. Indeed, when the Maharaja applied to leave India, his application was denied. The British officials wrote in explanation that even if "there is no evidence of active disloyalty, his words and actions evince a sympathy with the extremists... his picture has more than once appeared among portraits published by the extreme part of Nationalist heroes, etc."[36] Suddenly, Queen Victoria's center in the photographic collage is the seed of a nationalist program that germinates around her.

The Chitrashala instituted a nationalist program by way of its subjects as well as the media in which they were represented. While the Maharaja of Baroda and Justice Ranade's prints were based on photographs, the Chitrashala editors turned to other sources for leaders whose images preceded photography. The artists derived Malharrao Holkar's portrait from an illustration in Macdonald's *Memoir of... Nana Furnuwees*, for instance (fig. 144).[37] Macdonald, in turn, had used Maratha paintings from local collections in Satara as the source for his reproductive prints. For example, Holkar is in a similar pose to Shahu Maharaj smoking a hookah in a painting that D. B. Parasnis had

142 Poona Photographic Company, *H.H. Maharaja Sahib of Baroda*, after 1887. Photomontage, 28.7 × 21 cm. Anil Relia Collection, Ahmedabad

143 Poona Photographic Company, *Victoria Group*, after 1887. Photomontage, 33 × 27.4 cm. Anil Relia Collection, Ahmedabad

collected from the Satara region around 1900 (see fig. 75).[38] The Chitrashala artists probably pared down the original painting and added the wall molding and the curtain drawn to the right to make it contemporary, as they did with other prints of the Peshwas.

Similarly, the tinted lithograph of Narayanrao Peshwa (fig. 145) was based on an earlier work, possibly an original painting formerly housed in Satara's royal collections (fig. 146), the replica of it that a British official had commissioned in 1854, or another copy.[39] The multiple renditions of Narayanrao's portrait attest to its circulation in painted as well as printed form long before the Chitrashala's program of dissemination. Like that of Malharrao Holkar, the Chitrashala print of Narayanrao is not an exact copy of the painting. The artist reproduced the identifying aspects of the painted portrait – the profile and pose – nearly exactly, but updated the scene with decorative floor tiles, a thick swag of curtain, and glass-paned windows. The Chitrashala Press thus preserved a genealogy of portraits, but also of the history of portraiture in the Deccan, from eigh-

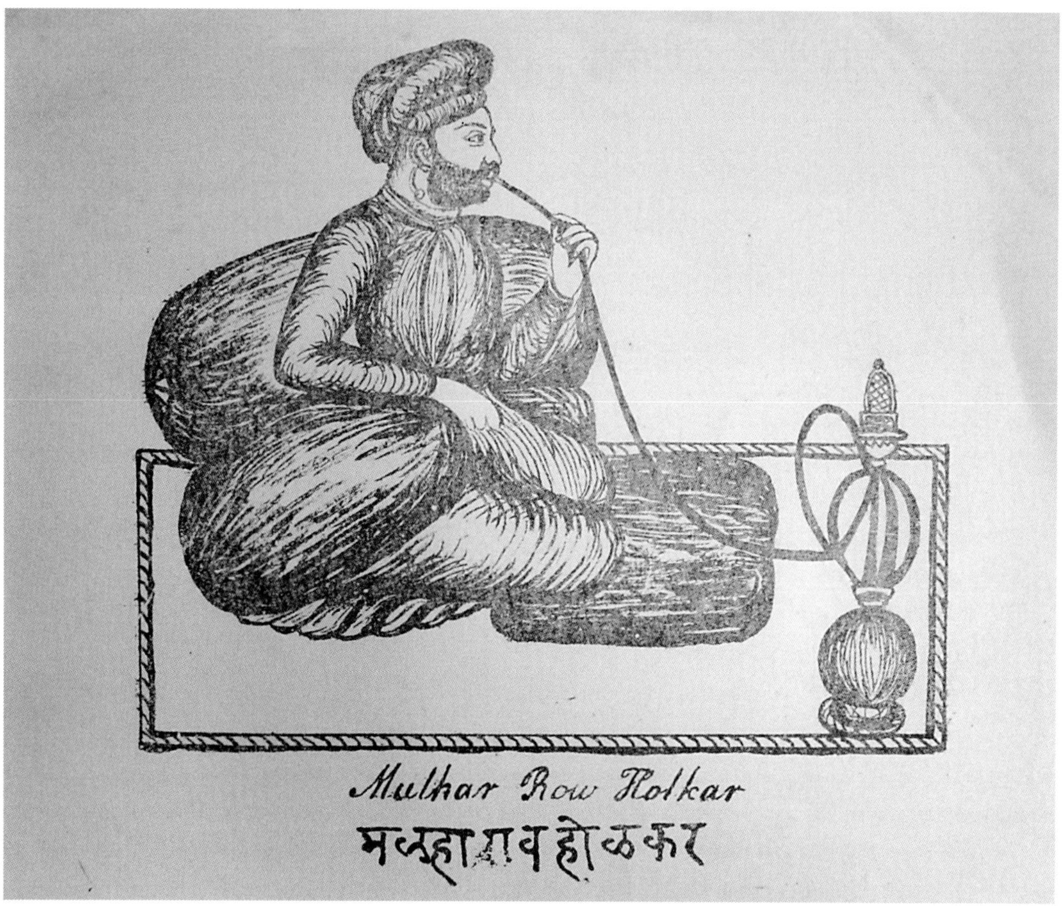

144 "Mulhar Row [Malharrao] Holkar," in Archibald Macdonald, *Memoir of the late Nana Furnuwees compiled from family records and extant works* (Bombay: American Mission Press, 1851). Lithograph on paper, 17.3 × 18.4 cm. Royal Asiatic Society of Great Britain and Ireland, London, RAS 091.001

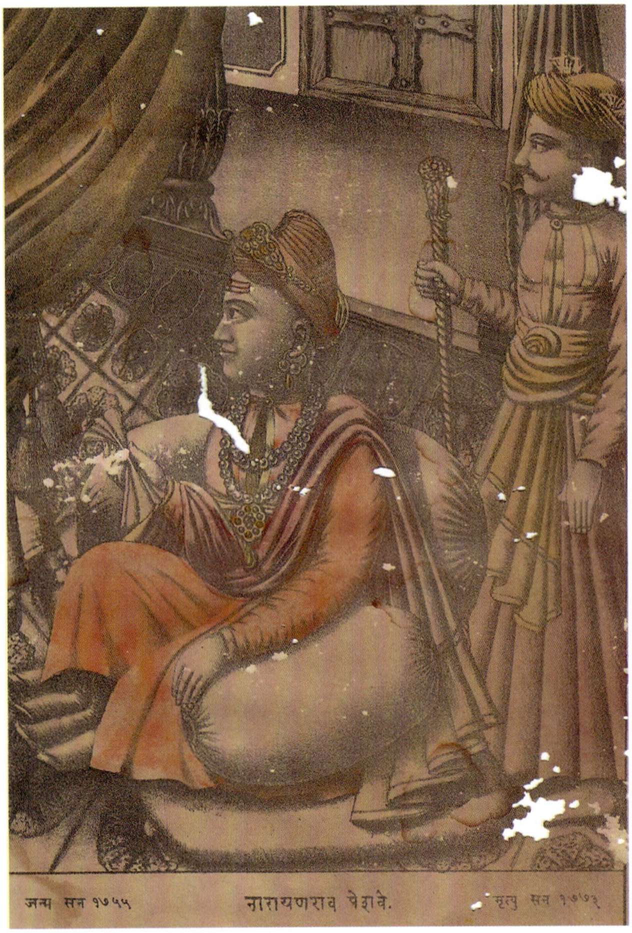

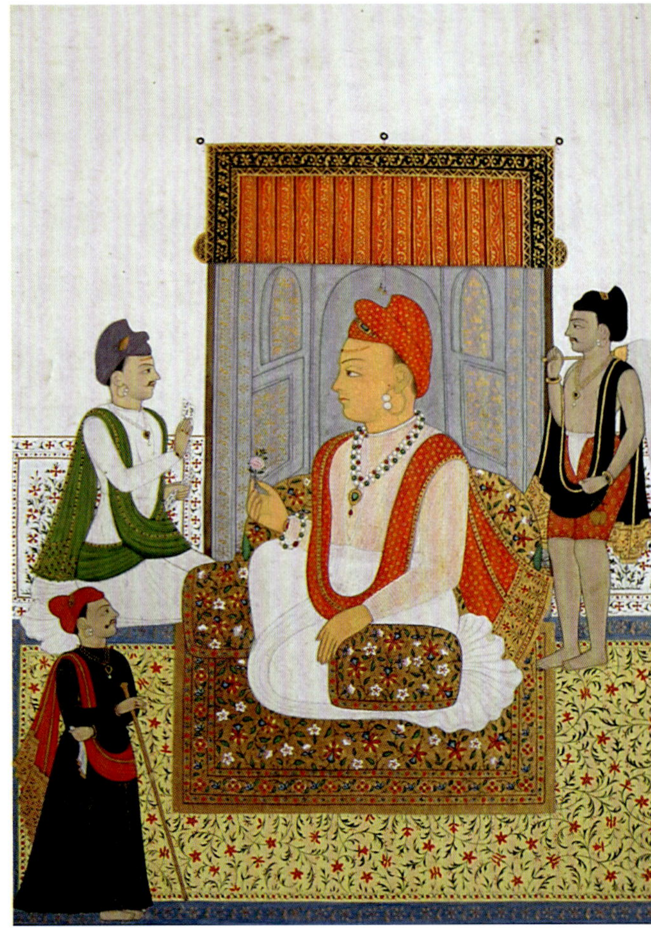

teenth-century Maratha portraiture, to the advent of British oil painting, to photography, and the lithographic print.

The intermediality of these images heightened their versatility as well as their prospects for diverse interpretation. The art historian Hermann Goetz, who was the Director of the Baroda Museum & Picture Gallery from 1939 to 1956, observed that the arts of the Marathas emblematized a route to "a strong national or social consciousness" in the subcontinent. This sensibility was not forged by "virgin purity," but through "chaotic agglomerations of cultural elements, national as well as foreign, contemporary as well as old ones." Only such mixtures "could assimilate . . . many influences into [a] self contained style of outspoken personality" and therefore be motivated toward anticolonial resistance.[40] This conceptualization of variety paralleled Justice Ranade's notion of a diverse confederacy as the key to political freedom, but it also proposed an aesthetic

145 *Narayanrao Peshwa*, Chitrashala Press, Poona, ca. 1885. Lithograph with hand coloring on paper, 22.7 × 16.5 cm. Dr. Prashant & Rashmi Tapadia Collection, Pune

146 Shivram Chitari, *Narayanrao Peshwa*, Maharashtra, late 18th century. Opaque watercolor on paper, 33 × 25.5 cm. History Museum, Dr. Babasaheb Ambedkar Marathwada University, Aurangabad

one. Not only did political mixture parallel a composite population and unify it, but it also afforded a type of camouflage.[41] While conforming to visual modes used by the British, these prints also contained historical and contemporary meanings to Marathas that allowed for the dissemination of variegated, at times highly politicized, messages.

The range of meanings that the Chitrashala prints insinuated was propagated by laymen. In a telling juxtaposition, an unknown fabricator pasted a photograph of Professor S. G. Jinsiwale, the late nineteenth-century conservative Hindu nationalist leader, to the upper right of a painting of the last Peshwa, Bajirao II, who was deposed by the British in 1818 (fig. 147). Bajirao II's image is nearly identical to the lithograph published in Macdonald's book and, of course, to the painting it was probably based on (now in the Bharat Itihas Sanshodhak Mandal, Pune), drawn in 1821 by Sayyid Ghulam Hasan Khan when Bajirao II was in exile in Brahmavarti in North India. Although the inspiration for the collage is unknown, the image seems to pictorialize a speech that Jinsiwale gave in 1897, in which he said

> that the reason why Shri Shivaji Maharajah should be considered superior to Caesar and Napoleon was that while the great men of Europe were actuated by ambition alone . . . the uncommon attributes displayed by our Maharajah, were not the blaze of the fire of ambition or discontent, but were the outcome of the terrible irritation at the ruin of his country and religion by foreigners.[42]

This collage-maker implied that it was those British foreigners who defeated Bajirao II in 1818 who should be ousted.

Nationalists in western India were not alone in turning to print to provide visual imagery in service of a movement. Their regional print culture paralleled that in Calcutta, another vibrant seat of production and blooming nationalism. In the middle of the nineteenth century, the graphic woodcuts known as Battala prints, after the region of Calcutta in which they were made, were concerned with contemporary themes and political commentary. However, their aesthetic drew from the living Kalighat tradition of painting rather than from reusing historical materials.[43] In the later nineteenth century, the Calcutta Art Studio, set up in 1878, the same year as the Chitrashala, produced lithographic portraits based on oil paintings of renowned Bengalis. Then in 1886, the art journal *Shilpa Pushpanjali* included similar images of men based on photographs.[44] As former students of the Government Art School, the founders of the Calcutta Art Studio brought together their training in Western illusionism and classical forms prevalent in academic art with the publication of images of Hindu gods.[45] The icons of deities, in particular, were not only popular but also carried explicit nationalist messages. However, there is little evidence that these nineteenth-century Bengali presses were interested in adapting an eighteenth-century regional aesthetic.[46]

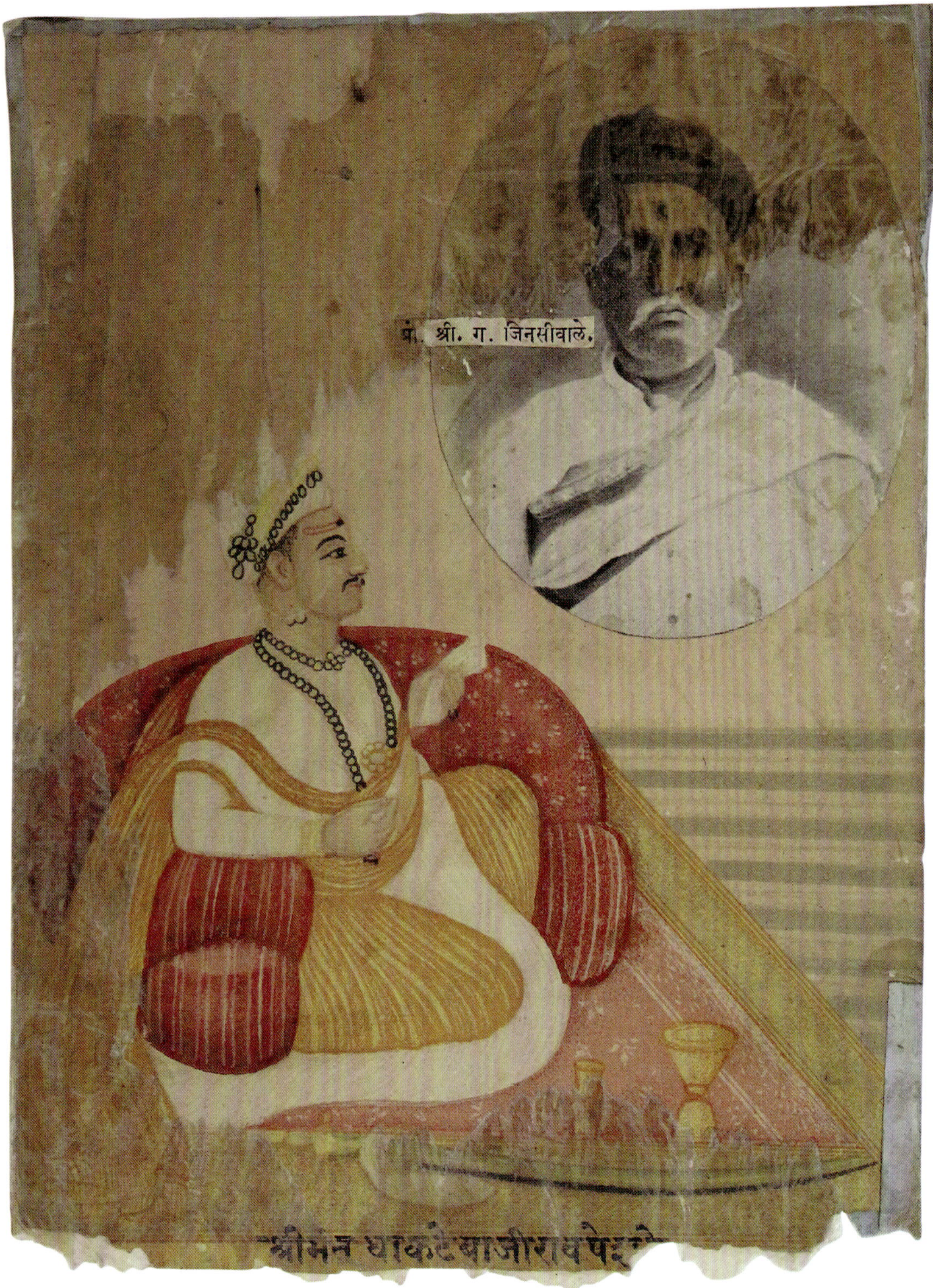

147 *Peshwa Bajirao II and Shri G. Jinsiwale*, Maharashtra, ca. 1900. Collage of painting and photograph, approx. 24 × 17 cm. Bharat Itihas Sanshodhak Mandal, Pune

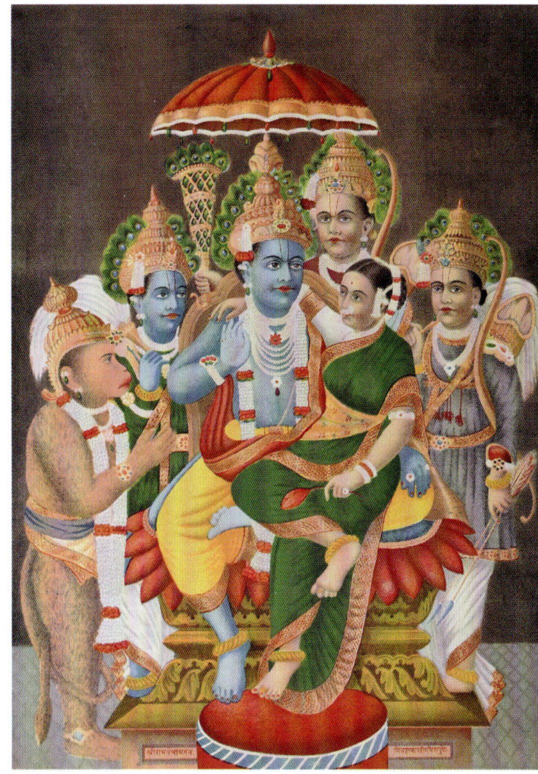

The Chitrashala's revivalist framework was notable, but it focused not only on the heroization of men but also a visualization of gods, which supported the founders' attention to a Hindu polity and proved lucrative. According to Kanitkar's *History of the Chitrashala Press*, contemporary portraits of lesser-known figures were unpopular. Therefore, one of the editors suggested that pictures of deities might be commercially viable, and others approved.[47] For the new design, the artist copied a painting of *Ram Panchayatan* in the Raja of Aundh's collection from a photograph, which sold two thousand copies in a month and secured a consumer base for the press (fig. 148).[48] Formally this picture relates to paintings on paper and walls from the Satara region, such as a painting from the Mate Ram Mandir (see fig. 106), and sculpted icons as well as their reproduction in British publications such as Moor's *Hindu Pantheon* (see Chapter Four).[49]

In their pictures of gods, the publishers at the Chitrashala used similar aesthetics as in their portraits: they looked to regional art production as their design source. The robust bodies, round faces, acorn-shaped crowns, and regional garments like the nine-yard sari all point to local forms of production. However, the profuse shadows, rosy cheeks, and receding perspective of the gray-blue floor, reflect Western publications like *The Hindu Pantheon* and training prevalent in art schools: this focused on reaching a scientific ideal through a staged curriculum of perspective and architectural drawing, freehand drawing as well as copying, and learning to enunciate figures with tone and shade.[50] The Chitrashala prints anticipate Raja Ravi Varma's depictions of gods and goddesses in the lithographic press he opened more than fifteen years later, in 1894. However, they have not yet smoothly transitioned from the local aesthetic of iconic deities to a Victorian-inspired green and brown verdant landscape.

Like the Chitrashala portraits of men, those of gods also contained political undertones or came to be used in that manner. Christopher Pinney has shown the range of negotiation and reuse of devotional imagery that the Chitrashala motivated toward a political end, such as prints of women setting parrots free that evoked a longing to be independent of British rule.[51] The Chitrashala never abandoned portraits, though, and

148 *Rama Enthroned with Sita Surrounded by Hanuman and Other Members of His Family (Ram Panchayatan)*, Chitrashala Press, Poona, ca. 1880s. Chromolithograph on paper, 50.8 × 35.6 cm. Anil Relia Collection, Ahmedabad

certainly not its political program. In the official report of the Calcutta exhibition of 1883–4 the chromolithographs from the "Chitrashala Press in Poona" were listed with their prices. They included portraits of saints such as Ramdas Swami (Rs.1,10), a dancing girl (Rs.1,8), and devotional images of the Ganapati Panchayatan (Rs.1,12) and the Ram Panchayatan (Rs.5). It also displayed famous men including the Nizam of Hyderabad (Rs.5), political activists such as Ganesh Vasudev Joshi (Rs.4), and intellectuals of the press, such as Chiplunkar (Rs.6).[52] The portrait of Chiplunkar carried the heaviest price tag, perhaps related to his recent death, in 1882. This itemized list shows that the prized prints exhibited included a variety of subjects, touching on religion, pleasure, and heroes though all with a distinct regional, if not explicitly political, focus. Ramdas Swami was the spiritual guru of Shivaji, Ganapati (Ganesha) the deity of the Peshwas, and Chiplunkar of course a founding nationalist figure, a self-titled "Shivaji of the Marathi language."[53]

These kinds of images undoubtedly participated in polemic, specifically around the image and history of Shivaji, the first Maratha king, whose image was revered across caste lines. The Chitrashala was one of the earliest, if not the first, to publish a portrait of Shivaji, though others proliferated, such as the well-known chromolithograph by Raja Ravi Varma (fig. 149).[54] A disapproving Bombay police notice of November 6, 1906 from Sholapur reported:

> The Pandharpur Industrial Exhibition was opened . . . on the 20th October. The Chief [of Miraj] delivered a speech exhorting the people to shake off their lethargy and emulate other countries in their efforts to foster home industries. The Honourable . . . B G Tilak . . . [was] present, but did not speak. Financially the exhibition is a complete failure and I look upon it as a pretext for assembling in Pandharpur a host of speakers to carry on a propaganda in Tilak's interest. Some of the exhibits are very good specimens of Native handicraft, but in the majority of cases the material used is not of country manufacture. Nearly every stall displays pictures of Shivaji and in the Fine Arts Gallery I counted seven paintings describing episodes of his life . . . to suit the Brahman version of the incident . . . .[55]

These pictures moved in a wide sphere of anticolonial activity and became incentives for nationalist action.

In Nasik before 1906, for example, the British reported that there was an association run by the conservative western Hindu nationalists Ganesh and Vinayak Savarkar. The report notes as evidence a photograph that showed members grouped around Vinayak Savarkar "in which four or five pictures of Shivaji . . . are prominently displayed." In front of these images, Savarkar spoke, according to the police, "to arouse the passion for independence and hatred of the foreign rulers of the country and to suggest how by means

149 Raja Ravi Varma, *Shivaji Maharaj*, Ravi Varma Press, Bombay, 1896. Chromolithograph on paper, 50.8 × 35.6 cm. Anil Relia Collection, Ahmedabad

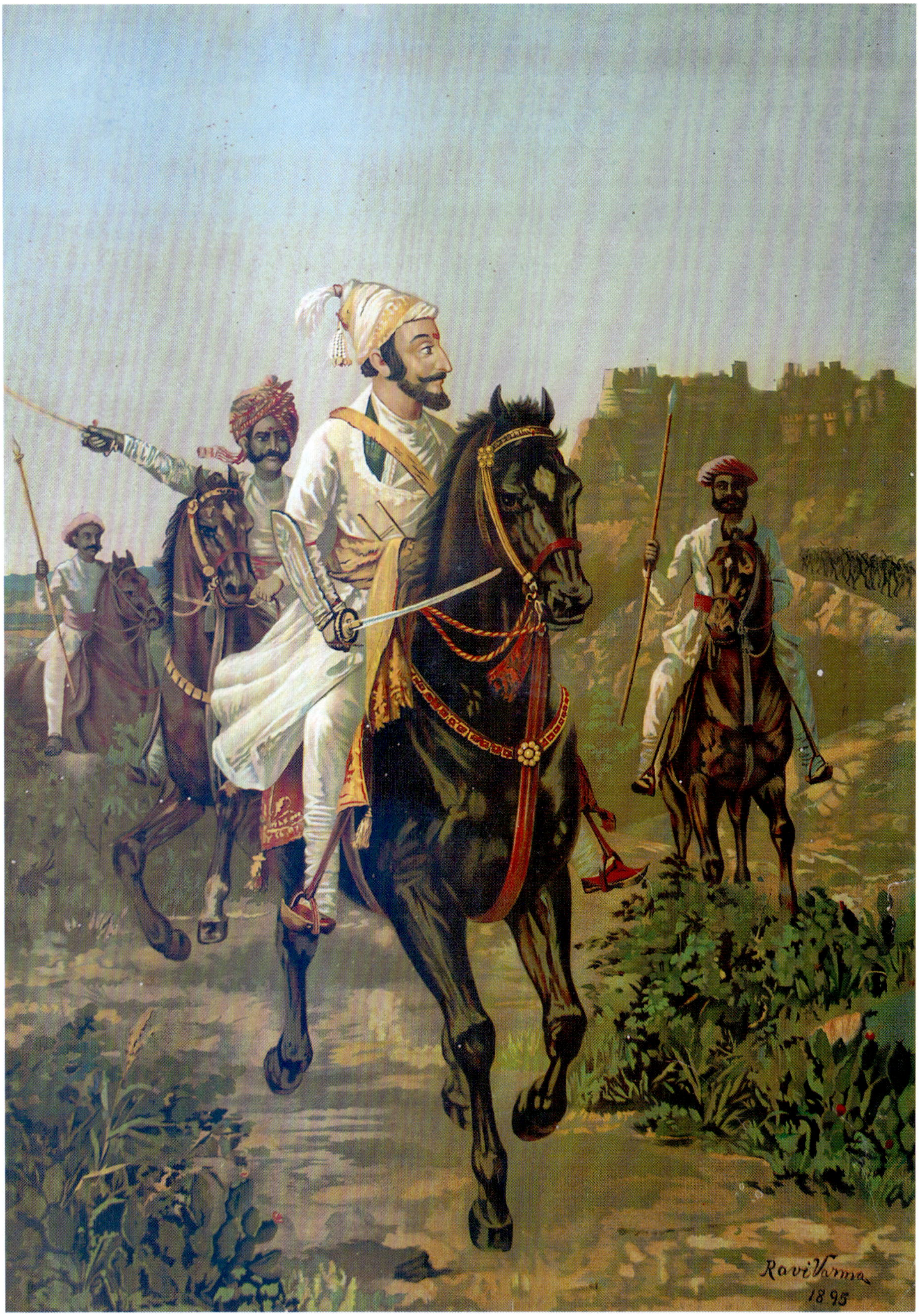
Ravi Varma
1895

of mental training and physical exercises, preparation might be made for successful revolt."[56] According to one testimony, Savarkar used Shivaji's image as an icon, taking an insurgent

> to a room and closed the door from the inside. He . . . placed a lamp with ghee in it on the mantelpiece, and put a picture of Shivaji on it. He poured water into the hollow of the deponent's palm . . . . He told him his duties were to be ready to wage war against the Government with such weapons as he might have, sacrificing life, family and possession.[57]

By 1916, unsurprisingly, the British had declared that "no pictures of humans could be carried and no names other than gods could be invoked in procession."[58]

From emulation to communalism to anticolonial violence, the use of Chitrashala Press images would vary, but they instigated a movement in western India in which printed portraits of heroes and gods provoked nationalist agitation. As scholars have written about the pivotal role that these and other images played in the independence movement, my goal here has been to reflect on how the late eighteenth-century mixtures of material and meaning within western Indian arts invited particular regenerations in the late nineteenth and early twentieth centuries.[59] The writings of western Indian nationalists, and the prints published by the Chitrashala Press, traced a path from the Maratha past – including their interactions with the Company and their education during the Raj – through biography, historical sources, and iconic portraits of heroes and Hindu gods to a future without British rule.

"ROOT-GRUBBING" HISTORY

Western Indian nationalists collected visually inspiring images of the past to imagine a political community, to use the terms of Benedict Anderson, and unify the populace.[60] They developed this history through research and writing and in the structure of production by interlocking the location, preservation, and publication of sources. Thus far, I have primarily focused on how Chiplunkar and others instigated a movement to collect historical Marathi texts, paintings, sculptures, textiles, and weapons, and how they distributed them in print from newspapers to journals and chromolithographs. Others, like the scholar V. K. Rajwade, turned to their conservation and study. In 1910, Rajwade founded a historical society, the Bharat Itihas Sanshodhak Mandal (BISM, colloquially known as the Mandal) in Poona, to store documents and promote a historical method to use them.[61]

At the Mandal, archival scholarship was self-consciously modeled on the nineteenth-century German historian Leopold von Ranke's concept of source-based history, with an emphasis placed on the historian's ability to find or refind political and social paths forward through facts.[62] Although Ranke's renowned student Karl Marx mocked him as a "root-grubbing" historian – one who merely accumulated facts without justifying the reason for their collection or attending to the overarching systems that connected them – this method could slyly allow for historical revisions.[63]

By unearthing new sources, scholars in western India could build alternatives to British colonial histories. Marathi-speaking scholars countered the characterization of Maratha civilization as devoid of art with a new alignment of proofs. For example, the scholar and editor V. K. Bhave followed the empirical method of the colonial state, but used archives beyond the reach of the British to write four volumes of social history on Maharashtra. In the process, he emended the colonial commentary on the era from one of decline to that of innovation.[64] In this light, a magazine like *Kavyetihas Sangraha* could simultaneously extol a "root grubbing" attention to individual letters, histories, poems, or paintings, and aggregate a cultural system from those accumulated items to support a nation. For part of Marx's critique was to acknowledge that historians not only gathered facts, but also made choices in the histories that they wrote.[65] History always has the capability of polemic; colonial educators did not anticipate that their positivist ideology, the "root-grubbing" history that they proffered, would initiate a countermovement that would participate in their empire's demise.

The purpose of the Mandal, and other research institutes founded in Maharashtra in this period, was to provide spaces, resources, and a community to conduct research. With these provisions, it was up to the researcher to find the document to translate, the painting to reproduce, or the history to write. The promise of the Mandal remains in its collections. Rare books and manuscripts, paintings, coins, and other materials are stored in steel cabinets, wrapped in cloth, laid flat in files, and organized and re-organized for access. In one of the artist Dayanita Singh's photographs of the Mandal, the central cabinet's handle is tilted from use and the items are documented numerically to be smudged out and re-written in chalk as they are taken out for study, returned, or rehoused (fig. 150). These steadfast cabinets wait, at a scale vaster than the single bulb that illuminates them, for whoever might come and call on their contents.

Other parts of the Mandal's structure aid the archive and support its products, including a library and gallery, study tables, an auditorium to present members' research, and a press and bookshop to publish and sell scholarship at a reasonable price. Those publications are stacked in the eaves and niches of the balcony at the top of the auditorium in another of Singh's photographs (fig. 151); they are placed in proximity to, even protected by, portraits of esteemed scholars who consulted them and who look down over those presenting their research to the audience below.

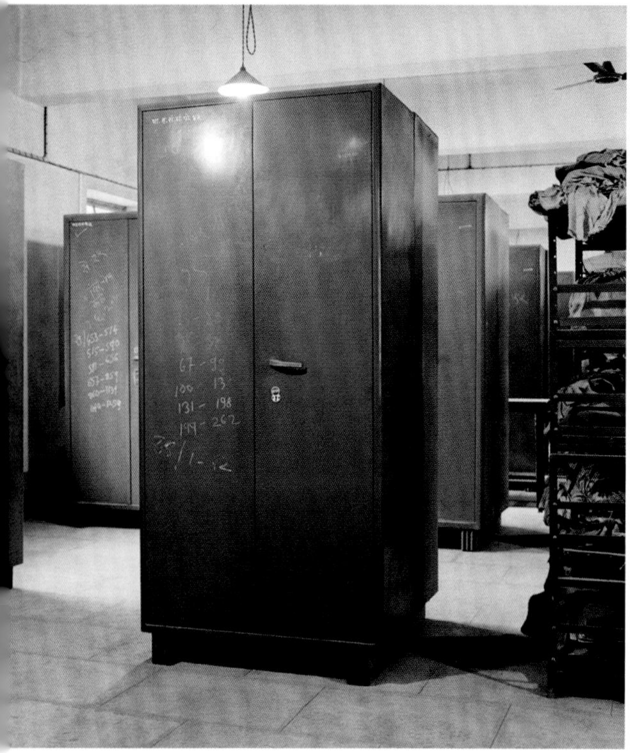

Here, one of Chiplunkar's goals for the Chitrashala becomes materially evident. He wrote that "we started our workshop so the figures of men famous in history would remain for a long time," like that of Justice Ranade who is seen framed in a Chitrashala portrait, or one based on it, above right of the fan in Singh's image.[66] But viewing such portraits close to the products made by those portrayed – the histories, newspapers, translations, laws, lectures, and others – and the sources that undergirded them, expands their meaning. This is evident even in the furniture at a similar society nearby, the Bhandarkar Oriental Research Institute, named after Sir Ramakrishna Gopal Bhandarkar, the scholar and translator of Sanskrit and other Indian texts, whose image is displayed to the left of Ranade in the Mandal's auditorium.

At Bhandarkar's Oriental Research Institute, founded soon after Ranade's in 1917 but whose collection of Indian manuscripts is based on that of the colonial government, its acronym BORI is carefully painted in white on the varnished wood of a card catalogue (fig. 152).[67] Placed flush with another cabinet facing the other direction, it still shares the other's mount: a series of four continuous glass and wood frames inset with printed portraits. The scholar's potential metamorphosis from a "root-grubbing" researcher consulting the card catalogue to a luminary portrayed in a picture frame rests in the empty chair in the foreground of Singh's photograph. The chair is just comfortable enough to sustain the body, elbows on the flowered tablecloth, to read the books that will be brought, to write a poem, or perhaps even the Indian constitution, as Dr. Babasaheb Ambedkar, who is displayed second from the left in the arch over the card catalogue, must have done in a similar library (though he did visit this one).

These are figures – heroes in the Chitrashala Press's language – to emulate as one pursues one's own research. They are individual, but also point to a community that comes into being through the joint endeavor of scholarship. This is an idealistic view of study, but in Maharashtra, at places like BORI or the Mandal, researching was connected to pride of place and of language, which also opened scholars to criticism. As Dipesh Chakrabarty has outlined, the prominent historian Sir Jadunath Sarkar determined that the historians associated with the Mandal in particular were imbued with "Maratha

150 Dayanita Singh, *Bharat Itihas Sanshodhak Mandal, Pune*, 2014

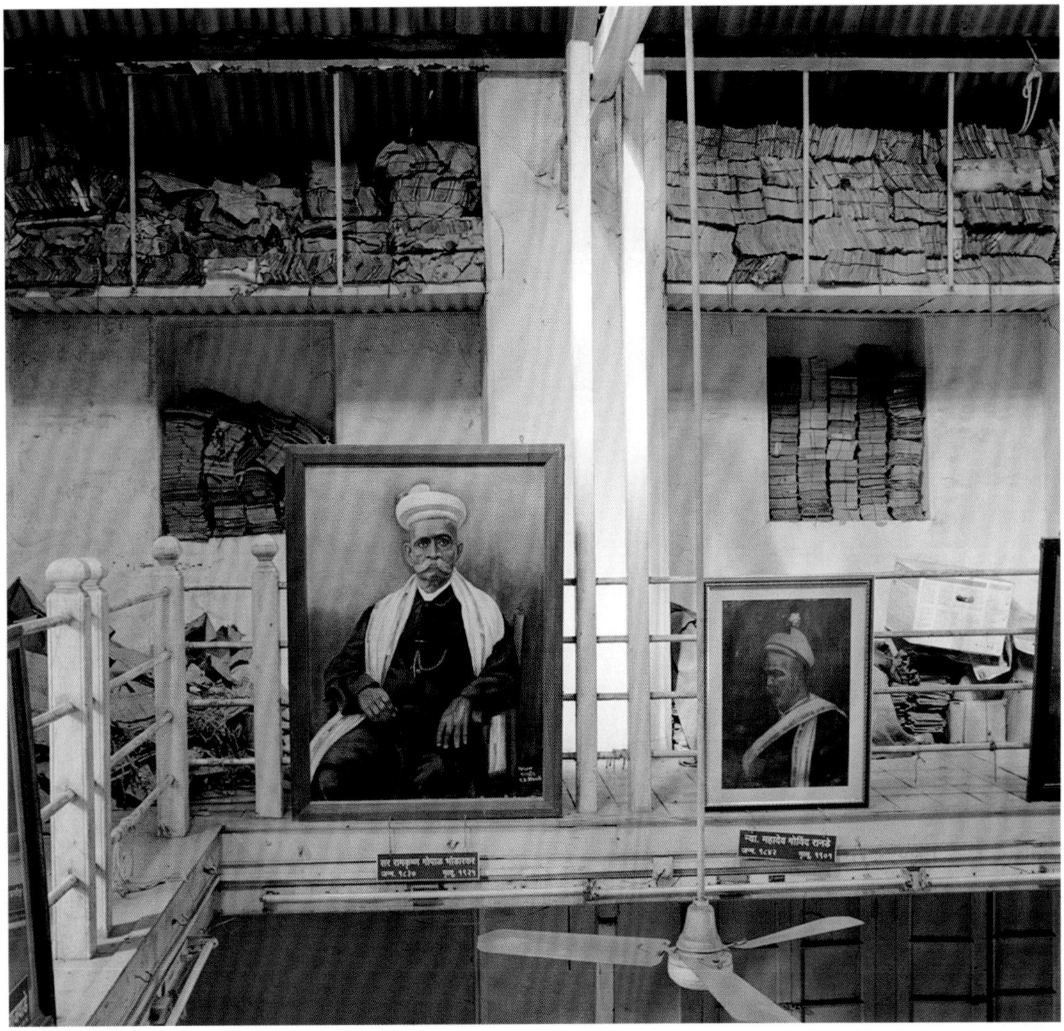

national sentiments." Sarkar disapproved of what he identified as a "pride in a particular [Maratha] identity" that governed the writing of Mandal historians. This pride countered the "impartial objectivity," which Sarkar considered to be at the foundation of the discipline of history.[68]

Sarkar's critique was directed at the Mandal, but it points to a divide that stretched over the nineteenth and twentieth centuries about the claims of historical writing.[69] For Rajwade also lauded the pursuit of objective fact, similarly to Chiplunkar, but neither hesitated to admit that they chose to pursue certain histories for subjective reasons. Their historical writing can be seen as simultaneously "root grubbing" and "shot through with chips of messianic time," in Walter Benjamin's phrase. For Benjamin, writing in the

151 Dayanita Singh, *Bharat Itihas Sanshodhak Mandal, Pune*, 2014

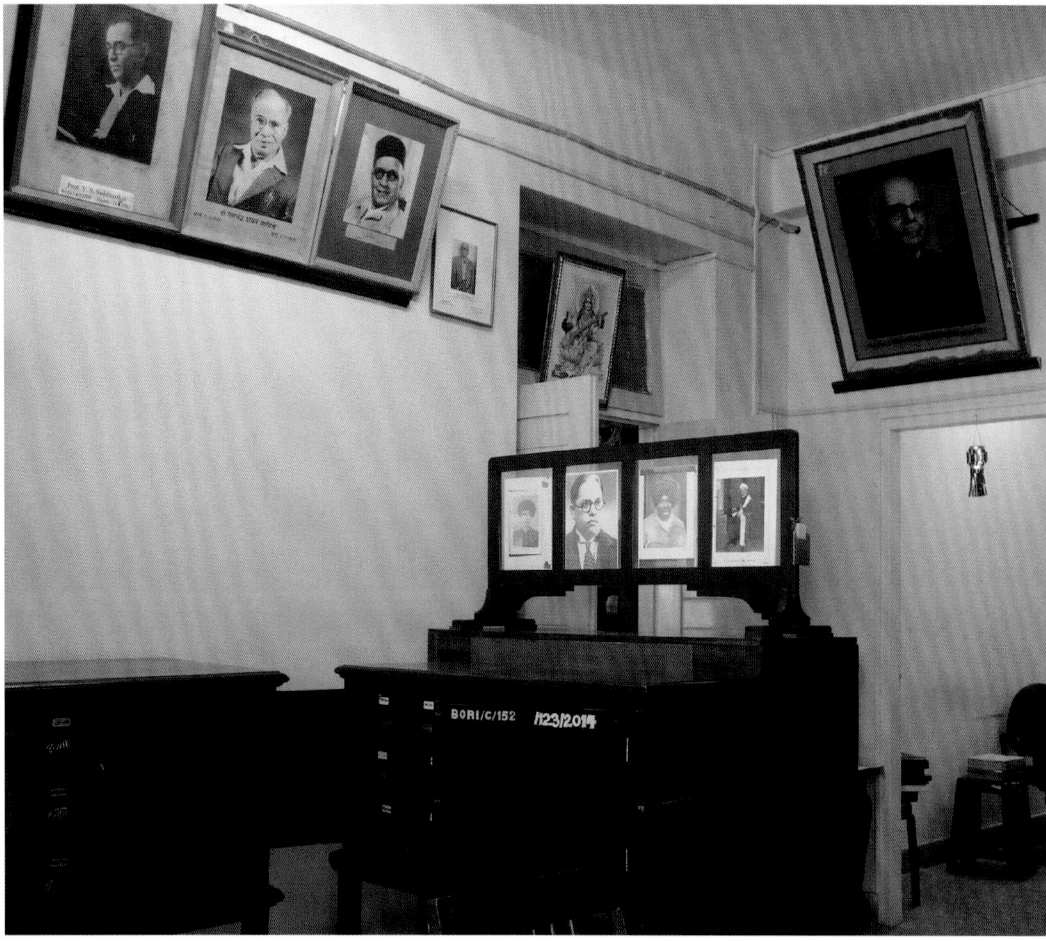

152 Dayanita Singh, *Bhandarkar Oriental Research Institute, Pune*, 2014

same period as the western Indian historians, a fact became "historical posthumously . . . through events that may be separated from it by thousands of years. A historian who takes this as his point of departure . . . grasps the constellation which his own era has formed with a definite earlier one."[70]

This critique of the writing of history as always of the present and the past has become standard, but the power accorded to the historian to regenerate the past in late nineteenth- and early twentieth-century western India also relates to a privacy at the heart of the country's nationalism. By cultivating a national culture in the spiritual "inner" domain, Indian nationalists, according to Partha Chatterjee, protected it from the material "outer" domain associated with colonialism and the imitation of "Western skills" in "the economy and of statecraft, of science and technology."[71] There is an intimacy, even a domesticity, to this approach toward the regeneration of history in order to generate a nation that ran across nationalist movements from eastern to western India, from reformist to extremist.[72] It is present in the portraits, in the furniture, in the archives, in the institutions founded then and witnessed in Dayanita Singh's photographs; it is still open to researchers today.

ON REGENERATION

I became aware of the late nineteenth-century history that I have been telling in this chapter over the course of my research in Maharashtra through the generosity of archivists, curators, and scholars at the Mandal, BORI, and other institutions who helped me with the late eighteenth-century materials that I consulted there. There were reasons why these materials were in state and community collections rather than national or colonial ones. Those items collected, commissioned, or plundered by the British were in the British Library, British Museum, Victoria and Albert Museum, and in regional archives, museums, and family collections in Britain, as one would expect, as well as in American collections, such as the Yale Center for British Art. But the complement to those items – the works collected, commissioned, or plundered by the Marathas – had neither been taken abroad nor removed to the Indian capital. They had either remained in family collections, like that of Nana Fadnavis, or had been collected and preserved by western Indian nationalists long before the nation had been founded, and thus stayed in a network of regional institutions. It became clear to me that the eighteenth-century history I was accessing in Maharashtra was filtered through the energies of late nineteenth-century nationalists, similar to how the histories present in Britain, and America by way of that country, were colonial ones that had been produced in eighteenth-century India and in nineteenth-century Britain after officials returned.

The network of archives that I consulted for this project, the figures who emerged from the records housed within them, and those people who helped me to locate and access materials undergird the history that I have written. Founded on individuals and their relationships with others, the model I have found useful for this art history is one of graft for a reason. The arts and documents in the archives attest to artists grafting works together, but I used the same method to join together the friends, superiors, employees, and mentors who were mentioned in one figure's archive with those other characters' independent records housed in different locations. The result is a patchwork of materials written, drafted, and gathered from a range of perspectives, which at certain junctures interlocked with others but at others left gaps. I have tried to leave the historical and archival grafts visible in this project, from those that fused relationships together to those that branched away from each other.

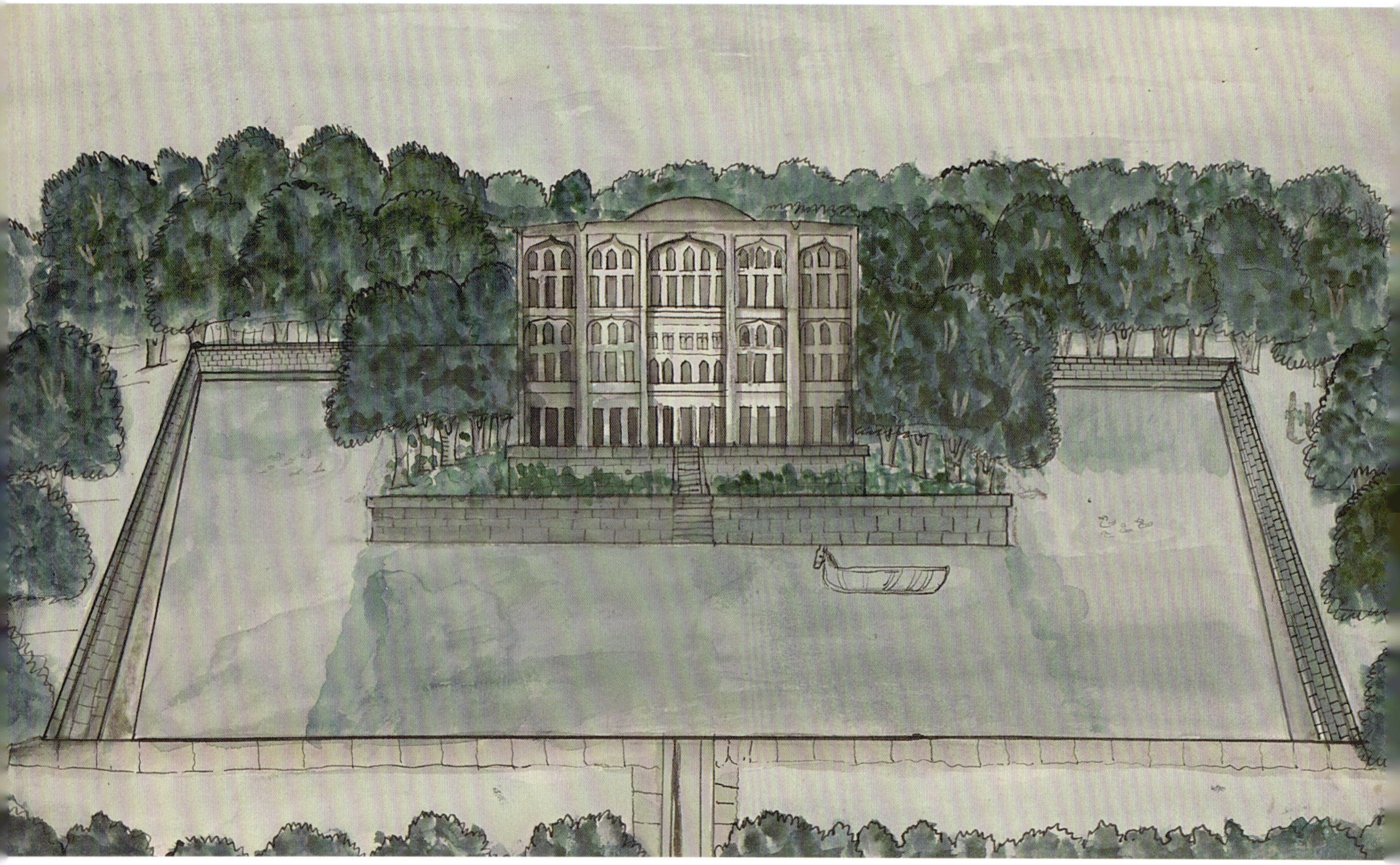

But there have also been traces – clues, if you will – that leave one wondering about all of the information that is neither written down or made visible, nor stored and maintained in archives.[73] These are the conversations and occurrences that happened in between the notes written and the sketches recorded, which would animate them. Consider Gangaram Tambat's drawing of Faria Bagh (fig. 153), which his Company patron Malet inscribed as a garden (*bagh*) near Ahmednagar sometime in the 1790s. From Malet's inscriptions and Gangaram's other employer James Wales's journals, as well as his own notes and drawings, we know that he traveled to Ahmednagar to draw his guru and his fellow devotees as well as himself in at least two self-portraits (see figs. 5 and 72), and it is likely that he sketched this palace on one of those trips.

There are snippets of information about Gangaram, as I discussed in Chapter Two, which are tempting to put together with his drawings to imagine the circumstances of

153 Gangaram Tambat, *Faria Bagh near Ahmednagar*, Maharashtra, ca. 1790–96. Watercolor, gouache, and graphite with pen and black ink on paper, 27.3 × 42.9 cm. Yale Center for British Art, New Haven, Connecticut, Paul Mellon Collection, B1977.14.22355

their production.[74] But we do not know his connection to Ahmednagar, whether this was the trip on which he declared that he would go without clothes so as to avoid being robbed by bandits,[75] or the name of his guru. Did he make multiple portraits of this respected person, some for Malet and others for his community – could these still be extant? Did his guru live near Faria Bagh, or did he go to the garden palace because of its beauty, or because Malet or Wales had instructed him to draw this historical building or any that he chanced upon during his travels?

I went to Ahmednagar, not because I thought that I could answer these questions, but because I wondered whether there might be more information available about Gangaram in a place that seemed dear to him. Dr. Bhave, the Secretary at the Mandal, put me in touch with a colleague, Bhushan Deshmukh, who took me to the museum where we pored over their library and collection. On a motor scooter, he showed me the famous sights in the region including Faria Bagh, where I was struck by the recognition that this was the same building that Gangaram had drawn, and the medieval Ahmednagar Fort that had served as a colonial-era jail. There Jawaharlal Nehru, the future prime minister of independent India, had been imprisoned and wrote *The Discovery of India* (1946), which offers his own meditation on nationalism. By this point, Bhushan too wanted to find out more about this eighteenth-century artist, so he wrote an article in a local newspaper and included one of Gangaram's self-portraits. Soon after, an architect and designer, Vilas Bhagirath Navgire, contacted him and I returned to Ahmednagar so that Bhushan and I could meet him. Vilas Bhagirath unfurled a drawing of his family tree: the brother of Gangaram's father Chintaman was his ancestor.

This meeting, which lay somewhere in between chance and the determination that propels research, made me all too aware of the information that floats in the interstices between records in an archive and can rarely be accessed. The fieldwork only resulted in a note in Chapter Two, but in my memory it was a trip full of meaning. Not only did I feel a connection to an artist whose works I adored and whose life I had been trying to piece together for years (a connection which I shared with two men and their families whom I would not have met otherwise), but I also became cognizant of the concurrent intersections between people from different temporalities. The person who I wanted to share this with was Dayanita Singh, whose photographs tell a parallel story of western India in this chapter, and whose sustained interest in file rooms, meandering sequences of events, and the animate natures of inanimate things converses with, and has inspired, my own.

When Dayanita came to the archives in Pune, I suggested that she visit Ahmednagar. The contact sheets that resulted are part of the constellation of this story (fig. 154a and b): there is Faria Bagh, buttressed at a later date than Gangaram's drawing, from a distance, then closer and closer until the attention is on the declarations of love scratched into the walls by "R.S." and others. There is a military tank museum, a tree, and a printing press with the plaster cast of a god and a wrought-iron window. There are power lines that intersect with the wall by the tree, the retreat from Faria Bagh, the difference between empty sky and architecture, whitewashed walls, a corridor between files, there are moods.

What Dayanita saw in these places, and what I took from my dialogues with her, like that with Bhushan Deshmukh and Vilas Bhagirath Navgire, with Dr. Bhave who led me to them and opened the possibilities of the Mandal to me, has made me conscious of my own subjectivity in what I choose to focus on in archives. Only certain types of items are stored in collections. Some people from the past continue to live through their material and textual remains, but there are others whose lives were lived outside of them. I have therefore endeavored to write a "root-grubbing" history of art in this book, but the sub-

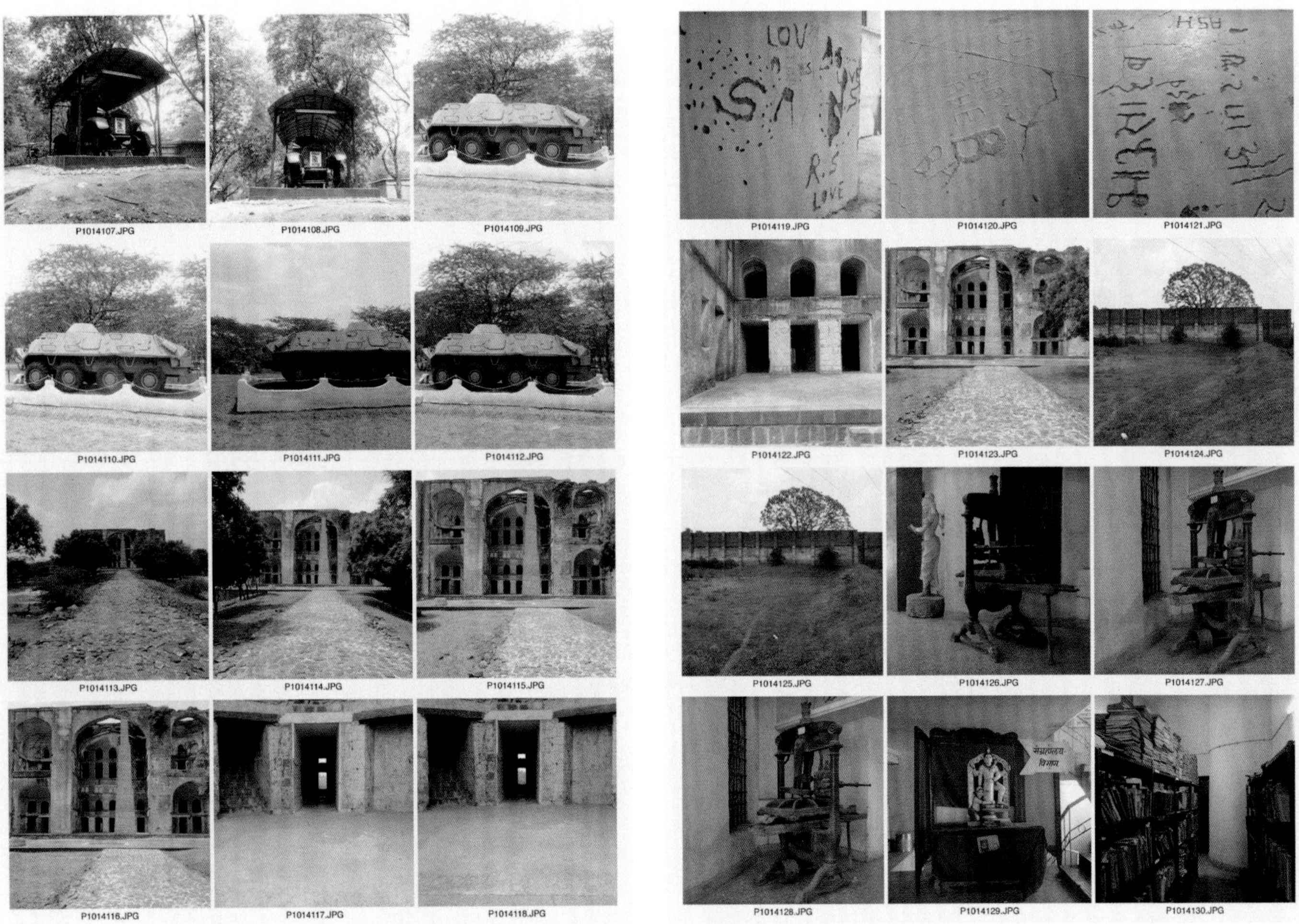

154 a and b Dayanita Singh, *Contact Sheets from Ahmednagar and Pune*, 2014

jectivities of the historical materials and my reckoning with them are also "shot through with messianic time."

I have also dwelled on the intersection of past and present temporalities because the materials on which I have focused from the eighteenth, and then the late nineteenth and early twentieth centuries, continue to be remade today. Communities, the press, and the modern nation-state have channeled these western Indian arts – and their diverse, branching histories – into a singular Hindu-oriented one. To revise such arts as telling only a fundamentalist history, the media and the public have again instrumentalized graft. The media joins sources from photographs to films, recordings, and audio as montaged truths; viewers collage, interpret, and reinterpret such images in endless cycles to foment communal, rather than nationalist, agitation that again and again results in religious violence and death.[76]

Graft in English and *kalam* in Marathi are words that explicate the violence and creativity inherent in artistic production as well as in the suture of wounds, the gain from conquest, and the joining of a bud to a tree be it supplementary, parasitic, or host to create new fruit. In the context of this book, I have used these terms to think about the eclectic processes that supported artistic practices and fused cultural traditions, in a period of empire-building tense with negotiations and military actions among the Marathas and Britain's East India Company in western India and from there across India and in Britain.

Many of these arts served as tools ingeniously made to move empire along – to aid in diplomacy, to accrue knowledge for imperial purposes, to solidify political realms, to wage war. They are the "art" which empire "follows," to return to the phrase that Blake wrote on Reynolds's *Works* (1798), discussed in Chapter Four. Blake sought an antidote to Reynolds and the Royal Academy, who trained the artists who in his opinion furnished a tyrannical empire. Similarly, the western Indian nationalists turned those arts into tools to resist it, and contemporary politicians reframe them to support a Hindu conception of the nation. Arts that perpetuate empires and are the foundation of nations can hide in the relationships to the past that they claim. We must be alert to the subtlety and insidiousness of their mixtures, but also to those stranger and more fragile arts (the scions that wither on the rootstock, the sutures that do not hold) that buck time and settle lightly, if at all, in the materials of history. These are arts that were made from multiples, and continue to sprout, but become harder and harder to follow and root.

Abbreviations

BISM	Bharat Itihas Sanshodhak Mandal, Pune
BL	British Library, London
BM	British Museum, London
BORI	Bhandarkar Oriental Research Institute, Pune
CSMVS	Chhatrapati Shivaji Maharaj Vastu Sangrahalaya, Mumbai
ODNB	*Oxford Dictionary of National Biography*, ed. H. C. G. Matthew and Brian Harrison; David Cannadine (Oxford: Oxford University Press, 2004)
V&A	Victoria and Albert Museum, London
Wales Archive	James Wales Archive, MSS 26, Yale Center for British Art, New Haven, Conn.
YCBA	Yale Center for British Art, New Haven, Conn.

Notes

INTRODUCTION

1 J. T. Molesworth, *A Dictionary, Marathi and English* (Bombay: Printed for the Government of Bombay, June, 1831), कलम (p. 166).

2 The alliance was made among the Marathas, the British East India Company, and the Nizam of Hyderabad. I focus on the interactions between the Marathas and the British. On the wider context see Stewart Gordon, *The Marathas 1600–1818* (Cambridge: Cambridge University Press, 1993), 154–73.

3 Besides the use of professional artists, like James Wales on the Company side and artists like Sabaji Anant and Shivram Chitari on the side of the Marathas, whom I shall introduce in due course, soldiers were trained in draftsmanship in order to survey lands and produce maps for military purposes; see Rosie Dias, "Memory and the Aesthetics of Military Experience: Viewing the Landscape of the Anglo-Mysore Wars," *Tate Papers*, no. 19 (Spring 2013): https://www.tate.org.uk/research/publications/tatepapers/19/memory-and-the-aesthetics-of-military-experience-viewing-the-landscape-of-the-anglomysore-wars (accessed February 10, 2019). On Maratha maps and cartographic practices see Susan Gole, *India within the Ganges* (New Delhi: Jayaprints, 1983), 18–21.

4 Edward Moor, *The Hindu Pantheon* (London: J. Johnson, 1810), 62.

5 Ibid., pl. 16, fig. 3.

6 *OED: Oxford English Dictionary Online* (Oxford University Press, 2020; accessed April 20, 2020), "graft, n." and "graff, n."; Adam Gacek, *The Arabic Manuscript Tradition: A Glossary of Technical Terms* (Leiden: Brill, 2008), "قلم" *qalam*, 65; Francis Joseph Steingass, "قلم" *qalam*, in *A Comprehensive Persian-English Dictionary* (London: Routledge & K. Paul, 1892), 986 in *Digital Dictionaries of South Asia*: https://dsal.uchicago.edu/dictionaries/steingass (accessed April 20, 2020).

7 Molesworth, *Dictionary*, कलम [*kalam*] (p. 166); *OED*, "graft, n." and "graff, n." On graft in relation to South Asian gardens, see Nicolas Roth, "Marigolds and Munshīs: Horticultural Writing and Garden Culture in Mughal South Asia" (Ph.D. diss., Harvard University, 2020). On graft in the context of gardens and empire see Jill H. Casid, *Sowing Empire: Landscape and Colonization* (Minneapolis and London: University of Minnesota Press, 2005).

8 *Merriam-Webster.com Dictionary*, Merriam-Webster, https://www.merriam-webster.com/dictionary/graft (accessed April 20, 2020), "graft."

9 Kaushik Roy, *War, Culture, and Society in Early Modern South Asia* (London: Routledge, 2011), 96; William Dalrymple, *The Anarchy* (London: Bloomsbury Publishing, 2019).

10 On colonial loss, see Aaron M. Hyman and Dana Leibsohn, "Washing the Archive," *Early American Literature* 55, no. 2 (2020): 419–44; Kate Smith, "Loss and Dispossession in the Long Eighteenth Century," Inaugural Lecture of the Material Culture in the Seventeenth and Eighteenth Century Research Cluster, University of Edinburgh (17 March 2020).

11 Molesworth, *Dictionary*, नविंशी कलम [*nirvamshi kalam*] (p. 582): "The ghost or spirit of a family that has become extinct. It haunts the family that now occupies its place and tenements."

12 For ch. 15.101 in a Marathi conception see Swami Kripananda, *Jnaneshwar's Gita* (Albany: State University of New York Press, 1989), 239.

13 Edward Said, *Culture and Imperialism* (New York: Vintage, 1994), 20.

14 Parul Dave Mukherji, "Whither Art History in a Globalizing World," *Art Bulletin* 96, no. 2 (June 2014): 154. On case studies, "new imperial" historians like Maya Jasanoff have also stressed that "personal encounters" and histories of collecting "offer a different perspective on the relationship of culture and imperialism . . . [they show] how power and culture intersected in tangled, contingent, sometimes self-contradictory ways"; Maya Jasanoff, *Edge of Empire: Lives, Culture, and Conquest in the East, 1750–1850* (New York: Vintage, 2007), 6; see also David Gilmour, *The British in India: A Social History of the Raj* (New York: Farrar, Straus and Giroux, 2018), 4; Stephen Howe, ed., *The New Imperial Histories Reader* (Abingdon and New York: Routledge, 2010).

15 Tim Barringer, Geoff Quilley, and Douglas Fordham, eds., *Art and the British Empire* (Manchester: Manchester University Press, 2007), 3. See also Tim Barringer, *Men at Work: Art and Labour in Victorian Britain* (New Haven and London: Yale University Press, 2005), "Colonial Gothic," 242–311; Douglas Fordham, *British Art and the Seven Years' War* (New Haven and London: Yale University Press, 2010); Geoff Quilley, *Empire to Nation: Art, History and the Visualization of Maritime Britain, 1768–1829* (New Haven and London: Yale University Press, 2011), among other scholars' work, which I detail below.

16 On the critique of Maratha art, see Hermann Goetz, *The Art of the Marathas and Its Problems*, Baroda State Museum Pamphlets (Baroda: Sadhana, 1946), 1–2; on the critique of British art in India see the Tate exhibition catalogue, Alison Smith, ed., *Artist and Empire: Facing Britain's Imperial Past* (London: Tate Publishing, 2015).

17 On eclecticism and its critics see Rudolf Wittkower, "Imitation, Eclecticism, and Genius," in *Aspects of the Eighteenth Century*, ed. Earl R. Wasserman (Baltimore: Johns Hopkins University Press, 1965), 143–61; Joan Wallach Scott, "Against Eclecticism," *Differences: A Journal of Feminist Cultural Studies* 16, no. 3 (2005): 114–37; Kristoffer Neville, "Winckelmann's Eclecticism," *Notes in the History of Art* 37, no. 4 (Summer 2018): 228–36; Daniel M. Unger, *Redefining Eclecticism in Early Modern Bolognese Painting* (Amsterdam: Amsterdam University Press, 2019). On British colonial critiques of Maratha arts see e.g. James Tod, *Annals and Antiquities of Rajasthan*, 2 vols. (1829–32; repr., London: Oxford University Press, 1920), vol. 1, 93, 154, 193, 472; James Forbes, *Oriental Memoirs: A Narrative of Seventeen Years*

Residence in India, 2nd edn., 2 vols. (London: Richard Bentley, 1834), vol. 1, 29. On early twentieth-century Indian historians' critiques see Sir Jadunath Sarkar, *Shivaji and His Times* (London: Longmans, Green, 1920), 6; V. K. Bhave, *Peshwekalin Maharashtra* [Maharashtra in the Peshwa Era. In Marathi] (1935; repr., Pune: Bharat Itihas Sanshodhak Mandal, 1975), 124–9. On the dismissal of British arts in India see Finbarr Barry Flood, "Correct Delineations and Promiscuous Outlines: Envisioning India at the Trial of Warren Hastings," *Art History* 29, no. 1 (February 2006): 47–78; Michael Willis, "Detritus to Treasure: Memory, Metonymy, and the Museum," in *Sacred Objects in Secular Spaces*, ed. Bruce M. Sullivan (London: Bloomsbury Academic, 2015), 148–9; Natasha Eaton, "Colonial Iconoclash: Mimetic Rivalry, Collecting and Idolatry Between India and Britain," in *Acquiring Cultures: Histories of World Art on Western Markets*, ed. Bénédicte Savoy, Charlotte Guichard, and Christine Howald (Berlin: De Gruyter, 2018), 31–46.

18 For an overview of the asymmetric, yet mutually constitutive, power dynamics between colonizer and colonized see Leela Gandhi, *Postcolonial Theory: A Critical Introduction* (New York: Columbia University Press, 2019). Although not in a colonial context, Cécile Fromont has provided a model for "spaces of correlation" that "are cultural creations such as narratives, artworks, or performances that offer a yet unspecified domain in which their creators can bring together ideas and forms belonging to radically different realms, confront them, and eventually turn them into interrelated parts of a new system of thought and expression"; Cécile Fromont, *The Art of Conversion: Christian Visual Culture in the Kingdom of Kongo* (Chapel Hill: University of North Carolina Press, 2014), 15.

19 See Homi K. Bhabha, *The Location of Culture* (London: Routledge, 1994), esp. "Of Mimicry and Man" (121–31) and "Signs Taken for Wonders" (145–74).

20 Although hybridity as a theoretical term has productively been used to understand colonial circumstances of cross-cultural mixture, it faces challenges when applied to artistic production, which is why I have chosen other terms to address mixture; see Carolyn Dean and Dana Leibsohn, "Hybridity and its Discontents: Considering Visual Culture in Colonial Spanish America," *Colonial Latin American Review* 12, no. 1 (2003): 5–35.

21 I have expanded on eclecticism's relationship to empire in a separate essay: Holly Shaffer, "Eclecticism and Empire, in Translation," *Modern Philology* 119, no. 1 (August 2021): 147–65. On cross-cultural artistic practice among the Mughals, see Kavita Singh, *Real Birds in Imagined Gardens: Mughal Painting between Persia and Europe* (Los Angeles: Getty Publications, 2017).

22 See Shaffer, "Eclecticism and Empire"; Neville, "Winckelmann's Eclecticism," 228–36; Scott, "Against Eclecticism," 114–37; Wittkower, "Imitation, Eclecticism," 143–61. Early modern writers explicitly promoted mixture. The Ottoman scholar Mustafa Ali even used the metaphor of graft for the mixture of ethnicities within the empire as "different species of fruitbearing tree mingled and mated" as a source of fine qualities, "like a princely pear," quoted in Cornell H. Fleischer, *Bureaucrat and Intellectual in the Ottoman Empire: The Historian Mustafa Ali (1541–1600)* (Princeton, N.J.: Princeton University Press, 1986), 254; I thank Emine Fetvaci for this reference. On a similar conception in British history see Wolfram Schmidgen, *Exquisite Mixture: The Virtues of Impurity in Early Modern England* (Princeton, N.J.: Princeton University Press, 2012); in art historiography see Éric Michaud, *Barbarian Invasions: A Genealogy of the History of Art*, trans. Nicholas Huckle (Cambridge, Mass.: MIT Press, 2019).

23 On colonialism, archival practice, and its perils for scholarship, see Saidiya Hartman, "Venus in Two Acts," *Small Axe* 12, issue 2 (June 2008): 1–14; Ann Laura Stoler, *Along the Archival Grain: Epistemic Anxiety and Colonial Common Sense* (Princeton, N.J.: Princeton University Press, 2009); Ricardo Roque and Kim A. Wagner, eds., *Engaging Colonial Knowledge: Reading European Archives in World History* (Basingstoke and New York: Palgrave Macmillan, 2012).

24 Gangaram's full name is Gangaram Chintaman Navgire Tambat. I use Gangaram Tambat here as his shortened full name, and Gangaram, rather than Tambat, to be consistent with other scholarship. South Asian artists are often known by their first rather than their last or caste name.

25 Robert Mabon, Journal (Maharashtra, ca. 1790–95), 1, James Wales Archive, MSS 26, Yale Center for British Art, New Haven, Conn. In a letter of entreaty to James Boswell in 1790, Mabon hints at the addictions that made him "deviate" from "the paths of virtue," including gambling and other habits that in his words, "hurried me from one degree of dissipation to another till at last I have brought myself to the lowest pitch of misery" and eventually, in a "Drunken frolick," landed him enlisted in the Company army and bound for India; Robert Mabon to James Boswell, November 15, 1790, Boswell Collection, GEN MSS 89: box 26, folder 634, Beinecke Rare Book and Manuscript Library, Yale University.

26 Nebahat Avcioğlu and Finbarr Barry Flood, "Introduction: Globalizing Cultures: Art and Mobility in the Eighteenth Century," *Ars Orientalis* 39 (2010): 11.

27 Meredith Martin and Daniela Bleichmar, "Objects in Motion in the Early Modern World," *Art History* 38, no. 4 (September 2015): 604–19.

28 E.g. Douglas Fordham, *Aquatint Worlds: Travel, Print and Empire* (New Haven and London: Paul Mellon Centre in association with Yale University Press, 2019); Mary Roberts, *Istanbul Exchanges: Ottomans, Orientalists, and Nineteenth-Century Visual Culture* (Oakland: University of California Press, 2015); Natasha Eaton, *Colour, Art and Empire: Visual Culture and the Nomadism of Representation* (London: I.B. Tauris, 2013). Others dynamically argue for transcultural programs but across the Atlantic or Pacific worlds, such as Elizabeth Kornhauser and Tim Barringer, *Thomas Cole's Journey: Atlantic Crossings* (New York: Metropolitan Museum of Art, 2018); J. M. Mancini, *Art and War in the Pacific World: Making, Breaking, and Taking from Anson's Voyage to the Philippine-American War* (Oakland: University of California Press, 2018); Edward S. Cooke, *Inventing Boston: Design, Production, and Consumption 1680–1720* (New Haven and London: Paul Mellon Centre in association with Yale University Press, 2019), building on such foundational work as Nicholas Thomas, *Entangled Objects: Exchange, Material Culture, and Colonialism in the Pacific* (Cambridge, Mass.: Harvard University Press, 1991).

29 Zoltán Biedermann, *(Dis)connected Empires: Imperial Portugal, Sri Lankan Diplomacy, and the Making of a Hapsburg Conquest in Asia* (Oxford: Oxford University Press, 2018); Sanjay Subrahmanyam, *Europe's India: Worlds, People, Empires* (Cambridge, Mass.: Harvard University Press, 2017); Sanjay Subrahmanyam, "Connected

Histories: Notes towards a Reconfiguration of Early Modern Eurasia," *Modern Asian Studies* 31, no. 3 (July 1997): 735–62.

30 On Maratha arts see M. S. Mate, "Maratha Architecture, 1650 A.D. to 1850 A.D." (Ph.D. diss., University of Poona, 1957); Usha Ranade and Kamal Chavan, *Tala Paintings* (Pune: Bharat Itihas Sanshodhak Mandal, 1976); Kamal Chavan, *Maratha Murals: Late Medieval Painting of the Deccan, 1650–1850 A.D.* (Delhi: B. R. Publishing, 1983); Usha Ranade, *Manuscript Illustrations of the Medieval Deccan* (Pune: B. R. Publishing, 1983); B. K. Apte, *Maratha Wall Paintings (Wai, Menavali, Satara, Pune)* (Bombay: Government Central Press, 1988); S. B. Deshmukh, *Maratha Painting* (Aurangabad: Marathwada University, 1992); Manoj Dani, *Battle of Panipat: In Light of Recently Discovered Paintings* (Pune: Monkey Hill Publications, 2021). On artistic interactions between the Marathas and the British see Douglas Fordham, "Costume Dramas: British Art at the Court of the Marathas," *Representations* 101 (Winter 2008): 57–85; Uday S. Kulkarni, *James Wales: Artist and Antiquarian in the Time of Peshwa Sawai Madhavrao* (Pune: Mula Mutha Publishers, 2019). On arts made in other Maratha regions see Satya Vrata Tripathi, *Mysteries of Love: Maratha Miniatures of the Rasamanjari* (New Delhi: National Museum, 2001); Indira Viswanathan Peterson, "Portraiture at the Tanjore Maratha Court," in *Portraits in Princely India, 1700–1947*, ed. Rosie Llewellyn-Jones (Mumbai: Marg, 2008), 44–57.

31 Barringer, Quilley, and Fordham, *Art and the British Empire*, 3.

32 E.g., in India see Richard H. Davis, *Lives of Indian Images* (Princeton, N.J.: Princeton University Press, 1997); Tapati Guha-Thakurta, *Monuments, Objects, Histories: Institutions of Art in Colonial and Postcolonial India* (New York: Columbia University Press, 2004); Hermione de Almeida and George Gilpin, *Indian Renaissance: British Romantic Art and the Prospect of India* (Aldershot: Ashgate, 2005); Romita Ray, *Under the Banyan Tree: Relocating the Picturesque in British India* (New Haven and London: Yale University Press, 2013). On other areas of the British Empire see Kornhauser and Barringer, *Thomas Cole's Journey*; Mancini, *Art and War*; Quilley, *Empire to Nation*; Fordham, *British Art and the Seven Years' War*; Tim Barringer, Gillian Forrester, and Barbaro Martinez Ruiz, eds., *Art and Emancipation in Jamaica* (New Haven and London: Yale University Press, 2007); Kay Dian Kriz, *Slavery, Sugar, and the Culture of Refinement* (New Haven and London: Yale University Press, 2008). Many of these works build on foundational scholarship on the British in India, and Indian art's place in Europe, such as Partha Mitter, *Much Maligned Monsters: A History of European Reactions to Indian Art* (Oxford: Clarendon Press, 1977); Vidya Dehejia with Pratapaditya Pal, *From Merchants to Emperors: British Artists and India* (Ithaca, N.Y.: Cornell University Press, 1986); C. A. Bayly, ed., *The Raj: India and the British, 1600–1947* (London: National Portrait Gallery, 1990).

33 Natasha Eaton, *Mimesis across Empires: Artworks and Networks in India, 1765–1860* (Durham, N.C.: Duke University Press, 2013).

34 Postcolonial scholarship, such as the work of Bernard Cohn and Nicholas Dirks (the "Chicago" school), has foregrounded the intertwined and imperial nature of Company officials' scholarly and artistic endeavors alongside their political, economic, and military purpose. More recent scholarship, known as the "collaborationist" or "Cambridge" school (led by C. A. Bayly), has added nuance to the postcolonial school of thought, arguing that knowledge was not just acquired in India, but also co-produced with Indians and in dialogue with Indigenous knowledge systems. This debate is from the perspective of British colonial control; my project seeks to offer a different perspective from a scenario where control was undecided, but arts (and therefore knowledge) for Indian and British rulers were being produced through collaboration and by different hosts. For a literature review of the intellectual exchange on knowledge production see Phillip B. Wagoner, "Precolonial Intellectuals and the Production of Colonial Knowledge," *Society for Comparative Study of Society and History* 45, no. 4 (October 2003): 783–814; Kapil Raj, *Relocating Modern Science: Circulation and the Construction of Knowledge in South Asia and Europe, 1650–1900* (Basingstoke and New York: Palgrave Macmillan, 2007). On Company arts see the defining texts of Mildred Archer, such as *Company Paintings: Indian Paintings of the British Period* (London: Victoria and Albert Museum, 1992), and the most recent intervention in William Dalrymple, ed., *Forgotten Masters: Indian Painting for the East India Company* (London: Wallace Collection, 2019).

35 Chanchal Dadlani, *From Stone to Paper: Architecture as History in Eighteenth-Century Mughal India* (New Haven and London: Yale University Press, 2019). On other innovative studies of transcultural artistic interactions in Mughal India see Malini Roy, "Idiosyncrasies in the Late Mughal Painting Tradition" (Ph.D. diss., SOAS, University of London, 2009); William Dalrymple and Yuthika Sharma, *Princes and Painters in Mughal Delhi, 1707–1857* (New York: Asia Society Museum, 2012); Yuthika Sharma, "Art in between Empires: Visual Culture and Artistic Knowledge in Late Mughal Delhi, 1748–1857" (Ph.D. diss., Columbia University, 2013).

36 See Debra Diamond, ed., *Garden and Cosmos: The Royal Paintings of Jodhpur* (London: Thames & Hudson, 2008); Molly Emma Aitken, *The Intelligence of Tradition in Rajput Court Painting* (New Haven and London: Yale University Press, 2010); Sugata Ray, *Climate Change and the Art of Devotion: Geoaesthetics in the Land of Krishna, 1550–1850* (Seattle: University of Washington Press, 2019); Dipti Khera, *The Place of Many Moods: Udaipur's Painted Lands and India's Eighteenth Century* (Princeton, N.J.: Princeton University Press, 2020).

37 Janaki Nair, *Mysore Modern: Rethinking the Region under Princely Rule* (New Delhi: Orient Blackswan, 2011), 36; see also Susan Stronge, *Tipu's Tigers* (London: Victoria and Albert Museum, 2009).

38 The Bahmani Sultanate (1347–1527) split into five kingdoms collectively known as the Deccan Sultanates, including the Nizam Shahi of Ahmednagar, Qutb Shahi of Golkonda, and Adil Shahi of Bijapur; see Gordon, *The Marathas*, 10–15; Prachi Deshpande, *Creative Pasts: Historical Memory and Identity in Western India, 1700–1960* (New Delhi: Permanent Black, 2007), 49–52.

39 George Michell and Mark Zebrowski, *Architecture and Art of the Deccan Sultanates* (Cambridge: Cambridge University Press, 1999), 55; Randolf G. S. Cooper, *The Anglo-Maratha Campaigns and the Contest for India* (Cambridge: Cambridge University Press, 2005), 21–31; see also P. N. Deshpande, "Maratha Forts and Siege Tactics," *Marg* 34, no. 2 (March 1981): 15–40.

40 In this book, I use the term Maratha to describe the political regime rather than the caste. Thus, the Peshwas are

included within the overarching category "Maratha" even though they are Brahmins by caste.

41 Margot C. Finn, "Material Turns in British History: Loot," *Transactions of the RHS* 28 (2018): 13–14; see also Gordon, *The Marathas*, 163–77.

42 K. G. Subramanyan, "Eclecticism II," in *The Creative Circuit* (Calcutta: Seagull, 1992), 48; see also Sir Joshua Reynolds, "Discourse II," in *Discourses on Art*, ed. Robert R. Wark (New Haven and London: Yale University Press, 1997), 36, who also uses soldiers as a metaphor for artists.

43 See Ian Copland et al., *A History of State and Religion in India* (London: Routledge, 2012), 142–61.

44 See Günther-Dietz Sontheimer, *Pastoral Deities in Western India*, trans. Anne Feldhaus (Oxford and New York: Oxford University Press, 1989); Anne Feldhaus, *Connected Places: Region, Pilgrimage, and Geographical Imagination in India* (Basingstoke and New York: Palgrave Macmillan, 2003); Christian Lee Novetzke, *Religion and Public Memory: A Cultural History of Saint Namdev in India* (New York: Columbia University Press, 2008).

45 Copland, *A History*, 154, 157; as these scholars point out, there were exceptions to inclusivity, particularly regarding cow protection and rhetoric against Muslims (156–7).

46 Ibid., 143; André Wink, *Land and Sovereignty in India: Agrarian Society and Politics under the Eighteenth-Century Maratha Svarajya* (Cambridge: Cambridge University Press, 1986), 7–8. On the "discourse of sovereignty" in Mughal culture, see Abhishek Kaicker, *The King and the People: Sovereignty and Popular Politics in Mughal Delhi* (Oxford: Oxford University Press, 2020), 9.

47 Wink, *Land and Sovereignty*, 7–8. On Maratha military power see Roy, *War, Culture, and Society*, 95–130.

48 Krishan Kumar, *Visions of Empire: How Five Imperial Regimes Shaped the World* (Princeton, N.J.: Princeton University Press, 2017), 6, 11.

49 Scholars have argued that the Marathas were a confederacy rather than an empire; see Gordon, *The Marathas*, 10–15.

50 See C. A. Bayly, *Imperial Meridian: The British Empire and the World, 1780–1830* (London: Longman, 1989); see also Dirk H. A. Kolff, *Naukar, Rajput, and Sepoy: The Ethnohistory of the Military Labour Market in Hindustan, 1450–1850* (Cambridge: University of Cambridge Press, 1990); John Darwin, *Unfinished Empire: The Global Expansion of Britain* (New York: Bloomsbury, 2013).

51 On the East India Company as a "military-fiscal" state, see John Brewer, *The Sinews of Power: War, Money, and the English State* (Cambridge, Mass.: Harvard University Press, 1990); Philip J. Stern, *The Company-State: Corporate Sovereignty and the Early Modern Foundations of the British Empire in India* (London: Oxford University Press, 2012); Rupali Mishra, *A Business of State: Commerce, Politics, and the Birth of the East India Company* (Cambridge, Mass.: Harvard University Press, 2018); Bayly, *Imperial Meridian*.

52 See Finn, "Material Turns," 13–14; G. J. Bryant, "Indigenous Mercenaries in the Service of European Imperialists: The Case of the Sepoys in the Early British Indian Army, 1750–1800," *War in History* 7, no. 1 (January 2000): 2–28.

53 See Christopher Pinney, *Photos of the Gods: The Printed Image and Political Struggle in India* (London: Reaktion, 2004); Daniel E. White, *From Little London to Little Bengal: Religion, Print, and Modernity in Early British India, 1793–1835* (Baltimore: Johns Hopkins University Press, 2013); Eaton, "Colonial Iconoclash," 31–46.

54 General information on Maratha politics can be accessed in sources like Gordon, *The Marathas*, 158–74.

1 "TAKE ALL OF THEM"

1 An earlier version of this chapter was published as "'Take all of them:' Eclecticism and the Arts of the Pune Court in India, 1760–1800," *Art Bulletin* 100, no. 2 (June 2018): 61–93. See John Briggs, "An Autobiographical Memoir of the Early Life of Nana Farnevís [*sic*]," *Transactions of the Royal Asiatic Society of Great Britain and Ireland* 2, no. 1 (1829): 95–108. Nana Fadnavis's autobiography was also published in Marathi: V. V. Khare, *Nana Phadnavisanche Charitra* [*Nana Fadnavis's Biography*] (1892; repr., Pune: Varda, 2012).

2 D. B. Parasnis, "Nana Fadnavis's Painting Collection and Delhi Craftsmanship," article no. 11, *Itihas Sangraha Aitihasik Tipane* [in Marathi] (Poona, 1908), 13–15.

3 Nana Fadnavis's name has been spelled different ways including Phadnis and Phadnavis.

4 Briggs, "Autobiographical Memoir," 98.

5 Ibid., 99–100.

6 A brief account of Fadnavis's collection is in Edward Moor, *The Hindu Pantheon* (London: J. Johnson, 1810), 431.

7 At least one other album of paintings was passed down through Nana Fadnavis's descendants and sold in 1973, which led to the division of its folios. It contained portraits, battle scenes, animal fights, Persian narratives, religious leaders, and gatherings of ascetics and character types, mostly from the Mughal era. Some of the works relate to the period when Fadnavis was in Delhi, including a drawing of the Mughal emperor Muhammad Shah (r. 1719–48) being carried on a palanquin; see A. C. Ardeshar, "Mughal Miniature Painting (with Illustrations from the Collection of Mr. A. C. Ardeshar of Bombay)," *Roopa-Lekha* 1, no. 2 (1940): 19–34; *Catalogue of Important Oriental Miniatures and a Mughal Manuscript: The Property of a Gentleman*, Sotheby's, New York, July 10, 1973, lots 1–40; two of these folios are now in the Bibliothèque Nationale de France, Estampes, Réserve od 44, ff. 14, 17; see Roselyne Hurel, *Miniatures et peintures indiennes*, vol. 1 (Paris: Bibliothèque Nationale de France, 2010), 109–10; one is in the San Diego Museum of Art (Faqir-ullah, *Muhammad Shah Carried in a Palanquin*, Mughal, ca. 1735, Edwin Binney 3rd Collection, acc. no. 1990.37); others have been on the market; see J. P. Losty, *A Prince's Eye: Imperial Mughal Paintings from a Princely Collection* (London: Francesca Galloway, 2013), 10, cat. no. 1A. For other references to this album see Toby Falk and Mildred Archer, *Indian Miniatures of the India Office Library* (London: Sotheby Parke Bernet, 1981), 122; William Dalrymple and Yuthika Sharma, *Princes and Painters in Mughal Delhi, 1707–1857* (New York: Asia Society Museum, 2012), 76–7; Yuthika Sharma, "From Miniatures to Monuments: Picturing Shah Alam's Delhi (1771–1806)," in *Indo-Muslim Cultures in Transition*, ed. Alka Patel and Karen Leonard (Leiden: Brill, 2012), 120.

8 According to CSMVS records, P. V. Mawjee and D. B. Parasnis purchased paintings from families in the Satara region in the early twentieth century, including an album of

paintings "with uniform size *hashias* [margins] with arabesque design in gold and a green border" from the descendants of Nana Fadnavis; see Madhav Gandhi, Sadashiv Gorakshkar, and Kalpana Desai, *Mirror of Beauty: Art Treasures from India* [Skonhetens Spegel: Konstkatter Fran Indien; in Swedish], Part 2 (Stockholm: Östasiatiska Museet, 1987), 3, cat. 76. Together two of the museum's published catalogs identify five paintings from both collections, but by measuring the pages (ca. 35 × 56 cm) and comparing the identical gold-designed borders edged in green and orange, there appear to be fifteen from P. V. Mawjee's collection and five from D. B. Parasnis's collection; see Gandhi, Gorakshkar, and Desai, *Mirror of Beauty*, cat. 76, 79, 80, 82; Kalpana Desai, *Jewels of the Crescent: Masterpieces of Chhatrapati Shivaji Maharaj Vastu Sangrahalaya formerly Prince of Wales Museum of Western India* (Ahmedabad: CSMVS with Mapin, 2002), cat. 85, 88, 90, 91; see also the unpublished Catalog of Miniature Paintings in the CSMVS, housed in the museum's library.

9 On the Mughals and Christian imagery, see Gauvin Bailey, "The Indian Conquest of Catholic Art: The Mughals, the Jesuits, and Imperial Mural Painting," *Art Journal* 57, no. 1 (Spring 1998): 24–30; Yael Rice, "Lines of Perception: European Prints and the Mughal *Kitabkhana*," in *Prints in Translation, 1450–1750: Image, Materiality, Space*, ed. Suzanne Karr Schmidt and Edward H. Wouk (London and New York: Routledge, 2017), 202–23.

10 The portrait of Muhammad Shah, ca. 1735 (acc. no. 15.288) is inscribed in Persian as Firdaus Aramgah, a name given to the emperor after his death.

11 These "modest" images stand in contrast to erotic ones popular in the period. Edward Moor discussed the latter in Daulatrao Scindia's collection, in *Oriental Fragments* (London: Smith, Elder, 1834), 149–50; for modern studies see e.g. Kavita Singh, "Congress of Kings: Notes on a Painting of Muhammad Shah Rangeela Having Sex," in *A Magical World: New Visions of Indian Painting*, ed. Molly Emma Aitken (Mumbai: Marg Publications, 2017), 38–49.

12 Briggs, "Autobiographical Memoir," 101. Sadashivrao Bhau's portrait is reproduced in Mark Zebrowski, *Deccani Painting* (Berkeley: University of California Press, 1983), 258.

13 See Malini Roy, "Battle of Panipat, 1761," Asian and African Studies Blog, British Library, posted September 10, 2015, https://blogs.bl.uk/asian-and-african/2015/09/battle-of-panipat-1761.html.

14 Briggs, "Autobiographical Memoir," 101.

15 V. K. Bhave, *Peshwekalin Maharashtra* [Maharashtra in the Peshwa Era; in Marathi] (1935; repr., Pune: Bharat Itihas Sanshodhak Mandal, 1975), 127.

16 "Secret Correspondence of the Court of the Peshwa Madhu Rao, from Year 1761–1772," *Transactions of the Royal Asiatic Society of Great Britain and Ireland* 2, no. 1 (March 1830): 125–6.

17 Inscribed Boge Raj [Bhojraj], *Madhavrao Peshwa*, second half of the 18th century, YCBA, B1977.14.22245; see Douglas Fordham, "Costume Dramas: British Art at the Court of the Marathas," *Representations* 101 (Winter 2008): 61–2. Bhojraj was also hired to paint pictures from the Ramayana and the Mahabharata on the walls of the Peshwa's mansion, or Shanivarwada; see D. B. Parasnis, "The Peshwa's Palace [Rajwada] in Poona," article no. 17, *Itihas Sangraha Aitihasik Safur Lekh* [Collection of history: expanded historical writings; in Marathi] (Poona, 1907–16), 53–5; D. B. Parasnis, *Poona in Bygone Days* (Bombay: Times Press, 1921), 8–9.

18 Mahadji Scindia's name has been spelled in various ways, including Shinde.

19 See John Malcolm, *A Memoir of Central India, including Malwa and Adjoining Provinces . . .*, 2nd edn., 2 vols. (London: Kingsbury, Parbury & Allen, 1824), vol. 1, 118–19; H. G. Keene, *Mádhav Ráo Sindhia, Otherwise Called Madhoji* (Oxford: Clarendon Press, 1891), 43–4; Uday S. Kulkarni, *Solstice at Panipat: 14 January 1761; An Authentic Account of the Panipat Campaign* (Pune: Mula Mutha, 2012), 224–5.

20 Stewart Gordon, *The Marathas 1600–1818* (Cambridge: Cambridge University Press, 1993), 157–8, 167–8. Scindia's troops included those led by the Savoyard general Benoît de Boigne; see Jérôme Boyé, *L'Extraordinaire aventure de Benoît de Boigne aux Indes* (Paris: C & D, 1996).

21 G. S. Sardesai, *New History of the Marathas*, 3 vols. (Bombay: Phoenix, 1946–8), vol. 3, 137–70.

22 Scindia is mentioned in Jaipur court poetry; see Krishnadatta Kavi, *Pratap Prakasa* [A contemporary account of life in the royal court at Jaipur in the late 18th century; in Hindi], ed. Gopal Narayan Bahura (Jaipur: Maharaja Sawai Man Singh II Museum Trust, 1983), 7–8.

23 Sir Jadunath Sarkar, *A History of Jaipur, c. 1503–1938* (1984; repr., New Delhi: Orient Blackswan, 2009), 256.

24 Parasnis, "Jaipur's Bhojraj Minegar," article no. 25, *Itihas Sangraha Aitihasik Tipane*, 38–9. Other rulers imported skilled craftsmen. In the mid-eighteenth century, Haidar Ali brought twenty-five families from the Saurashtrika caste of northern Gujarat who specialized in gold and silver embroidery from Tanjore to Mysore; see Anne Buddle, *Tigers around the Throne: The Court of Tipu Sultan (1750–99)* (London: Zamana Gallery, 1990), 34.

25 A record in the Jaipur court's painting workshop (*chitragrih/suratkhana*), now in Rajasthan State Archives, Bikaner, documents an exchange of paintings from the Jaipur administrator Raja Ayamal to the Maratha king Shahu in *shaka* year 1794 (1716 CE) for 350 rupees for an album, 350 rupees for 100 paintings, or at 3 rupees 8 anna per painting. I thank Molly Aitken for sharing this unpublished reference.

26 D. B. Parasnis, "Jaipur's King's Bhagvat," article no. 24, *Itihas Sangraha Aitihasik Tipane*, 37–8.

27 Ibid. Paintings entered the market due to war and defeat, such as after Ghulam Qadir Khan's sack of Delhi in 1788. In his treatise *Yadgar-i Bahaduri* (Memoirs of Bahadur), Bahadur Singh relates that Ghulam Qadir Khan's relatives sold the Mughal emperor Shah Alam II's "paintings and books like they were vegetables and crops." Bahadur also names Mahadji Scindia as a ruler akin to the Nawabs of Awadh who purchased single folio paintings and albums dispersed from the Mughal library; see Natalia di Pietrantonio, "Circuits of Exchange: Albums and the Art Market in 18th-Century Avadh," *Journal 18* 6 (October 2018), http://www.journal18.org/2846 (accessed March 25, 2021).

28 Parashar Dadaji was Nana Fadnavis's agent, and Anand Rao Gangadhar was Scindia's; Parasnis, "Nana Fadnavis's Painting Collection," 13–14; G. S. Sardesai, "Nana Fadnavis's Hobby of Collecting Paintings," in *Aitihasik Patrabodh* [Informative historical documents; in Marathi], comp. and ed. G. S. Sardesai (Bombay: Shri Samarth Prakashan, 1939), 95.

29 Parasnis, "Nana Fadnavis's Painting Collection," 13–14; also quoted in Sardesai, "Nana Fadnavis's Hobby," 93–4; see also Sharma, "From Miniatures to Monuments," 120. A fine Mughal equestrian portrait, probably of Peshwa Bajirao I (1700–1740) or Peshwa Balaji Bajirao (1720–1761), from P. V. Mawjee's collection in the CSMVS (15.257) is attributed to Nidhamal (fl. 1735–60), which indicates that this artist was prized by the Marathas.

30 Parasnis, "Nana Fadnavis's Painting Collection," 13–14; Sardesai, "Nana Fadnavis's Hobby," 93–4.

31 Bhave, *Peshwekalin Maharashtra*, 128.

32 Besides the paintings previously described, P. V. Mawjee purchased works from Fadnavis's descendants that include manuscripts with "golden border lines" of different prayers to gods (*stotra*), which he read at the time of "daily prayer"; love sonnets, Mughal paintings on ivory playing cards, and jade chess pieces are also mentioned; see *A Catalogue of Purshotam Vishram Mawjee Museum* (Bombay, n.d.), 14, 27, 29.

33 *A Dancer Balances a Bottle on Her Head*, Faizabad, ca. 1770, Chester Beatty Library, Dublin.

34 See G. S. Sardesai, ed., *Selections from the Peshwa Daftar* (hereafter *SPD*) [in Marathi], 46 vols. (Bombay: Government Central Press, 1934), vol. 32, 101, no. 182; 114–16, no. 196; B. K. Apte, *Maratha Wall Paintings (Wai, Menavali, Satara, Pune)* (Bombay: Government Central Press, 1988), 22. I thank Ashok Phadnis for providing information on the Fadnavis family temples, deities, lineage, and paintings, and for discussing the artworks with me.

35 See the albums of Hindu gods made for Antoine-Louis Polier in Awadh, British Library, London, OR.4769, OR.4770.

36 Sardesai, "Nana Fadnavis's Hobby," 93–4.

37 See Malini Roy, "William Beckford's Albums on Hindu Mythology," Asian and African Studies Blog, British Library, posted December 8, 2014, http://blogs.bl.uk/asian-and-african/2014/12/william-beckfords-albums-on-hindu-mythology.html.

38 See Isabella Nardi, *The Theory of Citrasutras in Indian Painting: A Critical Re-evaluation of Their Uses and Interpretations* (London: Routledge, 2006), 26. In the seventeenth century, the Maharashtrian Swami Ram Das wrote that pictures should be drawn on the walls of buildings; Ram Das, *Shri Samarth Granth Bhandar* [in Marathi], ed. L. R. Pangarkar (Bombay: Popular Prakashan, 1999), 432–3. Kamal Chavan, *Maratha Murals: Late Medieval Painting of the Deccan, 1650–1850 A.D.* (Delhi: B. R. Publishing, 1983), 7–15 offers an account of literary references to mural production in Maharashtra.

39 One temple was dedicated to Lakshmi-Vasudev (connected to Vishnu) and the other to Amruteshvar (connected to Shiva); Apte, *Maratha Wall Paintings*, 22. On the Peshwa and Nana Fadnavis's devotion to Hari-Hara, a combination of Vishnu and Shiva, see Sardesai, *SPD*, vol. 32, 101, no. 182; 114–16, no. 196.

40 See Professor Mustansir Dalvi's curator's note for the exhibition *Wadas of Maharashtra: Measured Drawings from Sir J. J. School of Art, Bombay, 1929–1946*, 2010, Archives of the Sir J. J. College of Architecture, Mumbai.

41 See Parasnis, *Poona in Bygone Days*, 29–31.

42 The sage is Yajnavalkya; Apte, *Maratha Wall Paintings*, 32.

43 On Dattatreya see Charles Pain with Eleanor Zelliot, "The God Dattatreya and the Datta Temples of Pune," in *The Experience of Hinduism: Essays on Religion in Maharashtra*, ed. Maxine Berntsen and Eleanor Zelliot (Albany: State University of New York Press, 1988), 95–108.

44 On the general history of the Chitpavan and their historical accounts, see Nicolas Dejenne, "Telling the History of the Sacred Ramakshetra in the Vadeshvaradayakavya," in *Time, History and the Religious Imaginary in South Asia*, ed. Anne Murphy (London: Routledge, 2011), 110–15.

45 P. V. Mawjee's collection included prayer books (*stotra*) from Nana Fadnavis's collection such as those by Upamanyu, a sage at Dhom; see *Catalogue of Mawjee Museum*, 14–16.

46 Govind Bhikaji Raste, a banker to the Peshwas, built this temple.

47 See Sardesai, *SPD*, vol. 32, 14, no. 26; see also M. S. Mate, *Temples and Legends of Maharashtra* (Bombay: Bharat Vidya Bhavan, 1962), 1–25; Laurence W. Preston, "Subregional Religious Centres in the History of Maharashtra: The Sites Sacred to Ganesh," in *Images of Maharashtra: A Regional Profile of India*, ed. N. K. Wagle (London: Curzon, 1980), 118–20; Anne Feldhaus, *Connected Places: Region, Pilgrimage, and Geographical Imagination in India* (Basingstoke and New York: Palgrave Macmillan, 2003), 140–48.

48 The mingling of history and myth typifies family histories, or *kula-vrittanta*, that trace a family's genealogy from a deity into the present; see Maureen L. Patterson, "Chitpavan Brahman Family Histories: Sources for a Study of Social Structure and Social Change in Maharashtra," in *Structure and Change in Indian Society*, ed. Milton Singer and Bernard S. Cohen (Chicago: Aldine, 1968), 397–412; Prachi Deshpande, *Creative Pasts: Historical Memory and Identity in Western India, 1700–1960* (New Delhi: Permanent Black, 2007), ch. 1; Dejenne, "Telling the History," 100–14.

49 See Holly Shaffer, "Towards a History of Maratha Painting in the Deccan," in *Dakhan 2018: Recent Studies on Indian Painting*, ed. John Seyller (Hyderabad: Jagdish and Kamla Mittal Museum of Indian Art, 2020), 77–108. On the nexus of painting traditions in central India, see Narmada Prasad Upadhyaya, *Geet Govinda: Paintings in Kanheri Style* (Ocean Township, N.J.: Mapin, 2006); Narmada Prasad Upadhyaya, *The Color's Fragrance: The Catalogue of the Stray Leaves and Illustrated Manuscripts in the Scindia Oriental Research Institute, Vikram University, Ujjain (MP)* (Harda: Shri Beni Madhava Prakashan Graha, 2011).

50 In the frieze of Vishnu's incarnations, Rama is portrayed as relieving Ahilya of the curse that turned her to stone, rather than in his more standard depiction as defeating Ravana; see Apte, *Maratha Wall Paintings*, 29.

51 Ibid., 23.

52 The artist was from Vittal Peth; Tulshibagh Daftar to Ramji Chitari, Letter 184: "Picture work from Tulshibagh (March 18, 1826)," *Traimasik* 32, nos. 1–4 [in Marathi] (Pune: Bharat Itihas Sanshodhak Mandal, January 1952): 240.

53 Sardesai, *SPD*, vol. 18, 34, nos. 56, 57.

54 Ibid. In Marathi *bhasma* can mean either golden dust or sacred ash, and *rogani* can mean oil or varnish. *Argaja*, which can be used for dying garments, in Persian and Urdu means "a perfume of a yellowish colour compounded of several scented ingredients (one receipt specifies sandal, rose-water, camphor, musk, ambergris, and butter as the ingredients)": J. T. Molesworth, *A dictionary, Marathi and English, 2nd edition, rev. and enl.* (Bombay: Printed for the Government , 1857), cited in Chavan, *Maratha Murals*, 6, 24; John Thompson Platts, *A*

Dictionary of Urdu, Classical Hindi, and English ([London]: Oxford University Press, 1960).

55 See George Michell, *Art and Architecture of Southern India: Vijayanagara and the Successor States, 1350–1750* (New York: Cambridge University Press, 1995); Anila Verghese and Anna Dallapiccola, *South India under Vijayanagara: Art and Archaeology* (Oxford: Oxford University Press, 2011). A figure of the door guardian Vijaya adorned the Kakare Wada and the Raj Wada, both in Satara.

56 Major Edward Moor purchased this painting in Poona between 1797 and 1805 and he returned with it to England.

57 Moor, *Hindu Pantheon*, 27–8. The Shanivarwada burnt down in 1827, and thus information about its interior is available only in texts and paintings; see Parasnis, "Peshwa's Palace," 53–5; Parasnis, *Poona in Bygone Days*, 8–9.

58 N. K. Wagle, "Heroes in the Caritra-Bakhar, Povada and Akhyana," in *The Concept of Hero in Indian Culture*, ed. Heidrun Brückner, Hugh van Skyhawk, and Claus Peter Zoller (New Delhi: Manohar, 2007), 219–22.

59 See Khare, *Nana Fadnavis's Biography*, 80–81.

60 Y. N. Kelkar, ed., *Aitihasik Powade* [in Marathi] (Pune: Diamond, 2008), 177, cited in Chetan Sahasrabudhe and Anurag Kashyap, "Festivals, Rituals, and Urban Landscape in Eighteenth-Century Maharashtra," *South Asian Studies* 32, no. 2 (2016): 160.

61 See Khare, *Nana Fadnavis's Biography*, 80–81.

62 D. B. Parasnis, "Savai Madhavrao's Eulogy," article no. 40, *Itihas Sangraha Prastavik Lekh (zunya aitihasik goshti)* [in Marathi] (Poona, 1907–16), 64.

63 On Poona's transformation into a sacred center under the Peshwas, see Parasnis, *Poona in Bygone Days*, 29–31; Sardesai, *SPD*, vol. 32, 14, no. 26; Preston, "Subregional Religious Centres," 118–20; Feldhaus, *Connected Places*, 140–48; Mate, *Temples and Legends of Maharashtra*, 1–25.

64 See Shivram Chitari, *Ganesha on an Elephant in Procession*, Maharashtra, 18th century, reproduced in S. B. Deshmukh, *Maratha Painting* (Aurangabad: Marathwada University, 1992), pl. VIII.

65 "Peshwyanchi Bakhar [History of the Peshwas]," in *Kavyetihas Sangraha* [Collection of poetry and history; in Marathi], no. 1, ed. Kashinath N. Sane and J. B. Modak (Poona: Shivaji Printing House, 1878), 167–72. Krishnaji Vinayak Sohoni, or another official to the Peshwas, probably composed this text around 1818 when Peshwa rule ceased; see Deshpande, *Creative Pasts*, 21. See also M. G. Dikshit, "Early Life of Peshwa Savai Madhavrao," *Bulletin of the Deccan College Research Institute* (Poona) 7, nos. 1–4 (December 1946): 231; Sahasrabudhe and Kashyap, "Festivals, Rituals," 160.

66 On the comparative construction of other eighteenth-century cities such as Lucknow, Jaipur, and Benares along royal and devotional axes, see Sandria B. Freitag, ed., *The Visual Turn: South Asia across the Disciplines* (Abingdon: Routledge, 2015); Madhuri Desai, *Banaras Reconstructed: Architecture and Sacred Space in a Hindu Holy City* (Seattle: University of Washington Press, 2017).

67 Indira Viswanathan Peterson, "The Sequence of King Śarabhendra's Sacred Places: Pilgrimage and Kingship in a Marathi Text from 19th-Century Thanjavur," in *Festschrift Heidrun Brückner*, ed. Anna Aurelia Esposito et al. (Wiesbaden: Harrassowitz, 2016), 275–81; see also Indira Viswanathan Peterson, "Portraiture at the Tanjore Maratha Court," in *Portraits in Princely India*, ed. Rosie Llewellyn-Jones (Mumbai: Marg, 2008), 44–57.

68 Vibhuti Sachdev and Giles Tillotson, *Building Jaipur: The Making of an Indian City* (London: Reaktion, 2002), 36–56. Nineteenth-century kings continued to relate divine with royal realms in Jaipur; see Sugata Ray, "Colonial Frames, 'Native' Claims: The Jaipur Economic and Industrial Museum," *The Art Bulletin* 96, no. 2 (2014): 196–212.

69 In August 1768, the British had given the Peshwa four small glass containers with a foreign scent, mirrors, twenty-four paintings of the sea, a silver cow, and a gold chain; Sardesai, *SPD*, vol. 22, 120, no. 208.

70 David J. Howlett, "Malet, Sir Charles Warre, first baronet (1753–1815)," *Oxford Dictionary of National Biography* (Oxford University Press, 2004; online edn. May 2009); Fordham, "Costume Dramas," 59, 80; Holly Shaffer, *Adapting the Eye: An Archive of the British in India* (New Haven, Conn.: Yale Center for British Art, 2011), 6–9.

71 Edward Moor decried the representation of the space as having "far more mythological ornaments than are actually in the room," perhaps due to its depiction during the annual festival of Ganesha; Moor, *Hindu Pantheon*, 174.

72 Charles Warre Malet, Memoranda Book, January 1791–March 1793, MSS Eur F149/67, pp. 67–8, Malet Collection: Papers of Sir Charles Warre Malet, India Office Records and Private Papers, British Library, cited in Fordham, "Costume Dramas," 80. For a transcription of Wales's journey to Poona and a chronicle of his work there, see Uday S. Kulkarni, *James Wales: Artist and Antiquarian in the Time of Peshwa Sawai Madhavrao* (Pune: Mula Mutha Publishers, 2019).

73 See D. B. Parasnis, *Savai Madhavarava Peshwyancha Darbara ani tya Veleche Pahile Ingraja Resident Sir Charles Malet* [The court of Peshwa Savai Madhavrao and the then English Resident Sir Charles Malet; in Marathi] (Mumbai: Tukaram Javaji Nirnaysagar Press, ca. 1867), chs. 4, 5. On European artists at Indian courts see Natasha Eaton, *Mimesis across Empires: Artworks and Networks in India, 1765–1860* (Durham, N.C.: Duke University Press, 2013); Deborah Hutton and Rebecca Tucker, "The Worldly Artist in the Seventeenth Century: The Travels of Cornelis Claesz. Heda," *Art History* 37, no. 5 (November 2014): 870, 878, 881.

74 C. A. Bayly, *Empire and Information: Intelligence Gathering and Social Communication in India* (Cambridge: Cambridge University Press, 1996), 31–2.

75 Fordham, "Costume Dramas," 57–85.

76 James Wales, "From Bombay to Poona, 1792," 19, James Wales Archive, YCBA.

77 The honor of *vakil-al mutlaq* had been conferred six years previously. Scindia also had other reasons to visit Poona, including to secure payment, to settle a dispute with other Maratha generals, and to check on Malet as the new Resident; see Sardesai, *New History*, vol. 3, 229–60; Sir Jadunath Sarkar, *Sindhia Regent of Delhi (Persian Records of Maratha History)* (Bombay: Director of Archives, 1954), 56; R. G. Pandey, *Mahadji Shinde and the Poona Durbar* (New Delhi: Oriental Publishers & Distributors, 1980), 95–8.

78 Sardesai, *New History*, vol. 3, 232.

79 C. W. Malet to Major William Palmer, Resident with Mhadjee Sindea, Poona, April 15, 1792, in G. S. Sardesai, *English Records of Maratha History: Poona Residency Correspondence*, vol. 2 (Bombay: Government Central Press, 1936), 233, no. 132.

80 A Devanagari inscription on the painting says: "the servant Sabaji Anant the painter" (*sevak sabaji anant musavir*); this is probably the same artist Sabaji who painted *Peshwa Savai Madhavrao Exercising with a Long Spear* (see fig. 30) and was employed by the Peshwa.

81 Wales, "From Bombay to Poona," 12–13, 17.

82 Wales to Captain Smith, July 7, 1792, ibid. Wales also wrote that he had received news of his daughter Nelly's death, after which he prepared for his wife's travel to India with their remaining children.

83 See ibid., 31; Nicholas Eastaugh et al., *The Pigment Compendium* (Oxford: Elsevier, 2004), s.v., "Green Earth."

84 Wales, "From Bombay to Poona," 14, 26.

85 James Wales, *Findlay, Esq. Aide-de-Camp to Sir Charles Malet*, Maharashtra, 1792, oil on board, 32 × 27 cm, Dillington House, Somerset, reproduced in *Oil Paintings in Public Ownership in Somerset* (London: Public Catalogue Foundation, 2008), 193, and online, https://artuk.org/discover/artworks/findlay-esq-aide-de-camp-to-sir-charles-malet-40499 (accessed June 17, 2021).

86 Wales, "From Bombay to Poona," 26, 30.

87 Ibid., 31.

88 On British miniatures, see Marcia Pointon, "'Surrounded with Brilliants': Miniature Portraits in Eighteenth-Century England," *The Art Bulletin* 83, no. 1 (March 2001): 48–77.

89 Parasnis, *Court of Peshwa Savai Madhavrao*, 66.

90 On Mughal paintings in Malet's collection see *Indian Woman in Red and Gold Dress*, YCBA, B1977.14.22432, published in Shaffer, *Adapting the Eye*, 25. On Mughal paintings with kneeling figures in Fadnavis's collection see Desai, *Jewels of the Crescent*, cat. 85, 91.

91 Joshua Reynolds, Discourse II: 81, quoted in Christine Bolus-Reichert, *The Age of Eclecticism: Literature and Culture in Britain, 1815–1885* (Columbus: Ohio State University Press, 2009), 33.

92 Joshua Reynolds, "Discourse VI," in *Discourses on Art*, ed. Robert R. Wark (New Haven and London: Paul Mellon Centre for Studies in British Art with Yale University Press, 1997), 110.

93 See Mildred Archer, "James Wales: Portrait Painter in Bombay and Poona, 1791–95," *Journal of the Indian Society of Oriental Art*, no. 8 (1977): 57–64; J. L. Caw, rev. Douglas Fordham, "Wales, James (1747–1795)," *ODNB* (2004).

94 See Lawrence Lipking, *The Ordering of the Arts in Eighteenth-Century England* (Princeton, N.J.: Princeton University Press, 1970), 164–207; John Barrell, *The Political Theory of Painting from Reynolds to Hazlitt* (New Haven and London: Yale University Press, 1986), 69–162.

95 Eaton, *Mimesis across Empires*, 171 argues that Johann Zoffany forged an Anglo-Indian *kalam* (style) specifically with reference to Mughal art at the Lucknow court, offering a fascinating parallel. In an Ottoman context, Jonathan Richardson (1667–1745) and Jean-Étienne Liotard (1702–1789) appropriated an "'Oriental' manière": Nebahat Avcioğlu and Finbarr Barry Flood, "Introduction: Globalizing Cultures: Art and Mobility in the Eighteenth Century," *Ars Orientalis* 39 (2010): 15; Kristel Smentek, "Looking East: Jean-Étienne Liotard, the Turkish Painter," ibid: 84–112.

96 Wales, "From Bombay to Poona," 49.

97 Parasnis, *Court of Peshwa Savai Madhavrao*, 67.

98 Wales, "From Bombay to Poona," 49.

99 Ibid., 55.

100 A description of the gifts in the "Peshwyanchi Bakhar" (162) includes a *jama*, long trousers (*vizar*), a textile for the waist (*patka*), strings of pearls, earrings, a bracelet, and an armband, some of which are depicted in the painting; Deshpande, *Creative Pasts*, 21.

101 See Robert Mabon, *Persian Sword Hilt Set with Diamonds*, 1792–5, YCBA, B1977.14.22270; Fordham, "Costume Dramas," 63–4.

102 For other examples see Deshmukh, *Maratha Painting*, 50–51.

103 In the Marathi historical treatise the "Peshwyanchi Bakhar," 166 the reconciliation occurred while Scindia and the Peshwa were boating. Scindia asked to lead both the administration and the military, but the Peshwa refused: "My right hand is Nana Fadnavis and my left hand is Mahadji Scindia. These two hands are with me. Until then the state's administration need not worry me." Colonel Palmer wrote a letter to Cornwallis on July 21, 1793 that confirmed the truce; see Sardesai, *New History*, vol. 3, 251–2.

104 Parasnis, *Court of Peshwa Savai Madhavrao*, 65–7.

105 James Wales, "Indian Antiquities" (notebook), James Wales Archive, box 1, folder 2, 5–6; James Wales, "Indian Antiquities" (journal), ibid., vol. 2, 30–32, 39. Other Indian rulers also fed the Maratha interest in optical technologies; the Nawab of Arcot sent a spyglass to Scindia as a gift; see Justin Biel, "Divide and Tolerate: Imperial Secularisms in Ireland, India, and Britain, 1774–1815" (Ph.D. diss., University of Minnesota, 2014), 199.

106 Wales, "From Bombay to Poona," 66. See Mabon's sketches at the YCBA, acc. nos. B1977.14.22281, B1977.14.22440, and by Wales in *The Other Side of the Verandah: Watercolours, Drawings, and Photographs of Anglo-Indian Interiors in the British Period 1800–1900*, exh. cat. (London: Eyre and Hobhouse, 1981).

107 Eaton, *Mimesis across Empires*, 178–82.

108 Charles Warre Malet, Letter Book, 56, 59, MSS Eur F149/1, Malet Collection, British Library, cited in Eaton, *Mimesis across Empires*, 179. For other examples of equestrian portraits see Deshmukh, *Maratha Painting*, pl. II; Rosemary Crill and Kapil Jariwala, *The Indian Portrait, 1560–1860* (Ahmedabad: Mapin Publishing, 2010); Llewellyn-Jones, *Portraits in Princely India*.

109 Jonathan Richardson, *The Works* (London: T. Davies, 1773), 7, quoted in Avcioğlu and Flood, "Introduction: Globalizing Cultures," 14.

110 Parasnis, *Court of Peshwa Savai Madhavrao*, 65.

111 The Mughal court similarly hired Dutch artists for skills in both "naturalism" and "psychological portraiture"; see Sanjay Subrahmanyam, "Roomful of Mirrors: The Artful Embrace of Mughals and Franks, 1550–1700," *Ars Orientalis* 39 (2010): 51. On the different facets of portraiture in Udaipur and Tanjore see Molly Emma Aitken, *The Intelligence of Tradition in Rajput Court Painting* (New Haven and London: Yale University Press, 2010), 118–19; Peterson, "Portraiture at the Tanjore Maratha Court," 50–53.

112 For other representations see Robert Mabon, *Sketches Illustrative of Oriental Manners and Customs* (Calcutta?: 1797?), pl. V; Fordham, "Costume Dramas," 64.

113 Eaton, *Mimesis across Empires*, 178–82.

114 The *arasemahal* may be akin to the North Indian *ai'na-khana* where pictures and curiosities were displayed; see Natasha Eaton, "Between Mimesis and Alterity: Art, Gift, and Diplomacy in Colonial India, 1770–1800," *Society for Comparative Study of Society and History* 46, no. 4 (October 2004): 184–5.

115 Wales also might have been ill: he had an eye infection in the first half of November: Wales, "Indian Antiquities" (journal), 33 (November 6–8, 1794).

116 Letters quoted in Parasnis, *Court of Peshwa Savai Madhavrao*, 66; Parasnis, *Poona in Bygone Days*, 69.

117 On the definition of *murti*, see Frederick M. Asher, "Indian Image / Image in India," in *What Is an Image?*, ed. James Elkins (State College: Pennsylvania State Press, 2011), 113.

118 James Mackintosh, 1805, quoted in Parasnis, *Poona in Bygone Days*, 66–7; Eaton, *Mimesis across Empires*, 182.

119 See S. Settar and Gunther-Dietz Sontheimer, eds., *Memorial Stones: A Study of Their Origin, Significance and Variety* (Dharwad: Institute of Indian Art History, Karnatak University, 1982); Padma Kaimal, "The Problem of Portraiture in South India, circa 870–970 AD," *Artibus Asiae* 59, nos. 1–2 (1999): 73–5. On Rajput and Maratha *chhatris* see Melia Belli, "Keeping Up with the Rajputs: Appropriation and the Articulation of Sacrality and Political Legitimacy in Scindia Funerary Art," *Archives of Asian Art* 61 (2011): 92.

120 Belli, "Keeping Up with the Rajputs," 100–02.

121 See Aitken, *Intelligence of Tradition*, ch. 3, "The Portrait as Gift"; Eaton, *Mimesis across Empires*, 178–82.

122 See Aitken, *Intelligence of Tradition*, 37–41.

123 See Vidya Dehejia, "The Very Idea of a Portrait," *Ars Orientalis* 28 (1998): 40–50; Kaimal, "Problem of Portraiture 870–970 AD," 59–133; Padma Kaimal, "The Problem of Portraiture in South India, circa 970–1000 AD," *Artibus Asiae* 60, no. 1 (2000): 139–79.

124 On the Nayaka period see Crispin Branfoot, "Royal Portrait Sculpture in the South Indian Temple," *South Asian Studies* 16, no. 1 (2000): 11–36. On the Maratha court in Tanjore see Peterson, "Portraiture at the Tanjore Maratha Court," 44–57. On the Mysore court see Janaki Nair, *Mysore Modern: Rethinking the Region under Princely Rule* (New Delhi: Orient Blackswan, 2011), 69–72.

125 At the Maratha court in Tanjore, Serfoji II hired John Flaxman to sculpt his marble portrait as a devotee. The sculpture's placement on the plinth of the previous ruler's throne transformed it into the public face of the king. Over time, Serfoji's portrait took on the gilded and jewel-encrusted status of an icon; Peterson, "Portraiture at the Tanjore Maratha Court," 44–57; Peterson, "Sequence of King Śarabhendra's Sacred Places," 275–81.

126 Fordham, "Costume Dramas," 62–6; Archer, *India and British Portraiture*, 333–55.

127 Wales, "From Bombay to Poona," 62, 66 (October 16, 1792).

128 Robert Mabon, "Journal," 6, James Wales Archive, box 1, folder 3.

129 Fordham, "Costume Dramas," 65–6.

130 Wales, "Indian Antiquities" (notebook), 1, 3.

131 See Tapati Guha-Thakurta, *The Making of a New "Indian" Art: Artists, Aesthetics, and Nationalism in Bengal, c. 1850–1920* (Cambridge: Cambridge University Press, 1992), 35–44; Christopher Pinney, *Photos of the Gods: The Printed Image and Political Struggle in India* (London: Reaktion, 2004).

132 Wales, "Indian Antiquities" (journal), 34 (November 14, 1794).

133 Mabon, "Journal," 1.

134 Wales, "Indian Antiquities" (journal), 27 (October 9, 1794), 46–7 (January 27, 1795).

135 Ibid., 24 (October 1, 1794), 25–7 (October 6, 1794).

136 I thank Manisha Patil for directing me to this portrait in Central Museum, Nagpur.

137 Wales, "Indian Antiquities" (journal), 37 (December 3, 1794).

138 Wales, "Indian Antiquities" (notebook), 2.

139 See the portraits of Portuguese governors in the Archaeological Survey of India, Goa, e.g. D. Fr. Miguel Rangel (acc-no-0169) or Manuel Mascarenhas Homem (acc-no-0119): http://museumsofindia.gov.in/repository/museum/gom_goa/collection/object_type/painting/0/1/10.

140 V. D. Divekar, *Sir Charles Warre Malet's Bequests at Chargot, England* (1976?), 4; this is an offprint from *Indian Archives* (January/June 1976) in the British Library.

141 There is a partially legible Persian inscription on the painting's border: "the painter [*musavir*] of magical forms Sabaji son of [Anantji?] . . . faithful servant of the ruler clothed in the creed"; and on the right: "from God's bounty . . . employee of his excellency Madhavrao Narayan . . . mounted"; I thank Prashant Keshavmurthy, Murad Khan Mumtaz, Leila El-Murr, and Sameer Ali for the translation. The second name of Sabaji is difficult to read; if the Persian vowels are reused it could be Anantji.

142 See Robert Mabon, *Sketch of an Elaborately Saddled Horse* and *Ornament for a Horse's Forelock*, both Poona, 1792–4, both watercolor and graphite with pen and black ink on paper, YCBA, B1977.14.22382 and B1977.14.22420.

143 Wales, "Indian Antiquities" (journal), 25 (October 6, 1794), 34 (November 14, 1794), 34 (November 16, 1794).

144 Wales listed prints he hoped to sell to the court: "Prints of the Royal Family," "Prints of Eminent Men," "Prints . . . after Sir P Lilly [Peter Lely] and Vandyke," "prints of beautiful women"; Wales, "Indian Antiquities" (notebook), 5–6.

145 Compositional precedents exist in paintings produced in the Deccan; see *Princely Deer Hunters*, Bijapur, ca. 1660–70, Stuart Carey Welch Collection, reproduced in Navina Najat Haidar and Marika Sardar, *Sultans of Deccan India 1500–1700: Opulence and Fantasy* (New York: Metropolitan Museum of Art, 2015), 151, cat. 68; Muttam, attrib., *Equestrian Portrait of Nasir Jang*, Aurangabad, ca. 1748–50, Salar Jung Museum (XXXI-20), reproduced in John Seyller and Jagdish Mittal, *Deccani Paintings, Drawings and Manuscripts* (Hyderabad: Jagdish and Kamla Mittal Museum of Indian Art, 2017), 190, fig. 23.

146 Wales, "Indian Antiquities" (journal), 36 (November, 27 1794). On Savai Madhavrao's fondness for deer see Parasnis, "A Specimen of Savai Madhavrao's Daily Routine," article no. 15, *Itihas Sangraha Aitihasik Tipane*, 19–21.

147 Aitken, *Intelligence of Tradition*, 113 has called this tension a "witness-effect" in Rajput paintings.

148 See n. 141 above.

149 On painters of "magical" forms see Gregory Minissale, *Images of Thought: Visuality in Islamic India* (Newcastle: Cambridge Scholars, 2009), 17, 48–9, 53.

2 A POONA ARTIST AT THE BRITISH RESIDENCY

1 Parvati Hill is named after the temple at the top dedicated by Maratha rulers to that goddess.

2 Indian artists often go by their first name rather than family or caste name. I use Gangaram, rather than Navgire and Tambat (castes of metalworkers) for this reason in the text and because Malet and Wales used it in their writings, often spelled as "Gungaram." I have chosen to use Gangaram Tambat as Gangaram's shortened name to be consistent with other scholarship.

3 See "Letter from Sir C. W. Malet, Bart., to the President, on the Subject of the Following Paper [Description of the Caves or Excavations, on the Mountain, About a Mile to the Eastward of the Town of Ellora]," hereafter "Description of the Caves," *Asiatick Researches* 6 (Calcutta, 1799): 382–3. Malet first hired Gangaram in 1790; he noted "Gangaram Painter" and "Gangaram" in his ledger; Charles Warre Malet, Journal and Ledger (January 21 and 31, 1790), 60, MSS Eur F149/79, Malet Collection, BL. Malet and Wales's archive is primarily in the YCBA and the BL; see Holly Shaffer, *Adapting the Eye: An Archive of the British in India, 1770–1830* (New Haven, Conn.: Yale Center for British Art, 2011).

4 See Mildred Archer, *Company Paintings: Indian Paintings of the British Period* (London: Victoria and Albert Museum, 1992).

5 William Jones, *The Works of Sir William Jones: A Discourse on the Institution of Society, for inquiring into the History, Civic and Natural, The Antiquities, Arts, Sciences and Literature, of Asia*, vol. 3 (London: John Stockdale, 1807), 5–6. Company officials repeated such sentiments, e.g. Robert Home, *Select Views in Mysore, the country of Tippoo Sultan* . . . (London: Mr. Bowyer, 1794), v–vii. On colonial knowledge and postcolonial scholarship see the Introduction of this book.

6 See Milo Beach, B. N. Goswamy, and Eberhard Fischer, eds., *Masters of Indian Painting* (Seattle: University of Washington Press, 2011); Henry Noltie, *Robert Wight and the Botanical Drawings of Rungiah and Govindoo*, 2 vols. (Edinburgh: Royal Botanic Garden, 2007); William Dalrymple, ed., *Forgotten Masters: Indian Painting for the East India Company* (London: Wallace Collection, 2019). On artist families see Tryna Lyons, *The Artists of Nathadwara: The Practice of Painting in Rajasthan* (Bloomington: Indiana University Press, 2004). On using colonial archives to decipher "written" and visual "traces of colonial lives" see Ann Laura Stoler, *Along the Archival Grain: Epistemic Anxiety and Colonial Common Sense* (Princeton, N.J.: Princeton University Press, 2009), 1–5.

7 *Indian Painting for British Patrons 1770–1860*, exh. cat. (London: Hazlitt, Gooden & Fox, February 27–March 28, 1991), cat. 5. Moor described Gangaram's pleasure in capturing "the placid serenity of the camel, and the ferocious confidence of the tiger" in his sculptures; Edward Moor, *A Narrative of the Operations of Captain Little's Detachment and of the Mahratta Army* . . . (London: J. Johnson, 1794), 366.

8 D. B. Parasnis, "The English Diplomat," article no. 35, *Itihas Sangraha Aitihasik Tipane* [in Marathi] (Poona, 1908), 53 noted that this bird was a *shajamurgh* and that a painter drew and titled it as such. In 1796, Gangaram drew an ostrich, which he titled *cheetlmurgh*; see YCBA, B1977.14.22310.

9 Charles Warre Malet, Memoranda (November 26, 1789), 59; (February 10, 1790), 85, MSS Eur F149/66.

10 Ibid. (August 6, 1790), 189–90.

11 Ibid. (August to December 1790), 190–244.

12 Hazlitt, Gooden & Fox, *Indian Painting*, cat. 5; see also *The British in India*, exh. cat. (Brighton Museum and Art Gallery, May 9–August 31, 1973); Koes Rookmaaker, "Records of an Animal Collection in Poona at the End of the Eighteenth Century," *Back When and Then* 2, no. 1 (August 1997): 2.

13 See Ebba Koch, "Jahangir as Francis Bacon's Ideal of the King as an Observer and Investigator of Nature," *Journal of the Royal Asiatic Society of Great Britain and Ireland* 19 (2009): 293–338.

14 P. K. Gode, "The Menagerie of the Peshwa," *Proceedings of the Deccan History Conference, First (Hyderabad) Session* (Hyderabad, 1945), 404.

15 James Wales, "Indian Antiquities" (journal), James Wales Archive, Rare Books and Manuscripts, YCBA, vol. 2 (November 27, 1794), 36; Robert Mabon, *Sketches Illustrative of Oriental Manners and Customs* (Calcutta?, 1797?), pl. III. *Poona Akhbars*, 3 vols. (Hyderabad: Central Records Office, Government of Andhra Pradesh, 1956), vol. 3, 42–4 detailed Savai Madhavrao's routine, which included regular sport with horses at the base of Parvati Hill.

16 V. V. Khare, *Nana Phadnavisanche Charitra* [*Nana Fadnavis's Biography*; in Marathi] (1892; repr., Pune: Varda, 2012), 81; M. G. Dikshit, "Early Life of Peshwa Savai Madhavrao," *Bulletin of the Deccan College Research Institute* (Poona; December 1946): 230, nos. 28–32.

17 G. S. Sardesai, ed., *Selections from the Peshwa Daftar* [in Marathi] (Bombay: Government Central Press, 1934), vol. 22, no. 232.

18 James Forbes, *Oriental Memoirs: A Narrative of Seventeen Years Residence in India*, 2nd edn., 2 vols. (London: Richard Bentley, 1834), vol. 2, 83; see Ch. 1 above for Savai Madhavrao's fondness for deer.

19 Dikshit, "Early Life," 230, nos. 28–30.

20 Parasnis collected this painting in western India in the early twentieth century, and identified the figure as Malet. Other Europeans had visited the Maratha court in Poona but, given Malet's longstanding relationship with the Peshwa and their passion for hunting and animals, Parasnis's attribution seems correct; D. B. Parasnis, *Poona in Bygone Days* (Bombay: Times Press, 1921), 130.

21 Moor, *A Narrative*, 366 described the "wild animals" in the Peshwa's possession as an accumulation of tribute.

22 Parasnis, *Poona in Bygone Days*, 130.

23 On Deccan Sultanate hunts and Sufi epics see Navina Najat Haidar and Marika Sardar, *Sultans of Deccan India: Opulence and Fantasy* (New York: Metropolitan Museum of Art, 2015), 151, cat. 68; 297–8, cat. 174; on Hindu icons see Kamal Chavan, *Maratha Murals: Late Medieval Painting of the Deccan, 1650–1850 A.D.* (Delhi: B. R. Publishing, 1983), 104–5, and Shivram Chitari's other paintings such as fig. 75. For British prints see George Bickham's engraving "A View of the Queens Statue, in the Gardens of

Earl Temple at Stow, in Buckinghamshire," in *Beauties of Stow* (London: Robert Sayer, Carington Bowles and John Bowles, 1753), collected by a Maratha family, now in the Bharat Itihas Sanshodhak Mandal, Pune.

24 Forbes, *Oriental Memoirs*, vol. 2, 243–4. Besides Malet's collection, prints were available in Poona at this time. James Wales noted these in his journals (see Ch. 1 above), and Lieut.-Col. Fitzclarens wrote in 1818 that he saw "several large English books of fine engravings" in the palace, quoted in D. B. Parasnis, "The Peshwa's Palace [Rajwada] in Poona," article no. 17, *Itihas Sangraha Aitihasik Safur Lekh* [Collection of history: expanded historical writings; in Marathi] (Poona, 1908–16), 59.

25 A Society of Gentlemen, *A New and Complete Dictionary of Arts and Sciences . . . engraved by Mr. Jefferys*, 2nd edn., 4 vols. (London: W. Owen, 1764), vol. 4, pl. CCXXXII, opp. p. 2773. There were many compendia of natural history in the period; see e.g. Denis Diderot et al., *L'Encyclopédie*, 28 vols. (Paris: André le Breton et al., 1751–72), vol. 14 (1765), 251, pl. 1, fig. 2; Georges Louis Leclerc, Comte de Buffon, *Histoire Naturelle*, 36 vols. (Paris: Imprimerie Royale, 1749–88), vol. 11, pl. 37, opp. p. 202. Such works also reused images: e.g. on the visual history of the rhinoceros see L. Rookmaaker, *Bibliography of a Rhinoceros* (Rotterdam: A. A. Balkema, 1983). Mughal and Deccan artists painted flora and fauna too: see Koch, "Jahangir as Bacon's Ideal," 293–338; BL, Or. 1621, al-Qazwini, *'Ajaib al Makhlukat*, Deccan (Bijapur?), 16th century, f. 156.

26 See the inscriptions on "The Figure of the Common Camel of Hindostan accurately taken from a Living One . . . ," BL, Add. Or. 4364.

27 James Wales, Loose Notes and Drawings, James Wales Archive, 46; Malet, "Description of the Caves," 382. It is likely that Gangaram's family of Navgire Tambat traces its roots to Ahmednagar as Gangaram's father's (Chintaman) brother's family tree remains extant with a descendant, Vilas Bhagirath Navgire. Gangaram's guru was also located in Ahmednagar. I thank Bhushan Deshmukh and Vilas Bhagirath Navgire for providing this information.

28 *Gazetteer of the Bombay Presidency*, vol. 18, part 1 (Poona) (Bombay: Government Central Press, 1885), 340.

29 In J. T. Molesworth's *A Dictionary, Marathi and English* (Bombay: Government of Bombay, June, 1831), तांबट or तांबटकर [tambata or tambatakara] is "A caste or an individual of it. They are coppersmiths." See also "Tambat" in *Maharashtra State Gazetteers, Ahmadnagar District* (Bombay: Gazetteers Department, Government of Maharashtra, 1976), http://164.100.185.107/gazetteer/home.html (accessed May 5, 2021), which notes that they "claim descent from Tvashta the divine architect and from one of the class of Panchals which is generally supposed to mean five crafts-men"; see also Isabella Nardi, *The Theory of Citrasutras in Indian Painting: A Critical Re-evaluation of Their Uses and Interpretations* (London: Routledge, 2006), 17 and 172.

30 As Vijaya Ramaswamy has argued in "Artisans in Vijayanagar Society," *Indian Economic and Social History Review* 22, no. 4 (1985): 417–44, artisans gained higher social status from the medieval period in western and southern India; as Abhishek Kaicker discusses regarding Mughal Delhi, *The King and the People: Sovereignty and Popular Politics in Mughal Delhi* (Oxford: Oxford University Press, 2020), artisans, among other "common people," emerged as political subjects. On caste see Nicholas Dirks, *Castes of Mind: Colonialism and the Making of Modern India* (Princeton, N.J.: Princeton University Press, 2001); on British perceptions of Brahmins in Maratha territories see Dominic Vendell, "Scribes and the Vocation of Politics in the Maratha Empire, 1707–1827" (Ph.D. diss., Columbia University, 2018).

31 See Edward S. Cooke, Jr., "Utensils," in *Britain and the World: Treasures from the Yale Center for British Art*, ed. Martina Droth et al. (New Haven and London: Yale University Press, 2019), 140–43; see also Jefferys, *New and Complete Dictionary*, vol. 2, "Joinery," 1810–11; Diderot, *L'Encyclopédie*, vol. 3 (plates), pl. IV, *Chaudronnier* (Coppersmithing).

32 I thank Prasad Boradkar, Edward S. Cooke, and Bhalchandra Kadu (a coppersmith in Poona) for deciphering these tools and the musical instruments as *tambat*-related; see also YCBA, B1977.14.22312.

33 Gangaram was paid for wax, "bormar," and paint; Malet, Journal and Ledger, August 31, 1792. The art historian Robert Skelton has noted that *dhuna* is an aromatic gum of the *sal* tree (*Shorea robusta*) that has been boiled with mustard oil to produce a shiny black malleable substance when warmed, and a firm one when cold; in Niall Hobhouse, *Indian Painting During the British Period*, exh. cat. (London: Hobhouse, September 9–27, 1986), cat. 5. According to Bhalchandra Kadu, coppersmiths use German red pitch and western Indian resins and waxes to chase in present practice; personal communication, September 2015.

34 Edward Moor, *The Hindu Pantheon* (London: J. Johnson, 1810), 44.

35 Ibid., 203. On the motif of *navanari kunjara*, see Kamal Chavan, "Chandwad Wall Paintings," *Traimasik* 18, issue 55, nos. 1–4 [in Marathi] (Pune, Bharat Itihas Sanshodhak Mandal, December 1976), 9–11; Robert J. Del Bontà, "Reinventing Nature: Mughal Composite Animal Painting," in *Flora and Fauna in Mughal Art*, ed. Som Prakash Verma (Mumbai: Marg Publishing, 1999), 69–82.

36 See Irawati Karvé, "Some Folk Songs of Maharashtra," *Bulletin of the Deccan College Research Institute* 1, no. 1 (Poona, 1939), 80–81; N. K. Wagle and A. R. Kulkarni, trans., *Vallabha's Parasharama Charitra: An Eighteenth-Century Maratha History of the Peshwas* (Bombay: Popular Prakashan, 1976), 154.

37 Mrs. Hervey quoted in Charlotte H. F. Smith and Michelle Stevenson, "Modeling Cultures: 19th Century Indian Clay Figures," *Museum Anthropology* 33, no. 1 (2010): 42.

38 See the clay sculptures of a Brahmin sacred bull (ST 40337), a laden bullock (ST 40348), and a dancing bear (ST 40785) in Museums Victoria; the last two were sent from Poona to be displayed in Britain's India Court at the 1880 Melbourne International Exhibition.

39 See Crispin Branfoot, "Tirumala Nayak's 'New Hall' and the European Study of the South Indian Temple," *Journal of the Royal Asiatic Society*, 3rd s., 11, no. 2 (July 2001): 213–14; Adam Blackader's models and drawings are now in the V&A and the Ashmolean Museum, Oxford.

40 Fig. 114 concerns the circularity of colonial knowledge production: Moor in *The Hindu Pantheon* (1810) reproduced images of the Hindu gods as descriptive of the religion, but the British were actually responsible for their manufacture. Wilkins's zinc sculptures are in the V&A.

41 Moor, *A Narrative*, 366.

42 James Wales, "From Bombay to Poona, 1792," 11, James Wales Archive.

43 On the cheetah, see Forbes, *Oriental Memoirs*, vol. 1, 169–74; there is a drawing of one by Malet's wife (Wales's daughter) Susannah: YCBA, B1977.14.22275.

44 Wales, "From Bombay to Poona" (Tuesday, August 12), 49.

45 E.g. Wales drew and labeled a buzzard as "the *tookdar* of the Persians, the *hubare* of the Arabs, the *kurdook* of the Deccan or the *bustard* of England"; James Wales, "Indian Antiquities" (notebook), 3, James Wales Archive.

46 Moor, *A Narrative*, 364.

47 Ibid.

48 I thank Charles, Muppet, and Henrietta Malet, Rory and Mira Guinness, and William Lyons for information about Charles Warre Malet and his Wilbury estate.

49 Wales, "Indian Antiquities," Mem 1st (undated list in one of Wales's journals), 3 discusses "A landscape for Sir Charles" that he had begun "at Poona."

50 V. D. Divekar, *Sir Charles Warre Malet's Bequests at Chargot, England* (1976?), 4.

51 See D. B. Parasnis, *Savai Madhavarava Peshwyancha Darbara ani tya Veleche Pahile Ingraja Resident Sir Charles Malet* [The court of Peshwa Savai Madhavrao and the then English Resident Sir Charles Malet; in Marathi] (Mumbai: Tukaram Javaji Nirnaysagar Press, ca. 1867), 63–5.

52 See Nikolas Pevsner, *Wiltshire* (Harmondsworth: Penguin Books, 1963), 510–11; Historic England, "Wilbury House" (List Entry Number: 1001245), https://historicengland.org.uk/listing/the-list/list-entry/1001245 (accessed December 16, 2019). I thank Mark Aronson, Chief Conservator at the Yale Center for British Art, for examining this painting with me.

53 See David J. Howlett, 'Malet, Sir Charles Warre, first baronet (1753–1815)', *Oxford Dictionary of National Biography* (Oxford University Press, 2004; online edn. May 2009). *Hobson-Jobson* defines Nabob "as a corruption and representative of Nawab" (a Mughal governor), and as an epithet for "Anglo-Indians who returned with fortunes from the East"; Sir Henry Yule, *Hobson-Jobson: A Glossary of Colloquial Anglo-Indian Words and Phrases . . .* (London: J. Murray, 1903), 610. William Dalrymple coined "White Mughal" as an alternative to stress British assimilation into India's courtly culture in *White Mughals* (London: Harper Perennial; New York: Penguin, 2004).

54 On paintings of flora and fauna in menageries in India, including of Sir Elijah and Lady Mary Impey, see Dalrymple, *Forgotten Masters*, 39–116. Company officials also transported their menageries to Britain: e.g. the first Governor-General of India, Warren Hastings, returned to England with exotic animals he had collected in the region, including a yak from Bhutan that he commissioned George Stubbs to paint on his estate in 1791; see Caroline Grigson, *Menagerie: The History of Exotic Animals in England, 1100–1837* (Oxford: Oxford University Press, 2016), 147–9.

55 Malet, Memoranda (September 6 and 7, 1791), MSS Eur F149/67.

56 David Price, *Memoirs of the Early Life and Service of a Field Officer, of the Retired List of the Indian Army* (London: W. H. Allen & Co., 1839), 268–9, cited in Parasnis, *Poona in Bygone Days*, 122.

57 Malet, Memoranda (September 7, 1791).

58 Rosalind O'Hanlon, "Military Sports and the History of the Martial Body in India," *Journal of the Economic and Social History of the Orient* 50, no. 4 (2007): 496–7.

59 "*A Pair of Indian Teak and Part-Painted Exercise Clubs*, late 18th century, 35 in. high (89 cm). Owned by Sir Charles Warre Malet, 1st Bt., (1752–1815)"; Christies Sale 7586, "West – East: The Niall Hobhouse Collection," London, May 22, 2008, lot 210.

60 See Molly Emma Aitken, *The Intelligence of Tradition in Rajput Court Painting* (New Haven and London: Yale University Press, 2010), 113.

61 S. V. Putambekar, "The Ajnapatra or Royal Edict," *Journal of Indian History* 8 (1929), 104, cited in O'Hanlon, "Military Sports," 510.

62 Khare, *Nana Fadnavis's Biography*, 81.

63 Parasnis, *Poona in Bygone Days*, 121–2. O'Hanlon, "Military Sports," 511 notes that "Gopikabai showed . . . interest in the education of boys of the family, reminding Savai Madhavrao in 1783 that he should go to the gymnasium every day, and take 4 or 5 boys . . . with one or two *jetti* to show them the wrestling throws."

64 On Narayan Peth see the inscription on Gangaram's drawing, YCBA, B1977.14.22296.

65 The *tambat* community seems to have been interested in wrestling: Bhalchandra Kadu has noted that *tambats* often practiced wrestling, including his father; personal communication, September 2015. Regarding a relationship between metalworking and wrestling, the *Maharashtra State Gazetteers*, http://164.100.185.107/gazetteer/people_castes.html, notes that the traditional ancestor of the "Ghisadis, or wandering blacksmiths . . . is said to have been called Ghisadi because he knew the *ghissa pench*, a special grip in wrestling and beat a great gymnast."

66 O'Hanlon, "Military Sports," 512.

67 See Dirk H. A. Kolff, *Naukar, Rajput and Sepoy: The Ethnohistory of the Military Labour Market in Hindustan, 1450–1850* (Cambridge: Cambridge University Press, 1990), 17–31; Joseph S. Alter, *The Wrestler's Body: Identity and Ideology in North India* (Berkeley: University of California Press, 1992); William R. Pinch, *Warrior Ascetics and Indian Empires* (Cambridge: Cambridge University Press, 2006); O'Hanlon, "Military Sports," 490–523.

68 Malet's ledger volumes from 1788 to 1794, MSS Eur F149/78–83, record that Malet paid "Gungaram" or "Gungaram Painter" three times during his first year of employment in 1789, and then about every other month for the next five years. The ledger skips two years (from July 1794 to August 1796), but then continues payment to Gangaram every two months through November 1796 with payments per item, such as for paintings of a tiger, a leopard, and a seaport and a map of Poona in October and November 1796; MSS Eur F149/84. Malet left Poona in February 1797 for Bombay and then Britain. Other employees by the name of "Gungaram" are mentioned in the ledgers, but they are addended with Coppersmith, Smith, and Miner. When Gangaram is named solely without "Painter" attached, he is being paid for paint, wax, or for making silver items. Other painters are also recorded as being paid between one and three times including Govinda, Bapoo, and Mairalla. These primarily correlate with the decoration of the Residency for the Peshwa's

visit in February 1790; Malet, Journal and Ledger, 80, 84, MSS Eur F149/79.

69 J. P. Losty, *Sita Ram's Views of India* (London: Thames & Hudson, 2015), 9, 22–3.

70 Henry William Tone, *Letter on the Marhattas* (1799); Edward Scott-Waring, *History of the Marhattoes* (1810). Moor also published a "Note on the Marathas" in his *Narrative* (1794), 430–34; see Jack Harrington, *Sir John Malcolm and the Creation of British India* (Basingstoke and New York: Palgrave Macmillan, 2010), 103–5.

71 Charles Warre Malet, "Notes (Maratta)," 10–12, MSS Eur F149/93, "Sketch of a Maratta," 54. Malet read widely for this task. He subscribed to *Asiatick Researches*; read Quentin Crauford's *Sketches Chiefly Relating to the History, Religion and Learning* (1790), which he copied verbatim; cited Alexander Dowe's *History of Hindostan* (1768) and William Francklin's *History of the reign of Shah Aulum* (1798); Malet, Journal and Ledger (August 1792–July 1793), 112, MSS Eur F149/82.

72 E.g., after Malet traveled to Ujjain to negotiate with Scindia, he wrote a description of his capital, "Description of Ugen, the capital of Mahadagee Scindia," *Oriental Repertory*, vol. 1, ed. Alexander Dalrymple (London, 1793), 265–8.

73 Malet, "Notes (Maratta)," 10–11; he collected Persian, Marathi, and English books that his son gave to the Royal Asiatic Society; Alexander Malet, "Catalogue of Persian MSS," *Transactions of the Royal Asiatic Society of Great Britain and Ireland* 2, no. 2 (July 1830): xxxiv–xxxv.

74 See *A Sewra or Juttee – A Kind of Hindu Monk*, Cambay, 18th century, YCBA, B1977.14.22398.

75 Malet, "Notes (Religion)," 10, MSS Eur F149/93.

76 Forbes, *Oriental Memoirs*, vol. 2, 163.

77 Ibid., 243–4.

78 Samira Sheikh, "A Gujarati Map and Pilot Book of the Indian Ocean, ca. 1750," *Imago Mundi* 61, no. 1 (2009), 75; Samira Sheikh, "Drawing Gujarat in the Eighteenth Century," "Uncommon Knowledge Three Ways," panel presentation, Association for Asian Studies Conference, Washington, D.C., March 2018. Sadanand Vyas made a detailed map of Gujarat, along with other works, for East India Company officials and signed his work; he is mentioned in Malet's memoranda, MSS Eur 149/93, 45.

79 Forbes, *Oriental Memoirs*, vol. 2, 243–4.

80 Ibid., vol. 1, 48.

81 Margot C. Finn, "Material Turns in British History: Loot," *Transactions of the Royal Historical Society* 28 (2018): 5.

82 On European reactions to Ellora, see Partha Mitter's groundbreaking *Much Maligned Monsters: A History of European Reactions to Indian Art* (Oxford: Clarendon Press, 1977).

83 Ibid., 41.

84 Malet, "Description of the Caves," 382–3.

85 See Mitter, *Much Maligned Monsters*, 120–23; Douglas Fordham, *Aquatint Worlds: Travel, Print, and Empire* (London and New Haven: Paul Mellon Centre with Yale University Press, 2019), 90–97.

86 Malet, "Description of the Caves," 382–3. On earlier British artists who drew Indian architecture see Pauline Rohatgi and Pheroza Godrej, eds., *Under the Indian Sun: British Landscape Artists* (Bombay: Marg, 1995); Geoff Quilley and John Bonehill, eds., *William Hodges 1744–1797: The Art of Exploration* (Greenwich: National Maritime Museum, 2004); Hermione de Almeida and George H. Gilpin, *Indian Renaissance: British Romantic Art and the Prospect of India* (Aldershot: Ashgate, 2005).

87 See Jones, *Works of Sir William Jones*, vol. 3, 5–6; Stephen Bann, "Antiquarianism, Visuality, and the Exotic Monument," in *Traces of India: Photography, Architecture, and the Politics of Representation, 1850–1900*, ed. Maria Antonella Pelizzari (New Haven and London: Yale University Press, 2003), 60–85.

88 Thomas Daniell and his nephew William were well-regarded artists and publishers of Indian architecture, and Wales's friends; they sketched together at Elephanta and Salsette; see Fordham, *Aquatint Worlds*, 59–117; de Almeida and Gilpin, *Indian Renaissance*, 192; Giles Tillotson, ed., *Vision and Landscape: Aquatints of India by Thomas and William Daniell* (Delhi: Delhi Art Gallery, 2019).

89 Fordham, *Aquatint Worlds*, 111–17; see also Mitter, *Much Maligned Monsters*, 108–12.

90 See James Forbes, *A Voyage from England to Bombay with Descriptions in Asia, Africa, and South America*, 13 vols. (1765–1800), vol. 6, YCBA, MSS 66; Richard H. Davis, *Lives of Indian Images* (Princeton, N.J.: Princeton University Press, 1997), 160–63; Elisabeth Fairman, "James Forbes," in *Paul Mellon's Legacy: A Passion for British Art* (New Haven, Conn. and London: Yale Center for British Art and Royal Academy of Arts with Yale University Press, 2007), 303, no. 130.

91 The British acquisition of these islands connects to the succession crisis at the Pune court after the assassination of Narayanrao Peshwa. In payment for British support, Raghunathrao (the Peshwa's uncle) ceded the islands. The British maintained them even after they and Raghunathrao were defeated by the Poona faction; Forbes, *Oriental Memoirs*, vol. 1, 307.

92 Ibid., 284, 277.

93 James Forbes, *Oriental Memoirs* (London: White, Cochrane and Co., 1813), vol. 1, iii.

94 De Almeida and Gilpin, *Indian Renaissance*, 42, 47; see also Pauline Rohatgi, "Early Impressions of the Islands: James Forbes and James Wales in Bombay 1766–95," in *Bombay to Mumbai: Changing Perspectives*, ed. Pauline Rohatgi, Pheroza Godrej, and Rahul Mehrotra (Mumbai: Marg Publications, 1997), 66.

95 Mildred Archer, "Works by William Alexander and James Wales," in *The Royal Asiatic Society: Its History and Treasures*, ed. Stuart Simmonds and Simon Digby (London: E. J. Brill, 1979), 119–25.

96 Charles Warre Malet, "Manuscript of Indian Dialects," 1785–86, MSS Eur F149/96; Malet, "Letter to Mr. Fleming to be laid before the Asiatic Society," 1795, Loose Notes and Drawings, YCBA.

97 Malet, Journal and Ledger (index), (August 1793–July 1794), 83–90, MSS Eur F149/83.

98 Malet, "Description of the Caves," 422; the interior drawing of "Biskurma" that relates to this text is YCBA, B1977.14.22323.

99 Malet, "Description of the Caves," 422.

100 Ibid., 382–3.

101 James Wales, "Prospectus for Oriental Antiquities," Loose Notes and Drawings, YCBA. Wales's journal, in comparison, is titled "Indian Antiquities." I use "Indian Antiquities" for Wales's project.

102 Ibid..

103 Wales, "Indian Antiquities" (journal), 29.

104 Ibid., 64, 68.

105 Malet, Memoranda (January 23–February 10, 1795), MSS Eur F149/68.

106 James Wales to Sir Joseph Banks, Bombay, July 25, 1794, BL, Add. 33979, ff. 235–6.

107 Wales, "Prospectus for *Oriental Antiquities*."

108 Wales, "Indian Antiquities" (journal), 29, 35.

109 Gangaram's drawings include an exterior view of Vishvakarma and Indra Sabha, 1793–5; they remain pasted in albums that Moor's son, Edward J. Moor, compiled from his father's collection (private collection).

110 Wales, "Indian Antiquities" (journal), 43, 60.

111 Wales, "Prospectus for *Oriental Antiquities*."

112 Wales, "Indian Antiquities" (journal), 50; he drew this or a like man, YCBA, B1977.14.22346.

113 Wales, "Indian Antiquities" (journal), 46.

114 Wales, Loose Notes and Drawings; see Ch. 1 above for a discussion of the Goan artist Josir, whom Wales employed and named in his journal as Josir, Jossi, and Josi; for consistency, I use Jossi.

115 Wales, "Indian Antiquities" (journal) (March 29, 1795), 73.

116 Captain George Millett, "A hasty but faithful account of a Tour to the Island and Caves of Salset, in company with the ingenious Mr. Wales," BL, MSS Eur K154 1795, 32.

117 Thomas Daniell, *Oriental Scenery*, vol. 5 or 6: "Hindoo Excavations in the Mountain of Ellora, near Aurungabad, in the Decan, in Twenty-Four Views" (London: the author, 1803–4), 3–4. The dates 1792 and 1793 might relate to Wales's investigations of other rock-carved temples, since he only went to Ellora in 1795.

118 See J. P. Losty, "'A very ingenious person': The Maratha Artist Gangaram Cintaman Tambat," Asian and African Studies Blog, BL, posted August 28, 2014, https://britishlibrary.typepad.co.uk/asian-and-african/2014/08/the-maratha-artist-gangaram-cintaman-tambat.html#sthash.nv7GtFbF.dpuf.

119 Gangaram Tambat, *Shiva and Parvati Playing Chaupar*, Ellora, 1793 or 1795, YCBA, B1977.14.22306.

120 Wales, Loose Notes and Drawings.

121 Gangaram Tambat, *Inside View of Indur Subha* (Indra Sabha), Ellora, 1793 or 1795, YCBA, B1977.14.22335.

122 An inscription on the back of fig. 57 notes: "Keylas, a Representation of one Side & the opposite scarp of the Mountain."

123 Wales, Loose Notes and Drawings, 46.

124 Wales and Malet both termed the site Ekvera because of the Hindu temple dedicated to the goddess Ekvera who was actively worshipped at the site. The British did not know this type of prayer hall was a Buddhist *chaitya* until ca. 1825; see Fordham, *Aquatint Worlds*, 69. Whether Gangaram recognized Karle as a Buddhist site is unknown. He identified Jain or "Sewra" temples at Ellora, even though the "people who showed them" said they were "Hindoo"; see YCBA, B1977.14.22340. If Malet had cited Gangaram, he would have avoided criticism by William H. Sykes, "An Account of the Caves of Ellora," *Transactions of the Literary Society of Bombay* 3 (1819–21): 265–323. Sykes, though, recognized only two religions: Hindu and Buddhist. In 1823, William Erskine identified the Jain temples; see Mitter, *Much Maligned Monsters*, 159–68; Philip Almond, *The British Discovery of Buddhism* (Cambridge: Cambridge University Press, 1988).

125 Gangaram Tambat, *Drawing of a Column from Ekvera* (Karle), Karle, ca. 1793, YCBA, B1977.14.22321.

126 Tapati Guha-Thakurta, *Monuments, Objects, Histories: Institutions of Art in Colonial and Postcolonial India* (New York: Columbia University Press, 2004), 8.

127 Henry Salt, *Twenty-Four Views in St. Helena, the Cape, India, Ceylon, the Red Sea, Abyssinia, and Egypt* (London: William Miller, 1809), pl. XIV.

128 Guha-Thakurta, *Monuments, Objects, Histories*, 7, 27, 10.

129 Giles Tillotson, "The Indian Picturesque: Images of India in British Landscape Painting, 1780–1880," in *The Raj: India and the British 1600–1947*, ed. C. A. Bayly (London: National Portrait Gallery Publications, 1990), 141–51.

130 The Daniells justified their accuracy via their use of technology as other British artists did in this period; see Finbarr Barry Flood, "Correct Delineations and Promiscuous Outlines: Envisioning India at the Trial of Warren Hastings," *Art History* 29, no. 1 (February 2006): 66.

131 De Almeida and Gilpin, *Indian Renaissance*, 192.

132 Wales, Loose Notes and Drawings.

133 Wales, "Indian Antiquities" (notebook), "Verrool Excavations Memorandums", 2.

134 Robert Mabon, Journal (Maharashtra, ca. 1790–95), 1, 3, James Wales Archive, MSS 26, YCBA. Wales, "Indian Antiquities" (journal), 86 noted that "the dark apartments in the Excavations were intended as dungeons for confining delinquents."

135 Edmund Burke, *A Philosophical Inquiry into the origins of our ideas of the sublime and beautiful* (London: R. and J. Dodsley, 1757), esp. VII–X.

136 Wales, "Description of the Excavation of Eckvera or Yeheve," Loose Notes and Drawings.

137 Malet, "Description of the Caves," 422; Thomas and William Daniell, *Oriental Scenery* (London: printed by the author, 1816), 40; this is a later edition, smaller in format, of the Daniells' series.

138 See Thomas Daniell after James Wales, "Ekvera," in *Antiquities of India* (London: T. Daniell, 1803), pl. 6, BL, P179.

139 Kapil Raj, *Relocating Modern Science: Circulation and the Construction of Knowledge in South Asia and Europe, 1650–1900* (Basingstoke and New York: Palgrave Macmillan, 2007), 13.

140 Yuthika Sharma, "In the Company of the Mughal Court: Delhi Painter Ghulam Ali Khan," in *Princes and Painters in Mughal Delhi, 1707–1857*, ed. William Dalrymple and Yuthika Sharma (New York: Asia Society Museum, 2012), 42.

141 Dipti Khera, *The Place of Many Moods: Udaipur's Painted Lands and India's Eighteenth Century* (Princeton, N.J.: Princeton University Press, 2020), 143.

142 Ibid., 117–45.

143 Shailka Mishra, "*Suratkhana* at Amber-Jaipur in the 18th Century: Paintings, Patronage, Practices" (Ph.D. diss., Jawaharlal Nehru University, 2015), 44; see also Molly Emma Aitken, "Colonial-Period Court Painting and the Case of Bikaner," *Archives of Asian Art* 67, no. 1 (April 2017): 25–59.

144 The "foreign and uncanny takes on meaning through material objects and practices" in this colonial context: Carolyn Dean and Dana Leibsohn, "Hybridity and its Discontents:

Considering Visual Culture in Colonial Spanish America," *Colonial Latin American Review* 12, no. 1 (2003): 6.

145 Gangaram is probably wearing one of two turbans that Malet gave him, one "for drawing from the life" the "Peshwas camel" (January 31, 1791) and one possibly for his Ellora drawings and perhaps the "orrery globe" for the Peshwa (June 30, 1793); Malet, Journal and Ledger, 82, MSS Eur F149/80.

146 BL online catalog, Add. Or. 4145, Malet Collection, India Office Selection Materials (Prints & Drawings). Malet paid Gangaram's guru twice, in December 1791 and in February 1794; Malet, Journal and Ledger (August 1791–July 1792), MSS Eur F149/81 and (August 1793–July 1794), MSS Eur F149/83.

147 See another of Gangaram's drawings of his guru, YCBA, B1977.14.22248.

148 See James Wales, attrib., *A Maribou at Gunnygaum*, 1795, YCBA, B1977.14.22346; Wales, "Indian Antiquities" (journal) (January 30 and February 7, 1795), 50, 65.

149 Wales, "Indian Antiquities" (journal), 50.

150 Bhagavad Gita, ch. 4:1; see Richard H. Davis, *The Bhagavad Gita: A Biography* (Princeton, N.J.: Princeton University Press, 2015), 23 for this episode.

151 This image could relate to Malet's "History of the Marathas" as the Bohras were merchants who controlled the opium trade between Burhanpur and Surat, and played an economic role across Gujarat, Malwa, and Maharashtra; see Moor, *A Narrative*, 340; Stewart Gordon, *Marathas, Marauders, and State Formation in Eighteenth-Century India* (Oxford: Oxford University Press, 1998), 173.

152 Parasnis, *Court of Peshwa Savai Madhavrao*, 66.

153 Mabon, *Oriental Manners*, 26–7, pl. XIX. For a history of European reactions to such penance, see Holly Shaffer, "The Bed of Nails: The Exotic Across Borders and Media," in *Yoga: The Art of Transformation*, ed. Debra Diamond (Washington, D.C.: Arthur M. Sackler Gallery, 2013), 250–57; see also Holly Shaffer, *Strange and Wondrous: Prints of India from the Robert J. Del Bontà Collection* (Washington, D.C.: Arthur M. Sackler Gallery, 2013), http://www.asia.si.edu/explore/del-bonta/; see also Mitter, *Much Maligned Monsters*.

154 Other artists translated European typologies in Indian contexts; see Robert L. Hardgrave, *Portrait of the Hindus: Balthazar Solvyns and the European Image of India, 1760–1824* (Oxford and New York: Oxford University Press, 2004).

155 See Catherine Asher, "Jaipur: City of Tolerance and Progress," *South Asia: Journal of South Asian Studies* 37, no. 3 (2014): 410–30. For another portrait of a holy man, see *Portrait of a Seated Shaivite Holy Man with Prayer Beads*, 18th century, Jaipur, Harvard Art Museums, Cambridge, Mass., 2009.202.19.

3 "MEN AND GODS, AND THINGS"

1 Edward Moor, *The Hindu Pantheon* (London: J. Johnson, 1810), 29. Based on the direction of her sway, this goddess could be Lakshmi's form as Bhudevi, who with Shridevi is one of Vishnu's two consorts.

2 In brief, after Peshwa Savai Madhavrao's untimely death in 1795, Bajirao II, the son of the former Peshwa's uncle and rival for rule, Raghunathrao, was appointed Peshwa; see Intro. above for earlier history. He allowed Daulatrao Scindia, the Maratha general who succeeded Mahadji Scindia, to imprison him and sack Poona in 1797; a year later Nana Fadnavis was released, but he died two years later in 1800.

3 Moor, *Hindu Pantheon*, 35, 47; Moor is referring to Blackwell's letter on the duality of Jupiter as father of gods and men, but he adds "things" to the equation; Thomas Blackwell, *Letters Concerning Mythology* (London, 1748), 140.

4 Edward Moor, *Hindu Infanticide* (London: J. Johnson, 1811), 227; *East India Military Calendar, containing the services of General and Field Officers of the Indian Army*, vol. 1 (London, 1823), 339–48; Thomas Seccombe, "Moor, Edward (1771–1848)," rev. J. B. Katz, *ODNB*, 2004.

5 Moor's descendant gave these objects, his publications, and catalogues to the BM in 1940. The bulk of his letters are still in family hands, and a few items are in Ipswich Museum and the Suffolk Records Office.

6 For a parallel, albeit later, case see Katrina Hill, "Collecting on Campaign: British Soldiers in China during the Opium Wars," *Journal of the History of Collections* 25, no. 2 (2013): 227–52.

7 *East India Military Calendar*, vol. 1, 339; Seccombe, "Moor, Edward."

8 Parshuram Bhau built Patwardhan Wada in Wai in the last quarter of the eighteenth century; his son probably commissioned its wall paintings around 1800 (see fig. 104).

9 Edward Moor, *A Narrative of the Operations of Captain Little's Detachment and of the Mahratta Army, commanded by Purseram Bhow, during the late confederacy in India against the Nawab Tippoo Sultan Bahadur* (London: J. Johnson, 1794); this map is more detailed than other published summaries of the routes in this region; however, the roads it charts follow those from ancient and medieval archaeology to the Mughals and Marathas; see Jean Deloche, *Transport and Communications in India Prior to Steam Locomotion*, vol. 1, trans. James Walker (Delhi: Oxford University Press, 1993), pt. I, esp. 66–81; Dilip K. Chakrabarti, *The Ancient Routes of the Deccan and Southern Peninsula* (New Delhi: Aryan Books International, 2010), 1–61.

10 *East India Military Calendar*, vol. 1, 339; Seccombe, "Moor, Edward."

11 See Anne Buddle, "The Tipu-Mania: Narrative Sketches of the Conquest of Mysore," *Marg* 40, no. 4 (September 1987): 53–70; Margot Finn, "Harem Histories and Princely Politics: Tipu Sultan, the Family and East India Company Rule," Neale Lecture, University College London, March 19, 2013, http://podcasts.ox.ac.uk/keywords/tipu-sultan.

12 Moor, *Narrative*, 239.

13 Temple towns are shown on such a map in the Biwalkar Collection, Deccan College Museum, Pune. Earlier maps follow similar patterns of showing road and water routes, fortified towns, and shrines; see Susan Gole, *India within the Ganges* (New Delhi: Jayaprints, 1983), 18–21.

14 Moor, *Narrative*, 56, including a procession of Shiva's abstract form, a *linga*, in "Baugoor."

15 Ibid., 262. James Wales drew a sketch of the "Cataract of Gocauk" for Moor, after a drawing of Lieut. Emmitt's, which confirms their association. Drawings by Gangaram Tambat are also still in Moor's albums compiled by his son, Edward J. Moor, here named the Edward J. Moor Collection (hereafter EJM Collection).

16 Ibid., 309, 339–41, 347–50.

17 Ibid., Appendix, 465–93, nos. 5–6; Moor also considered the coins and seals of Tipu Sultan, many of them bearing prayers of Muslim devotion, but the majority of his collection focuses on Hindu religious objects because of his persistent connection with the Marathas over the twenty years he spent in India. On pilgrimage and devotional material, and political routes see Sudipta Sen, *Empire of Free Trade: The East India Company and the Making of the Colonial Marketplace* (Philadelphia: University of Pennsylvania Press, 1998), 32–8.

18 Moor does not mention buying representations of the gods housed at Pandharpur and Jejuri in his *Narrative*, but he defined and illustrated them in *The Hindu Pantheon*, 415–21, noting that he received the information about these sites from the "Brahmans of Poona."

19 Moor, *Hindu Pantheon*, 1, 421–2.

20 Günther-Dietz Sontheimer, *Pastoral Deities in Western India*, trans. Anne Feldhaus (Oxford and New York: Oxford University Press, 1989), 154. There are many theories of Khandoba's origins; see M. N. Deshpande, "Some Aspects of Folk Religion in the Konkan and Desh Regions of Maharashtra," in *Maharashtra: Culture and Society*, ed. Günther-Dietz Sontheimer (New Delhi: Manohar, 1995), 171.

21 Moor, *Hindu Pantheon*, 421–2; see Deshpande, "Some Aspects," 171.

22 Günther-Dietz Sontheimer, "The Mallari/Khandoba Myth as Reflected in Folk Art and Ritual," *Anthropos* 79, no. 1/3 (1984): 162.

23 Moor, *Hindu Pantheon*, 421–2. *Tak*, Moor explained (423), "are impressions on thin plates of copper, embossed by steel or iron dies, for the accommodation, being very rude and cheap, of such pious persons as are not in circumstances to obtain the advantage of a domestic image. Kandeh Rao is met with in this form as often as any of his divine brotherhood." I thank Hemant Fanse for discussing the *tak* in his family's home shrine.

24 M. S. Mate, *Temples and Legends of Maharashtra* (Bombay: Bharatiya Vidya Bhavan, 1962), 189–93 relates the intertwined myths of Vithoba and Pandharpur.

25 Moor, *Hindu Pantheon*, 417–18; see R. C. Dhere, *The Rise of a Folk God: Vitthal of Pandharpur*, trans. Anne Feldhaus (Oxford and New York: Oxford University Press, 2011).

26 Mate, *Temples and Legends*, 193–9.

27 Ibid., 53–78.

28 For one of Moor's representations of Bhavani see BM, 1940,0716.37. On the "manifold guises" of the great goddess see Vidya Dehejia, *Devi: The Great Goddess* (Washington, D.C.: Arthur M. Sackler Gallery and Mapin Publishing, 1999), 13. On folk forms of Durga see Cornelia Mallebrein, *Die anderen Götter: Volks- und Stammesbronzen aus Indien* [The other gods: folk and tribal bronzes from India] (Cologne: Edition Braus, 1993), 210–21, 244–53; Cornelia Mallebrein, "In the Company of Gods: G.-D. Sontheimer and His Passion for Folk and Tribal Bronzes," in *In The Company of Gods: Essays in Memory of Günther-Dietz Sontheimer*, ed. Aditya Malik, Anne Feldhaus, and Heidrun Brückner (Delhi: Manohar, 2005), 381–4; Anne Feldhaus, *Connected Places: Region, Pilgrimage, and Geographical Imagination in India* (Basingstoke and New York: Palgrave Macmillan, 2003), 140–48.

29 See Cornelia Mallebrein, "Hidden Gods Within the House: House Shrines of the Kokna Tribe of Maharashtra," in *House and Home in Maharashtra*, ed. Irina Glushkova and Anne Feldhaus (Delhi: Oxford University Press, 1998): 215–41.

30 John Griffiths, "The Brass and Copper Wares of the Bombay Presidency," *Journal of Indian Art and Industry* 7 no. 55 (July 1896): 16; N. M. Joshi, *Urban Handicrafts of the Bombay Deccan* (Bombay: Gokhale Institute, 1936), 56–9. On brassware and the twentieth-century labor market see Tirthankar Roy, *Traditional Industry in the Economy of Colonial India* (Cambridge: Cambridge University Press, 1999), 128–54.

31 See BM, 1940,0716.96; K. C. Aryan, *Indian Folk Bronzes* (New Delhi: Rekha Prakshan, 1991), 50. On modern metalwork in Nasik see Priyansi Nimish Tambat and Ketaki Chandrakant Joshi, "Promoting Craft Entrepreneurship by Rejuvenating *Tambat* Craft in Old *Tambat Ali*, Nashik," *Journal of Heritage Management* 2, no. 1 (2017): 53–75.

32 Mallebrein, "Hidden Gods," 235–8.

33 Ibid., 200–21.

34 Moor, *Hindu Pantheon*, 1, 431.

35 *The East India Military Calendar*, vol. 1, 342; Stewart Gordon, *The Marathas 1600–1818* (Cambridge: Cambridge University Press, 1993), 154–73.

36 Men in the military, from a cadet in Bombay like Moor to Clive of Plassey, often collected and returned home with objects connected to their careers. Moor's album page covers the range of his material possessions and interests, similar to how Clive's chest of "Indian Curiosities" of bejeweled turban ornaments, inscribed weapons, and enameled hookahs did for his son, though Moor's were more humble, fitting his rank; see Maya Jasanoff, *Edge of Empire: Lives, Culture, and Conquest in the East, 1750–1850* (New York: Vintage, 2005), 41–2. On "scholar-dealers" see Ivan Gaskell, "Tradesmen as Scholars," in *Art History and Its Institutions: The Nineteenth Century*, ed. Elizabeth Mansfield (London: Routledge, 2002), 146–62.

37 Moor also discussed and reproduced these objects in *The Hindu Pantheon* and *Oriental Fragments*.

38 Raffi Gregorian, "Unfit for Service: British Law and Looting in India in the Mid-Nineteenth Century," *South Asia: Journal of South Asian Studies* 13, no. 1 (1990), 66. On Robert Clive's apportionment of "prize" after the Battle of Plassey see John Keay, *The Honourable Company: A History of the English East India Company* (New York: Macmillan, 1991), 320–27.

39 Gregorian, "Unfit for Service," 63–9; James L. Hevia, "Plunders, Markets, and Museums: The Biographies of Chinese Imperial Objects in Europe and North America," in *What's the Use of Art? Asian Visual and Material Culture in Context*, ed. Jan Mrázek and Morgan Pitelka (Honolulu: University of Hawaii Press, 2008), 131.

40 Edward Moor, *A Compilation of all the Government and General – Government – General – Brigade and Garrison Orders – Minutes of council – Commands of the Hon. Company – or Regulations, from whatever authority promulgated, from the year 1750 to the 31st of July 1801, that are now in force and operating on the Discipline or Expenditure of the Bombay Army* (Bombay: Courier and Gazette Presses, 1801), section XLIII, "Stores and Provisions . . ." (pp. 566–7).

41 Alexander Dirom, *A Narrative of the Campaign which terminated the war with Tippoo Sultan in 1792* (London: printed by W. Bulmar, 1793), 266–73.

42 The selling of pillage or prize was entwined with the cultivation of connoisseurship and profit, especially as prize sales and commercial, estate, and book auctions proliferated from the seventeenth century; see Brian Cowan, "Arenas of Connoisseurship: Auctioning Art in Late Stuart England," in *Art Markets in Europe: 1400–1800*, ed. Michael North and David Ormrod (Aldershot and Burlington, Vt.: Ashgate, 1998), 154–5; Richard Hill, *Prizes of War: The Naval Prize System in the Napoleonic Wars, 1793–1815* (Portsmouth: Royal Naval Publications, 1998), 139–89. On the cultural processes and societal impact of "surplus transfer[red]" through loot rather than trade see Maria Dolores Sánchez-Jáuregui and Scott Wilcox, eds., *The English Prize: The Capture of the Westmorland* (New Haven, Conn.: Yale Center for British Art, 2013); J. M. Mancini, *Art and War in the Pacific World: Making, Breaking, and Taking from Anson's Voyage to the Philippine-American War* (Oakland: University of California Press, 2018), 29.

43 Arthur Wellesley, ed., *Supplementary Despatches and Memoranda of Field Marshal Arthur, Duke of Wellington K.G.*, vol. 1 (London: J. Murray, 1858), 212.

44 David Price, *Memoirs of the Early Life and Service of a Field Officer* (London: W. H. Allen, 1839), 361, 436–51. On Tipu Sultan's items see Mohammad Moienuddin, *Sunset at Srirangapatam* (Hyderabad: Orient Longman, 2000), esp. 107–27.

45 Price, *Memoirs*, 440–42. These items included gems associated with icons in temples. For a novelist's later account of these tales see Wilkie Collins, *The Moonstone* (1868).

46 Richard H. Davis, "Three Styles in Looting India," *History and Anthropology* 6 (1994): 304–7; Susan Stronge, *Tipu's Tigers* (London: Victoria & Albert Museum, 2009), 43–59. On nineteenth-century parallels in China see Hevia, "Plunders, Markets, and Museums," 129–41; Christine Howald, "The Power of Provenance: Marketing and Pricing of Chinese Looted Art on the European Market (1860–62)," in *Acquiring Cultures: Histories of World Art on Western Markets*, ed. Bénédicte Savoy, Charlotte Guichard, and Christine Howald (Berlin: De Gruyter, 2018), 241–65.

47 See Alexander Allan, *Views in the Mysore Country* (London: Allan, 1794); Robert Colebrooke, *Twelve Views of Places in the Kingdom of Mysore, Country of Tippoo Sultan, from drawings taken on the spot* (London: Thomson, 1794); Robert Home, *Select Views in Mysore, the Country of Tippoo Sultan . . .* (London: Mr. Bowyer, 1794). Allan mentions the "military stores and provisions" gained, in so many words, in a line of the text in relation, but these are not seen in pls. II, III, IV, VI, X, XI, XII, XIV, XIX; Colebrooke discusses plunder in two of his twelve plates but only goes into depth about the bullion received from Tipu after his defeat; Home discusses the provisions of the forts conquered in relation to four plates and notes the gold and land gained in the final treaty. None show looting in their plates.

48 Mary A. Favret, *War at a Distance: Romanticism and the Making of Modern Wartime* (Princeton, N.J.: Princeton University Press, 2009), 187–229; Rosie Dias, "Memory and the Aesthetics of Military Experience: Viewing the Landscape of the Anglo-Mysore Wars," *Tate Papers*, no. 19 (Spring 2013): https://www.tate.org.uk/research/publications/tatepapers/19/memory-and-the-aesthetics-of-military-experience-viewing-the-landscape-of-the-anglomysore-wars, accessed February 10, 2019.

49 Moor, *Narrative*, 465–93, Appendix nos. 5–6.

50 British artists and tourists in eighteenth-century Rome similarly saw opportunities to excavate, purchase, and sell Greek and Roman antiquities for which the Pope issued licenses; see Ilaria Bignamini and Clare Hornsby, *Digging and Dealing in Eighteenth-Century Rome* (New Haven and London: Yale University Press, 2010).

51 Davis, "Three Styles," 304–7.

52 Charlotte Guichard and Bénédicte Savoy, "Acquiring Cultures and Trading Value in a Global World," in *Acquiring Cultures*, 5.

53 Edward Moor, *Oriental Fragments* (London: Smith, Elder and Co., 1834), 43. At Tipu Sultan's defeat the British realized that he had been collecting and preserving their books and goods, much like they did with his, such as Francis Buchanan's notes on botany, and a "wooden-turned spice box"; see Price, *Memoirs*, 443; Mark F. Watson and Henry J. Noltie, "Career, Collections, Reports and Publications of Dr. Francis Buchanan (Later Hamilton), 1762–1829: Natural History Studies in Nepal, Burma (Myanmar), Bangladesh and India (Part 1)," *Annals of Science* 73 (2016): 392–424.

54 Moor, *Oriental Fragments*, 149–50.

55 Ibid., 42. The books from Tipu's library and letters were sent to the East India Company's Library in London, Calcutta College, Oxford, and Cambridge; see Lucian Harris, "British Collecting of Indian Art and Artifacts" (Ph.D. diss., Sussex University, 2002), 208–10; Joshua Ehrlich, "Plunder and Prestige: Tipu Sultan's Library and the Making of British India," *South Asia: Journal of South Asian Studies* (2020): 478–92.

56 Margot C. Finn, "Material Turns in British History: Loot," *Transactions of the Royal Historical Society* 28 (2018): 15. On medieval looting see Finbarr Barry Flood, *Objects in Translation: Material Culture and Medieval "Hindu-Muslim" Encounter* (Princeton, N.J.: Princeton University Press, 2009); Davis, "Three Styles," 304–7.

57 Moor, *Hindu Pantheon*, 32–3.

58 Moor names other objects that he received in trying circumstances, such as a "marble brought from Indore, the capital of Holkar," which was sent to Moor "by a friend" during the "late war with the Mahrata confederates"; ibid., 263, pl. 30; it was "about two feet high, and half as broad" (160).

59 Ibid., 32–3. Ballaji or Vyankateshvara is housed in Tirupati, Andhra Pradesh. Besides the icon's value, the temple was a major source of revenue for the British after it came into their possession.

60 Ibid., 29, 32–3.

61 On the burial of deities by devotees see Ganesh C. Vad et al., eds., *Selections from the Satara Raja's and the Peshwa's Diaries* [in Marathi] (Pune: Deccan Vernacular Translation Society, 1902–6), vol. 1, letter 397; vol. 6, letter 482; Mate, *Temples and Legends*, 193–7.

62 On the transferral of bodily pain to a referent such as an object see the classic Elaine Scarry, *The Body in Pain* (Oxford and New York: Oxford University Press, 1995), 13–14, 124–33.

63 *East India Military Calendar*, vol. 1, 339; Seccombe, "Moor, Edward." In Moor's consultation with the renowned doctor Sir Everard Home about his injury, Home commented on the medical aspects of Moor's "curious case," but also on the soldier's wager between bullets and coins: "I shall not take any of your guineas – If you had had a good shake or two of

Tippoo's pagoda tree, it would have been another matter. – But as you have probably more of his lead in your bones than of his gold in your pocket – I shall extract only the grosser metal." The surgery was never performed, but the anecdote remains in Moor's albums, EJM Collection.

64 Price, *Memoirs*, 248; Moor, *Narrative*, 133. James Wales, *Bombay Views*, pl. 11, ca. 1792, rhymes a soldier's amputated leg with the cannon pointing out of the fort (YCBA).

65 See James Wales, "Subscription Book: A Remarkable Portrait," 6, BL, Malet Collection, MSS Eur F149/97; M. Felix Freshwater, "A Discussion of Nicolo Manuzzi (1639–1717) and the First Report of the Indian Rhinoplasty," *JPRAS: An International Journal of Surgical Reconstruction*, 63 (2010): 251–3; Nayana Sharma Mukherjee and Susmita Basu Majudar, "A Nose Lost and Honour Regained: The Indian Method of Rhinoplasty Revisited," *Proceedings of the Indian History Congress* 72, pt. 1 (2011): 968–77.

66 Moor, *Hindu Pantheon*, pl. 16, fig. 3.

67 Ibid., 55, 249.

68 Ibid., 1, 62, 431.

69 Mallebrein, "In the Company of Gods," 363–4.

70 An image of a god is consecrated through the rituals of *pratistha*; only if the proportions of that image are appropriate will it be considered auspicious; see Isabella Nardi, *The Theory of Citrasutras in Indian Painting: A Critical Re-evaluation of Their Uses and Interpretations* (London: Routledge, 2006), 25; Isabella Nardi, "Re-Evaluating the Role of Text in Indian Art: Towards a Shastric Analysis of the Image of Shri Nathji in Nathdvara Miniature Painting," *South Asia Research* 29, no. 2 (2009): 107; Crispin Branfoot, "Iconography and Images: Art," in *Brill's Encyclopedia of Hinduism*, vol. 2: *Texts, Rituals, Arts, Concepts*, ed. Knut A. Jacobsen (Leiden: Brill, 2010), 536–50.

71 Moor, *Hindu Pantheon*, 431.

72 Michael Willis, "Detritus to Treasure: Memory, Metonymy, and the Museum," in *Sacred Objects in Secular Spaces*, ed. Bruce M. Sullivan (London: Bloomsbury Academic, 2015), 148–9.

73 Thomas Wright, *The Life of Edward Fitzgerald* (London: Grant Richards, 1904), 47, 217.

74 Moor, *Hindu Pantheon*, 62, 63, 64, pl. 18.

75 John Seyller, "The Inspection and Valuation of Manuscripts in the Imperial Mughal Library," *Artibus Asiae* 57, no. 3/4 (1997): 243–349; Shailka Mishra, "*Suratkhana* at Amber-Jaipur in the 18th Century: Paintings, Patronage, Practices" (Ph.D. diss., Jawaharlal Nehru University, 2015), 70–73.

76 Seyller, "Inspection and Valuation," esp. 274–5, Table 1.

77 Mishra, "*Suratkhana* at Amber-Jaipur," 70–73.

78 Ibid., 77–93; Seyller, "Inspection and Valuation," 271; John Seyller, "For Love or Money: The Shaping of Historical Painting Collections in India," in *Intimate Worlds: Indian Paintings from the Alvin O. Bellak Collection*, ed. Darielle Mason (Ahmedabad: Mapin Publishing, 2001), 15; John Seyller, *Pearls of the Parrot of India: The Walters Art Museum Khamsa of Amir Khusraw of Delhi* (Baltimore, Md.: Walters Art Gallery, 2002), 16–17. On *dilli kalam* see Molly Emma Aitken, *The Intelligence of Tradition in Rajput Court Painting* (New Haven and London: Yale University Press, 2010), 74–103.

79 Mishra, "*Suratkhana* at Amber-Jaipur," 74, 87, noting that in 1725 a 40-rupee painting was just under the average price (45 Rs.) of a painting in a manuscript of the Mughal *Razmnama* that entered the Jaipur Royal Collection, and that in 1798 a 22 R. 4 anna painting of a goddess was enumerated as consisting of 14 R. for labor, 2 for pearls, and 6 R. 4 annas to grind the pearls.

80 Advertisement for *The Hindu Pantheon* (1810) drafted for the "India papers," EJM Collection.

81 Mishra, "*Suratkhana* at Amber-Jaipur," 100–01.

82 Ibid; Natalia di Pietrantonio, "Circuits of Exchange: Albums and the Art Market in 18th-Century Avadh," *Journal 18* 6 (Fall 2018), http://www.journal18.org/2846, noting a range of figures who presented paintings to Nawab Asaf al-Daula in Lucknow and served as intermediaries in the art market.

83 D. B. Parasnis, "Nana Fadnavis's Painting Collection and Delhi Craftsmanship" and "The Jaipur King's Bhagavata Purana," article nos. 11 and 24, *Itihas Sangraha Aitihasik Tipane* [Collection of history; in Marathi] (Poona, 1908), 13–15; 37–8.

84 Jasanoff, *Edge of Empire*, 69.

85 Mishra, "*Suratkhana* at Amber-Jaipur," 101–3.

86 Yuthika Sharma, "Art in between Empires: Visual Culture and Artistic Knowledge in Late Mughal Delhi, 1748–1857" (Ph.D. diss., Columbia University, 2013), 259–60. Jasanoff, *Edge of Empire*, 63 also describes the bazaar in Lucknow as a source of paintings for collectors such as Richard Johnson.

87 Moor, *Hindu Pantheon*, 189; see also Carolien Stolte, *Philip Angel's Deex-Autaers* (New Delhi: Manohar, 2012), 68–83; Robert J. Del Bontà, "Engraving India in 17th- and 18th-Century Europe," *Art in Print* 4, no. 4 (November–December 2014): 20–25. François Bernier, *Travels in the Mogul Empire* (Oxford University Press, 1916), 254–6, wrote that there were workshops for painting in the palace and in the bazaar, but that those artists in the bazaar were not paid well and under strict deadlines. Paintings were available for foreign purchase and were reproduced in print; see Stephanie Schrader, ed., *Rembrandt and the Inspiration of India* (Los Angeles: Getty Research Institute, 2018).

88 Portraits of Peshwa Bajirao II and Daulatrao Scindia, EJM Collection.

89 See Holly Shaffer, "Towards a History of Maratha Painting in the Deccan," in *Dakhan 2018: Recent Studies on Indian Painting*, ed. John Seyller (Hyderabad: Jagdish and Kamla Mittal Museum of Art, 2020), 77–108. Many of these painters were documented because of their work for British or French officials; see Mildred Archer, *Company Paintings: Indian Paintings of the British Period* (London: Victoria and Albert Museum, 1992); A. L. Dallapiccola, *South Indian Paintings* (Ahmedabad: Mapin Publishing, 2010).

90 Yael Rice, "Workshop as Network: A Case Study from Mughal South Asia," *Artl@s Bulletin* 6, no. 3 (2017): Article 4; John Seyller, "Farrukh Beg in the Deccan," *Artibus Asiae* 55, no. 3/4 (1995): 319–41; John Seyller, *Workshop and Patron in Mughal India* (Zurich: Artibus Asiae Publishers, 1999), 22–4; Pramod Chandra, "Ustad Salivahana and the Development of Popular Mughal Art," *Lalit Kala* 8 (1960): 25–46; Jasanoff, *Edge of Empire*, 69; Antoine Polier, *A European Experience of the Mughal Orient: The I'jaz-i Arsalani (Persian Letters 1772–1779) of Antoine-Louis Henri Polier*, trans. M. Alam and S. Alavi (Delhi: Oxford University Press, 2001); Malini Roy, "Some Unexpected Sources for Paintings by the Artist Mihr Chand (fl. c. 1759–86), Son of Ganga Ram," *South Asian Studies* 26, no. 1 (2010), 21–9.

91 Pauline Lunsingh Scheurleer, "Indian Miniatures for Europe: The Dutch Market in the 17th and 18th Centuries," in *Miniatur Geschichten: Die Sammlung Indischer Malerei Im Dresdner*

Kupferstich-Kabinett, ed. Monica Juneja and Petra Kuhlmann-Hodick (Dresden: Sandstein Verlag, 2017), 55–67.

92 Tryna Lyons, *The Artists of Nathadwara: The Practice of Painting in Rajasthan* (Bloomington: Indiana University Press, 2004), 32–3, 74–100, 127–67.

93 Molly Emma Aitken, "Pardah and Portrayal: Rajput Women as Subjects, Patrons, and Collectors," *Artibus Asiae* 62, no. 2 (2002): 250–51.

94 The Khasgivale and Raste families among others owned such series, now housed in Poona's Bharat Itihas Sanshodhak Mandal; see G. H. Khare, "Old Pictures from the Mandal," *Traimasik* 17, no. 1 [in Marathi] (Poona: Bharat Itihas Sanshodhak Mandal, 1959): 1–8.

95 For Moor's paintings of Jagannatha see Ipswich Museum, R1928-77-18AB, and BM, 1940,0713,0.151.

96 Mishra, "*Suratkhana* at Amber-Jaipur," 380–403 for gifts in Jaipur and to other courts, 403–19 for gifts specifically to the Marathas; see also Aitken, *Intelligence of Tradition*, ch. 1.

97 D. B. Parasnis, *Poona in Bygone Days* (Bombay: Times Press, 1921), 8–9. Bikaner court records detail that "Jaipurya" artists had been hired to paint palace murals as early as the 1750s in that jurisdiction; see Mira Seth, *Wall Paintings of Rajasthan* (New Delhi: National Museum, 2002), 327–8.

98 The painting of Krishna is inscribed as a gift (*nazar*); Maharaja Sawai Man Singh II Museum, Jaipur City Palace, AG 1895.76. On *nazar* see Mishra, "*Suratkhana* at Amber-Jaipur," 365–71.

99 See Maharaja Sawai Man Singh II Museum, AG 1864.76. Maji Shri Rathor was probably the daughter of Maharaja Bahadur Singh of Kishengarh who married Maharaja Sawai Prithvi Singh (1762–1778); Aitken, "Pardah and Portrayal," 251.

100 Ibid., 277–80.

101 For example, beyond the *baramasa* images, the paintings in Rathor's collection and Moor's in the BM show overlapping themes, palettes, and compositions; see Rathor's painting of Shrinathji (AG 1607.75) to Moor's (BM 1940,0713,0.113); the birth of Krishna (AG 1248.76) to BM 1940,0713,0.149; Rama and Sita with Lakshman and Hanuman (AG 1311.76; AG 1312.76; AG 1334.76) to BM 1940,0713,0.84; Radha and Krishna watching the moon (AG 941.76) to BM 1940,0713,0.92 and 1940,0713,0.62; Krishna and Radha with milk jars (AG 1894.76) to BM 1940,0713,0.61; Gajendra Moksha (AG 1897.76) to BM 1940,0713,0.102 and 1940,0713,0.68; Krishna Kaliya (AG 1900.76) to BM 1940,0713,0.109.

102 One painting, of Raga Hindol, is inscribed as in the collection of Maji Shri Rathor, AG 1892.76, with a like painting in Moor's, BM 1940,0713,0.94, and one on the same theme, BM 1940,0713,0.56.

103 Varunika Saraf, "A Market for Fakes: 'Miniature' Painting in Rajasthan, 1960–2000," *Marg* 69, no. 3 (March–June 2018): 54–63.

104 See *ragamala* paintings donated by the Khasgivale family in the BISM, nos. 1, 8, 15, 246.

105 Khare, "Old Pictures from the Mandal," 1–8.

106 Moor, *Hindu Pantheon*, 189.

107 Jiwaji Ganesh Khasgivale to the Peshwa, nos. 56 and 57, reproduced in G. S. Sardesai, ed., *Selections from the Peshwa Daftar* [in Marathi], 46 vols. (Bombay: Government Central Press, 1930–34), vol. 18, p. 34.

108 Tulshibagh Daftar to Ramji Chitari, Letter 184: "Picture work from Tulshibagh (March 18, 1826)," *Traimasik* 32, nos. 1–4 [in Marathi] (Pune: Bharat Itihas Sanshodhak Mandal, January 1952): 240; Vad, *Selections*, vol. 5 (Bajirao II): 240–43; see also Kamal Chavan, *Maratha Murals: Late Medieval Painting of the Deccan, 1650–1850 AD* (Delhi: B. R. Publishing, 1983), 6, 24.

109 Moor, *Hindu Pantheon*, 189.

110 Ibid., 130.

111 The same scenes welcomed the reader well into the nineteenth century, such as on wooden covers that would have protected the pages of such a manuscript (see fig. 99), and in printed works, such as the *Nandan Nam Sanvastarai* (Chitra-Prasarag Printing Press, 1892) now in the Mansingh Kumthekar Collection, Miraj. I thank Shreenand Bapat and Mansingh Kumthekar for discussing these manuscripts with me.

112 The Marathas across their realm followed common compositions, methods of portrayal, and subject matter, but their renditions varied in style depending on the region with which they were in contact, as seen in the differences between arts made in Nagpur and Poona; see Shaffer, "Towards a History," 77–108.

113 Moor, *Hindu Pantheon*, 425–8. See "Changdev taking darshan of the Poet-saint Jnaneshvar (Jnanadeva)" in the *Jnaneshvari*, Nagpur, 18th century, Virginia Museum of Fine Arts, Richmond; see Shaffer, "Towards a History," 101, fig. 22.

114 I thank Narmada Upadhyaya for his assistance in Indore, and the Scindia Oriental Research Institute, Ujjain.

115 For Indra in Moor's collection see BM 1974,0617,0.14.16; Dallapiccola, *South Indian Paintings*, 121–7, cat. 8. Some deities in this series do not find parallels in Moor's collection, such as Varuna "catching sinners in a fishing net," Subrahmanya Naga (which relates to snake and termite hill worship), and Vishnu reclining on the serpent Shesha.

116 Chavan, *Maratha Murals*, 7–15.

117 See BM 1940,0713,0.201.

118 I thank Tony K. Stewart and John Brockington for discussing the narrative in this painting with me.

119 Devadas, "Vyankatesh Stotra," in *Stotramala: A Garland of Hindu Prayers*, trans. Justin E. Abbott (Poona: Scottish Mission Industries, 1929), 79–80, 81–96.

120 Moor, *Hindu Pantheon*, 182.

121 Vad, *Selections*, vol. 8 (Savai Madhavrao), 300. The seventeenth-century Marathi poet Vaman Pandit narrated the *Dasavatara* in short poems that sought to offer a direct experience with the incarnations: "I bow before Vishnu who is in the form of a fish / A demon Shankha had taken the Vedas and entered the water, Hari killed him in the form of a fish"; Vaman Pandit, "Dasavatara," in *Kavyetihas Sangraha* [Collection of poetry and history; in Marathi], ed. Kashinath N. Sane (Poona: Shivaji Printing House, 1878–80), vol. 2, 60–61.

122 Meera Kosambi, *Gender and Performance: Marathi Theatre and Cinema Before Independence* (New Delhi: Routledge, 2015), 8–10.

123 Personal communication with Mr. Mate at Mate Ram Mandir, Satara, Maharashtra, 2014; with thanks to Mr. Mate and Ajit Salunkhe for facilitating this visit and others in Satara. See the series of these paintings in the Chhatrapati Shivaji Museum, Satara.

124 Woodman Taylor, "Picture Practice: Painting Programs, Manuscript Production, and Liturgical Performances at the

Kotah Royal Palace," in *Gods, Kings, and Tigers: The Art of Kotah* (Munich: Prestel, 1997), 61.

125 Moor, *Hindu Pantheon*, 330–31; see Jyotindra Jain, ed., *Picture Showmen: Insights into the Narrative Tradition in Indian Art* (Mumbai: Marg Publishing, 1998).

126 A. K. Ramanujan, "Three Hundred Ramayanas: Five Examples and Three Thoughts on Translation," in *The Collected Essays of A. K. Ramanujan*, ed. Vinay Dharwadker (Delhi: Oxford University Press, 1999), 134.

127 Edward Moor, Catalogue of the Oriental Cabinet of Major Moor, F.R.S., 6, Asia Department, BM, 1940,7013,0.254. Moor, *Hindu Pantheon*, 192–3, 329–31, refers to his Ramayana and the images in the sections on Rama and on Hanuman; he wrote that he was put off the translation idea after he learned that Mr. W. Carey had translated Valmiki's *Ramayana* (Serampore: Serampore Press, 1806).

128 Other pictures in Moor's *Ramayana* are also specific to the region, such as when Ahalya returns to her form as a woman from that of stone; see Ramanujan, "Three Hundred Ramayanas," 134–44, BM, 1940,0713,0.194; Günther Sontheimer, "The Ramayana in Contemporary Folk Traditions of Maharashtra," in *Essays on Religion, Literature and Law*, ed. Heidrunn Brückner, Anne Feldhaus, and Aditya Malik (New Delhi: Manohar, 2004), 385. The episode of Ahalya is depicted in the Nana Fadnavis Wada and Patwardhan Wada.

129 Krishna's adventures were also written in texts such as in the *Bhagavata Purana* and the *Harivamsa*. On storytelling see Joanna Williams, *The Two-Headed Deer: Illustrations of the Ramayana in Orissa* (Berkeley: University of California Press, 1996), 109–11.

130 See Jain, *Picture Showmen*; Joanna Williams, ed., *Kingdom of the Sun: Indian Court and Village Art from the Princely State of Mewar* (San Francisco: Asian Art Museum, 2007).

4 *THE HINDU PANTHEON*

1 For this chapter, I use all of Moor's personal material related to *The Hindu Pantheon* – his published copy, the proofs, the album of Haughton's drawings, and his handwritten catalogue – which are now housed in the British Museum, having been donated by Moor's descendant Mrs. A. G. Moor in 1940.

2 "111. The Hindu Pantheon" and "Notice of Moor's Hindu Pantheon," *Classical Journal* (June 1813), EJM Collection, 99. Moor's son, Edward J. Moor, structured the albums of his father's materials as a network of personalities and publications, which he further illustrated with portraits and newspaper clippings. On the tradition of albums and extra-illustration see Lucy Peltz, *Facing the Text: Extra-Illustration, Print Culture and Society in Britain, 1769–1840* (Manchester: Manchester University Press, 2017).

3 Images of Indian gods had been reproduced by Europeans since the fifteenth century; see Partha Mitter, *Much Maligned Monsters: A History of European Reactions to Indian Art* (Oxford: Clarendon Press, 1977).

4 See Sumit Guha, *History and Collective Memory in South Asia, 1200–2000* (Seattle: University of Washington Press, 2019), 120–25; and Daniel E. White, *From Little London to Little Bengal: Religion, Print, and Modernity in Early British India, 1793–1835* (Baltimore: Johns Hopkins University Press, 2013), 5–6.

5 Edward Moor, *The Hindu Pantheon* (London: J. Johnson, 1810), 1.

6 William Jones, "Introduction," *Asiatick Researches* 1 (Calcutta: The Company's Printing Office, 1788), iii–iv. Moor was elected a member of the Asiatic Society in 1796 and in 1803 published an essay on a "living deity" near Poona in its journal; "An Account of a Hereditary living Deity to whom devotion is paid by the Brahmans of Poona, &c.," *Asiatick Researches* 7 (1803): 383–97; see *East India Military Calendar, containing the services of General and Field Officers of the Indian Army*, vol. 1 (London, 1823), 343–4.

7 Moor, *Hindu Pantheon*, 72.

8 Ibid., 26; e.g. he cites (15–26) William Jones, "On the Gods of Greece, Italy and India," *Asiatick Researches* 1 (1788), 245–6 and Mr. Wilford, "On Egypt and other countries adjacent to the . . . Nile," *Asiatick Researches* 3 (printed verbatim from the Calcutta edition, London: Vernor and Hood, 1799), 375.

9 Moor, *Hindu Pantheon*, pls. 4, 10. On Stuart see Jörg Fisch, "A Solitary Vindicator of the Hindus: The Life and Writings of General Charles Stuart (1757/58–1828)," *Journal of the Royal Asiatic Society of Great Britain and Ireland* 117, no. 1 (January 1985): 41; Michael D. Willis, "Sculpture from India," in *A. W. Franks: Nineteenth-Century Collecting and the British Museum*, ed. Marjorie Caygill and John Cherry (London: British Museum Press, 1997), 253–5; Lucian Harris, "British Collecting of Indian Art and Artifacts" (Ph.D. diss., Sussex University, 2002), 264–70.

10 Moor, *Hindu Pantheon*, 26.

11 Ibid., 28–9; bronze cast, BM, 1940,0716.255.

12 Ibid., pl. 73; pl. 68 (Moor mislabeled the Jina as "Buddha"), BM, 1880.1551.

13 Edward Moor, *A Narrative of the Operations of Captain Little's Detachment and of the Mahratta Army . . . Against the Nawab Tippoo Sultan . . .* (London: J. Johnson, 1794).

14 W. Ramsay to Moor, May 9, 1794 and January 8, 1796, EJM Collection. The East India Company initially requested that Moor return the advance on the book, but then released the "bond"; see also Cornwallis to Moor, December 12, 1794, and Edward J. Moor, Summary, ibid.

15 Cornwallis to Moor, March 7, 1795 and March 27, 1796; Moor to the British Museum, October 19, 1836, ibid. See also Thomas Seccombe, "Moor, Edward (1771–1848)," rev. J. B. Katz, *ODNB*, 2004 online edn.

16 Moor, *Hindu Pantheon*, pl. 27; V&A, 681(IS).

17 Ibid., pls. 3, 13, 15, 48, 50–51, 71, 87, which publishers copied; see Thomas Robbins et al., *All Religions and Ceremonies*, vol. 2 (London: Oliver D. Cooke, 1823), opp. 48; "Culturgeschichte" (Cultural history) in Johann Georg Heck, *Systematischer Bilder-Atlas* (A systematic picture atlas) (Leipzig: F. A. Brockhaus, ca. 1850); George C. Birdwood, *Industrial Arts of India*, in 2 parts (London: Chapman and Hall, 1880), part I, pl. C.

18 For a comparison see Sarah Monks, "Making Love: Thomas Banks' Camadeva and the Discourses of British India c. 1790," *Visual Culture in Britain* 11, no. 2 (2010): 195–218.

19 See Graham Shaw, *Printing in Calcutta to 1800* (London: Bibliographical Society, 1981), 34–5; Miles Ogborn, *Indian Ink: Script and Print in the Making of the English East India Company* (Chicago: University of Chicago Press, 2007), 240–43. On the production of sculpture for Company officials see Ch. Three above.

20 See Kim Sloan, ed., *Enlightenment: Discovering the World in the Eighteenth Century* (London: British Museum Press, 2004), 215–21; Monks, "Making Love," 207.

21 Malet and Duncan built collections, commissioned illustrations, and wrote extensive notes but neither Malet published his research nor Duncan his "voluminous mass of Manuscripts," as Moor described the collection. Duncan's descendants requested Moor to sort and publish that "mass," but he was not able to do so; Edward Moor, *Oriental Fragments* (London: Smith, Elder and Co., 1834), 70.

22 Alexander Walker, "An Account of various Hindoo Deities," 8, MS. 13903 (from 1806) and "figures and Drawings," MS. 13816, Walker of Bowlands Papers, National Library of Scotland, Edinburgh.

23 Edward Moor, *Hindu Infanticide: an account of the measures adopted for suppressing the practice of the systematic murder by their parents of female infants* (London: J. Johnson, 1811). Moor and Walker could have encouraged each other in their common interests, but they do not seem to have shared materials. Walker, "Account of various Hindoo Deities," 8, wrote: "The collection was made at Baroda in 1806. It contains a very short and imperfect sketch of some of the principal Hindoo Gods.* [*The Hindoo Pantheon, the elaborate work of my friend Major Moor was not published until some years afterwards; in 1810]." This suggests that Walker did not know that Moor was pursuing publication, and, as Moor does not cite Walker in his book, that Moor was not aware of Walker's efforts. Sanjay Subrahmanyam, *Europe's India: Worlds, People, Empires* (Cambridge, Mass.: Harvard University Press, 2017), 268–83, implies that Moor followed Walker's lead.

24 On Colonel Gentil see Chanchal Dadlani, "Transporting India: The Gentil Album and Mughal Manuscript Culture," *Art History* 38, no. 4 (September 2015): 748–76; on Polier see Malini Roy, "William Beckford's Albums on Hindu Mythology," Asian and African Studies Blog, BL, posted December 8, 2014, https://blogs.bl.uk/asian-and-african/2014/12/william-beckfords-albums-on-hindu-mythology.htm.

25 On Colonel Mackenzie see Nicholas B. Dirks, *Castes of Mind: Colonialism and the Making of Modern India* (Princeton, N.J.: Princeton University Press, 2001); Jennifer Howes, *Illustrating India: The Early Colonial Investigations of Colin Mackenzie* (Oxford: Oxford University Press, 2010).

26 Draft of advertisement for *The Hindu Pantheon* for papers in India; agreement between Major Moor and J. Johnson for printing *The Hindu Pantheon*, EJM Collection. Moor's *Narrative* had a larger print run, at 1200, but was published in a smaller quarto size with only 8 plates plus maps at half the price (20 Rs). Johnson kept 750 copies in his shop at St Paul's Churchyard, London and gave Moor 500, which he shipped to India for subscribers in the civil, medical, and military establishments of the Company, primarily in Bombay, Madras, and Calcutta. Moor advertised for subscriptions and created relationships with people in India and Britain to make subscription lists, collect the cost of publication, and distribute the books, including Mr. Uhthoff, for whom he served as secretary in Poona in 1797–8, a Mr. Humphreys and Mr. Harvey in Calcutta, a Captain Hall near Cawnpore, and a Major Hart in Madras; Uhthoff to Moor, January 3, 1795; Humphreys to Moor, May 1, 1795, Letters, EJM Collection.

27 See Joseph Bell to Moor, November 1, 1809, EJM Collection.

28 See subscription lists for *Hindu Pantheon*, ibid.

29 Edward J. Moor, Summary, ibid.

30 Urs App, *The Birth of Orientalism* (Philadelphia: University of Pennsylvania Press, 2010), 4–6.

31 Edward Moor, Catalogue of the Oriental Cabinet of Major Moor, F.R.S. (1839), 5, BM, 1940,7013,0.254.

32 Moor, *Hindu Pantheon*, xii.

33 Ibid., 413–14; Moor, *Oriental Fragments*, 466–7.

34 Henry Thomas Colebrooke, "On the Vedas," *Asiatic Researches* 8 (printed verbatim from the Calcutta edition, London: Vernor, Hood and Sharpe, 1808), 397, quoted in Moor, *Hindu Pantheon*, 8; see 437–45 for Moor's views of the Vedas. After vol. 7, *Asiatick Researches* became *Asiatic Researches*.

35 Moor, *Hindu Pantheon*, 4.

36 Ibid., 2, 13, 439. On monism see App, *Birth of Orientalism*, 4–6.

37 On *aum*, also spelled *Om*, see Finnian McKean Moore Gerety, "This Whole World is Om: Song, Soteriology, and the Emergence of the Sacred Syllable" (Ph.D. diss., Harvard University, 2015), 209.

38 Moor, *Hindu Pantheon*, xii.

39 Jones, "On the Gods," 227.

40 Moor, *Hindu Pantheon*, 122, 138, 158 (noting that Ganesha is "lord of Ganas").

41 Ibid., 1–2. This glosses earlier seventeenth and eighteenth-century European interpretations of Asian religions as esoteric/exoteric; see App, *Birth of Orientalism*, 2–3. It also parallels Platonic notions of the division of *eidos* (form or idea) from *eidolon* (image or representation), and participates in colonial conceptions of "idolatry," which I will explore in the last section; see Swagato Ganguly, *Idolatry and the Idea of India: Visions of Horror, Allegories of Enlightenment* (London: Routledge, 2018), 2, 4.

42 Moor, *Hindu Pantheon*, 1–2.

43 Ibid., 151.

44 Jones, "On the Gods," 222–3, 242–3. Moor also borrowed Jones's disquisition on *aum*, and the relationship between the single divine and the multiple "illusory" deities.

45 See Phiroze Vasunia, *The Classics and Colonial India* (Oxford: Oxford University Press, 2013), 242–3. Jones shared this supposition with Jacob Bryant, *A New System or Analysis of Ancient Mythology* (London: P. Elmsly, 1773). On Jones's use of the metaphor of the sun to remove the "traces of idolatry" from "Hinduism's origin" see Ganguly, *Idolatry*, 30–31.

46 Moor, *Hindu Pantheon*, 277, referring to Jones, "On the Gods," 267.

47 On this approach's theological undercurrent see Urs App, "William Jones's Ancient Theology," *Sino-Platonic Papers* 191 (July 2009): 1–125. Such an approach was expanded by Friedrich Creuzer in *Symbolik und Mythologie der alten Völker* (1810) and by Hegel; see Mitter, *Much Maligned Monsters*, 202–20.

48 Jones, "On the Gods," 225. Jones stages this argument in the negative, but his purpose is to "weed" from his mind the "capital error" of the first few chapters of Genesis.

49 Warren Hastings, "Introduction," in *The Bhagvat-Geeta, or Dialogues of Krishna and Arjoon, translated from the original, in*

the Sanskreet, or ancient language of the Brahmans, trans. Charles Wilkins (London: C. Nourse, 1785), 9–10.

50 See Peter Funnell, "The Symbolic Language of Antiquity," in *The Arrogant Connoisseur: Richard Payne Knight*, ed. Michael Clarke and Nicholas Penny (Manchester: Manchester University Press, 1982), 50–64.

51 The inspiration for Knight's "Discourse" was the Society of Dilettanti, which printed the book. It was as steeped in irony and male society as in antiquarianism; see Bruce Redford, *Dilettanti: The Antic and the Antique in Eighteenth-Century England* (Los Angeles: J. Paul Getty Museum, 2008), 113–28.

52 This sculptural fragment from Charles Townley's collection entered the British Museum in 1805; see Willis, "Sculpture from India," 250; Mitter, *Much Maligned Monsters*, 87; Harris, "British Collecting," ch. 7.

53 Richard Payne Knight developed these ideas, with more material examples and toward a chronological history of art, in *An Inquiry into the Symbolical Language of Ancient Art and Mythology* (London, 1818); see Funnell, "Symbolic Language," 50–64.

54 Moor, *Narrative*, 395.

55 Moor, *Hindu Pantheon*, 179.

56 Ibid., 56, 147.

57 Ibid., 163–4.

58 "Moor's Hindu Pantheon," *Edinburgh Review* (1811), 313–14.

59 See "Ravana the divinity and giant who has ten heads and twenty arms," in *Dieux des Indiens, for missionaries in South India, 1688–1725* (Bibliothèque Nationale de France, Paris, OD 38).

60 "The god Indra or the Jupiter of the earth," in *Figures et Divinités de l'Inde, Coromandel Coast, 1720–30, owned by Charles-Adrian Picard* (Bibliothèque Nationale de France, OD 40).

61 Günther Sontheimer, "The Mallari/Khandoba Myth as Reflected in Folk Art and Ritual," *Anthropos* 79, no. 1/3 (1984): 167; Isabella Nardi, *The Theory of Citrasutras in Indian Painting: A Critical Re-evaluation of Their Uses and Interpretations* (London: Routledge, 2006), 3, 6.

62 [Charles] Grignion, "Medals of Goddesses," in John Bell, *Bell's New Pantheon, or, Historical dictionary of the gods, demi-gods, heroes and fabulous personages of antiquity* ... (London: J. Bell, 1790), pl. 1.

63 See John Bugg, ed., *The Joseph Johnson Letter Book* (Oxford: Oxford University Press, 2016), intro; see also David Weir, *Brahma in the West: William Blake and the Oriental Renaissance* (New York: State University of New York Press, 2003), 29.

64 Joseph Johnson to Edward Moor, letter no. 23, June 18, 1796, in Bugg, *Johnson Letter Book*, 22–3; original or copy pasted into the section on Johnson in Moor's albums, EJM Collection.

65 See Gerald P. Tyson, *Joseph Johnson: A Liberal Publisher* (Iowa City: University of Iowa Press, 1979); Bugg, *Johnson Letter Book*, xix–lxxxi. At this time "bookseller" also included the role of publisher and much else. According to Johnson, the job included "sourcing paper, organizing printing, arranging for the correction of the text, advertising, and distribution"; Bugg, *Johnson Letter Book*, xxvii–xxix.

66 Bugg, *Johnson Letter Book*, xix.

67 Weir, *Brahma in the West*, 49; see also P. J. Marshall, ed., *The British Discovery of Hinduism in the Eighteenth Century* (Cambridge: Cambridge University Press, 1970); Esther Bloch, Marianne Keppens, and Rajaram Hegde, *Rethinking Religion in India: The Colonial Construction of Hinduism* (London: Routledge, 2010).

68 Johnson to Moor, in Bugg, *Johnson Letter Book*, 22–3; J. Johnson to Lieutenant Moor of Bombay, London, June 18, 1796, EJM Collection. In the 1820s, Moor transformed this early bookselling practice into a literary agency that specialized in trade between London and India; Literary Agency Summary and Letters, EJM Collection.

69 Handwritten letter pasted next to a print of "Mr. Joseph Johnson engraved by W. Sharpe, from a portrait by Moses Haughton, in the possession of John Miles," EJM Collection. This dinner must have been on September 18, 1805, as William Godwin noted in his diary that day: "Dine at Johnson's, w. Fuseli, [John] Bonnycastle, [Anna Letitia] Barbaulds & major Moor: [William] Mulready calls. Ja Wt [James Wollstonecraft] dies"; "Diary entry for 18 September 1805," *The Diary of William Godwin*, ed. Victoria Myers, David O'Shaughnessy, and Mark Philp (Oxford: Oxford Digital Library, 2010), http://godwindiary.bodleian.ox.ac.uk/diary/1805-09-18.html (accessed May 5, 2021).

70 Weir, *Brahma in the West*, 74–86; the publication date is printed on most of the *Hindu Pantheon* plates.

71 Johann Winckelmann, *Reflections on the Paintings and Sculpture of the Greeks*, trans. Henry Fuseli (London: A. Millar, 1765), 4. On Neoplatonism see Christian Wildberg, "Neoplatonism," *The Stanford Encyclopedia of Philosophy* (Summer 2019), ed. Edward N. Zalta, https://plato.stanford.edu/archives/sum2019/entries/Neoplatonism/.

72 Henry Fuseli used the Latin phrase, *ut pictura poesis*, but attributed its origins to the Greek poet Simonides in "The Arts," *Analytical Review* 1, ed. Joseph Johnson (1788), 216.

73 Andrei Pop, *Antiquity, Theatre, and the Painting of Henry Fuseli* (Oxford: Oxford University Press, 2015), 2–3; Pop suggests the term "neopagan" as more descriptive of the discovery of a global antiquity than "neoclassical."

74 Henry Fuseli, attrib., "Art. IX. On the Gods of Greece, Italy, and India, written in 1784; and since revised; by the President," *Analytical Review* 6 (1790), 313, cited in Weir, *Brahma in the West*, 42.

75 Pop, *Antiquity*, 57; Monks, "Making Love," 195–218.

76 Deanna Petherbridge, "Some Thoughts on Flaxman and the Engraved Outlines," *Print Quarterly* 28, no. 4 (2011): 385.

77 For Flaxman's drawings of Indian and Egyptian works see e.g. Sketchbook 832/3, ff. 15–24, Fitzwilliam Museum, Cambridge, and Flaxman Collection, 3160, University College London Art Museum.

78 See Rosemary Sweet, *Antiquaries: The Discovery of the Past in Eighteenth-Century Britain* (London: Bloomsbury Academic, 2004). For a global perspective see Alain Schnapp, ed., *World Antiquarianism: Comparative Perspectives* (Los Angeles: Getty Research Institute, 2014).

79 Jason Edwards terms Flaxman's use of neoclassicism in imperial commissions "colonial cosmopolitanism"; Jason Edwards, "John Charles Felix Rossi's Cornwallis Monument (1807–11) and the Colonial-Cosmopolitanism of the British School," in *The British School of Sculpture, ca. 1760–1832*, ed. Jason Edwards and Sarah Burnage (London: Routledge, 2016), 189–92.

80 See Barbara Groseclose, *British Sculpture and the Company Raj: Church Monuments and Public Statuary in Madras, Calcutta, and*

Bombay to 1858 (Cranbury, N.J.: Associated University Presses, 1995), 13–14, 60–69.

81 Moor, Catalogue of the Oriental Cabinet, 44.

82 Ibid., 5.

83 This inscription is on BM, 1940,0713,0.246. "Outline four to a plate," often with the addition to "make very handsome," is on numerous paintings including 1940.0713,0.73, 0.80, 0.81, 0.86, 0.107, 0.109, 0.239–245.

84 BM, 1940,0713,0.239–246.

85 Another of Brahma, Vishnu, and Shiva remains in Moor's albums: it followed the lines of a South Indian painting, though the original is not extant in Moor's collection; BM, 1940,0713,0.248, Haughton's drawing of it (1940,0713,0.251), and Moor, *Hindu Pantheon*, pl. 5.

86 Moor, Catalogue of the Oriental Cabinet, 44.

87 The bronze sculpture is in the BM, 1940,0716.32.

88 On antiquarianism and veracity see Stephen Bann, "Antiquarianism, Visuality and the Exotic Monument," in *Traces of India: Photography, Architecture, and the Politics of Representation, 1850–1900*, ed. Maria Antonella Pelizzari (New Haven and London: Yale University Press, 2003), 60–85. Eighteenth-century art historians and physiognomists identified character as well as beauty in the contoured line on objects, e.g. Winckelmann, *Reflections*, 23; Johann Caspar Lavater, *Essays on Physiognomy*, trans. Thomas Holcroft (London, 1789); see David Bindman, *Ape to Apollo: Aesthetics and the Idea of Race in the 18th Century* (Ithaca, N.Y.: Cornell University Press, 2002).

89 Francois Pomey, *The Pantheon, representing the fabulous histories of the heathen gods, and most illustrious heroes ... translated by Andrew Tooke* (London: J. F. & C. Rivington et al., 1787), 1–5, 10–11.

90 Samuel Johnson defined "pantheon" as "a temple of all the gods" in his dictionary; "Pantheon," in *A Dictionary of the English Language* (1755, 1773), ed. Beth Rapp Young et al. (2021): https://johnsonsdictionaryonline.com (accessed May 6, 2021).

91 Robert Rosenblum, *The International Style of 1800* (New York: Garland, 1976). On the picturesque see Geoff Quilley, "William Hodges: Artist of Empire," in *William Hodges 1744–1797: The Art of Exploration*, ed. Geoff Quilley and John Bonehill (Greenwich: National Maritime Museum, 2004), 1–8; Tim Barringer, "The Visual Culture of the Plantation: Picturesque Prospects and the Labor of the Enslaved," in *Art and Emancipation in Jamaica*, ed. Timothy Barringer, Gillian Forrester, and Barbaro Martinez Ruiz (New Haven and London: Yale University Press, 2007), 40–63.

92 I thank Robert J. Del Bontà for the Paulinus reference.

93 See Moor, *Hindu Pantheon*, 189.

94 George Cumberland, *Thoughts on Outline, Sculpture, and the System that Guided the Ancient Artists in Composing their Figures and Groupes* ... (London, 1796), 1, 12, 28–9; Tilar Jenon Mazzeo, "Verbal Echoes of Cumberland's Thoughts on Outline, Sculpture, and the System that Guided the Ancients (1796) in Jerusalem," *Blake/An Illustrated Quarterly* 35, no. 1 (Summer 2001), 24–6.

95 Moor, *Hindu Pantheon*, 2, 1.

96 Cumberland, *Thoughts on Outline*, 1, 13.

97 Winckelmann, *Reflections*, 60–61.

98 Rosenblum, *International Style*, 48–9, argued that the linear style encouraged the transformation of what was "remote in time and space" into something "fantastic and visionary in subject matter."

99 John Flaxman, *Lectures on Sculpture* (London: John Murray, 1829), 52, pl. 13, 34–5, 41, 47–9.

100 Jones, "On the Gods," 221–5; Cumberland, *Thoughts on Outline*, 29; Moor, *Hindu Pantheon*, xi; discussed in Morton D. Paley, "Wonderful Originals: Blake and Ancient Sculpture," in *Blake in His Time*, ed. Robert N. Essick and Donald Pearce (Bloomington: Indiana University Press, 1978), 185–6. William Hodges also discussed Indian arts as preceding the Greek; *Travels in India during the years 1780, 1781, 1782, & 1783* (London: J. Edwards, 1793), 62–77.

101 Flaxman, *Lectures on Sculpture*, 52.

102 On Indian art's role in the European question of art's origins see Mitter, *Much Maligned Monsters*, 189–220.

103 On Flaxman, Blake, and details of the "Sculpture" essay see Rosamund A. Paice, "Encyclopedic Resistance: Blake, Rees's *Cyclopaedia*, and the Laocoön Separate Plate," *Blake: An Illustrated Quarterly* 37, no. 2 (Fall 2003): 44–62. Flaxman wrote that "Mr. Blake" was "the best engraver of outlines"; see G. E. Bentley, Jr., *William Blake in the Desolate Market* (Montreal: McGill-Queens University Press, 2016), 10.

104 John Flaxman, "Sculpture," in Rees's *Cyclopaedia*, vol. 4 (London: Longman, Hurst, Rees, Orme & Browne, 1819–20), pl. IV, for which Blake was paid £21; see Bentley, *Blake in the Desolate Market*, tab. 1.3. On the reduced number of co-authors of the essay see Paice, "Encyclopedic Resistance," 48; see also James Bogan, "Blake's Jupiter Olympius in Rees's *Cyclopaedia*," *Blake/An Illustrated Quarterly* 15, no. 4 (Spring 1982): 157, who considered Moor's print "hackwork."

105 Robert N. Essick, *William Blake's Commercial Book Illustrations* (Oxford: Clarendon Press, 1991), 110–12.

106 See the following for their alignment of engravings in Moor's *Hindu Pantheon* with Blake's work: Anthony Blunt, "Blake's Pictorial Imagination," *Journal of the Warburg and Courtauld Institutes* 6 (1943): 206; Joseph Burke, "The Eidetic and the Borrowed Image: An Interpretation of Blake's Theory and Practice of Art," in *In Honour of Daryl Lindsay: Essays and Studies*, ed. Franz Philipp and June Stewart (Melbourne: Oxford University Press, 1964), 119–25, 290, figs. 101–2; Hermione de Almeida and George H. Gilpin, *Indian Renaissance: British Romantic Art and the Prospect of India* (2005; London and New York: Routledge, 2016), 271–86; Weir, *Brahma in the West*, 74–86.

107 On stippling see Paice, "Encyclopedic Resistance," 51.

108 Paley, "Wonderful Originals," 66–80.

109 William Blake, *A Descriptive Catalogue of Pictures, Poetical and Historical Inventions* (London: J. Blake, 1809), 3, Copy D, Huntington Library, San Marino, Cal., http://www.blakearchive.org/ (accessed June 8, 2021), dual cat. nos. 1 and 2 on *The Spiritual Form of Nelson Guiding Leviathan* and *The Spiritual Form of Pitt, Guiding Behemoth*.

110 Blake, *Descriptive Catalogue*, 4; see also Paley, "Wonderful Originals," 186. Almeida and Gilpin, *Indian Renaissance*, 272, have suggestively proposed that Blake's visions of ancient works collapsed the prophet Ezekiel's vision of sculpted halls with the rock-carved temples of India as published in Daniell's *Oriental Scenery* with James Wales's prints of Ellora and Karle and discussed by James Forbes.

111 Blake, *Descriptive Catalogue*, 4.

112 Ibid., 1–7. William Blake, *The Spiritual Form of Pitt Guiding Behemoth*, ca. 1805–9, Tate, N01110, and *The Spiritual Form of Nelson Guiding Leviathan*, ca. 1805–9, Tate, N03006.

113 Almeida and Gilpin, *Indian Renaissance*, 276–9.

114 Blake also discusses the cyclical revival of "eternal principles" in later figures in his entry on the Pilgrims on their journey in the Canterbury Tales; *Descriptive Catalogue*, 21; see David Fallon, *Blake, Myth, and Enlightenment* (London: Palgrave Macmillan, 2017), 196.

115 *Bhagvat-Geeta*; Weir, *Brahma in the West*, 13, 39–42, argues that Blake had access to Wilkins's translation of the Gita (and other Asiatic Society texts, such as Jones's essay "On the Gods") from ca. 1790; he cites Blake's description of time in *Europe: A Prophecy*, 10.21–2, as "infinite / Shut up in finite revolutions."

116 Blake, *Descriptive Catalogue*, 59.

117 The phrase "ancient language of the Brahmans" is on the title page of Wilkins's book, *The Bhagvat-Geeta*. Blake's phrase seems to paraphrase Winckelmann: "Had Laocoon been covered with a garb becoming an antient sacrifice, his sufferings would have lost one half of their Expression"; cited in Morton D. Paley, *The Traveller in the Evening: The Last Works of William Blake* (Oxford: Oxford University Press, 2003), 59.

118 See Paley, "Wonderful Originals," 66–80, and *Traveller in the Evening*, 53–100.

119 Weir, *Brahma in the West*, 56; see BM, 1900,0824.211.

120 *Bhagvat-Geeta*, trans. Wilkins, 36–7.

121 See Blunt, "Blake's Pictorial Imagination," 206; Weir, *Brahma in the West*, 74–86, for other associations between Moor and Blake. Moor titles her "Devi," but the iconography is that of two elephants showering the goddess Lakshmi (*Gaja Lakshmi*), who is a form of the great goddess.

122 Weir, *Brahma in the West*, 76.

123 Company authors stressed poetic personification in early Hindu writings, summarily called Vedanta, and related them to the classical tradition of *ut pictura poesis*; on the former see App, *Birth of Orientalism*, 4–6; on the latter and Blake see W. J. T. Mitchell, *Blake's Composite Art* (Princeton, N.J.: Princeton University Press, 1978), 4–33.

124 Moor, *Hindu Pantheon*, 56.

125 William Blake, *Jerusalem: The Emanation of the Giant Albion*, ed. Morton D. Paley (Princeton, N.J.: Princeton University Press, 1991), 216.

126 Moor, *Hindu Pantheon*, 152, quotes Jones's "Hymn to Durga" in the text as well: "O Durga! Thou hast deign'd to shield / Man's feeble virtue with celestial might, / Gliding from yon jasper field; / And, on a lion borne, has brav'd the fight: / For when the demon Vice thy realms defy'd, / And arm'd with death each arched horn, / Thy golden lance, O goddess! mountain-born, / Touch'd but the pest – he roar'd, and died!"

127 On the sublime and pathos in *Jerusalem* see Morton D. Paley, *The Continuing City: William Blake's Jerusalem* (Oxford: Clarendon Press, 1983), 57–77.

128 David Bindman, "William Blake and Popular Religious Imagery," *Burlington Magazine* 128 (1986): 712–18; Esther Chadwick, "The Radical Print: British Art and Graphic Experiment in the Paper Age" (Ph.D. diss., Yale University, 2016), 220–22; see also Susanne Sklar, *Blake's Jerusalem as Visionary Theatre* (Oxford: Oxford University Press, 2011), 20–43.

129 Jones, "On the Gods," 222–3; see Weir, *Brahma in the West*, 57.

130 Blake, *Jerusalem*, ed. Paley, 296, pl. 99; Paley suggests the connection to and cites this passage in the *Bhagvat-Geeta*, trans. Wilkins, 75–6.

131 A similar formulation of compression might apply to the other Indic forms that pervade *Jerusalem*, e.g. with the female form on the lotus: Mitchell, *Blake's Composite Art*, 206–9, describes her as "Blake's genius for designing pictures as vortices which draw the reader inward, into a dialectic of ironies, ambiguities, paradoxes, and concentric unfoldings."

132 Saree Makdisi, *William Blake and the Impossible History of the 1790s* (Chicago: University of Chicago Press, 2002), 246. On Blake and history see David Worrall, "Blake's Jerusalem and the Visionary History of Britain," *Studies in Romanticism* 16, no. 2 (Spring 1977): 189–216.

133 Building on Bindman's work, Chadwick, "Radical Print," 212–59, has elaborated the idea that Blake's second Laocoön, ca. 1826, is related to Protestant broadsides like Garnet Terry's print "Prophetic Vision or Daniel's Great Image of the Mystical Body of Babylon," which drew on Indian sculpture to visualize biblical sculpture; see Bindman, "William Blake and Popular Religious Imagery," 712–18; David Bindman, *William Blake: His Art and Times* (London: Thames & Hudson, 1982), 165–7.

134 Sir Joshua Reynolds, *The Works of Sir Joshua Reynolds*, vol. 1 (London: T. Cadell, Jun. and W. Davies, 1798), contents page, BL, C.45.e.18-20, notes by William Blake.

135 W. J. T. Mitchell, "Empire and Objecthood," in *What Do Pictures Want? The Lives and Loves of Images* (Chicago: University of Chicago Press, 2005), 168; see also Hazard Adams, *Blake's Margins* (Jefferson, N.C.: McFarland, 2009), 109–38.

136 Moor, *Hindu Pantheon*, 427. On idolatry see Moshe Halbertal and Avishai Margalit, *Idolatry*, trans. Naomi Goldblum (Cambridge, Mass.: Harvard University Press, 1992).

137 Moor, *Hindu Pantheon*, 1–3.

138 Moor, *Oriental Fragments*, 70; see also Moor, *Hindu Infanticide*.

139 Moor, *Hindu Pantheon*, 419–20. Almeida and Gilpin, *Indian Renaissance*, 284–5, make the argument that Blake could have modeled the Christ figure in *Jerusalem* on Moor's.

140 Moor, *Hindu Pantheon*, 1–2, 419–20.

141 See White, *From Little London*, 5–6.

142 See Karen Chancey, "The Star in the East: The Controversy over Christian Missions to India, 1805–1813," *The Historian* 60, no. 3 (Spring 1998): 507–22.

143 Moor, *Hindu Pantheon*, 427–8.

144 See Homi K. Bhabha, "Signs Taken for Wonders: Questions of Ambivalence and Authority under a Tree outside Delhi, May 1817," in *The Location of Culture* (Milton Park: Routledge, 1994), 145–74; Penelope Carson, *The East India Company and Religion, 1698–1858* (Woodbridge: Boydell Press, 2012).

145 Mitter, *Much Maligned Monsters*, 1–3. Protestants also faced tensions with material forms, the worship of God, and idolatry, especially in their consideration of Catholicism; see Joseph Koerner, "The Icon as Iconoclash," in *Iconoclash: Beyond the Image Wars in Science, Religion, and Art*, ed. Bruno Latour and Peter Weibel (Cambridge, Mass.: MIT Press, 2002), 164–213.

146 Kenneth Curry, ed., *New Letters of Robert Southey*, 2 vols. (New York: Columbia University Press, 1965), vol. 1, 213, cited in White, *From Little London*, 56.

147 White, *From Little London*, 56, 61, 73–82; Natasha Eaton, "Colonial Iconoclash: Mimetic Rivalry, Collecting and Idolatry between India and Britain," in *Acquiring Cultures: Histories of World Art in Western Markets*, ed. Bénédicte Savoy, Charlotte Guichard, and Christine Howard (Berlin: De Gruyter, 2018), 31–46.

148 Etienne Alexander Rodriguez, *The Hindoo Pantheon* (Madras: American Mission Press, 1849), iii.

149 D. T. Barry, *Travelling Game of India: Amusing & Instructive* (Liverpool: Arthur Newling, 1858), 10.

150 *Books for the Children of India: A Paper for the Juvenile Friends of the Christian Vernacular Education Society for India* (London: W. M. Watts, 1865), EJM Collection.

151 Edward Moor, *The Hindu Pantheon*, 3rd edn., ed. W. O. Simpson (Madras: J. Higginbotham, 1864), x.

152 Ibid., ix; Moor, *Hindu Pantheon* (1810), 427–8.

153 Moor, *Hindu Pantheon* (1810), 145–68.

154 Ibid., 2.

155 Edward Moor, *The Hindu Pantheon*, 2nd edn., ed. A. O. Moor (London: Williams and Norgate, 1861), advertisement.

156 Dipti Khera, "'Designs to Suit Every Taste': P. Orr & Sons and Swami Silverware," in Vidya Dehejia, *Delight in Design: Indian Silver for the Raj* (Ahmedabad: Mapin, 2008), 23; see also F. W. Emery, *Hindoo Mythology: Popularly Treated: being an epitomized description of the various heathen deities illustrated on the silver swami tea service, presented as a memento of his visit to India to H. R. H. The Prince of Wales, K. G., G. C. S. I., by his Highness the Gaekwar of Baroda* (Madras: Printed by Gantz Brothers, 1875).

157 Khera, "'Designs to Suit Every Taste,'" 20–37.

158 Birdwood, *Industrial Arts*, part I, 125; Mitter, *Much Maligned Monsters*, 1–3.

159 Birdwood, *Industrial Arts*, part I, 46, 131, pls. C–L, 1–76; he offered a damning appraisal: "This is possibly why sculpture and painting are unknown, as fine arts, in India" (125); Mitter, *Much Maligned Monsters*, chs. 4 and 5.

160 This vase is similar to that which ended Moor's *Hindu Pantheon*, pl. 105.

161 Christopher Pinney, *Photos of the Gods: The Printed Image and Political Struggle in India* (London: Reaktion, 2004), 18.

162 "The Hindoo Pantheon" advertisement, in Birdwood, *Industrial Arts*, advertisement section, 5.

5 A MARATHA PRESS FOR INDEPENDENCE

1 Vishnushastri Chiplunkar, *Nibandhamala* [A Garland of essays; in Marathi] (1874–81), 2 vols. (Pune: Varada Books, 1993), vol. 2, 1195, n. 3. Chiplunkar inaugurated a nationalist era by founding and writing in Marathi and English magazines and newspapers in Poona, promoting new methods of education such as in the Deccan Education Society, and participating in political protest. Between 1874 and 1881 he edited and wrote the Marathi literary journal *Nibandhamala* and opened the Chitrashala Press, and the Arya Bhushan Press, in 1878. With Bal Ganghadar Tilak and Gopal Ganesh Agarkar, he published the English *Mahratta* and the Marathi *Kesari* newspapers, from 1880; see N. C. Kelkar, "Vishnushastri Chiplunkar," in *Indian Worthies* (Bombay: Manoranjak Grantha Prasarak Mandal, 1906), 119–63; "The Late Vishnushastri Chiplunkar: In Memoriam," *The Mahratta* (19 March 1882), cited in Veena Naregal, *Language Politics, Elites and the Public Sphere: Western India Under Colonialism* (London: Anthem Press, 2002), 209.

2 Christopher Pinney, *Photos of the Gods: The Printed Image and Political Struggle in India* (London: Reaktion, 2004), 46–58, has argued that Chiplunkar's *Nibandhamala* "exploded 'like a bombshell.'" He relates Chiplunkar's text with Chitrashala prints and nationalist agitation.

3 Thomas Carlyle instigated the founding of the National Portrait Gallery to offer a visual collection of the British nation's heroes; see Paul Barlow, "The Imagined Hero as Incarnate Sign: Thomas Carlyle and the Mythology of the 'National Portrait' in Victorian Britain," *Art History* 17, no. 4 (December 1994): 517–45.

4 On chromolithography see Michael Twyman, *A History of Chromolithography: Printed Colour for All* (London: British Library, 2013). On chromolithography in India see Christopher Pinney, "The Nation (Un)Pictured? Chromolithography and 'Popular' Politics in India, 1878–1995," *Critical Inquiry* 23, no. 4 (Summer 1997): 860–63; Pinney, *Photos of the Gods*, 14–19; Kajri Jain, *Gods in the Bazaar: The Economies of Indian Calendar Art* (Durham, N.C.: Duke University Press, 2007), 56–62. For the relationship of color to empire see Natasha Eaton, *Colour, Art and Empire: Visual Culture and the Nomadism of Representation* (London: I.B. Tauris, 2013).

5 Chiplunkar, "Essay on Lokman," in *Nibandhamala*, vol. 2, 1195, n. 3.

6 J. B. Modak and K. N. Sane, "Preface," *Kavyetihas Sangraha* [Collection of poetry and history; in Marathi] 1, no. 1 (Pune, 1878), 3. K. N. Sane, J. B. Modak, and Shankar Tukaram Shaligram started *Kavyetihas Sangraha* with the cooperation of Chiplunkar; see R. P. Kanitkar, *Chitrashalecha Itihas* [History of the Chitrashala; in Marathi] (Pune: Vasukaka Joshi Vikhvast Nidhi, 1975), 3. On history-writing in western India see Prachi Deshpande, *Creative Pasts: Historical Memory and Identity in Western India, 1700–1960* (New Delhi: Permanent Black, 2007); Sumit Guha, *History and Collective Memory in South Asia, 1200–2000* (Seattle: University of Washington Press, 2019), 83–175; and Sumit Guha, "Speaking Historically: The Changing Voices of Historical Narration in Western India, 1400–1900," *American Historical Review* 109, no. 4 (October 2004): 1084–103.

7 The title of this history was *Peshwyanchi bakhar*; it was probably written by Krishnaji Vinayak Sohoni ca. 1818; see Deshpande, *Creative Pasts*, 21.

8 Brahmins had dominated the administration in the Peshwa period, but they consolidated their power within the colonial system through English-language education, and by disseminating English and Marathi materials through the printing press and schools; see Deshpande, *Creative Pasts*, 78–82, chs. 3 and 4. This was in contrast to the majority of the lower-middle class who were Marathi-language educated, creating, as Naregal, *Language Politics*, esp. 6–21, describes, a linguistic split between the classes and the social and political leadership, which fueled dueling anticolonial and anticaste movements. See also Guha, *History and Collective Memory*, 152–68; Gordon Johnson, "Chitpavan Brahmins and Politics in Western India in the Late Nineteenth and Early Twentieth Centuries," in *Elites in South Asia*, ed. Edmund Leach and S. N. Mukherjee (Cambridge: Cambridge University Press, 1970), 95–118; Rosalind O'Hanlon,

Caste, Conflict, and Ideology: Mahatma Jotirao Phule and Low Caste Protest in Nineteenth-Century Western India (Cambridge: Cambridge University Press, 1985).

9 This portrait of Nana Fadnavis was probably painted by Wales and Jossi (as fig. 28 was of Scindia) and is presently in the Sangli Museum.

10 Modak and Sane, "Preface," 3.

11 Vishnushastri Chiplunkar quoted in Kanitkar, *History of the Chitrashala*, 1.

12 Deshpande, *Creative Pasts*, 72, chs. 3 and 4; see also Naregal, *Language Politics*; Rama Mantena, *The Origins of Modern Historiography in India* (New York: Palgrave Macmillan, 2012).

13 James Grant Duff, *History of the Mahrattas*, 3 vols. (London: Longman, 1826); Deshpande, *Creative Pasts*, 116.

14 Modak and Sane, *Kavyetihas Sangraha*, 1–7; see Guha, *History and Collective Memory*, 136–40.

15 A. R. Kulkarni, *Maratha Historiography* (Delhi: Manohar, 2006), pt. 2, 95–184; Deshpande, *Creative Pasts*, 116; Guha, *History and Collective Memory*, 118–75, esp. 137–40.

16 Modak and Sane, *Kavyetihas Sangraha*, 1–7; Deshpande, *Creative Pasts*, 99, 116. Vernacular printing created what Benedict Anderson termed an "imagined community" that formed a nation; *Imagined Communities: Reflections on the Origin and Spread of Nationalism* (London: Verso, 2006), ch. 3.

17 Rosalind O'Hanlon, "Maratha History as Polemic: Low Caste Ideology and Political Debate in Late Nineteenth-Century Western India," *Modern Asian Studies* 17, no. 1 (1983): 3–4.

18 Mahadev L. Apte, "Lokahitavadi and V. K. Chiplunkar: Spokesmen of Change in Nineteenth-Century Maharashtra," *Modern Asian Studies* 7, no. 2 (1973): 200–08; Richard Tucker, "Hindu Traditionalism and Nationalist Ideologies in Nineteenth-Century Maharashtra," *Modern Asian Studies* 10, no. 3 (1976): 345–8.

19 See Christophe Jaffrelot, *The Hindu Nationalist Movement in India* (New York: Columbia University Press, 1996); Christophe Jaffrelot, ed., *Hindu Nationalism: A Reader* (Princeton, N.J.: Princeton University Press, 2007).

20 See Apte, "Lokahitavadi and V. K. Chiplunkar," 193–208, for the concept of "traditionalist" to define Chiplunkar's multistranded thought.

21 Vishnushastri Chiplunkar, "Kavyetihas Sangraha," *Kavyetihas Sangraha* no. 49 (December 1880), repr. in Chiplunkar, *Nibandhamala*, vol. 1, 466–8. Carlyle's work percolated throughout Marathi publications, e.g. "Hero-worship," *Kesari*, June 1, 1897, which followed Carlyle's premise but discussed Shivaji as the hero; see Anil Samarth, *Shivaji and the Indian National Movement* (Bombay: Somaiya Publications, 1975), 41.

22 Chiplunkar, *Nibandhamala*, vol. 1, 466; vol. 2, 746–51. *The Mahratta*, August 21, 1882, noted that in a lecture one "Mr. Telang observed that the publication of Marathi Bakhars in the *Kavyetihas Sangraha* had given an impetus to the working of Biographies in the Marathi language," but that students needed guidance and education in the use of original sources.

23 Chiplunkar, "Kavyetihas Sangraha," 466–8. On Chiplunkar's prose see Apte, "Lokahitavadi and V. K. Chiplunkar," 193–208.

24 Chiplunkar, "Kavyetihas Sangraha," 466–8. On the varied interpretations of Shivaji by different strands of nationalists in western India see O'Hanlon, "Maratha History," 1–33.

25 Chiplunkar's nationalist polemic was not lost on the British, who by 1910 under the new India Press Act considered his essay *Amchya Deshachi Stithi* [The state of our country] (1881), seditious and confiscated it as evidence against the Samarth Vidyalaya school's "extremist" nationalist program; see M. R. Palande et al., eds., *Source Material for a History of the Freedom Movements in India (Collected from Bombay Government Records)* (hereafter BHFM), vol. 2 (Mumbai: Government of Maharashtra, 1958), 855–8.

26 See Captain A. Macdonald, *Memoir of the life of the late Nana Furnuwees compiled from family records and extant works* (Bombay: American Mission Press, 1851), pl. 1.

27 Kanitkar, *History of the Chitrashala*, 2.

28 For histories of chromolithography see n. 4 above.

29 Wales's practice was more like a workshop than an art school, as I discuss in Chs. One and Two, but it was perceived as an art school in the late nineteenth century; see D. B. Parasnis, *Poona in Bygone Days* (Bombay: Times Press, 1921), 53; Partha Mitter, *Art and Nationalism in Colonial India: Occidental Orientations* (Cambridge: Cambridge University Press, 1994), 30. The J. J. School of Art traces its lineage to this school with pride; *The Story of the J. J. School of Art, 1857–1957* (Bombay: Government Central Press, ca.1957), 12–13, 24.

30 Justice M. G. Ranade, *Rise of the Maratha Power* (New Delhi: Rakesh Press, 1961), 6–7. Other writers also attended to the legacy of Nana Fadnavis in this period; V. V. Khare, *Nana Phadnavisanche Charitra* [*Nana Fadnavis's Biography*; in Marathi] (1892; repr. Pune: Varda Press, 2012), 79; N. C. Kelkar, *Pleasures and Privileges of the Pen* (Poona: K. N. Kelkar, 1929), 79–89.

31 The historian Jadunath Sarkar, *House of Shivaji* (1940; Hyderabad: Orient Blackswan, e-edition 2012), ch. 24, wrote: "no other Indian race has produced such a galaxy of leaders in war and learning as Maratha history records. Is this the root cause of the fact that no other province of India in the closing sixty years of British rule has produced such constructive patriots of the modern civilized type as Maharashtra?"

32 Ranade, *Rise of the Maratha Power*, 7.

33 Sayajirao Gaekwad III received the Prince of Wales Gold Medal in 1875, the Kaiser-i-Hind Gold Medal in 1877, and the Knight Grand Commander of the Order of the Star of India in 1887.

34 See "His Highness Maharajah Sayaji Rao Gaekwar of Baroda, Nov. 1875," catalogue information, BL. On royal portrait photography in India and royal medals see Rosie Llewellyn-Jones, ed., *Portraits in Princely India, 1700–1947* (Mumbai: Marg, 2008).

35 For another example see "Collage of Queen Victoria with Photographers and Noblemen," ca. 1890s, discussed in Rahaab Allana, *Painted Photographs: Coloured Portraiture in India* (New Delhi: Alkazi Collection of Photography and Mapin, 2008), 9–34.

36 Hardinge of Penshurst et al. to the Marquis of Crewe, Secretary of State for India, November 1911, in Palande, *BHFM*, vol. 2, 579–80.

37 Macdonald, *Memoir*, 154, wrote that the "annexed picture" in his book was from an original "which is an exceedingly well painted picture in oils, preserved with great care at Manowley" (Menavali, near Wai, where Nana Fadnavis's ancestral home is located).

38 The majority of signed works by Shivram Chitari are in the History Museum at Dr. Babasaheb Ambedkar Marathwada University, Aurangabad; see Ch. One above; S. B. Deshmukh,

Maratha Painting (Aurangabad: Marathwada University, 1992), 45–52.

39 For the British-commissioned replica, see CSMVS, 27.6, discussed in their catalogue of paintings. Other 1854 paintings from Satara seem to be copies of paintings that Parasnis collected from Satara and Sangli, such as this one, which are now in the History Museum, Aurangabad; see T. V. Pathy, "Dattatreya Parasnis and His Collection," in *Marg: The Art of Chhatrapatis and Peshwas*, ed. Saryu Doshi, 34, no. 2 (1981): 91–2.

40 Hermann Goetz, *The Art of the Marathas and its Problems*, Baroda State Museum Pamphlets (Baroda: Sadhana Press, 1946), 2. Rabindranath Tagore and Jawaharlal Nehru also considered cosmopolitanism "a strategy of anti-colonial nationalism"; see Antoinette Burton, *The Postcolonial Careers of Santha Rama Rau* (Durham, N.C.: Duke University Press, 2007), 36, cited in Sonal Khullar, *Worldly Affiliations: Artistic Practice, National Identity, and Modernism in India, 1930–1990* (Berkeley: University of California Press, 2015), 25.

41 See Homi K. Bhabha, "Of Mimicry and Man: The Ambivalence of Colonial Discourse," in *Location of Culture* (London: Routledge, 1994), 121–31. In relation to the early modern period, Wolfram Schmidgen, *Exquisite Mixture: The Virtues of Impurity in Early Modern England* (Philadelphia: University of Pennsylvania Press, 2013), 1–23, has identified such an "exquisite mixture" as rendering the British nation possible.

42 S. G. Jinsiwale quoted in Narayan H. Kulkarnee, ed., *Chhatrapati Shivaji: Architect of Freedom* (Delhi: Chhatrapati Shivaji Smarak Samiti, 1975), Appendix I, 238.

43 See *Krishna Steals the Gopis' Clothes*, mid-19th century, hand colored woodblock print, collection of Anandita Ghosh. On Kalighat paintings, Battala prints, and the relationship between art and nationalism in Bengal see Tapati Guha-Thakurta, *The Making of a New "Indian" Art: Artists, Aesthetics and Nationalism in Bengal, c. 1850–1920* (Cambridge: Cambridge University Press, 1992), ch. 1.

44 *Shilpa Pushpanjali* was founded in 1886, and according to Guha-Thakurta, ibid., 154, "set out with the intention of placing before readers the artistic achievements of their forefathers" to inspire a present-day revitalization of artistic practice. Yet the art discussed was primarily associated with technical and vocational skills and matters of "correct" instruction.

45 Partha Mitter, "Mechanical Reproduction and the World of the Colonial Artist," *Contributions to Indian Sociology* 36, nos. 1–2 (February 2002): 17.

46 Guha-Thakurta, *Making of a New "Indian" Art*, 92–6.

47 Raoji Shridhar Gondhalakar suggested turning to deities and the artist Balkrishnapant Joshi approved; Kanitkar, *History of the Chitrashala*, 2.

48 Ibid., 2; *Ram Panchayatan* was painted by Bhiva Sutar.

49 Edward Moor, *The Hindu Pantheon* (London: J. Johnson, 1810), pls. 11, 57.

50 Mitter, *Art and Nationalism*, 34–5.

51 Christopher Pinney, "Iatrogenic Religion and Politics," in *Censorship in South Asia: Cultural Regulation from Sedition to Seduction*, ed. R. Kaur and W. Mazzarella (Bloomington: Indiana University Press, 2009), 34; see also Pinney, *Photos of the Gods*, 56–7.

52 *Official Report of the Calcutta International Exhibition, 1883–1884*, 2 vols. (Calcutta: Bengal Secretariat Press, 1885), vol. 2, 97.

53 Y. D. Phadke, *V. K. Chiploonkar* (New Delhi: National Book Trust, 1982), 66.

54 According to V. K. Rajwade, "Shivaji's Image (*Pratima*) from Malvan," in D. B. Parasnis, *Itihas Sangraha Aitihasik Safur Lekh* [Collection of history: expanded historical writings; in Marathi], vol. 1 (1908), 2, "Chiplunkar printed the first historical picture [of Shivaji] in the *Chitrashala*." It looked "exactly similar" to the Shivaji that illustrated Robert Orme's *Historical Fragments* published in 1805, which had in turn been reproduced in e.g. Macdonald's *Memoir* (1851). This is perhaps the image that Tilak used while rallying the population of Poona for the Shivaji memorial fund in December 1895. On Tilak see Richard I. Cashman, *The Myth of the Lokamanya: Tilak and Mass Politics in Maharashtra* (Berkeley: University of California Press, 1975).

55 Police notice, November 6, 1906, Bombay Presidency Police Abstract of Intelligence, repr. in Palande, *BHFM*, 614.

56 Extract from the Special Bench Judgment, Secret Abstract, 1911, C.I.D., Bombay, 153–82, repr. in Palande, *BHFM*, 395–6.

57 *The Times*, May 25, 1910, repr. in Palande, *BHFM*, 444–5. According to Sir James Mackintosh, quoted in Parasnis, *Poona in Bygone Days*, 66–7, James Wales's painting of Mahadji Scindia was venerated as an icon after his death in Scindia's Chhattri in Poona in 1805; see Ch. Two above.

58 British edict reported in *Kesari*, August 29, 1916, quoted in Cashman, *Myth of the Lokamanya*, 88.

59 On nationalist prints see Richard H. Davis, *Lives of Indian Images* (Princeton, N.J.: Princeton University Press, 1997); Pinney, *Photos of the Gods*; Jain, *Gods in the Bazaar*; Kama Maclean, *A Revolutionary History of Interwar India: Violence, Image, Voice and Text* (Oxford: Oxford University Press, 2015). In "Shivaji's Portrait," in *How Secular Is Art?* ed. Tapati Guha-Thakurta and Vazira Zamindar (Cambridge: Cambridge University Press, expected 2022), I discuss the portrait of Shivaji Maharaj, which came to define the western Indian nationalist movement.

60 Anderson, *Imagined Communities*.

61 See Guha, *History and Collective Memory*, 142–7; and M. R. Kantak, ed., *Rajwade and His Thoughts* (Pune: Bharat Itihas Sanshodhak Mandal, 1990).

62 Rajwade used Ranke's method of source-based history, but he promoted the use of Indigenous languages, such as Marathi, for historical writing in comparison to English; see Dipesh Chakrabarty, *The Calling of History: Sir Jadunath Sarkar and His Empire of Truth* (Chicago: University of Chicago Press, 2015), 59, 63, 135–6.

63 Paul Blackledge, *Reflections on a Marxist Theory of History* (Manchester: Manchester University Press, 2006), 23–4.

64 See e.g. V. K. Bhave, *Peshwekalin Maharashtra* [Maharashtra in the Peshwa era; in Marathi] (1935; Pune: Bharat Itihas Sanshodhak Mandal, 1975), on the Peshwa era.

65 Blackledge, *Reflections on a Marxist Theory*, 23–4.

66 Kanitkar, *History of the Chitrashala*, 1.

67 While similar in concept to the Mandal, the Bhandarkar Oriental Research Institute (BORI) differed in its colonial roots; in 1866, the Government of Bombay instituted a program to collect manuscripts from across India, which was administered by Elphinstone College in Bombay before being transferred to Deccan College in Poona, and then BORI after it was founded in 1917.

68 Chakrabarty, *Calling of History*, 162–3; 115–26. Sarkar had other criticisms of the Mandal historians: while he often used similar methods, Sarkar lamented their secret ways of acquiring documents from families, and the limited access to such materials that they gave to scholars outside of their scholarly BISM/Mandal community.

69 The question of history is at the center of Marx's critique of Ranke, as discussed in Blackledge, *Reflections on a Marxist Theory*, 23–4, as well as in India; see Chakrabarty, *Calling of History*; Deshpande, *Creative Pasts*; Mantena, *Origins of Modern Historiography*. In general see Daniel Little, "Philosophy of History," in *Stanford Encyclopedia of Philosophy* (Summer 2017), ed. Edward N. Zalta, https://plato.stanford.edu/archives/sum2017/entries/history/ (accessed April 17, 2020).

70 Walter Benjamin, "Theses on the Philosophy of History," in *Illuminations*, trans. Harry Zohn (New York: Harcourt, 1968), 263. Anderson, *Imagined Communities*, 24–6, drew on Benjamin's theses in his theory of nationalism; he understood messianic time as "a simultaneity of past and future in an instantaneous present" that intersected with "homogenous, empty time" marked by clock and calendar, by newspaper and novel, which allowed for the "nation" to be imagined through faith in "steady, anonymous, simultaneous activity."

71 Partha Chatterjee, *The Nation and Its Fragments* (Princeton, N.J.: Princeton University Press, 1994), 6. Postcolonial theorists have proposed intimacy, as well as care and repair, as antidotes to colonial logic; see Hazel Carby, *Imperial Intimacies: A Tale of Two Islands* (New York: Penguin Random House, 2019); Leela Gandhi, *Postcolonial Theory: A Critical Introduction* (New York: Columbia University Press, 2019), 177–213.

72 On Bengal see Chatterjee, *Nation and Its Fragments*, 6; on western and central India, and the relationship between intimacy and Hindu nationalism, known as Hindutva, see Vinayak Chaturvedi, "Vinayak & Me: 'Hindutva' and the Politics of Naming," *Social History* 28, no. 2 (May 2003): 155–73.

73 Scholars have long questioned the status of archival information, and in colonial contexts, the lives of the colonized or enslaved people who are left out of records or exist sparingly, hauntingly, in a reference or two. On the former see Michel Foucault, *The Order of Things: An Archaeology of Human Knowledge* (New York: Pantheon Books, 1970); Jacques Derrida, *Archive Fever: A Freudian Impression* (Chicago: University of Chicago Press, 1996); Carolyn Steedman, *Dust: The Archive and Cultural History* (Manchester: Manchester University Press, 2001); on the latter see Guha, *History and Collective Memory*; and Ann Laura Stoler, *Along the Archival Grain: Epistemic Anxiety and Colonial Common Sense* (Princeton, N.J.: Princeton University Press, 2009); on methods to confront absences see Saidiya Hartman, "Venus in Two Acts," *Small Axe* 26, no. 12.2 (June 2008): 1–14, particularly the concept of "critical fabulation."

74 In the first few months of 1795, Gangaram traveled with Wales to Ellora. On their return journey in March, Wales noted that he saw 'Baby maal' or Bibi Mahal through his "spy glass" in the environs of Ahmednagar. This is one of the possible times that Gangaram could have drawn Faria Bagh; James Wales, Indian Antiquities (journal), 69–72, James Wales Archive.

75 Ibid., 50.

76 The literature on the construction of contemporary images and their political and entertainment potential is vast; in brief see the MIT Press Essential Knowledge Series such as Limor Shifman, *Memes in Digital Culture* (2013), Michael Buckland, *Information and Society* (2017); Lee McIntyre, *Post-Truth* (2018). I have considered the relationship between contemporary and early twentieth-century western Indian art and nationalism in "The Indian Evidence Act: Contemporary Art and Nationalism," *Third Text* 30, nos. 5–6 (2017): 437–55.

Bibliography

ARCHIVES AND MANUSCRIPTS

Beinecke Rare Book and Manuscript Library, Yale University
Boswell Collection, GEN MSS 89
Bhandarkar Oriental Research Institute, Pune
Manuscript and Paintings Collection
Bharat Itihas Sanshodhak Mandal, Pune
Manuscript and Paintings Collection
Bibliothèque Nationale de France, Paris
Dieux des Indiens [Gods of India], 1688–1725, OD 38
Figures et Divinités de l'Inde [Figures and divinities of India], 1720–30, OD 40
British Library, London
Malet Collection, MSS Eur F149; Add. Or. 4145; Add. Or. 4364; Add. 33979, ff. 235–6; MSS Eur K154 1795; Or. 1621
British Museum, London
Moses Haughton drawings for *The Hindu Pantheon*, 1805–10, 1940,0713,0.251
Edward Moor Collection, 1940,0713,0.1–.250; 1940,0716.1–.361
Edward Moor, proof of *The Hindu Pantheon*, 1810, 1940,0713,0.252
——, Catalogue of the Oriental Cabinet of Major Moor, F.R.S., 1940,0713,0.254
Chhatrapati Shivaji Maharaj Vastu Sangrahalaya, Mumbai
P. V. Mawjee Collection
D. B. Parasnis Collection
Fitzwilliam Museum, Cambridge
John Flaxman Sketchbook, 832/3
History Museum, Dr. Babasaheb Ambedkar Marathwada University, Aurangabad
Paintings Collection
Huntington Library, Art Collections, and Botanical Gardens, San Marino, California
William Blake, *A Descriptive Catalogue of Pictures, Poetical and Historical Inventions*. London: J. Blake, 1809. Copy D, http://www.blakearchive.org
Ipswich Museum
Reverend Edward J. Moor Collection
Sir J. J. College of Architecture, University of Mumbai
Wadas of Maharashtra Archive
Raja Dinkar Kelkar Museum, Pune
Paintings Collection
Mansingh Kumthekar Collection, Miraj
Edward J. Moor Collection
Albums of Major Edward Moor's letters, paintings, and other materials
National Library of Scotland, Edinburgh
Walker of Bowlands Papers, MS 13816, MS 13903
Royal Asiatic Society of Great Britain and Ireland, London
William Jones Collection
Alexander Malet Collection
Maharaja Sawai Man Singh II Museum, City Palace, Jaipur
Maji Shri Rathor Collection
Smithsonian Institution, Washington, D.C.
Freer Gallery of Art and Arthur M. Sackler Archives, Robert J. Del Bontà Collection
Tate, London
William Blake Collection, N01110, N03006
University College London
Art Museum, Flaxman Gallery and Collection
Victoria and Albert Museum, London
South Asian Department, Photographic Archives
Charles Wilkins Collection
Yale Center for British Art, New Haven, Connecticut
William Blake, *Jerusalem*, 1804–20, Bentley Copy E, B1992.8.1
James Forbes Archive, MSS 66
James Wales Archive, MSS 26

COMPILATIONS OF HISTORICAL DOCUMENTS

Kavyetihas Sangraha [Collection of poetry and history; in Marathi; monthly journal]. Ed. Kashinath N. Sane and J. B. Modak. Poona: Shivaji Printing House, 1878–89

Palande, M. R., et al., eds. *Source Material for a History of the Freedom Movements in India (Collected from Bombay Government Records)*. Vol. 2. Mumbai: Government of Maharashtra, 1958

Parasnis, D. B. *Itihas Sangraha* [Collection of history; in Marathi]. Poona, 1907–16

Poona Akhbars. 3 vols. Hyderabad: Central Records Office, Government of Andhra Pradesh, 1956

Sardesai, G. S. *Poona Affairs, 1786–1797 (Malet's Embassy): English Records of Maratha History. Poona Residency Correspondence*, vol. 2. Bombay: Government Central Press, 1936

——, ed. *Selections from the Peshwa Daftar* [in Marathi]. 46 vols. Bombay: Government Central Press, 1930–34

Sarkar, Sir Jadunath. *Sindhia Regent of Delhi (Persian Records of Maratha History)*. Bombay: Director of Archives, 1954

Vad, Ganesh C., et al., eds. *Selections from the Satara Rajas' and the Peshwas' Diaries* [in Marathi], 9 vols. Poona: Deccan Vernacular Translation Society, 1902–11

PUBLISHED SOURCES

Abbott, Justin E., trans. *Stotramala: A Garland of Hindu Prayers*. Poona: Scottish Mission Industries, 1929

Adams, Hazard. *Blake's Margins*. Jefferson, N.C.: McFarland, 2009

Aitken, Molly Emma. *The Intelligence of Tradition in Rajput Court Painting*. New Haven and London: Yale University Press, 2010

——. "Colonial-Period Court Painting and the Case of Bikaner." *Archives of Asian Art* 67, no. 1 (April 2017): 25–59
——. "Pardah and Portrayal: Rajput Women as Subjects, Patrons, and Collectors." *Artibus Asiae* 62, no. 2 (2002): 247–80
——, ed. *A Magical World: New Visions of Indian Painting*. Mumbai: Marg, 2017
Allan, Alexander. *Views in the Mysore Country*. London: Allan, 1794
Allana, Rahaab. *Painted Photographs: Coloured Portraiture in India*. New Delhi: Alkazi Collection of Photography and Mapin, 2008
Almeida, Hermione de, and George H. Gilpin. *Indian Renaissance: British Romantic Art and the Prospect of India*. 2005; London and New York: Routledge, 2016
Almond, Philip. *The British Discovery of Buddhism*. Cambridge: Cambridge University Press, 1988
Alter, Joseph S. *The Wrestler's Body: Identity and Ideology in North India*. Berkeley: University of California Press, 1992
Anderson, Benedict. *Imagined Communities: Reflections on the Origin and Spread of Nationalism*. London: Verso, 2006
App, Urs. *The Birth of Orientalism*. Philadelphia: University of Pennsylvania Press, 2010
——. "William Jones's Ancient Theology." *Sino-Platonic Papers* 191 (July 2009): 1–125
Apte, B. K. *Maratha Wall Paintings (Wai, Menavali, Satara, Pune)*. Bombay: Government Central Press, 1988
Apte, Mahadev L. "Lokahitavadi and V. K. Chiplunkar: Spokesmen of Change in Nineteenth-Century Maharashtra." *Modern Asian Studies* 7, no. 2 (1973): 193–208
Archer, Mildred. *Company Paintings: Indian Paintings of the British Period*. London: Victoria and Albert Museum, 1992
——. "James Wales: Portrait Painter in Bombay and Poona, 1791–95." *Journal of the Indian Society of Oriental Art* no. 8 (1977): 57–64
——. "Works by William Alexander and James Wales." In *The Royal Asiatic Society: Its History and Treasures*. Ed. Stuart Simmonds and Simon Digby. Leiden: Brill, 1979, 119–25
Ardeshar, A. C. "Mughal Miniature Painting (with Illustrations from the Collection of Mr. A. C. Ardeshar of Bombay)." *Roopa-Lekha* 1, no. 2 (1940): 19–34
Aryan, K. C. *Indian Folk Bronzes*. New Delhi: Rekha Prakshan, 1991
Asher, Catherine. "Jaipur: City of Tolerance and Progress." *South Asia: Journal of South Asian Studies* 37, no. 3 (2014): 410–30
Asher, Frederick M. "Indian Image / Image in India." In *What Is an Image?* Ed. James Elkins. State College: Pennsylvania State University Press, 2011, 109–13
Avcioğlu, Nebahat, and Finbarr Barry Flood. "Introduction: Globalizing Cultures: Art and Mobility in the Eighteenth Century." *Ars Orientalis* 39 (2010): 7–38
Bahura, Gopal Narayan. *Literary Heritage of the Rulers of Amber and Jaipur: With an Index to the Register of Manuscripts in the Pothikhana of Jaipur (I. Khasmohor Collection)*. Jaipur: Maharaja Sawai Man Singh II Museum, 1976
Bailey, Gauvin. "The Indian Conquest of Catholic Art: The Mughals, the Jesuits, and Imperial Mural Painting." *Art Journal* 57, no. 1 (Spring 1998): 24–30
Bann, Stephen. "Antiquarianism, Visuality, and the Exotic Monument." In *Traces of India: Photography, Architecture, and the Politics of Representation, 1850–1900*. Ed. Maria Antonella Pelizzari. New Haven and London: Yale University Press, 2003, 60–85
Barlow, Paul. "The Imagined Hero as Incarnate Sign: Thomas Carlyle and the Mythology of the 'National Portrait' in Victorian Britain." *Art History* 17, no. 4 (December 1994): 517–45
Barrell, John. *The Political Theory of Painting from Reynolds to Hazlitt*. New Haven and London: Yale University Press, 1986
Barringer, Timothy. *Men at Work: Art and Labour in Victorian Britain*. New Haven and London: Yale University Press, 2005
——, Geoff Quilley, and Douglas Fordham, eds. *Art and the British Empire*. Manchester: Manchester University Press, 2007
——, Gillian Forrester, and Barbaro Martinez Ruiz, eds. *Art and Emancipation in Jamaica*. New Haven and London: Yale University Press, 2007
Barry, D. T. *Travelling Game of India: Amusing & Instructive*. Liverpool: Arthur Newling, 1858
Bayly, C. A. *Empire and Information: Intelligence Gathering and Social Communication in India*. Cambridge: Cambridge University Press, 1996
——. *Imperial Meridian: The British Empire and the World, 1780–1830*. London: Longman, 1989
——, ed. *The Raj: India and the British, 1600–1947*. London: National Portrait Gallery, 1990
Beach, Milo, B. N. Goswamy, and Eberhard Fischer, eds. *Masters of Indian Painting*. Seattle: University of Washington Press, 2011
Bell, John. *Bell's New Pantheon, or, Historical dictionary of the gods, demi-gods, heroes and fabulous personages of antiquity*.... London: J. Bell, 1790
Belli, Melia. "Keeping Up with the Rajputs: Appropriation and the Articulation of Sacrality and Political Legitimacy in Scindia Funerary Art." *Archives of Asian Art* 61 (2011): 91–106
Benjamin, Walter. "Theses on the Philosophy of History." In *Illuminations*. Trans. Harry Zohn. New York: Harcourt, 1968, 253–64
Bentley, G. E., Jr. *William Blake in the Desolate Market*. Montreal: McGill-Queens University Press, 2016
Bernier, François. *Travels in the Mogul Empire*. Oxford: Oxford University Press, 1916
Bhabha, Homi K. *The Location of Culture*. London: Routledge, 1994
The Bhagvat-Geeta, or Dialogues of Krishna and Arjoon, translated from the original, in the Sanskreet, or ancient language of the Brahmans. Trans. Charles Wilkins. London: C. Nourse, 1785
Bhave, V. K. *Peshwekalin Maharashtra* [Maharashtra in the Peshwa era; in Marathi]. 1935; repr., Pune: Bharat Itihas Sanshodhak Mandal, 1975
Biedermann, Zoltán. *(Dis)connected Empires: Imperial Portugal, Sri Lankan Diplomacy, and the Making of a Hapsburg Conquest in Asia*. Oxford: Oxford University Press, 2018
Biel, Justin. "Divide and Tolerate: Imperial Secularisms in Ireland, India, and Britain, 1774–1815." Ph.D. diss., University of Minnesota, 2014
Bignamini, Ilaria, and Clare Hornsby. *Digging and Dealing in Eighteenth-Century Rome*. New Haven and London: Yale University Press, 2010
Bindman, David. *Ape to Apollo: Aesthetics and the Idea of Race in the 18th Century*. Ithaca, N.Y.: Cornell University Press, 2002

——. *William Blake: His Art and Times*. London: Thames & Hudson, 1982
——. "William Blake and Popular Religious Imagery." *Burlington Magazine* 128 (1986): 712–18
Birdwood, George C. *Industrial Arts of India*. London: Chapman and Hall, 1880
Blackledge, Paul. *Reflections on a Marxist Theory of History*. Manchester: Manchester University Press, 2006
Blackwell, Thomas. *Letters Concerning Mythology*. London, 1748
Blake, William. *Jerusalem: The Emanation of the Giant Albion* (1804–ca. 1820). Ed. Morton D. Paley. Princeton, N.J.: Princeton University Press, 1991
Bloch, Esther, Marianne Keppens, and Rajaram Hegde. *Rethinking Religion in India: The Colonial Construction of Hinduism*. London: Routledge, 2010
Blunt, Anthony. "Blake's Pictorial Imagination." *Journal of the Warburg and Courtauld Institutes* 6 (1943): 190–212
Bogan, James. "Blake's Jupiter Olympius in Rees's *Cyclopaedia*." *Blake/An Illustrated Quarterly* 15, no. 4 (Spring 1982): 156–63
Bolus-Reichert, Christine. *The Age of Eclecticism: Literature and Culture in Britain, 1815–1885*. Columbus: Ohio State University Press, 2009
Books for the Children of India: A Paper for the Juvenile Friends of the Christian Vernacular Education Society for India. London: W. M. Watts, 1865
Boyé, Jérôme. *L'Extraordinaire aventure de Benoît de Boigne aux Indes*. Paris: C & D, 1996
Branfoot, Crispin. "Iconography and Images: Art." In *Brill's Encyclopedia of Hinduism*, vol. 2: *Texts, Rituals, Arts, Concepts*. Ed. Knut A. Jacobsen. Leiden: Brill, 2010, 536–50
——. "Tirumala Nayaka's 'New Hall' and the European Study of the South Indian Temple." *Journal of the Royal Asiatic Society*, 3rd s., 11, no. 2 (July 2001): 191–217
——. "Royal Portrait Sculpture in the South Indian Temple." *South Asian Studies* 16, no. 1 (2000): 11–36
Brewer, John. *The Sinews of Power: War, Money, and the English State*. Cambridge, Mass.: Harvard University Press, 1990
Briggs, John. "An Autobiographical Memoir of the Early Life of Nana Farnevís." *Transactions of the Royal Asiatic Society of Great Britain and Ireland* 2, no. 1 (1829): 95–108
The British in India, exh. cat. Brighton Museum and Art Gallery, May 9–August 31, 1973
Bryant, G. J. "Indigenous Mercenaries in the Service of European Imperialists: The Case of the Sepoys in the Early British Indian Army, 1750–1800." *War in History* 7, no. 1 (January 2000): 2–28
Bryant, Jacob. *A New System or Analysis of Ancient Mythology*. London: P. Elmsly, 1773
Buddle, Anne. *Tigers around the Throne: The Court of Tipu Sultan (1750–99)*. London: Zamana Gallery, 1990
——. "The Tipu-Mania: Narrative Sketches of the Conquest of Mysore." *Marg* 40, no. 4 (September 1987): 53–70
Bugg, John, ed. *The Joseph Johnson Letter Book*. Oxford: Oxford University Press, 2016
Burke, Edmund. *A Philosophical Inquiry into the origins of our ideas of the sublime and beautiful*. London: R. and J. Dodsley, 1757
Burke, Joseph. "The Eidetic and the Borrowed Image: An Interpretation of Blake's Theory and Practice of Art." In *In Honour of Daryl Lindsay: Essays and Studies*. Ed. Franz Philipp and June Stewart. Melbourne: Oxford University Press, 1964, 110–27
Burton, Antoinette. *The Postcolonial Careers of Santha Rama Rau*. Durham, N.C.: Duke University Press, 2007
Carby, Hazel. *Imperial Intimacies: A Tale of Two Islands*. New York: Penguin Random House, 2019
Carlyle, Thomas. *On Heroes, Hero-Worship, and the Heroic in History*. London: James Fraser, 1841
Carson, Penelope. *The East India Company and Religion, 1698–1858*. Woodbridge: Boydell Press, 2012
Cashman, Richard I. *The Myth of the Lokamanya: Tilak and Mass Politics in Maharashtra*. Berkeley: University of California Press, 1975
Casid, Jill H. *Sowing Empire: Landscape and Colonization*. Minneapolis and London: University of Minnesota Press, 2005
Catalogue of Important Oriental Miniatures and a Mughal Manuscript: The Property of a Gentleman. Sotheby's, New York, July 10, 1973
A Catalogue of Purshotam Vishram Mawjee Museum. Bombay, n.d.
Caw, J. L. "Wales, James (1747–1795)." Rev. Douglas Fordham. ODNB, 2004
Chadwick, Esther. "The Radical Print: British Art and Graphic Experiment in the Paper Age." Ph.D. diss., Yale University, 2016
Chakrabarti, Dilip K. *The Ancient Routes of the Deccan and Southern Peninsula*. New Delhi: Aryan Books International, 2010
Chakrabarty, Dipesh. *The Calling of History: Sir Jadunath Sarkar and His Empire of Truth*. Chicago: University of Chicago Press, 2015
Chancey, Karen. "The Star in the East: The Controversy over Christian Missions to India, 1805–1813." *The Historian* 60, no. 3 (Spring 1998): 507–22
Chandra, Pramod. "Ustad Salivahana and the Development of Popular Mughal Art." *Lalit Kala* 8 (1960): 25–46
Chatterjee, Partha. *The Nation and Its Fragments*. Princeton, N.J.: Princeton University Press, 1994
Chaturvedi, Vinayak. "Vinayak & Me: 'Hindutva' and the Politics of Naming." *Social History* 28, no. 2 (May 2003): 155–73
Chavan, Kamal. *Maratha Murals: Late Medieval Painting of the Deccan, 1650–1850 A.D.* Delhi: B. R. Publishing, 1983
——. "Chandwad Wall Paintings." *Traimasik* 18, issue 55, nos. 1–4 [in Marathi] (Pune: Bharat Itihas Sanshodhak Mandal, December 1976): 9–11
Chiplunkar, Vishnushastri. *Nibandhamala* [A Garland of Essays; in Marathi] (1874–81). 2 vols. Pune: Varada Books, 1993
Colebrooke, Henry Thomas. "On the Vedas." *Asiatic Researches* 8 (printed verbatim from the Calcutta edition, London: Vernor, Hood and Sharpe, 1808): 377–497
Colebrooke, Robert. *Twelve Views of Places in the Kingdom of Mysore, Country of Tippoo Sultan, from drawings taken on the spot*. London: Thomson, 1793
Cooke, Edward S. *Inventing Boston: Design, Production, and Consumption 1680–1720*. London and New Haven: Paul Mellon Centre with Yale University Press, 2019
——. "Utensils." In *Britain and the World: Treasures from the Yale Center for British Art*. Ed. Martina Droth et al.. New Haven and London: Yale University Press, 2019, 140–43

Cooper, Randolf G. S. *The Anglo-Maratha Campaigns and the Contest for India*. Cambridge: Cambridge University Press, 2005

Copland, Ian, Ian Mabbett, Asim Roy, Kate Brittlebank, and Adam Bowles. *A History of State and Religion in India*. London: Routledge, 2012

Cowan, Brian. "Arenas of Connoisseurship: Auctioning Art in Late Stuart England." In *Art Markets in Europe: 1400–1800*. Ed. Michael North and David Ormrod. Aldershot and Burlington, Vt.: Ashgate, 1998, 153–86

Crill, Rosemary, and Kapil Jariwala. *The Indian Portrait, 1560–1860*. Ahmedabad: Mapin, 2010

Cumberland, George. *Thoughts on Outline, Sculpture, and the System that Guided the Ancient Artists in Composing their Figures and Groupes* .... London, 1796

Curry, Kenneth, ed. *New Letters of Robert Southey*. 2 vols. New York: Columbia University Press, 1965

Dadlani, Chanchal. *From Stone to Paper: Architecture as History in Eighteenth-Century Mughal India*. New Haven and London: Yale University Press, 2019

——. "Transporting India: The Gentil Album and Mughal Manuscript Culture." *Art History* 38, no. 4 (September 2015): 748–76

Dallapiccola, A. L. *South Indian Paintings*. Ahmedabad: Mapin, 2010

Dalrymple, William. *The Anarchy*. London: Bloomsbury, 2019

——. *White Mughals*. London: Harper Perennial; New York: Penguin, 2004

——, ed. *Forgotten Masters: Indian Painting for the East India Company*. London: Wallace Collection, 2019

——, and Yuthika Sharma. *Princes and Painters in Mughal Delhi, 1707–1857*. New York: Asia Society Museum, 2012

Dani, Manoj. *Battle of Panipat: In Light of Recently Discovered Paintings*. Pune: Monkey Hill Publications, 2021

Daniell, Thomas. *Antiquities of India*. London: T. Daniell, 1803

——. *Oriental Scenery*, 6 vols. London: T. Daniell, 1795–1808

——. *Oriental Scenery*, 6 parts in 2 vols. London: T. Daniell, 1812–16

Darwin, John. *Unfinished Empire: The Global Expansion of Britain*. New York: Bloomsbury, 2013

Das, Ram. *Shri Samarth Granth Bhandar* [in Marathi]. Ed. L. R. Pangarkar. Bombay: Popular Prakashan, 1999

Davis, Richard H. *The Bhagavad Gita: A Biography*. Princeton, N.J.: Princeton University Press, 2015

——. *Lives of Indian Images*. Princeton, N.J.: Princeton University Press, 1997

——. "Three Styles in Looting India." *History and Anthropology* 6 (1994): 293–317

Dean, Carolyn, and Dana Leibsohn. "Hybridity and its Discontents: Considering Visual Culture in Colonial Spanish America." *Colonial Latin American Review* 12, no. 1 (2003): 5–35

Dehejia, Vidya. *Devi: The Great Goddess*. Washington, D.C.: Arthur M. Sackler Gallery and Mapin Publishing, 1999

——. "The Very Idea of a Portrait." *Ars Orientalis* 28 (1998): 40–50

——, with Pratapaditya Pal. *From Merchants to Emperors: British Artists and India*. Ithaca, N.Y.: Cornell University Press, 1986

Dejenne, Nicolas. "Telling the History of the Sacred Ramakshetra in the Vadeshvaradayakavya." In *Time, History and the Religious Imaginary in South Asia*. Ed. Anne Murphy. London: Routledge, 2011, 110–15

Del Bontà, Robert J. "Engraving India in 17th- and 18th-Century Europe." *Art in Print* 4, no. 4 (November–December 2014): 20–25

——. "Reinventing Nature: Mughal Composite Animal Painting." In *Flora and Fauna in Mughal Art*. Ed. Som Prakash Verma. Mumbai: Marg Publishing, 1999, 69–82

Deloche, Jean. *Transport and Communications in India Prior to Steam Locomotion*, vol. 1. Trans. James Walker. Delhi: Oxford University Press, 1993

Derrida, Jacques. *Archive Fever: A Freudian Impression*. Trans. Eric Prenowitz. Chicago: University of Chicago Press, 1996

Desai, Kalpana. *Jewels of the Crescent: Masterpieces of Chhatrapati Shivaji Maharaj Vastu Sangrahalaya formerly Prince of Wales Museum of Western India*. Ahmedabad: Chhatrapati Shivaji Maharaj Vastu Sangrahalaya with Mapin, 2002

Desai, Madhuri. *Banaras Reconstructed: Architecture and Sacred Space in a Hindu Holy City*. Seattle: University of Washington Press, 2017

Desai, Vishakha. "Reflections of the Past in the Present: Copying Processes in Indian Painting." In *Perceptions of South Asia's Visual Past*. Ed. Catherine B. Asher and Thomas R. Metcalf. New Delhi: American Institute of Indian Studies, 1994

Deshmukh, S. B. *Maratha Painting*. Aurangabad: Marathwada University, 1992

Deshpande, M. N. "Some Aspects of Folk Religion in the Konkan and Desh Regions of Maharashtra." In *Maharashtra: Culture and Society*. Ed. Günther-Dietz Sontheimer. New Delhi: Manohar, 1995, 165–80

Deshpande, P. N. "Maratha Forts and Siege Tactics." *Marg* 34, no. 2 (March 1981): 15–40

Deshpande, Prachi. *Creative Pasts: Historical Memory and Identity in Western India, 1700–1960*. New Delhi: Permanent Black, 2007

Deshpande, S. R. *Wai: Kala ani Sanskruti (Wai: art and culture)*. Wai: Paryavaran Maithri Sanstha, 2011

Dhere, R. C. *The Rise of a Folk God: Vitthal of Pandharpur*. Trans. Anne Feldhaus. Oxford and New York: Oxford University Press, 2011

Diamond, Debra, ed. *Garden and Cosmos: The Royal Paintings of Jodhpur*. London: Thames & Hudson, 2008

——, ed. *Yoga: The Art of Transformation*. Washington, D.C.: Arthur M. Sackler Gallery, 2013

Dias, Rosie. "Memory and the Aesthetics of Military Experience: Viewing the Landscape of the Anglo-Mysore Wars." *Tate Papers* 19 (Spring 2013): https://www.tate.org.uk/research/publications/tate-papers/19

Diderot, Denis, et al. *Encyclopédie, ou dictionnaire raisonné des sciences, des arts et des métiers*. 28 vols. Paris: André le Breton et al., 1751–72

Dikshit, M. G. "Early Life of Peshwa Savai Madhavrao." *Bulletin of the Deccan College Research Institute* (Poona; December 1946): 225–48

Dirks, Nicholas. *Castes of Mind: Colonialism and the Making of Modern India*. Princeton, N.J.: Princeton University Press, 2001

Dirom, Alexander. *A Narrative of the Campaign which terminated the war with Tippoo Sultan in 1792*. London: printed by W. Bulmar, 1793

Divekar, V. D. *Sir Charles Warre Malet's Bequests at Chargot, England*. Published by the Indian Archives in Jan. / June 1976

Doshi, Saryu, ed. *The Art of Chhatrapatis and Peshwas*. *Marg* 34, no. 2 (March 1981)

——. *Maharashtra: Traditions in Art*. *Marg* 36, no. 4 (September 1983)

Droth, Martina, Michael Hatt, and Nathan Flis, eds. *Britain in the World: Treasures from the Yale Center for British Art*. New Haven and London: Yale University Press, 2019

Duff, James Grant. *The History of the Mahrattas*. 3 vols. London: Longman, 1826

East India Military Calendar, containing the services of General and Field Officers of the Indian Army. Vol. 1. London, 1823

Eastaugh, Nicholas, et al. *The Pigment Compendium*. Oxford: Elsevier, 2004

Eaton, Natasha. *Colour, Art and Empire: Visual Culture and the Nomadism of Representation*. London: I.B. Tauris, 2013

——. *Mimesis across Empires: Artworks and Networks in India, 1765–1860*. Durham, N.C.: Duke University Press, 2013

——. "Between Mimesis and Alterity: Art, Gift, and Diplomacy in Colonial India, 1770–1800." *Society for Comparative Study of Society and History* 46, no. 4 (October 2004): 816–44

——. "Colonial Iconoclash: Mimetic Rivalry, Collecting and Idolatry Between India and Britain." In Savoy, Guichard, and Howald, *Acquiring Cultures*, 31–46

Edwards, Jason. "John Charles Felix Rossi's Cornwallis Monument (1807–11) and the Colonial-Cosmopolitanism of the British School." In *The British School of Sculpture, ca. 1760–1832*. Ed. Jason Edwards and Sarah Burnage. London: Routledge, 2016, 188–209

Ehrlich, Joshua. "Plunder and Prestige: Tipu Sultan's Library and the Making of British India." *South Asia: Journal of South Asian Studies* (2020): 478–92

Emery, F. W. *Hindoo Mythology: Popularly Treated: being an epitomized description of the various heathen deities illustrated on the silver swami tea service, presented as a memento of his visit to India to H. R. H. The Prince of Wales, K. G., G. C. S. I., by his Highness the Gaekwar of Baroda*. Madras: Printed by Gantz Brothers, 1875

Erle, Sibylle. *Blake, Lavater and Physiognomy*. London: Legenda, 2010

Essick, Robert N. *William Blake's Commercial Book Illustrations*. Oxford: Clarendon Press, 1991

Falk, Toby, and Mildred Archer. *Indian Miniatures of the India Office Library*. London: Sotheby Parke Bernet, 1981

Fallon, David. *Blake, Myth, and Enlightenment*. London: Palgrave Macmillan, 2017

Favret, Mary A. *War at a Distance: Romanticism and the Making of Modern Wartime*. Princeton, N.J.: Princeton University Press, 2009

Feldhaus, Anne. *Connected Places: Region, Pilgrimage, and Geographical Imagination in India*. Basingstoke and New York: Palgrave Macmillan, 2003

Feldman, Marian H. *Communities of Style: Portable Luxury Arts, Identity, and Collective Memory in the Iron Age Levant*. Chicago: University of Chicago Press, 2014

Finn, Margot C. "Material Turns in British History: Loot." *Transactions of the Royal Historical Society* 28 (2018): 5–32

Fisch, Jörg. "A Solitary Vindicator of the Hindus: The Life and Writings of General Charles Stuart (1757/58–1828)," *Journal of the Royal Asiatic Society of Great Britain and Ireland* 117, no. 1 (January 1985): 35–57

Flaxman, John. *Lectures on Sculpture*. London: John Murray, 1829

——. "Sculpture." In Abraham Rees, *The Cyclopaedia; or Universal Dictionary of Arts, Sciences, and Literature*. Vol. 4. London: Longman, Hurst, Rees, Orme & Browne, 1819–20, 62–100

Fleischer, Cornell H. *Bureaucrat and Intellectual in the Ottoman Empire: The Historian Mustafa Ali (1541–1600)*. Princeton, N.J.: Princeton University Press, 1986

Flood, Finbarr Barry. *Objects in Translation: Material Culture and Medieval "Hindu-Muslim" Encounter*. Princeton, N.J.: Princeton University Press, 2009

——. "Correct Delineations and Promiscuous Outlines: Envisioning India at the Trial of Warren Hastings." *Art History* 29, no. 1 (February 2006): 47–78

Forbes, James. *Oriental Memoirs*. 4 vols. London: White, Cochrane and Co., 1813

——. *Oriental Memoirs: A Narrative of Seventeen Years Residence in India*. 2nd edn., 2 vols. London: Richard Bentley, 1834

Fordham, Douglas. *Aquatint Worlds: Travel, Print and Empire*. New Haven and London: Paul Mellon Centre with Yale University Press, 2019

——. *British Art and the Seven Years' War*. New Haven and London: Yale University Press, 2010

——. "Costume Dramas: British Art at the Court of the Marathas." *Representations* 101 (Winter 2008): 57–85

Foucault, Michel. *The Order of Things: An Archaeology of Human Knowledge*. Translation from the French. New York: Pantheon Books, 1970

Freitag, Sandria B., ed. *The Visual Turn: South Asia across the Disciplines*. Abingdon: Routledge, 2015

Freshwater, M. Felix. "A Discussion of Nicolo Manuzzi (1639–1717) and the First Report of the Indian Rhinoplasty." *JPRAS: An International Journal of Surgical Reconstruction* 63 (2010): 251–3

Fromont, Cécile. *The Art of Conversion: Christian Visual Culture in the Kingdom of Kongo*. Chapel Hill: University of North Carolina Press, 2014

Funnell, Peter. "The Symbolic Language of Antiquity." In *The Arrogant Connoisseur: Richard Payne Knight*. Ed. Michael Clarke and Nicholas Penny. Manchester: Manchester University Press, 1982, 50–64

Fuseli, Henry (writing as "Simonides"). "The Arts," *Analytical Review* 1. Edited by Joseph Johnson (1788): 216

——, attrib. "Art. IX. On the Gods of Greece, Italy, and India, written in 1784; and since revised; by the President." *Analytical Review* 6 (1790): 313

Gacek, Adam. "قلم" (*qalam*). In *The Arabic Manuscript Tradition: A Glossary of Technical Terms*. Leiden: Brill, 2008

Gandhi, Leela. *Postcolonial Theory: A Critical Introduction*. New York: Columbia University Press, 2019

Gandhi, Madhav, Sadashiv Gorakshkar, and Kalpana Desai. *Mirror of Beauty: Art Treasures from India* [Skonhetens spegel: konstkatter fran Indien; in Swedish], Part 2. Stockholm: Östasiatiska Museet, the Museum of Far Eastern Antiquities, 1987

Ganguly, Swagato. *Idolatry and the Idea of India: Visions of Horror, Allegories of Enlightenment*. London: Routledge, 2018

Gaskell, Ivan. "Tradesmen as Scholars." In *Art History and Its Institutions: The Nineteenth Century*. Ed. Elizabeth Mansfield. London: Routledge, 2002, 146–62

Gazetteer of the Bombay Presidency, vol. 18, part 1 (Poona). Bombay: Government Central Press, 1885

Gerety, Finnian McKean Moore, "This Whole World is Om: Song, Soteriology, and the Emergence of the Sacred Syllable." Ph.D. diss., Harvard University, 2015

Gilmour, David. *The British in India: A Social History of the Raj*. London: Allen Lane; New York: Farrar, Straus and Giroux, 2018

Gode, P. K. "The Menagerie of the Peshwa." *Proceedings of the Deccan History Conference, First (Hyderabad) Session*. Hyderabad, 1945, 403–7

Godwin, William. *The Diary of William Godwin*. Ed. Victoria Myers, David O'Shaughnessy, and Mark Philp. Oxford: Oxford Digital Library, 2010, http://godwindiary.bodleian.ox.ac.uk/

Goetz, Hermann. *The Art of the Marathas and Its Problems*. Baroda State Museum Pamphlets. Baroda: Sadhana Press, 1946

Gokhale, Balkrishna Govind. *Poona in the Eighteenth Century: An Urban History*. New Delhi: Oxford University Press, 1988

Gole, Susan. *India within the Ganges*. New Delhi: Jayaprints, 1983

Gordon, Stewart. *The Marathas 1600–1818*. Cambridge: Cambridge University Press, 1993

——. *Marathas, Marauders, and State Formation in Eighteenth-Century India*. Oxford: Oxford University Press, 1998

Gregorian, Raffi. "Unfit for Service: British Law and Looting in India in the Mid-Nineteenth Century." *South Asia: Journal of South Asian Studies* 13, no. 1 (1990): 63–84

Griffiths, John. "The Brass and Copper Wares of the Bombay Presidency." *Journal of Indian Art and Industry* 7 no. 55 (July 1896): 13–22

Grigson, Caroline. *Menagerie: The History of Exotic Animals in England, 1100–1837*. Oxford: Oxford University Press, 2016

Groseclose, Barbara. *British Sculpture and the Company Raj: Church Monuments and Public Statuary in Madras, Calcutta, and Bombay to 1858*. Cranbury, N.J.: Associated University Presses, 1995

Guha, Sumit. *History and Collective Memory in South Asia, 1200–2000*. Seattle: University of Washington Press, 2019

——. "Speaking Historically: The Changing Voices of Historical Narration in Western India, 1400–1900." *American Historical Review* 109, no. 4 (October 2004): 1084–103

Guha-Thakurta, Tapati. *The Making of a New "Indian" Art: Artists, Aesthetics, and Nationalism in Bengal, c. 1850–1920*. Cambridge: Cambridge University Press, 1992

——. *Monuments, Objects, Histories: Institutions of Art in Colonial and Postcolonial India*. New York: Columbia University Press, 2004

Guichard, Charlotte, and Bénédicte Savoy. "Acquiring Cultures and Trading Value in a Global World." In Savoy, Guichard, and Howald, *Acquiring Cultures*, 1–8

Haidar, Navina Najat, and Marika Sardar. *Sultans of Deccan India 1500–1700: Opulence and Fantasy*. New York: Metropolitan Museum of Art, 2015

Halbertal, Moshe, and Avishai Margalit. *Idolatry*. Trans. Naomi Goldblum. Cambridge, Mass.: Harvard University Press, 1992

Hardgrave, Robert L. *Portrait of the Hindus: Balthazar Solvyns and the European Image of India, 1760–1824*. Oxford and New York: Oxford University Press, 2004

Harrington, Jack. *Sir John Malcolm and the Creation of British India*. Basingstoke and New York: Palgrave Macmillan, 2010

Harris, Lucian. "British Collecting of Indian Art and Artifacts." Ph.D. diss., University of Sussex, 2002

Hartman, Saidiya. "Venus in Two Acts." *Small Axe* 26, no. 12.2 (June 2008): 1–14

Head, Raymond. *Catalogue of Paintings, Drawings, Engravings and Busts in the Collection of the Royal Asiatic Society*. London: Routledge, 1991

Heck, Johann Georg, ed. *Systematischer Bilder-Atlas*. Leipzig: F. A. Brockhaus, ca. 1850

Hevia, James L. "Plunders, Markets, and Museums: The Biographies of Chinese Imperial Objects in Europe and North America." In *What's the Use of Art? Asian Visual and Material Culture in Context*. Ed. Jan Mrázek and Morgan Pitelka. Honolulu: University of Hawaii Press, 2008, 129–41

Hill, Katrina. "Collecting on Campaign: British Soldiers in China during the Opium Wars." *Journal of the History of Collections* 25, no. 2 (2013): 227–52

Hill, Richard. *Prizes of War: The Naval Prize System in the Napoleonic Wars, 1793–1815*. Portsmouth: Royal Naval Publications, 1998

"111. [Review of] The Hindu Pantheon" and "Notice of Moor's Hindu Pantheon," *Classical Journal* (June 1813)

Historic England. "Wilbury House." https://historicengland.org.uk/listing/the-list/list-entry/1001245

Hobhouse, Niall. *Indian Painting During the British Period*. Exh. cat. London: Hobhouse, 1986

Hodges, William. *Travels in India during the years 1780, 1781, 1782, & 1783*. London: J. Edwards, 1793

Home, Robert. *Select Views in Mysore, the Country of Tippoo Sultan . . . .* London: Mr. Bowyer, 1794

Howald, Christine. "The Power of Provenance: Marketing and Pricing of Chinese Looted Art on the European Market (1860–62)." In Savoy, Guichard, and Howald, *Acquiring Cultures*, 241–65

Howe, Stephen, ed. *The New Imperial Histories Reader*. London: Routledge, 2010

Howes, Jennifer. *Illustrating India: The Early Colonial Investigations of Colin Mackenzie*. Oxford: Oxford University Press, 2010

Howlett, David J. "Malet, Sir Charles Warre, first baronet (1753–1815)."ODNB, 2004; online edn. May 2009

Hurel, Roselyne. *Miniatures et peintures indiennes*. Vol. 1. Paris: Bibliothèque Nationale de France, 2010

Hutton, Deborah, and Rebecca Tucker. "The Worldly Artist in the Seventeenth Century: The Travels of Cornelis Claesz. Heda." *Art History* 37, no. 5 (November 2014), 860–89

Hyman, Aaron M., and Dana Leibsohn. "Washing the Archive." *Early American Literature* 55, no. 2 (2020): 419–44

Indian Painting for British Patrons 1770–1860. Exh. cat. London: Hazlitt, Gooden & Fox, 1991

Jaffrelot, Christophe. *The Hindu Nationalist Movement in India*. New York: Columbia University Press, 1996

——, ed., *Hindu Nationalism: A Reader*. Princeton, N.J.: Princeton University Press, 2007

Jain, Jyotindra, ed. *Picture Showmen: Insights into the Narrative Tradition in Indian Art*. Mumbai: Marg Publishing, 1998

Jain, Kajri. *Gods in the Bazaar: The Economies of Indian Calendar Art.* Durham, N.C.: Duke University Press, 2007

Jasanoff, Maya. *Edge of Empire: Lives, Culture, and Conquest in the East, 1750–1850.* New York: Vintage, 2007

Jefferys, Thomas. *A New and Complete Dictionary of Arts and Sciences . . . engraved by Mr. Jefferys.* 4 vols. 2nd edn. London: W. Owen, 1764

Johnson, Gordon. "Chitpavan Brahmins and Politics in Western India in the Late Nineteenth and Early Twentieth Centuries." In *Elites in South Asia.* Ed. Edmund Leach and S. N. Mukherjee. Cambridge: Cambridge University Press, 1970, 95–118

Johnson, Samuel. *A Dictionary of the English Language.* 1755, 1773. Ed. Beth Rapp Young et al., 2021. https://johnsonsdictionaryonline.com

Jones, William. *The Works of Sir William Jones: A Discourse on the Institution of Society, for inquiring into the History, Civic and Natural, the Antiquities, Arts, Sciences and Literature, of Asia.* Vol. 3. London: John Stockdale, 1807

——. "Introduction" and "On the Gods of Greece, Italy and India." *Asiatick Researches* 1 (Calcutta: The Company's Printing Office, 1788): iii–xvi; 221–75

Joshi, N. M. *Urban Handicrafts of the Bombay Deccan.* Bombay: Gokhale Institute, 1936

Kaicker, Abhishek. *The King and the People: Sovereignty and Popular Politics in Mughal Delhi.* Oxford: Oxford University Press, 2020

Kaimal, Padma. "The Problem of Portraiture in South India, circa 870–970 AD." *Artibus Asiae* 59, nos. 1–2 (1999): 59–133

——. "The Problem of Portraiture in South India, circa 970–1000 AD." *Artibus Asiae* 60, no. 1 (2000): 139–79

Kanitkar, R. P. *Chitrashalecha Itihas* [History of the Chitrashala; in Marathi]. Pune: Vasukaka Joshi Vikhvast Nidhi, 1975

Kantak, M. R., ed. *Rajwade and His Thoughts.* Pune: Bharat Itihas Sanshodhak Mandal, 1990

Karvé, Irawati. "Some Folk Songs of Maharashtra." *Bulletin of the Deccan College Research Institute* 1, no. 1 (Poona, 1939): 79–95

Kavi, Krishnadatta. *Pratap Prakasa* [A contemporary account of life in the royal court at Jaipur in the late 18th century; in Hindi]. Ed. Gopal Narayan Bahura. Jaipur: Maharaja Sawai Man Singh II Museum Trust, 1983

Keay, John. *The Honourable Company: A History of the English East India Company.* New York: Macmillan, 1991

Keene, H. G. *Mádhav Ráo Sindhia, Otherwise Called Madhoji.* Oxford: Clarendon Press, 1891

Kelkar, N. C. *Pleasures and Privileges of the Pen.* Poona: K. N. Kelkar, 1929

——. "Vishnushastri Chiplunkar." In *Indian Worthies.* Bombay: Manoranjak Grantha Prasarak Mandal, 1906, 119–63

Kesari newspaper [in Marathi], 1897, 1916

Khare, G. H. "Old Pictures from the Mandal." *Traimasik* 17, no. 1 [in Marathi] (Poona: Bharat Itihas Sanshodhak Mandal, 1959): 1–8

Khare, V. V. *Nana Phadnavisanche Charitra* [*Nana Fadnavis's Biography*; in Marathi]. 1892; repr., Pune: Varda, 2012

Khera, Dipti. *The Place of Many Moods: Udaipur's Painted Lands and India's Eighteenth Century.* Princeton, N.J.: Princeton University Press, 2020

——. "'Designs to Suit Every Taste': P. Orr & Sons and Swami Silverware." In Vidya Dehejia, *Delight in Design: Indian Silver for the Raj.* Ahmedabad: Mapin, 2008, 20–37

Khullar, Sonal. *Worldly Affiliations: Artistic Practice, National Identity, and Modernism in India, 1930–1990.* Berkeley: University of California Press, 2015

Knight, Richard Payne. *An Inquiry into the Symbolical Language of Ancient Art and Mythology.* London, 1818

Koch, Ebba. "Jahangir as Francis Bacon's Ideal of the King as an Observer and Investigator of Nature." *Journal of the Royal Asiatic Society of Great Britain and Ireland* 19 (2009): 293–338

Koerner, Joseph. "The Icon as Iconoclash." In *Iconoclash: Beyond the Image Wars in Science, Religion, and Art.* Ed. Bruno Latour and Peter Weibel. Cambridge, Mass.: MIT Press, 2002, 164–213

Kolff, Dirk H. A. *Naukar, Rajput, and Sepoy: The Ethnohistory of the Military Labour Market in Hindustan, 1450–1850.* Cambridge: Cambridge University Press, 1990

Kornhauser, Elizabeth, and Tim Barringer. *Thomas Cole's Journey: Atlantic Crossings.* New York: Metropolitan Museum of Art, 2018

Kosambi, Meera. *Gender and Performance: Marathi Theatre and Cinema Before Independence.* New Delhi: Routledge, 2015

Kripananda, Swami. *Jnaneshwar's Gita.* Albany: State University of New York Press, 1989

Kriz, Kay Dian. *Slavery, Sugar, and the Culture of Refinement.* New Haven and London: Yale University Press, 2008

Kulkarnee, Narayan H., ed. *Chhatrapati Shivaji: Architect of Freedom.* Delhi: Chhatrapati Shivaji Smarak Samiti, 1975

Kulkarni, A. R. *Maratha Historiography.* Delhi: Manohar, 2006

Kulkarni, Uday S. *Solstice at Panipat: 14 January 1761; An Authentic Account of the Panipat Campaign.* Pune: Mula Mutha Publishers, 2012

——. *James Wales: Artist and Antiquarian in the Time of Peshwa Sawai Madhavrao.* Pune: Mula Mutha Publishers, 2019

Kumar, Krishan. *Visions of Empire: How Five Imperial Regimes Shaped the World.* Princeton, N.J.: Princeton University Press, 2017

Lavater, Johann Caspar. *Essays on Physiognomy.* Trans. Thomas Holcroft. London, 1789

Leclerc, Georges Louis, Comte de Buffon. *Histoire Naturelle.* (Paris: Imprimerie Royale, 1749–88). Vol. 11

Lipking, Lawrence. *The Ordering of the Arts in Eighteenth-Century England.* Princeton, N.J.: Princeton University Press, 1970

Llewellyn-Jones, Rosie. *Portraits in Princely India, 1700–1947.* Mumbai: Marg, 2008

Losty, J. P. *A Prince's Eye: Imperial Mughal Paintings from a Princely Collection.* London: Francesca Galloway, 2013

——. *Sita Ram's Views of India.* London: Thames & Hudson, 2015

——. "'A very ingenious person': The Maratha Artist Gangaram Cintaman Tambat." Asian and African Studies Blog, British Library, August 28, 2014, https://britishlibrary.typepad.co.uk/asian-and-african/2014/08/the-maratha-artist-gangaram-cintaman-tambat.html#sthash.nv7GtFbF.dpuf

Lyons, Tryna. *The Artists of Nathadwara: The Practice of Painting in Rajasthan.* Bloomington: Indiana University Press, 2004

Mabon, Robert. *Sketches Illustrative of Oriental Manners and Customs.* Calcutta? 1797?

Macdonald, Captain A. *Memoir of the life of the late Nana Furnuwees compiled from family records and extant works*. Bombay: American Mission Press, 1851

Maclean, Kama. *A Revolutionary History of Interwar India: Violence, Image, Voice and Text*. Oxford: Oxford University Press, 2015

Maharashtra State Gazetteers, Ahmadnagar District. Bombay: Gazetteers Department, Government of Maharashtra, 1976

Mahratta newspaper, 1882

Makdisi, Saree. *William Blake and the Impossible History of the 1790s*. Chicago: University of Chicago Press, 2002

Malcolm, John. *A Memoir of Central India, including Malwa and Adjoining Provinces* .... 2 vols. 2nd edn. London: Kingsbury, Parbury & Allen, 1824

Malet, Alexander. "Catalogue of Persian MSS." *Transactions of the Royal Asiatic Society of Great Britain and Ireland* 2, no. 2 (July 1830): xxxiv–xxxv

Malet, Charles Warre. "Description of Ugen, the Capital of Mahadagee Scindia." In *Oriental Repertory*. Vol. 1. Ed. Alexander Dalrymple. London, 1793, 265–8

——. "Letter from Sir C. W. Malet, Bart., to the President, on the Subject of the Following Paper [Description of the Caves or Excavations, on the Mountain, About a Mile to the Eastward of the Town of Ellora]." *Asiatick Researches* 6 (Calcutta: Asiatic Society of Bengal, 1799): 382–423

Mallebrein, Cornelia. *Die anderen Götter: Volks-und Stammesbronzen aus Indien* [The other gods: folk and tribal bronzes from India]. Cologne: Edition Braus, 1993

——. "Hidden Gods Within the House: House Shrines of the Kokna Tribe of Maharashtra." In *House and Home in Maharashtra*. Ed. Irina Glushkova and Anne Feldhaus. Delhi: Oxford University Press, 1998, 215–41

——. "In the Company of Gods: G.-D. Sontheimer and His Passion for Folk and Tribal Bronzes." In *In the Company of Gods: Essays in Memory of Günther-Dietz Sontheimer*. Ed. Aditya Malik, Anne Feldhaus, and Heidrun Brückner. Delhi: Manohar, 2005, 363–93

Mancini, J. M. *Art and War in the Pacific World: Making, Breaking, and Taking from Anson's Voyage to the Philippine-American War*. Oakland: University of California Press, 2018

Mantena, Rama. *The Origins of Modern Historiography in India*. New York: Palgrave Macmillan, 2012

Marshall, P. J., ed. *The British Discovery of Hinduism in the Eighteenth Century*. Cambridge: Cambridge University Press, 1970

Martin, Meredith, and Daniela Bleichmar. "Objects in Motion in the Early Modern World." *Art History* 38, no. 4 (September 2015): 604–19

Mate, M. S. *Temples and Legends of Maharashtra*. Bombay: Bharat Vidya Bhavan, 1962

——. "Maratha Architecture, 1650 A.D. to 1850 A.D." Ph.D. diss., University of Poona, 1957

Mazzeo, Tilar Jenon. "Verbal Echoes of Cumberland's *Thoughts on Outline, Sculpture, and the System that Guided the Ancients* (1796) in *Jerusalem*." *Blake/An Illustrated Quarterly* 35, no. 1 (Summer 2001): 24–6

Paul Mellon's Legacy: A Passion for British Art. New Haven, Conn. and London: Yale Center for British Art and Royal Academy of Arts with Yale University Press, 2007

Michaud, Éric. *Barbarian Invasions: A Genealogy of the History of Art*. Trans. Nicholas Huckle. Cambridge, Mass.: MIT Press, 2019

Michell, George. *Art and Architecture of Southern India: Vijayanagara and the Successor States, 1350–1750*. New York: Cambridge University Press, 1995

——, and Mark Zebrowski. *Architecture and Art of the Deccan Sultanates*. Cambridge: Cambridge University Press, 1999

Minissale, Gregory. *Images of Thought: Visuality in Islamic India*. Newcastle: Cambridge Scholars, 2009

Mishra, Rupali. *A Business of State: Commerce, Politics, and the Birth of the East India Company*. Cambridge, Mass.: Harvard University Press, 2018

Mishra, Shailka. "*Suratkhana* at Amber-Jaipur in the 18th Century: Paintings, Patronage, Practices." Ph.D. diss., Jawaharlal Nehru University, 2015

Mitchell, W. J. T. *Blake's Composite Art*. Princeton, N.J.: Princeton University Press, 1978

——. *What Do Pictures Want? The Lives and Loves of Images*. Chicago: University of Chicago Press, 2005

Mitter, Partha. *Art and Nationalism in Colonial India: Occidental Orientations*. Cambridge: Cambridge University Press, 1994

——. *Much Maligned Monsters: A History of European Reactions to Indian Art*. Oxford: Clarendon Press, 1977

——. "Mechanical Reproduction and the World of the Colonial Artist." *Contributions to Indian Sociology* 36, nos. 1–2 (February 2002): 1–31

Moienuddin, Mohammad. *Sunset at Srirangapatam*. Hyderabad: Orient Longman, 2000

Molesworth, J. T. *A dictionary, Marathi and English, 2nd edition, rev. and enl.* Bombay: Printed for the Government, 1857

Monks, Sarah. "Making Love: Thomas Banks' Camadeva and the Discourses of British India c. 1790." *Visual Culture in Britain* 11, no. 2 (2010): 195–218

Moor, Edward. *A Compilation of all the Government and General – Government – General – Brigade and Garrison Orders – Minutes of council – Commands of the Hon. Company – or Regulations, from whatever authority promulgated, from the year 1750 to the 31st of July 1801, that are now in force and operating on the Discipline or Expenditure of the Bombay Army*. Bombay: Courier and Gazette Presses, 1801

——. *Hindu Infanticide: an account of the measures adopted for suppressing the practice of the systematic murder by their parents of female infants*. London: J. Johnson, 1811

——. *The Hindu Pantheon*. London: J. Johnson, 1810

——. *The Hindu Pantheon*. 2nd edn. Ed. A. O. Moor. London: Williams and Norgate, 1861

——. *The Hindu Pantheon*. 3rd edn. Ed. W. O. Simpson. Madras: J. Higginbotham, 1864

——. *A Narrative of the Operations of Captain Little's Detachment and of the Mahratta Army, commanded by Purseram Bhow, during the late confederacy in India against the Nawab Tippoo Sultan Bahadur*. London: J. Johnson, 1794

——. *Oriental Fragments*. London: Smith, Elder and Co., 1834

——. "An Account of a Hereditary living Deity to whom devotion is paid by the Brahmans of Poona, &c." *Asiatick Researches* 7 (1803): 383–97

"Moor's *Hindu Pantheon*." *Edinburgh Review* (1811), 313–30

Mukherjee, Nayana Sharma, and Susmita Basu Majudar. "A Nose Lost and Honour Regained: The Indian Method of Rhinoplasty Revisited." *Proceedings of the Indian History Congress* 72, pt. 1 (2011): 968–77

Mukherji, Parul Dave. "Whither Art History in a Globalizing World." *Art Bulletin* 96, no. 2 (June 2014): 151–5

Nair, Janaki. *Mysore Modern: Rethinking the Region under Princely Rule*. New Delhi: Orient Blackswan, 2011

Nardi, Isabella. *The Theory of Citrasutras in Indian Painting: A Critical Re-evaluation of Their Uses and Interpretations*. London: Routledge, 2006

——. "Re-Evaluating the Role of Text in Indian Art: Towards a Shastric Analysis of the Image of Shri Nathji in Nathdvara Miniature Painting." *South Asia Research* 29, no. 2 (2009): 99–126

Naregal, Veena. *Language Politics, Elites and the Public Sphere: Western India Under Colonialism*. London: Anthem Press, 2002

Neville, Kristoffer. "Winckelmann's Eclecticism." *Notes in the History of Art* 37, no. 4 (Summer 2018): 228–36

Noltie, Henry. *Robert Wight and the Botanical Drawings of Rungiah and Govindoo*. 2 vols. Edinburgh: Royal Botanic Garden, 2007

Novetzke, Christian Lee. *Religion and Public Memory: A Cultural History of Saint Namdev in India*. New York: Columbia University Press, 2008

Official Report of the Calcutta International Exhibition, 1883–1884. 2 vols. Calcutta: Bengal Secretariat Press, 1885

Ogborn, Miles. *Indian Ink: Script and Print in the Making of the English East India Company*. Chicago: University of Chicago Press, 2007

O'Hanlon, Rosalind. *Caste, Conflict, and Ideology: Mahatma Jotirao Phule and Low Caste Protest in Nineteenth-Century Western India*. Cambridge: Cambridge University Press, 1985

——. "Maratha History as Polemic: Low Caste Ideology and Political Debate in Late Nineteenth-Century Western India." *Modern Asian Studies* 17, no. 1 (1983): 1–33

——. "Military Sports and the History of the Martial Body in India." *Journal of the Economic and Social History of the Orient* 50, no. 4 (2007): 490–523

Orme, Edward. *Historical Fragments of the Mogul empire, of the Morattoes, and of the English*. London: F. Wingrave, 1805

The Other Side of the Verandah: Watercolours, Drawings, and Photographs of Anglo-Indian Interiors in the British Period 1800–1900. Exh. cat. London: Eyre and Hobhouse, 1981

Paice, Rosamund A. "Encyclopedic Resistance: Blake, Rees's *Cyclopaedia*, and the Laocoön Separate Plate." *Blake: An Illustrated Quarterly* 37, no. 2 (Fall 2003): 44–62

Pain, Charles, with Eleanor Zelliot. "The God Dattatreya and the Datta Temples of Pune." In *The Experience of Hinduism: Essays on Religion in Maharashtra*. Ed. Maxine Berntsen and Eleanor Zelliot. Albany: State University of New York Press, 1988, 95–108

Paley, Morton D. *The Continuing City: William Blake's Jerusalem*. Oxford: Clarendon Press, 1983

——. *The Traveller in the Evening: The Last Works of William Blake*. Oxford: Oxford University Press, 2003

——. "Wonderful Originals: Blake and Ancient Sculpture." In *Blake in His Time*. Ed. Robert N. Essick and Donald Pearce. Bloomington: Indiana University Press, 1978, 170–97

Pandey, R. G. *Mahadji Shinde and the Poona Durbar*. New Delhi: Oriental Publishers & Distributors, 1980

Pandit, Vaman. "Dasavatara," *Kavyetihas Sangraha* [Collection of poetry and history; in Marathi] 1 (Poona; 1878): 60–61

Parasnis, D. B. *Poona in Bygone Days*. Bombay: Times Press, 1921

——. *Savai Madhavarava Peshwyancha Darbara ani tya Veleche Pahile Ingraja Resident Sir Charles Malet* [The court of Peshwa Savai Madhavrao and the then English Resident Sir Charles Malet; in Marathi]. Mumbai: Tukaram Javaji Nirnaysagar Press, ca. 1867

Pathy, T. V. "Dattatreya Parasnis and His Collection." *Marg: The Art of Chhatrapatis and Peshwas*, ed. Saryu Doshi, 34, no. 2 (1981): 91–2

Patterson, Maureen L. "Chitpavan Brahman Family Histories: Sources for a Study of Social Structure and Social Change in Maharashtra." In *Structure and Change in Indian Society*. Ed. Milton Singer and Bernard S. Cohen. Chicago: Aldine, 1968, 397–412

Peltz, Lucy. *Facing the Text: Extra-Illustration, Print Culture and Society in Britain, 1769–1840*. Manchester: Manchester University Press, 2017

"Peshwyanchi Bakhar [History of the Peshwas]." *Kavyetihas Sangraha* [Collection of poetry and history; in Marathi], no. 1. Ed. Kashinath N. Sane and J. B. Modak (Poona: Shivaji Printing House, 1878): 1–240

Peterson, Indira Viswanathan. "Portraiture at the Tanjore Maratha Court." In *Portraits in Princely India, 1700–1947*. Ed. Rosie Llewellyn-Jones. Mumbai: Marg, 2008, 44–57

——. "The Sequence of King Śarabhendra's Sacred Places: Pilgrimage and Kingship in a Marathi Text from 19th-Century Thanjavur." In *Festschrift Heidrun Brückner*. Ed. Anna Aurelia Esposito et al. Wiesbaden: Harrassowitz, 2016, 275–81

Petherbridge, Deanna. "Some Thoughts on Flaxman and the Engraved Outlines." *Print Quarterly* 28, no. 4 (2011): 385–91

Pevsner, Nikolas. *Wiltshire*. Harmondsworth: Penguin, 1963

Phadke, Y. D. *V. K. Chiploonkar*. New Delhi: National Book Trust, 1982

Pietrantonio, Natalia di. "Circuits of Exchange: Albums and the Art Market in 18th-Century Avadh." *Journal 18* 6 (October 2018), http://www.journal18.org/2846

Pinch, William R. *Warrior Ascetics and Indian Empires*. Cambridge: Cambridge University Press, 2006

Pinney, Christopher. *Photos of the Gods: The Printed Image and Political Struggle in India*. London: Reaktion, 2004

——. "Iatrogenic Religion and Politics." In *Censorship in South Asia: Cultural Regulation from Sedition to Seduction*. Ed. R. Kaur and W. Mazzarella. Bloomington: Indiana University Press, 2009, 29–62

——. "The Nation (Un)Pictured? Chromolithography and 'Popular' Politics in India, 1878–1995." *Critical Inquiry* 23, no. 4 (Summer 1997): 834–67

Platts, John Thompson. *A Dictionary of Urdu, Classical Hindi, and English*. London: Oxford University Press, 1960

Pointon, Marcia. "'Surrounded with Brilliants': Miniature Portraits in Eighteenth-Century England." *Art Bulletin* 83, no. 1 (March 2001): 48–77

Polier, Antoine. *A European Experience of the Mughal Orient: The I'jaz-i Arsalani (Persian Letters 1772–1779) of Antoine-Louis Henri Polier*. Trans. M. Alam and S. Alavi. Delhi: Oxford University Press, 2001

Pomey, François. *The Pantheon, representing the fabulous histories of the heathen gods, and most illustrious heroes . . . translated by Andrew Tooke*. London: J. F. & C. Rivington et al., 1787

Pop, Andrei. *Antiquity, Theatre, and the Painting of Henry Fuseli.* Oxford: Oxford University Press, 2015

Preston, Laurence W. "Subregional Religious Centres in the History of Maharashtra: The Sites Sacred to Ganesh." In *Images of Maharashtra: A Regional Profile of India.* Ed. N. K. Wagle. London: Curzon, 1980, 102–28

Price, David. *Memoirs of the Early Life and Service of a Field Officer, of the Retired List of the Indian Army.* London: W. H. Allen, 1839

Quilley, Geoff. *Empire to Nation: Art, History and the Visualization of Maritime Britain, 1768–1829.* New Haven and London: Yale University Press, 2011

——, and John Bonehill, eds. *William Hodges 1744–1797: The Art of Exploration.* Greenwich: National Maritime Museum, 2004

Raj, Kapil. *Relocating Modern Science: Circulation and the Construction of Knowledge in South Asia and Europe, 1650–1900.* Basingstoke and New York: Palgrave Macmillan, 2007

Rajwade, V. K. "Shivaji's Image (*Pratima*) from Malvan." *Itihas Sangraha Aitihasik Safur Lekh* [Collection of history: expanded historical writings; in Marathi], 1 (1908): 1–4

Ramanujan, A. K. "Three Hundred Ramayanas: Five Examples and Three Thoughts on Translation." In *The Collected Essays of A. K. Ramanujan.* Ed. Vinay Dharwadker. Delhi: Oxford University Press, 1999, 131–60

Ramaswamy, Vijaya. "Artisans in Vijayanagar Society." *Indian Economic and Social History Review* 22, no. 4 (1985): 417–44

Ranade, Justice M. G. *Rise of the Maratha Power.* New Delhi: Rakesh, 1961

Ranade, Usha. *Manuscript Illustrations of the Medieval Deccan.* Pune: B. R. Publishing, 1983

——, and Kamal Chavan. *Tala Paintings.* Pune: Bharat Itihas Sanshodhak Mandal, 1976

Ray, Romita. *Under the Banyan Tree: Relocating the Picturesque in British India.* New Haven and London: Yale University Press, 2013

Ray, Sugata. *Climate Change and the Art of Devotion: Geoaesthetics in the Land of Krishna, 1550–1850.* Seattle: University of Washington Press, 2019

——. "Colonial Frames, 'Native' Claims: The Jaipur Economic and Industrial Museum." *Art Bulletin* 96, no. 2 (2014): 196–212

Redford, Bruce. *Dilettanti: The Antic and the Antique in Eighteenth-Century England.* Los Angeles: J. Paul Getty Museum, 2008

Reynolds, Sir Joshua. *Discourses on Art.* Ed. Robert R. Wark. New Haven and London: Paul Mellon Centre for Studies in British Art with Yale University Press, 1997

——. *The Works of Sir Joshua Reynolds.* Vol. 1. London: T. Cadell, Jun. and W. Davies, 1798

Rice, Yael. "Lines of Perception: European Prints and the Mughal *Kitabkhana.*" In *Prints in Translation, 1450–1750: Image, Materiality, Space.* Ed. Suzanne Karr Schmidt and Edward H. Wouk. London and New York: Routledge, 2017, 202–23

——. "Workshop as Network: A Case Study from Mughal South Asia." *Artl@s Bulletin* 6, no. 3 (2017): Article 4

Robbins, Thomas, et al. *All Religions and Ceremonies.* Vol. 2. London: Oliver D. Cooke, 1823

Roberts, Mary. *Istanbul Exchanges: Ottomans, Orientalists, and Nineteenth-Century Visual Culture.* Oakland: University of California Press, 2015

Rodriguez, Etienne Alexander. *The Hindoo Pantheon.* Madras: American Mission Press, 1849

Rohatgi, Pauline. "Early Impressions of the Islands: James Forbes and James Wales in Bombay 1766–95." In *Bombay to Mumbai: Changing Perspectives.* Ed. Pauline Rohatgi, Pheroza Godrej, and Rahul Mehrotra. Mumbai: Marg Publications, 1997, 58–77

——, and Pheroza Godrej, eds. *Under the Indian Sun: British Landscape Artists.* Bombay: Marg, 1995

Rookmaaker, L. C. *Bibliography of a Rhinoceros.* Rotterdam: A. A. Balkema, 1983

——. "Records of an Animal Collection in Poona at the End of the Eighteenth Century." *Back When and Then* 2, no. 1 (August 1997): 2

Roque, Ricardo, and Kim A. Wagner, eds. *Engaging Colonial Knowledge: Reading European Archives in World History.* Basingstoke and New York: Palgrave Macmillan, 2012

Rosenblum, Robert. *The International Style of 1800.* New York: Garland, 1976

Roth, Nicolas. "Marigolds and Munshīs: Horticultural Writing and Garden Culture in Mughal South Asia." Ph.D. dissertation, Harvard University, 2020

Roy, Kaushik. *War, Culture, and Society in Early Modern South Asia.* London: Routledge, 2011

Roy, Malini. "Some Unexpected Sources for Paintings by the Artist Mihr Chand (fl. c. 1759–86), Son of Ganga Ram." *South Asian Studies* 26, no. 1 (2010): 21–9

——. "Battle of Panipat, 1761." Asian and African Studies Blog, British Library, September 10, 2015. https://blogs.bl.uk/asian-and-african/2015/09/battle-of-panipat-1761.html

——. "William Beckford's Albums on Hindu Mythology." Asian and African Studies Blog, British Library, December 8, 2014. https://blogs.bl.uk/asian-and-african/2014/12/william-beckfords-albums-on-hindu-mythology.htm

——. "Idiosyncrasies in the Late Mughal Painting Tradition." Ph.D. diss., SOAS, University of London, 2009

Roy, Tirthankar. *Traditional Industry in the Economy of Colonial India.* Cambridge: Cambridge University Press, 1999

Sachdev, Vibhuti, and Giles Tillotson. *Building Jaipur: The Making of an Indian City.* London: Reaktion, 2002

Sahasrabudhe, Chetan, and Anurag Kashyap. "Festivals, Rituals, and Urban Landscape in Eighteenth-Century Maharashtra." *South Asian Studies* 32, no. 2 (2016): 155–65

Said, Edward. *Culture and Imperialism.* New York: Vintage, 1994

Salt, Henry. *Twenty-Four Views in St. Helena, the Cape, India, Ceylon, the Red Sea, Abyssinia, and Egypt.* London: William Miller, 1809

Samarth, Anil. *Shivaji and the Indian National Movement.* Bombay: Somaiya Publications, 1975

Sánchez-Jáuregui, Maria Dolores, and Scott Wilcox, eds. *The English Prize: The Capture of the Westmorland.* New Haven, Conn.: Yale Center for British Art, 2013

Saraf, Varunika. "A Market for Fakes: 'Miniature' Painting in Rajasthan, 1960–2000." *Marg* 69, no. 3 (March–June 2018): 54–63

Sardesai, G. S. *Marathi Riyasat* [The Maratha power; in Marathi]. 8 vols. 1948–57; Mumbai: Popular Prakashan, rev. edn., 1989

——. *New History of the Marathas.* 3 vols. Bombay: Phoenix, 1948

——. "Nana Fadnavis's Hobby of Collecting Paintings." In *Aitihasik Patrabodh* [Informative historical documents; in Marathi]. Comp. and ed. G. S. Sardesai. Bombay: Shri Samarth Prakashan, 1939, 93–5

Sarkar, Sir Jadunath. *A History of Jaipur, c. 1503–1938*. 1984; repr., New Delhi: Orient Blackswan, 2009
——. *House of Shivaji* (1940). Hyderabad: Orient Blackswan, e-edition 2012
——. *Shivaji and His Times*. London: Longmans, Green, 1920
Savoy, Bénédicte, Charlotte Guichard, and Christine Howald, eds. *Acquiring Cultures: Histories of World Art on Western Markets*. Berlin: De Gruyter, 2018
Scarry, Elaine. *The Body in Pain*. Oxford and New York: Oxford University Press, 1995
Scheurleer, Pauline Lunsingh. "Indian Miniatures for Europe: The Dutch Market in the 17th and 18th Centuries." In *Miniatur Geschichten: Die Sammlung Indischer Malerei im Dresdner Kupferstich-Kabinett*. Ed. Monica Juneja and Petra Kuhlmann-Hodick. Dresden: Sandstein, 2017, 55–67
Schmidgen, Wolfram. *Exquisite Mixture: The Virtues of Impurity in Early Modern England*. Philadelphia: University of Pennsylvania Press, 2013
Schnapp, Alain, ed. *World Antiquarianism: Comparative Perspectives*. Los Angeles: Getty Research Institute, 2014
Schrader, Stephanie, ed. *Rembrandt and the Inspiration of India*. Los Angeles: Getty Center, 2018
Scott, Joan Wallach. "Against Eclecticism." *Differences: A Journal of Feminist Cultural Studies* 16, no. 3 (2005): 114–37
Seccombe, Thomas. "Moor, Edward (1771–1848)." Rev. J. B. Katz. *ODNB*, 2004
"Secret Correspondence of the Court of the Peshwa Madhu Rao, from Year 1761–1772." *Transactions of the Royal Asiatic Society of Great Britain and Ireland* 2, no. 1 (March 1830): 109–65
Sen, Sudipta. *Empire of Free Trade: The East India Company and the Making of the Colonial Marketplace*. Philadelphia: University of Pennsylvania Press, 1998
Seth, Mira. *Wall Paintings of Rajasthan*. New Delhi: National Museum, 2002
Settar, S., and Günther-Dietz Sontheimer, eds. *Memorial Stones: A Study of Their Origin, Significance and Variety*. Dharwad: Institute of Indian Art History, Karnatak University, 1982
Seyller, John. *Pearls of the Parrot of India: The Walters Art Museum Khamsa of Amir Khusraw of Delhi*. Baltimore, Md.: Walters Art Museum, 2002
——. *Workshop and Patron in Mughal India*. Zurich: Artibus Asiae Publishers, 1999
——. "Farrukh Beg in the Deccan." *Artibus Asiae* 55, no. 3/4 (1995): 319–41
——. "For Love or Money: The Shaping of Historical Painting Collections in India." In *Intimate Worlds: Indian Paintings from the Alvin O. Bellak Collection*. Ed. Darielle Mason. Ahmedabad: Mapin Publishing, 2001, 12–21
——. "The Inspection and Valuation of Manuscripts in the Imperial Mughal Library." *Artibus Asiae* 57, no. 3/4 (1997): 243–349
——, and Jagdish Mittal. *Deccani Paintings, Drawings and Manuscripts*. Hyderabad: Jagdish and Kamla Mittal Museum of Indian Art, 2017
Shaffer, Holly. *Adapting the Eye: An Archive of the British in India*. New Haven, Conn.: Yale Center for British Art, 2011
——. *Strange and Wondrous: Prints of India from the Robert J. Del Bontà Collection*. Washington, D.C.: Arthur M. Sackler Gallery, 2013. http://www.asia.si.edu/explore/del-bonta/
——. "The Bed of Nails: The Exotic Across Borders and Media." In *Yoga: The Art of Transformation*. Ed. Debra Diamond. Washington, D.C.: Arthur M. Sackler Gallery, 2013, 250–57
——. "Eclecticism and Empire, in Translation." *Modern Philology* 119, no. 1 (August 2021): 147–65
——. "An Ecology of Picture-Rhythms (Talamala) in Western India, circa 1800." *Art History* 44, no. 4 (September 2021): 710–40
——. "The Indian Evidence Act: Contemporary Art and Nationalism." *Third Text* 30, nos. 5–6 (2017): 437–55
——. "Shivaji's Portrait." In *How Secular Is Art?* Ed. Tapati Guha-Thakurta and Vazira Zamindar. Cambridge: Cambridge University Press, forthcoming
——. "'Take all of them:' Eclecticism and the Arts of the Pune Court in India, 1760–1800." *Art Bulletin* 100, no. 2 (June 2018): 61–93
——. "Towards a History of Maratha Painting in the Deccan." In *Dakhan 2018: Recent Studies on Indian Painting*. Ed. John Seyller. Hyderabad: Jagdish and Kamla Mittal Museum of Indian Art, 2020, 77–108
Sharma, Yuthika. "Art in between Empires: Visual Culture and Artistic Knowledge in Late Mughal Delhi, 1748–1857." Ph.D. diss., Columbia University, 2013
——. "From Miniatures to Monuments: Picturing Shah Alam's Delhi (1771–1806)." In *Indo-Muslim Cultures in Transition*. Ed. Alka Patel and Karen Leonard. Leiden: Brill, 2012, 111–38
——. "In the Company of the Mughal Court: Delhi Painter Ghulam Ali Khan." In *Princes and Painters in Mughal Delhi, 1707–1857*. Ed. William Dalrymple and Yuthika Sharma. New York: Asia Society Museum, 2012, 41–51
Shaw, Graham. *Printing in Calcutta to 1800*. London: Bibliographical Society, 1981
Sheikh, Samira. *Forging a Region: Sultans, Traders, and Pilgrims in Gujarat, 1200–1500*. New Delhi: Oxford University Press, 2010
——. "A Gujarati Map and Pilot Book of the Indian Ocean, ca. 1750." *Imago Mundi* 61, no. 1 (2009): 67–83
Shirgaonkar, Varsha S. *Eighteenth Century Deccan: Cultural History of the Peshwas*. New Delhi: Aryan Books, 2010
Singh, Dayanita. *File Room*. Göttingen: Steidl, 2013
Singh, Kavita. *Real Birds in Imagined Gardens: Mughal Painting between Persia and Europe*. Los Angeles: Getty Publications, 2017
——. "Congress of Kings: Notes on a Painting of Muhammad Shah Rangeela Having Sex." In *A Magical World: New Visions of Indian Painting*. Ed. Molly Emma Aitken. Mumbai: Marg Publications, 2017, 38–49
Sklar, Susanne. *Blake's Jerusalem as Visionary Theatre*. Oxford: Oxford University Press, 2011
Sloan, Kim, ed. *Enlightenment: Discovering the World in the Eighteenth Century*. London: British Museum Press, 2004
Smentek, Kristel. "Looking East: Jean-Étienne Liotard, the Turkish Painter." *Ars Orientalis* 39 (2010): 84–112
Smith, Alison, ed. *Artist and Empire: Facing Britain's Imperial Past*. London: Tate Publishing, 2015
Smith, Charlotte H. F., and Michelle Stevenson. "Modeling Cultures: 19th Century Indian Clay Figures." *Museum Anthropology* 33, no. 1 (2010): 37–48
Smith, Kate. "Loss and Dispossession in the Long Eighteenth Century." Inaugural Lecture of the Material Culture in the

Seventeenth and Eighteenth Century Research Cluster, University of Edinburgh (17 March 2020)

Sontheimer, Günther-Dietz. *Pastoral Deities in Western India*. Trans. Anne Feldhaus. Oxford and New York: Oxford University Press, 1989

——. "The Mallari/Khandoba Myth as Reflected in Folk Art and Ritual." *Anthropos* 79, no. 1/3 (1984): 155–70

——. "The Ramayana in Contemporary Folk Traditions of Maharashtra." In *Essays on Religion, Literature and Law*. Ed. Heidrunn Brückner, Anne Feldhaus, and Aditya Malik. New Delhi: Manohar, 2004, 383–99

Steedman, Carolyn. *Dust: The Archive and Cultural History*. Manchester: Manchester University Press, 2001

Steingass, Joseph. *A Comprehensive Persian-English Dictionary*. London: Routledge & K. Paul, 1892

Stern, Philip J. *The Company-State: Corporate Sovereignty and the Early Modern Foundations of the British Empire in India*. London: Oxford University Press, 2012

Stoler, Ann Laura. *Along the Archival Grain: Epistemic Anxiety and Colonial Common Sense*. Princeton, N.J.: Princeton University Press, 2009

Stolte, Carolien. *Philip Angel's Deex-Autaers: Vaisnava mythology from manuscript to book market in the context of the Dutch East India Company, c.1600–1672*. New Delhi: Manohar, 2012

The Story of the J. J. School of Art, 1857–1957. Bombay: Government Central Press, ca. 1957

Stronge, Susan. *Tipu's Tigers*. London: Victoria and Albert Museum, 2009

Stuart, Charles. *Vindication of the Hindoos, from the Aspersions of Claudius Buchanan*. . . . London: R. and J. Rodwell, 1808

Subrahmanyam, Sanjay. *Europe's India: Worlds, People, Empires*. Cambridge, Mass.: Harvard University Press, 2017

——. "Connected Histories: Notes towards a Reconfiguration of Early Modern Eurasia." *Modern Asian Studies* 31, no. 3 (July 1997): 735–62

——. "Roomful of Mirrors: The Artful Embrace of Mughals and Franks, 1550–1700." *Ars Orientalis* 39 (2010): 39–83

Subramanyan, K. G. *The Creative Circuit*. Calcutta: Seagull, 1992

Sweet, Rosemary. *Antiquaries: The Discovery of the Past in Eighteenth-Century Britain*. London: Bloomsbury Academic, 2004

Sykes, William H. "An Account of the Caves of Ellora." In *Transactions of the Literary Society of Bombay* 3 (1819–21): 265–323

Tambat, Priyansi Nimish, and Ketaki Chandrakant Joshi. "Promoting Craft Entrepreneurship by Rejuvenating *Tambat* Craft in Old *Tambat Ali*, Nashik." *Journal of Heritage Management* 2, no. 1 (2017): 53–75

Taylor, Woodman. "Picture Practice: Painting Programs, Manuscript Production, and Liturgical Performances at the Kotah Royal Palace." In *Gods, Kings, and Tigers: The Art of Kotah*. Ed. Stuart Carey Welch. Munich: Prestel, 1997, 61–72

Thomas, Nicholas. *Entangled Objects: Exchange, Material Culture, and Colonialism in the Pacific*. Cambridge, Mass.: Harvard University Press, 1991

Tillotson, Giles. "The Indian Picturesque: Images of India in British Landscape Painting, 1780–1880." In *The Raj: India and the British 1600–1947*. Ed. C. A. Bayly. London: National Portrait Gallery Publications, 1990, 141–51

——, ed. *Vision and Landscape: Aquatints of India by Thomas and William Daniell*. Delhi: Delhi Art Gallery, 2019

Tod, James. *Annals and Antiquities of Rajasthan*. 2 vols. 1829–32; repr., London: Oxford University Press, 1920

Tripathi, Satya Vrata. *Mysteries of Love: Maratha Miniatures of the Rasamanjari*. New Delhi: National Museum, 2001

Tucker, Richard. "Hindu Traditionalism and Nationalist Ideologies in Nineteenth-Century Maharashtra." *Modern Asian Studies* 10, no. 3 (1976): 321–48

Tulshibagh Daftar to Ramji Chitari. Letter 184: "Picture work from Tulshibagh (March 18, 1826)." *Traimasik* 32, nos. 1–4 [in Marathi] (Pune: Bharat Itihas Sanshodhak Mandal, January 1952): 240

Twyman, Michael. *A History of Chromolithography: Printed Colour for All*. London: British Library, 2013

Tyson, Gerald P. *Joseph Johnson: A Liberal Publisher*. Iowa City: University of Iowa Press, 1979

Unger, Daniel M. *Redefining Eclecticism in Early Modern Bolognese Painting*. Amsterdam: Amsterdam University Press, 2019

Upadhyaya, Narmada Prasad. *The Color's Fragrance: The Catalogue of the Stray Leaves and Illustrated Manuscripts in the Scindia Oriental Research Institute, Vikram University, Ujjain (MP)*. Harda: Shri Beni Madhava Prakashan Graha, 2011

——. *Geet Govinda: Paintings in Kanheri Style*. Ocean Township, N.J.: Mapin, 2006

Vasunia, Phiroze. *The Classics and Colonial India*. Oxford: Oxford University Press, 2013

Vendell, Dominic. "Scribes and the Vocation of Politics in the Maratha Empire, 1707–1827." Ph.D. diss., Columbia University, 2018

Verghese, Anila, and Anna Dallapiccola. *South India under Vijayanagara: Art and Archaeology*. Oxford: Oxford University Press, 2011

Wagle, N. K. "Heroes in the Caritra-Bakhar, Povada and Akhyana." In *The Concept of Hero in Indian Culture*. Ed. Heidrun Brückner, Hugh van Skyhawk, and Claus Peter Zoller. New Delhi: Manohar, 2007, 219–36

——, and A. R. Kulkarni, trans. *Vallabha's Parasharama Charitra: An Eighteenth-Century Maratha History of the Peshwas*. Bombay: Popular Prakashan, 1976

Wagoner, Phillip B. "Precolonial Intellectuals and the Production of Colonial Knowledge." *Society for Comparative Study of Society and History* 45, no. 4 (October 2003): 783–814

Watson, Mark F., and Henry J. Noltie. "Career, Collections, Reports and Publications of Dr. Francis Buchanan (Later Hamilton), 1762–1829: Natural History Studies in Nepal, Burma (Myanmar), Bangladesh and India (Part 1)." *Annals of Science* 73 (2016): 392–424

Weir, David. *Brahma in the West: William Blake and the Oriental Renaissance*. New York: State University of New York Press, 2003

Wellesley, Arthur, ed. *Supplementary Despatches and Memoranda of Field Marshal Arthur, Duke of Wellington K.G*. Vol. 1. London: J. Murray, 1858

White, Daniel E. *From Little London to Little Bengal: Religion, Print, and Modernity in Early British India, 1793–1835*. Baltimore: Johns Hopkins University Press, 2013

Wilford, Lieutenant Francis. "On Egypt and other countries adjacent to the . . . Nile." *Asiatick Researches* 3 (printed verbatim from the Calcutta edition, London: Vernor and Hood, 1799): 295–462

Williams, Joanna. *The Two-Headed Deer: Illustrations of the Ramayana in Orissa*. Berkeley: University of California Press, 1996

——, ed. *Kingdom of the Sun: Indian Court and Village Art from the Princely State of Mewar*. San Francisco: Asian Art Museum, 2007

Willis, Michael. "Detritus to Treasure: Memory, Metonymy, and the Museum." In *Sacred Objects in Secular Spaces*. Ed. Bruce M. Sullivan. London: Bloomsbury Academic, 2015, 145–52

——. "Sculpture from India." In *A. W. Franks: Nineteenth-Century Collecting and the British Museum*. Ed. Marjorie Caygill and John Cherry. London: British Museum Press, 1997, 250–61

Winckelmann, Johann. *Reflections on the Paintings and Sculpture of the Greeks*. Trans. Henry Fuseli. London: A. Millar, 1765

Wink, André. *Land and Sovereignty in India: Agrarian Society and Politics under the Eighteenth-Century Maratha Svarajya*. Cambridge: Cambridge University Press, 1986

Wittkower, Rudolf. "Imitation, Eclecticism, and Genius." In *Aspects of the Eighteenth Century*. Ed. Earl R. Wasserman. Baltimore: Johns Hopkins University Press, 1965, 143–61

Worrall, David. "Blake's Jerusalem and the Visionary History of Britain." *Studies in Romanticism* 16, no. 2 (Spring 1977): 189–216

Wright, Thomas. *The Life of Edward Fitzgerald*. London: Grant Richards, 1904

Yule, Sir Henry. *Hobson-Jobson: A Glossary of Colloquial Anglo-Indian Words and Phrases*. . . . London: J. Murray, 1903

Zebrowski, Mark. *Deccani Painting*. Berkeley: University of California Press, 1983

Picture Credits

Images have been provided by and are reproduced courtesy of the owners or custodians of the works of art. Images for which additional photographic credit is due are listed below.

Image courtesy Göttingen State and University Library: 1; © The Trustees of the British Museum: 2, 46, 78, 81, 82a and b, 85, 86, 89, 91, 92, 93, 94, 95, 96, 98, 100, 102, 103, 105, 108, 109, 110, 111, 112, 113, 116, 117, 119, 121a and b, 122, 123, 127, 129, 132; Photograph by the author, courtesy Bharat Itihas Sanshodhak Mandal, Pune: 3, 4, 74, 97, 147; © Laura Grey Studio: 6; Courtesy of the Trustees of the Chhatrapati Shivaji Maharaj Vastu Sangrahalaya formerly Prince of Wales Museum of Western Mumbai. Not to be reproduced without prior permission of the Trustees: 7; © The British Library Board: 8 (Johnson Album 66,3), 26 (Foster 826), 29 (T 39881(3)), 55 (X432/6(19)), 63 (P178), 64 (X432/5(2)), 65 (X432/6(24)), 66 (X432/5(16), 68 (P181), 69 (P180), 71 (X432/6(7)), 72 (Add. Or. 4145); Courtesy Maharaja Sawai Man Singh II Museum Trust, The City Palace, Jaipur: 9; Photograph by the author, reproduced with permission of the Phadnis Family: 10, 13, 14, 15, 16, 17, 18; Photograph by the author, reproduced with permission of Sir J. J. College of Architecture, Mumbai: 11, 12; Photograph courtesy Colchester and Ipswich Museum Service: 19; Photo © Tate [2021]: 20; Photograph by the author, from a photograph in the Photographic Archives, South Asian Department, Victoria and Albert Museum, London: 21; © Islamic Arts Museum Malaysia: 23; Photograph courtesy Royal Asiatic Society of Great Britain and Ireland, London: 25, 144; Photograph by the author, courtesy of the Directorate of Archaeology and Museums, Maharashtra State: 28; Photograph courtesy Raja Dinkar Kelkar Museum, Pune. Not to be reproduced without prior permission from the museum: 30, 49; Photograph courtesy Malini Roy and Cam Sharp Jones © The British Library Board, F872: 37; Photograph courtesy the History Museum, Dr. Babasaheb Ambedkar Marathwada University, Aurangabad: 38, 75, 146; Photograph by Tamara Sears: 53, 58; Photographs courtesy of the General Collection, Beinecke Rare Book and Manuscript Library, Yale University, New Haven, Connecticut: 54, 118, 124; © Christie's Images Limited [2022]: 67; Photograph courtesy Lewis Walpole Library, Yale University, New Haven, Connecticut: 79; Photograph courtesy Hanna Holborn Gray Special Collections Research Center, University of Chicago Library: 80; Photograph by the author: 83, 87, 90, 99, 101, 104, 106, 107, 126, 138; Reproduced with permission from SUNY Press: 84; Courtesy Brown University Library: 88, 136; © Victoria & Albert Museum: 114, 137; Reproduced by permission of the National Library of Scotland: 115; From the Rare Book Division, New York Public Library (*OLV): 125; Courtesy of Freer Gallery of Art and Arthur M. Sackler Gallery Archives, Gift of Robert J. Del Bontà, 2014 and 2015, FSA.A2014.06-00001: 133; Victoria and Albert Museum, London, National Art Library: 134, 135; Photograph courtesy Anil Relia Collection, Ahmedabad: 139, 142, 143, 148, 149; Photograph courtesy Dr. Prashant & Rashmi Tapadia Collection, Pune: 140, 141, 145; © Dayanita Singh: 150, 151, 152, 154a and b

Index

Italic page numbers refer to illustrations.